D0936282

Object-Oriented Software Engineering

Stephen R. Schach
Vanderbilt University

 **Higher Education**

Boston   Burr Ridge, IL   Dubuque, IA   New York   San Francisco   St. Louis
Bangkok   Bogotá   Caracas   Kuala Lumpur   Lisbon   London   Madrid   Mexico City
Milan   Montreal   New Delhi   Santiago   Seoul   Singapore   Sydney   Taipei   Toronto

The McGraw-Hill Companies

McGraw-Hill
Higher Education

OBJECT-ORIENTED SOFTWARE ENGINEERING

Some ancillaries, including electronic and print components, may not be available to customers outside the United States.

This book is printed on acid-free paper.

1 2 3 4 5 6 7 8 9 0 DOC/DOC 0 9 8 7

ISBN   978–0–07–352333–0
MHID   0–07–352333–X

Global Publisher: *Raghothaman Srinivasan*
Executive Editor: *Michael Hackett*
Director of Development: *Kristine Tibbetts*
Developmental Editor: *Lora Kalb*
Senior Managing Editor: *Faye Schilling*
Executive Marketing Manager: *Michael Weitz*
Lead Production Supervisor: *Sandy Ludovissy*
Lead Media Project Manager: *Judi David*
Associate Media Producer: *Christina Nelson*
Designer: *John Joran/Brenda Rolwes*
Cover Design: *Studio Montage, St. Louis*
 (USE) Cover Image: *Royalty-Free/Getty Images*
Compositor: *Aptara*
Typeface: 10/12 *Times Roman*
Printer: *R. R. Donnelley Crawfordsville, IN*

Library of Congress Cataloging-in-Publication Data

Schach, Stephen R.
   Object-oriented software engineering / Stephen Schach. —1st ed.
      p.   cm.
   Includes index.
   ISBN 978-0-07-352333-0 — ISBN 0-07-352333-X (hard copy : alk. paper)
      1. Software engineering.   2. Object-oriented programming (Computer science)   I. Title.
QA76.758.S3185   2008
005.1'17--dc22

                                                                2007021842

www.mhhe.com

To Jackson

Preface

The wheel has turned full circle.

In 1988, I wrote a textbook entitled *Software Engineering*. Virtually the only mention of the object-oriented paradigm in that book was one section that described object-oriented design.

By 1994, the object-oriented paradigm was starting to gain acceptance in the software industry, so I wrote a textbook called *Classical and Object-Oriented Software Engineering*. Six years later, however, the object-oriented paradigm had become more important than the classical paradigm. To reflect this change, I switched the order of the two topics in the title of the textbook I wrote in 2000, and called it *Object-Oriented and Classical Software Engineering*.

Nowadays, use of the classical paradigm is largely restricted to maintaining legacy software. Students learn C++ or Java as their first programming language, and object-oriented languages are used in subsequent computer science and computer engineering courses. Students expect that, when they graduate, they will work for a company that uses the object-oriented paradigm. The object-oriented paradigm has all but squeezed out the classical paradigm. And that is why I have written a textbook entitled *Object-Oriented Software Engineering*.

Features of This Book

- The Unified Process is still largely the methodology of choice for object-oriented software development. Throughout this book, the student is therefore exposed to both the theory and the practice of the Unified Process.
- In Chapter 1 ("The Scope of Object-Oriented Software Engineering"), the strengths of the object-oriented paradigm are analyzed in depth.
- The iterative-and-incremental life-cycle model has been introduced as early as possible, namely, in Chapter 2 ("Software Life-Cycle Models"). Agile processes are also discussed in this chapter.
- In Chapter 3 ("The Software Process"), the workflows (activities) and processes of the Unified Process are introduced, and the need for two-dimensional life-cycle models is explained.
- A wide variety of ways of organizing software teams are presented in Chapter 4 ("Teams"), including teams for agile processes and for open-source software development.
- Chapter 5 ("Tools of the Trade") includes information on important classes of CASE tools.
- The importance of continual testing is stressed in Chapter 6 ("Testing").
- Objects are the focus of attention in Chapter 7 ("From Modules to Objects").
- In Chapter 8 ("Reusability and Portability"), design patterns have been stressed.
- The new IEEE standard for software project management plans is presented in Chapter 9 ("Planning and Estimating").

- Chapter 10 ("The Requirements Workflow"), Chapter 11 ("The Analysis Workflow"), Chapter 12 ("The Design Workflow"), and Chapter 13 ("The Implementation Workflow") are largely devoted to the workflows (activities) of the Unified Process.

- The material in Chapter 13 ("The Implementation Workflow") clearly distinguishes between implementation and integration.

- The importance of postdelivery maintenance is stressed in Chapter 14 ("Postdelivery Maintenance").

- Chapter 15 ("More on UML") provides additional material on UML to prepare the student thoroughly for employment in the software industry. This chapter is of particular use to instructors who utilize this book for the two-semester software engineering course sequence. In the second semester, in addition to developing the team-based term project or a capstone project, the student can acquire additional knowledge of UML, beyond what is needed for this book.

- There are two running case studies. The MSG Foundation case study and the elevator problem case study have been developed using the Unified Process. Java and C++ implementations are available online at **www.mhhe.com/schach**.

- In addition to the two running case studies that are used to illustrate the complete life cycle, seven mini case studies highlight specific topics, such as the moving-target problem, stepwise refinement, design patterns, and postdelivery maintenance.

- I stress the importance of documentation, maintenance, reuse, portability, testing, and CASE tools. It is no use teaching students the latest ideas unless they appreciate the importance of the basics of object-oriented software engineering.

- Attention is paid to object-oriented life-cycle models, object-oriented analysis, object-oriented design, management implications of the object-oriented paradigm, and the testing and maintenance of object-oriented software. Metrics for the object-oriented paradigm also are included. In addition, many briefer references are made to objects, a paragraph or even only a sentence in length. The reason is that the object-oriented paradigm is not just concerned with how the various workflows are performed but rather permeates the way we think about software engineering. Object technology pervades this book.

- The software process underlies the book as a whole. To control the process, we have to be able to measure what is happening to the project. Accordingly, there is an emphasis on metrics. With regard to process improvement, there is material on the capability maturity model (CMM), ISO/IEC 15504 (SPICE), and ISO/IEC 12207; the people capability maturity model (P–CMM) has been included in the chapter on teams.

- The book is language independent; the few code examples are presented in C++ and Java, and I have made every effort to smooth over language-dependent details and ensure that the code examples are equally clear to C++ and Java users. For example, instead of using cout for C++ output and System.out.println for Java output, I have utilized the pseudocode instruction *print*. (The one exception is the second case study, where complete implementation details are given in both C++ and Java.)

- This book contains over 600 references. I have selected current research papers as well as classic articles and books whose message remains fresh and relevant. There is no question that object-oriented software engineering is a rapidly moving field, and students therefore need to know the latest results and where in the literature to find them. At the same time, today's cutting-edge research is based on yesterday's truths, and I see no reason to exclude an older reference if its ideas are as applicable today as they originally were.

- With regard to prerequisites, it is assumed that the reader is familiar with one high-level object-oriented programming language such as C++ or Java. In addition, the reader is expected to have taken a course in data structures.

How This Book Is Organized

This book is written for both the traditional one-semester and the newer two-semester software engineering curriculum, now growing in popularity. In the traditional one-semester (or one-quarter) course, the instructor has to rush through the theoretical material to provide the students the knowledge and skills needed for the term project as soon as possible. The need for haste is so that the students can commence the term project early enough to complete it by the end of the semester. To cater to a one-semester, project-based software engineering course, Part 2 of this book covers the software life cycle, workflow by workflow, and Part 1 contains the theoretical material needed to understand Part 2. For example, Part 1 introduces the reader to CASE, metrics, and testing; each chapter of Part 2 contains a section on CASE tools for that workflow, a section on metrics for that workflow, and a section on testing during that workflow. Part 1 is kept short to enable the instructor to start Part 2 relatively early in the semester. Furthermore, the last two chapters of Part 1 (Chapters 8 and 9) may be postponed, and then taught in parallel with Part 2. As a result, the class can begin developing the term project as soon as possible.

We turn now to the two-semester software engineering curriculum. More and more computer science and computer engineering departments are realizing that the overwhelming preponderance of their graduates find employment as software engineers. As a result, many colleges and universities have introduced a two-semester (or two-quarter) software engineering sequence. The first course is largely theoretical (but often includes a small project of some sort). The second course comprises a major team-based term project. This is usually a capstone project. When the term project is in the second course, there is no need for the instructor to rush to start Part 2.

Therefore, an instructor teaching a one-semester (or one-quarter) sequence using this book covers most of Chapters 1 through 7 and then starts Part 2 (Chapters 10 through 15). Chapters 8 and 9 can be taught in parallel with Part 2 or at the end of the course while the students are implementing the term project. When teaching the two-semester sequence, the chapters of the book are taught in order; the class now is fully prepared for the team-based term project that it will develop in the following semester.

To ensure that the key software engineering techniques of Part 2 truly are understood, each is presented twice. First, when a technique is introduced, it is illustrated by means of the elevator problem. The elevator problem is the correct size for the reader to be able to see the technique applied to a complete problem, and it has enough subtleties to highlight both the strengths and weaknesses of the technique being taught. Then, the relevant portion of the MSG Foundation case study is presented. This detailed solution provides the second illustration of each technique.

The Problem Sets

This book has five types of problems. First, there are running object-oriented analysis and design projects at the end of Chapters 10, 11, and 12. These have been included because the only way to learn how to perform the requirements, analysis, and design workflows is from extensive hands-on experience.

Second, the end of each chapter contains a number of exercises intended to highlight key points. These exercises are self-contained; the technical information for all the exercises can be found in this book.

Third, there is a software term project. It is designed to be solved by students working in teams of three, the smallest number of team members that cannot confer over a standard telephone. The term project comprises 14 separate components, each tied to the relevant chapter. For example, design is the topic of Chapter 12, so in that chapter the component of the term project is concerned with software design. By breaking a large project into smaller, well-defined pieces, the instructor can monitor the progress of the class more closely. The structure of the term project is such that an instructor may freely apply the 14 components to any other project that he or she chooses.

Because this book has been written for use by graduate students as well as upper-class undergraduates, the fourth type of problem is based on research papers in the software engineering literature. In each chapter, an important paper has been chosen. The student is asked to read the paper and answer a question relating to its contents. Of course, the instructor is free to assign any other research paper; the For Further Reading section at the end of each chapter includes a wide variety of relevant papers.

The fifth type of problem relates to the case study. This type of problem has been included in response to a number of instructors who feel that their students learn more by modifying an existing product than by developing a new product from scratch. Many senior software engineers in the industry agree with that viewpoint. Accordingly, each chapter in which the case study is presented has problems that require the student to modify the case study in some way. For example, in one chapter the student is asked what the effect would have been of performing the steps of the object-oriented analysis in a different order. To make it easy to modify the source code of the case study, it is available on the World Wide Web at www.mhhe.com/schach.

The website also has material for instructors, including a complete set of PowerPoint lecture notes, and detailed solutions to all the exercises as well as to the term project.

Material on UML

This book makes substantial use of the Unified Modeling Language (UML). If the students do not have previous knowledge of UML, this material may be taught in two ways. I prefer to teach UML on a just-in-time basis; that is, each UML concept is introduced just before it is needed. The following table describes where the UML constructs used in this book are introduced.

Construct	Section in Which the Corresponding UML Diagram is Introduced
Class diagram, note, inheritance (generalization), aggregation, association, navigation triangle	Section 7.7
Use case	Section 10.4.3
Use-case diagram, use-case description	Section 10.7
Stereotype	Section 11.4
Statechart	Section 11.9
Interaction diagram (sequence diagram, communication diagram)	Section 11.18

Alternatively, Chapter 15 contains an introduction to UML, including material above and beyond what is needed for this book. Chapter 15 may be taught at any time; it does not depend on material in the first 14 chapters. The topics covered in Chapter 15 are given in the following table:

Construct	Section in Which the Corresponding UML Diagram is Introduced
Class diagram, aggregation, multiplicity, composition, generalization, association	Section 15.2
Note	Section 15.3
Use-case diagram	Section 15.4
Stereotype	Section 15.5
Interaction diagram	Section 15.6
Statechart	Section 15.7
Activity diagram	Section 15.8
Package	Section 15.9
Component diagram	Section 15.10
Deployment diagram	Section 15.11

Acknowledgments

I should like to thank the reviewers of this book:

Michael A. Aars,
Baylor University
Keith S. Decker,
University of Delaware
Xiaocong Fan,
The Pennsylvania State University
Adrian Fiech,
Memorial University
Sudipto Ghosh,
Colorado State University

Anita Kuchera,
Rensselaer Polytechnic Institute
Matthew R. McBride,
Southern Methodist University
Michael McCracken,
Georgia Institute of Technology
Rick Mercer,
University of Arizona
Richard J. Povinelli,
Marquette University

David C. Rine,
George Mason University
Keng Siau,
University of Nebraska-Lincoln

John Sturman,
Rensselaer Polytechnic Institute
Levent Yilmaz,
Auburn University

I warmly thank three individuals who have also made significant contributions to previous books I have written. First, Kris Irwin provided a complete solution to the term project, including implementing it in both Java and C++. Second, Jeff Gray implemented the MSG Foundation case study. Third, Lauren Ryder was a coauthor of the *Instructor's Solution Manual* and contributor to the PowerPoint slides.

I turn now to McGraw-Hill. I am truly grateful to Senior Managing Editor Faye Schilling for her willingness to take over the role of production manager mid-project. I am also most appreciative of her readiness to modify the schedule when needed. Developmental Editor Lora Kalb was a pillar of strength from start to finish; it was a real pleasure to work with Lora again. I also warmly thank copyeditor Lucy Mullins, proofreader Dorothy Wendell, and Production Manager Joyce Berendes. Finally, I am grateful to Brenda Rolwes in coordinating with cover designer Jenny Hobein from Studio Montage. Jenny transformed a photograph of Sydney Harbour Bridge into a striking cover.

I would like to thank the numerous instructors from all over the world who sent me e-mail regarding my other books. I look forward with anticipation to receiving instructors' feedback on this book also. My e-mail address is srs@vuse.vanderbilt.edu.

Students, too, continue to be most helpful. Once more I thank my students at Vanderbilt University for their provocative questions and constructive suggestions, both inside and outside the classroom. I also am most appreciative of the questions and comments e-mailed to me by students from all over the world. As with my previous books, I look forward keenly to student feedback on this book, too.

Finally, as always, I thank my family for their continual support. As with all my previous books, I did my utmost to try to ensure that family commitments took precedence over writing. However, when deadlines loomed, this was sometimes not possible. At such times, they were always understanding, and for this I am most grateful.

It is my privilege to dedicate my fourteenth book to my grandson, Jackson, with love.

Stephen R. Schach

Contents

PART ONE
INTRODUCTION TO OBJECT-
ORIENTED SOFTWARE
ENGINEERING   1

Chapter 1
The Scope of Object-Oriented Software
Engineering   3

        Learning Objectives   3
1.1   Historical Aspects   4
1.2   Economic Aspects   7
1.3   Maintenance Aspects   8
        1.3.1   The Modern View of
        *   Maintenance   9*
        1.3.2   The Importance of Post-
        *   delivery Maintenance   11*
1.4   Requirements, Analysis, and
        Design Aspects   13
1.5   Team Development Aspects   15
1.6   Why There Is No Planning Phase   16
1.7   Why There Is No Testing Phase   17
1.8   Why There Is No Documentation Phase   18
1.9   The Object-Oriented Paradigm   18
1.10   Terminology   20
1.11   Ethical Issues   24
        Chapter Review   25
        For Further Reading   25
        Key Terms   26
        Problems   27
        References   28

Chapter 2
Software Life-Cycle Models   32

        Learning Objectives   32
2.1   Software Development in Theory   32
2.2   Winburg Mini Case Study   33
2.3   Lessons of the Winburg Mini Case Study   37
2.4   Teal Tractors Mini Case Study   37
2.5   Iteration and Incrementation   38
2.6   Winburg Mini Case Study Revisited   42
2.7   Risks and Other Aspects of Iteration
        and Incrementation   43

2.8   Managing Iteration and Incrementation   46
2.9   Other Life-Cycle Models   47
        2.9.1   Code-and-Fix Life-Cycle Model   47
        2.9.2   Waterfall Life-Cycle Model   48
        2.9.3   Rapid-Prototyping Life-Cycle
        *   Model   50*
        2.9.4   Open-Source Life-Cycle Model   51
        2.9.5   Agile Processes   54
        2.9.6   Synchronize-and-Stabilize
        *   Life-Cycle Model   57*
        2.9.7   Spiral Life-Cycle Model   57
2.10   Comparison of Life-Cycle Models   61
        Chapter Review   62
        For Further Reading   63
        Key Terms   64
        Problems   64
        References   65

Chapter 3
The Software Process   68

        Learning Objectives   68
3.1   The Unified Process   70
3.2   Iteration and Incrementation   72
3.3   The Requirements Workflow   73
3.4   The Analysis Workflow   74
3.5   The Design Workflow   76
3.6   The Implementation Workflow   77
3.7   The Test Workflow   78
        3.7.1   Requirements Artifacts   78
        3.7.2   Analysis Artifacts   79
        3.7.3   Design Artifacts   79
        3.7.4   Implementation Artifacts   79
3.8   Postdelivery Maintenance   81
3.9   Retirement   82
3.10   The Phases of the Unified Process   82
        3.10.1   The Inception Phase   83
        3.10.2   The Elaboration Phase   85
        3.10.3   The Construction Phase   86
        3.10.4   The Transition Phase   86
3.11   One- versus Two-Dimensional Life-Cycle
        Models   87
3.12   Improving the Software Process   89
3.13   Capability Maturity Models   89

3.14 Other Software Process Improvement
     Initiatives   92
3.15 Costs and Benefits of Software Process
     Improvement   93
     Chapter Review   95
     For Further Reading   95
     Key Terms   96
     Problems   97
     References   97

Chapter 4
Teams   101

     Learning Objectives   101
4.1 Team Organization   101
4.2 Democratic Team Approach   103
     *4.2.1 Analysis of the Democratic Team
            Approach   104*
4.3 Chief Programmer Team Approach   104
     4.3.1 The New York Times Project   106
     *4.3.2 Impracticality of the Chief
            Programmer Team Approach   107*
4.4 Beyond Chief Programmer and Democratic
     Teams   107
4.5 Synchronize-and-Stabilize Teams   111
4.6 Teams for Agile Processes   112
4.7 Open-Source Programming Teams   112
4.8 People Capability Maturity Model   113
4.9 Choosing an Appropriate Team
     Organization   114
     Chapter Review   115
     For Further Reading   115
     Key Terms   115
     Problems   116
     References   116

Chapter 5
The Tools of The Trade   118

     Learning Objectives   118
5.1 Stepwise Refinement   118
     *5.1.1 Stepwise Refinement Mini
            Case Study   119*
5.2 Cost–Benefit Analysis   124
5.3 Software Metrics   126
5.4 CASE   127

5.5 Taxonomy of CASE   128
5.6 Scope of CASE   130
5.7 Software Versions   133
     5.7.1 Revisions   134
     5.7.2 Variations   134
5.8 Configuration Control   135
     *5.8.1 Configuration Control during
            Postdelivery Maintenance   137*
     5.8.2 Baselines   138
     *5.8.3 Configuration Control during
            Development   138*
5.9 Build Tools   138
5.10 Productivity Gains with CASE
     Technology   139
     Chapter Review   141
     For Further Reading   141
     Key Terms   141
     Problems   142
     References   143

Chapter 6
Testing   145

     Learning Objectives   145
6.1 Quality Issues   146
     6.1.1 Software Quality Assurance   147
     6.1.2 Managerial Independence   147
6.2 Non-Execution-Based Testing   148
     6.2.1 Walkthroughs   149
     6.2.2 Managing Walkthroughs   149
     6.2.3 Inspections   150
     *6.2.4 Comparison of Inspections and
            Walkthroughs   152*
     *6.2.5 Strengths and Weaknesses of
            Reviews   153*
     6.2.6 Metrics for Inspections   153
6.3 Execution-Based Testing   153
6.4 What Should Be Tested?   154
     6.4.1 Utility   155
     6.4.2 Reliability   155
     6.4.3 Robustness   156
     6.4.4 Performance   156
     6.4.5 Correctness   157
6.5 Testing versus Correctness Proofs   158
     6.5.1 Example of a Correctness Proof   158
     *6.5.2 Correctness Proof Mini Case
            Study   162*

6.5.3 Correctness Proofs and Software Engineering 163
6.6 Who Should Perform Execution-Based Testing? 166
6.7 When Testing Stops 167
Chapter Review 167
For Further Reading 168
Key Terms 168
Problems 169
References 170

Chapter 7
From Modules to Objects 173

Learning Objectives 173
7.1 What Is a Module? 174
7.2 Cohesion 176
7.2.1 Coincidental Cohesion 177
7.2.2 Logical Cohesion 178
7.2.3 Temporal Cohesion 178
7.2.4 Procedural Cohesion 179
7.2.5 Communicational Cohesion 179
7.2.6 Functional Cohesion 180
7.2.7 Informational Cohesion 180
7.2.8 Cohesion Example 181
7.3 Coupling 181
7.3.1 Content Coupling 182
7.3.2 Common Coupling 183
7.3.3 Control Coupling 185
7.3.4 Stamp Coupling 185
7.3.5 Data Coupling 186
7.3.6 Coupling Example 187
7.3.7 The Importance of Coupling 188
7.4 Data Encapsulation 189
7.4.1 Data Encapsulation and Development 191
7.4.2 Data Encapsulation and Maintenance 192
7.5 Abstract Data Types 197
7.6 Information Hiding 199
7.7 Objects 201
7.8 Inheritance, Polymorphism, and Dynamic Binding 205
7.9 The Object-Oriented Paradigm 207
Chapter Review 210
For Further Reading 211
Key Terms 211

Problems 212
References 212

Chapter 8
Reusability and Portability 215

Learning Objectives 215
8.1 Reuse Concepts 216
8.2 Impediments to Reuse 218
8.3 Reuse Case Studies 219
8.3.1 Raytheon Missile Systems Division 220
8.3.2 European Space Agency 221
8.4 Objects and Reuse 222
8.5 Reuse during Design and Implementation 222
8.5.1 Design Reuse 222
8.5.2 Application Frameworks 224
8.5.3 Design Patterns 224
8.5.4 Software Architecture 226
8.5.5 Component-Based Software Engineering 227
8.6 More on Design Patterns 227
8.6.1 FLIC Mini Case Study 228
8.6.2 Adapter Design Pattern 229
8.6.3 Bridge Design Pattern 230
8.6.4 Iterator Design Pattern 233
8.6.5 Abstract Factory Design Pattern 233
8.7 Categories of Design Patterns 235
8.8 Strengths and Weaknesses of Design Patterns 237
8.9 Reuse and Postdelivery Maintenance 238
8.10 Portability 239
8.10.1 Hardware Incompatibilities 239
8.10.2 Operating System Incompatibilities 240
8.10.3 Numerical Software Incompatibilities 241
8.10.4 Compiler Incompatibilities 241
8.11 Why Portability? 244
8.12 Techniques for Achieving Portability 245
8.12.1 Portable System Software 246
8.12.2 Portable Application Software 246
8.12.3 Portable Data 247
8.12.4 Web-Based Applications 248
Chapter Review 249
For Further Reading 249

Key Terms   250
Problems   250
References   252

Chapter 9
Planning and Estimating   256

Learning Objectives   256
9.1   Planning and the Software Process   257
9.2   Estimating Duration and Cost   258
   9.2.1   *Metrics for the Size of a Product*   260
   9.2.2   *Techniques of Cost Estimation*   263
   9.2.3   *Intermediate COCOMO*   265
   9.2.4   *COCOMO II*   269
   9.2.5   *Tracking Duration and Cost Estimates*   270
9.3   Estimation Issues   270
9.4   Components of a Software Project Management Plan   271
9.5   Software Project Management Plan Framework   272
9.6   IEEE Software Project Management Plan   274
9.7   Planning Testing   277
9.8   Training Requirements   278
9.9   Documentation Standards   279
9.10   CASE Tools for Planning and Estimating   279
9.11   Testing the Software Project Management Plan   280
   Chapter Review   280
   For Further Reading   280
   Key Terms   281
   Problems   282
   References   283

PART TWO
THE WORKFLOWS OF THE SOFTWARE LIFE CYCLE   286

Chapter 10
The Requirements Workflow   287

Learning Objectives   287
10.1   Determining What the Client Needs   288

10.2   Overview of the Requirements Workflow   289
10.3   Understanding the Domain   289
10.4   The Business Model   290
   10.4.1   *Interviewing*   290
   10.4.2   *Other Techniques*   291
   10.4.3   *Use Cases*   292
10.5   Initial Requirements   293
10.6   Initial Understanding of the Domain: The MSG Foundation Case Study   294
10.7   Initial Business Model: The MSG Foundation Case Study   297
10.8   Initial Requirements: The MSG Foundation Case Study   300
10.9   Continuing the Requirements Workflow: The MSG Foundation Case Study   302
10.10   Revising the Requirements: The MSG Foundation Case Study   304
10.11   The Test Workflow: The MSG Foundation Case Study   312
10.12   What Are Object-Oriented Requirements?   321
10.13   Rapid Prototyping   321
10.14   Human Factors   322
10.15   Reusing the Rapid Prototype   324
10.16   CASE Tools for the Requirements Workflow   324
10.17   Metrics for the Requirements Workflow   325
10.18   Challenges of the Requirements Workflow   325
   Chapter Review   327
   For Further Reading   327
   Key Terms   327
   Case Study Key Terms   328
   Problems   328
   References   329

Chapter 11
The Analysis Workflow   331

Learning Objectives   331
11.1   The Specification Document   332
11.2   Informal Specifications   333
11.3   Correctness Proof Mini Case Study Redux   334

11.4 The Analysis Workflow 335
11.5 Extracting the Entity Classes 337
11.6 The Elevator Problem 338
11.7 Functional Modeling: The Elevator Problem Case Study 338
11.8 Entity Class Modeling: The Elevator Problem Case Study 340
    11.8.1 Noun Extraction 341
    11.8.2 CRC Cards 343
11.9 Dynamic Modeling: The Elevator Problem Case Study 344
11.10 The Test Workflow: The Elevator Problem Case Study 347
11.11 Extracting the Boundary and Control Classes 351
11.12 The Initial Functional Model: The MSG Foundation Case Study 352
11.13 The Initial Class Diagram: The MSG Foundation Case Study 354
11.14 The Initial Dynamic Model: The MSG Foundation Case Study 357
11.15 Revising the Entity Classes: The MSG Foundation Case Study 359
11.16 Extracting the Boundary Classes: The MSG Foundation Case Study 360
11.17 Extracting the Control Classes: The MSG Foundation Case Study 361
11.18 Use-Case Realization: The MSG Foundation Case Study 362
    11.18.1 Estimate Funds Available for Week Use Case 362
    11.18.2 Manage an Asset Use Case 369
    11.18.3 Update Estimated Annual Operating Expenses Use Case 373
    11.18.4 Produce a Report Use Case 375
11.19 Incrementing the Class Diagram: The MSG Foundation Case Study 380
11.20 The Software Project Management Plan: The MSG Foundation Case Study 382
11.21 The Test Workflow: The MSG Foundation Case Study 382
11.22 The Specification Document in the Unified Process 382
11.23 More on Actors and Use Cases 383
11.24 CASE Tools for the Analysis Workflow 385

11.25 Challenges of the Analysis Workflow 385
Chapter Review 386
For Further Reading 386
Key Terms 387
Case Study Key Terms 387
Problems 387
References 389

Chapter 12
The Design Workflow 392
Learning Objectives 392
12.1 Object-Oriented Design 393
12.2 Object-Oriented Design: The Elevator Problem Case Study 397
12.3 Object-Oriented Design: The MSG Foundation Case Study 400
12.4 The Design Workflow 402
12.5 The Test Workflow: Design 404
12.6 The Test Workflow: The MSG Foundation Case Study 405
12.7 Formal Techniques for Detailed Design 405
12.8 Real-Time Design Techniques 406
12.9 CASE Tools for Design 407
12.10 Metrics for Design 408
12.11 Challenges of the Design Workflow 409
Chapter Review 410
For Further Reading 410
Key Terms 411
Problems 411
References 412

Chapter 13
The Implementation Workflow 414
Learning Objectives 414
13.1 Choice of Programming Language 414
13.2 Good Programming Practice 417
    13.2.1 Use of Consistent and Meaningful Variable Names 417
    13.2.2 The Issue of Self-Documenting Code 418
    13.2.3 Use of Parameters 420
    13.2.4 Code Layout for Increased Readability 421
    13.2.5 Nested **if** *Statements 421*

13.3   Coding Standards   422
13.4   Code Reuse   423
13.5   Integration   423
   13.5.1   Top-down Integration   424
   13.5.2   Bottom-up Integration   426
   13.5.3   Sandwich Integration   426
   13.5.4   Integration Techniques   428
   13.5.5   Management of Integration   428
13.6   The Implementation Workflow   429
13.7   The Implementation Workflow: The MSG Foundation Case Study   429
13.8   The Test Workflow: Implementation   429
13.9   Test Case Selection   430
   13.9.1   Testing to Specifications versus Testing to Code   430
   13.9.2   Feasibility of Testing to Specifications   430
   13.9.3   Feasibility of Testing to Code   431
13.10 Black-Box Unit-Testing Techniques   433
   13.10.1   Equivalence Testing and Boundary Value Analysis   434
   13.10.2   Functional Testing   435
13.11 Black-Box Test Cases: The MSG Foundation Case Study   436
13.12 Glass-Box Unit-Testing Techniques   436
   13.12.1   Structural Testing: Statement, Branch, and Path Coverage   438
   13.12.2   Complexity Metrics   440
13.13 Code Walkthroughs and Inspections   441
13.14 Comparison of Unit-Testing Techniques   441
13.15 Cleanroom   442
13.16 Testing Issues   443
13.17 Management Aspects of Unit Testing   445
13.18 When to Rewrite Rather than Debug a Code Artifact   446
13.19 Integration Testing   447
13.20 Product Testing   448
13.21 Acceptance Testing   449
13.22 The Test Workflow: The MSG Foundation Case Study   450
13.23 CASE Tools for Implementation   450
   13.23.1   CASE Tools for the Complete Software Process   450
   13.23.2   Integrated Development Environments   451

   13.23.3   Environments for Business Applications   452
   13.23.4   Public Tool Infrastructures   452
   13.23.5   Potential Problems with Environments   452
13.24 CASE Tools for the Test Workflow   453
13.25 Metrics for the Implementation Workflow   453
13.26 Challenges of the Implementation Workflow   454
   Chapter Review   455
   For Further Reading   455
   Key Terms   456
   Problems   457
   References   459

Chapter 14
Postdelivery Maintenance   462

   Learning Objectives   462
14.1   Development and Maintenance   462
14.2   Why Postdelivery Maintenance Is Necessary   464
14.3   What Is Required of Postdelivery Maintenance Programmers?   465
14.4   Postdelivery Maintenance Mini Case Study   467
14.5   Management of Postdelivery Maintenance   468
   14.5.1   Defect Reports   468
   14.5.2   Authorizing Changes to the Product   469
   14.5.3   Ensuring Maintainability   470
   14.5.4   Problem of Repeated Maintenance   471
14.6   Maintenance Issues   471
14.7   Postdelivery Maintenance Skills versus Development Skills   474
14.8   Reverse Engineering   474
14.9   Testing during Postdelivery Maintenance   475
14.10 CASE Tools for Postdelivery Maintenance   476
14.11 Metrics for Postdelivery Maintenance   477
14.12 Postdelivery Maintenance: The MSG Foundation Case Study   477
14.13 Challenges of Postdelivery Maintenance   477

Chapter Review   478
For Further Reading   478
Key Terms   479
Problems   479
References   480

Chapter 15
More on UML   482

Learning Objectives   482
15.1   UML Is *Not* a Methodology   483
15.2   Class Diagrams   483
     15.2.1   Aggregation   484
     15.2.2   Multiplicity   485
     15.2.3   Composition   486
     15.2.4   Generalization   487
     15.2.5   Association   487
15.3   Notes   488
15.4   Use-Case Diagrams   488
15.5   Stereotypes   488
15.6   Interaction Diagrams   489
15.7   Statecharts   491
15.8   Activity Diagrams   494
15.9   Packages   496
15.10   Component Diagrams   497
15.11   Deployment Diagrams   497
15.12   Review of UML Diagrams   498
15.13   UML and Iteration   498
Chapter Review   498
For Further Reading   499
Key Terms   499
Problems   499
References   500

Bibliography   501

Appendix A
Term Project: Osric's Office Appliances and Decor   524

Appendix B
Software Engineering Resources   528

Appendix C
The Requirements Workflow: The MSG Foundation Case Study   530

Appendix D
The Analysis Workflow: The MSG Foundation Case Study   531

Appendix E
Software Project Management Plan: The MSG Foundation Case Study   532

Appendix F
The Design Workflow: The MSG Foundation Case Study   537

Appendix G
The Implementation Workflow: The MSG Foundation Case Study (C++ Version)   542

Appendix H
The Implementation Workflow: The MSG Foundation Case Study (Java Version)   543

Appendix I
The Test Workflow: The MSG Foundation Case Study   544

The following are registered trademarks:

ADF	Java	Requisite Pro
Analyst/Designer	JBuilder	Rhapsody
Ant	JUnit	Rose
Apache	Linux	SBC Communications
Apple	Lotus 1-2-3	SilkTest
AS/400	Lucent Technologies	SLAM
AT&T	MacApp	Software through Pictures
Bachman Product Set	Macintosh	Solaris
Bell Laboratories	Macintosh Toolbox	SourceSafe
Borland	MacProject	SPARCstation
Bugzilla	Microsoft	Sun
Capability Maturity Model	Motif	Sun Enterprise
ClearCase	MS-DOS	Sun Microsystems
ClearQuest	MVS/360	Sun ONE Java Studio
CMM	Natural	System Architect
Coca-Cola	Netscape	Together
CORBA	*New York Times*	UNIX
CppUnit	Object C	VAX
CVS	Objective-C	Visual Component Library
DataFlex	ObjectWindows Library	Visual C++
DB2	1-800-flowers.com	Visual J++
Eclipse	Oracle	VM/370
e-Components	Oracle Developer Suite	VMS
Emeraude	OS/360	*Wall Street Journal*
Enterprise JavaBeans	OS/370	WebSphere
eServer	OS/VS2	Win32
Excel	Palm Pilot	Windows 95
Firefox	Parasoft	Windows 2000
Focus	Post-it Note	Windows NT
Ford	PowerBuilder	X11
FoxBASE	PREfix	Xrunner
GCC	PREfast	XUnit
Hewlett-Packard	Project	Zip disk
IBM	PureCoverage	ZIP Code
IMS/360	PVCS	zSeries
Internet Explorer	QARun	
Jackpot Source Code Metrics	Rational	

Introduction to Object-Oriented Software Engineering

The first nine chapters of this book play a dual role: They introduce the reader to the object-oriented software process, and they provide the foundation for the material in the second half of the book, where the workflows (activities) of object-oriented software development are described.

The software process is the way we produce software. It starts with concept exploration and ends when the product is finally decommissioned. During this period, the product goes through a series of steps such as requirements, analysis (specification), design, implementation, integration, postdelivery maintenance, and ultimately, retirement. The software process includes the tools and techniques we use to develop and maintain software, as well as the software professionals involved.

Chapter 1, "The Scope of Object-Oriented Software Engineering," points out that techniques for software production must be cost effective and promote constructive interaction between the members of the software production team. The importance of objects is stressed throughout the book, starting with this chapter.

A variety of different software life-cycle models are discussed in detail in Chapter 2, "Software Life-Cycle Models." These include the evolution-tree model, the waterfall model, the rapid-prototyping model, the synchronize-and-stabilize model, the open-source model, the agile process model, the spiral model, and most important of all, the iterative-and-incremental model (the model that underlies much of object-oriented software engineering). To enable the reader to decide on an appropriate life-cycle model for a specific project, the various life-cycle models are compared and contrasted.

"The Software Process" is the title of Chapter 3. The emphasis in this chapter is on the Unified Process, currently the most promising way of developing software. Agile processes, an alternative approach to software development gaining in popularity, are also treated in detail. Open-source software is also discussed in some depth. The chapter concludes with material on software process improvement.

Chapter 4 is entitled "Teams." Today's projects are too large to be completed by a single individual within the given time constraints. Instead, a team of software professionals collaborate on the project. The major topic of this chapter is how teams should be organized so that team members work together productively. Various ways of organizing teams are discussed, including democratic teams, chief programmer teams, synchronize-and-stabilize teams, open-source teams, and agile process teams.

A software engineer needs to be able to use a number of different tools, both analytical and practical. In Chapter 5, "The Tools of the Trade," the reader is introduced to a variety of software engineering tools. One such tool is stepwise refinement, a technique for decomposing a large problem into smaller, more tractable problems. Another tool is cost–benefit analysis, a technique for determining whether a software project is financially feasible. Then, computer-aided software engineering (CASE) tools are described. A CASE tool is a software product that assists software engineers to develop and maintain software. Finally, to manage the software process, it is necessary to measure various quantities to determine whether the project is on track. These measures (metrics) are critical to the success of a project.

The last two topics of Chapter 5, CASE tools and metrics, are treated in detail in Chapters 10 through 13, which describe the specific workflows of the software life cycle. There is a discussion of the CASE tools that support each workflow, as well as a description of the metrics needed to manage that workflow adequately.

In Chapter 6, "Testing," discusses the concepts underlying testing. The consideration of testing techniques specific to each workflow of the software life cycle is deferred until Chapters 10 through 14.

Chapter 7, "From Modules to Objects," gives a detailed explanation of classes and objects, and why the object-oriented paradigm is proving more successful than the classical paradigm. The concepts of this chapter are utilized in the rest of the book, particularly Chapter 10, "The Requirements Workflow"; Chapter 11, "The Analysis Workflow"; and Chapter 12, "The Design Workflow."

The ideas of Chapter 7 are extended in Chapter 8, "Reusability and Portability." It is important to be able to write reusable software that can be ported to a variety of different hardware. The first part of the chapter is devoted to reuse; the topics include a variety of reuse case studies as well as reuse strategies such as patterns and frameworks. Portability is the second major topic; portability strategies are presented in some depth. A recurring theme of this chapter is the role of objects in achieving reusability and portability.

The last chapter in Part 1 is Chapter 9, "Planning and Estimating." Before starting a software project, it is essential to plan the entire operation in detail. Once the project begins, management must closely monitor progress, noting deviations from the plan and taking corrective action where necessary. Also, it is vital that the client be provided accurate estimates of how long the project will take and how much it will cost. Different estimation techniques are presented, including function points and COCOMO II. A detailed description of a software project management plan is given. The material of this chapter is utilized in Chapter 11 ('The Analysis Workflow") because the major planning effort takes place at the end of the analysis workflow.

Chapter 1

The Scope of Object-Oriented Software Engineering

Learning Objectives

After studying this chapter, you should be able to

- Define what is meant by object-oriented software engineering.
- Explain why the object-oriented paradigm is now so widely accepted.
- Discuss the implications of the various aspects of software engineering.
- Describe the modern view of maintenance.
- Discuss the importance of continual planning, testing, and documentation.
- Appreciate the importance of adhering to a code of ethics.

A well-known story tells of an executive who received a computer-generated bill for $0.00. After having a good laugh with friends about "idiot computers," the executive tossed the bill away. A month later, a similar bill arrived, this time marked 30 days. Then came the third bill. The fourth bill arrived a month later, accompanied by a message hinting at possible legal action if the bill for $0.00 was not paid at once.

The fifth bill, marked 120 days, did not hint at anything—the message was rude and forthright, threatening all manner of legal actions if the bill was not immediately paid. Fearful of his organization's credit rating in the hands of this maniacal machine, the executive called an acquaintance who was a software engineer and related the whole sorry story. Trying not to laugh, the software engineer told the executive to mail a check for $0.00. This had the desired effect, and a receipt for $0.00 was received a few days later. The executive meticulously filed it away in case at some future date the computer might allege that $0.00 was still owed.

This well-known story has a less well-known sequel. A few days later, the executive was summoned by his bank manager. The banker held up a check and asked, "Is this your check?"

The executive agreed that it was.

"Would you mind telling me why you wrote a check for $0.00?" asked the banker.

So the whole story was retold. When the executive had finished, the banker turned to him and she quietly asked, "Have you any idea what your check for $0.00 did to *our* computer system?"

A computer professional can laugh at this story, albeit somewhat nervously. After all, every one of us has designed or implemented a product that, in its original form, would have resulted in the equivalent of sending dunning letters for $0.00. Up to now, we have always caught this sort of fault during testing. But our laughter has a hollow ring to it, because at the back of our minds is the fear that someday we will not detect the fault before the product is delivered to the customer.

A decidedly less humorous software fault was detected on November 9, 1979. The Strategic Air Command had an alert scramble when the worldwide military command and control system (WWMCCS) computer network reported that the Soviet Union had launched missiles aimed toward the United States [Neumann, 1980]. What actually happened was that a simulated attack was interpreted as the real thing, just as in the movie *WarGames* some 5 years later. Although the U.S. Department of Defense understandably has not given details about the precise mechanism by which test data were taken for actual data, it seems reasonable to ascribe the problem to a software fault. Either the system as a whole was not designed to differentiate between simulations and reality, or the user interface did not include the necessary checks for ensuring that end users of the system would be able to distinguish fact from fiction. In other words, a software fault, if indeed the problem was caused by software, could have brought civilization as we know it to an unpleasant and abrupt end. (See Just in Case You Wanted to Know Box 1.1 for information on disasters caused by other software faults.)

Whether we are dealing with billing or air defense, much of our software is delivered late, over budget, and with residual faults, and does not meet the client's needs. Software engineering is an attempt to solve these problems. In other words, **software engineering** is a discipline whose aim is the production of fault-free software, delivered on time and within budget, that satisfies the client's needs. Furthermore, the software must be easy to modify when the user's needs change.

The scope of software engineering is extremely broad. Some aspects of software engineering can be categorized as mathematics or computer science; other aspects fall into the areas of economics, management, or psychology. To display the wide-reaching realm of software engineering, we now examine five different aspects.

1.1   Historical Aspects

It is a fact that electric power generators fail, but far less frequently than payroll products. Bridges sometimes collapse but considerably less often than operating systems. In the belief that software design, implementation, and maintenance could be put on the same footing as traditional engineering disciplines, a NATO study group in 1967 coined the term *software engineering*. The claim that building software is similar to other engineering tasks

In the case of the WWMCCS network, disaster was averted at the last minute. However, the consequences of other software faults have been fatal. For example, between 1985 and 1987, at least two patients died as a consequence of severe overdoses of radiation delivered by the Therac-25 medical linear accelerator [Leveson and Turner, 1993]. The cause was a fault in the control software.

Also, during the 1991 Gulf War, a Scud missile penetrated the Patriot antimissile shield and struck a barracks near Dhahran, Saudi Arabia. In all, 28 Americans were killed and 98 wounded. The software for the Patriot missile contained a cumulative timing fault. The Patriot was designed to operate for only a few hours at a time, after which the clock was reset. As a result, the fault never had a significant effect and therefore was not detected. In the Gulf War, however, the Patriot missile battery at Dhahran ran continuously for over 100 hours. This caused the accumulated time discrepancy to become large enough to render the system inaccurate.

During the Gulf War, the United States shipped Patriot missiles to Israel for protection against the Scuds. Israeli forces detected the timing problem after only 8 hours and immediately reported it to the manufacturer in the United States. The manufacturer corrected the fault as quickly as it could, but tragically, the new software arrived the day after the direct hit by the Scud [Mellor, 1994].

Fortunately, it is extremely rare for death or serious injury to be caused by a software fault. However, one fault can cause major problems for thousands and thousands of people. For example, in February 2003, a software fault resulted in the U.S. Treasury Department mailing 50,000 Social Security checks that had been printed without the name of the beneficiary, so the checks could not be deposited or cashed [St. Petersburg Times Online, 2003]. In April 2003, borrowers were informed by SLM Corp. (commonly known as Sallie Mae) that the interest on their student loans had been miscalculated as a consequence of a software fault from 1992 but detected only at the end of 2002. Nearly 1 million borrowers were told that they would have to pay more, either in the form of higher monthly payments or extra interest payments on loans extending beyond their original 10-year terms [GJSentinel.com, 2003]. Both faults were quickly corrected, but together they resulted in nontrivial financial consequences for about a million people.

A failed software project with widespread negative consequences was the Virtual Case File (VCF), developed by the United States Federal Bureau of Investigation (FBI) between 2000 and 2005. When the project was finally abandoned in disarray, $170 million of taxpayers' money had been wasted [Goldstein, 2005]. The FBI has been forced to continue to use its outdated Automated Case Support (ACS) system, hampering its activities.

was endorsed by the 1968 NATO Software Engineering Conference held in Garmisch, Germany [Naur, Randell, and Buxton, 1976]. This endorsement is not too surprising; the very name of the conference reflected the belief that software production should be an engineering-like activity (but see Just in Case You Wanted to Know Box 1.2). A conclusion of the conferees was that software engineering should use the philosophies and paradigms of established engineering disciplines to solve what they termed the **software crisis**, namely, that the quality of software generally was unacceptably low and that deadlines and budgets were not being met.

Despite many software success stories, an unacceptably large proportion of software products still are being delivered late, over budget, and with residual faults. For example, the Standish Group is a research firm that analyzes software development projects. Their

As stated in Section 1.1, the aim of the Garmisch conference was to make software development as successful as traditional engineering. But by no means are all traditional engineering projects successful. For example, consider bridge building.

In July 1940, construction of a suspension bridge over the Tacoma Narrows in Puget Sound, Washington State, was completed. Soon after, it was discovered that the bridge swayed and buckled dangerously in windy conditions. Approaching cars would alternately disappear into valleys and then reappear as that part of the bridge rose again. From this behavior, the bridge was given the nickname "Galloping Gertie." Finally, on November 7, 1940, the bridge collapsed in a 42 mile per hour wind; fortunately, the bridge had been closed to all traffic some hours earlier. The last 15 minutes of its life were captured on film, now stored in the U.S. National Film Registry.

A somewhat more humorous bridge construction failure was observed in January 2004. A new bridge was being built over the Upper Rhine River near the German town of Laufenberg, to connect Germany and Switzerland. The German half of the bridge was designed and constructed by a team of German engineers; the Swiss half by a Swiss team. When the two parts were connected, it immediately became apparent that the Swiss half was some 21 inches (54 centimeters) lower than the German half. Major reconstruction was needed to correct the problem, which was caused by wrongly correcting for the fact that "sea level" is taken by Swiss engineers to be the average level of the Mediterranean Sea, whereas German engineers use the North Sea. To compensate for the difference in sea levels, the Swiss side should have been raised 10.5 inches. Instead, it was lowered 10.5 inches, resulting in the gap of 21 inches [Spiegel Online, 2004].

study of 9236 development projects completed in 2004 is summarized in Figure 1.1 [Hayes, 2004]. Only 29 percent of the projects were successfully completed, whereas 18 percent were canceled before completion or were never implemented. The remaining 53 percent of the projects were completed and installed on the client's computer. However, those projects were over budget, late, or had fewer features and functionality than initially specified. In other words, during 2004, less than one in three software development projects was successful; more than half the projects displayed one or more symptoms of the software crisis.

The financial implications of the software crisis are horrendous. In a survey conducted by the Cutter Consortium [2002], the following was reported:

Figure 1.1
The outcomes of over 9000 development projects completed in 2004.

Source: [Hayes, 2004].

- An astounding 78 percent of information technology organizations have been involved in disputes that ended in litigation.
- In 67 percent of those cases, the functionality or performance of the software products as delivered did not meet up to the claims of the software developers.
- In 56 percent of those cases, the promised delivery date slipped several times.
- In 45 percent of those cases, the faults were so severe that the software product was unusable.

It is clear that far too little software is delivered on time, within budget, fault free, and meeting its client's needs. To achieve these goals, a software engineer has to acquire a broad range of skills, both technical and managerial. These skills have to be applied not just to programming but to every step of software production, from requirements to postdelivery maintenance.

That the software crisis still is with us, some 40 years later, tells us two things. First, the software production process, while resembling traditional engineering in many respects, has its own unique properties and problems. Second, the software crisis perhaps should be renamed the **software depression**, in view of its long duration and poor prognosis.

We now consider economic aspects of software engineering.

1.2   Economic Aspects

A software organization currently using coding technique CT_{old} discovers that new coding technique CT_{new} would result in code being produced in only nine-tenths of the time needed by CT_{old} and, hence, at nine-tenths the cost. Common sense seems to dictate that CT_{new} is the appropriate technique to use. In fact, although common sense certainly dictates that the faster technique is the technique of choice, the economics of software engineering may imply the opposite.

- One reason is the cost of introducing new technology into an organization. The fact that coding is 10 percent faster when technique CT_{new} is used may be less important than the costs incurred in introducing CT_{new} into the organization. It may be necessary to complete two or three major projects before recouping the cost of training. Also, while attending courses on CT_{new}, software personnel are unable to do productive work. Even when they return, a steep learning curve may be involved; it may take many months of practice with CT_{new} before software professionals become as proficient with CT_{new} as they currently are with CT_{old}. Therefore, initial projects using CT_{new} may take far longer to complete than if the organization had continued to use CT_{old}. All these costs need to be taken into account when deciding whether to change to CT_{new}.
- A second reason why the economics of software engineering may dictate that CT_{old} be retained is the maintenance consequence. Coding technique CT_{new} indeed may be 10 percent faster than CT_{old} and the resulting code may be of comparable quality from the viewpoint of satisfying the client's current needs. But the use of technique CT_{new} may result in code that is difficult to maintain, making the cost of CT_{new} higher over the life of the product. Of course, if the software developer is not responsible for any postdelivery maintenance, then, from the viewpoint of just that developer, CT_{new} is a more attractive proposition. After all, the use of CT_{new} would cost 10 percent less. The

client should insist that technique CT_{old} be used and pay the higher initial costs with the expectation that the total lifetime cost of the software will be lower. Unfortunately, often the sole aim of both the client and the software provider is to produce code as quickly as possible. The long-term effects of using a particular technique generally are ignored in the interests of short-term gain. Applying economic principles to software engineering requires the client to choose techniques that reduce long-term costs.

This example deals with coding, which constitutes less than 10 percent of the software development effort. The economic principles, however, apply to all other aspects of software production as well.

We now consider the importance of maintenance.

1.3   Maintenance Aspects

In this section, we describe maintenance within the context of the software life cycle. A *life-cycle model* is a description of the steps that should be performed when building a software product. Many different life-cycle models have been proposed; several of them are described in Chapter 2. Because it is almost always easier to perform a sequence of smaller tasks than one large task, the overall life-cycle model is broken into a series of smaller steps, called *phases*. The number of phases varies from model to model—from as few as four to as many as eight. In contrast to a life-cycle model, which is a theoretical description of what should be done, the actual series of steps performed on a specific software product, from concept exploration through final retirement, is termed the *life cycle* of that product. In practice, the phases of the life cycle of a software product may not be carried out exactly as specified in the life-cycle model, especially when time and cost overruns are encountered. It has been claimed that more software projects have gone wrong from lack of time than for all other reasons combined [Brooks, 1975].

Until the end of the 1970s, most organizations were producing software using as their life-cycle model what now is termed the *waterfall model*. There are many variations of this model, but by and large, a product developed using this life-cycle model goes through the six phases shown in Figure 1.2. These phases probably do not correspond exactly to the phases of any one particular organization, but they are sufficiently close to most practices for the purposes of this book. Similarly, the precise name of each phase varies from organization to organization. The names used here for the various phases have been chosen to be as general as possible in the hope that the reader will feel comfortable with them.

Figure 1.2
The six phases of the waterfall life-cycle model.

1. Requirements phase
2. Analysis (specification) phase
3. Design phase
4. Implementation phase
5. Postdelivery maintenance
6. Retirement

1. *Requirements phase.* During the **requirements phase**, the concept is explored and refined, and the client's requirements are elicited.

2. *Analysis (specification) phase.* The client's requirements are analyzed and presented in the form of the **specification document**, "what the product is supposed to do." The **analysis phase** sometimes is called the **specification phase**. At the end of this phase, a plan is drawn up, the **software project management plan**, describing the proposed software development in full detail.

3. *Design phase.* The specifications undergo two consecutive design processes during the **design phase**. First comes **architectural design**, in which the product as a whole is broken down into components, called **modules**. Then, each module is designed; this process is termed **detailed design**. The two resulting **design documents** describe "how the product does it."

4. *Implementation phase.* The various components undergo **coding** and testing (**unit testing**) separately. Then, the components of the product are combined and tested as a whole; this is termed **integration**. When the developers are satisfied that the product functions correctly, it is tested by the client (**acceptance testing**). The **implementation phase** ends when the product is accepted by the client and installed on the client's computer. (We see in Chapter 13 that coding and integration should be performed in parallel.)

5. Postdelivery maintenance. The product is used to perform the tasks for which it was developed. During this time, it is maintained. **Postdelivery maintenance** includes all changes to the product once the product has been delivered and installed on the client's computer and passes its acceptance test. Postdelivery maintenance includes **corrective maintenance** (or **software repair**), which consists of the removal of residual faults while leaving the specifications unchanged, as well as **enhancement** (or software update), which consists of changes to the specifications and the implementation of those changes. There are, in turn, two types of enhancement. The first is **perfective maintenance**, changes that the client thinks will improve the effectiveness of the product, such as additional functionality or decreased response time. The second is **adaptive maintenance**, changes made in response to changes in the environment in which the product operates, such as a new hardware/operating system or new government regulations. (For an insight into the three types of postdelivery maintenance, see Just in Case You Wanted to Know Box 1.3.)

6. *Retirement.* **Retirement** occurs when the product is removed from service. This occurs when the functionality provided by the product no longer is of any use to the client organization.

Now we examine the definition of *maintenance* in greater detail.

1.3.1   The Modern View of Maintenance

In the 1970s, software production was viewed as consisting of two distinct activities performed sequentially: *development* followed by *maintenance*. Starting from scratch, the software product was developed, and then installed on the client's computer. Any change to

One of the most widely quoted results in software engineering is that 17.4 percent of the postdelivery maintenance effort is corrective in nature; 18.2 percent is adaptive; 60.3 percent is perfective; and 4.1 percent can be categorized as "other." This result is taken from a paper published in 1978 [Lientz, Swanson, and Tompkins, 1978].

However, the result in that paper was not derived from *measurements* on maintenance data. Instead, the authors conducted a survey of maintenance managers who were asked to *estimate* how much time was devoted to each category within their organization as a whole and state how confident they felt about their estimate. More specifically, the participating software maintenance managers were asked whether their response was based on reasonably accurate data, minimal data, or no data; 49.3 percent stated that their answer was based on reasonably accurate data, 37.7 percent on minimal data, and 8.7 percent on no data.

In fact, one should seriously question whether any respondents had "reasonably accurate data" regarding the percentage of time devoted to the categories of maintenance included in the survey; most of them probably did not have even "minimal data." In that survey, participants were asked to state what percentage of maintenance consisted of items like "emergency fixes" or "routine debugging"; from this raw information, the percentage of adaptive, corrective, and perfective maintenance was deduced. Software engineering was just starting to emerge as a discipline in 1978, and it was the exception for software maintenance managers to collect the detailed information needed to respond to such a survey. Indeed, in modern terminology, in 1978 virtually every organization was still at CMM level 1 (see Section 3.13).

Hence, we have strong grounds for questioning whether the actual distribution of postdelivery maintenance activities back in 1978 was anything like the estimates of the managers who took part in the survey. The distribution of maintenance activities is certainly nothing like that today. For example, results on actual maintenance data for the Linux kernel [Schach et al., 2002] and the gcc compiler [Schach et al., 2003b] show that at least 50 percent of postdelivery maintenance is corrective, as opposed to the 17.4 percent figure of the survey.

---

the software after installation on the client's computer and acceptance by the client, whether to fix a residual fault or extend the functionality, constituted maintenance [IEEE 610.12, 1990]. This approach can be described as the ***development-then-maintenance model***.

This was a ***temporal definition***; that is, an activity was classified as development or maintenance depending on when it was performed. Suppose that a fault in the software was detected and corrected a day after the software was installed. By definition, this constituted maintenance. But if the identical fault was detected and corrected the day before the software was installed, in terms of the definition, this constituted development. Now suppose that a software product had just been installed but the client wanted to increase the functionality of the software product. That would be described as "perfective maintenance." However, if the client wanted the same change to be made just before the software product was installed, this would be development. Again, there is no difference whatsoever between the nature of the two activities, but one was considered to be development, the other perfective maintenance.

In addition to such inconsistencies, two other reasons explain why the development-then-maintenance model is unrealistic today:

1. Nowadays, it is certainly not unusual for construction of a product to take a year or more. During this time, the client's requirements may well change. For example, the client might insist that the product now be implemented on a faster microprocessor, which has just become available. Alternatively, the client organization may have expanded into Belgium while development was under way, and the product now has to be modified so it also can handle sales in Belgium. To see how a change in requirements can affect the software life cycle, suppose that the client's requirements change while the design is being developed. The software engineering team has to suspend development and modify the specification document to reflect the changed requirements. Furthermore, it then may be necessary to modify the design as well, if the changes to the specifications necessitate corresponding changes to those portions of the design already completed. Only when these changes have been made can development proceed. In other words, developers have to perform "maintenance" long before the product is installed.

2. A second problem with the development-then-maintenance model arose because, some 30 years ago, a development team built a target product starting from scratch. In contrast, as a consequence of the high cost of software production today, wherever possible developers try to reuse parts of existing software products in the software product to be constructed (reuse is discussed in detail in Chapter 8). Therefore, the development-then-maintenance model is inappropriate today because reuse is so widespread.

A more realistic way of looking at maintenance is that given in the standard for life-cycle processes published by the International Organization for Standardization (ISO) and the International Electrotechnical Commission (IEC). That is, maintenance is the process that occurs when "software undergoes modifications to code and associated documentation due to a problem or the need for improvement or adaptation" [ISO/IEC 12207, 1995]. In terms of this **operational definition**, maintenance occurs whenever a fault is fixed or the requirements change, irrespective of whether this takes place before or after installation of the product. The Institute for Electrical and Electronics Engineers (IEEE) and the Electronic Industries Alliance (EIA) subsequently adopted this definition [IEEE/EIA 12207.0-1996, 1998] when IEEE standards were modified to comply with ISO/IEC 12207. (See Just in Case You Wanted to Know Box 1.4 for more on ISO.)

In this book, the term *postdelivery maintenance* refers to the 1990 IEEE definition of maintenance as any change to the software after it has been delivered and installed on the client's computer, and *modern maintenance* or just **maintenance** refers to the 1995 ISO/IEC definition of corrective, perfective, or adaptive activities performed at any time. Postdelivery maintenance is therefore a subset of (modern) maintenance.

1.3.2   The Importance of Postdelivery Maintenance

It is sometimes said that only bad software products undergo postdelivery maintenance. In fact, the opposite is true: Bad products are thrown away, whereas good products are repaired and enhanced, for 10, 15, or even 20 years. Furthermore, a software product is a model of the real world, and the real world is perpetually changing. As a consequence, software has to be maintained constantly for it to remain an accurate reflection of the real world.

The International Organization for Standardization (ISO) is a network of the national standards institutes of 147 countries, with a central secretariat based in Geneva, Switzerland. ISO has published over 13,500 internationally accepted standards, ranging from standards for photographic film speed ("ISO number") to many of the standards presented in this book. For example, ISO 9000 is discussed in Chapter 3.

ISO is not an acronym. It is derived from the Greek word ισος, meaning "equal," the root of the English prefix iso- found in words such as *isotope, isobar,* and *isosceles*. The International Organization for Standardization chose ISO as the short form of its name to avoid having multiple acronyms arising from the translation of the name "International Organization for Standardization" into the languages of the different member countries. Instead, to achieve international standardization, a universal short form of its name was chosen.

For instance, if the sales tax rate changes from 6 to 7 percent, almost every software product that deals with buying or selling has to be changed. Suppose the product contains the C++ statement

const float SALES_TAX = 6.0;

or the equivalent Java statement

public static final float SALES_TAX = **(float)** 6.0;

declaring that SALES_TAX[1] is a floating-point constant initialized to the value **6.0**. In this case, maintenance is relatively simple. With the aid of a text editor the value **6.0** is replaced by **7.0** and the code is recompiled and relinked. However, if instead of using the name SALES_TAX, the actual value **6.0** has been used in the product wherever the value of the sales tax is invoked, then such a product is extremely difficult to modify. For example, there may be occurrences of the value **6.0** in the source code that should be changed to **7.0** but are overlooked or instances of **6.0** that do not refer to sales tax but incorrectly are changed to **7.0**. Finding these faults almost always is difficult and time consuming. In fact, with some software, it might be less expensive in the long run to throw away the product and recode it rather than try to determine which of the many constants need to be changed and how to make the modifications.

The real-time real world also is constantly changing. The missiles with which a jet fighter is armed may be replaced by a new model, requiring a change to the weapons control component of the associated avionics system. A six-cylinder engine is to be offered as an option in a popular four-cylinder automobile; this implies changing the onboard computers that control the fuel injection system, timing, and so on.

But just how much time (= money) is devoted to postdelivery maintenance? The pie chart in Figure 1.3(a) shows that, some 30 years ago, approximately two-thirds of total software costs went to postdelivery maintenance; the data were obtained by averaging information from various sources, including [Elshoff, 1976; Daly, 1977; Zelkowitz, Shaw, and Gannon, 1979; and Boehm, 1981]. Later data show that an even larger proportion is devoted to postdelivery maintenance. Many organizations devote 70–80 percent or more of their software budget to postdelivery maintenance [Yourdon, 1992; Hatton, 1998], as shown in Figure 1.3(b).

---

[1] A common convention in object-oriented programming languages like C++ and Java is for names of constants to be in uppercase letters, with component words separated by underscores.

Figure 1.3
Approximate average cost percentages of development and postdelivery maintenance (a) between 1976 and 1981 and (b) between 1992 and 1998.

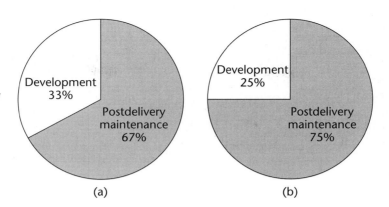

(a)   (b)

Now consider again the software organization currently using coding technique CT_{old} that learns that CT_{new} will reduce coding time by 10 percent. Even if CT_{new} has no adverse effect on maintenance, an astute software manager will think twice before changing coding practices. The entire staff has to be retrained, new software development tools purchased, and perhaps additional staff members hired who are experienced in the new technique. However, coding together with unit testing consumes on average only 34 percent of development costs [Grady, 1994], and development costs (as shown in Figure 1.3(b)) constitute only 25 percent of the total software costs. So, all this expense and disruption has to be endured for a decrease of at most 10 percent of 34 percent of 25 percent or 0.85 percent of total software costs.

Now suppose a new technique that reduces postdelivery maintenance costs by 10 percent is developed. This probably should be introduced at once, because on average, it will reduce overall costs by 7.5 percent. The overhead involved in changing to this technique is a small price to pay for such large overall savings.

Because postdelivery maintenance is so important, a major aspect of software engineering consists of those techniques, tools, and practices that lead to a reduction in postdelivery maintenance costs.

1.4   Requirements, Analysis, and Design Aspects

Software professionals are human and therefore sometimes make a mistake while developing a product. As a result, there will be a fault in the software. If the mistake is made while eliciting the requirements, the resulting fault will probably also appear in the specifications, the design, and the code. Clearly, the earlier we correct a fault, the better.

The relative costs of fixing a fault at various phases in the software life cycle are shown in Figure 1.4 [Boehm, 1981]. The figure reflects data from IBM [Fagan, 1974], GTE [Daly, 1977], the Safeguard project [Stephenson, 1976], and some smaller TRW projects [Boehm, 1980]. The solid line in Figure 1.4 is the best fit for the data relating to the larger projects, and the dashed line is the best fit for the smaller projects. For each of the phases of the software life cycle, the corresponding relative cost to detect and correct a fault is depicted in Figure 1.5. Each step on the solid line in Figure 1.5 is constructed by taking the corresponding point on the solid straight line of Figure 1.4 and plotting the data on a linear scale.

Figure 1.4
The relative cost of fixing a fault at each phase of the software life cycle. The solid line is the best fit for the data relating to the larger software projects, and the dashed line is the best fit for the smaller software projects.

Source: Barry Boehm, Software Engineering Economics, © 1981, p. 40. Adapted by permission of Prentice Hall, Inc., Englewood Cliffs, NJ.

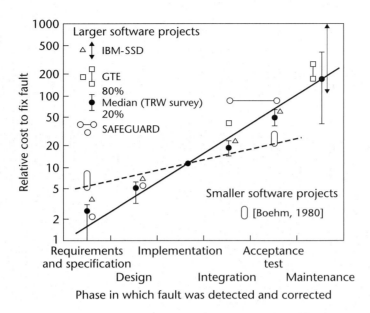

Suppose it costs $40 to detect and correct a specific fault during the design phase. From the solid line in Figure 1.5 (projects between 1974 and 1980), that same fault would cost only about $30 to fix during the analysis phase. But, during postdelivery maintenance, that fault would cost around $2000 to detect and correct. Newer data show that now it is even more important to detect faults early. The dashed line in Figure 1.5 shows the cost of detecting and correcting a fault during the development of system software for the IBM AS/400 [Kan et al., 1994]. On average, the same fault would have cost $3680 to fix during postdelivery maintenance of the AS/400 software.

The reason that the cost of correcting a fault increases so steeply is related to what has to be done to correct a fault. Early in the development life cycle, the product essentially exists only on paper, and correcting a fault may simply mean making a change to a document. The other extreme is a product already delivered to a client. At the very least, correcting a fault at that time means editing the code, recompiling and relinking it, and then carefully testing that the problem is solved. Next, it is critical to check that making the change has not created a new problem elsewhere in the product. All the relevant documentation, including manuals, needs to be updated. Finally, the corrected product must be delivered and reinstalled. The moral of the story is this: We must find faults early or else it will cost us money. We therefore should employ techniques for detecting faults during the requirements and analysis (specification) phases.

There is a further need for such techniques. Studies have shown [Boehm, 1979] that between 60 and 70 percent of all faults detected in large projects are requirements, analysis, or design faults. Newer results from inspections bear out this preponderance of requirements, analysis, or design faults (an inspection is a meticulous examination of a document by a team, as described in Section 6.2.3). During 203 inspections of Jet Propulsion Laboratory software for the NASA unmanned interplanetary space program, on average, about 1.9

Figure 1.5
The solid line depicts the points on the solid line of Figure 1.4 plotted on a linear scale. The dashed line depicts newer data.

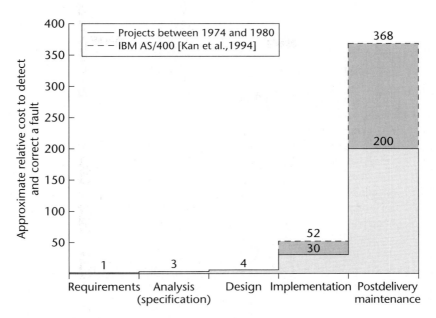

faults were detected per page of a specification document, 0.9 faults per page of a design, but only 0.3 faults per page of code [Kelly, Sherif, and Hops, 1992].

Therefore it is important that we improve our requirements, analysis, and design techniques, not only so that faults can be found as early as possible but also because requirements, analysis, and design faults constitute such a large proportion of all faults. Just as the example in Section 1.3 showed that reducing postdelivery maintenance costs by 10 percent reduces overall costs by about 7.5 percent, reducing requirements, analysis, and design faults by 10 percent reduces the overall number of faults by 6–7 percent.

That so many faults are introduced early in the software life cycle highlights another important aspect of software engineering: techniques that yield better requirements, specifications, and designs. Most software is produced by a team of software engineers rather than by a single individual responsible for every aspect of the development and maintenance life cycle. We now consider the implications of this.

1.5   Team Development Aspects

The cost of hardware continues to decrease rapidly. A mainframe computer of the 1950s that cost in excess of a million preinflation dollars was considerably less powerful in every way than a laptop computer of today costing less than $1000. As a result, organizations easily can afford hardware that can run large products, that is, products too large to be written by one person within the allowed time constraints. For example, if a product has to be delivered within 18 months but would take a single software professional 15 years to complete, then the product must be developed by a team. However, team development leads to interfacing problems among code components and communication problems among team members.

For example, Jeff and Juliet code methods p and q, respectively, where method p calls method q. When Jeff codes p, he writes a call to q with five arguments in the argument list. Juliet codes q with five arguments, but in a different order from those of Jeff. Some software tools, such as the Java interpreter and loader, detect such a type violation but only if the interchanged arguments are of different types; if they are of the same type, then the problem may not be detected for a long period of time. It may be debated that this is a design problem, and if the methods had been more carefully designed, this problem would not have happened. That may be true, but in practice a design often is changed after coding commences, but notification of a change may not be distributed to all members of the development team. Therefore, when a design that affects two or more programmers has been changed, poor communication can lead to the interface problems Jeff and Juliet experienced. This sort of problem is less likely to occur when only one individual is responsible for every aspect of the product, as was the case before powerful computers that can run huge products became affordable.

But interfacing problems are merely the tip of the iceberg when it comes to problems that can arise when software is developed by teams. Unless the team is properly organized, an inordinate amount of time can be wasted in conferences between team members. Suppose that a product takes a single programmer 1 year to complete. If the same task is assigned to a team of six programmers, the time for completing the task frequently is closer to 1 year than the expected 2 months, and the quality of the resulting code may well be lower than if the entire task had been assigned to one individual (see Section 4.1). Because a considerable proportion of today's software is developed and maintained by teams, the scope of software engineering must include techniques for ensuring that teams are properly organized and managed.

As has been shown in the preceding sections, the scope of software engineering is extremely broad. It includes every step of the software life cycle, from requirements to postdelivery retirement. It also includes human aspects, such as team organization; economic aspects; and legal aspects, such as copyright law. All these aspects implicitly are incorporated in the definition of software engineering given at the beginning of this chapter, that software engineering is a discipline whose aim is the production of fault-free software delivered on time, within budget, and satisfying the user's needs.

We return to the waterfall phases of Figure 1.2 to ask why there is no planning, testing, or documentation phase.

1.6   Why There Is No Planning Phase

Clearly it is impossible to develop a software product without a plan. Accordingly, it appears to be essential to have a ***planning phase*** at the very beginning of the project.

The key point is that, until it is known exactly what is to be developed, there is no way an accurate detailed plan can be drawn up. Therefore, three types of planning activities take place when a software product is developed using the waterfall model:

1. At the beginning of the project, preliminary planning takes place for managing the requirements and analysis phases.

2. Once what is going to be developed is known precisely, the *software project management plan* (SPMP) is drawn up. This includes the budget, staffing requirements,

and detailed schedule. The earliest we can draw up the project management plan is when the specification document has been approved by the client, that is, at the end of the analysis phase. Until that time, planning has to be preliminary and partial.

3. All through the project, management needs to monitor the SPMP and be on the watch for any deviation from the plan.

For example, suppose that the SPMP for a specific project states the project as a whole will take 16 months and that the design phase will take 4 of those months. After a year, management notices that the project as a whole seems to be progressing considerably slower than anticipated. A detailed investigation shows that, so far, 8 months have been devoted to the design, which is still far from complete. The project almost certainly will have to be abandoned, and the funds spent to date are wasted. Instead, management should have tracked progress by phase, and noticed, after at most 2 months, a serious problem in the design. At that time, a decision could have been made how best to proceed. The usual initial step in such a situation is to call in a consultant to determine if the project is feasible and whether the design team is competent to carry out the task or the risk of proceeding is too great. Based on the report of the consultant, various alternatives are now considered, including reducing the scope of the target product and then designing and implementing a less ambitious one. Only if all other alternatives are considered unworkable does the project have to be canceled. In the case of the specific project, this cancellation would have taken place some 6 months earlier if management had monitored the plan closely, saving a considerable sum of money.

In conclusion, there is no separate planning phase. Instead, planning activities are carried out all through the life cycle. However, there are times when planning activities predominate. These include the beginning of the project (preliminary planning) and directly after the specification document has been signed off on by the client (software project management plan).

1.7   Why There Is No Testing Phase

It is essential to check a software product meticulously after it has been developed. Accordingly, it is reasonable to ask why there is no testing phase after the product has been implemented.

Unfortunately, checking a software product once it is ready to be delivered to the client is far too late. For instance, if there is a fault in the specification document, this fault will have been carried forward into the design and implementation. There are times in the process when testing is carried out almost to the total exclusion of other activities. This occurs toward the end of each phase (**verification**) and is especially true before the product is handed over to the client (**validation**). Although there are times when testing predominates, there should never be times when no testing is being performed. If testing is treated as a separate **testing phase**, then there is a very real danger that testing will not be carried out constantly throughout every phase of the product development and maintenance process.

But, even this is not enough. What is needed is continual checking of a software product. Meticulous checking should be an automatic accompaniment of every software development and maintenance activity. Conversely, a separate testing phase is incompatible with the goal of ensuring that a software product is as fault free as possible at all times.

Every software development organization should contain an independent group whose primary responsibility is to ensure that the delivered product is what the client needs and that the product has been built correctly in every way. This group is called the *software quality assurance* (SQA) group. The **quality** of software is the extent to which it meets its specifications. Quality and software quality assurance are described in more detail in Chapter 6, as is the role of SQA in setting and enforcing standards.

1.8   Why There Is No Documentation Phase

Just as there should never be a separate planning phase or testing phase, there also should never be a separate **documentation phase**. On the contrary, at all times, the documentation of a software product must be complete, correct, and up to date. For instance, during the analysis phase, the specification document must reflect the current version of the specifications and similarly for the other phases.

1. One reason why it is essential to ensure that the documentation is always up to date is the large turnover in personnel in the software industry. For example, suppose that the design documentation has not been kept current and the chief designer leaves to take another job. It is now extremely hard to update the design document to reflect all the changes made while the system was being designed.

2. It is almost impossible to perform the steps of a specific phase unless the documentation of the previous phase is complete, correct, and up to date. For instance, an incomplete specification document must inevitably result in an incomplete design and then in an incomplete implementation.

3. It is virtually impossible to test whether a software product is working correctly unless documents are available that state how that software product is supposed to behave.

4. Maintenance is almost impossible unless there is a complete and correct set of documentation that describes precisely what the current version of the product does.

Therefore, just as there is no separate planning phase or testing phase, there is no separate documentation phase. Instead, planning, testing, and documentation should be activities that accompany all other activities while a software product is being constructed.

Now we examine the object-oriented paradigm.

1.9   The Object-Oriented Paradigm

Before 1975, most software organizations used no specific techniques; each individual worked his or her own way. Major breakthroughs were made between approximately 1975 and 1985, with the development of the so-called **structured** or **classical paradigm**. The techniques constituting the classical paradigm include structured systems analysis [Gane and Sarsen, 1979], structured programming, and structured testing (Section 13.12.2). These techniques seemed extremely promising when first used. However, as time passed, they proved to be somewhat less successful in two respects:

1. The techniques sometimes were unable to cope with the increasing size of software products. That is, the classical techniques were adequate when dealing with small-scale products (typically 5000 lines of code) or even medium-scale products of 50,000 lines of code. Today, however, large-scale products of 500,000 lines of code are relatively common; even products of 5 million or more lines of code are not considered unusual. However, the classical techniques frequently could not scale up sufficiently to handle the development of today's larger products.

2. The classical paradigm did not live up to earlier expectations during postdelivery maintenance. A major driving force behind the development of the classical paradigm 30 years ago was that, on average, two-thirds of the software budget was being devoted to postdelivery maintenance (see Figure 1.3(a)). Unfortunately, the classical paradigm has not solved this problem; as pointed out in Section 1.3.2, many organizations still spend 70–80 percent or more of their time and effort on postdelivery maintenance [Yourdon, 1992; Hatton, 1998].

A major reason for the limited success of the classical paradigm is that classical techniques are either operation oriented or attribute (data) oriented but not both. In contrast, the **object-oriented paradigm** considers both attributes and operations to be equally important. A simplistic way of looking at an object is as a unified software artifact that incorporates both the attributes and the operations performed on the attributes (an **artifact** is a component of a software product, such as a specification document, a code module, or a manual). This definition of an object is incomplete and is fleshed out later in the book, once *inheritance* has been considered in detail (Section 7.8). Nevertheless, the definition captures much of the essence of an object.

The object-oriented paradigm has many strengths:

1. The object-oriented paradigm supports information hiding, a mechanism for ensuring that implementation details are local to an object (see Section 7.6 for more details). Consequently, if during maintenance implementation details are changed within an object, information hiding ensures that no other parts of the product need to be modified to ensure consistency. Accordingly, the object-oriented paradigm makes maintenance quicker and easier, and the chance of introducing a **regression fault** (that is, a fault inadvertently introduced into one part of a product as a consequence of making an apparently unrelated change to another part of the product) is greatly reduced.

2. In addition to maintenance, the object-oriented paradigm also makes development easier. In many instances, an object has a physical counterpart. For example, a bank account object in a bank product corresponds to an actual bank account in the bank for which the product is being written. As will be shown in Part 2, modeling plays a major role in the object-oriented paradigm. The close correspondence between the objects in a product and their counterparts in the real world should lead to better-quality software.

3. Well-designed objects are independent units. As stated at the beginning of this section, an object encompasses both attributes and the operations performed on the attributes. If all the operations performed on the attributes of an object are included in that object, then the object can be considered a conceptually independent entity. Everything in the product that relates to the portion of the real

world modeled by that object can be found in the object itself. This conceptual independence sometimes is termed **encapsulation** (Section 7.4). But there is an additional form of independence, physical independence. In a well-designed object, information hiding ensures that implementation details are hidden from everything outside that object. The only allowable form of communication is sending a message to the object to carry out a specific operation. The way that the operation is carried out is entirely the responsibility of the object itself. For this reason, object-oriented design sometimes is referred to as **responsibility-driven design** [Wirfs-Brock, Wilkerson, and Wiener, 1990] or **design by contract** [Meyer, 1992]. (For another view of responsibility-driven design, see Just in Case You Wanted to Know Box 1.5, derived from an example in [Budd, 2002].)

4. A product built using the classical paradigm is implemented as a set of modules, but conceptually it is essentially a single unit. This is one reason why the classical paradigm has been less successful when applied to larger products. In contrast, when the object-oriented paradigm is used correctly, the resulting product consists of a number of smaller, largely independent units. The object-oriented paradigm reduces the level of complexity of a software product and hence simplifies both development and maintenance.

5. The object-oriented paradigm promotes reuse; because objects are independent entities, they can be utilized in future products. This reuse of objects reduces the time and cost of both development and maintenance, as explained in Chapter 8.

However, the object-oriented paradigm is by no means a panacea of all ills:

1. Like all approaches to software production, the object-oriented paradigm has to be used correctly; it is just as easy to misuse the object-oriented paradigm as any other paradigm.

2. When correctly applied, the object-oriented paradigm can solve some (but not all) of the problems of the classical paradigm.

3. The object-oriented paradigm has some problems of its own, as described in Section 7.9.

4. The object-oriented paradigm is the best approach available today. However, like all technologies, it is certain to be superseded by a superior technology in the future.

Throughout this book, strengths and weaknesses of the object-oriented paradigm are pointed out within the context of the specific topic under discussion. That is, material analyzing the object-oriented paradigm does not appear in one single place but rather is spread over the entire book.

We now define a number of software engineering terms.

1.10 Terminology

The **client** is the individual who wants a product to be built (developed). The **developers** are the members of a team responsible for building that product. The developers may be responsible for every aspect of the process, from the requirements onward, or they may be responsible for only the implementation of an already designed product.

Both the client and developers may be part of the same organization. For example, the client may be the head actuary of an insurance company and the developers a team headed by the vice-president for software development of that insurance company. This

Suppose that you live in New Orleans, and you want to send a Mother's Day bouquet to your mother in Chicago. One strategy would be to consult the Chicago yellow pages (on the World Wide Web), determine which florist is located closest to your mother's apartment, and place your order with that florist. A more convenient way is to order the flowers at 1-800-flowers.com, leaving the total responsibility for delivering the flowers to that company. It is irrelevant where 1-800-flowers.com is physically located or which florist is given your order to deliver. In any event, the company does not divulge that information, an instance of information hiding.

In exactly the same way, when a message is sent to an object, not only is it entirely irrelevant how the request is carried out, but the unit that sends the message is not even allowed to know the internal structure of the object. The object itself is entirely responsible for every detail of carrying out the message.

---

is termed **internal software development**. On the other hand, with **contract software** the client and developers are members of totally independent organizations. For instance, the client may be a senior official in the Department of Defense and the developers employees of a major defense contractor specializing in software for weapons systems. On a much smaller scale, the client may be an accountant in a one-person practice and the developer a student who earns income by writing software on a part-time basis.

The third party involved in software production is the **user**. The user is the person or persons on whose behalf the client has commissioned the product and who will utilize the software. In the insurance company example, the users may be insurance agents, who will use the software to select the most appropriate policy. In some instances, the client and the user are the same person (for example, the accountant discussed previously).

As opposed to expensive custom software written for one client, multiple copies of software, such as word processors or spreadsheets, are sold at much lower prices to a large numbers of buyers. That is, the manufacturers of such software (such as Microsoft or Borland) recover the cost of developing a product by volume selling. This type of software usually is called **commercial off-the-shelf (COTS) software**. The earlier term for this type of software was **shrink-wrapped software**, because the box containing the CD or diskettes, the manuals, and the license agreement almost always was shrink-wrapped. Nowadays, COTS software often is downloaded over the World Wide Web—there is no box to shrink-wrap. For this reason, COTS software nowadays sometimes is referred to as **clickware**. COTS software is developed for "the market"; that is, there are no specific clients or users until the software has been developed and is available for purchase.

Open-source software is becoming extremely popular. An open-source software product is developed and maintained by a team of volunteers and may be downloaded and used free of charge by anyone. Widely used open-source products include the Linux operating system, the Firefox Web browser, and the Apache Web server. The term open source refers to the availability of the source code to all, unlike most commercial products where only the executable version is sold. Because any user of an open-source product can scrutinize the source code and report faults to the developers, many open-source software products are of high quality. The expected consequence of the public nature of faults in open-source software was formalized by Raymond in *The Cathedral and the Bazaar* as *Linus's Law*, named after Linus Torvalds, the creator of Linux [Raymond, 2000]. **Linus's Law** states that "given enough eyeballs, all bugs are shallow." In other words, if enough individuals scrutinize the source code of an open-source software product, someone should be able to locate that fault and suggest how to fix it. A related principle is "Release early. Release often" [Raymond, 2000]. That is, open-source developers tend to spend less time on testing than closed-source developers, preferring to release a new version of a product virtually as soon as it is finished, leaving much of the responsibility for testing to users.

A word used on almost every page of this book is **software**. Software consists of not just code in machine-readable form but also all the documentation that is an intrinsic component of every project. Software includes the specification document, the design document, legal and accounting documents of all kinds, the software project management plan, and other management documents as well as all types of manuals.

Since the 1970s, the difference between a **program** and a **system** has become blurred. In the "good old days," the distinction was clear. A program was an autonomous piece of code, generally in the form of a deck of punched cards that could be executed. A system was a related collection of programs. A system might consist of programs P, Q, R, and S. Magnetic tape T1 was mounted, and then program P was run. It caused a deck of data cards to be read in and produced as output tapes T2 and T3. Tape T2 then was rewound, and program Q was run, producing tape T4 as output. Program R now merged tapes T3 and T4 into tape T5; T5 served as input for program S, which printed a series of reports.

Compare that situation with a product, running on a machine with a front-end communications processor and a back-end database manager, that performs real-time control of a steel mill. The single piece of software controlling the steel mill does far more than the old-fashioned system, but in terms of the traditional definitions of program and system, this software undoubtedly is a program. To add to the confusion, the term *system* now is also used to denote the hardware–software combination. For example, the flight control system in an aircraft consists of both the in-flight computers and the software running on them. Depending on who is using the term, the flight control system also may include the controls, such as the joystick, that send commands to the computer and the parts of the aircraft, such as the wing flaps, controlled by the computer. Furthermore, within the context of traditional software development, the term **systems analysis** refers to the first two phases (requirements and analysis phases) and **systems design** refers to the third phase (design phase).

To minimize confusion, this book uses the term **product** to denote a nontrivial piece of software. There are two reasons for this convention. The first is simply to obviate the program versus system confusion by using a third term. The second reason is more important. This book deals with the **process** of software production, and the end result of a process is termed a *product*. Finally, the term *system* is used in its modern sense, that is, the combined hardware and software, or as part of universally accepted phrases, such as operating system and management information system.

Two words widely used within the context of software engineering are *methodology* and *paradigm*. In the 1970s, the word **methodology** began to be used in the sense of "a way of developing a software product"; the word actually means the "science of methods."

Then, in the 1980s, the word ***paradigm*** became a major buzzword of the business world, as in the phrase, "It's a whole new paradigm." The software industry soon started using the word *paradigm* in phrases like object-oriented paradigm and classical (or structured) paradigm to mean "a style of software development." This was another unfortunate choice of terminology, because a paradigm is a model or a pattern. Erudite readers offended by this corruption of the English language are warmly invited to take up the cudgels of linguistic accuracy on the author's behalf; he is tired of tilting at windmills.

A methodology or a paradigm applies to the process as a whole. In contrast, a ***technique*** is applicable to a portion of the software process. Examples include coding techniques, documentation techniques, and planning techniques.

When a programmer makes a ***mistake***, the consequence of that mistake is a ***fault*** in the code. Executing the software product then results in a ***failure***, that is, the observed incorrect behavior of the product as a consequence of the fault. An ***error*** is the amount by which a result is incorrect. The terms *mistake*, *fault*, *failure*, and *error* are defined in IEEE Standard 610.12, "A Glossary of Software Engineering Terminology" [IEEE 610.12, 1990], reaffirmed in 2002 [IEEE Standards, 2003]. The word ***defect*** is a generic term that refers to a fault, failure, or error. In the interests of precision, in this book we therefore minimize use of the umbrella term *defect*.

One term that is avoided as far as possible is ***bug*** (the history of this word is in Just in Case You Wanted to Know Box 1.6). The term *bug* nowadays is simply a euphemism for a *fault*. Although there generally is no real harm in using euphemisms, the word bug has overtones that are not conducive to good software production. Specifically, instead of saying, "I made a mistake," a programmer will say, "A bug crept into the code" (not *my* code but *the* code), thereby transferring responsibility for the mistake from the programmer to the bug. No one blames a programmer for coming down with a case of influenza, because the flu is caused by the flu bug. Referring to a mistake as a bug is a way of casting off responsibility. In contrast, the programmer who says, "I made a mistake," is a computer professional who takes responsibility for his or her actions.

Considerable confusion surrounds object-oriented terminology. For example, in addition to the term ***attribute*** for a data component of an object, the term ***state variable*** sometimes is used in the object-oriented literature. In Java, the term is ***instance variable***. In C++ the term ***field*** is used, and in Visual Basic .NET, the term is ***property***. With regard to the implementation of the operations of an object, the term *method* usually is used; in C++, however, the term is ***member function***. In C++, a ***member*** of an object refers to either an attribute ("field") or a method. In Java, the term *field* is used to denote either an attribute ("instance variable") or a method. To avoid confusion, wherever possible, the generic terms *attribute* and *method* are used in this book.

Fortunately, some terminology is widely accepted. For example, when a method within an object is invoked, this almost universally is termed ***sending a message*** to the object.

Finally, we define the topic of this book. At the beginning of this chapter, we defined software engineering as "a discipline whose aim is the production of fault-free software, delivered on time and within budget, that satisfies the client's needs. Furthermore, the software must be easy to modify when the user's needs change." ***Object-oriented software engineering*** is a discipline that utilizes the object-oriented paradigm to achieve the aims of software engineering.

The first use of the word *bug* to denote a fault is attributed to computer pioneer Rear Admiral Grace Murray Hopper (1906–92). On September 9, 1945, a moth flew into the Mark II computer that Hopper and her colleagues used at Harvard and lodged between the contact plates of a relay. Consequently, there was actually a bug in the system. Hopper taped the bug to the log book and wrote, "First actual case of bug being found." The log book, with moth still attached, is in the Naval Museum at the Naval Surface Weapons Center, in Dahlgren, Virginia.

Although this may have been the first use of *bug* in a computer context, the word was used in engineering slang in the 19th century [Shapiro, 1994]. For example, Thomas Alva Edison wrote on November 18, 1878, "This thing gives out and then that—'Bugs'—as such little faults and difficulties are called ..." [Josephson, 1992]. One of the definitions of *bug* in the 1934 Edition of *Webster's New English Dictionary* is, "A defect in apparatus or its operation." It is clear from Hopper's remark that she, too, was familiar with the use of the word in that context; otherwise, she would have explained what she meant.

1.11   Ethical Issues

We conclude this chapter on a cautionary note. Software products are developed and maintained by humans. If those individuals are hard working, intelligent, sensible, up to date, and above all, *ethical*, then the chances are good that the way that the software products they develop and maintain will be satisfactory. Unfortunately, the converse is equally true.

Most societies for professionals have a code of **ethics** to which all its members must adhere. The two major societies for computer professionals, the Association for Computing Machinery (ACM) and the Computer Society of the Institute of Electrical and Electronics Engineers (IEEE-CS) jointly approved a Software Engineering Code of Ethics and Professional Practice as the standard for teaching and practicing software engineering [IEEE/ACM, 1999]. It is lengthy, so a short version, consisting of a preamble and eight principles, was also produced. Here is the short version:

Software Engineering Code of Ethics and Professional Practice[2] (Version 5.2)
as recommended by the IEEE-CS/ACM Joint Task Force on
Software Engineering Ethics and Professional Practices
Short Version
Preamble

The short version of the code summarizes aspirations at a high level of abstraction; the clauses that are included in the full version give examples and details of how these aspirations change the way we act as software engineering professionals. Without the aspirations, the details can become legalistic and tedious; without the details, the aspirations can become high sounding but empty; together, the aspirations and the details form a cohesive code.

Software engineers shall commit themselves to making the analysis, specification, design, development, testing and maintenance of software a beneficial and respected profession. In accordance with their commitment to the health, safety, and welfare of the public, software engineers shall adhere to the following Eight Principles:

[2] © 1999 by the Institute of Electrical and Electronics Engineers, Inc., and the Association for Computing Machinery, Inc.

1. *Public*—Software engineers shall act consistently with the public interest.
2. *Client and Employer*—Software engineers shall act in a manner that is in the best interests of their client and employer consistent with the public interest.
3. *Product*—Software engineers shall ensure that their products and related modifications meet the highest professional standards possible.
4. *Judgment*—Software engineers shall maintain integrity and independence in their professional judgment.
5. *Management*—Software engineering managers and leaders shall subscribe to and promote an ethical approach to the management of software development and maintenance.
6. *Profession*—Software engineers shall advance the integrity and reputation of the profession consistent with the public interest.
7. *Colleagues*—Software engineers shall be fair to and supportive of their colleagues.
8. *Self*—Software engineers shall participate in lifelong learning regarding the practice of their profession and shall promote an ethical approach to the practice of the profession.

The codes of ethics of other societies for computer professionals express similar sentiments. It is vital for the future of our profession that we adhere rigorously to such codes of ethics.

In Chapter 2, we examine various life-cycle models that are relevant to the object-oriented paradigm.

Chapter Review

Software engineering is defined (Section 1.1) as a discipline whose aim is the production of fault-free software that satisfies the user's needs and is delivered on time and within budget. To achieve this goal, appropriate techniques have to be used throughout software production, including when performing analysis (specification) and design (Section 1.4) and postdelivery maintenance (Section 1.3). Software engineering addresses all the steps of the software life cycle and incorporates aspects of many different areas of human knowledge, including economics (Section 1.2) and the social sciences (Section 1.5). There is no separate planning phase (Section 1.6), no testing phase (Section 1.7), and no documentation phase (Section 1.8). The object-oriented paradigm is discussed in Section 1.9. Next, in Section 1.10, the terminology used in this book is explained. Finally, ethical issues are discussed in Section 1.11.

For Further Reading

The earliest source of information on the scope of software engineering is [Boehm, 1976]. For an analysis of the extent to which software engineering can be considered to be a true engineering discipline, see [Wasserman, 1996] and [Ebert, Matsubara, Pezzé, and Bertelsen, 1997]. The future of software engineering is discussed in [Brereton et al., 1999; Kroeker et al., 1999; and Finkelstein, 2000]. The current state of the practice of software engineering is described in a variety of articles in the November/December 2003 issue of *IEEE Software*.

For a view on the importance of postdelivery maintenance in software engineering and how to plan for it, see [Parnas, 1994]. The unreliability of software and the resulting risks (especially in safety-critical systems) are discussed in [Mellor, 1994] and [Neumann, 1995]. Software development for COTS-based products is the subject of [Brownsword, Oberndorf, and Sledge, 2000]. Acquiring COTS components is described in [Ulkuniemi and Seppanen, 2004] and in [Keil and Tiwana, 2005].

Risks in enterprise systems are described in [Scott and Vessey, 2002] and in information systems in general in [Longstaff, Chittister, Pethia, and Haimes, 2000]. A modern view of the software crisis appears in [Glass, 1998]. Zvegintzov [1998] explains just how little accurate data on software engineering practice actually are available.

The fact that mathematics underpins software engineering is stressed in [Devlin, 2001]. The importance of economics in software engineering is discussed in [Boehm, 1981; Baetjer, 1996; and Boehm and Huang, 2003]. The November/December 2002 issue of *IEEE Software* contains a number of articles on software engineering economics.

Two standard works on the social sciences and software engineering are [Weinberg, 1971] and [Shneiderman, 1980]. Neither book requires prior knowledge of psychology or the behavioral sciences in general. A newer book on the topic is [DeMarco and Lister, 1987].

Brooks's [1975] timeless work, *The Mythical Man-Month*, is a highly recommended introduction to the realities of software engineering. The book includes sections on all the topics mentioned in this chapter.

An excellent introduction to open-source software is [Raymond, 2000]. Paulsen, Succi, and Eberlein [2004] present an empirical study comparing open- and closed-source software products. Reuse of open-source components is described in [Madanmohan and De', 2004]. A variety of articles on open-source software appears in the January/February 2004 issue of *IEEE Software* and in issue No. 2, 2005, of *IBM Systems Journal*.

Excellent introductions to the object-oriented paradigm include [Meyer, 1997] and [Budd, 2002]. A balanced perspective of the paradigm is given in [Radin, 1996]. Khan, Al-A'ali, and Girgis [1995] explain the differences between the classical and object-oriented paradigms. Three successful projects carried out using the object-oriented paradigm are described in [Capper, Colgate, Hunter, and James, 1994], with a detailed analysis. A survey of the attitudes of 150 experienced software developers toward the object-oriented paradigm is reported in [Johnson, 2000]. Lessons learned from developing large-scale object-oriented products are presented in [Maring, 1996] and [Fichman and Kemerer, 1997]. Potential pitfalls of the object-oriented paradigm are described in [Webster, 1995].

Key Terms

acceptance testing 9
adaptive maintenance 9
analysis phase 9
architectural design 9
artifact 19
attribute 23
bug 23
classical paradigm 18
clickware 21
client 20
coding 9
commercial-off-the-shelf
   (COTS) software 21
contract software 21
corrective maintenance 9
defect 23
design by contract 20

design document 9
design phase 9
detailed design 9
developer 20
development-then-
   maintenance model 10
documentation phase 18
encapsulation 20
enhancement 9
error 23
ethics 24
failure 23
fault 23
field 23
implementation phase 9
instance variable 23
integration 9

internal software
   development 21
life cycle 8
life-cycle model 8
Linus's Law 22
maintenance 11
member 23
member function 23
methodology 22
mistake 23
module 9
object-oriented
   paradigm 19
object-oriented software
   engineering 23
open-source software 21

operational definition
   (of maintenance) 11
paradigm 23
perfective maintenance 9
phase 8
planning phase 16
postdelivery
   maintenance 9
process 22
product 22
program 22
property 23
quality 18
regression fault 19
requirements phase 9

responsibility-driven
   design 20
retirement 9
sending a message 23
shrink-wrapped
   software 21
software 22
software crisis 5
software depression 7
software engineering 4
software project
   management plan 9
software repair 9
specification document 9
specification phase 9

state variable 23
structured paradigm 18
system 22
systems analysis 22
systems design 22
technique 23
temporal definition
   (of maintenance) 10
testing phase 17
unit testing 9
user 21
validation 17
verification 17
waterfall model 8

Problems

1.1   You are in charge of automating a large bakery. The cost of developing the software has been estimated to be $425,000. Approximately how much additional money will be needed for postdelivery maintenance of the software?

1.2   Is there a way of reconciling the original temporal definition of maintenance with the modern operational definition we now use? Explain your answer.

1.3   You are a software-engineering consultant. The chief information officer of a regional gasoline distribution corporation wants you to develop a software product that will carry out all the accounting functions of the company and provide online information to the head office staff regarding orders and inventory in the various company storage tanks. Computers are required for 21 accounting clerks, 15 order clerks, and 37 storage tank clerks. In addition, 14 managers need access to the data. The company is willing to pay $30,000 for the hardware and the software together and wants the complete software product in 4 weeks. What do you tell the chief information officer? Bear in mind that your company wants his corporation's business, no matter how unreasonable his request.

1.4   You are a vice-admiral in the Velorian Navy. It has been decided to call in a software development organization to develop the control software for a new generation of ship-to-ship missiles. You are in charge of supervising the project. In order to protect the government of Veloria, what clauses do you include in the contract with the software developers?

1.5   You are a software engineer whose job is to supervise the development of the software in Problem 1.4. List ways your company can fail to satisfy the contract with the navy. What are the probable causes of such failures?

1.6   Seven months after delivery, a fault is detected in the software of a product that analyzes DNA using the Stein–Röntgen reagent. The cost of fixing the fault is $16,700. The cause of the fault is an ambiguous sentence in the specification document. Approximately how much would it have cost to have corrected the fault during the analysis phase?

1.7   Suppose that the fault in Problem 1.6 had been detected during the implementation phase. Approximately how much would it have cost to have fixed it then?

1.8   You are the president of an organization that builds large-scale software. You show Figure 1.5 to your employees, urging them to find faults early in the software life cycle. Someone responds that it is unreasonable to expect anyone to remove faults before they have entered the product. For example, how can anyone remove a fault while the design is being produced if the fault in question is a coding fault? What do you reply?

1.9   Describe a situation in which the client, developer, and user are the same person.

1.10   What problems can arise if the client, developer, and user are the same person? How can these problems be solved?

1.11   What potential advantages accrue if the client, developer, and user are the same person?

1.12   Look up the word *system* in a dictionary. How many different definitions are there? Write down those definitions that are applicable within the context of software engineering.

1.13   It is your first day at your first job. Your manager hands you a program listing and says, "See if you can find the bug." What do you reply?

1.14   You are in charge of developing the product in Problem 1.1. Will you use the object-oriented paradigm or the classical paradigm? Give reasons for your answer.

1.15   Instead of implementing component c9 of a software product, the developers decide to buy a COTS component with the same specifications as component c9. What are the advantages and disadvantages of this approach?

1.16   Instead of implementing component c37 of a software product, the developers decide to utilize an open-source component with the same specifications as component c37. What are the advantages and disadvantages of this approach?

1.17   (Term Project) Suppose that the product for Osric's Office Appliances and Decor of Appendix A has been implemented exactly as described. Now Osric wants the product to be modified so that the priority of a customer in the queue can be manually changed. In what ways will the existing product have to be changed? Would it be better to discard everything and start again from scratch?

1.18   (Readings in Software Engineering) Your instructor will distribute copies of [Schach et al., 2003b]. What is your opinion of the relative merits of results based on managers' estimates compared to results computed from actual data?

References

[Baetjer, 1996] H. BAETJER, *Software as Capital: An Economic Perspective on Software Engineering,* IEEE Computer Society Press, Los Alamitos, CA, 1996.

[Boehm, 1976] B. W. BOEHM, "Software Engineering," *IEEE Transactions on Computers* **C-25** (December 1976), pp. 1226–41.

[Boehm, 1979] B. W. BOEHM, "Software Engineering, R & D Trends and Defense Needs," in: *Research Directions in Software Technology,* P. Wegner (Editor), The MIT Press, Cambridge, MA, 1979.

[Boehm, 1980] B. W. BOEHM, "Developing Small-Scale Application Software Products: Some Experimental Results," *Proceedings of the Eighth IFIP World Computer Congress,* October 1980, pp. 321–26.

[Boehm, 1981] B. W. BOEHM, *Software Engineering Economics,* Prentice Hall, Englewood Cliffs, NJ, 1981.

[Boehm and Huang, 2003] B. BOEHM AND L. G. HUANG, "Value-Based Software Engineering: A Case Study," *IEEE Computer* **36** (March 2003), pp. 33–41.

[Brereton et al., 1999] P. BRERETON, D. BUDGEN, K. BENNETT, M. MUNRO, P. LAYZELL, L. MACAULAY, D. GRIFFITHS, AND C. STANNETT, "The Future of Software," *Communications of the ACM* **42** (December 1999), pp. 78–84.

[Brooks, 1975] F. P. BROOKS, Jr., *The Mythical Man-Month: Essays on Software Engineering,* Addison-Wesley, Reading, MA, 1975; Twentieth Anniversary Edition, Addison-Wesley, Reading, MA, 1995.

[Brownsword, Oberndorf, and Sledge, 2000] L. Brownsword, T. Oberndorf, and C. A. Sledge, "Developing New Process for COTS-Based Systems," *IEEE Software* **17** (July/August 2000), pp. 40–47.

[Budd, 2002] T. A. Budd, *An Introduction to Object-Oriented Programming*, 3rd ed., Addison-Wesley, Reading, MA, 2002.

[Capper, Colgate, Hunter, and James, 1994] N. P. Capper, R. J. Colgate, J. C. Hunter, and M. F. James, "The Impact of Object-Oriented Technology on Software Quality: Three Case Histories," *IBM Systems Journal* **33** (No. 1, 1994), pp. 131–57.

[Cutter Consortium, 2002] Cutter Consortium, "78% of IT Organizations Have Litigated," *The Cutter Edge*, www.cutter.com/research/2002/edge020409.html[3], April 09, 2002.

[Daly, 1977] E. B. Daly, "Management of Software Development," *IEEE Transactions on Software Engineering* **SE-3** (May 1977), pp. 229–42.

[DeMarco and Lister, 1987] T. DeMarco and T. Lister, *Peopleware: Productive Projects and Teams*, Dorset House, New York, 1987.

[Devlin, 2001] K. Devlin, "The Real Reason Why Software Engineers Need Math," *Communications of the ACM* **44** (October 2001), pp. 21–22.

[Ebert, Matsubara, Pezzé, and Bertelsen, 1997] C. Ebert, T. Matsubara, M. Pezzé, and O. W. Bertelsen, "The Road to Maturity: Navigating between Craft and Science," *IEEE Software* 14 (November/December 1997), pp. 77–88.

[Elshoff, 1976] J. L. Elshoff, "An Analysis of Some Commercial PL/I Programs," *IEEE Transactions on Software Engineering* **SE-2** (June 1976), pp. 113–20.

[Fagan, 1974] M. E. Fagan, "Design and Code Inspections and Process Control in the Development of Programs," Technical Report IBM-SSD TR 21.572, IBM Corporation, December 1974.

[Fichman and Kemerer, 1997] R. G. Fichman and C. F. Kemerer, "Object Technology and Reuse: Lessons from Early Adopters," *IEEE Computer* **30** (July 1997), pp. 47–57.

[Finkelstein, 2000] A. Finkelstein (Editor), *The Future of Software Engineering*, IEEE Computer Society Press, Los Alamitos, CA, 2000.

[Gane and Sarsen, 1979] C. Gane and T. Sarsen, *Structured Systems Analysis: Tools and Techniques*, Prentice Hall, Englewood Cliffs, NJ, 1979.

[GJSentinel.com, 2003] "Sallie Mae's Errors Double Some Bills," www.gjsentinel.com/news/content/coxnet/headlines/0522_salliemae.html, May 22, 2003.

[Glass, 1998] R. L. Glass, "Is There Really a Software Crisis?" *IEEE Software* **15** (January/February 1998), pp. 104–5.

[Goldstein, 2005] H. Goldstein, "Who Killed the Virtual Case File?" *IEEE Spectrum* **43** (September 2005), pp. 24–35.

[Grady, 1994] R. B. Grady, "Successfully Applying Software Metrics," *IEEE Computer* **27** (September 1994), pp. 18–25.

[Hatton, 1998] L. Hatton, "Does OO Sync with How We Think?" *IEEE Software* **15** (May/June 1998), pp. 46–54.

[Hayes, 2004] F. Hayes, "Chaos is Back," *Computerworld*, www.computerworld.com/managementtopics/management/project/story/0,10801,97283,00.html, November 8, 2004.

[IEEE 610.12, 1990] *A Glossary of Software Engineering Terminology*, IEEE 610.12-1990, Institute of Electrical and Electronic Engineers, Inc., 1990.

[IEEE Standards, 2003] "Products and Projects Status Report," standards.ieee.org/db/status/status.txt, June 3, 2003.

[IEEE/ACM, 1999] "Software Engineering Code of Ethics and Professional Practice, Version 5.2, as Recommended by the IEEE-CS/ACM Joint Task Force on Software Engineering Ethics and Professional Practice," www.computer.org/tab/seprof/code.htm, 1999.

[IEEE/EIA 12207.0-1996, 1998] "IEEE/EIA 12207.0-1996 Industry Implementation of International Standard ISO/IEC 12207:1995," Institute of Electrical and Electronic Engineers, Electronic Industries Alliance, New York, 1998.

---

[3] This and the other Web addresses cited in this book were correct at the time of going to press. However, Web addresses tend to change all too frequently and without prior or subsequent notification. If this happens, the reader should use a search engine to locate the new Web address.

[ISO/IEC 12207, 1995] "ISO/IEC 12207:1995, Information Technology—Software Life-Cycle Processes," International Organization for Standardization, International Electrotechnical Commission, Geneva, 1995.

[Johnson, 2000] R. A. JOHNSON, "The Ups and Downs of Object-Oriented System Development," *Communications of the ACM* **43** (October 2000), pp. 69–73.

[Josephson, 1992] M. JOSEPHSON, *Edison, A Biography*, John Wiley and Sons, New York, 1992.

[Kan et al., 1994] S. H. KAN, S. D. DULL, D. N. AMUNDSON, R. J. LINDNER, AND R. J. HEDGER, "AS/400 Software Quality Management," *IBM Systems Journal* **33** (No. 1, 1994), pp. 62–88.

[Keil and Tiwana, 2005] M. KEIL AND A. TIWANA, "Beyond Cost: The Drivers of COTS Application Value," IEEE Software 22 (May/June 2005), pp. 64–69.

[Kelly, Sherif, and Hops, 1992] J. C. KELLY, J. S. SHERIF, AND J. HOPS, "An Analysis of Defect Densities Found during Software Inspections," *Journal of Systems and Software* **17** (January 1992), pp. 111–17.

[Khan, Al-A'ali, and Girgis, 1995] E. H. KHAN, M. AL-A'ALI, AND M. R. GIRGIS, "Object-Oriented Programming for Structured Procedural Programming," *IEEE Computer* **28** (October 1995), pp. 48–57.

[Kroeker et al., 1999] K. K. KROEKER, L. WALL, D. A. TAYLOR, C. HORN, P. BASSETT, J. K. OUSTERHOUT, M. L. GRISS, R. M. SOLEY, J. WALDO, AND C. SIMONYI, "Software [R]evolution: A Roundtable," *IEEE Computer* **32** (May 1999), pp. 48–57.

[Leveson and Turner, 1993] N. G. LEVESON AND C. S. TURNER, "An Investigation of the Therac-25 Accidents," *IEEE Computer* **26** (July 1993), pp. 18–41.

[Lientz, Swanson, and Tompkins, 1978] B. P. LIENTZ, E. B. SWANSON, AND G. E. TOMPKINS, "Characteristics of Application Software Maintenance," *Communications of the ACM* **21** (June 1978), pp. 466–71.

[Longstaff, Chittister, Pethia, and Haimes, 2000] T. A. LONGSTAFF, C. CHITTISTER, R. PETHIA, AND Y. Y. HAIMES, "Are We Forgetting the Risks of Information Technology?" *IEEE Computer* **33** (December 2000), pp. 43–51.

[Madanmohan and De', 2004] T. R. MADANMOHAN AND R. DE', "Open Source Reuse in Commercial Firms," *IEEE Software* **21** (November/December 2004), pp. 62–69.

[Maring, 1996] B. MARING, "Object-Oriented Development of Large Applications," *IEEE Software* **13** (May 1996), pp. 33–40.

[Mellor, 1994] P. MELLOR, "CAD: Computer-Aided Disaster," Technical Report, Centre for Software Reliability, City University, London, July 1994.

[Meyer, 1992] B. MEYER, "Applying 'Design by Contract'," *IEEE Computer* **25** (October 1992), pp. 40–51.

[Meyer, 1997] B. MEYER, *Object-Oriented Software Construction*, 2nd ed., Prentice Hall, Upper Saddle River, NJ, 1997.

[Naur, Randell, and Buxton, 1976] P. NAUR, B. RANDELL, AND J. N. BUXTON (Editors), *Software Engineering: Concepts and Techniques: Proceedings of the NATO Conferences*, Petrocelli-Charter, New York, 1976.

[Neumann, 1980] P. G. NEUMANN, Letter from the Editor, *ACM SIGSOFT Software Engineering Notes* **5** (July 1980), p. 2.

[Neumann, 1995] P. G. NEUMANN, *Computer-Related Risks*, Addison-Wesley, Reading, MA, 1995.

[Parnas, 1994] D. L. PARNAS, "Software Aging," *Proceedings of the 16th International Conference on Software Engineering*, Sorrento, Italy, May 1994, pp. 279–87.

[Paulson, Succi, and Eberlein, 2004] J. W. PAULSON, G. SUCCI, AND A. EBERLEIN, "An Empirical Study of Open-Source and Closed-Source Software Products," *IEEE Transactions on Software Engineering* **30** (April 2004), pp. 246–56.

[Radin, 1996] G. RADIN, "Object Technology in Perspective," *IBM Systems Journal* **35** (No. 2, 1996), pp. 124–26.

[Raymond, 2000] E. S. RAYMOND, *The Cathedral and the Bazaar: Musings on Linux and Open Source by an Accidental Revolutionary*, O'Reilly & Associates, Sebastopol, CA, 2000; also available at www.catb.org/~esr/writings/cathedral-bazaar/cathedral-bazaar/.

[Schach et al., 2002] S, R. Schach, B. Jin, D. R. Wright, G. Z. Heller, and A. J. Offutt, "Maintainability of the Linux Kernel," *IEE Proceedings—Software* **149** (February 2002), pp. 18–23.

[Schach et al., 2003b] S. R. Schach, B. Jin, G. Z. Heller, L. Yu, and J. Offutt, "Determining the Distribution of Maintenance Categories: Survey versus Measurement," *Empirical Software Engineering* **8** (December 2003), pp. 351–66.

[Scott and Vessey, 2002] J. E. Scott and I. Vessey, "Managing Risks in Enterprise Systems Implementations," *Communications of the ACM* **45** (April 2002), pp. 74–81.

[Shapiro, 1994] F. R. Shapiro, "The First Bug," *Byte* **19** (April 1994), p. 308.

[Shneiderman, 1980] B. Shneiderman, *Software Psychology: Human Factors in Computer and Information Systems*, Winthrop Publishers, Cambridge, MA, 1980.

[Spiegel Online, 2004] "Rheinbrücke mit Treppe—54 Zentimeter Höhenunterschied," www.spiegel.de/panorama/0,1518,281837,00.html.

[St. Petersburg Times Online, 2003] "Thousands of Federal Checks Uncashable," www.sptimes.com/2003/02/07/Worldandnation/Thousands_of_federal_.shtml, February 07, 2003.

[Stephenson, 1976] W. E. Stephenson, "An Analysis of the Resources Used in Safeguard System Software Development," Bell Laboratories, Draft Paper, August 1976.

[Ulkuniemi and Seppanen, 2004] P. Ulkuniemi, and V. Seppanen, "COTS Component Acquisition in an Emerging Market," *IEEE Software* **21** (November/December 2004), pp. 76–82.

[Wasserman, 1996] A. I. Wasserman, "Toward a Discipline of Software Engineering," *IEEE Software* **13** (November/December 1996), pp. 23–31.

[Webster, 1995] B. F. Webster, *Pitfalls of Object-Oriented Development*, M&T Books, New York, 1995.

[Weinberg, 1971] G. M. Weinberg, *The Psychology of Computer Programming*, Van Nostrand Reinhold, New York, 1971.

[Wirfs-Brock, Wilkerson, and Wiener, 1990] R. Wirfs-Brock, B. Wilkerson, and L. Wiener, *Designing Object-Oriented Software*, Prentice Hall, Englewood Cliffs, NJ, 1990.

[Yourdon, 1992] E. Yourdon, *The Decline and Fall of the American Programmer*, Yourdon Press, Upper Saddle River, NJ, 1992.

[Zelkowitz, Shaw, and Gannon, 1979] M. V. Zelkowitz, A. C. Shaw, and J. D. Gannon, *Principles of Software Engineering and Design,* Prentice Hall, Englewood Cliffs, NJ, 1979.

[Zvegintzov, 1998] N. Zvegintzov, "Frequently Begged Questions and How to Answer Them," *IEEE Software* **15** (January/February 1998), pp. 93–96.

Chapter 2

Software Life-Cycle Models

Learning Objectives

After studying this chapter, you should be able to

- Describe how software products are developed in practice.
- Understand the evolution-tree life-cycle model.
- Appreciate the negative impact of change on software products.
- Utilize the iterative-and-incremental life-cycle model.
- Comprehend the impact of Miller's Law on software production.
- Describe the strengths of the iterative-and-incremental life-cycle model.
- Realize the importance of mitigating risks early.
- Describe agile processes, including extreme programming.
- Compare and contrast a variety of other life-cycle models.

Chapter 1 describes how software products would be developed in an ideal world. The theme of this chapter is what happens in practice. As will be explained, there are vast differences between theory and practice.

2.1 Software Development in Theory

In an ideal world, a software product is developed as described in Chapter 1. As depicted schematically in Figure 2.1, the system is developed from scratch; ∅ denotes the empty set. (See Just in Case You Wanted to Know Box 2.1 if you want to know the origin of the term *from scratch*.) First the client's Requirements are determined, and then the Analysis is performed. When the

The term *from scratch*, meaning "starting with nothing," comes from 19th century sports terminology. Before roads (and running tracks) were paved, races had to be held on open ground. In many cases, the starting line was a scratch in the sand. A runner who had no advantage or handicap had to start from that line, that is, "from [the] scratch."

The term *scratch* has a different sporting connotation nowadays. A "scratch golfer" is one whose golfing handicap is zero.

Figure 2.1
Idealized software development.

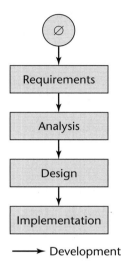

analysis artifacts are complete, the **Design** is produced. This is followed by the **Implementation** of the complete software product, which is then installed on the client's computer.

However, software development is considerably different in practice for two reasons. First, software professionals are human and therefore make mistakes. Second, the client's requirements can change while the software is being developed. In this chapter, both these issues are discussed in some depth, but first we present a mini case study, based on the case study in [Tomer and Schach, 2000], that illustrates the issues involved.

Mini Case Study

2.2 Winburg Mini Case Study

To reduce traffic congestion in downtown Winburg, Indiana, the mayor convinces the city to set up a public transportation system. Bus-only lanes are to be established, and commuters will be encouraged to "park and ride"; that is, to park their cars in suburban parking lots and then take buses from there to work and back at a cost of one dollar per ride. Each bus is to have a fare machine that accepts only dollar bills. Passengers insert a bill into the slot as they enter the bus. Sensors inside the fare machine scan the bill, and the software in the machine uses an image recognition algorithm to decide whether the passenger has indeed inserted a valid dollar bill into the slot. It is important that the fare machine be accurate because, once the news gets out that any piece of paper will do the trick, fare income will plummet to effectively zero. Conversely, if the machine regularly rejects valid dollar bills, passengers will be reluctant to use the buses. In addition, the fare machine must be rapid. Passengers will be equally reluctant to use the buses if the machine spends 15 seconds coming to a decision regarding the validity of a dollar bill—it would take even a relatively small number of passengers many minutes to board a bus. Therefore, the requirements for the fare machine software include an average response time of less than 1 second, and an average accuracy of at least 98 percent.

Episode 1 The first version of the software is implemented.

Episode 2 Tests show that the required constraint of an average response time of 1 second for deciding on the validity of a dollar bill is not achieved. In fact, on average, it takes 10 seconds to get a response. Senior management discovers the cause. It seems that, to get the required 98 percent accuracy, a programmer has been instructed by her manager to use double-precision numbers for all mathematical calculations. As a result, every operation takes at least twice as long as it would with the usual single-precision numbers. The result is that the program is much slower than it should be, resulting in the long response time. Calculations then show that, despite what the manager told the programmer, the stipulated 98 percent accuracy can be attained even if single-precision numbers are used. The programmer starts to make the necessary changes to the implementation.

Episode 3 Before the programmer can complete her work, further tests of the system show that, even if the indicated changes to the implementation were made, the system would still have an average response time of over 4.5 seconds, nowhere near the stipulated 1 second. The problem is the complex image recognition algorithm. Fortunately, a faster algorithm has just been discovered, so the fare machine software is redesigned and rewritten using the new algorithm. This results in the average response time being successfully achieved.

Episode 4 By now, the project is considerably behind schedule and way over budget. The mayor, a successful entrepreneur, has the bright idea of asking the software development team to try to increase the accuracy of the dollar bill recognition component of the system as much as possible, to sell the resulting package to vending machine companies. To meet this new requirement, a new design is adopted that improves the average accuracy to over 99.5 percent. Management decides to install that version of the software in the fare machines. At this point, development of the software is complete. The city is later able to sell its system to two small vending machine companies, defraying about one-third of the cost overrun.

Epilogue A few years later, the sensors inside the fare machine become obsolete and need to be replaced by a newer model. Management suggests taking advantage of the change to upgrade the hardware at the same time. The software professionals point out that changing the hardware means that new software also is needed. They suggest rewriting the software in a programming language. At the time of writing, the project is

6 months behind schedule and 25 percent over budget. However, everyone involved is confident that the new system will be more reliable and of higher quality, despite "minor discrepancies" in meeting its response time and accuracy requirements.

Figure 2.2 depicts the **evolution-tree life-cycle model** of the mini case study. The leftmost boxes represent Episode 1. As shown in the figure, the system was developed from scratch ($\emptyset$). The requirements (Requirements$_1$), analysis (Analysis$_1$), design (Design$_1$), and implementation (Implementation$_1$) followed in turn. Next, as previously described, trials of the first version of the software showed that the average response time of 1 second could not be achieved and the implementation had to be modified. The modified implementation appears in Figure 2.2 as Implementation$_2$. However, Implementation$_2$ was never completed. That is why the rectangle representing Implementation$_2$ is drawn with a dotted line.

In Episode 3, the design had to be changed. Specifically, a faster image recognition algorithm was used. The modified design (Design$_3$) resulted in a modified implementation (Implementation$_3$).

Finally, in Episode 4, the requirements were changed (Requirements$_4$) to increase the accuracy. This resulted in modified specifications (Analysis$_4$), modified design (Design$_4$) and modified implementation (Implementation$_4$).

In Figure 2.2, the solid arrows denote development, and the dashed arrows denote maintenance. For example, when the design is changed in Episode 3, Design$_3$ replaced Design$_1$ as the design of Analysis$_1$.

The evolution-tree model is an example of a **life-cycle model** (or **model**, for short), that is, the series of steps to be performed while the software product is developed and maintained. Another life-cycle model that can be used for the mini case study is the **waterfall life-cycle model** [Royce, 1970]; a simplified version of the

Figure 2.2 The evolution-tree life-cycle model for the Winburg mini case study. (The rectangle drawn with a dotted line denotes the implementation that was not completed.)

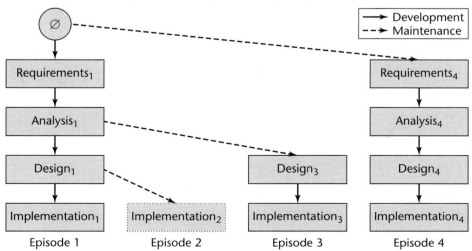

waterfall model is depicted in Figure 2.3. This life-cycle model can be viewed as the linear model of Figure 2.1 with feedback loops. Then, if a fault is found during the design that was caused by a fault in the requirements, following the dashed upward arrows, the software developers can backtrack from the design up to the analysis and hence to the requirements and make the necessary corrections there. Then, they move down to the analysis, correct the specification document to reflect the corrections to the requirements, and in turn, correct the design document. Design activities can now resume where they were suspended when the fault was discovered. Again, the solid arrows denote development; the dashed arrows, maintenance.

The waterfall model can certainly be used to represent the Winburg mini case study, but, unlike the evolution-tree model of Figure 2.2, it cannot show the order of events. The evolution-tree model has a further advantage over the waterfall model. At the end of each episode we have a **baseline**, that is, a complete set of artifacts (recall that an **artifact** is a constituent component of a software product). There are four baselines in Figure 2.2. They are

At the end of Episode 1: Requirements$_1$, Analysis$_1$, Design$_1$, Implementation$_1$
At the end of Episode 2: Requirements$_1$, Analysis$_1$, Design$_1$, Implementation$_2$
At the end of Episode 3: Requirements$_1$, Analysis$_1$, Design$_3$, Implementation$_3$
At the end of Episode 4: Requirements$_4$, Analysis$_4$, Design$_4$, Implementation$_4$

The first baseline is the initial set of artifacts; the second baseline reflects the modified (but never completed) Implementation$_2$ of Episode 2, together with the unchanged requirements, analysis, and design of Episode 1. The third baseline is the same as the first baseline but with the design and implementation changed. The fourth baseline is the complete set of new artifacts shown in Figure 2.2. We revisit the concept of a baseline in Chapters 5 and 14.

Figure 2.3
A simplified version of the waterfall life-cycle model.

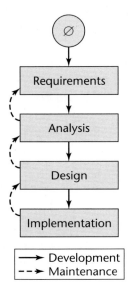

2.3   Lessons of the Winburg Mini Case Study

The Winburg mini case study depicts the development of a software product that goes awry for a number of unrelated causes, such as a poor implementation strategy (the unnecessary use of double-precision numbers) and the decision to use an algorithm that was too slow. In the end, the project was a success. However, the obvious question is, Is software development really as chaotic in practice? In fact, the mini case study is far less traumatic than many, if not the majority of, software projects. In the Winburg mini case study, there were only two new versions of the software because of faults (the inappropriate use of double-precision numbers and the utilization of an algorithm that could not meet the response time requirement), and only one new version because of a change made by the client (the need for increased accuracy).

Why are so many changes to a software product needed? First, as previously stated, software professionals are human and therefore make mistakes. Second, a software product is a model of the real world, and the real world is continually changing. This issue is discussed at greater length in the Section 2.4.

Mini Case Study

2.4   *Teal Tractors Mini Case Study*

Teal Tractors, Inc., sells tractors in most areas of the United States. The company has asked its software division to develop a new product that can handle all aspects of its business. For example, the product must be able to handle sales, inventory, and commissions paid to the sales staff, as well as providing all necessary accounting functions. While this software product is being implemented, Teal Tractors buys a Canadian tractor company. The management of Teal Tractors decides that, to save money, the Canadian operations are to be integrated into the U.S. operations. That means that the software has to be changed before it is completed:

1. It must be modified to handle additional sales regions.
2. It must be extended to handle those aspects of the business that are handled differently in Canada, such as taxes.
3. It must be extended to handle two different currencies, U.S. dollars and Canadian dollars.

Teal Tractors is a rapidly growing company with excellent future prospects. The takeover of the Canadian tractor company is a positive development, one that may well lead to even greater profits in future years. But, from the viewpoint of the software division, the purchase of the Canadian company could be disastrous. Unless the requirements, analysis, and design have been performed with a view to incorporating possible future extensions, the work involved in adding the Canadian sales regions may be so great that it might be more effective to discard everything done to date and start from scratch. The reason is that changing the product at this stage is similar to trying to fix a software product late in its life cycle (see Figure 1.5). Extending the software to handle aspects specific to the Canadian market, as well as Canadian currency, may be equally hard.

Even if the software has been well thought out and the original design is indeed extensible, the design of the resulting patched-together product cannot be as cohesive as it would have been if it had been developed from the very beginning to cater to both the United States and Canada. This can have severe implications for future maintenance.

The software division of Teal Tractors is a victim of the **moving-target problem**. That is, while the software is being developed, the requirements change. It does not matter that the reason for the change is otherwise extremely worthwhile. The fact is that the takeover of the Canadian company could well be detrimental to the quality of the software being developed.

In some cases, the reason for the moving target is less benign. Sometimes a powerful senior manager within an organization keeps changing his or her mind regarding the functionality of a software product being developed. In other cases, there is **feature creep**, a succession of small, almost trivial, additions to the requirements. But, whatever the reason may be, frequent changes, no matter how minor they may seem, are harmful to the health of a software product. It is important that a software product be designed as a set of components that are as independent as possible, so that a change to one part of the software does not induce a fault in an apparently unrelated part of the code, a so-called **regression fault**. When numerous changes are made, the effect is to induce dependencies within the code. Finally, there are so many dependencies that virtually any change induces one or more regression faults. At that time, the only thing that can be done is to redesign the entire software product and reimplement it.

Unfortunately, there is no known solution to the moving-target problem. With regard to positive changes to requirements, growing companies are always going to change, and these changes have to be reflected in the mission-critical software products of the company. As for negative changes, if the individual calling for those changes has sufficient clout, nothing can be done to prevent the changes being implemented, to the detriment of the further maintainability of the software product.

2.5   Iteration and Incrementation

As a consequence of both the moving-target problem and the need to correct the inevitable mistakes made while a software product is being developed, the life cycle of actual software products resembles the evolution-tree model of Figure 2.2 or the waterfall model of Figure 2.3, rather than the idealized chain of Figure 2.1. One consequence of this reality is that it does not make much sense to talk about (say) "*the* analysis phase." Instead, the operations of the analysis phase are spread out over the life cycle. Similarly, Figure 2.2 shows four different versions of the implementation, one of which (Implementation$_2$) was never completed because of the moving-target problem.

Consider successive versions of an artifact, for example, the specification document or a code module. From this viewpoint, the basic process is iterative. That is, we produce the first version of the artifact, then we revise it and produce the second version, and so on. Our intent is that each version is closer to our target than its predecessor and finally we construct a version that is satisfactory. **Iteration** is an intrinsic aspect of software engineering, and iterative life-cycle models have been used for over 30 years [Larman and Basili, 2003]. For example, the waterfall model, which was first put forward in 1970, is iterative (but not incremental).

A second aspect of developing real-world software is the restriction imposed on us by **Miller's Law**. In 1956, George Miller, a professor of psychology, showed that, at any one time, we humans are capable of concentrating on only approximately seven chunks (units of information) [Miller, 1956]. However, a typical software artifact has far more than seven chunks. For example, a code artifact is likely to have considerably more than seven variables, and a requirements document is likely to have many more than seven requirements. One way we humans handle this restriction on the amount of information we can handle at any one time is to use **stepwise refinement**. That is, we concentrate on those aspects that are currently the most important and postpone until later those aspects that are currently less critical. In other words, every aspect is eventually handled but in order of current importance. This means that we start off by constructing an artifact that solves only a small part of what we are trying to achieve. Then, we consider further aspects of the problem and add the resulting new pieces to the existing artifact. For example, we might construct a requirements document by considering the seven requirements we consider the most important. Then, we would consider the seven next most important requirements, and so on. This is an incremental process. **Incrementation** is also an intrinsic aspect of software engineering; incremental software development is over 45 years old [Larman and Basili, 2003].

In practice, iteration and incrementation are used in conjunction with one another. That is, an artifact is constructed piece by piece (incrementation), and each increment goes through multiple versions (iteration). These ideas are illustrated in Figure 2.2, which represents the life cycle for the Winburg mini case study (Sections 2.2 and 2.3). As shown in that figure, there is no single "requirements phase" as such. Instead, the client's requirements are extracted and analyzed twice, yielding the original requirements (Requirements$_1$) and the modified requirements (Requirements$_4$). Similarly, there is no single "implementation phase," but rather four separate episodes in which the code is produced and then modified.

These ideas are generalized in Figure 2.4, which reflects the basic concepts underlying the **iterative-and-incremental life-cycle model** [Jacobson, Booch, and Rumbaugh, 1999]. The figure shows the development of a software product in four increments, labeled Increment A, Increment B, Increment C, and Increment D. The horizontal axis is time, and the vertical axis is person-hours (one person-hour is the amount of work that one person can do in 1 hour), so the shaded area under each curve is the total effort for that increment.

It is important to appreciate that Figure 2.4 depicts just one possible way a software product can be decomposed into increments. Another software product may be constructed in just 2 increments, whereas a third may require 13. Furthermore, the figure is not intended to be an accurate representation of precisely how a software product is developed. Instead, it shows how the emphasis changes from iteration to iteration.

The sequential phases of Figure 2.1 are artificial constructs. Instead, as explicitly reflected in Figure 2.4, we must acknowledge that different **workflows** (activities) are performed over the entire life cycle. There are five **core workflows**, the **requirements workflow, analysis workflow, design workflow, implementation workflow**, and **test workflow**, and, as stated in the previous sentence, all five are performed over the life cycle of a software product. However, there are times when one workflow predominates over the other four.

Figure 2.4   The construction of a software product in four increments.

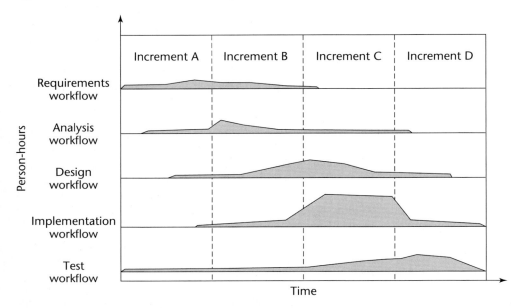

For example, at the beginning of the life cycle, the software developers extract an initial set of requirements. In other words, at the beginning of the iterative-and-incremental life cycle, the requirements workflow predominates. These requirements artifacts are extended and modified during the remainder of the life cycle. During that time, the other four workflows (analysis, design, implementation, and test) predominate. In other words, the requirements workflow is the major workflow at the beginning of the life cycle, but its relative importance decreases thereafter. Conversely, the implementation and test workflows occupy far more of the time of the members of the software development team toward the end of the life cycle than they do at the beginning.

Planning and documentation activities are performed throughout the iterative-and-incremental life cycle. Furthermore, testing is a major activity during each iteration, and particularly at the end of each iteration. In addition, the software as a whole is thoroughly tested once it has been completed; at that time, testing and then modifying the implementation in the light of the outcome of the various tests is virtually the sole activity of the software team. This is reflected in the test workflow of Figure 2.4.

Figure 2.4 shows four increments. Consider Increment A, depicted by the column on the left. At the beginning of this increment, the requirements team members determine the client's requirements. Once most of the requirements have been determined, the first version of part of the analysis can be started. When sufficient progress has been made with the analysis, the first version of the design can be started. Even some coding is often done during this first increment, perhaps in the form of a proof-of-concept prototype to test the feasibility of part of the proposed software product. Finally, as previously mentioned, planning, testing, and documentation activities start on Day One and continue from then on, until the software product is finally delivered to the client.

Similarly, the primary concentration during Increment B is on the requirements and analysis workflows, and then on the design workflow. The emphasis during Increment C is first on the design workflow, and then on the implementation workflow and test workflow. Finally, during Increment D, the implementation workflow and test workflow dominate.

As reflected in [Grady, 1994], about one-fifth of the total effort is devoted to the requirements and analysis workflows (together), another one-fifth to the design workflow, and about three-fifths to the implementation workflow. The relative total sizes of the shaded areas in Figure 2.4 reflect these values.

There is iteration during each increment of Figure 2.4. This is shown in Figure 2.5, which depicts three iterations during Increment B. (Figure 2.5 is an enlarged view of the second column of Figure 2.4.) As shown in Figure 2.5, each iteration involves all five workflows but again in varying proportions.

Again, it must be stressed that Figure 2.5 is not intended to show that every increment involves exactly three iterations. The number of iterations varies from increment to increment. The purpose of Figure 2.5 is to show the iteration within each increment and repeat that all five workflows (requirements, analysis, design, implementation, and testing, together with planning and documentation) are carried out during almost every iteration, although in varying proportions each time.

As previously explained, Figure 2.4 reflects the incrementation intrinsic to the development of every software product. Figure 2.5 explicitly displays the iteration that underlies incrementation. Specifically, Figure 2.5 depicts three consecutive iterative steps, as opposed to one large incrementation. In more detail, Iteration B.1 consists of requirements, analysis, design, implementation, and test workflows, represented by the leftmost dashed

Figure 2.5
The three iterations of Increment B of the iterative-and-incremental life-cycle model of Figure 2.4.

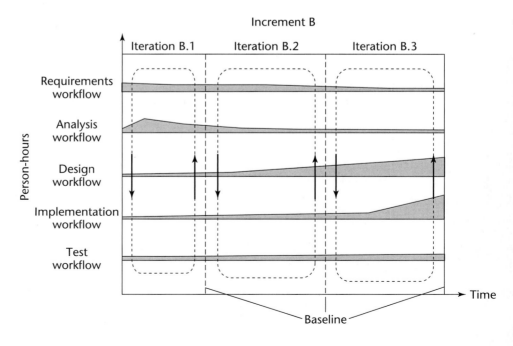

rectangle with rounded corners. The iteration continues until the artifacts of each of the five workflows are satisfactory.

Next, all five sets of artifacts are iterated in Iteration B.2. This second iteration is similar in nature to the first. That is, the requirements artifacts are improved, which in turn triggers improvements to the analysis artifacts, and so on, as reflected in the second iteration of Figure 2.5, and similarly for the third iteration.

The process of iteration and incrementation starts at the beginning of Increment A and continues until the end of Increment D. The completed software product is then installed on the client's computer.

2.6   Winburg Mini Case Study Revisited

Figure 2.6 shows the evolution-tree model of the Winburg mini case study (Figure 2.2) superimposed on the iterative-and-incremental model (the test workflow is not shown because the evolution-tree model assumes continual testing, explained in Section 1.7). Figure 2.6 sheds additional light on the nature of incrementation:

Figure 2.6 The evolution-tree life-cycle model for the Winburg mini case study (Figure 2.2) superimposed on the iterative-and-incremental life-cycle model.

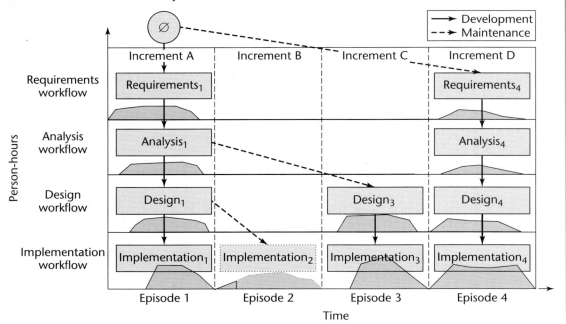

- Increment A corresponds to Episode 1, Increment B corresponds to Episode 2, and so on.
- From the viewpoint of the iterative-and-incremental model, two of the increments do not include all four workflows. In more detail, Increment B (Episode 2) includes only the implementation workflow, and Increment C (Episode 3) includes only the design workflow and the implementation workflow. The iterative-and-incremental model does not require that every workflow be performed during every increment.
- Furthermore, in Figure 2.4 most of the requirements workflow is performed in Increment A and Increment B, whereas in Figure 2.6 it is performed in Increment A and Increment D. Also, in Figure 2.4 most of the analysis is performed in Increment B, whereas in Figure 2.6 the analysis workflow is performed in Increment A and Increment D. This accentuates that neither Figure 2.4 nor Figure 2.6 represents the way every software product is built. Instead, each figure shows the way that one particular software product is built, highlighting the underlying iteration and incrementation.
- The small size and abrupt termination of the implementation workflow during Increment B (Episode 2) of Figure 2.6 shows that Implementation$_2$ was not completed. The piece with a dotted line reflects the part of the implementation workflow that was not performed.
- The three dashed arrows of the evolution-tree model show that each increment constitutes maintenance of the previous increment. In this example, the second and third increments are instances of corrective maintenance. That is, each increment corrects faults in the previous increment. As previously explained, Increment B (Episode 2) corrects the implementation workflow by replacing double-precision variables with the usual single-precision variables. Increment C (Episode 3) corrects the design workflow by using a faster image recognition algorithm, thereby enabling the response time requirement to be met. Corresponding changes then have to be made to the implementation workflow. Finally, in Increment D (Episode 4) the requirements are changed to stipulate improved overall accuracy, an instance of perfective maintenance. Corresponding changes are then made to the analysis workflow, design workflow, and implementation workflow.

2.7   Risks and Other Aspects of Iteration and Incrementation

Another way of looking at iteration and incrementation is that the project as a whole is divided into smaller mini projects (or increments). Each mini project extends the requirements, analysis, design, implementation, and testing artifacts. Finally, the resulting set of artifacts constitutes the complete software product.

In fact, each mini project consists of more than just extending the artifacts. It is essential to check that each artifact is correct (the test workflow) and make any necessary changes to the relevant artifacts. This process of checking and modifying, then rechecking and remodifying, and so on, is clearly iterative in nature. It continues until the members of the development team are satisfied with all the artifacts of the current mini project (or increment). When that happens, they proceed to the next increment.

Comparing Figure 2.3 (the waterfall model) with Figure 2.5 (view of the iterations within Increment B) shows that each iteration can be viewed as a small but complete waterfall model. That is, during each iteration the members of the development team go through the requirements, analysis, design, and implementation phases on a specific portion of the software product. From this viewpoint, the iterative-and-incremental model of Figures 2.4 and 2.5 can be viewed as a consecutive series of waterfall models.

The iterative-and-incremental model has many strengths:

1. Multiple opportunities are offered for checking that the software product is correct. Every iteration incorporates the test workflow, so every iteration is another chance to check all the artifacts developed up to this point. The later faults are detected and corrected, the higher is the cost, as shown in Figure 1.5. Unlike the waterfall model, each of the many iterations of the iterative-and-incremental model offers a further opportunity to find faults and correct them, thereby saving money.

2. The robustness of the underlying architecture can be determined relatively early in the life cycle. The ***architecture*** of a software product includes the various component artifacts and how they fit together. An analogy is the architecture of a cathedral, which might be described as Romanesque, Gothic, or Baroque, among other possibilities. Similarly, the architecture of a software product might be described as object-oriented (Chapter 7), pipes and filters (UNIX or Linux components), or client–server (with a central server providing file storage for a network of client computers). The architecture of a software product developed using the iterative-and-incremental model must have the property that it can be extended continually (and, if necessary, easily changed) to incorporate the next increment. Being able to handle such extensions and changes without falling apart is called ***robustness***. Robustness is an important quality during development of a software product; it is vital during post-delivery maintenance. So, if a software product is to last through the usual 12, 15, or more years of postdelivery maintenance, the underlying architecture has to be robust. When an iterative-and-incremental model is used, it soon becomes apparent whether or not the architecture is robust. If, in the course of incorporating (say) the third increment, it is clear that the software developed to date has to be drastically reorganized and large parts rewritten, then it is clear that the architecture is not sufficiently robust. The client must decide whether to abandon the project or start again from scratch. Another possibility is to redesign the architecture to be more robust, and then reuse as much of the current artifacts as possible before proceeding to the next increment. Another reason why a robust architecture is so important is the moving-target problem (Section 2.4). It is all but certain that the client's requirements will change, either because of growth within the client's organization or because the client keeps changing his or her mind as to what the target software has to do. The more robust the architecture, the more resilient to change the software will be. It is not possible to design an architecture that can cope with too many drastic changes. But, if the required changes are reasonable in scope, a robust architecture should be capable of incorporating those changes without having to be drastically restructured.

3. The iterative-and-incremental model enables us to ***mitigate risks*** early. ***Risks*** are invariably involved in software development and maintenance. In the Winburg mini case study, for example, the original image recognition algorithm was not fast enough; there is an ever-present risk that a completed software product will not meet its time constraints. Developing a software product incrementally enables us to mitigate such risks early in the life cycle. For example, suppose a new local area network (LAN) is being developed and there is concern that the current network hardware is inadequate for the new software product. Then, the first one or two iterations are directed toward constructing those parts of the software that interface with the network hardware. If it turns out that, contrary to the developers' fears, the network has the necessary capability, the developers can proceed with the project, confident that this risk has been mitigated. On the other hand, if the network indeed cannot cope with the additional traffic that the new LAN generates, this is reported to the client early in the life cycle, when only a small proportion of the budget has been spent. The client can now decide whether to cancel the project, extend the capabilities of the existing network, buy a new and more powerful network, or take some other action.

4. We always have a working version of the software. Suppose a software product is developed using the idealized life-cycle model of Figure 2.1. Only at the very end of the project is there a working version of the software product. In contrast, when the iterative-and-incremental life-cycle model is used, at the end of each iteration, there is a working version of part of the overall target software product. The client and the intended users can experiment with that version and determine what changes are needed to ensure that the future complete implementation meets their needs. These changes can be made to a subsequent increment, and the client and users can then determine if further changes are needed. A variation on this is to deliver partial versions of the software product, not only for experimentation but to smooth the introduction of the new software product in the client organization. Change is almost always perceived as a threat. All too frequently, users fear that the introduction of a new software product within the workplace will result in them losing their jobs to a computer. However, introducing a software product gradually can have two benefits. First, the understandable fear of being replaced by a computer is diminished. Second, it is generally easier to learn the functionality of a complex software product if that functionality is introduced stepwise over a period of months, rather than as a whole.

5. There is empirical evidence that the iterative-and-incremental life-cycle works. The pie chart of Figure 1.1 shows the results of the report from The Standish Group on projects completed in 2004 [Hayes, 2004]. In fact, this report (the so-called CHAOS Report—see Just in Case You Wanted to Know Box 2.2) is produced every 2 years. Figure 2.7 shows the results for 1994 through 2004. The percentage of successful products increased steadily from 16 percent in 1994 to 34 percent in 2002, but then decreased to 29 percent in 2004. In both the 2002 [Softwaremag.com, 2004] and 2004 [Hayes, 2004] reports, one of the factors associated with the successful projects was the use of an iterative process. (The reasons given for the decrease in the percentage of successful projects in 2004 included more large projects than in 2002, use of the waterfall model, lack of user involvement, and lack of support from senior executives [Hayes, 2004].)

The term *CHAOS* is an acronym. For some unknown reason, The Standish Group keeps the acronym top secret. They state [Standish, 2003]:

Only a few people at The Standish Group, and any one of the 360 people who received and saved the T-shirts we gave out after they completed the first survey in 1994, know what the CHAOS letters represent.

Figure 2.7
Results of the Standish Group CHAOS Report from 1994 to 2004.

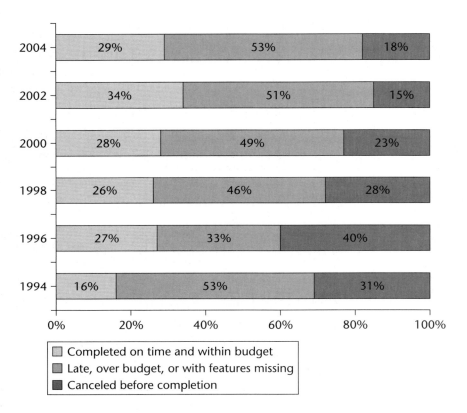

2.8   Managing Iteration and Incrementation

At first glance, the iterative-and-incremental model of Figures 2.4 and 2.5 looks totally chaotic. Instead of the orderly progression from requirements to implementation of the waterfall model (Figure 2.3), it appears that developers do whatever they like, perhaps some coding in the morning, an hour or two of design after lunch, and then half an hour of specifying before going home. That is *not* the case. On the contrary, the iterative-and-incremental model is as regimented as the waterfall model, because as previously pointed out, developing a software product using the iterative-and-incremental model is nothing more or less than developing a series of smaller software products, all using the waterfall model.

In more detail, as shown in Figure 2.3, developing a software product using the waterfall model means successively performing the requirements, analysis, design, and implementation phases (in that order) on the software product as a whole. If a problem is encountered, the feedback loops of Figure 2.3 (dashed arrows) are followed; that is, iteration (maintenance) is performed. However, if the same software product is developed using the iterative-and-incremental model, the software product is treated as a set of increments. For each increment in turn, the requirements, analysis, design, and implementation phases (in that order) are repeatedly performed *on that increment* until it is clear that no further iteration is needed. In other words, the project as a whole is broken up into a series of waterfall mini projects. During each mini project, iteration is performed as needed, as shown in Figure 2.5. Therefore, the reason the previous paragraph stated that the iterative-and-incremental model is as regimented as the waterfall model is because the iterative-and-incremental model *is* the waterfall model, applied successively.

2.9   Other Life-Cycle Models

We now consider a number of life-cycle models that are used in conjunction with the object-oriented paradigm. We begin with the infamous code-and-fix model.

2.9.1   Code-and-Fix Life-Cycle Model

It is unfortunate that so many products are developed using what might be termed the **code-and-fix life-cycle model**. The product is implemented without requirements or specifications, or any attempt at design. Instead, the developers simply throw code together and rework it as many times as necessary to satisfy the client. This approach is shown in Figure 2.8, which clearly displays the absence of requirements, specifications, and design. Although this approach may work well on short programming exercises 100 or 200 lines long, the code-and-fix model is totally unsatisfactory for products of any reasonable size. Figure 1.5 shows that the cost of changing a software product is relatively small if the

Figure 2.8
The code-and-fix life-cycle model.

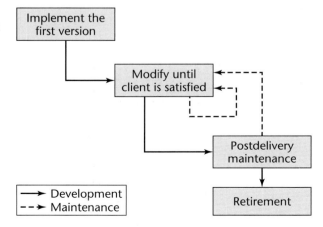

change is made during the requirements, analysis, or design phases but grows unacceptably large if changes are made after the product has been coded or, worse, if it has already been delivered and installed on the client's computer. Hence, the cost of the code-and-fix approach is actually far greater than the cost of a properly specified and meticulously designed product. In addition, maintenance of a product can be extremely difficult without specification or design documents, and the chances of a regression fault occurring are considerably greater. Instead of the code-and-fix approach, it is essential that, before development of a product begins, an appropriate life-cycle model be chosen.

Regrettably, all too many projects use the code-and-fix model. The problem is particularly acute in organizations that measure progress solely in terms of lines of code, so members of the software development team are pressured into churning out as many lines of code as possible, starting on Day One of the project. The code-and-fix model is the easiest way to develop software—and by far the worst way.

A simplified version of the waterfall model was presented in Section 2.2. We now consider that model in more detail.

2.9.2   Waterfall Life-Cycle Model

The **waterfall life-cycle model** was first put forward by Royce [1970]. Figure 2.9 shows the feedback loops for maintenance while the product is being developed, as reflected in Figure 2.3, the simplified waterfall model. Figure 2.9 also shows the feedback loops for postdelivery maintenance.

A critical point regarding the waterfall model is that no phase is complete until the documentation for that phase has been completed and the products of that phase have been approved by the software quality assurance (SQA) group. This carries over into modifications;

Figure 2.9
The full waterfall life-cycle model.

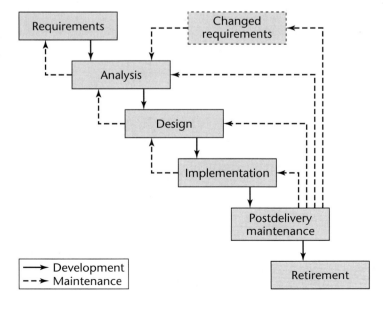

if the products of an earlier phase have to be changed as a consequence of following a feed-back loop, that earlier phase is deemed to be complete only when the documentation for the phase has been modified and the modifications have been checked by the SQA group.

Inherent in every phase of the waterfall model is testing. Testing is not a separate phase to be performed only after the product has been constructed, nor is it to be performed only at the end of each phase. Instead, as stated in Section 1.7, testing should proceed continually throughout the software process. In particular, during maintenance, it is necessary to ensure not only that the modified version of the product still does what the previous version did—and still does it correctly (regression testing)—but that it also satisfies any new requirements imposed by the client.

The waterfall model has many strengths, including the enforced disciplined approach—the stipulation that documentation be provided at each phase and the requirement that all the products of each phase (including the documentation) be meticulously checked by SQA. However, the fact that the waterfall model is documentation driven can also be a weakness. To see this, consider the following two somewhat bizarre scenarios.

First, Joe and Jane Johnson decide to build a house. They consult with an architect. Instead of showing them sketches, plans, and perhaps a scale model, the architect gives them a 20-page single-spaced typed document describing the house in highly technical terms. Even though both Joe and Jane have no previous architectural experience and hardly understand the document, they enthusiastically sign it and say, "Go right ahead, build the house!"

Another scenario is as follows. Mark Marberry buys his suits by mail order. Instead of mailing him pictures of their suits and samples of available cloths, the company sends Mark a written description of the cut and the cloth of their products. Mark then orders a suit solely on the basis of a written description.

The preceding two scenarios are highly unlikely. Nevertheless, they typify precisely the way software is often constructed using the waterfall model. The process begins with the specifications. In general, specification documents are long, detailed, and quite frankly, boring to read. The client is usually inexperienced in the reading of software specifications, and this difficulty is compounded by the fact that specification documents are usually written in a style with which the client is unfamiliar. The difficulty is even worse when the specifications are written in a formal (mathematical) specification language like Z [Spivey, 1992]. Nevertheless, the client proceeds to sign off on the specification document, whether properly understood or not. In many ways there is little difference between Joe and Jane Johnson contracting to have a house built from a written description that they only partially comprehend and clients approving a software product described in terms of a specification document that they only partially understand.

Mark Marberry and his mail-order suits may seem bizarre in the extreme, but that is precisely what happens when the waterfall model is used in software development. The first time that the client sees a working product is only after the entire product has been coded. Small wonder that software developers live in fear of the sentence, "I know this is what I asked for, but it isn't really what I wanted."

What has gone wrong? There is a considerable difference between the way a client understands a product as described by the specification document and the actual product. The specifications exist only on paper; the client therefore cannot really understand what the product itself will be like. The waterfall model, depending as it does so crucially on written specifications, can lead to the construction of products that simply do not meet the clients' real needs.

In fairness it should be pointed out that, just as an architect can help a client understand what is to be built by providing scale models, sketches, and plans, so the software engineer can use graphical techniques, such as UML diagrams (Chapter 15), to communicate with the client. The problem is that these graphical aids do not describe how the finished product will work. For example, there is a considerable difference between a flowchart (a diagrammatic description of a product) and the working product itself. In Chapters 10 and 11 we describe a solution to the problem that the specification document generally does not describe a product in a way that enables the client to determine whether the proposed product meets his or her needs.

We now examine rapid prototyping, used in object-oriented software engineering as described in Section 10.14.

2.9.3   Rapid-Prototyping Life-Cycle Model

A **rapid prototype** is a working model that is functionally equivalent to a subset of the product. For example, if the target product is to handle accounts payable, accounts receivable, and warehousing, then the rapid prototype might consist of a product that performs the screen handling for data capture and prints the reports, but does no file updating or error handling. A rapid prototype for a target product that is to determine the concentration of an enzyme in a solution might perform the calculation and display the answer, but without doing any validation or reasonableness checking of the input data.

The first step in the **rapid-prototyping life-cycle model** depicted in Figure 2.10 is to build a rapid prototype and let the client and future users interact and experiment with the rapid prototype. Once the client is satisfied that the rapid prototype indeed does most of what is required, the developers can draw up the specification document with some assurance that the product meets the client's real needs.

Figure 2.10
The rapid-prototyping life-cycle model.

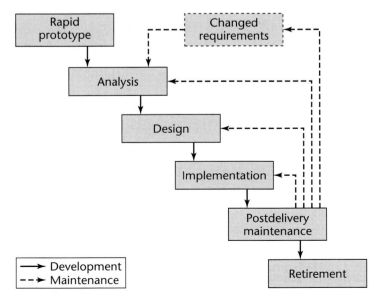

Having constructed the rapid prototype, the software process continues as shown in Figure 2.10. A major strength of the rapid-prototyping model is that the development of the product is essentially linear, proceeding from the rapid prototype to the delivered product; the feedback loops of the waterfall model (Figure 2.9) are less likely to be needed in the rapid-prototyping model. There are a number of reasons for this. First, the members of the development team use the rapid prototype to construct the specification document. Because the working rapid prototype has been validated through interaction with the client, it is reasonable to expect that the resulting specification document will be correct. Second, consider the design. Even though the rapid prototype has (quite rightly) been hurriedly assembled, the design team can gain insight from it—at worst it will be of the "how not to do it" variety. Again, the feedback loops of the waterfall model are less likely to be needed here.

Implementation comes next. In the waterfall model, implementation of the design sometimes leads to design faults coming to light. In the rapid-prototyping model, the fact that a preliminary working version of the software product has already been built tends to lessen the need to repair the design during or after implementation. The prototype has given some insights to the design team, even though it may reflect only partial functionality of the complete target product.

Once the product has been accepted by the client and installed, postdelivery maintenance begins. Depending on the specific maintenance task that has to be performed, the cycle is reentered either at the requirements, analysis, design, or implementation phase.

An essential aspect of a rapid prototype is embodied in the word *rapid*. The developers should endeavor to construct the rapid prototype as rapidly as possible to speed up the software development process. After all, the sole use of the rapid prototype is to determine what the client's real needs are; once this has been determined, the rapid prototype implementation is discarded but the lessons learned are retained and used in subsequent development phases. For this reason, the internal structure of the rapid prototype is not relevant. What is important is that the prototype be built rapidly and modified rapidly to reflect the client's needs. Therefore, speed is of the essence.

The use of rapid prototyping within the context of the Unified Process is described in Chapter 10.

2.9.4   Open-Source Life-Cycle Model

Almost all successful **open-source software** projects go through two informal phases. First, a single individual has an idea for a program, such as an operating system (Linux), a Net browser (Firefox), or a Web server (Apache). He or she builds an initial version, which is then made available for distribution free of charge to anyone who would like a copy; nowadays, this is done via the Internet, at sites like SourceForge.net and FreshMeat.net. If someone downloads a copy of the initial version and thinks that the program fulfills a need, he or she will start to use that program.

If there is sufficient interest in the program, the project moves gradually into informal phase two. Users become co-developers, in that some users report defects and others suggest ways of fixing those defects. Some users put forward ideas for extending the program, and others implement those ideas. As the program expands in functionality, yet other users port the program so that it can run on additional operating system/hardware combinations.

A key aspect is that individuals work on an open-source project in their spare time on a voluntary basis; they are not paid to participate.

Now look more closely at the three activities of the second informal phase:

1. Reporting and correcting defects is corrective maintenance.
2. Adding additional functionality is perfective maintenance.
3. Porting the program to a new environment is adaptive maintenance.

In other words, the second informal phase of the open-source life-cycle model consists solely of postdelivery maintenance, as shown in Figure 2.11. In fact, the term *co-developers* in the second paragraph of this section should rather be *co-maintainers*.

There are a number of key differences between closed-source and open-source software life-cycle models:

- Closed-source software is maintained and tested by teams of employees of the organization that owns the software. Users sometimes submit defect reports. However, these are restricted to **failure reports** (reports of observed incorrect behavior); users have no access to the source code, so they cannot possibly submit **fault reports** (reports that describe where the source code is incorrect and how to correct it).

   In contrast, open-source software is generally maintained by unpaid volunteers. Users are strongly encouraged to submit defect reports. Although all users have access to the source code, only the minority have the inclination and the time, as well as the necessary skills, to peruse the source code and submit fault reports ("fixes"); most defect reports are therefore failure reports. There is generally a **core group** of dedicated maintainers who take responsibility for managing the open-source project. Some members of the **peripheral group**, that is, the users who are not members of the core group, choose to submit defect reports from time to time. The members of the core group are responsible for ensuring that these defects are corrected. In more detail, when a fault report is submitted, a core group member checks that the fix indeed solves the problem and modifies the source code appropriately. When a failure report is submitted, a member of the core group will either personally determine the fix or assign that task to another volunteer, often a member of the peripheral group who is eager to become more involved in the open-source project. Again, the power to install the fix in the software is restricted to members of the core group.

Figure 2.11
The open-source life-cycle model.

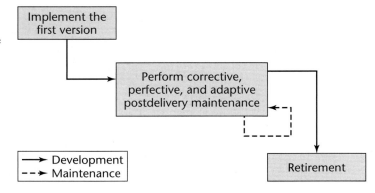

- New versions of closed-source software are typically released roughly once a year. Each new version is carefully checked by the software quality assurance group before release, and a wide variety of test cases are run.

   In contrast, a dictum of the open-source movement is "Release early. Release often" [Raymond, 2000]. That is, the core group releases a new version of an open-source product as soon as it is ready, which may be a month or even only a day after the previous version was released. This new version is released after minimal testing; it is assumed that more extensive testing will be performed by the members of the peripheral group. A new version may be installed by literally hundreds of thousands of users within a day or two of its release. These users do not run test cases as such. However, in the course of utilizing the new version on their computer, they encounter failures, which they report via e-mail. In this way, faults in the new version (as well as deeper faults in previous versions) come to light and are corrected.

Comparing Figures 2.8, 2.10, and 2.11, we see that the open-source life-cycle model has features in common with both the code-and-fix model and the rapid-prototyping model. In all three life-cycle models, an initial working version is produced. In the case of the rapid-prototyping model, this initial version is discarded, and the target product is then specified and designed before being coded. In both the code-and-fix and open-source life-cycle models, the initial version is reworked until it becomes the target product. Accordingly, in an open-source project, there are generally no specifications or design.

Bearing in mind the great importance of having specifications and designs, how have some open-source projects been so successful? In the closed-source world, some software professionals are more skilled and some are less skilled (see Section 9.2). The challenge of producing open-source software has attracted some of the finest software experts. In other words, an open-source project can be successful, despite the lack of specifications or design, if the skills of the individuals who work on that project are so superb that they can function effectively without specifications or design. However, notwithstanding the abilities of the members of the core group, eventually a point will be reached when the open-source product is no longer maintainable [Yu, Schach, Chen, and Offutt, 2004].

The open-source life-cycle model is restricted in its applicability. On the one hand, the open-source model has been extremely successful when used for certain infrastructure software projects, such as operating systems (Linux, OpenBSD, Mach, Darwin), Web browsers (Firefox, Netscape), compilers (gcc), Web servers (Apache), or database management systems (MySQL). On the other hand, it is hard to conceive of open-source development of a software product to be used in one commercial organization. A key to open-source software development is that the members of both the core group and the periphery are users of the software being developed. Consequently, the open-source life-cycle model is inapplicable unless a wide range of users consider the target product to be useful to them.

At the time of this writing, there are more than 175,000 open-source projects at Source-Forge.net and FreshMeat.net. About half them have never even attracted a team to work on the project. Of those where work has started, the overwhelming preponderance have never been completed and are unlikely to ever progress much further. But when the open-source model has worked, it has sometimes been incredibly successful. The open-source products listed in parentheses in the previous paragraph are extremely widely used; most of them are utilized on a regular basis by literally millions of users.

Explanations for the success of the open-source life-cycle model are presented in Chapter 4 within the context of team organizational aspects of open-source software projects.

2.9.5   Agile Processes

Extreme programming [Beck, 2000] is a somewhat controversial new approach to software development based on the iterative-and-incremental model. The first step is that the software development team determines the various features (***stories***) the client would like the product to support. For each such feature, the team informs the client how long it will take to implement that feature and how much it will cost. This first step corresponds to the requirements and analysis workflows of the iterative-and-incremental model (Figure 2.4).

The client selects the features to be included in each successive build using cost–benefit analysis (Section 5.2), that is, on the basis of the time and the cost estimates provided by the development team as well as the potential benefits of the feature to his or her business. The proposed build is broken down into smaller pieces termed **tasks**. A programmer first draws up test cases for a task; this is termed ***test-driven development (TDD)***. Two programmers work together on one computer (***pair programming***) [Williams, Kessler, Cunningham, and Jeffries, 2000], implementing the task and ensuring that all the test cases work correctly. The two programmers alternate typing every 15 or 20 minutes; the programmer who is not typing carefully checks the code while it is being entered by his or her partner. The task is then integrated into the current version of the product. Ideally, implementing and integrating a task should take no more than a few hours. In general, a number of pairs will implement tasks in parallel, so integration takes place essentially continuously. Team members change coding partners daily, if possible; learning from the other team members increases everyone's skill level. The TDD test cases used for the task are retained and utilized in all further integration testing.

Some drawbacks to pair programming have been observed in practice [Drobka, Noftz, and Raghu, 2004]. For example, pair programming requires large blocks of uninterrupted time, and software professionals can have difficulty in finding 3- to 4-hour blocks of time. In addition, pair programming does not always work well with shy or overbearing individuals, or with two inexperienced programmers.

A number of features of extreme programming (XP) are somewhat different to the way that software is usually developed:

- The computers of the XP team are set up in the center of a large room lined with small cubicles.
- A client representative works with the XP team at all times.
- No individual can work overtime for two successive weeks.
- There is no specialization. Instead, all members of the XP team work on requirements, analysis, design, code, and testing.
- There is no overall design step before the various builds are constructed. Instead, the design is modified while the product is being built. This procedure is termed ***refactoring***. Whenever a test case will not run, the code is reorganized until the team is satisfied that the design is simple, straightforward, and runs all the test cases satisfactorily.

Two acronyms now associated with extreme programming are YAGNI ("you aren't gonna need it") and DTSTTCPW ("do the simplest thing that could possibly work"). In other words, a principle of extreme programming is to minimize the number of features; there is no need to build a product that does any more than what the client actually needs.

Extreme programming is one of a number of new paradigms that are collectively referred to as ***agile processes***. Seventeen software developers (later dubbed the Agile Alliance) met at a Utah ski resort for two days in February 2001 and produced the *Manifesto for Agile Software Development* [Beck et al., 2001]. Many of the participants had previously authored their own software development methodologies, including Extreme Programming [Beck, 2000], Crystal [Cockburn, 2001], and Scrum [Schwaber, 2001]. Consequently, the Agile Alliance did not prescribe a specific life-cycle model, but rather laid out a group of underlying principles that were common to their individual approaches to software development.

Agile processes are characterized by considerably less emphasis on analysis and design than in almost all other modern life-cycle models. Implementation starts much earlier in the life cycle, because working software is considered more important than detailed documentation. Responsiveness to changes in requirements is another major goal of agile processes, and so is the importance of collaborating with the client.

One of the principles in the *Manifesto* is to deliver working software frequently, ideally every 2 or 3 weeks. One way of achieving this is to use ***timeboxing*** [Jalote, Palit, Kurien, and Peethamber, 2004], which has been used for many years as a time management technique. A specific amount of time is set aside for a task, and the team members then do the best job they can during that time. Within the context of agile processes, typically 3 weeks are set aside for each iteration. On the one hand, it gives the client confidence to know that a new version with additional functionality will arrive every 3 weeks. On the other hand, the developers know that they will have 3 weeks (but no more) to deliver a new iteration without client interference of any kind; once the client has chosen the work for an iteration, it cannot be changed or increased. However, if it is impossible to complete the entire task in the timebox, the work may be reduced ("descoped"). In other words, agile processes demand fixed time, not fixed features.

Another common feature of agile processes is to have a short meeting at a regular time each day. All team members have to attend the meeting. Making all the participants stand in a circle, rather than sit around a table, helps to ensure that the meeting lasts no more than the stipulated 15 minutes. Each team member in turn answers five questions:

1. What have I done since yesterday's meeting?
2. What am I working on today?
3. What problems are preventing me from achieving this?
4. What have we forgotten?
5. What did I learn that I would like to share with the team?

The aim of the ***stand-up meeting*** is to raise problems, not solve them; solutions are found at follow-up meetings, preferably held directly after the stand-up meeting. Like timeboxing, stand-up meetings are a successful management technique now utilized within the context of agile processes. Both timeboxed iterations and stand-up meetings are instances of two basic principles that underlie all agile methods: communication, and satisfying the client's needs as quickly as possible.

Agile processes have been successfully used on a number of small-scale projects. However, agile processes have not yet been used widely enough to determine whether this approach will fulfill its early promise. Furthermore, even if agile processes turn out to be good for small-scale software products, that does not necessarily mean that they can be used for medium- or large-scale software products, as will now be explained.

To appreciate why many software professionals have expressed doubts about agile processes within the context of medium- and especially large-scale software products [Reifer, Maurer, and Erdogmus, 2003], consider the following analogy by Grady Booch [2000]. Anyone can successfully hammer together a few planks to build a doghouse, but it would be foolhardy to build a three-bedroom home without detailed plans. In addition, skills in plumbing, wiring, and roofing are needed to build a three-bedroom home, and inspections are essential. (That is, being able to build small-scale software products does not necessarily mean that one has the skills for building medium-scale software products.) Furthermore, the fact that a skyscraper is the height of 1000 doghouses does not mean that one can build a skyscraper by piling 1000 doghouses on top of one another. In other words, building large-scale software products requires even more specialized and sophisticated skills than those needed to cobble together small-scale software products.

A key determinant in deciding whether agile processes are indeed a major breakthrough in software engineering will be the cost of future postdelivery maintenance (Section 1.3.2). That is, if the use of agile processes results in a reduction in the cost of postdelivery maintenance, XP and other agile processes will become widely adopted. On the other hand, refactoring is an intrinsic component of agile processes. As previously explained, the product is not designed as a whole; instead, the design is developed incrementally, and the code is reorganized whenever the current design is unsatisfactory for any reason. This refactoring then continues during postdelivery maintenance. If the design of a product when it passes its acceptance test is open-ended and flexible, then perfective maintenance should be easy to achieve at a low cost. However, if the design has to be refactored whenever additional functionality is added, then the cost of postdelivery maintenance of that product will be unacceptably high. As a consequence of the newness of the approach, as yet only a small amount of experimental data exist on development using agile processes, and almost none on maintenance. However, preliminary data indicate that refactoring can consume a large percentage of the overall cost [Li and Alshayeb, 2002].

Nevertheless, experiments have shown that certain features of agile processes work well. For example, Williams, Kessler, Cunningham, and Jeffries [2000] have shown that pair programming leads to the development of higher-quality code in a shorter time, with greater job satisfaction. Accordingly, even if agile processes as a whole prove to be disappointing, some features of agile processes may be adopted as mainstream software engineering practices in the future.

The *Manifesto for Agile Software Development* essentially claims that agile processes are superior to more disciplined processes like the Unified Process (Chapter 3). Skeptics respond that proponents of agile processes are little more than hackers. However, there is a middle ground. The two approaches are not incompatible; it is possible to incorporate proven features of agile processes within the framework of disciplined processes. This integration of the two approaches is described in books such as the one by Boehm and Turner [2003].

In conclusion, agile processes appear to be a useful approach to building small-scale software products when the client's requirements are vague. In addition, some of the features of agile processes can be effectively utilized within the context of other life-cycle models.

2.9.6   Synchronize-and-Stabilize Life-Cycle Model

Microsoft, Inc., is the world's largest manufacturer of COTS software. The majority of its packages are built using a version of the iterative-and-incremental model that has been termed the ***synchronize-and-stabilize life-cycle model*** [Cusumano and Selby, 1997].

The requirements analysis phase is conducted by interviewing numerous potential clients for the package and extracting a list of features of highest priority to the clients. A specification document is now drawn up. Next, the work is divided into three or four builds. The first build consists of the most critical features, the second build consists of the next most critical features, and so on. Each build is carried out by a number of small teams working in parallel. At the end of each day, all the teams ***synchronize***; that is, they put the partially completed components together and test and debug the resulting product. ***Stabilization*** is performed at the end of each of the builds. Any remaining faults that have been detected so far are fixed, and they now ***freeze*** the build; that is, no further changes will be made to the specifications.

The repeated synchronization step ensures that the various components always work together. Another advantage of this regular execution of the partially constructed product is that the developers obtain early insight into the operation of the product and can modify the requirements if necessary during the course of a build. The life-cycle model can even be used if the initial specification is incomplete. The synchronize-and-stabilize model is considered further in Section 4.5, where team organizational details are discussed.

Finally we describe the spiral model, which is risk-driven; controlling risk is an essential aspect of the Unified Process.

2.9.7   Spiral Life-Cycle Model

As stated in Section 2.5, an element of risk is always involved in the development of software. For example, key personnel can resign before the product has been adequately documented. The manufacturer of hardware on which the product is critically dependent can go bankrupt. Too much, or too little, can be invested in testing and quality assurance. After spending hundreds of thousands of dollars on developing a major software product, technological breakthroughs can render the entire product worthless. An organization may research and develop a database management system, but before the product can be marketed, a lower-priced, functionally equivalent package is announced by a competitor. The components of a product may not fit together when integration is performed. For obvious reasons, software developers try to minimize such risks wherever possible.

One way of minimizing certain types of risk is to construct a prototype. As described in Section 2.9.3, one approach to reducing the risk that the delivered product will not satisfy the client's real needs is to construct a rapid prototype during the requirements phase. During subsequent phases, other sorts of prototypes may be appropriate. For example, a telephone company may devise a new, apparently highly effective algorithm for routing calls through a long-distance network. If the product is implemented but does not work as expected, the telephone company will have wasted the cost of developing the product. In addition, angry or inconvenienced customers may take their business elsewhere. This outcome can be avoided by constructing a proof-of-concept prototype to handle only the routing of calls and testing it on a simulator. In this way, the actual system is not disturbed;

and for the cost of implementing just the routing algorithm, the telephone company can determine whether it is worthwhile to develop an entire network controller incorporating the new algorithm.

A proof-of-concept prototype is not a rapid prototype constructed to be certain that the requirements have been accurately determined, as described in Section 2.9.3. Instead, it is more like an engineering prototype, that is, a scale model constructed to test the feasibility of construction. If the development team is concerned whether a particular part of the proposed software product can be constructed, a **proof-of-concept prototype** is constructed. For example, the developers may be concerned whether a particular computation can be performed quickly enough. In that case, they build a prototype to test the timing of just that computation. Or they may be worried that the font they intend to use for all screens will be too small for the average user to read without eyestrain. In this instance, they construct a prototype to display a number of different screens and determine by experiment whether the users find the font uncomfortably small.

The idea of minimizing risk via the use of prototypes and other means is the idea underlying the **spiral life-cycle model** [Boehm, 1988]. A simplified way of looking at this life-cycle model is as a waterfall model with each phase preceded by risk analysis, as shown in Figure 2.12. Before commencing each phase, an attempt is made to mitigate (control) the risks. If it is impossible to mitigate all the significant risks at that stage, then the project is immediately terminated.

Figure 2.12
A simplified version of the spiral life-cycle model.

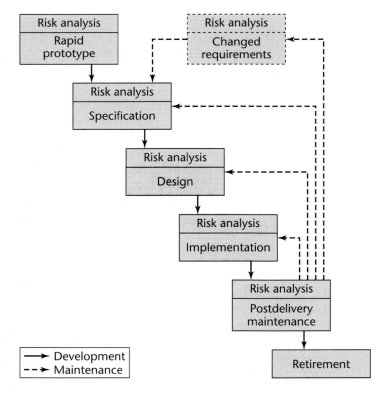

Prototypes can be used effectively to provide information about certain classes of risk. For example, timing constraints can generally be tested by constructing a prototype and measuring whether the prototype can achieve the necessary performance. If the prototype is an accurate functional representation of the relevant features of the product, then measurements made on the prototype should give the developers a good idea as to whether the timing constraints can be achieved.

Other areas of risk are less amenable to prototyping, for example, the risk that the software personnel necessary to build the product cannot be hired or that key personnel may resign before the project is complete. Another potential risk is that a particular team may not be competent enough to develop a specific large-scale product. A successful contractor who builds single-family homes would probably not be able to build a high-rise office complex. In the same way, there are essential differences between small-scale and large-scale software, and prototyping is of little use. This risk cannot be mitigated by testing team performance on a much smaller prototype, in which team organizational issues specific to large-scale software cannot arise. Another area of risk for which prototyping cannot be employed is evaluating the delivery promises of a hardware supplier. A strategy the developer can adopt is to determine how well previous clients of the supplier have been treated, but past performance is by no means a certain predictor of future performance. A penalty clause in the delivery contract is one way of trying to ensure that essential hardware is delivered on time, but what if the supplier refuses to sign an agreement that includes such a clause? Even with a penalty clause, late delivery may occur and eventually lead to legal action that can drag on for years. In the meantime, the software developer may have gone bankrupt because nondelivery of the promised hardware caused nondelivery of the promised software. In short, whereas prototyping helps reduce risk in some areas, in other areas it is at best a partial answer, and in still others it is no answer at all.

The full spiral model is shown in Figure 2.13. The radial dimension represents cumulative cost to date, and the angular dimension represents progress through the spiral. Each cycle of the spiral corresponds to a phase. A phase begins (in the top left quadrant) by determining objectives of that phase, alternatives for achieving those objectives, and constraints imposed on those alternatives. This process results in a strategy for achieving those objectives. Next, that strategy is analyzed from the viewpoint of risk. Attempts are made to mitigate every potential risk, in some cases by building a prototype. If certain risks cannot be mitigated, the project may be terminated immediately; under some circumstances, however, a decision could be made to continue the project but on a significantly smaller scale. If all risks are successfully mitigated, the next development step is started (bottom right quadrant). This quadrant of the spiral model corresponds to the waterfall model. Finally, the results of that phase are evaluated and the next phase is planned.

The spiral model has been used successfully to develop a wide variety of products. In one set of 25 projects in which the spiral model was used in conjunction with other means of increasing productivity, the productivity of every project increased by at least 50 percent over previous productivity levels and by 100 percent in most of the projects [Boehm, 1988]. To be able to decide whether the spiral model should be used for a given project, the strengths and weaknesses of the spiral model are now assessed.

The spiral model has a number of strengths. The emphasis on alternatives and constraints supports the reuse of existing software (Section 8.1) and the incorporation of software quality as a specific objective. In addition, a common problem in software development is

Figure 2.13   Full spiral life-cycle model.

Source: [Boehm, 1988] (© 1988 IEEE)

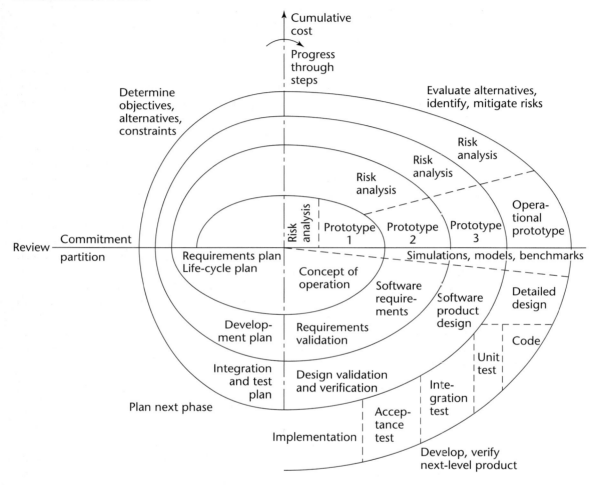

determining when the products of a specific workflow have been adequately tested. Spending too much time on testing is a waste of money, and delivery of the product may be unduly delayed. Conversely, if too little testing is performed, then the delivered software may contain residual faults, resulting in unpleasant consequences for the developers. The spiral model answers this question in terms of the risks that would be incurred by not doing enough testing or by doing too much testing. Perhaps most important, within the structure of the spiral model, postdelivery maintenance is simply another cycle of the spiral; there is essentially no distinction between postdelivery maintenance and development. Therefore, the problem that postdelivery maintenance is sometimes maligned by ignorant software professionals does not arise, because postdelivery maintenance is treated the same way as development.

There are restrictions on the applicability of the spiral model. Specifically, in its present form, the model is intended exclusively for internal development of large-scale software [Boehm, 1988]. Consider an internal project, that is, one where the developers and client are members of the same organization. If risk analysis leads to the conclusion that the project should be terminated, then in-house software personnel can simply be reassigned to a different project. However, once a contract has been signed between a development organization and an external client, an attempt by either side to terminate that contract can lead to a breach-of-contract lawsuit. Therefore, in the case of contract software, all risk analysis must be performed by both client and developers before the contract is signed, not as in the spiral model.

A second restriction on the spiral model relates to the size of the project. Specifically, the spiral model is applicable to only large-scale software. It makes no sense to perform risk analysis if the cost of performing the risk analysis is comparable to the cost of the project as a whole, or if performing the risk analysis would significantly affect the profit potential. Instead, the developers should first decide how much is at risk and then how much risk analysis, if any, to perform.

A major strength of the spiral model is that it is risk driven, but this can also be a weakness. Unless the software developers are skilled at pinpointing the possible risks and analyzing the risks accurately, there is a real danger that the team may believe that all is well at a time when the project, in fact, is headed for disaster. Only if the members of the development team are competent risk analysts should management decide to use the spiral model.

Overall, however, the major weakness of the spiral model, as well as the waterfall model and the rapid-prototyping model, is that it assumes that software is developed in discrete phases. In reality, however, software development is iterative and incremental, as reflected in the evolution-tree model (Section 2.2) or the iterative-and-incremental model (Section 2.5).

2.10   Comparison of Life-Cycle Models

Nine different software life-cycle models have been examined with special attention paid to some of their strengths and weaknesses. The code-and-fix model (Section 2.9.1) should be avoided. The waterfall model (Section 2.9.2) is a known quantity. Its strengths are understood, and so are its weaknesses. The rapid-prototyping model (Section 2.9.3) was developed as a reaction to a specific perceived weakness in the waterfall model, namely, that the delivered product may not be what the client really needs. However, there is still insufficient evidence that this approach is superior to the waterfall model in other respects. The open-source life-cycle model has been incredibly successful in a small number of cases when used to construct infrastructure software (Section 2.9.4). Agile processes (Section 2.9.5) are a set of controversial new approaches that, so far, appear to work, but for only small-scale software. The synchronize-and-stabilize model (Section 2.9.6) has been used with great success by Microsoft, but as yet there is no evidence of comparable success in other corporate cultures. Yet another alternative is to use the spiral model (Section 2.9.7), but only if the developers are adequately trained in risk analysis and risk resolution. The evolution-tree model (Section 2.2) and the iterative-and-incremental model (Section 2.5) are closest to the way that software is produced in the real world. An overall comparison appears in Figure 2.14.

Figure 2.14 Comparison of life-cycle models described in this chapter, including the section in which each is defined.

Life-Cycle Model	Strengths	Weaknesses
Evolution-tree model (Section 2.2)	Closely models real-world software production Equivalent to the iterative-and-incremental model	
Iterative-and-incremental life-cycle model (Section 2.5)	Closely models real-world software production Underlies the Unified Process	
Code-and-fix life-cycle model (Section 2.9.1)	Fine for short programs that require no maintenance	Totally unsatisfactory for nontrivial programs
Waterfall life-cycle model (Section 2.9.2)	Disciplined approach Document driven	Delivered product may not meet client's needs
Rapid-prototyping life-cycle model (Section 2.9.3)	Ensures that the delivered product meets the client's needs	Not yet proven beyond all doubt
Open-source life-cycle model (Section 2.9.4)	Has worked extremely well in a small number of instances	Limited applicability Usually does not work
Agile processes (Section 2.9.5)	Works well when the client's requirements are vague	Appears to work on only small-scale projects
Synchronize-and-stabilize life-cycle model (Section 2.9.6)	Future users' needs are met Ensures that components can be successfully integrated	Has not been widely used other than at Microsoft
Spiral life-cycle model (Section 2.9.7)	Risk driven	Can be used for only large-scale, in-house products Developers have to be competent in risk analysis and risk resolution

Each software development organization should decide on a life-cycle model that is appropriate for that organization, its management, its employees, and its software process and should vary the life-cycle model depending on the features of the specific product currently under development. Such a model incorporates appropriate aspects of the various life-cycle models, utilizing their strengths and minimizing their weaknesses.

Chapter Review

There are significant differences between the way that software is developed in theory (Section 2.1) and the way it is developed in practice. The Winburg mini case study is used to introduce the evolution-tree model (Section 2.2). Lessons of this mini case study, especially that requirements change, are presented in Section 2.3. Change is discussed in greater detail in Section 2.4, where the moving-target problem is presented using the Teal Tractors mini case study. In Section 2.5, the importance of iteration and incrementation in real-world software engineering is stressed, and the iterative-and-incremental model is presented. The Winburg mini case study is then re-examined in Section 2.6 to illustrate the equivalence of the evolution-tree model and the iterative-and-incremental model. In Section 2.7, the strengths of the iterative-and-incremental model are presented, particularly that it enables us to resolve risks early. Management of the iterative-and-incremental model is discussed in Section 2.8. A number of different life-cycle models are now described, including the code-and-fix life-cycle model (Section 2.9.1), waterfall life-cycle model (Section 2.9.2), rapid-prototyping life-cycle model (Section 2.9.3), open-source life-cycle model (Section 2.9.4), agile processes (Section 2.9.5), synchronize-and-stabilize life-cycle model (Section 2.9.6), and spiral life-cycle model (Section 2.9.7). In Section 2.10, these life-cycle models are compared and suggestions are made regarding the choice of a life-cycle model for a specific project.

For Further Reading

The waterfall model was first put forward in [Royce, 1970]. An analysis of the waterfall model is given in the first chapter of [Royce, 1998].

For an introduction to rapid prototyping, a suggested book is [Connell and Shafer, 1989].

The synchronize-and-stabilize model is outlined in [Cusumano and Selby, 1997] and described in detail in [Cusumano and Selby, 1995]. Insight into the synchronize-and-stabilize model can be obtained from [McConnell, 1996]. The spiral model is explained in [Boehm, 1988], and its application to the TRW Software Productivity System appears in [Boehm et al., 1984].

Extreme programming is described in [Beck, 2000]; refactoring is the subject of [Fowler et al., 1999]. The *Manifesto for Agile Software Development* may be found at [Beck et al., 2001]. Books have been published on a variety of agile methods, including [Cockburn, 2001] and [Schwaber, 2001]. Agile methods are advocated in [Highsmith and Cockburn, 2001; Boehm, 2002; DeMarco and Boehm, 2002; and Boehm and Turner, 2003], whereas the case against agile methods is presented in [Stephens and Rosenberg, 2003]. Refactoring is surveyed in [Mens and Tourwe, 2004]. The use of XP in four mission-critical projects is described in [Drobka, Noftz, and Raghu, 2004]. Issues that can arise when introducing agile processes within an organization that currently is using traditional methodologies are discussed in [Nerur, Mahapatra, and Mangalaraj, 2005]. A number of papers on extreme programming appear in the May/June 2003 issue of *IEEE Software*, including [Murru, Deias, and Mugheddu, 2003] and [Rasmusson, 2003], both of which describe successful projects developed using extreme programming. The effectiveness of test-driven development is discussed in [Erdogmus, Morisio, and Torchiano, 2005]. The June 2003 issue of *IEEE Computer* contains several articles on agile processes. The May/June 2005 issue of *IEEE Software* has four articles on agile processes, especially [Ceschi, Sillitti, Succi, and De Panfilis, 2005] and [Karlström and Runeson, 2005].

Risk analysis is described in [Ropponen and Lyttinen, 2000; Longstaff, Chittister, Pethia, and Haimes, 2000; and Scott and Vessey, 2002]. The May/June 1997 issue of *IEEE Software* contains 10 articles on risk management.

A major iterative and incremental model is described in detail in [Jacobson, Booch, and Rumbaugh, 1999]. However, many other iterative and incremental models have been put forward over the past 30 years, as recounted in [Larman and Basili, 2003]. The use of an incremental model to build an air-traffic control system is discussed in [Goth, 2000]. An iterative approach to re-engineering legacy systems is given in [Bianchi, Caivano, Marengo, and Visaggio, 2003].

Many other life-cycle models have been put forward. For example, Rajlich and Bennett [2000] describe a maintenance-oriented life-cycle model. The July/August 2000 issue of *IEEE Software* has a variety of papers on software life-cycle models, including [Williams, Kessler, Cunningham, and Jeffries, 2000] which describes an experiment on pair programming, one component of agile methods.

The proceedings of the International Software Process Workshops are a useful source of information on life-cycle models. [ISO/IEC 12207, 1995] is a widely accepted standard for software life-cycle processes.

Key Terms

agile process 55
analysis workflow 39
architecture 44
artifact 36
baseline 36
code-and-fix life-cycle
    model 47
core group 52
core workflow 39
design workflow 39
evolution-tree life-cycle
    model 35
extreme programming 54
failure report 52
fault report 52
feature creep 38
freeze 57
implementation
    workflow 39

incrementation 39
iteration 38
iterative-and-incremental
    life-cycle model 39
life-cycle model 35
Miller's Law 39
mitigate risk 45
model 35
moving-target problem 38
open-source software 51
pair programming 54
peripheral group 52
proof-of-concept
    prototype 58
rapid prototype 50
rapid-prototyping life-cycle
    model 50
refactoring 54
regression fault 38

requirements workflow 39
risk 45
robustness 44
spiral life-cycle model 58
stabilization 57
stand-up meeting 55
stepwise refinement 39
story 54
synchronize 57
synchronize-and-stabilize
    life-cycle model 57
task 54
test-driven development
    (TDD) 54
test workflow 39
timeboxing 55
waterfall life-cycle
    model 35, 48
workflow 39

Problems

2.1   Represent the Winburg mini case study of Section 2.3 using the waterfall model. Is this more or less effective than the evolution-tree model? Explain your answer.

2.2   Assume that the programmer in the Winburg mini case study had used single-precision numbers from the beginning. Draw the resulting evolution tree.

2.3   What is the connection between Miller's Law and stepwise refinement?

2.4   Does stepwise refinement correspond to iteration or incrementation?

2.5   How are a workflow, an artifact, and a baseline related?

2.6   What is the connection between the waterfall model and the iterative-and-incremental model?

2.7   Suppose you have to build a product to determine the inverse of 653.8231 to five decimal places. Once the product has been implemented and tested, it will be thrown away. Which life-cycle model would you use? Give reasons for your answer.

2.8   You are a software engineering consultant and have been called in by the vice-president for finance of a corporation that manufactures and sells boots. She wants your organization to build a product that will monitor the company's stock, starting with the purchasing of the leather and keeping track of the boots as they are manufactured, distributed to the individual stores, and sold to customers. What criteria would you use in selecting a life-cycle model for the project?

2.9   List the risks involved in developing the software of Problem 2.8. How would you attempt to mitigate each risk?

2.10   Your development of the stock control product for the bootwear chain is so successful that your organization decides that it must be rewritten as a package to be sold to a variety of different organizations that manufacture and sell products via their own retailers. The new product must therefore be portable and easily adapted to new hardware and/or operating systems.

How would the criteria you use in selecting a life-cycle model for this project differ from those in your answer to Problem 2.7?

2.11 Describe the sort of product that would be an ideal application for open-source software development.

2.12 Now describe the type of situation where open-source software development is inappropriate.

2.13 Describe the sort of product that would be an ideal application for an agile process.

2.14 Now describe the type of situation where an agile process is inappropriate.

2.15 Describe the sort of product that would be an ideal application for the spiral model.

2.16 Now describe the type of situation where the spiral model is inappropriate.

2.17 (Term Project) Which software life-cycle model would you use for the Osric's Office Appliances and Decor product described in Appendix A? Give reasons for your answer.

References 2.18 (Readings in Software Engineering) Your instructor will distribute copies of [Mens and Tourwe, 2004]. What are the implications of this paper for agile processes?

[Beck, 2000] K. BECK, *Extreme Programming Explained: Embrace Change,* Addison-Wesley Longman, Reading, MA, 2000.

[Beck et al., 2001] K. BECK, M. BEEDLE, A. COCKBURN, W. CUNNINGHAM, M. FOWLER, J. GRENNING, J. HIGHSMITH, A. HUNT, R. JEFFRIES, J. KERN, B. MARICK, R. C. MARTIN, S. MELLOR, K. SCHWABER, J. SUTHERLAND, D. THOMAS, AND A. VAN BENNEKUM, *Manifesto for Agile Software Development*, agilemanifesto.org, 2001.

[Bianchi, Caivano, Marengo, and Visaggio, 2003] A. BIANCHI, D. CAIVANO, V. MARENGO, AND G. VISAGGIO, "Iterative Reengineering of Legacy Systems," *IEEE Transactions on Software Engineering* **29** (March 2003), pp. 225–41.

[Boehm, 1988] B. W. BOEHM, "A Spiral Model of Software Development and Enhancement," *IEEE Computer* **21** (May 1988), pp. 61–72.

[Boehm, 2002] B. W. BOEHM, "Get Ready for Agile Methods, with Care," *IEEE Computer* **35** (January 2002), pp. 64–69.

[Boehm and Turner, 2003] B. BOEHM AND R. TURNER, *Balancing Agility and Discipline: A Guide for the Perplexed*, Addison-Wesley Professional, Boston, MA, 2003.

[Boehm et al., 1984] B. W. BOEHM, M. H. PENEDO, E. D. STUCKLE, R. D. WILLIAMS, AND A. B. PYSTER, "A Software Development Environment for Improving Productivity," *IEEE Computer* **17** (June 1984), pp. 30–44.

[Booch, 2000] G. BOOCH, "The Future of Software Engineering," keynote address, International Conference on Software Engineering, Limerick, Ireland, May 2000.

[Ceschi, Sillitti, Succi, and De Panfilis, 2005] M. CESCHI, A. SILLITTI, G. SUCCI, AND S. DE PANFILIS, "Project Management in Plan-Based and Agile Companies," *IEEE Software* **22** (May/June 2005), pp. 21–27.

[Cockburn, 2001] A. COCKBURN, *Agile Software Development*, Addison-Wesley Professional, Reading, MA, 2001.

[Connell and Shafer, 1989] J. L. CONNELL AND L. SHAFER, *Structured Rapid Prototyping: An Evolutionary Approach to Software Development*, Yourdon Press, Englewood Cliffs, NJ, 1989.

[Cusumano and Selby, 1995] M. A. CUSUMANO AND R. W. SELBY, *Microsoft Secrets: How the World's Most Powerful Software Company Creates Technology, Shapes Markets, and Manages People*, The Free Press/Simon and Schuster, New York, 1995.

[Cusumano and Selby, 1997] M. A. CUSUMANO AND R. W. SELBY, "How Microsoft Builds Software," *Communications of the ACM* **40** (June 1997), pp. 53–61.

[DeMarco and Boehm, 2002] T. DEMARCO AND B. BOEHM, "The Agile Methods Fray," *IEEE Computer* **35** (June 2002), pp. 90–92.

[Drobka, Noftz, and Raghu, 2004] J. DROBKA, D. NOFTZ, AND R. RAGHU, "Piloting XP on Four Mission-Critical Projects," *IEEE Software* **21** (November/December 2004), pp. 70–75.

[Erdogmus, Morisio, and Torchiano, 2005] H. ERDOGMUS, M. MORISIO, AND M. TORCHIANO, "On the Effectiveness of the Test-First Approach to Programming," *IEEE Transactions on Software Engineering* **31** (March 2005), pp. 226–237.

[Fowler et al., 1999] M. FOWLER WITH K. BECK, J. BRANT, W. OPDYKE, AND D. ROBERTS, *Refactoring: Improving the Design of Existing Code*, Addison-Wesley, Reading, MA, 1999.

[Goth, 2000] G. GOTH, "New Air Traffic Control Software Takes an Incremental Approach," *IEEE Software* **17** (July/August 2000), pp. 108–111.

[Grady, 1994] R. B. GRADY, "Successfully Applying Software Metrics," *IEEE Computer* **27** (September 1994), pp. 18–25.

[Hayes, 2004] F. HAYES, "Chaos Is Back," *Computerworld*, www.computerworld.com/managementtopics/management/project/story/0,10801,97283,00.html, November 8, 2004.

[Highsmith and Cockburn, 2001] J. HIGHSMITH AND A. COCKBURN, "Agile Software Development: The Business of Innovation," *IEEE Computer* **34** (September 2001), pp. 120–122.

[ISO/IEC 12207, 1995] "ISO/IEC 12207:1995, Information Technology—Software Life-Cycle Processes," International Organization for Standardization, International Electrotechnical Commission, Geneva, 1995.

[Jacobson, Booch, and Rumbaugh, 1999] I. JACOBSON, G. BOOCH, AND J. RUMBAUGH, *The Unified Software Development Process*, Addison-Wesley, Reading, MA, 1999.

[Jalote, Palit, Kurien, and Peethamber, 2004] P. JALOTE, A. PALIT, P. KURIEN AND V. T. PEETHAMBER, "Timeboxing: A Process Model for Iterative Software Development," *Journal of Systems and Software* **70** (February 2004), pp. 117–27.

[Karlström and Runeson, 2005] D. KARLSTRÖM AND P. RUNESON, "Combining Agile Methods with Stage-Gate Project Management," *IEEE Software* **22** (May/June 2005), pp. 43–49.

[Larman and Basili, 2003] C. LARMAN AND V. R. BASILI, "Iterative and Incremental Development: A Brief History," *IEEE Computer* **36** (June 2003), pp. 47–56.

[Li and Alshayeb, 2002] W. LI AND M. ALSHAYEB, "An Empirical Study of XP Effort," *Proceedings of the 17th International Forum on COCOMO and Software Cost Modeling*, Los Angeles, October 2002.

[Longstaff, Chittister, Pethia, and Haimes, 2000] T. A. LONGSTAFF, C. CHITTISTER, R. PETHIA, AND Y. Y. HAIMES, "Are We Forgetting the Risks of Information Technology?" *IEEE Computer* **33** (December 2000), pp. 43–51.

[McConnell, 1996] S. MCCONNELL, "Daily Build and Smoke Test," *IEEE Software* **13** (July/August 1996), pp. 144, 143.

[Mens and Tourwe, 2004] T. MENS AND T. TOURWE, "A Survey of Software Refactoring," *IEEE Transactions on Software Engineering* **30** (February 2004), pp. 126–39.

[Miller, 1956] G. A. MILLER, "The Magical Number Seven, Plus or Minus Two: Some Limits on Our Capacity for Processing Information," *The Psychological Review* **63** (March 1956), pp. 81–97; reprinted in: www.well.com/user/smalin/miller.html.

[Murru, Deias, and Mugheddu, 2003] O. MURRU, R. DEIAS, AND G. MUGHEDDU, "Assessing XP at a European Internet Company," *IEEE Software* **20** (May/June, 2003), pp. 37–43.

[Nerur, Mahapatra, and Mangalaraj, 2005] S. NERUR, R. MAHAPATRA, AND G. MANGALARAJ, "Challenges of Migrating to Agile Methodologies," *Communications of the ACM* **48** (May 2005), pp. 72–78.

[Rajlich and Bennett, 2000] V. RAJLICH AND K. H. BENNETT, "A Staged Model for the Software Life Cycle," *IEEE Computer* **33** (July 2000), pp. 66–71.

[Rasmussen, 2003] J. RASMUSSON, "Introducing XP into Greenfield Projects: Lessons Learned," *IEEE Software* **20** (May/June, 2003), pp. 21–29.

[Raymond, 2000] E. S. RAYMOND, *The Cathedral and the Bazaar: Musings on Linux and Open Source by an Accidental Revolutionary*, O'Reilly & Associates, Sebastopol, CA, 2000; also available at www.catb.org/~esr/writings/cathedral-bazaar/cathedral-bazaar/.

[Reifer, Maurer, and Erdogmus, 2003] D. REIFER, F. MAURER, AND H. ERDOGMUS, "Scaling Agile Methods," *IEEE Software* **20** (July/August 2004), pp. 12–14.

[Ropponen and Lyttinen, 2000] J. ROPPONEN AND K. LYTTINEN, "Components of Software Development Risk: How to Address Them? A Project Manager Survey," *IEEE Transactions on Software Engineering* **26** (February 2000), pp. 96–111.

[Royce, 1970] W. W. ROYCE, "Managing the Development of Large Software Systems: Concepts and Techniques," *1970 WESCON Technical Papers, Western Electronic Show and Convention*, Los Angeles, August 1970, pp. A/1-1–A/1-9; reprinted in: *Proceedings of the 11th International Conference on Software Engineering*, Pittsburgh, May 1989, IEEE, pp. 328–38.

[Royce, 1998] W. ROYCE, *Software Project Management: A Unified Framework*, Addison-Wesley, Reading, MA, 1998.

[Schwaber, 2001] K. SCHWABER, *Agile Software Development with Scrum*, Prentice Hall, Upper Saddle River, NJ, 2001.

[Scott and Vessey, 2002] J. E. SCOTT AND I. VESSEY, "Managing Risks in Enterprise Systems Implementations," *Communications of the ACM* **45** (April 2002), pp. 74–81.

[Softwaremag.com, 2004] "Standish: Project Success Rates Improved Over 10 Years," www.softwaremag.com/L.cfm?Doc=newsletter/2004-01-15/Standish, January 15, 2004.

[Spivey, 1992] J. M. SPIVEY, *The Z Notation: A Reference Manual*, Prentice Hall, New York, 1992.

[Standish, 2003] STANDISH GROUP INTERNATIONAL, "Introduction," www.standishgroup.com/chaos/introduction.pdf, 2003.

[Stephens and Rosenberg, 2003] M. STEPHENS AND D. ROSENBERG, *Extreme Programming Refactored: The Case against XP*, Apress, Berkeley, CA, 2003.

[Tomer and Schach, 2000] A. TOMER AND S. R. SCHACH, "The Evolution Tree: A Maintenance-Oriented Software Development Model," in: *Proceedings of the Fourth European Conference on Software Maintenance and Reengineering (CSMR 2000)*, Zürich, Switzerland, February/March 2000, pp. 209–14.

[Williams, Kessler, Cunningham, and Jeffries, 2000] L. WILLIAMS, R. R. KESSLER, W. CUNNINGHAM, AND R. JEFFRIES, "Strengthening the Case for Pair Programming," *IEEE Software* **17** (July/August 2000), pp. 19–25.

[Yu, Schach, Chen, and Offutt, 2004] L. YU, S. R. SCHACH, K. CHEN, AND J. OFFUTT, "Categorization of Common Coupling and Its Application to the Maintainability of the Linux Kernel," *IEEE Transactions on Software Engineering* **30** (October 2004), pp. 694–706.

3

The Software Process

Learning Objectives

After studying this chapter, you should be able to

- Explain why two-dimensional life-cycle models are important.
- Describe the five core workflows of the Unified Process.
- List the artifacts tested in the test workflow.
- Describe the four phases of the Unified Process.
- Explain the difference between the workflows and the phases of the Unified Process.
- Appreciate the importance of software process improvement.
- Describe the capability maturity model (CMM).

The software process is the way we produce software. It incorporates the methodology (Section 1.11) with its underlying software life-cycle model (Chapter 2) and techniques, the tools we use (Sections 5.4 through 5.10), and most important of all, the individuals building the software.

Different organizations have different software processes. For example, consider the issue of documentation. Some organizations consider the software they produce to be self-documenting, that is, the product can be understood simply by reading the source code. Other organizations, however, are documentation intensive. They punctiliously draw up specifications and check them methodically. Then they perform design activities painstakingly, check and recheck their designs before coding commences, and give extensive descriptions of each code artifact to the programmers. Test cases are preplanned, the result of each test run is logged, and the test data are meticulously filed away. Once the product has been delivered and installed on the client's computer, any suggested change must be proposed in writing, with detailed reasons for making the change. The proposed change can be made only with written authorization, and the modification is not integrated into the product until the documentation has been updated and the changes to the documentation approved.

Intensity of testing is another measure by which organizations can be compared. Some organizations devote up to half their software budgets to testing software, whereas others feel that only the user can thoroughly test a product. Consequently, some companies devote minimal time and effort to testing the product but spend a considerable amount of time fixing problems reported by users.

Postdelivery maintenance is a major preoccupation of many software organizations. Software that is 10, 15, or even 20 years old is continually enhanced to meet changing needs; in addition, residual faults continue to appear, even after the software has been successfully maintained for many years. Almost all organizations move their software to newer hardware every 3 to 5 years; this, too, constitutes postdelivery maintenance.

In contrast, yet other organizations essentially are concerned with research, leaving development—let alone maintenance—to others. This applies particularly to university computer science departments, where graduate students build software to prove that a particular design or technique is feasible. The commercial exploitation of the validated concept is left to other organizations. (See Just in Case You Wanted to Know Box 3.1 regarding the wide variation in the ways different organizations develop software.)

However, regardless of the exact procedure, the software development process is structured around the five workflows of Figure 2.4: requirements, analysis (specification), design, implementation, and testing (but see Just in Case You Wanted to Know Box 3.2). In this chapter, these workflows are described, together with potential challenges that may arise during each workflow. Solutions to the challenges associated with the production of software usually are nontrivial, and the rest of this book is devoted to describing suitable techniques. In the first part of this chapter, only the challenges are highlighted, but the reader is guided to the relevant sections or chapters for solutions. Accordingly, this part of the chapter not only is an overview of the software process, but a guide to much of the rest of the book. The chapter concludes with national and international initiatives to improve the software process.

We now examine the Unified Process.

The terminology of the Unified Process has been changed in order to be consistent with the Object Management Group's (OMG) Software Process Engineering Metamodel (SPEM), a standard for defining processes [OMG, 2005]. The old term *workflow* has been replaced by the new term *discipline*. The meaning of the term workflow has been slightly changed; it is now a specific sequence of activities. Accordingly, each Unified Process discipline now comprises a (new) workflow.

This modification of terminology has, not surprisingly, caused widespread confusion. Most software engineers therefore continue to use the term workflow as before. Accordingly, I have done the same throughout this book.

Another change has been to split the old requirements workflow into two workflows: the business modeling workflow and the (new) requirements workflow. Again, this is most confusing, so I have continued to include business modeling as part of the requirements workflow.

3.1   The Unified Process

As stated at the beginning of this chapter, methodology is one component of a software process. The primary object-oriented methodology today is the **Unified Process**. As explained in Just in Case You Wanted to Know Box 3.3, the Unified "Process" is actually a methodology, but the name Unified Methodology already had been used as the name of the first version of the **Unified Modeling Language (UML)**. The three precursors of the Unified Process (OMT, Booch's method, and Objectory) are no longer supported, and the other object-oriented methodologies have had little or no following. As a result, the Unified Process is usually the primary choice today for object-oriented software production. Fortunately, as will be demonstrated in Part 2 of this book, the Unified Process is an excellent object-oriented methodology in almost every way.

The Unified Process is not a specific series of steps that, if followed, result in the construction of a software product. In fact, no such single "one size fits all" methodology could exist because of the wide variety of types of software products. For example, there are many different application domains, such as insurance, aerospace, and manufacturing. Also, a methodology for rushing a COTS package to market ahead of its competitors is different from one used to construct a high-security electronic funds transfer network. In addition, the skills of software professionals can vary widely.

Instead, the Unified Process should be viewed as an adaptable methodology. That is, it is modified for the specific software product to be developed. As will be seen in Part 2, some features of the Unified Process are inapplicable to small- and even medium-scale software. However, much of the Unified Process is used for software products of all sizes. The emphasis in this book is on this common subset of the Unified Process, but aspects of the Unified Process applicable to only large-scale software also are discussed, to ensure that the issues that need to be addressed when larger software products are constructed are thoroughly appreciated.

Until about 10 years ago, the most popular object-oriented software development methodologies were object modeling technique (OMT) [Rumbaugh et al., 1991] and Grady Booch's method [Booch, 1994]. OMT was developed by Jim Rumbaugh and his team at the General Electric Research and Development Center in Schenectady, New York, whereas Grady Booch developed his method at Rational, Inc., in Santa Clara, California. All object-oriented software development methodologies essentially are equivalent, so the differences between OMT and Booch's method are small. Nevertheless, there always was a friendly rivalry between the supporters of the two camps.

This changed in October 1994, when Rumbaugh joined Booch at Rational. The two methodologists immediately began to work together to develop a methodology that would combine OMT and Booch's method. When a preliminary version of their work was published, it was pointed out that they had not developed a methodology but merely a notation for representing an object-oriented software product. The name *Unified Methodology* was quickly changed to *Unified Modeling Language* (UML). In 1995, they were joined at Rational by Ivar Jacobson, author of the Objectory methodology. Booch, Jacobson, and Rumbaugh, affectionately called the "Three Amigos" (after the 1986 John Landis movie *Three Amigos!* with Chevy Chase and Steve Martin), then worked together. Version 1.0 of UML, published in 1997, took the software engineering world by storm. Until then, there had been no universally accepted notation for the development of a software product. Almost overnight UML was used all over the world. The Object Management Group (OMG), an association of the world's leading companies in object technology, took the responsibility for organizing an international standard for UML, so that every software professional would use the same version of UML, thereby promoting communication among individuals within an organization as well as companies worldwide. UML [Booch, Rumbaugh, and Jacobson, 1999] is today the unquestioned international standard notation for representing object-oriented software products.

An orchestral score shows which musical instruments are needed to play the piece, the notes each instrument is to play and when it is to play them, as well as a whole host of technical information such as the key signature, tempo, and loudness. Could this information be given in English, rather than a diagram? Probably, but it would be impossible to play music from such a description. For example, there is no way a pianist and a violinist could perform a piece described as follows: "The music is in march time, in the key of B minor. The first bar begins with the A above middle C on the violin (a quarter note). While this note is being played, the pianist plays a chord consisting of seven notes. The right hand plays the following four notes: E sharp above middle C ..."

It is clear that, in some fields, a textual description simply cannot replace a diagram. Music is one such field; software development is another. And for software development, the best modeling language available today is UML.

Taking the software engineering world by storm with UML was not enough for the Three Amigos. Their next endeavor was to publish a complete software development methodology that unified their three separate methodologies. This unified methodology was first called the *Rational Unified Process* (RUP); *Rational* is in the name of the methodology not because the Three Amigos considered all other approaches to be irrational, but because at that time all three were senior managers at Rational, Inc. (Rational was bought by IBM in 2003). In their book on RUP [Jacobson, Booch, and Rumbaugh, 1999], the name *Unified Software Development Process* (USDP) was used. The term *Unified Process* is generally used today, for brevity.

3.2 Iteration and Incrementation

The object-oriented paradigm uses modeling throughout. A ***model*** is a set of UML diagrams that represent one or more aspects of the software product to be developed. (UML diagrams are introduced in Chapter 7.) Recall that UML stands for Unified *Modeling* Language. That is, UML is the tool that we use to represent (model) the target software product. A major reason for using a graphical representation like UML is best expressed by the old proverb, a picture is worth a thousand words. UML diagrams enable software professionals to communicate with one another more quickly and more accurately than if only verbal descriptions were used.

The object-oriented paradigm is an iterative and incremental methodology. Each workflow consists of a number of steps, and to carry out that workflow, the steps of the workflow are repeatedly performed until the members of the development team are satisfied that they have an accurate UML model of the software product they want to develop. That is, even the most experienced software professionals iterate and reiterate until they are finally satisfied that the UML diagrams are correct. The implication is that software engineers, no matter how outstanding they may be, almost never get the various work products right the first time. How can this be?

The nature of software products is such that virtually everything has to be developed iteratively and incrementally. After all, software engineers are human, and therefore subject to Miller's Law (Section 2.5). That is, it is impossible to consider everything at the same time, so just seven or so chunks (units of information) are handled initially. Then, when the next set of chunks is considered, more knowledge about the target software product is gained, and the UML diagrams are modified in the light of this additional information. The process continues in this way until eventually the software engineers are satisfied that all the models for a given workflow are correct. In other words, initially the best possible UML diagrams are drawn in the light of the knowledge available at the beginning of the workflow. Then, as more knowledge about the real-world system being modeled is gained, the diagrams are made more accurate (iteration) and extended (incrementation). Accordingly, no matter how experienced and skillful a software engineer may be, he or she repeatedly iterates and increments until satisfied that the UML diagrams are an accurate representation of the software product to be developed.

Ideally, by the end of this book, the reader would have the software engineering skills necessary for constructing the large, complex software products for which the Unified Process was developed. Unfortunately, there are three reasons why this is not feasible:

1. Just as it is not possible to become an expert on calculus or a foreign language in one single course, gaining proficiency in the Unified Process requires extensive study and, more important, unending practice in object-oriented software engineering.

2. The Unified Process was developed primarily for use in developing large, complex software products. To be able to handle the many intricacies of such software products, the Unified Process is itself large. It would be hard to cover every aspect of the Unified Process in a textbook of this size.

3. To teach the Unified Process, it is necessary to present a case study that illustrates the features of the Unified Process. To illustrate the features that apply to large software products, such a case study would have to be large. For example, just the specifications typically would take over 1000 pages.

For these three reasons, this book presents most, but not all, of the Unified Process.

The five ***core workflows*** of the Unified Process (requirements workflow, analysis workflow, design workflow, implementation workflow, and test workflow) and their challenges are now discussed.

3.3   The Requirements Workflow

Software development is expensive. The development process usually begins when the client approaches a development organization with regard to a software product that, in the opinion of the client, is either essential to the profitability of his or her enterprise or somehow can be justified economically. The aim of the ***requirements workflow*** is for the development organization to determine the client's needs.

The first task of the development team is to acquire a basic understanding of the ***application domain*** (***domain*** for short), that is, the specific environment in which the target software product is to operate. The domain could be banking, automobile manufacturing, or nuclear physics.

At any stage of the process, if the client stops believing that the software will be cost effective, development will terminate immediately. Throughout this chapter the assumption is made that the client feels that the cost is justified. Therefore, a vital aspect of software development is the ***business model***, a document that demonstrates the cost-effectiveness of the target product. (In fact, the "cost" is not always purely financial. For example, military software often is built for strategic or tactical reasons. Here, the cost of the software is the potential damage that could be suffered in the absence of the weapon being developed.)

At an initial meeting between client and developers, the client outlines the product as he or she conceptualizes it. From the viewpoint of the developers, the client's description of the desired product may be vague, unreasonable, contradictory, or simply impossible to achieve. The task of the developers at this stage is to determine exactly what the client needs and to find out from the client what constraints exist.

- A major constraint is almost always the ***deadline***. For example, the client may stipulate that the finished product must be completed within 14 months. In almost every application domain, it is now commonplace for a target software product to be mission critical. That is, the client needs the software product for core activities of his or her organization, and any delay in delivering the target product is detrimental to the organization.

- A variety of other constraints often are present such as ***reliability*** (for example, the product must be operational 99 percent of the time or the mean time between failures must be at least 4 months). Another common constraint is the size of the executable load image (for example, it has to run on the client's personal computer or on the hardware inside the satellite).

- The ***cost*** is almost invariably an important constraint. However, the client rarely tells the developers how much money is available to build the product. Instead, a common practice is that, once the specifications have been finalized, the client asks the developers to name their price for completing the project. Clients follow this bidding procedure in the hope that the amount of the developers' bid is lower than the amount the client has budgeted for the project.

The preliminary investigation of the client's needs sometimes is called **concept exploration**. In subsequent meetings between members of the development team and the client team, the functionality of the proposed product is successively refined and analyzed for technical feasibility and financial justification.

Up to now, everything seems to be straightforward. Unfortunately, the requirements workflow frequently is performed inadequately. When the product finally is delivered to the user, perhaps a year or two after the specifications have been signed off on by the client, the client may say to the developers, "I know that this is what I asked for, but it isn't really what I wanted." What the client asked for and, therefore, what the developers thought the client wanted, was not what the client actually *needed*. There can be a number of reasons for this predicament. First, the client may not truly understand what is going on in his or her own organization. For example, it is no use asking the software developers for a faster operating system if the cause of the current slow turnaround is a badly designed database. Or, if the client operates an unprofitable chain of retail stores, the client may ask for a financial management information system that reflects such items as sales, salaries, accounts payable, and accounts receivable. Such a product will be of little use if the real reason for the losses is shrinkage (theft by employees and shoplifting). If that is the case, then a stock control system rather than a financial management information system is required.

But the major reason why the client frequently asks for the wrong product is that software is complex. If it is difficult for a software professional to visualize a piece of software and its functionality, the problem is far worse for a client who is barely computer literate. As will be shown in Chapter 10, the Unified Process can help in this regard; the many UML diagrams of the Unified Process assist the client in gaining the necessary detailed understanding of what needs to be developed.

3.4   The Analysis Workflow

The aim of the **analysis workflow** is to analyze and refine the requirements to achieve the detailed understanding of the requirements essential for developing a software product correctly and maintaining it easily. At first sight, however, there is no need for an analysis workflow. Instead, an apparently simpler way to proceed would be to develop a software product by continuing with further iterations of the requirements workflow until the necessary understanding of the target software product has been obtained.

The key point is that the output of the requirements workflow must be totally comprehended by the client. In other words, the artifacts of the requirements workflow must be expressed in the language of the client, that is, in a natural (human) language such as English, Armenian, or Zulu. But all natural languages, without exception, are somewhat imprecise and lend themselves to misunderstanding. For example, consider the following paragraph:

> *A part record and a plant record are read from the database. If it contains the letter A directly followed by the letter Q, then calculate the cost of transporting that part to that plant.*

At first sight, this requirement seems perfectly clear. But to what does *it* (the second word in the second sentence) refer: the part record, the plant record, or the database?

Ambiguities of this kind cannot arise if the requirements are expressed (say) in a mathematical notation. However, if a mathematical notation is used for the requirements, then the client is unlikely to understand much of the requirements. As a result, there may well be miscommunication between the client and developers regarding the requirements, and consequently, the software product developed to satisfy those requirements may not be what the client needs.

The solution is to have two separate workflows. The requirements workflow is couched in the language of the client; the analysis workflow, in a more precise language that ensures that the design and implementation workflows are correctly carried out. In addition, more details are added during the analysis workflow, details not relevant to the client's understanding of the target software product but essential for the software professionals who will develop the software product. For example, the initial state of a statechart (Section 11.9) would surely not concern the client in any way but has to be included in the specifications if the developers are to build the target product correctly.

The specifications of the product constitute a contract. The software developers are deemed to have completed the contract when they deliver a product that satisfies the acceptance criteria of the specifications. For this reason, the specifications should not include imprecise terms like s*uitable, convenient, ample*, or *enough*, or similar terms that sound exact but in practice are equally imprecise, such as *optimal* or *98 percent complete*. Whereas contract software development can lead to a lawsuit, there is no chance of the specifications forming the basis for legal action when the client and developers are from the same organization. Nevertheless, even in the case of internal software development, the specifications always should be written as if they will be used as evidence in a trial.

More important, the specifications are essential for both testing and maintenance. Unless the specifications are precise, there is no way to determine whether they are correct, let alone whether the implementation satisfies the specifications. And it is hard to change the specifications unless some document states exactly what the specifications currently are.

When the Unified Process is used, there is no specification document in the usual sense of the term. Instead, a set of UML artifacts are shown to the client, as described in Chapter 11. These UML artifacts constitute a more precise description of the target product than can be achieved with a natural language specification.

During the analysis workflow, the architecture of the product is determined. That is, the product is decomposed into relatively independent components (classes), each with its own data (attributes) and operations (methods). The attributes are determined during the analysis phase. However, for reasons explained in Section 11.25, the methods are added to the classes during the design phase.

Once the client has approved the specifications, detailed planning and estimating commences. No client authorizes a software project without knowing in advance how long the project will take and how much it will cost. From the viewpoint of the developers, these two items are just as important. If the developers underestimate the cost of a project, then the client pays the agreed-upon fee, which may be significantly less than the developers' actual cost. Conversely, if the developers overestimate what the project costs, then the client may turn down the project or have the job done by other developers whose estimate is more reasonable. Similar issues arise with regard to duration estimates. If the developers underestimate how long completing a project will take, then the resulting late delivery of the product, at best, results in a loss of confidence by the client. At worst, lateness penalty clauses in the contract are invoked, causing the developers to suffer financially. Again, if the developers overestimate how long it will take for the product to be delivered, the client may well award the job to developers who promise faster delivery.

For the developers, merely estimating the duration and total cost is not enough. The developers need to assign the appropriate personnel to the various workflows of the development process. For example, the implementation team cannot start until the relevant design artifacts have been approved by the software quality assurance (SQA) group, and the design team is not needed until the analysis team has completed its task. In other words, the developers have to plan ahead. A software project management plan (SPMP) must be drawn up that reflects the separate workflows of the development process and shows which members of the development organization are involved in each task, as well as the deadlines for completing each task.

The earliest that such a detailed plan can be drawn up is when the specifications have been finalized. Before that time, the project is too amorphous for complete planning. Some aspects of the project certainly must be planned right from the start, but until the developers know exactly what is to be built, they cannot specify all aspects of the plan for building it.

Therefore, once the specifications have been approved by the client, preparation of the software project management plan commences. Major components of the plan are the **_deliverables_** (what the client is going to get), the **_milestones_** (when the client gets them), and the **_budget_** (how much it is going to cost).

The plan describes the software process in fullest detail. It includes aspects such as the life-cycle model to be used, the organizational structure of the development organization, project responsibilities, managerial objectives and priorities, the techniques and CASE tools to be used, and detailed schedules, budgets, and resource allocations. Underlying the entire plan are the duration and cost estimates; techniques for obtaining such estimates are described in Section 9.2.

The analysis workflow is described in Chapter 11. A major artifact of the analysis workflow is the software project management plan. An explanation of how to draw up the SPMP is given in Sections 9.4 though 9.6.

Now the design workflow is examined.

3.5   The Design Workflow

The specifications of a product spell out *what* the product is to do; the design shows *how* the product is to do it. More precisely, the aim of the **_design workflow_** is to refine the artifacts of the analysis workflow until the material is in a form that can be implemented by the programmers.

As described in Section 3.4, during the analysis workflow the target product is decomposed into classes and the attributes of each class are extracted. During the design workflow, the design team determines the internal structure of the product. The methods are extracted and assigned to the classes. In particular, the interface of each method (that is, the arguments passed to the method and the arguments returned by the method) must be specified in detail. For example, a method might measure the water level in a nuclear reactor and cause an alarm to sound if the level is too low. A method in an avionics product might take as input two or more sets of coordinates of an incoming enemy missile, compute its trajectory, and invoke another method to advise the pilot as to possible evasive action. Another important aspect of the design workflow is choosing appropriate algorithms for each method.

Turning now to the data, the attributes are extracted during the analysis workflow (Section 3.4). However, the formats of the attributes are determined during the design workflow. For example, suppose attribute grossProfit is extracted during the analysis workflow. During the design workflow, the design team determines that this attribute should be represented by an eight-digit integer, because the largest possible gross profit that the product could conceivably have to handle is $99,999,999. Similarly, the values of attribute statusOfPressureValve might be determined to be open, closed, disconnected, or inoperable.

The design team must keep a meticulous record of the design decisions that are made. This information is essential for two reasons:

1. While the product is being designed, a dead end will be reached at times and the design team must backtrack and redesign certain pieces. Having a written record of why specific decisions were made assists the team when this occurs and helps it get back on track.

2. The second reason is to facilitate future enhancements (postdelivery maintenance). Ideally, the design of the product should be open-ended, meaning that future enhancements can be done by adding new classes or replacing existing classes without affecting the design as a whole. Of course, in practice, this ideal is difficult to achieve. Deadline constraints in the real world are such that designers struggle against the clock to complete a design that satisfies the original specifications, without worrying about any later enhancements. If future enhancements (to be added after the product is delivered to the client) are included in the specifications, then these must be allowed for in the design, but this situation is extremely rare. In general, the specifications, and hence the design, deal with only present requirements. In addition, while the product is still being designed, there is no way to determine all possible future enhancements. Finally, if the design has to take *all* future possibilities into account, at best it will be unwieldy; at worst, it will be so complicated that implementation is impossible. So the designers have to compromise, putting together a design that can be extended in many reasonable ways without the need for total redesign. But, in a product that undergoes major enhancement, the time will come when the design simply cannot handle further changes. When this stage is reached, the product must be redesigned as a whole. The task of the redesign team is considerably easier if the team members are provided a record of the reasons for all the original design decisions.

3.6   The Implementation Workflow

The aim of the ***implementation workflow*** is to implement the target software product in the chosen implementation language(s). A small software product is sometimes implemented by the designer. In contrast, a large software product is partitioned into smaller subsystems, which are then implemented in parallel by coding teams. The subsystems, in turn, consist of **code artifacts** implemented by an individual programmer.

Usually, the only documentation given a programmer is the relevant design artifact, the design of the class he or she is to implement. The design usually provides enough information for the programmer to implement the code artifact without too much difficulty. If there are any problems, they can quickly be cleared up by consulting the responsible designer.

However, there is no way for the individual programmer to know if the overall architecture (Section 2.7) is correct. Only when integration of individual code artifacts commences do the shortcomings of the design as a whole start coming to light.

Suppose that a number of code artifacts have been implemented and integrated and the parts of the product integrated so far appear to be working correctly. Suppose further that a programmer has correctly implemented artifact a45, but when this artifact is integrated with the other existing artifacts, the product fails. The cause of the failure lies not in artifact a45 itself, but rather in the way that artifact a45 interacts with the rest of the product. Nevertheless, in this type of situation the programmer who just coded artifact a45 tends to be blamed for the failure. This is unfortunate, because the programmer has simply followed the instructions provided by the designer and implemented the artifact exactly as described in the design for that artifact. The members of the programming team are rarely shown the "big picture," that is, the overall architecture, let alone asked to comment on it. Although it is grossly unfair to expect an individual programmer to be aware of the implications for the product as a whole of a specific artifact, this unfortunately happens in practice all too often. This is yet another reason why it is so important for the design to be correct in every respect.

The correctness of the design (as well as of the other artifacts) is checked as part of the test workflow.

3.7   The Test Workflow

As shown in Figure 2.4, in the Unified Process, testing is carried out in parallel with the other workflows, starting from the beginning. There are two major aspects to testing:

1. Every developer and maintainer is personally responsible for ensuring that his or her work is correct. Therefore, a software professional has to test and retest each artifact he or she develops or maintains.

2. Once the software professional is convinced that an artifact is correct, it is handed over to the software quality assurance group for independent testing, as described in Chapter 6.

The nature of the **test workflow** changes depending on the artifacts being tested. However, a feature important to all artifacts is traceability.

3.7.1   Requirements Artifacts

If the requirements artifacts are to be testable over the life cycle of the software product, then one property they must have is **traceability**. For example, it must be possible to trace every item in the analysis artifacts back to a requirements artifact and similarly for the design artifacts and the implementation artifacts. If the requirements have been presented methodically, properly numbered, cross-referenced, and indexed, then the developers should have little difficulty tracing through the subsequent artifacts and ensuring that they are indeed a true reflection of the client's requirements. When the work of the members of the requirements team is subsequently checked by the SQA group, traceability simplifies the SQA group's task, too.

3.7.2   Analysis Artifacts

As pointed out in Chapter 1, a major source of faults in delivered software is faults in the specifications that are not detected until the software has been installed on the client's computer and used by the client's organization for its intended purpose. Both the analysis team and the SQA group must therefore check the analysis artifacts assiduously. In addition, they must ensure that the specifications are feasible; for example, that a specific hardware component is fast enough or that the client's current online disk storage capacity is adequate to handle the new product. An excellent way of checking the analysis artifacts is by means of a review. Representatives of the analysis team and of the client are present. The meeting usually is chaired by a member of the SQA group. The aim of the review is to determine whether the analysis artifacts are correct. The reviewers go through the analysis artifacts, checking to see if there are any faults. Walkthroughs and inspections are two types of reviews, and they are described in Section 6.2.

We turn now to the checking of the detailed planning and estimating that takes place once the client has signed off on the specifications. Whereas it is essential that every aspect of the SPMP be meticulously checked by the development team and then by the SQA group, particular attention must be paid to the plan's duration and cost estimates. One way to do this is for management to obtain two (or more) independent estimates of both duration and cost when detailed planning starts, and then reconcile any significant differences. With regard to the SPMP document, an excellent way to check it is by a review similar to the review of the analysis artifacts. If the duration and cost estimates are satisfactory, the client will give permission for the project to proceed.

3.7.3   Design Artifacts

As mentioned in Section 3.7.1, a critical aspect of testability is traceability. In the case of the design, this means that every part of the design can be linked to an analysis artifact. A suitably cross-referenced design gives the developers and the SQA group a powerful tool for checking whether the design agrees with the specifications and whether every part of the specifications is reflected in some part of the design.

Design reviews are similar to the reviews that the specifications undergo. However, in view of the technical nature of most designs, the client usually is not present. Members of the design team and the SQA group work through the design as a whole as well as through each separate design artifact, ensuring that the design is correct. The types of faults to look for include logic faults, interface faults, lack of exception handling (processing of error conditions), and most important, nonconformance to the specifications. In addition, the review team always should be aware of the possibility that some analysis faults were not detected during the previous workflow. A detailed description of the review process is given in Section 6.2.

3.7.4   Implementation Artifacts

Each component should be tested while it is being implemented (desk checking); and after it has been implemented, it is run against test cases. This informal testing is done by the programmer. Thereafter, the quality assurance group tests the component methodically; this is termed **unit testing**. A variety of unit-testing techniques are described in Chapter 13.

In addition to running test cases, a code review is a powerful, successful technique for detecting programming faults. Here, the programmer guides the members of the review team through the listing of the component. The review team must include an SQA representative. The procedure is similar to reviews of specifications and designs described previously. As in all the other workflows, a record of the activities of the SQA group are kept as part of the test workflow.

Once a component has been coded, it must be combined with the other coded components so that the SQA group can determine whether the (partial) product as a whole functions correctly. The way in which the components are integrated (all at once or one at a time) and the specific order (from top to bottom or from bottom to top in the component interconnection diagram or class hierarchy) can have a critical influence on the quality of the resulting product. For example, suppose the product is integrated bottom up. A major design fault, if present, will show up late, necessitating an expensive rewrite. Conversely, if the components are integrated top down, then the lower-level components usually do not receive as thorough a testing as would be the case if the product were integrated bottom up. These and other problems are discussed in detail in Chapter 13. A detailed explanation is given there as to why coding and integration must be performed in parallel.

The purpose of this ***integration testing*** is to check that the components combine correctly to achieve a product that satisfies its specifications. During integration testing, particular care must be paid to testing the component interfaces. It is important that the number, order, and types of formal arguments match the number, order, and types of actual arguments. This strong type checking [van Wijngaarden et al., 1975] is best performed by the compiler and linker. However, many languages are not strongly typed; when such a language is used, checking the interfaces must be done by members of the SQA group.

When the integration testing has been completed (that is, when all the components have been coded and integrated), the SQA group performs ***product testing***. The functionality of the product as a whole is checked against the specifications. In particular, the constraints listed in the specifications must be tested. A typical example is whether the response time has been met. Because the aim of product testing is to determine whether the specifications have been correctly implemented, many of the test cases can be drawn up once the specifications are complete.

Not only must the correctness of the product be tested but also its robustness. That is, intentionally erroneous input data are submitted to determine whether the product will crash or whether its error-handling capabilities are adequate for dealing with bad data. If the product is to be run together with the client's currently installed software, then tests also must be performed to check that the new product will have no adverse effect on the client's existing computer operations. Finally, a check must be made as to whether the source code and all other types of documentation are complete and internally consistent. Product testing is discussed in Section 13.20. On the basis of the results of the product test, a senior manager in the development organization decides whether the product is ready to be released to the client.

The final aspect of integration testing is ***acceptance testing***. The software is delivered to the client, who tests it on the actual hardware, using actual data as opposed to test data. No matter how methodical the development team or the SQA group might be, there is a significant difference between test cases, which by their very nature are artificial, and actual data. A software product cannot be considered to satisfy its specifications until the product has passed its acceptance test. More details about acceptance testing are given in Section 13.21.

In the case of COTS software (Section 1.10), as soon as product testing is complete, versions of the complete product are supplied to selected possible future clients for testing on site. The first such version is termed the ***alpha release***. The corrected alpha release is called the ***beta release***; in general, the beta release is intended to be close to the final version. (The terms *alpha release* and *beta release* are generally applied to all types of software products, not just COTS.)

Faults in COTS software usually result in poor sales of the product and huge losses for the development company. So that as many faults as possible come to light as early as possible, developers of COTS software frequently give alpha or beta releases to selected companies, in the expectation that on-site tests will uncover any latent faults. In return, the alpha and beta sites frequently are promised free copies of the delivered version of the software. Risks are involved for a company participating in alpha or beta testing. In particular, alpha releases can be fault laden, resulting in frustration, wasted time, and possible damage to databases. However, the company gets a head start in using the new COTS software, which can give it an advantage over its competitors. A problem occurs sometimes when software organizations use alpha testing by potential clients in place of thorough product testing by the SQA group. Although alpha testing at a number of different sites usually brings to light a large variety of faults, there is no substitute for the methodical testing that the SQA group can provide.

3.8   Postdelivery Maintenance

Postdelivery maintenance is not an activity grudgingly carried out after the product has been delivered and installed on the client's computer. On the contrary, it is an integral part of the software process that must be planned for from the beginning. As explained in Section 3.5, the design, as far as is feasible, should take future enhancements into account. Coding must be performed with future maintenance kept in mind. After all, as pointed out in Section 1.3, more money is spent on postdelivery maintenance than on all other software activities combined. It therefore is a vital aspect of software production. Postdelivery maintenance must never be treated as an afterthought. Instead, the entire software development effort must be carried out in such a way as to minimize the impact of the inevitable future postdelivery maintenance.

A common problem with postdelivery maintenance is documentation or, rather, lack of it. In the course of developing software against a time deadline, the original analysis and design artifacts frequently are not updated and, consequently, are almost useless to the maintenance team. Other documentation such as the database manual or the operating manual may never be written, because management decided that delivering the product to the client on time was more important than developing the documentation in parallel with the software. In many instances, the source code is the only documentation available to the maintainer. The high rate of personnel turnover in the software industry exacerbates the maintenance situation, in that none of the original developers may be working for the organization at the time when maintenance is performed. Postdelivery maintenance frequently is the most challenging aspect of software production for these reasons and the additional reasons given in Chapter 14.

Turning now to testing, there are two aspects to testing changes made to a product when postdelivery maintenance is performed. The first is checking that the required changes have been implemented correctly. The second aspect is ensuring that, in the course of making the required changes to the product, no other inadvertent changes were made. Therefore, once the programmer has determined that the desired changes have been implemented, the product must be tested against previous test cases to make certain that the functionality of the rest of the product has not been compromised. This procedure is called *regression testing*. To assist in regression testing, it is necessary that all previous test cases be retained, together with the results of running those test cases. Testing during postdelivery maintenance is discussed in greater detail in Chapter 14.

A major aspect of postdelivery maintenance is a record of all the changes made, together with the reason for each change. When software is changed, it has to be regression tested. Therefore, the regression test cases are a central form of documentation.

3.9   Retirement

The final stage in the software life cycle is *retirement*. After many years of service, a stage is reached when further postdelivery maintenance no longer is cost effective.

- Sometimes, the proposed changes are so drastic that the design as a whole would have to be changed. In such a case, it is less expensive to redesign and recode the entire product.
- So many changes may have been made to the original design that interdependencies inadvertently have been built into the product, and even a small change to one minor component might have a drastic effect on the functionality of the product as a whole.
- The documentation may not have been adequately maintained, thereby increasing the risk of a regression fault to the extent that it would be safer to recode than maintain.
- The hardware (and operating system) on which the product runs is to be replaced; it may be more economical to rewrite from scratch than to modify.

In each of these instances the current version is replaced by a new version, and the software process continues.

True retirement, on the other hand, is a somewhat rare event that occurs when a product has outgrown its usefulness. The client organization no longer requires the functionality provided by the product, and it finally is removed from the computer.

3.10   The Phases of the Unified Process

Figure 3.1 differs from Figure 2.4 in that the labels of the increments have been changed. Instead of Increment A, Increment B, and so on, the four increments are now labeled Inception phase, Elaboration phase, Construction phase, and Transition phase. In other words, the phases of the Unified Process correspond to increments.

Although in theory the development of a software product could be performed in any number of increments, development in practice often seems to consist of four increments. The increments or phases are described in Sections 3.10.1 through 3.10.4, together with the deliverables of each phase, that is, the artifacts that should be completed by the end of that phase.

Figure 3.1
The core
workflows and
the phases of
the Unified
Process.

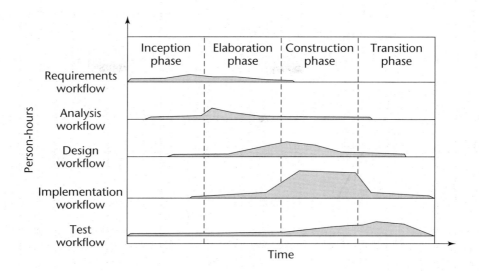

Every step performed in the Unified Process falls into one of five core workflows and *also* into one of four phases, the inception phase, elaboration phase, construction phase, and transition phase. The various steps of these four phases are already described in Sections 3.3 through 3.7. For example, building a business model is part of the requirements workflow (Section 3.3). It is also part of the inception phase. Nevertheless, each step has to be considered twice, as will be explained.

Consider the requirements workflow. To determine the client's needs, one of the steps is, as just stated, to build a business model. In other words, within the framework of the requirements workflow, building a business model is presented within a *technical* context. In Section 3.10.1, a description is presented of building a business model within the framework of the inception phase, the phase in which management decides whether or not to develop the proposed software product. That is, building a business model shortly is presented within an *economic* context (Section 1.2).

At the same time, there is no point in presenting each step twice, both times at the same level of detail. Accordingly, the inception phase is described in depth to highlight the difference between the technical context of the workflows and the economic context of the phases, but the other three phases are simply outlined.

3.10.1   The Inception Phase

The aim of the ***inception phase*** is to determine whether it is worthwhile to develop the target software product. In other words, the primary aim of this phase is to determine whether the proposed software product is economically viable.

Two steps of the requirements workflow are to understand the domain and build a business model. Clearly, there is no way the developers can give any kind of opinion regarding a possible future software product unless they first understand the domain in which they are considering developing the target software product. It does not matter if the domain is a television network, a machine tool company, or a hospital specializing in liver disease—if the developers do not fully understand the domain, little reliance can be placed on what they subsequently build. Hence, the first step is to obtain domain knowledge. Once the developers have a full comprehension of the domain, the second step is to build a business model. In other words, the first need is to understand the domain itself, and the second need is to understand precisely how the client organization operates in that domain.

Now the scope of the target project has to be delimited. For example, consider a proposed software product for a new highly secure ATM network for a nationwide chain of banks. The size of the business model of the banking chain as a whole is likely to be huge. To determine what the target software product should incorporate, the developers have to focus on only a subset of the business model, namely, the subset covered by the proposed software product. Therefore, delimiting the scope of the proposed project is the third step.

Now the developers can begin to make the initial business case. The questions that need to be answered before proceeding with the project include [Jacobson, Booch, and Rumbaugh, 1999]:

- Is the proposed software product cost effective? That is, will the benefits to be gained as a consequence of developing the software product outweigh the costs involved? How long will it take to obtain a return on the investment needed to develop the proposed software product? Alternatively, what will be the cost to the client if he or she decides not to develop the proposed software product? If the software product is to be sold in the marketplace, have the necessary marketing studies been performed?

- Can the proposed software product be delivered in time? That is, if the software product is delivered late to the market, will the organization still make a profit or will a competitive software product obtain the lion's share of the market? Alternatively, if the software product is to be developed to support the client organization's own activities (presumably including mission-critical activities), what is the impact if the proposed software product is delivered late?

- What risks are involved in developing the software product, and how can these risks be mitigated? Do the team members who will develop the proposed software product have the necessary experience? Is new hardware needed for this software product and, if so, is there a risk that it will not be delivered in time? If so, is there a way to mitigate that risk, perhaps by ordering backup hardware from another supplier? Are software tools (Chapter 5) needed? Are they currently available? Do they have all the necessary functionality? Is it likely that a COTS package (Section 1.11) with all (or almost all) the functionality of the proposed custom software product will be put on the market while the project is under way, and how can this be determined?

By the end of the inception phase the developers need answers to these questions so that the initial business case can be made.

The next step is to identify the risks. There are three major risk categories:

1. *Technical risks.* Examples of technical risks were just listed.
2. *Not getting the requirements right.* This risk can be mitigated by performing the requirements workflow correctly—see Chapter 10.
3. *Not getting the architecture right.* The architecture may not be sufficiently robust. (Recall from Section 2.7 that the architecture of a software product consists of the various components and how they fit together, and that the property of being able

to handle extensions and changes without falling apart is its robustness.) In other words, while the software product is being developed, there is a risk that trying to add the next piece to what has been developed so far might require the entire architecture to be redesigned from scratch. An analogy would be to build a house of cards, only to find the entire edifice tumbling down when an additional card is added.

The risks need to be ranked so that the critical risks are mitigated first.

As shown in Figure 3.1, a small amount of the analysis workflow is performed during the inception phase. All that is usually done is to extract the information needed for the design of the architecture. This design work is also reflected in Figure 3.1.

Turning now to the implementation workflow, during the inception phase frequently no coding is performed. However, on occasion, it is necessary to build a proof-of-concept prototype to test the feasibility of part of the proposed software product, as described in Section 2.9.7.

The test workflow commences at the start of the inception phase. The major aim here is to ensure that the requirements are accurately determined.

Planning is an essential part of every phase. In the case of the inception phase, the developers have insufficient information at the beginning of the phase to plan the entire development, so the only planning done at the start of the project is the planning for the inception phase itself. For the same reason, a lack of information, the only planning that can meaningfully be done at the end of the inception phase is to plan for just the next phase, the elaboration phase.

Documentation, too, is an essential part of every phase. The deliverables of the inception phase include [Jacobson, Booch, and Rumbaugh, 1999]:

- The initial version of the domain model.
- The initial version of the business model.
- The initial version of the requirements artifacts.
- A preliminary version of the analysis artifacts.
- A preliminary version of the architecture.
- The initial list of risks.
- The initial use cases (see Chapter 10).
- The plan for the elaboration phase.
- The initial version of the business case.

Obtaining the last item, the initial version of the business case, is the overall aim of the inception phase. This initial version incorporates a description of the scope of the software product as well as financial details. If the proposed software product is to be marketed, the business case includes revenue projections, market estimates, and initial cost estimates. If the software product is to be used in-house, the business case includes the initial cost-benefit analysis (Section 5.2).

3.10.2 The Elaboration Phase

The aim of the ***elaboration phase*** is to refine the initial requirements, refine the architecture, monitor the risks and refine their priorities, refine the business case, and produce the software project management plan. The reason for the name *elaboration phase* is clear; the major activities of this phase are refinements or elaborations of the previous phase.

Figure 3.1 shows that these tasks correspond to all but completing the requirements workflow (Chapter 10), performing virtually the entire analysis workflow (Chapter 11), and then starting the design of the architecture (Section 8.5.4).

The deliverables of the elaboration phase include [Jacobson, Booch, and Rumbaugh, 1999]:

- The completed domain model.
- The completed business model.
- The completed requirements artifacts.
- The completed analysis artifacts.
- An updated version of the architecture.
- An updated list of risks.
- The software project management plan (for the remainder of the project).
- The completed business case.

3.10.3   The Construction Phase

The aim of the ***construction phase*** is to produce the first operational-quality version of the software product, the so-called beta release (Section 3.7.4). Consider Figure 3.1 again. Even though the figure is only a symbolic representation of the phases, it is clear that the emphasis in this phase is on implementation and testing the software product. That is, the various components are coded and unit tested. The code artifacts are then compiled and linked (integrated) to form subsystems, which are integration tested. Finally, the subsystems are combined into the overall system, which is product tested. This was described in Section 3.7.4.

The deliverables of the construction phase include [Jacobson, Booch, and Rumbaugh, 1999]:

- The initial user manual and other manuals, as appropriate.
- All the artifacts (beta release versions).
- The completed architecture.
- The updated risk list.
- The software project management plan (for the remainder of the project).
- If necessary, the updated business case.

3.10.4   The Transition Phase

The aim of the ***transition phase*** is to ensure that the client's requirements have indeed been met. This phase is driven by feedback from the sites at which the beta version has been installed. (In the case of a custom software product developed for a specific client, there is just one such site.) Faults in the software product are corrected. Also, all the manuals are completed. During this phase, it is important to try to discover any previously unidentified risks. (The importance of uncovering risks even during the transition phase is highlighted in Just in Case You Wanted to Know Box 3.4.)

The deliverables of the transition phase include [Jacobson, Booch, and Rumbaugh, 1999]:

- All the artifacts (final versions).
- The completed manuals.

A real-time system frequently is more complex than most people, even its developers, realize. As a result, sometimes subtle interactions take place among components that even the most skilled testers usually would not detect. An apparently minor change therefore can have major consequences.

A famous example of this is the fault that delayed the first space shuttle orbital flight in April 1981 [Garman, 1981]. The space shuttle avionics are controlled by four identical synchronized computers. Also, an independent fifth computer is ready for backup in case the set of four computers fails. Two years earlier, a change had been made to the module that performs initialization before the avionics computers are synchronized. An unfortunate side effect of this change was that a record containing a time just slightly later than the current time was erroneously sent to the data area used for synchronization of the avionics computers. The time sent was sufficiently close to the actual time for this fault not to be detected. About 1 year later, the time difference was slightly increased, just enough to cause a 1 in 67 chance of a failure. Then, on the day of the first space shuttle launch, with hundreds of millions of people watching on television all over the world, the synchronization failure occurred and three of the four identical avionics computers were synchronized one cycle late relative to the first computer.

A fail-safe device that prevents the independent fifth computer from receiving information from the other four computers unless they are in agreement had the unanticipated consequence of preventing initialization of the fifth computer, and the launch had to be postponed. An all too familiar aspect of this incident was that the fault was in the initialization module, a module that apparently had no connection whatsoever with the synchronization routines.

Unfortunately, this was by no means the last real-time software fault affecting a space launch. For example, in April 1999, a Milstar military communications satellite was hurled into a uselessly low orbit at a cost of $1.2 billion; the cause was a software fault in the upper stage of the Titan 4 rocket [*Florida Today*, 1999].

Not just space launches are affected by real-time faults but landings, too. In May 2003, a Soyuz TMA-1 spaceship launched from the international space station landed 300 miles off course in Kazakhstan after a ballistic descent. The cause of the landing problems was, yet again, a real-time software fault [CNN.com, 2003].

3.11   One- versus Two-Dimensional Life-Cycle Models

A classical life-cycle model (like the waterfall model of Section 2.9.2) is a one-dimensional model, as represented by the single axis in Figure 3.2(a). Underlying the Unified Process is a two-dimensional life-cycle model, as represented by the two axes in Figure 3.2(b).

The one-dimensional nature of the waterfall model is clearly reflected in Figure 2.3. In contrast, Figure 2.2 shows the evolution-tree model of the Winburg mini case study. This model is two-dimensional and should therefore be compared to Figure 3.2(b).

Are the additional complications of a two-dimensional model necessary? The answer was given in Chapter 2, but this is such an important issue that it is repeated here. When developing a software product, in an ideal world, the requirements workflow would be completed before proceeding to the analysis workflow. Similarly, the analysis workflow would be completed before starting the design workflow, and so on. In reality, however, all but the most trivial software products are too large to handle as

Figure 3.2
Comparison of (a) a classical one-dimensional life-cycle model and (b) the two-dimensional Unified Process life-cycle model.

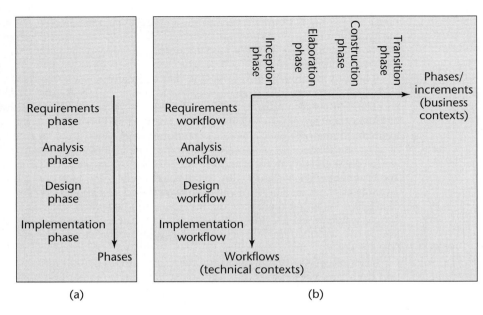

a single unit. Instead, the task has to be divided into increments (phases), and within each increment the developers have to iterate until they have completed the task under construction. As humans, we are limited by Miller's Law [Miller, 1956], which states that we can actively process only seven concepts at a time. We therefore cannot deal with software products as a whole, but instead we have to break those systems into subsystems. Even subsystems can be too large at times—components may be all that we can handle until we have a fuller understanding of the software product as a whole.

The Unified Process is the best solution to date for treating a large problem as a set of smaller, largely independent subproblems. It provides a framework for incrementation and iteration, the mechanism used to cope with the complexity of large software products.

Another challenge that the Unified Process handles well is the inevitable changes. One aspect of this challenge is changes in the client's requirements while a software product is being developed, the so-called moving-target problem (Section 2.4).

For all these reasons, the Unified Process is currently the best methodology available. However, in the future, the Unified Process will doubtless be superseded by some new methodology. Today's software professionals are looking beyond the Unified Process to the next major breakthrough. After all, in virtually every field of human endeavor, the discoveries of today are often superior to anything that was put forward in the past. The Unified Process is sure to be superseded, in turn, by the methodologies of the future. The important lesson is that, based on *today's* knowledge, the Unified Process appears to be better than the other alternatives currently available.

The remainder of this chapter is devoted to national and international initiatives aimed at process improvement.

3.12   Improving the Software Process

Our global economy depends critically on computers and hence on software. For this reason, the governments of many countries are concerned about the software process. For example, in 1987, a task force of the U.S. Department of Defense (DoD) reported, "After two decades of largely unfulfilled promises about productivity and quality gains from applying new software methodologies and technologies, industry and government organizations are realizing that their fundamental problem is the inability to manage the software process" [Brooks et al., 1987].

In response to this and related concerns, the DoD founded the Software Engineering Institute (SEI) and set it up at Carnegie Mellon University in Pittsburgh on the basis of a competitive procurement process. A major success of the SEI has been the capability maturity model (CMM) initiative. Related software process improvement efforts include the ISO 9000-series standards of the International Organization for Standardization, and ISO/IEC 15504, an international software improvement initiative involving more than 40 countries. We begin by describing the CMM.

3.13   Capability Maturity Models

The **capability maturity models** of the SEI are a related group of strategies for improving the software process, irrespective of the actual life-cycle model used. (The term **maturity** is a measure of the goodness of the process itself.) The SEI has developed CMMs for software (SW–CMM), for management of human resources (P–CMM; the *P* stands for "people"), for systems engineering (SE–CMM), for integrated product development (IPD–CMM), and for software acquisition (SA–CMM). There are some inconsistencies between the models, and an inevitable level of redundancy. Accordingly, in 1997, it was decided to develop a single integrated framework for maturity models, capability maturity model integration (CMMI), which incorporates all five existing capability maturity models. Additional disciplines may be added to CMMI in the future [SEI, 2002].

For reasons of space, only one capability maturity model, SW–CMM, is examined here, and an overview of the P–CMM is given in Section 4.8. The SW–CMM was first put forward in 1986 by Watts Humphrey [1989]. Recall that a software process encompasses the activities, techniques, and tools used to produce software. It therefore incorporates both technical and managerial aspects of software production. Underlying the SW–CMM is the belief that the use of new software techniques in itself will not result in increased productivity and profitability, because our problems are caused by how we manage the software process. The strategy of the SW–CMM is to improve the management of the software process in the belief that improvements in technique are a natural consequence. The resulting improvement in the process as a whole should result in better-quality software and fewer software projects that suffer from time and cost overruns.

Bearing in mind that improvements in the software process cannot occur overnight, the SW–CMM induces change incrementally. More specifically, five levels of maturity are defined, and an organization advances slowly in a series of small evolutionary steps toward the higher levels of process maturity [Paulk, Weber, Curtis, and Chrissis, 1995]. To understand this approach, the five levels now are described.

Maturity Level 1. Initial Level

At the ***initial level***, the lowest level, essentially no sound software engineering management practices are in place in the organization. Instead, everything is done on an ad hoc basis. A specific project that happens to be staffed by a competent manager and a good software development team may be successful. However, the usual pattern is time and cost overruns caused by a lack of sound management in general and planning in particular. As a result, most activities are responses to crises rather than preplanned tasks. In level-1 organizations, the software process is unpredictable, because it depends totally on the current staff; as the staff changes, so does the process. As a consequence, it is impossible to predict with any accuracy such important items as the time it will take to develop a product or the cost of that product.

It is unfortunate that the vast majority of software organizations all over the world are still level-1 organizations.

Maturity Level 2. Repeatable Level

At the ***repeatable level***, basic software project management practices are in place. Planning and management techniques are based on experience with similar products, hence, the name *repeatable*. At level 2, measurements are taken, an essential first step in achieving an adequate process. Typical measurements include the meticulous tracking of costs and schedules. Instead of functioning in a crisis mode, as in level 1, managers identify problems as they arise and take immediate corrective action to prevent them from becoming crises. The key point is that, without measurements, it is impossible to detect problems before they get out of hand. Also, measurements taken during one project can be used to draw up realistic duration and cost schedules for future projects.

Maturity Level 3. Defined Level

At the ***defined level***, the process for software production is fully documented. Both the managerial and technical aspects of the process are clearly defined, and continual efforts are made to improve the process wherever possible. Reviews (Section 6.2) are used to achieve software quality goals. At this level, it makes sense to introduce new technology, such as CASE environments (Section 5.5), to increase quality and productivity further. In contrast, "high tech" only makes the crisis-driven level-1 process even more chaotic.

Although a number of organizations have attained maturity levels 2 and 3, few have reached levels 4 or 5. The two highest levels therefore are targets for the future.

Maturity Level 4. Managed Level

A ***managed-level*** organization sets quality and productivity goals for each project. These two quantities are measured continually, and corrective action is taken when there are unacceptable deviations from the goal. Statistical quality controls [Deming, 1986; Juran, 1988] are in place to enable management to distinguish a random deviation from a meaningful violation of quality or productivity standards. (A simple example of a statistical quality control measure is the number of faults detected per 1000 lines of code. A corresponding objective is to reduce this quantity over time.)

Maturity Level 5. Optimizing Level

The goal of an **optimizing-level** organization is continuous process improvement. Statistical quality and process control techniques are used to guide the organization. The knowledge gained from each project is utilized in future projects. The process therefore incorporates a positive feedback loop, resulting in a steady improvement in productivity and quality.

These five maturity levels are summarized in Figure 3.3, which also shows the key process areas associated with each maturity level. To improve its software process, an organization first attempts to gain an understanding of its current process, and then formulates the intended process. Next, actions to achieve this process improvement are determined and ranked in priority. Finally, a plan to accomplish this improvement is drawn up and executed. This series of steps is repeated, with the organization successively improving its software process; this progression from level to level is reflected in Figure 3.3. Experience with the capability maturity model has shown that advancing a complete maturity level usually takes from 18 months to 3 years, but moving from level 1 to level 2 can sometimes take 3 or even 5 years. This is a reflection of how difficult it is to instill a methodical approach in an organization that up to now has functioned on a purely ad hoc and reactive basis.

For each maturity level, the SEI has highlighted a series of **key process areas (KPAs)** that an organization should target in its endeavor to reach the next maturity level. For example, as shown in Figure 3.3, the KPAs for level 2 (repeatable level) include configuration management (Section 5.8), software quality assurance (Section 6.1.1), project planning (Chapter 9), project tracking (Section 9.2.5), and requirements management (Chapter 10). These areas cover the basic elements of software management: Determine the client's needs (requirements management), draw up a plan (project planning), monitor deviations from that plan (project tracking), control the various pieces that make up the software product (configuration management), and ensure that the product is fault free (quality assurance). Within each KPA is a group of between two and four related goals that, if achieved, result in that maturity level being attained. For example, one project planning goal is the development of a plan that appropriately and realistically covers the activities of software development.

At the highest level, maturity level 5, the KPAs include fault prevention, technology change management, and process change management. Comparing the KPAs of the two levels, it is clear that a level-5 organization is far in advance of one at level 2. For example, a level-2 organization is concerned with software quality assurance, that is, with detecting and correcting faults (software quality is discussed in more detail in Chapter 6). In contrast, the process of a level-5 organization incorporates fault prevention, that is, trying to ensure that no faults are in the software in the first place. To aid an organization to reach the higher maturity levels, the SEI has developed a series of questionnaires that form the basis for an assessment by an SEI team. The purpose of the assessment is to highlight current shortcomings in the organization's software process and to indicate ways in which the organization can improve its process.

The CMM program of the Software Engineering Institute was sponsored by the U.S. Department of Defense. One of the original goals of the CMM program was to raise the quality of defense software by evaluating the processes of contractors who produce software for the DoD and awarding contracts to those contractors who demonstrate a mature process. The U.S. Air Force stipulated that any software development organization that wished to be an Air Force contractor had to conform to SW–CMM level 3 by 1998, and

Figure 3.3
The five levels
of the capability
maturity model
and their key
process areas
(KPAs).

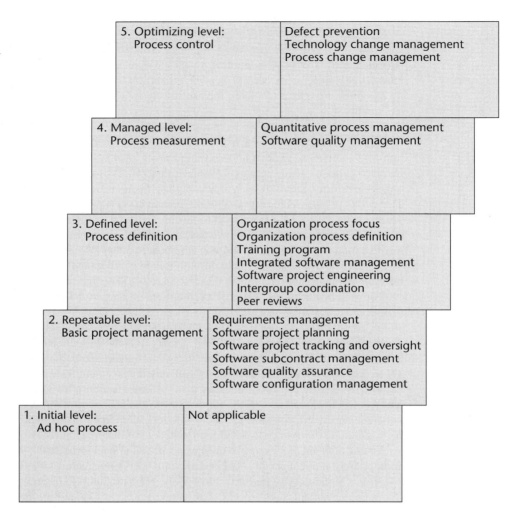

5. Optimizing level: Process control	Defect prevention Technology change management Process change management
4. Managed level: Process measurement	Quantitative process management Software quality management
3. Defined level: Process definition	Organization process focus Organization process definition Training program Integrated software management Software project engineering Intergroup coordination Peer reviews
2. Repeatable level: Basic project management	Requirements management Software project planning Software project tracking and oversight Software subcontract management Software quality assurance Software configuration management
1. Initial level: Ad hoc process	Not applicable

the DoD as a whole subsequently issued a similar directive. As a result, pressure is put on organizations to improve the maturity of their software processes. However, the SW–CMM program has moved far beyond the limited goal of improving DoD software and is being implemented by a wide variety of software organizations that wish to improve software quality and productivity.

3.14   Other Software Process Improvement Initiatives

A different attempt to improve software quality is based on the **_International Organization for Standardization_ (ISO)** 9000-series standards, a series of five related standards applicable to a wide variety of industrial activities, including design, development, production, installation, and servicing; ISO 9000 certainly is not just a software standard.

Within the ISO 9000 series, standard **ISO 9001** [1987] for quality systems is the standard most applicable to software development. Because of the broadness of ISO 9001, ISO has published specific guidelines to assist in applying ISO 9001 to software: **ISO 9000-3** [1991]. (For more information on ISO, see Just in Case You Wanted to Know Box 1.4.)

ISO 9000 has a number of features that distinguish it from the CMM [Dawood, 1994]. ISO 9000 stresses documenting the process in both words and pictures to ensure consistency and comprehensibility. Also, the ISO 9000 philosophy is that adherence to the standard does not guarantee a high-quality product but rather reduces the risk of a poor-quality product. ISO 9000 is only part of a quality system. Also required are management commitment to quality, intensive training of workers, and setting and achieving goals for continual quality improvement. ISO 9000-series standards have been adopted by over 60 countries, including the United States, Japan, Canada, and the countries of the European Union (EU). This means, for example, that if a U.S. software organization wishes to do business with a European client, the U.S. organization must first be certified as ISO 9000 compliant. A certified registrar (auditor) has to examine the company's process and certify that it complies with the ISO standard.

Following their European counterparts, more and more U.S. organizations are requiring ISO 9000 certification. For example, General Electric Plastic Division insisted that 340 vendors achieve the standard by June 1993 [Dawood, 1994]. It is unlikely that the U.S. government will follow the EU lead and require ISO 9000 compliance for non-U.S. companies that wish to do business with organizations in the United States. Nevertheless, pressures both within the United States and from its major trading partners ultimately may result in significant worldwide ISO 9000 compliance.

ISO/IEC 15504 is an international process improvement initiative, like ISO 9000. The initiative was formerly known as **SPICE**, an acronym formed from Software Process Improvement Capability dEtermination. Over 40 countries actively contributed to the SPICE endeavor. SPICE was initiated by the British Ministry of Defence (MOD) with the long-term aim of establishing SPICE as an international standard (MOD is the UK counterpart of the U.S. DoD, which initiated the CMM). The first version of SPICE was completed in 1995. In July 1997, the SPICE initiative was taken over by a joint committee of the International Organization for Standardization and the International Electrotechnical Commission. For this reason, the name of the initiative was changed from SPICE to ISO/IEC 15504, or 15504 for short.

3.15   Costs and Benefits of Software Process Improvement

Does implementing software process improvement lead to increased profitability? Results indicate that this indeed is the case. For example, the Software Engineering Division of Hughes Aircraft in Fullerton, California, spent nearly $500,000 between 1987 and 1990 for assessments and improvement programs [Humphrey, Snider, and Willis, 1991]. During this 3-year period, Hughes Aircraft moved up from maturity level 2 to level 3, with every expectation of future improvement to level 4 and even level 5. As a consequence of improving its process, Hughes Aircraft estimated its annual savings to be of the order of $2 million. These savings accrued in a number of ways, including decreased overtime hours, fewer crises, improved employee morale, and lower turnover of software professionals.

Comparable results have been reported at other organizations. For example, the Equipment Division at Raytheon moved from level 1 in 1988 to level 3 in 1993. A twofold increase in productivity resulted, as well as a return of $7.70 for every dollar invested in the process improvement effort [Dion, 1993]. As a consequence of results like these, the capability maturity models are being applied relatively widely within the U.S. software industry and abroad.

For example, Tata Consultancy Services in India used both the ISO 9000 framework and CMM to improve its process [Keeni, 2000]. Between 1996 and 2000, the errors in effort estimation decreased from about 50 percent to only 15 percent. The effectiveness of reviews (that is, the percentage of faults found during reviews) increased from 40 to 80 percent. The percentage of effort devoted to reworking projects dropped from nearly 12 percent to less than 6 percent.

Motorola Government Electronics Division (GED) has been actively involved in SEI's software process improvement program since 1992 [Diaz and Sligo, 1997]. Figure 3.4 depicts 34 GED projects, categorized according to the maturity level of the group that developed each project. As can be seen from the figure, the relative duration (that is, the duration of a project relative to a baseline project completed before 1992) decreased with increasing maturity level. Quality was measured in terms of faults per million equivalent assembler source lines (MEASL); to be able to compare projects implemented in different languages, the number of lines of source code was converted into the number of equivalent lines of assembler code [Jones, 1996]. As shown in Figure 3.4, quality increased with increasing maturity level. Finally, productivity was measured as MEASL per person-hour. For reasons of confidentiality, Motorola does not publish actual productivity figures, so Figure 3.4 reflects productivity relative to the productivity of a level-2 project. (No quality or productivity figures are available for the level-1 projects because these quantities cannot be measured when the team is at level 1.)

As a consequence of published studies such as those described in this section and those listed in the For Further Reading section of this chapter, more and more organizations worldwide are realizing that process improvement is cost effective.

An interesting side effect of the process improvement movement has been the interaction between software process improvement initiatives and software engineering standards. For example, in 1995 the International Organization for Standardization published ISO/IEC 12207, a full life-cycle software standard [ISO/IEC 12207, 1995]. Three years later, a U.S.

Figure 3.4 Results of 34 Motorola GED projects (MEASL stands for "million equivalent assembler source lines"). Source: [Diaz and Sligo, 1997] (© 1997, IEEE).

CMM Level	Number of Projects	Relative Decrease in Duration	Faults per MEASL Detected during Development	Relative Productivity
Level 1	3	1.0	—	—
Level 2	9	3.2	890	1.0
Level 3	5	2.7	411	0.8
Level 4	8	5.0	205	2.3
Level 5	9	7.8	126	2.8

There are constraints on the speed of hardware because electrons cannot travel faster than the speed of light. In a famous article entitled "No Silver Bullet," Brooks [1986] suggested that inherent problems exist in software production, and that these problems can never be solved because of analogous constraints on software. Brooks argued that intrinsic properties of software, such as its complexity, the fact that software is invisible and unvisualizable, and the numerous changes to which software is typically subjected over its lifetime, make it unlikely that there will ever be an order-of-magnitude increment (or "silver bullet") in software process improvement.

version of the standard [IEEE/EIA 12207, 1998] was published by the Institute of Electrical and Electronic Engineers (IEEE) and the Electronic Industries Alliance (EIA). This version incorporates U.S. software "best practices," many of which can be traced back to CMM. To achieve compliance with IEEE/EIA 12207, an organization must be at or near CMM capability level 3 [Ferguson and Sheard, 1998]. Also, ISO 9000-3 now incorporates parts of ISO/IEC 12207. This interplay between software engineering standards organizations and software process improvement initiatives surely will lead to even better software processes.

Another dimension of software process improvement appears in Just in Case You Wanted to Know Box 3.5.

Chapter Review

After some preliminary definitions, the Unified Process is introduced in Section 3.1. The importance of iteration and incrementation is described in Section 3.2. Now the core workflows of the Unified Process are explained in detail; the requirements workflow (Section 3.3), analysis workflow (Section 3.4), design workflow (Section 3.5), implementation workflow (Section 3.6), and test workflow (Section 3.7). The various artifacts tested during the test workflow are described in Sections 3.7.1 through 3.7.4. Postdelivery maintenance is discussed in Section 3.8, and retirement in Section 3.9. The relationship between the workflows and the phases of the Unified Process is analyzed in Section 3.10, and a detailed description is given of the four phases of the Unified Process: the inception phase (Section 3.10.1), the elaboration phase (Section 3.10.2), the construction phase (Section 3.10.3), and the transition phase (Section 3.10.4). The importance of two-dimensional life-cycle models is discussed in Section 3.11.

The last part of the chapter is devoted to software process improvement (Section 3.12). Details are given of various national and international software improvement initiatives, including the capability maturity models (Section 3.13), and ISO 9000 and ISO/IEC 15504 (Section 3.14). The cost-effectiveness of software process improvement is discussed in Section 3.15.

For Further Reading

The review articles in the For Further Reading section of Chapter 1 [Brooks, 1975; Boehm, 1976; Wasserman, 1996; and Ebert, Matsubara, Pezzé, and Bertelsen, 1997] also highlight the problems associated with the software process. The March/April 2003 issue of *IEEE Software* contains a number of articles on the software process, including [Eickelmann and Anant, 2003], a discussion of statistical process control. Practical applications of statistical process control are described in [Weller, 2000] and [Florac, Carleton, and Barnard, 2000].

With regard to testing during each workflow, a good general source is [Beizer, 1990]. More specific references are given in Chapter 6 of this book and in the For Further Reading section at the end of that chapter.

A detailed description of the original SEI capability maturity model is given in [Humphrey, 1989]. Capability maturity model integration is described in [SEI, 2002]. [Humphrey [1996] describes a personal software process (PSP); results of applying the PSP appear in [Ferguson et al., 1997]. Some potential problems with the PSP are discussed in [Johnson and Disney, 1998]. The PSP and the team software process (TSP) are described in [Humphrey, 1999]. The results of an experiment to measure the effectiveness of PSP training are presented in [Prechelt and Unger, 2000]. Extensions needed to the Unified Process for it to comply with CMM levels 2 and 3 are presented in [Manzoni and Price, 2003]. Implementing SW–CMM in a small organization is described in [Guerrero and Eterovic, 2004]. The July/August 2000 issue of *IEEE Software* has three papers on software process maturity, and there are four papers on the PSP in the November/December 2000 issue of *IEEE Software*.

An overview of SEI software process assessments appears in [Herbsleb et al., 1997]. A number of articles have been written on industry experiences from the viewpoint of a specific company that introduced the SEI process improvement program; typical examples include Shlumberger [Wohlwend and Rosenbaum, 1993] and Raytheon [Haley, 1996]. The impact of SEI on the software industry is discussed in [Saiedian and Kuzara, 1995] and [Johnson and Brodman, 2000]. An interesting view of the CMM is given in [Bamberger, 1997]. [Bamford and Deibler, 1993b] is a detailed comparison of ISO 9000 and the CMM; an overview appears in [Bamford and Deibler, 1993a]. Paulk [1995] details another comparison. Pitterman [2000] describes how a group at Telecordia Technologies reached level 5; a study of how a Computer Sciences Corporation group attained level 5 appears in [McGarry and Decker, 2002]. Insights into the nature of level-5 organizations appear in [Eickelmann, 2003]. Cost–benefit analysis of software process improvement is described in [van Solingen, 2004]. An empirical investigation of the key factors for success in software process improvement is presented in [Dybå, 2005].

Problems of software product improvement appear in [Conradi and Fuggetta, 2002]. The results of 18 different software process improvement initiatives conducted at Ericsson are described in [Borjesson and Mathiassen, 2004]. A wealth of information on the CMM is available at the SEI CMM website www.sei.cmu.edu. The ISO/IEC 15504 (SPICE) home page is at www.sei.cmu.edu/technology/process/spice/.

A comparison between CMM and IEEE/EIA 12207 is given in [Ferguson and Sheard, 1998], and a comparison between CMM and Six Sigma (another approach to process improvement) appears in [Murugappan and Keeni, 2003]. A repository containing the results of some 400 software improvement experiments is described in [Blanco, Gutiérrez, and Satriani, 2001].

Key Terms

acceptance testing 80
alpha release 81
analysis workflow 74
application domain 73
beta release 81
budget 76
business model 73
capability maturity model (CMM) 89
code artifact 77
concept exploration 74
construction phase 86
core workflow 73
cost 73
deadline 73
defined level 90
deliverable 76

design workflow 76
domain 73
elaboration phase 85
implementation workflow 77
inception phase 83
initial level 90
integration testing 80
International Organization for Standardization (ISO) 92
ISO 9000-3 93
ISO 9001 93
ISO/IEC 15504 93
key process area (KPA) 91
managed level 90
maturity 89

milestone 76
model 72
optimizing level 91
product testing 80
regression testing 82
reliability 73
repeatable level 90
requirements workflow 73
retirement 82
SPICE 93
test workflow 78
traceability 78
transition phase 86
Unified Modeling Language (UML) 70
Unified Process 70
unit testing 79

Problems   3.1   Consider the requirements workflow and the analysis workflow. Would it make more sense to combine these two activities into one workflow than to treat them separately?

3.2   More testing is performed during the implementation workflow than in any other workflow. Would it be better to divide this workflow into two separate workflows, one incorporating the nontesting aspects, the other all the testing?

3.3   Maintenance is the most important activity of software production and the most difficult to perform. Nevertheless, it is looked down on by many software professionals, and maintenance programmers often are paid less than developers. Do you think that this is reasonable? If not, how would you try to change it?

3.4   Why do you think that, as stated in Section 3.9, true retirement is a rare event?

3.5   Because of a fire at Elmer's Software, all documentation for a product is destroyed just before it is delivered. What is the impact of the resulting lack of documentation?

3.6   You have just purchased Antedeluvian Software Developers, an organization on the verge of bankruptcy because the company is at maturity level 1. What is the first step you will take to restore the organization to profitability?

3.7   Section 3.13 states that it makes little sense to introduce CASE environments within organizations at maturity level 1 or 2. Explain why this is so.

3.8   What is the effect of introducing CASE tools (as opposed to environments) within organizations with a low maturity level?

3.9   Maturity level 1, the initial level, refers to an absence of good software engineering management practices. Would it not have been better for the SEI to have labeled the initial level as maturity level 0?

3.10   (Term Project) What differences would you expect to find if the Osric's Office Appliances and Decor product of Appendix A were developed by an organization at CMM level 1, as opposed to an organization at level 5?

3.11   (Readings in Software Engineering) Your instructor will distribute copies of [Eickelmann, 2003]. Would you choose to work in a level-5 organization? Explain your answer.

References   [Bamberger, 1997] J. BAMBERGER, "Essence of the Capability Maturity Model," *IEEE Computer* **30** (June 1997), pp. 112–14.

[Bamford and Deibler, 1993a] R. C. BAMFORD AND W. J. DEIBLER, II, "Comparing, Contrasting ISO 9001 and the SEI Capability Maturity Model," *IEEE Computer* **26** (October 1993), pp. 68–70.

[Bamford and Deibler, 1993b] R. C. BAMFORD AND W. J. DEIBLER, II, "A Detailed Comparison of the SEI Software Maturity Levels and Technology Stages to the Requirements for ISO 9001 Registration," Software Systems Quality Consulting, San Jose, CA, 1993.

[Beizer, 1990] B. BEIZER, *Software Testing Techniques*, 2nd ed., Van Nostrand Reinhold, New York, 1990.

[Blanco, Gutiérrez, and Satriani, 2001] M. BLANCO, P. GUTIÉRREZ, AND G. SATRIANI, "SPI Patterns: Learning from Experience," *IEEE Software* **18** (May/June 2001), pp. 28–35.

[Boehm, 1976] B. W. BOEHM, "Software Engineering," *IEEE Transactions on Computers* **C-25** (December 1976), pp. 1226–41.

[Booch, 1994] G. BOOCH, *Object-Oriented Analysis and Design with Applications*, 2nd ed., Benjamin/Cummings, Redwood City, CA, 1994.

[Booch, Rumbaugh, and Jacobson, 1999] G. BOOCH, J. RUMBAUGH, AND I. JACOBSON, *The UML Users Guide*, Addison-Wesley, Reading, MA, 1999.

[Borjesson and Mathiassen, 2004] A. BORJESSON AND L. MATHIASSEN, "Successful Process Implementation," *IEEE Software* **21** (July/August 2004), pp. 36–44.

[Brooks, 1975] F. P. BROOKS, Jr., *The Mythical Man-Month: Essays on Software Engineering*, Addison-Wesley, Reading, MA, 1975; Twentieth Anniversary Edition, Addison-Wesley, Reading, MA, 1995.

[Brooks, 1986] F. P. BROOKS, JR., "No Silver Bullet," in: *Information Processing '86*, H.-J. Kugler (Editor), Elsevier North-Holland, New York, 1986; reprinted in *IEEE Computer* **20** (April 1987), pp. 10–19.

[Brooks et al., 1987] F. P. BROOKS, V. BASILI, B. BOEHM, E. BOND, N. EASTMAN, D. L. EVANS, A. K. JONES, M. SHAW, AND C. A. ZRAKET, "Report of the Defense Science Board Task Force on Military Software," Department of Defense, Office of the Under Secretary of Defense for Acquisition, Washington, DC, September 1987.

[CNN.com, 2003] "Russia: Software Bug Made Soyuz Stray," edition.cnn.com/2003/TECH/space/05/06/soyuz.landing.ap/.

[Conradi and Fuggetta, 2002] R. CONRADI AND A. FUGGETTA, "Improving Software Process Improvement," *IEEE Software* **19** (July/August 2002), pp. 92–99.

[Dawood, 1994] M. DAWOOD, "It's Time for ISO 9000," *CrossTalk* (March 1994), pp. 26–28.

[Deming, 1986] W. E. DEMING, *Out of the Crisis*, MIT Center for Advanced Engineering Study, Cambridge, MA, 1986.

[Diaz and Sligo, 1997] M. DIAZ AND J. SLIGO, "How Software Process Improvement Helped Motorola," *IEEE Software* **14** (September/October 1997), pp. 75–81.

[Dion, 1993] R. DION, "Process Improvement and the Corporate Balance Sheet," *IEEE Software* **10** (July 1993), pp. 28–35.

[Dybå, 2005] T. DYBÅ, "An Empirical Investigation of the Key Factors for Success in Software Process Improvement," *IEEE Transactions in Software Engineering* **31** (May 2005), pp. 410–24.

[Ebert, Matsubara, Pezzé, and Bertelsen, 1997] C. EBERT, T. MATSUBARA, M. PEZZÉ, AND O. W. BERTELSEN, "The Road to Maturity: Navigating between Craft and Science," *IEEE Software* **14** (November/December 1997), pp. 77–88.

[Eickelmann, 2003] N. EICKELMANN, "An Insider's View of CMM Level 5," *IEEE Software* **20** (July/August 2003), pp. 79–81.

[Eickelmann and Anant, 2003] N. EICKELMANN AND A. ANANT, "Statistical Process Control: What You Don't Know Can Hurt You!" *IEEE Software* **20** (March/April 2003), pp. 49–51.

[Ferguson and Sheard, 1998] J. FERGUSON AND S. SHEARD, "Leveraging Your CMM Efforts for IEEE/EIA 12207," *IEEE Software* **15** (September/October 1998), pp. 23–28.

[Ferguson et al., 1997] P. FERGUSON, W. S. HUMPHREY, S. KHAJENOORI, S. MACKE, AND A. MATVYA, "Results of Applying the Personal Software Process," *IEEE Computer* **30** (May 1997), pp. 24–31.

[Florac, Carleton, and Barnard, 2000] W. A. FLORAC, A. D. CARLETON, AND J. BARNARD, "Statistical Process Control: Analyzing a Space Shuttle Onboard Software Process," *IEEE Software* **17** (July/August 2000), pp. 97–106.

[*Florida Today*, 1999] "Milstar Satellite Lost during Air Force Titan 4b Launch from Cape," *Florida Today*, www.floridatoday.com/space/explore/uselv/titan/b32/, June 5, 1999.

[Garman, 1981] J. R. GARMAN, "The 'Bug' Heard 'Round the World," *ACM SIGSOFT Software Engineering Notes* **6** (October 1981), pp. 3–10.

[Guerrero and Eterovic, 2004] F. GUERRERO AND Y. ETEROVIC, "Adopting the SW-CMM in a Small IT Organization," *IEEE Software* **21** (July/August 2004), pp. 29–35.

[Haley, 1996] T. J. HALEY, "Raytheon's Experience in Software Process Improvement," *IEEE Software* **13** (November 1996), pp. 33–41.

[Herbsleb et al., 1997] J. HERBSLEB, D. ZUBROW, D. GOLDENSON, W. HAYES, AND M. PAULK, "Software Quality and the Capability Maturity Model," *Communications of the ACM* **40** (June 1997), pp. 30–40.

[Humphrey, 1989] W. S. HUMPHREY, *Managing the Software Process*, Addison-Wesley, Reading, MA, 1989.

[Humphrey, 1996] W. S. HUMPHREY, "Using a Defined and Measured Personal Software Process," *IEEE Software* **13** (May 1996), pp. 77–88.

[Humphrey, 1999] W. S. HUMPHREY, "Pathways to Process Maturity: The Personal Software Process and Team Software Process," *SEI Interactive* **2** (No. 4, December 1999), interactive.sei.cmu. edu/Features/1999/June/Background/Background.jun99.htm.

[Humphrey, Snider, and Willis, 1991] W. S. HUMPHREY, T. R. SNIDER, AND R. R. WILLIS, "Software Process Improvement at Hughes Aircraft," *IEEE Software* **8** (July 1991), pp. 11–23.

[IEEE/EIA 12207, 1998] "IEEE/EIA 12207.0-1996 Industry Implementation of International Standard ISO/IEC 12207:1995," Institute of Electrical and Electronic Engineers, Electronic Industries Alliance, New York, 1998.

[ISO 9000-3, 1991] "ISO 9000-3, Guidelines for the Application of ISO 9001 to the Development, Supply, and Maintenance of Software," International Organization for Standardization, Geneva, 1991.

[ISO 9001, 1987] "ISO 9001, Quality Systems—Model for Quality Assurance in Design/Development, Production, Installation, and Servicing," International Organization for Standardization, Geneva, 1987.

[ISO/IEC 12207, 1995] "ISO/IEC 12207:1995, Information Technology—Software Life-Cycle Processes," International Organization for Standardization, International Electrotechnical Commission, Geneva, 1995.

[Jacobson, Booch, and Rumbaugh, 1999] I. JACOBSON, G. BOOCH, AND J. RUMBAUGH, *The Unified Software Development Process*, Addison-Wesley, Reading, MA, 1999.

[Johnson and Brodman, 2000] D. JOHNSON AND J. G. BRODMAN, "Applying CMM Project Planning Practices to Diverse Environments," *IEEE Software* **17** (July/August 2000), pp. 40–47.

[Johnson and Disney, 1998] P. M. JOHNSON AND A. M. DISNEY, "The Personal Software Process: A Cautionary Tale," *IEEE Software* **15** (November/December 1998), pp. 85–88.

[Jones, 1996] C. JONES, *Applied Software Measurement*, McGraw-Hill, New York, 1996.

[Juran, 1988] J. M. JURAN, *Juran on Planning for Quality*, Macmillan, New York, 1988.

[Keeni, 2000] G. KEENI, "The Evolution of Quality Processes at Tata Consultancy Services," *IEEE Software* **17** (July/August 2000), pp. 79–88.

[Manzoni and Price, 2003] L. V. MANZONI AND R. T. PRICE, "Identifying Extensions Required by RUP (Rational Unified Process) to Comply with CMM (Capability Maturity Model) Levels 2 and 3," *IEEE Transactions on Software Engineering* **29** (February 2003), pp. 181–92.

[McGarry and Decker, 2002] F. MCGARRY AND B. DECKER, "Attaining Level 5 in CMM Process Maturity," *IEEE Software* **19** (2002), pp. 87–96.

[Miller, 1956] G. A. MILLER, "The Magical Number Seven, Plus or Minus Two: Some Limits on Our Capacity for Processing Information," *The Psychological Review* **63** (March 1956), pp. 81–97. Reprinted in: www.well.com/user/smalin/miller.html.

[Murugappan and Keeni, 2003] M. MURUGAPPAN AND G. KEENI, "Blending CMM and Six Sigma to Meet Business Goals," *IEEE Software* **20** (March/April 2003), pp. 42–48.

[OMG, 2005] "Software Process Engineering Metamodel Specification," Version 2.0, August 2005, www.omg.org/cgi-bin/doc?formal/05-07-04.

[Paulk, 1995] M. C. PAULK, "How ISO 9001 Compares with the CMM," *IEEE Software* **12** (January 1995), pp. 74–83.

[Paulk, Weber, Curtis, and Chrissis, 1995] M. C. PAULK, C. V. WEBER, B. CURTIS, AND M. B. CHRISSIS, *The Capability Maturity Model: Guidelines for Improving the Software Process*, Addison-Wesley, Reading, MA, 1995.

[Pitterman, 2000] B. PITTERMAN, "Telecordia Technologies: The Journey to High Maturity," *IEEE Software* **17** (July/August 2000), pp. 89–96.

[Prechelt and Unger, 2000] L. PRECHELT AND B. UNGER, "An Experiment Measuring the Effects of Personal Software Process (PSP) Training," *IEEE Transactions on Software Engineering* **27** (May 2000), pp. 465–72.

[Rumbaugh et al., 1991] J. RUMBAUGH, M. BLAHA, W. PREMERLANI, F. EDDY, AND W. LORENSEN, *Object-Oriented Modeling and Design*, Prentice Hall, Englewood Cliffs, NJ, 1991.

[Saiedian and Kuzara, 1995] H. SAIEDIAN AND R. KUZARA, "SEI Capability Maturity Model's Impact on Contractors," *IEEE Computer* **28** (January 1995), pp. 16–26.

[SEI, 2002] "CMMI Frequently Asked Questions (FAQ)," Software Engineering Institute, Carnegie Mellon University, Pittsburgh, June 2002.

[van Solingen, 2004] R. VAN SOLINGEN, "Measuring the ROI of Software Process Improvement," *IEEE Software* **21** (May/June 2004), pp. 32–38.

[van Wijngaarden et al., 1975] A. VAN WIJNGAARDEN, B. J. MAILLOUX, J. E. L. PECK, C. H. A. KOSTER, M. SINTZOFF, C. H. LINDSEY, L. G. L. T. MEERTENS, AND R. G. FISKER, "Revised Report on the Algorithmic Language ALGOL 68," *Acta Informatica* **5** (1975), pp. 1–236.

[Wasserman, 1996] A. I. WASSERMAN, "Toward a Discipline of Software Engineering," *IEEE Software* **13** (November/December 1996), pp. 23–31.

[Weller, 2000] E. F. WELLER, "Practical Applications of Statistical Process Control," *IEEE Software* **18** (May/June 2000), pp. 48–55.

[Wohlwend and Rosenbaum, 1993] H. WOHLWEND AND S. ROSENBAUM, "Software Improvements in an International Company," *Proceedings of the 15th International Conference on Software Engineering*, Baltimore, MD, May 1993, pp. 212–20.

Chapter 4

Teams

Learning Objectives

After studying this chapter, you should be able to

- Explain the importance of a well-organized team.
- Describe how modern hierarchical teams are organized.
- Analyze the strengths and weaknesses of a variety of different team organizations.
- Appreciate the issues that arise when choosing an appropriate team organization.

Without competent, well-trained software engineers, a software project is doomed to failure. However, having the right people is not enough; teams must be organized in such a way that the team members can work productively in cooperation with one another. Team organization is the subject of this chapter.

4.1 Team Organization

Most products are too large to be completed by a single software professional within the given time constraints. As a result, the product must be assigned to a group of professionals organized as a ***team***. For example, consider the analysis workflow. To specify the target product within 2 months, it may be necessary to assign the task to three analysis specialists organized as a team under the direction of the analysis manager. Similarly, the design task may be shared between members of the design team.

Suppose now that a product has to be coded within 3 months, even though 1 person-year of coding is involved (a person-year is the amount of work that can be done by one person in 1 year). The solution is apparently simple: If one programmer can code the product in 1 year, four programmers can do it in 3 months.

This, of course, does not work. In practice, the four programmers may take nearly a year, and the quality of the resulting product well may be lower than if one programmer had coded the entire product. The reason is that some tasks can be shared, but others must be done individually. For instance, if one farmhand can pick a strawberry field in 10 days, the same strawberry field can be picked by 10 farmhands in 1 day. On the other hand, one elephant can produce a calf in 22 months, but this feat cannot possibly be accomplished in 1 month by 22 elephants.

In other words, tasks like strawberry picking can be fully shared; others, like elephant production, cannot be shared at all. Unlike elephant production, it is possible to share implementation tasks between members of a team by distributing the coding among the team members. However, team programming also is unlike strawberry picking in that team members have to interact with one another in a meaningful and effective way. For example, suppose Sheila and Harry have to code two modules, m1 and m2. A number of things can go wrong. For instance, both Sheila and Harry may code m1 and ignore m2. Or Sheila may code m1, and Harry may code m2. But when m1 calls m2, it passes four arguments; Harry has coded m2 in such a way that it requires five arguments. Or the order of the arguments in m1 and m2 may be different. Or the order may be the same, but the data types may be slightly different. Such problems usually are caused by a decision made while the design workflow is performed that is not propagated throughout the development organization. The issue has nothing whatsoever to do with the technical competency of the programmers. Team organization is a managerial issue; management must organize the programming teams so that each team is highly productive.

A different type of difficulty that arises from team development of software is shown in Figure 4.1. Three channels of communication exist between the three computer professionals working on the project. Now, suppose that the work is slipping, a deadline is rapidly approaching, and the task is not nearly complete. The obvious thing to do is to add a fourth professional to the team. But the first thing that must happen when the fourth professional joins the team is for the other three to explain in detail what has been accomplished to date and what is still incomplete. In other words, adding personnel to a late software project makes it even later. This principle is known as ***Brooks's Law*** after Fred Brooks who observed it while managing the development of OS/360 [Brooks, 1975], an operating system for IBM 360 mainframe computers.

In a large organization, teams are used in every workflow of software production, but especially when the implementation workflow is performed; during that workflow, programmers work independently on separate code artifacts. Accordingly, the implementation

Figure 4.1
Communication paths between three computer professionals (solid lines) and when a fourth professional joins them (dashed lines).

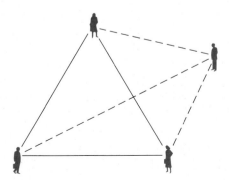

Some 40 years ago, when software was still input on punched cards, all too many program-mers regarded "bugs" in software in the same light as insects that would invade their card deck unless prevented from doing so. This attitude was amusingly lampooned by the marketing of an aerosol spray named *Shoo-Bug*. The instructions on the label solemnly explained that spraying one's card deck with Shoo-Bug would ensure that no bugs could possibly infest the code. Of course, the spray can contained nothing but air.

workflow is a prime candidate for sharing the task among several computer professionals. In some smaller organizations, one individual may be responsible for the requirements, analysis, and design, after which the implementation is done by a team of two or three programmers. Because teams are used most heavily when performing the implementation workflow, the problems of team organization are felt most acutely during implementation. In the remainder of this chapter, team organization therefore is presented within the context of implementation, even though the problems and their solutions are equally applicable to all the other workflows.

There are two extreme approaches to programming-team organization, democratic teams and chief programmer teams. The approach taken here is to describe each of the two approaches, highlight its strengths and weaknesses, and then suggest other ways of organizing a programming team that incorporate the best features of the two extremes.

4.2   Democratic Team Approach

The democratic team organization was first described by Weinberg in 1971 [Weinberg, 1971]. The basic concept underlying the democratic team is ***egoless programming***. Weinberg points out that programmers can be highly attached to their code. Sometimes, they even name their modules after themselves: They therefore see their modules as an ex-tension of themselves. The difficulty with this is that a programmer who sees a module as an extension of his or her ego is certainly not going to try to find all the faults in "his" code or "her" code. And, if there is a fault, it is termed a *bug*, like some insect that crept unasked into the code and could have been prevented if only the code had been guarded more zeal-ously against invasion (see Just in Case You Wanted to Know Box 4.1).

Weinberg's solution to the problem of programmers being too closely attached to their own code is egoless programming. The social environment must be restructured and so must programmer values. Every programmer must encourage the other members of the team to find faults in his or her code. The presence of a fault must not be considered some-thing bad but a normal and accepted event; the attitude of the reviewer should be apprecia-tion at being asked for advice, rather than ridicule of the programmer for making coding mistakes. The team as a whole therefore develops an ethos, a group identity; and modules belong to the team as a whole rather than to any one individual.

A group of up to 10 egoless programmers constitutes a ***democratic team***. Weinberg warns that management may have difficulty working with such a team. After all, consider the managerial career path. When a programmer is promoted to a management position, his or her fellow programmers are not promoted and must strive to attain the higher level at the next round of promotions. In contrast, a democratic team is a group working for a common cause with no single leader, with no programmers trying to get promoted to the next level. What is important is team identity and mutual respect.

Weinberg tells of a democratic team that developed an outstanding product. Management decided to give a cash award to the team's nominal manager (by definition, a democratic team has no leader). He refused to accept it personally, saying that it had to be shared equally among all members of the team. Management thought that he was angling for more money and that the team (and especially its nominal manager) had some rather unorthodox ideas. Management forced the nominal manager to accept the money, which he then divided equally among the team. Next, the entire team resigned and joined another company as a team.

The strengths and weaknesses of democratic teams are now presented.

4.2.1 Analysis of the Democratic Team Approach

A major strength of the democratic team approach is the positive attitude toward the finding of faults. The more found, the happier are the members of a democratic team. This positive attitude leads to more rapid detection of faults and hence to high-quality code. But there are some major problems. As pointed out previously, managers may have difficulty accepting egoless programming. In addition, a programmer with, say, 15 years of experience is likely to resent having his or her code appraised by fellow programmers, especially beginners.

Weinberg feels that egoless teams spring up spontaneously and cannot be imposed from outside. Little experimental research has been done on democratic programming teams, but the experience of Weinberg is that democratic teams are enormously productive. Mantei [1981] has analyzed the democratic team organization using arguments based on theories of and experiments on group organization in general rather than specifically on programming teams. She points out that decentralized groups work best when the problem is difficult and suggests that democratic teams should function well in a research environment. It has been my experience that a democratic team also works well in an industrial setting when a hard problem must be solved. On a number of occasions I have been a member of democratic teams that have sprung up spontaneously among computer professionals with research experience. But, once the task has been reduced to the implementation of a hard-won solution, the team must then be reorganized in a more hierarchical fashion, such as the chief programmer team approach described in Section 4.3.

4.3 Chief Programmer Team Approach

Consider the six-person team shown in Figure 4.2, with 15 two-person communication channels. In fact, the total number of two-, three-, four-, five-, and six-person groups is 57. This multiplicity of communication channels is the major reason why a six-person team structured as in Figure 4.2 is unlikely to be able to perform 36 person-months of work in 6 months; many hours are wasted in meetings involving two or more team members at a time.

Now consider the six-person team shown in Figure 4.3. Again, there are six programmers, but now only five lines of communication. This is the basic concept behind what now is termed the ***chief programmer team***. A related idea was put forward by Brooks [1975], who drew the analogy of a chief surgeon directing an operation. The surgeon is assisted by other

Figure 4.2
Communication
paths between
six computer
professionals.

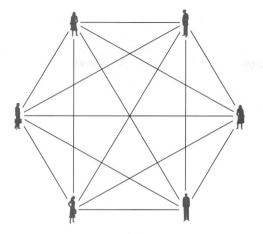

Figure 4.3
The structure
of a chief
programmer
team.

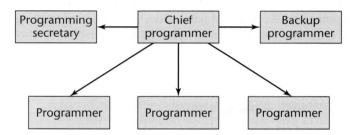

surgeons, the anesthesiologist, and a variety of nurses. In addition, when necessary, the team uses experts in other areas, such as cardiologists or nephrologists. This analogy highlights two key aspects of a chief programmer team. The first is **specialization**: Each member of the team carries out only those tasks for which he or she has been trained. The second aspect is **hierarchy**: The chief surgeon directs the actions of all the other members of the team and is responsible for every aspect of the operation.

The chief programmer team concept was formalized by Mills [Baker, 1972]. A chief programmer team, as described by Baker some 30 years ago, is shown in Figure 4.3. It consisted of the chief programmer, who was assisted by the backup programmer, the programming secretary, and from one to three programmers. When necessary, the team was assisted by specialists in other areas, such as legal or financial matters, or the job control language (JCL) statements used to give operating system commands to the mainframe computers of that era. The **chief programmer** was both a successful manager and a highly skilled programmer who designed the architecture and any critical or complex sections of the program. The other team members worked on the detailed design and the coding, under the direction of the chief programmer. As shown in Figure 4.3, no lines of communication existed between the programmers; all interfacing issues were handled by the chief programmer. Finally, the chief programmer reviewed the work of the other team members, because the chief programmer was personally responsible for every line of code.

The position of **backup programmer** was necessary only because the chief programmer was human and could therefore become ill, fall under a bus, or change jobs. Therefore, the backup programmer had to be as competent as the chief programmer in every respect and had to know as much about the project as the chief programmer. In addition, to free the chief programmer to concentrate on the design of the architecture, the backup programmer did black-box test case planning (Section 13.10) and other tasks independent of the design process.

The word *secretary* has a number of meanings. On the one hand, a secretary assists a busy executive by answering the telephone, typing correspondence, and so on. But when we talk about the American Secretary of State or the British Foreign Secretary, we refer to one of the most senior members of the Cabinet. The ***programming secretary*** was not a part-time clerical assistant but a highly skilled, well-paid, central member of a chief programmer team. The programming secretary was responsible for maintaining the project production library, the documentation of the project. This included source code listings, JCL, and test data. The programmers handed their source code to the secretary, who was responsible for its conversion to machine-readable form, compilation, linking, loading, execution, and running test cases. ***Programmers*** therefore did nothing but program. All other aspects of their work were handled by the programming secretary. (Because the programming secretary maintained the project production library, some organizations used the title ***librarian***.)

Recall that what is described here are Mills's and Baker's original ideas, dating back to 1971, when keypunches still were widely used. Coding no longer is done that way. Programmers now have their own terminals or workstations in which they enter their code, edit it, test it, and so on. A modern version of the chief programmer team is described in Section 4.4.

4.3.1   The New York Times Project

The chief programmer team concept was first used in 1971 by IBM to automate the clipping file ("morgue") of the *New York Times*. The clipping file contains abstracts and full articles from the *New York Times* and other publications. Reporters and other members of the editorial staff use this information bank as a reference source.

The facts of the project are astounding. For example, 83,000 lines of code (LOC) were written in 22 calendar months, an effort of 11 person-years. After the first year, only the file maintenance system consisting of 12,000 LOC had been written. Most of the code was written in the last 6 months. Only 21 faults were detected in the first 5 weeks of acceptance testing; only 25 further faults were detected in the first year of operation. Principal programmers averaged one detected fault and 10,000 LOC per person-year. The file maintenance system, delivered 1 week after coding was completed, operated 20 months before a single fault was detected. Almost half the subprograms, usually 200 to 400 lines of PL/I, a language developed by IBM, were correct on the first compilation [Baker, 1972].

Nevertheless, after this fantastic success, no comparable claims for the chief programmer team concept have been made. Yes, many successful projects have been carried out using chief programmer teams, but the figures reported, although satisfactory, are not as impressive as those obtained for the *New York Times* project. Why was the *New York Times* project such a success, and why have similar results not been obtained on other projects?

One possible explanation is that this was a prestige project for IBM. It was the first real trial for PL/I. An organization known for its superb software experts, IBM set up a team comprising what can only be described as its crème de la crème from one division.

Second, technical backup was extremely strong. PL/I compiler writers were on hand to assist the programmers in every way they could, and JCL experts assisted with the job control language. A third possible explanation was the expertise of the chief programmer, F. Terry Baker. He is what is now called a ***superprogrammer***, a programmer whose output is four or five times that of an average good programmer. In addition, Baker is a superb manager and leader, and his skills, enthusiasm, and personality could be the reasons underlying the success of the project.

If the chief programmer is competent, then the chief programmer team organization works well. Although the remarkable success of the *New York Times* project has not been repeated, many successful projects have employed variants of the chief programmer approach. The reason for the phrase *variants of the approach* is that the chief programmer team as described in [Baker, 1972] is impractical in many ways.

4.3.2   Impracticality of the Chief Programmer Team Approach

Consider the chief programmer, a combination of a highly skilled programmer and successful manager. Such individuals are difficult to find due to a shortage of highly skilled programmers as well as a shortage of successful managers; and the job description of a chief programmer requires both abilities. Also, the qualities needed to be a highly skilled programmer appear to be different from those needed to be a successful manager; therefore, the chances of finding a chief programmer are small.

If chief programmers are hard to find, backup programmers are as rare as hen's teeth. After all, the backup programmer is expected to be as good as the chief programmer but has to take a back seat and a lower salary while waiting for something to happen to the chief programmer. Few top programmers or top managers would accept such a role.

A programming secretary also is difficult to find. Software professionals are notorious for their aversion to paperwork, and the programming secretary is expected to do nothing but paperwork all day.

Therefore, chief programmer teams, at least as proposed by Baker, are impractical to implement. Democratic teams also were shown to be impractical but for different reasons. Furthermore, neither technique seems to be able to handle products that require 20, let alone 120, programmers for the implementation workflow. What is needed is a way of organizing programming teams that uses the strengths of democratic teams and chief programmer teams and can be extended to the implementation of larger products.

4.4   Beyond Chief Programmer and Democratic Teams

Democratic teams have a major strength: a positive attitude toward finding faults. A number of organizations use chief programmer teams in conjunction with code reviews (Section 6.2), creating a potential pitfall. The chief programmer is personally responsible for every line of code and, therefore, must be present during all code reviews. However, a chief programmer also is a manager and, as explained in Chapter 6, reviews should not be used for any sort of performance appraisal. So, because the chief programmer is also the manager responsible for the primary evaluation of the team members, it is strongly inadvisable for that individual to be present at a code review.

Figure 4.4
The structure
of a modern
programming
team.

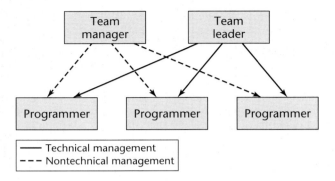

The way out of this contradiction is to remove much of the managerial role from the chief programmer. After all, the difficulty of finding one individual who is both a highly skilled programmer and successful manager has been pointed out. Instead, the chief programmer should be replaced by two individuals: a ***team leader*** in charge of the technical aspects of the team's activities and a ***team manager*** responsible for all nontechnical managerial decisions. The structure of the resulting team is shown in Figure 4.4. It is important to realize that this organizational structure does not violate the fundamental managerial principle that no employee should report to more than one manager. The areas of responsibility are clearly delineated. The team leader is responsible for only technical management. Consequently, budgetary and legal issues are not handled by the team leader nor are performance appraisals. On the other hand, the team leader has sole responsibility on technical issues. The team manager therefore has no right to promise, say, that the product will be delivered within 4 weeks; promises of that sort have to be made by the team leader. The team leader naturally participates in all code reviews; after all, he or she is personally responsible for every aspect of the code. At the same time, the team manager is not permitted at a review, because programmer performance appraisal is a function of the team manager. Instead, the team manager acquires knowledge of the technical skills of each programmer in the team during regularly scheduled team meetings.

Before implementation begins, it is important to demarcate clearly those areas that appear to be the responsibility of both the team manager and the team leader. For example, consider the issue of annual leave. The situation can arise that the team manager approves a leave application because leave is a nontechnical issue, only to find the application vetoed by the team leader because a deadline is approaching. The solution to this and related issues is for higher management to draw up a policy regarding areas that both the team manager and the team leader consider to be their responsibility.

What about larger projects? This approach can be scaled up as shown in Figure 4.5, which shows the technical managerial organizational structure; the nontechnical side is similarly organized. Implementation of the product as a whole is under the direction of the project leader. The programmers report to their team leaders, and the team leaders report to the project leader. For even larger products, additional levels can be added to the hierarchy.

Another way of drawing on the best features of both democratic and chief programmer teams is to decentralize the decision-making process where appropriate. The resulting channels of communication are shown in Figure 4.6. This scheme is useful for the sorts of

Figure 4.5 The technical managerial organizational structure for larger projects.

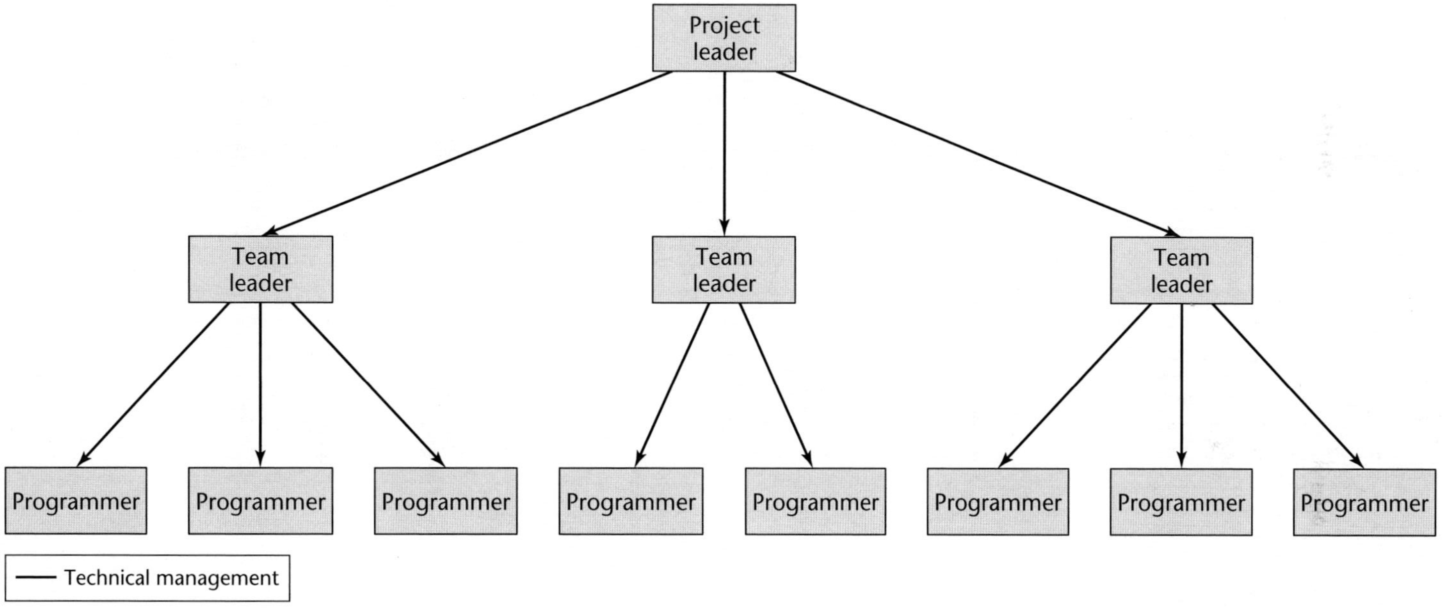

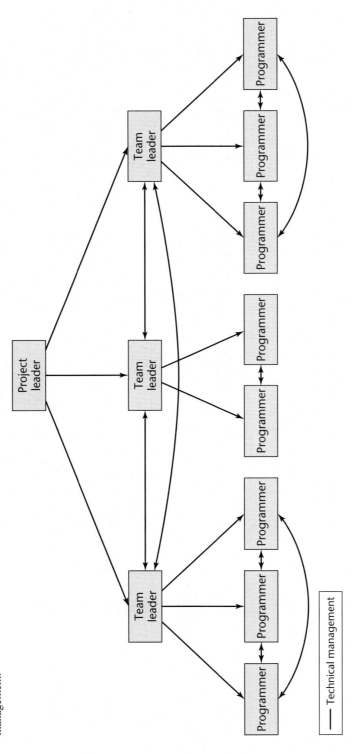

Figure 4.6 The decentralized decision-making version of the team organization of Figure 4.5 showing the communication channels for technical management.

problems for which the democratic approach is good, that is, in a research environment or whenever a hard problem requires the synergistic effect of group interaction for its solution. Notwithstanding the decentralization, the arrows from level to level still point downward; allowing programmers to dictate to the project leader can lead only to chaos.

4.5   Synchronize-and-Stabilize Teams

An alternative approach to team organization is the synchronize-and-stabilize team utilized by Microsoft [Cusumano and Selby, 1997]. Microsoft builds large products; for example, Windows 2000 consists of more than 30 million lines of code, built by over 3000 programmers and testers, reusing much of Windows NT 4.0 [Business Week Online, 1999]. Team organization is a vital aspect of the successful construction of a product of this size.

The synchronize-and-stabilize life-cycle model was described in Section 2.9.6. The success of this model is largely a consequence of the way the teams are organized. Each of the three or four sequential builds of the synchronize-and-stabilize model is constructed by a number of small parallel teams led by a manager and consisting of between three and eight developers together with three to eight testers who work one-to-one with the developers. The team is provided the specifications of its overall task; individual team members then are given the freedom to design and implement their portions of that task as they wish. The reason that this does not rapidly devolve into hacker-induced chaos is the synchronization step performed each day: The partially completed components are tested and debugged on a daily basis. Accordingly, even though individual creativity and autonomy are nurtured, the individual components always work together.

The strength of this approach is that, on the one hand, individual programmers are encouraged to be creative and innovative, a characteristic of a democratic team. On the other hand, the daily synchronization step ensures that the hundreds of developers work together toward a common goal without requiring the communication and coordination characteristic of a chief programmer team (Figure 4.3).

Microsoft developers must follow very few rules, but one of them is that they must adhere strictly to the time laid down to enter their code into the product database for that day's synchronization. Cusumano and Selby [1997] liken this to telling children that they can do what they like all day but have to be in bed by 9 P.M. Another rule is that, if a developer's code prevents the product from being compiled for that day's synchronization, the problem must be fixed immediately so that the rest of the team can test and debug that day's work.

Will use of the synchronize-and-stabilize model and associated team organization guarantee that every other software organization will be as successful as Microsoft? This is extremely unlikely. Microsoft, Inc., is more than just the synchronize-and-stabilize model. It is an organization consisting of a highly talented set of managers and software developers with an evolved group ethos. Merely using the synchronize-and-stabilize model does not magically turn an organization into another Microsoft. At the same time, the use of many of the features of the model in other organizations could lead to process improvement. On the other hand, it has been suggested that the synchronize-and-stabilize model is simply a way of allowing a group of hackers to develop large products and that Microsoft's success is due to superb marketing, rather than quality software.

4.6   Teams for Agile Processes

Section 2.9.5 gives an overview of agile processes [Beck et al., 2001]. In this section, we describe how teams are organized when agile processes are used.

A somewhat unusual feature of agile processes is that all code is written by a team of two programmers sharing a single computer; this is referred to as ***pair programming*** [Williams, Kessler, Cunningham, and Jeffries, 2000]. The reasons for this approach include:

- As explained in Section 2.9.5, pair programmers first draw up test cases and then implement that piece of code (***task***). As explained in Section 6.6, it is highly inadvisable for a programmer to test his or her own code. Agile processes get around this problem by having one pair programmer in a team draw up the test cases for a task and the other pair programmer jointly implement the code using those test cases.

- In a more conventional life-cycle model, when a developer leaves a project, all the knowledge accumulated by that developer leaves as well. In particular, the software on which that developer was working may not yet have been documented and may have to be redeveloped from scratch. In contrast, if one member of a pair programming team leaves, the other is sufficiently knowledgeable to continue working on the same part of the software with a new pair programmer. Furthermore, the presence of the test cases assists in highlighting a fault, should the new team accidentally damage the software by making an ill-advised modification.

- Working closely in pairs enables a less experienced software professional to acquire the skills of the more experienced team member.

- As mentioned in Section 2.9.5, all the computers used by the various pair teams are placed together in the middle of a large room. This promotes group ownership of code, a positive feature of egoless teams (Section 4.2).

So, even though the idea of two programmers working together on the same computer may seem somewhat unusual, the practice has distinct advantages.

4.7   Open-Source Programming Teams

It is surprising that *any* open-source projects have succeeded, let alone that some of the most successful software products ever were developed using the open-source life-cycle model. After all, open-source projects are generally staffed by teams of unpaid volunteers. They communicate asynchronously (via e-mail), with no team meetings and no managers—informality reigns in every respect. Furthermore, no specifications or designs exist; in fact, documentation of any kind is extremely rare, even in mature projects. But despite these virtually insurmountable obstacles, a small number of open-source projects such as Linux and Apache have attained the highest levels of success.

Individuals volunteer to take part in an open-source project for two main reasons: for the sheer enjoyment of accomplishing a worthwhile task or for the learning experience.

- In order to attract volunteers to an open-source project and keep them interested, it is essential that at all times they view the project as "worthwhile." Individuals are unlikely to devote a considerable portion of their spare time to a project unless they truly believe that the project will succeed and that the product will be widely utilized. Participants will start to drift away if they start viewing the project as futile.

- With regard to the second reason, many software professionals join an open-source project in order to gain skills in a technology that is new to them, such as a modern programming language or an operating system with which they are unfamiliar. They can then leverage the knowledge they gain to obtain a promotion within their own organization or acquire a better position in another organization. After all, employers frequently view experience gained working on a large, successful open-source project as more desirable than acquiring additional academic qualifications. Conversely, there is no point in devoting months of hard work to a project that ultimately fails.

In other words, unless a project is viewed at all times as a winner, it will not attract and retain volunteers to work on that project. Furthermore, the members of the open-source team must at all times feel that they are making a contribution. For all these reasons, it is essential that the key individual behind an open-source project be a superb motivator. Unless this is the case, the project is doomed to inevitable failure.

Another prerequisite for successful open-source development is the skills of the team members. As explained in detail in Section 9.2, large differences in skill levels have been observed between programmers. Bearing in mind the obstacles to successful open-source software production listed in the first paragraph of this section, there is virtually no way that an open-source project can succeed unless the members of the core group (Section 2.9.4) are top-caliber individuals with finely honed skills of the highest order. Such top-class individuals will thrive in almost any environment, including one as unstructured as an open-source team.

In other words, an open-source project succeeds because of the nature of the target product, the personality of the instigator, and the talents of the members of the core group. The way that a successful open-source team is organized is essentially irrelevant.

4.8   People Capability Maturity Model

The people capability maturity model (P–CMM) describes best practices for managing and developing the workforce of an organization [Curtis, Helfey, and Miller, 2002]. As with the software capability maturity model, SW–CMM (Section 3.13), an organization progresses through five maturity levels with the aim of continuously improving individual skills and engendering effective teams.

Every maturity level has its own **key process areas (KPAs)**, each of which needs to be addressed satisfactorily before an organization can be deemed to have attained that maturity level. For example, for level 2, the managed level, the KPAs are staffing, communication and coordination, work environment, performance management, training and development, and compensation. In contrast, the KPAs for level 5, the optimizing level, are continuous capability improvement, organizational performance alignment, and continuous workforce innovation.

The SW–CMM is a framework for improving an organization's software process—no specific process or methodology is recommended. In the same way, the P–CMM is a framework for improving an organization's processes for managing and developing its workforce, and no specific approach to team organization is put forward.

4.9   Choosing an Appropriate Team Organization

A comparison of the various types of team organization appears in Figure 4.7, which also shows the section in which each team organization is described. Unfortunately, no one solution solves the problem of programming team organization or, by extension, the problem of organizing teams for all the other workflows. The optimal way of organizing a team depends on the product to be built, previous experience with various team structures, and most important, the culture of the organization. For example, if senior management is uncomfortable with decentralized decision making, then it will not be implemented.

In practice, most teams are currently organized as described in Section 4.4. That is, some variant of the chief programmer team is the usual practice.

Not much research has been done on software development team organization, and many of the generally accepted principles are based on research on group dynamics in

Figure 4.7
Comparison of approaches to team organization and the section in this chapter in which each is described.

Team Organization	Strengths	Weaknesses
Democratic teams (Section 4.2)	High-quality code as consequence of positive attitude to finding faults Particularly good with hard problems	Experienced staff resent their code being appraised by beginners Cannot be externally imposed
Classical chief programmer teams (Section 4.3)	Major success of *New York Times* project	Impractical
Modified chief programmer teams (Section 4.3.1)	Many successes	No successes comparable to the *New York Times* project
Modern hierarchical programming teams (Section 4.4)	Team manager/team leader structure obviates need for chief programmer Scales up Supports decentralization when needed	Problems can arise unless areas of responsibility of the team manager and the team leader are clearly delineated
Synchronize-and-stabilize teams (Section 4.5)	Encourages creativity Ensures that a huge number of developers can work toward a common goal	No evidence so far that this method can be utilized outside Microsoft
Agile process teams (Section 4.6)	Programmers do not test their own code Knowledge is not lost if one programmer leaves Less-experienced programmers can learn from others Group ownership of code	Still too little evidence regarding efficacy
Open-source teams (Section 4.7)	A few projects are extremely successful	Narrowly applicable Must be led by a superb motivator Requires top caliber participants

general and not on software development teams. Even when studies on software teams have been conducted, the sample sizes have generally been small, so the results have not been convincing.

Until experimental results on team organization have been obtained within the software industry, it will not be easy to determine the optimal team organization for a specific product.

Chapter Review

The issue of team organization (Section 4.1) is approached by first considering democratic teams (Section 4.2) and chief programmer teams (Section 4.3). The success of the *New York Times* project (Section 4.3.1) is contrasted with the impracticality of chief programmer teams (Section 4.3.2). A team organization that uses the strengths of both approaches is suggested in Section 4.4. Synchronize-and-stabilize teams (used by Microsoft) are described in Section 4.5. Teams for agile processes are discussed in Section 4.6 and for open-source software in Section 4.7. The people capability maturity model (P–CMM) is described in Section 4.8. Finally, Section 4.9 describes the factors involved in choosing the optimal team organization for a given project.

For Further Reading

Three timeless works on team organization are [Weinberg, 1971; Baker, 1972; and Brooks, 1975]. Newer books on the subject include [DeMarco and Lister, 1987] and [Cusumano and Selby, 1995]. An interesting description of how team interactions evolve is found in [Mackey, 1999]. Articles on team organization and management can be found in the October 1993 issue of the *Communications of the ACM*. Chapter 11 of [Royce, 1998] contains useful information on the roles played by team members. A promising approach is the use of personality type analysis in selecting team members; see, for example, [Gorla and Lam, 2004].

Synchronize and-stabilize teams are outlined in [Cusumano and Selby, 1997] and described in detail in [Cusumano and Selby, 1995]. Insight into synchronize-and-stabilize teams can be obtained from [McConnell, 1996]. Extreme programming teams are described in [Beck, 2000]. The May/June 2003 issue of *IEEE Software* includes a number of papers on extreme programming, especially [Reifer, 2003] and [Murru, Deias, and Mugheddue, 2003]. Other views on agile processes are expressed in [Boehm, 2002] and [DeMarco and Boehm, 2002], and in the May/June 2005 issue of *IEEE Software*. Williams, Kessler, Cunningham, and Jeffries [2000] describe an experiment on pair programming, one component of extreme programming. Strengths and weaknesses of pair programming are described in [Drobka, Noftz, and Raghu, 2004]. P–CMM is described in [Curtis, Hefley, and Miller, 2002].

Key Terms

backup programmer 105	hierarchy 105	specialization 105
Brooks's Law 102	key process area (KPA) 113	superprogrammer 107
chief programmer 105	librarian 106	task 112
chief programmer team 104	pair programming 112	team 101
democratic team 103	programmer 106	team leader 108
egoless programming 103	programming secretary 106	team manager 108

Problems

4.1   How would you organize a team to develop a payroll project? Explain your answer.

4.2   How would you organize a team for developing state-of-the-art military communications software? Explain your answer.

4.3   You have just started a new software company. All your employees are recent college graduates; this is their first programming job. Is it possible to implement democratic teams in your organization, and if so, how?

4.4   A student programming team is organized as a democratic team. What can be deduced about the students in the team?

4.5   A student programming team is organized as a chief programming team. What can be deduced about the students in the team?

4.6   To compare two different team organizations, TO_1 and TO_2, within a large software company, the following experiment is proposed. The same software product will be built by two different teams, one organized according to TO_1 and the other according to TO_2. The company estimates that each team will take about 18 months to build the product. Give three reasons why this experiment is impractical and unlikely to yield meaningful results.

4.7   Why do programming teams for agile processes have to share a computer?

4.8   What are the differences between a democratic team and an open-source team?

4.9   Would you like to work in an organization that uses synchronize-and-stabilize teams? Explain your answer.

4.10 (Term Project) What type of team organization would be appropriate for developing Osric's Office Appliances and Decor product described in Appendix A?

4.11 (Readings in Software Engineering) Your instructor will distribute copies of [Drobka, Noftz, and Raghu, 2004]. Would you like to be a member of an extreme programming team? Explain your answer.

References

[Baker, 1972] F. T. BAKER, "Chief Programmer Team Management of Production Programming," *IBM Systems Journal* **11** (No. 1, 1972), pp. 56–73.

[Beck, 2000] K. BECK, *Extreme Programming Explained: Embrace Change*, Addison-Wesley Longman, Reading, MA, 2000.

[Beck et al., 2001] K. BECK, M. BEEDLE, A. COCKBURN, W. CUNNINGHAM, M. FOWLER, J. GRENNING, J. HIGHSMITH, A. HUNT, R. JEFFRIES, J. KERN, B. MARICK, R. C. MARTIN, S. MELLOR, K. SCHWABER, J. SUTHERLAND, D. THOMAS, AND A. VAN BENNEKUM, *Manifesto for Agile Software Development*, agilemanifesto.org, 2001.

[Boehm, 2002] B. W. BOEHM, "Get Ready for Agile Methods, with Care," *IEEE Computer* **35** (January 2002), pp. 64–69.

[Brooks, 1975] F. P. BROOKS, JR., *The Mythical Man-Month: Essays in Software Engineering*, Addison-Wesley, Reading, MA, 1975; Twentieth Anniversary Edition, Addison-Wesley, Reading, MA, 1995.

[Business Week Online, 1999] *Business Week Online*, www.businessweek.com/1999/99_08/b3617025.htm, February 2, 1999.

[Curtis, Hefley, and Miller, 2002] B. CURTIS, W. E. HEFLEY, AND S. A. MILLER, *The People Capability Maturity Model: Guidelines for Improving the Workforce*, Addison-Wesley, Reading, MA, 2002.

[Cusumano and Selby, 1995] M. A. CUSUMANO AND R. W. SELBY, *Microsoft Secrets: How the World's Most Powerful Software Company Creates Technology, Shapes Markets, and Manages People*, The Free Press/Simon and Schuster, New York, 1995.

[Cusumano and Selby, 1997] M. A. CUSUMANO AND R. W. SELBY, "How Microsoft Builds Software," *Communications of the ACM* 40 (June 1997), pp. 53–61.

[DeMarco and Boehm, 2002] T. DEMARCO AND B. BOEHM, "The Agile Methods Fray," *IEEE Computer* **35** (June 2002), pp. 90–92.

[DeMarco and Lister, 1987] T. DEMARCO AND T. LISTER, *Peopleware: Productive Projects and Teams*, Dorset House, New York, 1987.

[Drobka, Noftz, and Raghu, 2004] J. DROBKA, D. NOFTZ, AND R. RAGHU, "Piloting XP on Four Mission-Critical Projects," *IEEE Software* **21** (November/December 2004), pp. 70–75.

[Gorla and Lam, 2004] N. GORLA AND Y. W. LAM, "Who Should Work with Whom?" *Communications of the ACM* **47** (June 2004), pp. 79–82.

[Mackey, 1999] K. MACKEY, "Stages of Team Development," *IEEE Software* **16** (July/August 1999), pp. 90–91.

[Mantei, 1981] M. MANTEI, "The Effect of Programming Team Structures on Programming Tasks," *Communications of the ACM* **24** (March 1981), pp. 106–13.

[McConnell, 1996] S. MCCONNELL, "Daily Build and Smoke Test," *IEEE Software* **13** (July/August 1996), pp. 144, 143.

[Murru, Deias, and Mugheddue, 2003] O. MURRU, R. DEIAS, AND G. MUGHEDDUE, "Assessing XP at a European Internet Company," *IEEE Software* **20** (May/June 2003), pp. 37–43.

[Reifer, 2003] D. REIFER, "XP and the CMM," *IEEE Software* **20** (May/June 2003), pp. 14–15.

[Royce, 1998] W. ROYCE, *Software Project Management: A Unified Framework,* Addison-Wesley, Reading, MA, 1998.

[Weinberg, 1971] G. M. WEINBERG, *The Psychology of Computer Programming*, Van Nostrand Reinhold, New York, 1971.

[Williams, Kessler, Cunningham, and Jeffries, 2000] L. WILLIAMS, R. R. KESSLER, W. CUNNINGHAM, AND R. JEFFRIES, "Strengthening the Case for Pair Programming," *IEEE Software* 17 (July/August 2000), pp. 19–25.

Chapter 5

The Tools of the Trade

Learning Objectives

After studying this chapter, you should be able to

- Appreciate the importance of stepwise refinement and utilize it in practice.
- Apply cost–benefit analysis.
- Select appropriate software metrics.
- Discuss the scope and taxonomy of CASE.
- Describe version-control tools, configuration-control tools, and build tools.
- Understand the importance of CASE.

Software engineers need two types of tools. First are the analytical tools used in software development, such as stepwise refinement and cost-benefit analysis. Then come the software tools, that is, products that assist the teams of software engineers in developing and maintaining software. These usually are termed **CASE** tools (CASE is an acronym that stands for computer-aided software engineering). This chapter is devoted to these two types of tools of the trade, first theoretical (analytical) tools and then software (CASE) tools. We begin with stepwise refinement.

5.1 Stepwise Refinement

Stepwise refinement, introduced in Section 2.5, is a problem-solving technique that underlies many software engineering techniques. **Stepwise refinement** can be defined as a means to postpone decisions on details until as late as possible to concentrate on the important issues. As a consequence of Miller's Law (Section 2.5), we can concentrate on only approximately seven chunks (units of information) at a time. Accordingly, we use stepwise refinement to defer nonessential decisions until later while focusing on the key issues.

As will be seen during the course of this book, stepwise refinement underlies many analysis techniques, design and implementation techniques, and even testing and integration techniques. Stepwise refinement is of critical importance within the context of the object-oriented paradigm, because the underlying life-cycle model is iterative and incremental.

The following mini case study illustrates how stepwise refinement can be used in the design of a product.

Mini Case Study

5.1.1   *Stepwise Refinement Mini Case Study*

The mini case study presented in this section may seem almost trivial in that it involves updating a sequential master file, a common operation in many application areas. This choice of a simple, familiar problem is to enable you to concentrate on stepwise refinement rather than on the application domain.

Design a product to update the sequential master file containing name and address data for the monthly magazine, *True Life Software Disasters.* There are three types of transactions: insertions, modifications, and deletions, with transaction codes 1, 2, and 3, respectively. The transaction types are:

Type 1: INSERT (a new subscriber into the master file)

Type 2: MODIFY (an existing subscriber record)

Type 3: DELETE (an existing subscriber record)

Transactions are sorted into alphabetical order by name of subscriber. If more than one transaction is performed for a given subscriber, the transactions for that subscriber are sorted so that insertions occur before modifications and modifications before deletions.

The first step in designing a solution is to set up a typical file of input transactions, such as that shown in Figure 5.1. The file contains five records: DELETE Brown, INSERT Harris, MODIFY Jones, DELETE Jones, and INSERT Smith. (It is not unusual to perform both a modification and a deletion of the same subscriber in one run.)

Figure 5.1
Input transaction records for the sequential master file update.

Transaction Type	Name	Address
3	Brown	
1	Harris	2 Oak Lane, Townsville
2	Jones	Box 345, Tarrytown
3	Jones	
1	Smith	1304 Elm Avenue, Oak City

Figure 5.2
A representation
of the sequential
master file
update.

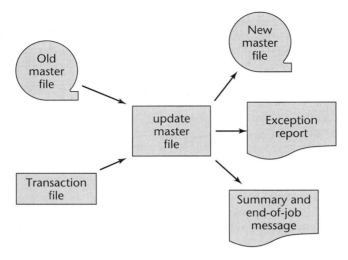

Figure 5.3
First refinement
of the design.

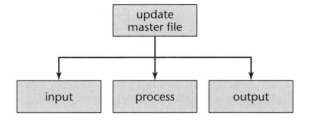

The problem may be represented as shown in Figure 5.2. There are two input files:

1. Old master file name and address records
2. Transaction file

and three output files:

3. New master file name and address records
4. Exception report
5. Summary and end-of-job message

To begin the design process, the starting point is the single box update master file shown in Figure 5.3. This box can be decomposed into three boxes, input, process, and output. The assumption is that, when process requires a record, our level of competence is such that the correct record can be produced at the right time. Similarly, we are capable of writing the correct record to the correct file at the right time. Therefore, the technique is to separate out the input and output aspects and concentrate on the process. What is this process? To determine what it does, consider the example shown in Figure 5.4. The key of the first transaction record (Brown) is compared with the key of the first old master file record (Abel). Because Brown comes after Abel, the Abel record is written to the new master file, and the next old master file record (Brown) is

Figure 5.4
The transaction file, old master file, new master file, and exception report.

Transaction file

3	Brown
1	Harris
2	Jones
3	Jones
1	Smith

Old master file

Abel
Brown
James
Jones
Smith
Townsend

New master file

Abel
Harris
James
Smith
Townsend

Exception report

Smith

Figure 5.5
A diagrammatic representation of the process.

Transaction record key = old master file record key	1. INSERT: Print error message 2. MODIFY: Change master file record 3. DELETE: *Delete master file record
Transaction record key > old master file record key	Copy old master file record onto new master file
Transaction record key < old master file record key	1. INSERT: Write transaction record to new master file 2. MODIFY: Print error message 3. DELETE: Delete master file

*Deletion of a master file record is implemented by not copying the record onto the new master file.

read. In this case, the key of the transaction record matches the key of the old master file record, and because the transaction type is 3 (DELETE), the Brown record must be deleted. This is implemented by not copying the Brown record onto the new master file. The next transaction record (Harris) and old master file record (James) are read, overwriting the Brown records in their respective buffers. Harris comes before James and, therefore, is inserted into the new master file; the next transaction record (Jones) is read. Because Jones comes after James, the James record is written to the new master file, and the next old master file record is read; this is Jones. As can be seen from the transaction file, the Jones record is to be modified and then deleted, so the next transaction record (Smith) and the next old master file record (also Smith) are read. Unfortunately, the transaction type is 1 (INSERT), but Smith already is in the master file. So there is an error of some sort in the data, and the Smith record is written to the exception report. To be more precise, the Smith transaction record is written to the exception report, and the Smith old master file record is written to the new master file.

Now that the process is understood, it may be represented as in Figure 5.5. Next, the process box of Figure 5.3 may be refined, resulting in the second refinement shown in Figure 5.6. The dashed lines to the input and output boxes denote that decisions as to how to handle input and output have been deferred until a later refinement. The remainder of the figure is the flowchart of the process, or rather,

Figure 5.6   The second refinement of the design.

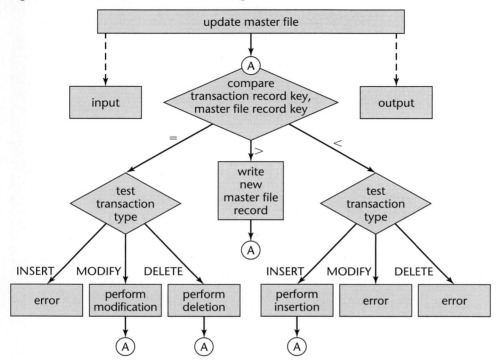

an early refinement of the flowchart. As already pointed out, input and output have been deferred. Also, there is no provision for an end-of-file condition, nor has it yet been specified what to do when an error condition is encountered. The strength of stepwise refinement is that these and similar problems can be solved in later refinements.

The next step is to refine the input and output boxes of Figure 5.6, resulting in Figure 5.7. End-of-file conditions still have not been handled nor has the writing of the end-of-job message. Again, these can be done at a later iteration. What is critical, however, is that the design of Figure 5.7 has a major fault. To see this, consider the situation with regard to the data of Figure 5.4 when the current transaction is 2 Jones, that is, modify Jones, and the current old master file record is Jones. In the design of Figure 5.7, because the key of the transaction record is the same as the key of the old master file record, the leftmost path is followed to the test transaction type decision box. Because the current transaction type is MODIFY, the old master file record is modified and written to the new master file, and the next transaction record is read. This record is 3 Jones, that is, delete Jones. But the modified Jones record has already been written to the new master file.

The reader may wonder why an incorrect refinement deliberately is presented. The point is that, when using stepwise refinement, it is necessary to check each successive refinement before proceeding to the next. If a particular refinement turns out to be

Figure 5.7   The third refinement of the design (the design has a major fault).

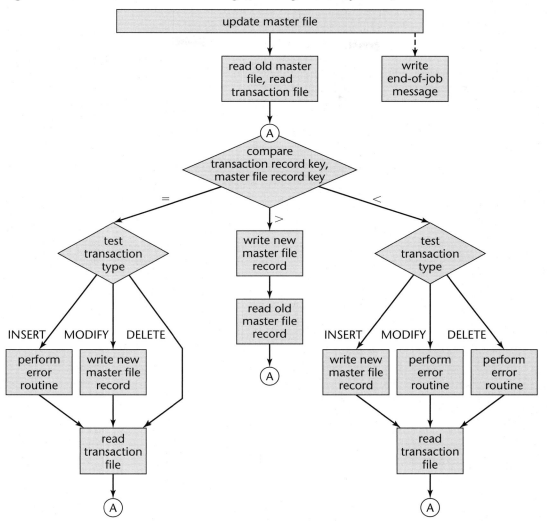

faulty, it is not necessary to restart the process from the beginning but merely to go back to the previous refinement and proceed from there. In this instance, the second refinement (Figure 5.6) is correct, so it may be used as the basis for another attempt at a third refinement. This time, the design uses level-1 **_lookahead_**; that is, a transaction record is processed only after the next transaction record has been analyzed. The details are left as an exercise; see Problem 5.1.

In the fourth refinement, details that have been ignored up to now, such as opening and closing files, have to be introduced. With stepwise refinement, such details are handled last, after the logic of the design has been fully developed. Obviously, it is impossible to execute the product without opening and closing files. However, what is important here is the stage in the design process at which such details as file openings and closings are handled. While the design is being developed, the seven or so chunks on which the designer can concentrate at once should *not* include details like opening and closing files. File openings and closings have nothing to do with the design itself; they are merely implementation details that are part of any design. However, in later refinements, opening and closing files becomes vital. In other words, stepwise refinement can be considered a technique for setting the priorities of the various problems that have to be solved within a workflow. Stepwise refinement ensures that every problem is solved and each is solved at the appropriate time, without having to handle more than 7 ± 2 chunks at any one time.

The term *stepwise refinement* was first introduced by Wirth [1971]. In the preceding mini case study, stepwise refinement was applied to a flowchart, whereas Wirth applied the technique to pseudocode. The specific representation to which stepwise refinement is applied is not important; stepwise refinement is a general technique that can be used for every workflow and with almost every representation.

Miller's Law is a fundamental restriction on the mental powers of humans. Because we cannot fight our nature, we must live with it, accepting our limitations and doing the best we can under the circumstances.

The power of stepwise refinement is that it helps the software engineer concentrate on the relevant aspects of the current development task and ignore details that, although essential in the overall scheme, need not be considered, and in fact should be ignored, until later. Unlike a divide-and-conquer technique, in which the problem as a whole is decomposed into subproblems of essentially equal importance, in stepwise refinement, the importance of a particular aspect of the problem changes from refinement to refinement. Initially, a particular issue may be irrelevant, but later that same issue is of critical importance. The challenge with stepwise refinement is deciding which issues must be handled in the current refinement and which postponed until a later refinement.

Like stepwise refinement, cost–benefit analysis is a fundamental theoretical software engineering technique used throughout the software life cycle. This technique is described in Section 5.2.

5.2   Cost–Benefit Analysis

One way of determining whether a possible course of action would be profitable is to compare estimated future benefits against projected future costs. This is termed **cost–benefit analysis**. As an example of cost–benefit analysis within the computer context, consider how Krag Central Electric Company (KCEC) decided in 1965 whether or not to computerize its billing system. Billing was being done manually by 80 clerks who mailed bills every 2 months to KCEC customers. Computerization would require KCEC to buy or lease the necessary software and hardware, including data-capture equipment for recording the input data on punch cards or magnetic tape.

One advantage of computerization would be that bills could be mailed monthly instead of every 2 months, improving the company's cash flow considerably. Furthermore, the 80 billing clerks would be replaced by 11 data-capture clerks. As shown in Figure 5.8,

Figure 5.8
Cost–benefit
analysis data
for KCEC.

Benefits		Costs	
Salary savings (7 years)	1,575,000	Hardware and software (7 years)	1,250,000
Improved cash flow (7 years)	875,000	Conversion cost (first year only)	350,000
		Explanations to customers (first year only)	125,000
Total benefits	$2,450,000	Total costs	$1,725,000

salary savings over the next 7 years were estimated to be $1.575 million, and improved cash flow was projected to be worth $875,000. The total benefits therefore were estimated at $2.45 million. On the other hand, a complete data processing department would have to be set up, staffed by well-paid computer professionals. Over a 7-year period, costs were estimated as follows. The cost of hardware and software, including postdelivery mainte-nance, was estimated to be $1.25 million. In the first year, there would be a conversion cost of $350,000, and the cost of explaining the new system to customers was estimated at an additional $125,000. Total costs were estimated at $1.725 million, about $750,000 less than the estimated benefits for that 7-year period. KCEC immediately decided to computerize.

Cost–benefit analysis is not always straightforward. On the one hand, a management con-sultant can estimate salary savings, an accountant can project cash flow improvements, net present value (NPV) can be used to handle the change in the cost of money, and a software engineering consultant can estimate the costs of hardware, software, and conversion. But how are we to determine the cost of dealing with customers trying to adjust to computerization? How can we measure the benefits of inoculating an entire population against measles? And how can we make estimates regarding a market window, that is, the benefit of being first on the market with a new product or the cost of not being the first (and hence losing customers)?

The point is that tangible benefits are easy to measure, but intangible benefits can be hard to quantify directly. A practical way of assigning a dollar value to intangible benefits is to make **assumptions**. These assumptions always must be stated in conjunction with the resulting estimates of the benefits. After all, managers have to make decisions. If no data are available, then making assumptions from which such data can be determined usually is the best that can be done under the circumstances. This approach has the further advantage that, if someone else reviewing the data and the underlying assumptions can come up with better assumptions, then better data can be produced and the associated intangible benefits can be computed more accurately. The same technique can be used for intangible costs.

Cost–benefit analysis is a fundamental technique in deciding whether a client should computerize his or her business, and if so, in what way. The costs and benefits of various alternative strategies are compared. For example, a product for storing the results of drug trials can be implemented in a number of different ways, including flat files and various database management systems. For each possible strategy, the costs and benefits are com-puted, and the one for which the difference between benefits and costs is the largest is selected as the optimal strategy.

The final theoretical tool described in this chapter is software metrics.

5.3   Software Metrics

As explained in Section 3.13, without measurements (or ***metrics***) it is impossible to detect problems early in the software process, before they get out of hand. In this way, metrics can serve as an early warning system for potential problems. A wide variety of metrics can be used. For example, lines of code (LOC) is one way of measuring the size of a product (see Section 9.2.1). If LOC measurements are taken at regular intervals, they provide a measure of how fast the project is progressing. In addition, the number of faults per 1000 lines of code is a measure of software quality. After all, it is of little use if a programmer consistently turns out 2000 lines of code a month but half of them have to be thrown away because they are unacceptable. Accordingly, LOC in isolation is not a very meaningful metric.

Once the product has been installed on the client's computer, a metric such as mean time between failures provides management an indication of its reliability. If a certain product fails every other day, its quality is clearly lower than that of a similar product that on average runs for 9 months without a failure.

Certain metrics can be applied throughout the software process. For example, for each workflow, we can measure the effort in person-months (1 person-month is the amount of work done by one person in 1 month). Staff turnover is another important metric. High turnover adversely affects current projects because it takes time for a new employee to learn the relevant facts about the project (see Section 4.1). In addition, new employees may have to be trained in aspects of the software process; if new employees are less educated in software engineering than the individuals they replace, then the process as a whole may suffer. Of course, cost is an essential metric that must also be monitored continually throughout the entire process.

A number of different metrics are described in this book. Some are ***product metrics;*** they measure some aspect of the product itself, such as its size or its reliability. Others are ***process metrics*** used by the developers to deduce information about the software process. A typical metric of this kind is the efficiency of fault detection during development, that is, the ratio of the number of faults detected during development to the total number of faults detected in the product over its lifetime.

Many metrics are specific to a given workflow. For example, lines of code cannot be used before the implementation workflow, and the number of faults detected per hour in reviewing specifications is relevant to only the analysis workflow. In subsequent chapters describing each of the various workflows of the software process, the metrics relevant to that workflow are discussed.

A cost is involved in gathering the data needed to compute the values of metrics. Even if the data gathering is fully automated, the CASE tool (Section 5.4) that accumulates the required information is not free and interpreting the output from the tool consumes human resources. Bearing in mind that hundreds (if not thousands) of metrics have been put forward, an obvious question is, What should a software organization measure? There are five essential, fundamental metrics:

1. Size (in lines of code or, better, in a more meaningful metric, such as those of Section 9.2.1)
2. Cost (in dollars)

As explained in Section 1.11, for software engineers the term *system* is frequently used to mean a software–hardware combination. The field of **systems engineering** spans a wide range of activities, starting with defining the client's needs and requirements until they have been fully implemented in the constructed system. Subsequently, after the system has been delivered to the client, following successful acceptance tests, it undergoes extensive modifications throughout its entire life cycle, to remove defects or add needed improvements or adaptations [Tomer and Schach, 2002].

Accordingly, there are strong similarities between systems engineering and software engineering. It is therefore not surprising that, for systems engineers, the acronym CASE stands for "computer-aided systems engineering." Because of the major role often played by software in systems engineering, within the context of systems engineering it is sometimes hard to know which version of the CASE acronym is meant.

3. Duration (in months)
4. Effort (in person-months)
5. Quality (number of faults detected)

Each of these metrics must be measured by workflow. On the basis of the data from these fundamental metrics, management can identify problems within the software organization, such as high fault rates during the design workflow or code output that is well below the industry average. Once problem areas have been highlighted, a strategy to correct these problems can be considered. To monitor the success of this strategy, more-detailed metrics can be introduced. For example, it may be deemed appropriate to collect data on the fault rates of each programmer or to conduct a survey of user satisfaction. Consequently, in addition to the five fundamental metrics, more detailed data gathering and analysis should be performed only toward a specific objective.

Finally, one aspect of metrics is still fairly controversial. Questions have been raised as to the validity of some popular metrics; these issues are discussed in Section 13.12.2. Although it is agreed that we cannot control the software process unless we can measure it, there is still some disagreement as to precisely what should be measured [Fenton and Pfleeger, 1997].

We now turn from theoretical tools to software (CASE) tools.

5.4   CASE

During the development of a software product, a number of very different operations have to be carried out. Typical activities include estimating resource requirements, drawing up the specification document, performing integration testing, and writing the user manual. Unfortunately, none of these activities, nor the others in the software process, can be fully automated and performed by a computer without human intervention.

However, computers can *assist* every step of the way. The title of this section, "CASE," stands for computer-aided (or computer-assisted) software engineering (but see Just in Case You Wanted to Know Box 5.1). Computers can help by carrying out much of the drudge work associated with software development, including the creation and organization of artifacts of all kinds, such as plans, contracts, specifications, designs, source code, and management information. Documentation is essential for software development and maintenance, but the majority of individuals involved in software development are not fond of creating or updating documentation. Maintaining diagrams on the computer is especially useful as it allows changes to be made with ease.

But CASE is not restricted to assisting with documentation. In particular, computers can assist software engineers to cope with the complexity of software development, especially in managing all the details. CASE involves all aspects of computer support for software engineering. At the same time, it is important to remember that CASE stands for computer-*aided* software engineering, and not computer-*automated* software engineering—no computer yet can replace a human with respect to development or maintenance of software. For the foreseeable future at least, the computer must remain a tool of the software professional.

5.5   Taxonomy of CASE

The simplest form of CASE is the software **tool**, a product that assists in just one aspect of the production of software. CASE tools currently are being used with every workflow of the life cycle. For example, a variety of tools are on the market, many of them for use with personal computers, that assist in the construction of graphical representations of software products, such as flowcharts and UML diagrams. CASE tools that help the developer during the earlier workflows of the process (the requirements, analysis, and design workflows) sometimes are termed **upperCASE** or **front-end tools**, whereas those that assist with the implementation workflow and postdelivery maintenance are termed **lowerCASE** or **back-end tools**. Figure 5.9(a) represents a CASE tool that assists with part of the requirements workflow.

An important class of CASE tools is the **data dictionary**, a computerized list of all data defined within the product. A large product contains tens (if not hundreds) of thousands of data items, and the computer is ideal for storing information such as variable names and types, and the location where each is defined, as well as procedure names and parameters and their types. An important part of every data dictionary entry is a description of the item; for example, This method takes as input the body weight of the newborn infant and computes the appropriate dosage of the drug or List of aircraft arrival times sorted with earliest times first.

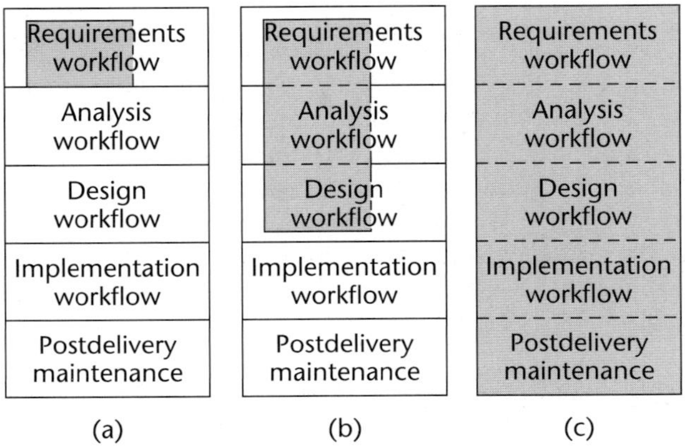

Figure 5.9
A representation of (a) a tool, (b) a workbench, and (c) an environment.

(a)	(b)	(c)
Requirements workflow	Requirements workflow	Requirements workflow
Analysis workflow	Analysis workflow	Analysis workflow
Design workflow	Design workflow	Design workflow
Implementation workflow	Implementation workflow	Implementation workflow
Postdelivery maintenance	Postdelivery maintenance	Postdelivery maintenance

The power of a data dictionary can be enhanced by combining it with a **consistency checker**, a tool to check that every data item in the specification document is reflected in the design and, conversely, every item in the design has been defined in the specification document.

Another use of a data dictionary is to provide the data for report generators and screen generators. A **report generator** is used to generate the code needed for producing a report. A **screen generator** is used to assist the software developer in producing the code for a data capture screen. Suppose that a screen is being designed to enter the weekly sales at each branch of a chain of book stores. The branch number is a four-digit integer in the range 1000–4500 or 8000–8999, entered on the screen three lines from the top. This information is given to the screen generator. The screen generator then automatically generates code to display the string BRANCH NUMBER _ _ _ _ three lines from the top and position the cursor at the first underline character. As the user enters each digit, it is displayed; and the cursor moves on to the next underline. The screen generator also generates code for checking that the user enters only digits and that the resulting four-digit integer is in the specified range. If the data entered are invalid or the user presses the ? key, help information is displayed.

Use of such generators can result in the implementation being quickly constructed. Furthermore, a graphical representation tool combined with a data dictionary, consistency checker, report generator, and screen generator constitute a requirements, analysis, and design **workbench** that supports the first three core workflows. An example of a commercial workbench that incorporates all these features is Software through Pictures.[1]

Another class of workbench is a requirements management workbench. Such a workbench allows systems analysts to organize and track the requirements of a software development project. RequisitePro is a commercial example of such a workbench.

A CASE workbench therefore is a collection of tools that together support one or two activities, where an **activity** is a related collection of tasks. For example, the coding activity includes editing, compiling, linking, testing, and debugging. An activity is not the same as a workflow of a life-cycle model. In fact, the tasks of an activity can even cross workflow boundaries. For example, a project management workbench is used for every workflow of the project, and a coding workbench can be used for building a proof-of-concept prototype, as well as for the implementation workflow and postdelivery maintenance. Figure 5.9(b) represents a workbench of upperCASE tools. The workbench includes the requirements workflow tool of Figure 5.9(a), as well as tools for parts of the analysis and design workflows.

Continuing the progression of CASE technology from tools to workbenches, the next item is the CASE environment. Unlike the workbench, which supports one or two activities, an **environment** supports the complete software process or, at the very least, a large portion of the software process [Fuggetta, 1993]. Figure 5.9(c) depicts an environment that supports all aspects of all workflows of the life cycle. Environments are discussed in greater detail in Chapter 13.

Having set up a CASE taxonomy (tools, workbenches, and environments), the scope of CASE now is considered.

---

[1] The fact that a specific CASE tool is cited in this book in no way implies any form of endorsement of that CASE tool by the author or publisher. Each CASE tool mentioned in this book has been included because it is a typical example of the class of CASE tools of which it is an instance.

5.6   Scope of CASE

As mentioned previously, the need to have accurate and up-to-date documentation available at all times is a primary reason for implementing CASE technology. For example, suppose that specifications are produced manually. A member of the development team has no way of telling whether a particular specification document is the current version or an older version. There is no way of knowing if the handwritten changes on that document are part of the current specification or merely a suggestion later rejected. On the other hand, if the specifications of the product are produced using a CASE tool, then at any time, there is only one copy of the specifications, the online version accessed via the CASE tool. Then, if the specifications are changed, members of the development team easily can access the document and be sure that they are seeing the current version. In addition, the consistency checker will flag any design changes without corresponding changes to the specification document.

Programmers also need **online documentation**. For example, online help information must be provided for the operating system, editor, programming language, and so on. In addition, programmers have to consult manuals of many kinds, such as editor manuals and programming manuals. It is highly desirable that, wherever possible, these manuals be available online. Apart from the convenience of having everything at one's fingertips, it generally is quicker to query by computer than to try to find the appropriate manual and plow through it to find the needed item. In addition, it usually is much easier to update an online manual than to try to find all hard-copy versions of a manual within an organization and make the necessary page changes. As a result, online documentation is likely to be more accurate than hard-copy versions of the same material—another reason for providing online documentation to programmers. An example of such online documentation is the UNIX *manual* pages [Sobell, 1995]. CASE also can assist with communication among team members. **E-mail** is as much a part of an office today as a computer or a fax machine. There are many advantages to e-mail. From the viewpoint of software production, storing copies of all e-mail relevant to a specific project in a particular mailbox provides a written record of the decisions made during the project. This can be used to resolve conflicts that may arise later. Many CASE environments and some CASE workbenches now incorporate e-mail systems. In other organizations, the e-mail system is implemented via a World Wide Web browser such as Netscape or Firefox. Other tools that are equally essential are **spreadsheets** and **word processors**.

The term **coding tools** refers to CASE tools such as text editors, debuggers, and pretty printers designed to simplify the programmer's task, reduce the frustration many programmers experience in their work, and increase programmer productivity. Before discussing such tools, three definitions are required. **Programming-in-the-small** refers to software development at the level of the code of a single module, whereas **programming-in-the-large** is software development at the module level [DeRemer and Kron, 1976]. The latter includes aspects such as designing the architecture and integration. **Programming-in-the-many** refers to software production by a team. At times, the team works at the module level; at times, at the code level. Accordingly, programming-in-the-many incorporates aspects of both programming-in-the-large and programming-in-the-small.

A ***structure editor*** is a text editor that "understands" the implementation language. That is, a structure editor can detect a syntax fault as soon as it has been keyed in by the programmer, speeding the implementation because time is not wasted on futile compilations. Structure editors exist for a wide variety of languages, operating systems, and hardware. Because a structure editor has knowledge of the programming language, it is easy to incorporate a ***pretty printer*** (or ***formatter***) into the editor to ensure that the code always has a good visual appearance. For example, a pretty printer for C++ ensures that each is } indented the same amount as its corresponding {. Reserved words are automatically put in boldface so that they stand out, and indentation has been designed to aid readability. Nowadays, structure editors of this kind form part of numerous programming workbenches, such as Visual C++ and JBuilder.

Now consider the problem of invoking a method within the code, only to discover at linkage time that either the method does not exist or it has been wrongly specified in some way. What is needed is for the structure editor to support ***online interface checking***. That is, just as the structure editor has information regarding the name of every variable declared by the programmer, so it must also know the name of every method defined within the product. For example, if the programmer enters a call such as

average = dataArray.computeAverage (numberOfValues);

but method computeAverage has not yet been defined, then the editor immediately responds with a message such as

Method computeAverage not known

At this point, the programmer is given two choices, either to correct the name of the method or to declare a new method named computeAverage. If the second option is chosen, the programmer also must specify the arguments of the new method. Argument types must be supplied when declaring a new method because the major reason for having online interface checking is precisely to be able to check full interface information, not just the names of methods. A common fault is for method p to call method q passing, say, four arguments, whereas method q has been specified with five arguments. It is more difficult to detect the fault when the call correctly uses four arguments, but two of the arguments are transposed. For example, the declaration of method q might be

void q (**float** floatVar, **int** intVar, string s1, string s2)

whereas the call is

q (intVar, floatVar, s1, s2);

The first two arguments have been transposed in the call statement. Java compilers and linkers detect this fault but only when they are invoked later. In contrast, an online interface checker immediately detects this and similar faults. In addition, if the editor has a help facility, the programmer can request online information as to the precise arguments of method q before attempting to code the call to q. Better yet, the editor should generate a template for the call, showing the type of each argument. The programmer merely has to replace each formal argument by an actual argument of the correct type.

A major advantage of online interface checking is that hard-to-detect faults caused by calling methods with the wrong number of arguments or arguments of the wrong type are immediately flagged. Online interface information is important for the efficient production of high-quality software, particularly when the software is produced by a team (programming-in-the-many). It is essential that online interface information regarding all code artifacts be available to all programming team members at all times. Furthermore, if one programmer changes the interface of method vaporCheck, perhaps by changing the type of one argument from **int** to **float** or by adding an additional argument, then every component that calls vaporCheck must automatically be disabled until the relevant call statements have been altered to reflect the new state of affairs.

Even with a ***syntax-directed editor*** incorporating an online interface checker, the programmer still has to exit from the editor and invoke the compiler and linker. Clearly, there can be no compilation faults, but the compiler still has to be invoked to perform code generation. Then the linker has to be called. Again, the programmer can be sure that all external references will be satisfied as a consequence of the presence of the online interface checker, but the linker still is needed to link the product. The solution to this is to incorporate an ***operating system front end*** within the editor. That is, a programmer should be able to give operating system commands from within the editor. To cause the editor to invoke the compiler, linker, loader, and any other system software needed to cause the code artifact to be executed, the programmer should be able to type a single command, named go or run, or use the mouse to choose the appropriate icon or menu selection. In UNIX, this can be achieved by using the *make* command (Section 5.9) or by invoking a shell script [Sobell, 1995]. Such front ends can be implemented in other operating systems, as well.

One of the most frustrating computing experiences is for a product to execute for a second or so and then terminate abruptly, printing a message such as

Overflow at 506

The programmer is working in a high-level language such as Java or C++ not a low-level language like assembler or machine code. But when debugging support is of the Overflow at 506 variety, the programmer is forced to examine machine code core dumps, assembler listings, linker listings, and a variety of similar low-level documentation, thereby destroying the whole advantage of programming in a high-level language.

A similar situation arises when the only information provided is the infamous UNIX message

Core dumped

or the equally uninformative

Segmentation fault

Here again, the user is forced to examine low-level information.

In the event of a failure, the message shown in Figure 5.10 is a great improvement over the earlier terse error messages. The programmer immediately can see that the method failed because of an attempt to divide by 0. Even more useful is for the operating system to enter edit mode and automatically display the line at which the failure was detected, line 6, together with the preceding and following four or five lines. The programmer probably can then see what caused the failure and make the necessary changes.

Another type of source-level debugging is tracing. Before the advent of CASE tools, programmers had to insert appropriate print statements into their code by hand that, at

Figure 5.10
Output from
a source-level
debugger.

> OVERFLOW ERROR
>   Class: cyclotronEnergy
>   Method: performComputation
>   Line 6:   newValue = (oldValue + tempValue) / tempValue;
>   oldValue = 3.9583   tempValue = 0.0000

execution time, would indicate the line number and the values of relevant variables. This now can be done by giving commands to a ***source-level debugger*** that automatically causes trace output to be produced. Even better is an ***interactive source-level debugger***. Suppose that the value of variable escapeVelocity seems to be incorrect and that method computeTrajectory seems to be faulty. Using the interactive source-level debugger, the programmer can set breakpoints in the code. When a breakpoint is reached, execution stops and debugging mode is entered. The programmer now asks the debugger to trace the variable escapeVelocity and the method computeTrajectory. That is, every time the value of escapeVelocity subsequently is either used or changed, execution again halts. The programmer then has the option of entering further debugging commands, for example, to request that the value of a specific variable be displayed. Alternatively, the programmer may choose to continue execution in debugging mode or return to normal execution mode. The programmer similarly can interact with the debugger whenever the method computeTrajectory is entered or exited. Such an interactive source-level debugger offers almost every conceivable type of assistance to the programmer when a product fails. The UNIX debugger *dbx* is an example of such a CASE tool.

As pointed out many times, it is essential that documentation of all kinds be available online. In the case of programmers, all documentation they might need should be accessible from within the editor.

What has now been described—a structure editor with online interface checking capabilities, operating system front end, source-level debugger, and online documentation—constitutes an adequate and effective programming workbench.

This sort of workbench is by no means new. All these features were supported by the FLOW software development workbench as far back as 1980 [Dooley and Schach, 1985]. Therefore, what has been put forward as a minimal but essential programming workbench does not require many years of research before a prototype can be tentatively produced. Quite the contrary, the necessary technology has been in place for over 20 years, and it is somewhat surprising that there are programmers who still implement code the "old-fashioned way," instead of using a commercial development environment like Sun Java Studio (which can be downloaded free) or an open-source development environment such as Eclipse.

An essential tool, especially when software is developed by a team, is a version-control tool.

5.7   Software Versions

Whenever a product is maintained, there will be at least two ***versions*** of the product: the old version and the new version. Because a product is composed of code artifacts, there will also be two or more versions of each of the component artifacts that have been changed.

Version control is described first within the context of postdelivery maintenance, and then broadened to include earlier parts of the process.

5.7.1   Revisions

Suppose a product has been installed at a number of different sites. If a fault is found in an artifact, then that artifact has to be fixed. After appropriate changes have been made, there will be two versions of the artifact, the old version and the new version intended to replace it. The new version is termed a *revision*. The presence of multiple versions apparently is easy to solve—any old versions should be thrown away, leaving just the correct one. But that would be most unwise. Suppose that the previous version of the artifact was revision n, and that the new version is revision $n + 1$. First, there is no guarantee that revision $n + 1$ is any more correct than revision n. Even though revision $n + 1$ may have been thoroughly tested by the software quality assurance group, both in isolation and linked to the rest of the product, there may be disastrous consequences when the new version of the product is run by the user on actual data. Revision n must be kept for a second reason. The product may have been distributed to a variety of sites, and not all of them may have installed revision $n + 1$. If a fault report is received from a site still using revision n, then to analyze this new fault, it is necessary to configure the product in exactly the same way it is configured at the user's site, that is, incorporating revision n of the artifact. It therefore is necessary to retain a copy of every revision of each artifact.

As described in Section 1.3, perfective maintenance is performed to extend the functionality of a product. In some instances, new artifacts are written; in other cases, existing artifacts are changed to incorporate this additional functionality. These new versions also are revisions of existing artifacts. So are artifacts changed when performing adaptive maintenance; that is, changes that are made to the product in response to changes in the environment in which the product operates. As with corrective maintenance, all previous versions must be retained because issues arise not just during postdelivery maintenance but from implementation onward. After all, once an artifact has been coded, it continually undergoes changes as a consequence of faults being detected and corrected. As a result, there are numerous versions of every artifact, and it is vital to have some sort of control to ensure that every member of the development team knows which is the current version of a given artifact. Before we can present a solution to this problem, a further complication must be taken into account.

5.7.2   Variations

Consider the following example. Most computers support more than one type of printer. For example, a personal computer may support an ink-jet printer and a laser printer. The operating system therefore must contain two *variations* of the printer driver, one for each type of printer. Unlike revisions, each of which is written specifically to replace its predecessor, variations are designed to coexist. Another situation where variations are needed is when a product is to be ported to a variety of different operating systems and hardware. A different variation of many of the artifacts may have to be produced for each operating system–hardware combination.

Versions are schematically depicted in Figure 5.11, which shows both revisions and variations. To complicate matters further, in general, there are multiple revisions of each variation. For a software organization to avoid drowning in a morass of multiple versions, a CASE tool is needed.

Figure 5.11
A schematic
representation
of multiple
versions of
artifacts,
showing
(a) revisions and
(b) variations.

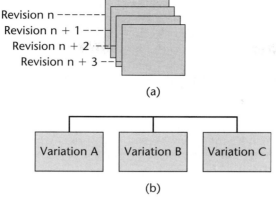

(a)

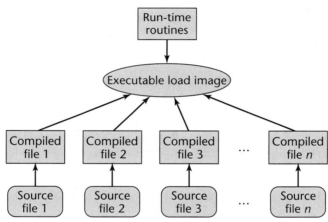

(b)

Figure 5.12
Components of
an executable
load image.

5.8   Configuration Control

The code for every artifact exists in three forms. First is the source code, nowadays generally written in a high-level language like C++ or Java. Next comes the object code, produced by compiling the source code. In this book, because of possible confusion of the word *object,* we refer to object code as *compiled code.* Finally, the compiled code for each artifact is combined with run-time routines to produce an executable load image. This is shown in Figure 5.12. The programmer can use various different versions of each artifact. The specific version of each artifact from which a given version of the complete product is built is called the ***configuration*** of that version of the product.

Suppose that a programmer is given a test report from the SQA group stating that an artifact failed on a specific set of test data. One of the first things to do is attempt to re-create the failure. But how can the programmer determine which revisions of which variations went into the version of the product that crashed? Unless a configuration-control tool (described in the following discussion) is used, the only way to pinpoint the cause of the failure is to look at the executable load image, in octal or hexadecimal format, and compare

Figure 5.13   Multiple revisions and variations. (a) Four revisions of artifact acknowledgeMessage. (b) Two variations of artifact printerDriver, with three revisions of variation printerDriver (laser).

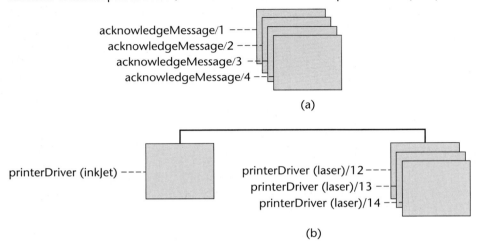

it to the compiled code, also in octal or hexadecimal. Specifically, the various versions of the source code have to be compiled and compared to the compiled code that went into the executable load image. Although this can be done, it can take a long time, particularly if the product has dozens (if not hundreds) of code artifacts, each with multiple versions. Therefore, two problems must be solved when dealing with multiple versions. First, we must distinguish between versions so that the correct version of each code artifact is compiled and linked to the product. Second, there is the inverse problem: Given an executable load image, determine which version of each of its components went into it.

The first item needed to solve this problem is a version-control tool. Many operating systems, particularly for mainframe computers, support version control. But many do not, in which case a separate version-control tool is needed. A common technique used in version control is for the name of each file to consist of two pieces, the file name itself and the revision number. For example, an artifact that acknowledges receipt of a message has revisions acknowledgeMessage/1, acknowledgeMessage/2, and so on, as depicted in Figure 5.13(a). A programmer then can specify exactly which revision is needed for a given task.

With regard to multiple variations (slightly changed versions that fulfill the same role in different situations), one useful notation is to have a basic file name, followed by a variation name in parentheses [Babich, 1986]. Accordingly, two printer drivers are given the names printerDriver (inkJet) and printerDriver (laser).

Of course, there will be multiple revisions of each variation, such as printerDriver (laser)/12, printerDriver (laser)/13, and printerDriver (laser)/14. This is depicted in Figure 5.13(b).

A version-control tool is the first step toward being able to manage multiple versions. Once it is in place, a detailed record (or ***derivation***) of every version of the product must be kept. The derivation contains the name of each source code element, including the variation and revision; the versions of the various compilers and linkers used; the name of the person who constructed the product; and of course, the date and the time at which it was constructed.

Version control is a great help in managing multiple versions of artifacts and the product as a whole. But more than just version control is needed, because of additional problems associated with maintaining multiple variations.

Consider the two variations printerDriver (inkJet) and printerDriver (laser). Suppose that a fault is found in printerDriver (inkJet), and suppose that the fault occurs in a part of the artifact common to both variations. Then it is necessary to fix not only printerDriver (inkJet) but also printerDriver (laser). In general, if there are v variations of an artifact, all v of them have to be fixed. Not only that, they have to be fixed in exactly the same way.

One solution to this problem is to store just one variation, say, printerDriver (inkJet). Then any other variation is stored in terms of the list of changes that have to be made to go from the original to that variation. The list of differences is termed a *delta*. What is stored is one variation and $v - 1$ deltas. Variation printerDriver (laser) is retrieved by accessing printerDriver (inkJet) and applying the delta. A change made just to printerDriver (laser) is implemented by changing the appropriate delta. However, any change made to printerDriver (inkJet), the original variation, automatically applies to all the other variations.

A **configuration-control tool** can automatically manage multiple variations. But **configuration control** goes beyond multiple variations. A configuration-control tool also can handle problems caused by development and maintenance by teams, as described in Section 5.8.1.

5.8.1   Configuration Control during Postdelivery Maintenance

All sorts of difficulties can arise when more than one programmer simultaneously maintains a product. For example, suppose each of two programmers is assigned a different fault report on a Monday morning. By coincidence, both localize the fault they are to fix to different parts of the same artifact mDual. Each programmer makes a copy of the current version of the artifact, mDual/16, and they start to work on the faults. The first programmer fixes the first fault, has the changes approved, and replaces the artifact, now called mDual/17. A day later the second programmer fixes the second fault, has the changes approved, and installs artifact mDual/18. Unfortunately, revision 17 contains the changes of only the first programmer, whereas revision 18 contains those of only the second programmer. None of the changes of the first programmer are in mDual/18, because the second programmer made changes to mDual/16, instead of to mDual/17.

Although the idea of each programmer making individual copies of an artifact is far better than both working together on the same piece of software, clearly it is inadequate for maintenance by a team. What is needed is some mechanism that allows only one user at a time to change an artifact.

5.8.2   Baselines

The maintenance manager must set up a **baseline**, a configuration (set of versions) of all the artifacts in the product. When trying to find a fault, a maintenance programmer puts copies of any needed artifacts into his or her **private workspace**. In this private workspace, the programmer can change anything at all without having an impact on any other programmer in any way, because all changes are made to the programmer's private copy; the baseline version is left untouched.

Once it has been decided which artifact has to be changed to fix the fault, the programmer **freezes** the current version of the artifact he or she is going to alter. No other programmer may make changes to any frozen version. After the maintenance programmer has made changes and they have been tested, the new version of the artifact is installed, thereby modifying the baseline. The previous version, now frozen, is retained because it may be needed in the future, as explained previously, but it cannot be altered. Once a new version has been installed, any other maintenance programmer can freeze the new version and make changes to it. The resulting artifact, in turn, becomes the next baseline version. A similar procedure is followed if two or more artifacts have to be changed simultaneously.

This scheme solves the problem with artifact mDual. Both programmers make private copies of mDual/16 and use those copies to analyze the respective faults that they have been assigned to fix. The first programmer decides what changes to make, freezes mDual/16 and makes those changes to repair the first fault. After the changes have been tested, the resulting revision, mDual/17, becomes the baseline version. In the meantime, the second programmer has found the second fault by experimenting with a private copy of mDual/16. However, changes cannot now be made to mDual/16 because it was frozen by the first programmer. Once mDual/17 becomes the baseline, it is frozen by the second programmer whose changes are made to mDual/17. The resulting artifact now is installed as mDual/18, a version that incorporates the changes of both programmers. Revisions mDual/16 and mDual/17 are retained for possible future reference, but they can never be altered.

5.8.3   Configuration Control during Development

While an artifact is in the process of being coded, versions are changing too rapidly for configuration control to be helpful. Once coding of the artifact has been completed, it should immediately be tested informally by its programmer, as described in Section 6.6. During this informal testing, the artifact again passes through numerous versions. When the programmer is satisfied, the artifact is handed over to the SQA group for methodical testing. As soon as the artifact has been passed by the SQA group, it is ready to be integrated into the product. From then on, it should be subject to the same configuration-control procedures as those of postdelivery maintenance. Any change to an integrated artifact can have an impact on the product as a whole in the same way as a change made during postdelivery maintenance. Therefore, configuration control is needed not only during postdelivery maintenance but also during implementation. Furthermore, management cannot monitor the development process adequately unless every artifact is subject to configuration control as soon as is reasonable, that is, after it has been passed by the SQA group. When configuration control is properly applied, management is aware of the status of every artifact and can take early corrective action if project deadlines seem to be slipping.

PVCS is a popular, commercially available configuration-control tool. Microsoft SourceSafe is a configuration-control tool for personal computers. The three major UNIX version-control tools are *sccs* (source code control system) [Rochkind, 1975]; *rcs* (revision control system) [Tichy, 1985]; and *cvs* (concurrent versions system) [Loukides and Oram, 1997], which is an open-source configuration management tool. (Open-source software is described in Section 1.10.)

5.9   Build Tools

If a software organization does not wish to purchase a complete configuration-control tool, then at the very least, a version-control tool must be used in conjunction with a **build tool**, that is, a tool that assists in selecting the correct version of each compiled-code artifact to be linked to form a specific version of the product. At any time, multiple variations and revisions of each artifact are in the product library. All version-control tools assist users in distinguishing among different versions of artifacts of source code. But keeping track of compiled code is more difficult, because some version-control tools do not attach revision numbers to compiled versions.

To cope with this, some organizations automatically compile the latest version of each artifact every night, thereby ensuring that all the compiled code is up to date. Although this technique works, it can be extremely wasteful of computer time because frequently a large number of unnecessary compilations are performed. The UNIX tool *make* can solve this problem [Feldman, 1979]. For each executable load image, the programmer sets up a Makefile specifying the hierarchy of the source and compiled files that go into that particular configuration; such a hierarchy is shown in Figure 5.12. More complex dependencies, such as included files in C++, also can be handled by *make*. When invoked by a programmer, the tool works as follows: UNIX, like virtually every other operating system, attaches a date and time stamp to each file. Suppose that the stamp on a source file is Friday, June 6, at 11:24 A.M., whereas the stamp on the corresponding compiled file is Friday, June 6, at 11:40 A.M. Then it is clear that the source file has not been changed since the compiled file was created by the compiler. On the other hand, if the date and time stamp on the source file is later than that on the compiled file, then *make* calls the appropriate compiler or assembler to create a version of the compiled file that corresponds to the current version of the source file.

Next, the date and time stamp on the executable load image is compared to those on every compiled file in that configuration. If the executable load image was created later than all the compiled files, then there is no need to relink. But if a compiled file has a later stamp than that of the load image, then the load image does not incorporate the latest version of that compiled file. In this case, *make* calls the linker and constructs an updated load image.

In other words, *make* checks whether the load image incorporates the current version of every artifact. If so, then nothing further is done and no CPU time is wasted on needless compilations and linkage. If not, then *make* calls the relevant system software to create an up-to-date version of the product.

In addition, *make* simplifies the task of building a compiled file. The user need not specify each time what artifacts are to be used and how they are to be connected, because this information already is in the Makefile. Therefore, a single *make* command is all that is needed to build a product with hundreds of artifacts and ensure that the complete product is put together correctly.

Tools like *make* have been incorporated into an endless variety of programming environments, including JBuilder and Visual C++. An open-source version of *make* is Ant (a product of the Apache project).

5.10   Productivity Gains with CASE Technology

Reifer (as reported in [Myers, 1992]) conducted an investigation into productivity gains as a consequence of introducing CASE technology. He collected data from 45 companies in 10 industries. Half the companies were in the field of information systems, 25 percent in scientific areas, and 25 percent in real-time aerospace. Average annual productivity gains varied from 9 percent (real-time aerospace) to 12 percent (information systems). If only productivity gains are considered, then these figures do not justify the cost of $125,000 per user of introducing CASE technology. However, the companies surveyed felt that the justification for CASE is not merely increased productivity but also shorter development time and improvement in software quality. In other words, the introduction of CASE environments boosted productivity, although less than some proponents of CASE technology have claimed. Nevertheless, other, equally important reasons were given for introducing CASE technology into a software organization, such as faster development, fewer faults, better usability, easier maintenance, and improved morale.

Newer results on the effectiveness of CASE technology from over 100 development projects at 15 Fortune 500 companies reflect the importance of training and the software process [Guinan, Cooprider, and Sawyer, 1997]. When teams using CASE were given training in application development in general as well as tool-specific training, user satisfaction increased and development schedules were met. However, when training was not provided, software was delivered late and users were less satisfied. Also, performance increased by 50 percent when teams used CASE tools in conjunction with a structured methodology. These results support the assertion in Section 3.13 that CASE environments should not be used by groups at maturity levels 1 or 2. To put it bluntly, a fool with a tool is still a fool [Guinan, Cooprider, and Sawyer, 1997]. The final figure in this chapter, Figure 5.14, is an alphabetical list of the theoretical tools and CASE tools described in this chapter, together with the section in which each is described.

Figure 5.14
Summary of the theoretical (analytical) tools and software (CASE) tools presented in this chapter and the section in which each is described.

Analytical Tools
Cost–benefit analysis (Section 5.2)
Metrics (Section 5.3)
Stepwise refinement (Section 5.1)

CASE Taxonomy
Environment (Section 5.5)
LowerCASE tool (Section 5.5)
UpperCASE tool (Section 5.5)
Workbench (Section 5.5)

CASE Tools
Build tool (Section 5.9)
Coding tool (Section 5.6)
Configuration-control tool
(Section 5.8)
Consistency checker (Section 5.5)
Data dictionary (Section 5.5)
E-mail (Section 5.6)
Interface checker (Section 5.6)
Online documentation (Section 5.6)
Operating system front end
(Section 5.6)
Pretty printer (Section 5.6)
Report generator (Section 5.5)
Screen generator (Section 5.5)
Source-level debugger (Section 5.6)
Spreadsheet (Section 5.6)
Structure editor (Section 5.6)
Version-control tool (Section 5.7)
Word processor (Section 5.6)
World Wide Web browser (Section 5.6)

Chapter Review

First, a number of analytical tools are presented. Stepwise refinement, based on Miller's Law, is described in Section 5.1 and illustrated by means of an example in Section 5.1.1. Another analytical tool, cost-benefit analysis, is presented in Section 5.2. Software metrics are introduced in Section 5.3.

Computer-aided software engineering (CASE) is defined in Section 5.4, and the taxonomy and scope of CASE are described in Sections 5.5 and 5.6, respectively. A variety of CASE tools are next described. When large products are constructed, version-control tools, configuration-control tools, and build tools are essential; these are presented in Sections 5.7 through 5.9. Productivity gains, as a consequence of the use of CASE technology, are described in Section 5.10.

For Further Reading

For further information regarding Miller's Law and his theory of how the brain operates on chunks, consult [Tracz, 1979] and [Moran, 1981] as well as Miller's original paper [Miller, 1956].

Wirth's [1971] paper on stepwise refinement is a classic of its kind and deserves detailed study. Equally significant from the viewpoint of stepwise refinement are the books by Dijkstra [1976] and Wirth [1975]. Stepwise design of real-time systems is described in [Kurki-Suonio, 1993].

Studies of tool evaluation are presented in [Kitchenham, Pickard, and Pfleeger, 1995]. The extent to which CASE is used in the software industry is described in [Sharma and Rai, 2000].

In this book, CASE tools for the separate workflows of the software process are described in the chapters on each workflow. For information on workbenches or CASE environments, consult the For Further Reading section of Chapter 13.

[Whitgift, 1991] is a good introduction to configuration management. Newer articles include [van der Hoek, Carzaniga, Heimbigner, and Wolf, 2002; Mens, 2002; and Walrad and Strom, 2002]. The proceedings of the International Workshops on Software Configuration Management are a useful source of information.

There are many excellent books on cost–benefit analysis, including [Gramlich, 1997]. Cost–benefit analysis of software product lines (Section 8.5.4) is discussed in [Bockle et al., 2004]. Van Solingen [2004] presents cost–benefit analysis of software process improvement.

Important books on metrics include [Shepperd, 1996] and [Fenton and Pfleeger, 1997]. Jones [1994] highlights unworkable and invalid metrics that nevertheless continue to be mentioned in the literature. The validity of object-oriented metrics is discussed in [El Emam, Benlarbi, Goel, and Rai, 2001] and [Alshayeb and Li, 2003]. The March/April 1997 issue of *IEEE Software* contains a number of papers on metrics, including [Pfleeger, Jeffrey, Curtis, and Kitchenham, 1997], an assessment of software measurement. Kilpi [2001] describes how a metrics program was implemented at Nokia. Metrics for COTS-based systems are presented in [Sedigh-Ali and Paul, 2001].

A number of articles from the Seventh International Software Metrics Symposium appear in the November 2001 issue of *IEEE Transactions on Software Engineering;* of particular interest is [Briand and Wüst, 2001].

Key Terms

activity 129	configuration control 137	environment 129
assumption 125	configuration-control	formatter 131
back-end tool 128	tool 137	freeze 137
baseline 137	consistency checker 129	front-end tool 128
build tool 138	cost–benefit analysis 124	interactive source-level
CASE 118	data dictionary 128	debugger 133
coding tool 130	derivation 136	lookahead 123
configuration 135	e-mail 130	lowerCASE tool 128

metrics 126
online documentation 130
online interface checker 131
operating system front
  end 132
pretty printer 131
private workspace 137
process metric 126
product metric 126
programming-in-the-
  large 130

programming-in-the-
  many 130
programming-in-the-
  small 130
report generator 129
revision 134
screen generator 129
source-level debugger 133
spreadsheet 130
stepwise refinement 118
structure editor 131

syntax-directed editor 132
systems engineering 127
tool 128
upperCASE tool 128
variation 134
version 133
word processor 130
workbench 129

Problems   5.1   Consider the effect of introducing lookahead to the design of the corrected third refinement of the sequential master file update problem. That is, before processing a transaction the next transaction must be read. If both transactions apply to the same master file record, then the decision regarding the processing of the current transaction depends on the type of the next transaction. Draw up a 3×3 table with the rows labeled by the type of the current transaction and the columns labeled by the type of the next transaction and fill in the action to be taken in each instance. For example, two successive insertions of the same record clearly are an error. But two modifications may be perfectly valid; for example, a subscriber can change address more than once in a given month. Now develop a flowchart for the third refinement that incorporates lookahead.

5.2   Check whether your answer to Problem 5.1 can correctly handle a modification transaction followed by a deletion transaction, both transactions being applied to the same master file record. If not, modify your answer.

5.3   Check whether your answer to Problem 5.1 also can handle correctly an insertion followed by a modification followed by a deletion, all applied to the same master file record. If not, modify your answer.

5.4   Check whether your answer to Problem 5.1 can also correctly handle n insertions, modifications, or deletions, $n > 2$, all applied to the same master file record. If not, modify your answer.

5.5   The last transaction record has no successor. Check whether your flowchart for Problem 5.1 takes this into account and processes the last transaction record correctly. If not, modify your answer.

5.6   In some applications, an alternative to lookahead can be achieved by cleverly ordering the transactions. For example, the original problem caused by a modification followed by a deletion of the same master file record could have been solved by processing a deletion before a modification. This would have resulted in the master file being written correctly and an error message appearing in the exception report. Investigate whether there is an ordering of the transactions that can solve all the difficulties listed in Problems 5.2 through 5.4.

5.7   A new form of gastrointestinal disease is sweeping the country of Concordia. Like histoplasmosis, it is transmitted as an airborne fungus. Although the disease is almost never fatal, an attack is extremely painful and the sufferer is unable to work for about 2 weeks. The government of Concordia wishes to determine how much money, if any, to spend on attempting to eradicate the disease. The committee charged with advising the Department of Public Health is considering four aspects of the problem: health care costs (Concordia provides free health care to all its citizens), loss of earnings (and hence loss of taxes), pain and discomfort, and gratitude toward the government. Explain how cost–benefit analysis can assist the committee. For each benefit or cost, suggest how a dollar estimate for that benefit or cost could be obtained.

5.8   Does a one-person software production organization need a version-control tool, and if so, why?

5.9   Does a one-person software production organization need a configuration-control tool, and if so, why?

5.10   You are the manager in charge of the software that controls the navigation system for a midget submarine. Three different user-reported faults have to be fixed, and you assign one each to Paul, Quentin, and Rachel. A day later you learn that, to implement each of the three fixes, the same four artifacts must be changed. However, your configuration-control tool is inoperative, so you will have to manage the changes yourself. How will you do it?

5.11   Which of the case tools listed in Figure 5.14 promote stepwise refinement during software development? Justify your answer.

5.12   (Term Project) What types of CASE tools would be appropriate for developing the Osric's Office Appliances and Decor product described in Appendix A?

5.13   (Readings in Software Engineering) Your instructor will distribute copies of [Wirth, 1971]. List the differences between Wirth's approach and the approach to stepwise refinement presented in this chapter.

References

[Alshayeb and Li, 2003] M. ALSHAYEB AND W. LI, "An Empirical Validation of Object-Oriented Metrics in Two Different Iterative Software Processes," *IEEE Transactions on Software Engineering* **29** (November 2003), pp. 1043–49.

[Babich, 1986] W. A. BABICH, *Software Configuration Management: Coordination for Team Productivity,* Addison-Wesley, Reading, MA, 1986.

[Bockle et al., 2004] G. BOCKLE, P. CLEMENTS, J. D. MCGREGOR, D. MUTHIG, AND K. SCHMID, "Calculating ROI for Software Product Lines," *IEEE Software* **21** (May/June 2004), pp. 23–31.

[Briand and Wüst, 2001] L. C. BRIAND AND J. WÜST, "Modeling Development Effort in Object-Oriented Systems Using Design Properties," *IEEE Transactions on Software Engineering* **27** (November 2001), pp. 963–86.

[DeRemer and Kron, 1976] F. DEREMER AND H. H. KRON, "Programming-in-the-Large versus Programming-in-the-Small," *IEEE Transactions on Software Engineering* **SE-2** (June 1976), pp. 80–86.

[Dijkstra, 1976] E. W. DIJKSTRA, *A Discipline of Programming*, Prentice Hall, Englewood Cliffs, NJ, 1976.

[Dooley and Schach, 1985] J. W. M. DOOLEY AND S. R. SCHACH, "FLOW: A Software Development Environment Using Diagrams," *Journal of Systems and Software* **5** (August 1985), pp. 203–19.

[El Emam, Benlarbi, Goel, and Rai, 2001] K. EL EMAM, S. BENLARBI, N. GOEL, AND S. N. RAI, "The Confounding Effect of Class Size on the Validity of Object-Oriented Metrics," *IEEE Transactions on Software Engineering* **27** (July 2001), pp. 630–50.

[Feldman, 1979] S. I. FELDMAN, "Make—A Program for Maintaining Computer Programs," *Software—Practice and Experience* **9** (April 1979), pp. 225–65.

[Fenton and Pfleeger, 1997] N. E. FENTON AND S. L. PFLEEGER, *Software Metrics: A Rigorous and Practical Approach*, 2nd ed., IEEE Computer Society, Los Alamitos, CA, 1997.

[Fuggetta, 1993] A. FUGGETTA, "A Classification of CASE Technology," *IEEE Computer* **26** (December 1993), pp. 25–38.

[Gramlich, 1997] E. M. GRAMLICH, *A Guide to Benefit–Cost Analysis*, 2nd ed., Waveland Books, Prospect Heights, IL, 1997.

[Guinan, Cooprider, and Sawyer, 1997] P. J. GUINAN, J. G. COOPRIDER, AND S. SAWYER, "The Effective Use of Automated Application Development Tools," *IBM Systems Journal* **36** (No. 1, 1997), pp. 124–39.

[Jones, 1994] C. JONES, "Software Metrics: Good, Bad, and Missing," *IEEE Computer* **27** (September 1994), pp. 98–100.

[Kilpi, 2001] T. KILPI, "Implementing a Software Metrics Program at Nokia," *IEEE Software* **18** (November/December 2001), pp. 72–76.

[Kitchenham, Pickard, and Pfleeger, 1995] B. KITCHENHAM, L. PICKARD, AND S. L. PFLEEGER. "Case Studies for Method and Tool Evaluation," *IEEE Software* **12** (July 1995), pp. 52–62.

[Kurki-Suonio, 1993] R. KURKI-SUONIO, "Stepwise Design of Real-Time Systems," *IEEE Transactions on Software Engineering* **19** (January 1993), pp. 56–69.

[Loukides and Oram, 1997] M. K. LOUKIDES AND A. ORAM, *Programming with GNU Software*, O'Reilly and Associates, Sebastopol, CA, 1997.

[Mens, 2002] T. MENS, "A State-of-the-Art Survey on Software Merging," *IEEE Transactions on Software Engineering* **28** (May 2002), pp. 449–62.

[Miller, 1956] G. A. MILLER, "The Magical Number Seven, Plus or Minus Two: Some Limits on Our Capacity for Processing Information," *The Psychological Review* **63** (March 1956), pp. 81–97. Reprinted at: www.well.com/user/smalin/miller.html.

[Moran, 1981] T. P. MORAN (Editor), Special Issue: The Psychology of Human-Computer Interaction, *ACM Computing Surveys* **13** (March 1981).

[Myers, 1992] W. MYERS, "Good Software Practices Pay off—or Do They?" *IEEE Software* **9** (March 1992), pp. 96–97.

[Pfleeger, Jeffrey, Curtis, and Kitchenham, 1997] S. L. PFLEEGER, R. JEFFREY, B. CURTIS, AND B. KITCHENHAM, "Status Report on Software Measurement," *IEEE Software* **14** (March/April 1997), pp. 33–44.

[Rochkind, 1975] M. J. ROCHKIND, "The Source Code Control System," *IEEE Transactions on Software Engineering* **SE-1** (October 1975), pp. 255–65.

[Sedigh-Ali and Paul, 2001] S. SEDIGH-ALI AND R. A. PAUL, "Software Engineering Metrics for COTS-Based Systems," *IEEE Computer* **34** (May 2001), pp. 44–50.

[Sharma and Rai, 2000] S. SHARMA AND A. RAI, "CASE Deployment in IS Organizations," *Communications of the ACM* **43** (January 2000), pp. 80–88.

[Shepperd, 1996] M. SHEPPERD, *Foundations of Software Measurement*, Prentice Hall, Upper Saddle River, NJ, 1996.

[Sobell, 1995] M. G. SOBELL, *A Practical Guide to the UNIX System*, 3rd ed., Benjamin/Cummings, Menlo Park, CA, 1995.

[Tichy, 1985] W. F. TICHY, "RCS—A System for Version Control," *Software—Practice and Experience* **15** (July 1985), pp. 637–54.

[Tomer and Schach, 2002] A. TOMER AND S. R. SCHACH, "A Three-Dimensional Model for System Design Evolution," *Systems Engineering* **5** (No. 4, 2002), pp. 264–73.

[Tracz, 1979] W. J. TRACZ, "Computer Programming and the Human Thought Process," *Software—Practice and Experience* **9** (February 1979), pp. 127–37.

[van der Hoek, Carzaniga, Heimbigner, and Wolf, 2002] A. VAN DER HOEK, A. CARZANIGA, D. HEIMBIGNER, AND A. L. WOLF, "A Testbed for Configuration Management Policy Programming," *IEEE Transactions on Software Engineering* **28** (January 2002), pp. 79–99.

[van Solingen, 2004] R. VAN SOLINGEN, "Measuring the ROI of Software Process Improvement," *IEEE Software* **21** (May/June 2004), pp. 32–38.

[Walrad and Strom, 2002] C. WALRAD AND D. STROM, "The Importance of Branching Models in SCM," *IEEE Computer* **35** (September 2002), pp. 31–38.

[Whitgift, 1991] D. WHITGIFT, *Methods and Tools for Software Configuration Management*, John Wiley and Sons, New York, 1991.

[Wirth, 1971] N. WIRTH, "Program Development by Stepwise Refinement," *Communications of the ACM* 14 (April 1971), pp. 221–27.

[Wirth, 1975] N. WIRTH, *Algorithms + Data Structures = Programs,* Prentice Hall, Englewood Cliffs, NJ, 1975.

Chapter

Testing

Learning Objectives

After studying this chapter, you should be able to

- Describe quality assurance issues.
- Describe how to perform non-execution-based testing (inspections) of artifacts.
- Describe the principles of execution-based testing.
- Explain what needs to be tested.

Classical software life-cycle models all too frequently included a separate testing phase, after integration and before postdelivery maintenance. Nothing could be more dangerous from the viewpoint of trying to achieve high-quality software. Testing is an integral component of the software process and an activity that must be carried out throughout the life cycle: During the requirements workflow, the requirements must be checked; during the analysis workflow, the specifications must be checked; and the software production management plan must undergo similar scrutiny. The design workflow requires meticulous checking at every stage. During the implementation workflow, each code artifact certainly must be tested; and the product as a whole needs testing when it has been fully integrated. After passing the acceptance test, the product is installed and postdelivery maintenance begins. And hand in hand with maintenance goes repeated checking of modified versions of the product.

In other words, it is not sufficient to test the product of a workflow merely at the end of that workflow. For example, consider the design workflow. The members of the design team must consciously and conscientiously check the design while they develop it. It is not much use for the team to develop the complete design artifacts only to find, weeks or months later, that a mistake made early in the process necessitates redesigning almost the entire product. Therefore, continual testing must be carried out by the development team while it performs each workflow, in addition to more methodical testing at the end of each workflow.

The terms *verification* and *validation* were introduced in Section 1.7. **Verification** refers to the process of determining whether a workflow has been correctly carried out; this takes place at the end of each workflow. On the other hand, **validation** is the intensive evaluation process that takes place just before the product is delivered to the client. Its purpose is to determine whether the product as a whole satisfies its specifications. Even though both terms are defined in the IEEE software engineering glossary [IEEE 610.12, 1990] in this way, and notwithstanding the common usage of the term **V & V** to denote testing, the words *verification* and *validation* are used as little as possible in this book. One reason is that, as explained in Section 6.5, the word *verification* has another meaning within the context of testing. A second reason is that the phrase *verification and validation* (V & V) implies that the process of checking a workflow can wait until the end of that workflow. On the contrary, it is essential that this checking be carried out in parallel with all software development and maintenance activities. Therefore, to avoid the undesirable implications of the phrase *V & V*, the term **testing** is used. A second reason why we use the word *testing* is that this is the terminology of the Unified Process. For example, the fifth core workflow is the **test workflow**.

Essentially there are two types of testing: execution-based testing and non-execution-based testing. For example, it is impossible to execute a written specification document; the only alternatives are to review it as carefully as possible or subject it to some form of analysis. However, once there is executable code, it becomes possible to run test cases, that is, to perform execution-based testing. Nevertheless, the existence of code does not preclude non-execution-based testing, because as will be explained, methodically reviewing code uncovers at least as many faults as running test cases. In this chapter, the principles of both execution-based and non-execution-based testing are described. These principles are applied in Chapters 10 through 14, where a description is given of each workflow of the process model and the specific testing practices applicable to it. The first two faults described in Just in Case You Wanted to Know Box 1.1 led to fatal consequences. Fortunately, in most cases, the result of delivering software with residual faults is considerably less catastrophic. Nevertheless, the importance of testing cannot be stressed too strongly.

6.1   Quality Issues

We begin this section by expanding on the definitions of Section 1.10 that relate to testing. A **fault** is injected into the software when a human makes a **mistake** [IEEE 610.12, 1990]. One mistake on the part of a software professional may cause several faults; conversely, various mistakes may cause the identical fault. A **failure** is the observed incorrect behavior of the software product as a consequence of a fault, and the **error** is the amount by which a result is incorrect [IEEE 610.12, 1990]. A specific failure may be caused by several faults, and some faults may never cause a failure. The word **defect** is a generic term for a fault, failure, or error.

Now we turn to quality issues. The term *quality* frequently is misunderstood when used within the software context. After all, quality implies excellence of some sort, but this unfortunately is infrequently the meaning intended by software engineers. To put it bluntly, all that many software development organizations can achieve is merely to get the software

The use of the term *quality* to denote "adheres to specifications" (as opposed to "excellent" or "luxurious") is the practice in fields such as engineering and manufacturing. Consider, for example, the quality control manager at a Coca-Cola bottling plant. The job of that quality control manager is to ensure that every bottle or can that leaves the production line satisfies the specifications for Coca-Cola in every way. There is no attempt to produce "excellent" Coca-Cola or "luxurious" Coca-Cola; the sole aim is to be certain that each bottle or can of Coca-Cola stringently adheres to the company's formula (specifications) for that carbonated beverage.

The word *quality* is used identically in the automobile industry. Quality Is Job One is a former slogan of the Ford Motor Company. In other words, the aim of Ford is to ensure that every car that comes off a Ford production line adheres rigorously to the specifications for that car; in common software engineering parlance, the car must be "bug free" in every way.

---

to function correctly—excellence is an order of magnitude more than what is generally possible for organizations at CMM level 1 (Section 3.13).

The **quality** of software is the extent to which the product satisfies its specifications (see Just in Case You Wanted to Know Box 6.1). However, this is not enough. For example, to ensure that a product can be easily maintained, the product must be well designed and meticulously coded. Therefore, it is necessary that software have high quality, but this is by no means sufficient.

The task of every software professional is to ensure high-quality software at all times. That is, each developer and maintainer is personally responsible for checking that his or her work is correct. Quality is not something added afterward by the **software quality assurance (SQA)** group but rather must be built in by the developers from the very beginning. One role of the SQA group is to ensure that the developers are indeed doing high-quality work. The SQA group has additional responsibilities, too, as described in Section 6.1.1.

6.1.1   Software Quality Assurance

As previously stated, one aspect of the role of the SQA group is to test that the developers' product is correct. More precisely, once the developers have completed a workflow and carefully checked their work, members of the SQA group have to ensure that the workflow has indeed been carried out correctly. Also, when the product is complete and the developers are confident that the product as a whole is correct, the SQA group has to make sure that this is so. However, software quality assurance goes further than just testing (or V & V) at the end of a workflow or the end of the development process. SQA applies to the software process itself. For example, the responsibilities of the SQA group include the development of the various standards to which the software must conform as well as the establishment of the monitoring procedures for ensuring compliance with those standards. In brief, the role of the SQA group is to ensure the quality of the software process and thereby ensure the quality of the product.

6.1.2   Managerial Independence

It is important to have **managerial independence** between the development team and the SQA group. That is, development should be under one manager, SQA under a different manager, and neither manager should be able to overrule the other. The reason is that, all too frequently, serious defects are found in a product as the delivery deadline approaches. The software organization must now choose between two unsatisfactory options. Either the product can be released on time but full of faults, leaving the client to struggle with faulty software, or the developers can fix the software but deliver it late. No matter what, the client probably will lose confidence in the software organization. The decision to deliver faulty software on time should not be made by the manager responsible for development, nor should the SQA manager be able to make the decision to perform further testing and deliver the product late. Instead, both managers should report to a more senior manager who can decide which choice would be in the best interests of both the software development organization and the client.

At first sight, having a separate SQA group would appear to add considerably to the cost of software development, but this is not so. The additional cost is relatively small compared to the resulting benefit—higher-quality software. Without an SQA group, every member of the software development organization would have to be involved to some extent with quality assurance activities. Suppose an organization has 100 software professionals and each devotes about 30 percent of his or her time to quality assurance activities. Instead, the 100 individuals should be divided into two groups, with 70 individuals performing software development and the other 30 people responsible for SQA. The same amount of time is devoted to SQA, the only additional expense being a manager to lead the SQA group. Quality assurance now can be performed by an independent group of specialists, leading to products of higher quality than when SQA activities are performed throughout the organization.

In the case of an extremely small software company (four employees or fewer), it may simply not be economically viable to have a separate SQA group. The best that can be done under such circumstances is to ensure that the analysis artifacts are checked by someone other than the person responsible for producing those artifacts and similarly for the design artifacts, code artifacts, and so on. The reason for this is explained in Section 6.2.

6.2   Non-Execution-Based Testing

Testing software without running test cases is termed ***non-execution-based testing***. Examples of non-execution-based testing methods include reviewing software (carefully reading through it) and analyzing software mathematically (Section 6.5).

It is not a good idea for the person responsible for drawing up a document to be the only one responsible for reviewing it. Almost everyone has blind spots that allow faults to creep into the document, and those same blind spots prevent the faults from being detected on review. Therefore, the review task must be assigned to someone other than the original author of the document. In addition, having only one reviewer may not be adequate; we all have had the experience of reading through a document many times while failing to detect a blatant spelling mistake that a second reader picks up almost immediately. This is one principle underlying review techniques like walkthroughs or inspections. In both types of review, a document (such as a specification document or design document) is painstakingly checked by a team of software professionals with a broad range of skills. The strength of a review by a team of experts is that the different skills of the participants increase the chances of finding a fault. In addition, a team of skilled individuals working together often generates a synergistic effect.

Walkthroughs and inspections are two types of reviews. The fundamental difference between them is that walkthroughs have fewer steps and are less formal than inspections.

6.2.1   Walkthroughs

A walkthrough team should consist of four to six individuals. An analysis walkthrough team should include at least one representative from the team responsible for drawing up the specifications, the manager responsible for the analysis workflow, a client representative, a representative of the team that will perform the next workflow of the development (in this instance the design team), and a representative of the software quality assurance group. For reasons that will be explained in Section 6.2.2, the SQA group member should chair the walkthrough.

The members of the walkthrough team should, as far as possible, be experienced senior technical staff members because they tend to find the important faults. That is, they detect the faults that would have a major negative impact on the project [R. New, personal communication, 1992].

The material for the walkthrough must be distributed to the participants well in advance to allow for thorough preparation. Each reviewer should study the material and develop two lists: a list of items the reviewer does not understand and a list of items the reviewer believes are incorrect.

6.2.2   Managing Walkthroughs

The walkthrough should be chaired by the SQA representative because the SQA representative has the most to lose if the walkthrough is performed poorly and faults slip through. In contrast, the representative responsible for the analysis workflow may be eager to have the specification document approved as quickly as possible to start some other task. The client representative may decide that any faults not detected at the review probably will show up during acceptance testing and be fixed at that time at no cost to the client organization. But the SQA representative has the most at stake: The quality of the product is a direct reflection of the professional competence of the SQA group.

The person leading the walkthrough guides the other members of the walkthrough team through the document to uncover any faults. It is not the task of the team to correct faults, but merely to record them for later correction. There are four reasons for this:

1. A correction produced by a committee (that is, the walkthrough team) within the time constraints of the walkthrough is likely to be lower in quality than a correction produced by an individual trained in the necessary techniques.

2. A correction produced by a walkthrough team of five individuals takes at least as much time as a correction produced by one person and, therefore, costs five times as much when the salaries of the five participants are considered.

3. Not all items flagged as faults actually are incorrect. In accordance with the dictum, "If it ain't broke, don't fix it," it is better for faults to be analyzed methodically and corrected only if there really is a problem, rather than have a team attempt to "fix" something that is completely correct.

4. There simply is not enough time in a walkthrough to both detect and correct faults. No walkthrough should last longer than 2 hours. The time should be spent detecting and recording faults, not correcting them.

There are two ways of conducting a walkthrough. The first is participant driven. Participants present their lists of unclear items and items they think are incorrect. The representative of the analysis team must respond to each query, clarifying what is unclear to the reviewer and either agreeing that indeed there is a fault or explaining why the reviewer is mistaken.

The second way of conducting a review is document driven. A person responsible for the document, either individually or as part of a team, walks the participants through that document, with the reviewers interrupting either with their prepared comments or comments triggered by the presentation. This second approach is likely to be more thorough. In addition, it generally leads to the detection of more faults because the majority of faults at a document-driven walkthrough are spontaneously detected by the presenter. Time after time, the presenter will pause in the middle of a sentence, his or her face will light up, and a fault, one that has lain dormant through many readings of the document, suddenly becomes obvious. A fruitful field for research by a psychologist would be to determine why verbalization so often leads to fault detection during walkthroughs of all kinds, including requirements walkthroughs, analysis walkthroughs, design walkthroughs, plan walkthroughs, and code walkthroughs. Not surprisingly, the more thorough document-driven review is the technique prescribed in the IEEE Standard for Software Reviews [IEEE 1028, 1997].

The primary role of the walkthrough leader is to elicit questions and facilitate discussion. A walkthrough is an interactive process; it is not supposed to be one-sided instruction by the presenter. It also is essential that the walkthrough not be used as a means of evaluating the participants. If that happens, the walkthrough degenerates into a point-scoring session and does not detect faults, no matter how well the session leader tries to run it. It has been suggested that the manager who is responsible for the document being reviewed should be a member of the walkthrough team. If this manager also is responsible for the annual evaluations of the members of the walkthrough team (and particularly of the presenter), the fault detection capabilities of the team will be compromised, because the primary motive of the presenter will be to minimize the number of faults that show up. To prevent this conflict of interests, the person responsible for a given workflow should not also be directly responsible for evaluating any member of the walkthrough team for that workflow.

6.2.3   Inspections

Inspections were first proposed by Fagan [1976] for testing designs and code. An **inspection** goes far beyond a walkthrough and has five formal steps.

1. An **overview** of the document to be inspected (requirements, specification, design, code, or plan) is given by one of the individuals responsible for producing that document. At the end of the overview session, the document is distributed to the participants.

2. In the **preparation**, the participants try to understand the document in detail. Lists of fault types found in recent inspections, with the fault types ranked by frequency, are excellent aids. These lists help team members concentrate on the areas where the most faults have occurred.

3. To begin the inspection, one participant walks through the document with the inspection team, ensuring that every item is covered and that every branch is taken at least once. Then fault finding commences. As with walkthroughs, the purpose is to

find and document the faults, not to correct them. Within one day the leader of the inspection team (the ***moderator***) must produce a written report of the inspection to ensure meticulous follow-through.

4. In the ***rework***, the individual responsible for the document resolves all faults and problems noted in the written report.

5. In the ***follow-up***, the moderator must ensure that every issue raised has been resolved satisfactorily, by either fixing the document or clarifying items incorrectly flagged as faults. All fixes must be checked to ensure that no new faults have been introduced [Fagan, 1986]. If more than 5 percent of the material inspected has been reworked, then the team must reconvene for a 100 percent reinspection.

The inspection should be conducted by a team of four. For example, in the case of a design inspection, the team consists of a moderator, designer, implementer, and tester. The moderator is both manager and leader of the inspection team. There must be a representative of the team responsible for the current workflow as well as a representative of the team responsible for the next workflow. The designer is a member of the team that produced the design, whereas the implementer is responsible, either individually or as part of a team, for translating the design into code. Fagan suggests that the tester be any programmer responsible for setting up test cases; it is, of course, preferable that the tester be a member of the SQA group. The IEEE standard recommends a team of between three and six participants [IEEE 1028, 1997]. Special roles are played by the moderator, the ***reader*** who leads the team through the design, and the ***recorder*** responsible for producing a written report of the detected faults.

An essential component of an inspection is the checklist of potential faults. For example, the checklist for a design inspection should include items such as these: Is each item of the specification document adequately and correctly addressed? For each interface, do the actual and formal arguments correspond? Have error-handling mechanisms been adequately identified? Is the design compatible with the hardware resources or does it require more hardware than actually is available? Is the design compatible with the software resources; for example, does the operating system stipulated in the analysis artifacts have the functionality required by the design?

An important component of the inspection procedure is the record of fault statistics. Faults must be recorded by severity (major or minor; an example of a major fault is one that causes premature termination or damages a database) and fault type. In the case of a design inspection, typical fault types include interface faults and logic faults. This information can be used in a number of useful ways:

• The number of faults in a given product can be compared with averages of faults detected at the same stage of development in comparable products, giving management an early warning that something is amiss and allowing timely corrective action to be taken.

• If inspecting two or three code artifacts results in the discovery of a disproportionate number of faults of a particular type, management can begin checking other code artifacts and take corrective action.

• If the inspection of a particular code artifact reveals far more faults than were found in any other code artifact in the product, there is usually a strong case for redesigning that artifact from scratch and implementing the new design.

- Information regarding the number and types of faults detected at an inspection of a design artifact aids the team performing the code inspection of the implementation of that artifact at a later stage.

The first experiment of Fagan [1976] was performed on a systems product. One hundred person-hours were devoted to inspections, at a rate of two 2-hour inspections per day by a four-person team. Of all the faults found during the development of the product, 67 percent were located by inspections before unit testing was started. Furthermore, during the first 7 months after the product was installed, 38 percent fewer faults were detected in the inspected product than in a comparable product reviewed using informal walkthroughs.

Fagan [1976] conducted another experiment on an applications product and found that 82 percent of all detected faults were discovered during design and code inspections. A useful side effect of the inspections was that programmer productivity rose because less time had to be spent on unit testing. Using an automated estimating model, Fagan determined that, as a result of the inspection process, the savings on programmer resources were 25 percent despite the time that had to be devoted to the inspections. In a different experiment Jones [1978] found that over 70 percent of detected faults could be detected by conducting design and code inspections.

Subsequent studies have produced equally impressive results. In a 6000-line business data processing application, 93 percent of all detected faults were found during inspections [Fagan, 1986]. As reported in [Ackerman, Buchwald, and Lewski, 1989], the use of inspections rather than testing during the development of an operating system decreased the cost of detecting a fault by 85 percent; in a switching system product, the decrease was 90 percent [Fowler, 1986]. At the Jet Propulsion Laboratory (JPL), on average, each 2-hour inspection exposed 4 major faults and 14 minor faults [Bush, 1990]. Translated into dollar terms, this meant a savings of approximately $25,000 *per inspection.* Another JPL study [Kelly, Sherif, and Hops, 1992] showed that the number of faults detected decreased exponentially by classical phase. In other words, with the aid of inspections, faults can be detected early in the software process. The importance of this early detection is reflected in Figure 1.5.

One advantage that code inspections have over running test cases (execution-based testing) is that the testers need not deal with failures. It frequently happens that, when a product under test is executed, it fails. The fault that caused the failure must now be located and fixed before execution-based testing can continue. In contrast, a fault found in the code during non-execution-based testing is logged and the review continues.

A risk of the inspection process is that, like the walkthrough, it might be used for performance appraisal. The danger is particularly acute in the case of inspections because of the detailed fault information available. Fagan dismisses this fear by stating that, over a period of 3 years, he knew of no IBM manager who used such information against a programmer, or as he put it, no manager tried to "kill the goose that lays the golden eggs" [Fagan, 1976]. However, if inspections are not conducted properly, they may not be as wildly successful as they have been at IBM. Unless top management is aware of the potential problem, misuse of inspection information is a distinct possibility.

6.2.4   Comparison of Inspections and Walkthroughs

Superficially, the difference between an inspection and a walkthrough is that the inspection team uses a checklist of queries to aid it in finding the faults. But the difference goes deeper than that. A walkthrough is a two-step process: preparation followed by team analysis of the document. An inspection is a five-step process: overview, preparation, inspection, rework, and follow-up;

and the procedure to be followed in each step is formalized. Examples of such formalization are the methodical categorization of faults and the use of that information in inspection of the documents of the succeeding workflows as well as in inspections of future products.

The inspection process takes much longer than a walkthrough. Is inspection worth the additional time and effort? The data of Section 6.2.3 clearly indicate that inspections are a powerful, cost-effective tool to detect faults.

6.2.5   Strengths and Weaknesses of Reviews

There are two major strengths of a ***review*** (walkthrough or inspection). First, a review is an effective way to detect a fault; second, faults are detected early in the software process, that is, before they become expensive to fix. For example, design faults are detected before implementation commences and coding faults are found before the artifact is integrated into the product.

However, the effectiveness of a review can be reduced if the software process is inadequate. First, large-scale software is extremely hard to review unless it consists of smaller, largely independent components. A strength of the object-oriented paradigm is that, if correctly carried out, the resulting product consists of largely independent pieces. Second, a design review team sometimes has to refer to the analysis artifacts; a code review team often needs access to the design documents. Unless the documentation of the previous workflows is complete, updated to reflect the current version of the project, and available online, the effectiveness of review teams is severely hampered.

6.2.6   Metrics for Inspections

To determine the effectiveness of inspections, a number of different metrics can be used. The first is the ***inspection rate***. When specifications and designs are inspected, the number of pages inspected per hour can be measured; for code inspections, an appropriate metric is lines of code inspected per hour. A second metric is the ***fault density***, measured in faults per page inspected or faults per 1000 lines of code (KLOC) inspected. This metric can be subdivided into major faults per unit of material and minor faults per unit of material. Another useful metric is the ***fault detection rate***, that is, the number of major and minor faults detected per hour. A fourth metric is the ***fault detection efficiency***, that is, the number of major and minor faults detected per person-hour.

Although the purpose of these metrics is to measure the effectiveness of the inspection process, the results instead may reflect deficiencies of the development team. For example, if the fault detection rate suddenly rises from 20 faults per thousand lines of code to 30, this does not necessarily mean that the inspection team has suddenly become 50 percent more efficient. Another explanation could be that the quality of code has decreased and there simply are more faults to be detected.

Having discussed non-execution-based testing, the next topic is execution-based testing.

6.3   Execution-Based Testing

It has been claimed that testing is a demonstration that faults ("bugs") are not present. Even though some organizations spend up to 50 percent of their software budget on testing, delivered "tested" software is notoriously unreliable.

The reason for this contradiction is simple. As Dijkstra put it, "Program testing can be a very effective way to show the presence of bugs, but it is hopelessly inadequate for showing their absence" [Dijkstra, 1972]. What Dijkstra is saying is that, if a product is executed with test data and the output is wrong, then the product definitely contains a fault. But, if the output is correct, then there still may be a fault in the product; the only information that can be deduced from that particular test is that the product runs correctly on that particular set of test data.

6.4   What Should Be Tested?

To be able to describe what properties should be tested, it is first necessary to give a precise description of ***execution-based testing***. According to Goodenough [1979], execution-based testing is a process of inferring certain behavioral properties of a product based, in part, on the results of executing the product in a known environment with selected inputs. This definition has three troubling implications.

1. First, the definition states that testing is an inferential process. The tester takes the product, runs it with known input data, and examines the output. The tester has to infer what, if anything, is wrong with the product. From this viewpoint, testing is comparable to trying to find the proverbial black cat in a dark room, but without knowing whether or not a cat is in the room in the first place. The tester has few clues to help find any faults; perhaps 10 or 20 sets of inputs and corresponding outputs, possibly a user fault report, and thousands of lines of code. From this, the tester has to deduce if there is a fault and, if so, what it is.

2. A problem with the definition arises from the phrase in a *known environment*. We never really can know our environment, either the hardware or the software. We never can be certain that the operating system is functioning correctly or that the run-time routines are correct. An intermittent hardware fault may lie in the main memory of the computer. So what is observed as the behavior of the product in fact may be a correct product interacting with a faulty compiler or faulty hardware or some other faulty component of the environment.

3. Another worrisome part of the definition of execution-based testing is the phrase *with selected inputs*. In the case of a real-time system, frequently no control is possible over the inputs to the system. Consider avionics software. The flight control system has two types of inputs. The first type of input is what the pilot wants the aircraft to do. If the pilot pulls back on the joystick to climb or opens the throttle to increase the speed of the aircraft, these mechanical motions are transformed into digital signals sent to the flight control computer. The second type of input is the current physical state of the aircraft, such as its altitude, speed, and the elevation of the wing flaps. The flight control software uses the values of such quantities to compute what signals should be sent to the components of the aircraft, such as the wing flaps and the engines, to implement the pilot's directives. Whereas the pilot's inputs easily can be set to any desired values simply by setting the aircraft's controls appropriately, the inputs corresponding to the current physical state of the aircraft cannot be manipulated so easily. In fact, there is no way one can force the aircraft to provide "selected inputs."

How then can such a real-time system be tested? The answer is to use a simulator. A **simulator** is a working model of the environment in which the product, in this case the flight control software, executes. The flight control software can be tested by causing the simulator to send selected inputs to the flight control software. The simulator has controls that allow the operator to set an input variable to any selected value. If the purpose of the test is to determine how the flight control software performs if one engine catches fire, then the controls of the simulator are set so that the inputs sent to the flight control software are indistinguishable from the inputs that would be sent if an engine of the actual aircraft were on fire. The output is analyzed by examining the output signals sent from the flight control software to the simulator. But, at best, a simulator can be a good approximation of a faithful model of some aspect of the system; it never can be the system itself. Using a simulator means that, whereas there indeed is a "known environment," there is little likelihood that this known environment is in every way identical to the actual environment in which the product will be installed.

The preceding definition of *testing* speaks of "behavioral properties." What behavioral properties must be tested? An obvious answer is, Test whether the product functions correctly. But, as will be shown, correctness is neither necessary nor sufficient. Before discussing correctness, four other behavioral properties are considered: utility, reliability, robustness, and performance [Goodenough, 1979].

6.4.1   Utility

Utility is the extent to which a user's needs are met when a correct product is used under conditions permitted by its specifications. In other words, a product that is functioning correctly is now subjected to inputs that are valid in terms of the specifications. The user may test, for example, how easy the product is to use, whether the product performs useful functions, and whether the product is cost effective compared to competing products. Irrespective of whether the product is correct or not, these vital issues have to be tested. If the product is not cost effective, then there is no point in buying it. And unless the product is easy to use, it will not be used at all or it will be used incorrectly. Therefore, when considering buying an existing product (including shrink-wrapped software), the utility of the product should be tested first, and if the product fails on that score, testing should stop.

6.4.2   Reliability

Another aspect of a product that must be tested is its reliability. **Reliability** is a measure of the frequency and criticality of product failure; recall that a failure is an unacceptable effect or behavior, under permissible operating conditions, that occurs as a consequence of a fault. In other words, it is necessary to know how often the product fails (**mean time between failures**) and how bad the effects of that failure can be. When a product fails, an important issue is how long it takes, on average, to repair it (**mean time to repair**). But, often more important is how long it takes to repair the *results* of the failure. This last point frequently is overlooked. Suppose that the software running on a communications front end fails, on average, only once every 6 months; but when it fails, it completely wipes out a database. At best, the database can be reinitialized to its status when the last checkpoint dump was taken, and the audit trail can then be used to put the database into a state that is virtually up to date. But, if this recovery process takes the better part of 2 days, during which time the database and communications front end are inoperative, then the reliability of the product is low, notwithstanding that the mean time between failures is 6 months.

An embedded computer is an integral part of a larger system whose primary purpose is not computation. The function of embedded software is to control the device in which the computer is embedded. Military examples include a network of avionics computers on board a warplane or a computer built into an intercontinental ballistic missile. The embedded computer in the nose cone of a missile controls only that missile; it cannot be used, say, for printing the payroll checks for the soldiers on the missile base.

More familiar examples are the computer chip in a digital watch or a washing machine. Again, the chip in a washing machine is used exclusively to control the washing machine. There is no way that the owner of that washing machine could use the chip to balance a checkbook.

6.4.3   Robustness

Another aspect of every product that requires testing is its robustness. Although it is difficult to come up with a precise definition, **robustness** essentially is a function of a number of factors, such as the range of operating conditions, the possibility of unacceptable results with valid input, and the acceptability of effects when the product is given invalid input. A product with a wide range of permissible operating conditions is more robust than a more-restrictive product. A robust product should not yield unacceptable results when the input satisfies its specifications; for example, giving a valid command should not have disastrous consequences. A robust product should not crash when the product is *not* used under permissible operating conditions. To test for this aspect of robustness, test data that do not satisfy the input specifications are deliberately entered, and the tester determines how badly the product reacts. For example, when the product solicits a name, the tester may reply with a stream of unacceptable characters, such as control-A escape-% ?$#@. If the computer responds with a message such as Incorrect data—Try again or, better, informs the user as to why the data do not conform to what was expected, it is more robust than a product that crashes whenever the data deviate even slightly from what is required.

6.4.4   Performance

Performance is another aspect of the product that must be tested. For example, it is essential to know the extent to which the product meets its constraints with regard to response time or space requirements. For an embedded computer system such as an onboard computer in a handheld antiaircraft missile, the space constraints of the system may be such that only 128 megabytes (MB) of main memory are available for the software. No matter how excellent the software may be, if it needs 256 MB of main memory, then it cannot be used at all. (For more information on embedded software, see Just in Case You Wanted to Know Box 6.2.)

Real-time software is characterized by hard time constraints, that is, time constraints of such a nature that, if a constraint is not met, information is lost. For example, a nuclear reactor control system may have to sample the temperature of the core and process the data every 10th of a second. If the system is not fast enough to handle interrupts from the temperature sensor every 10th of a second, then data are lost, and there is no way of ever recovering the data; the next time the system receives temperature data, it will be the current temperature, not the reading that was missed. If the reactor is on the point of a meltdown, then it is critical that all relevant information be both received and processed as laid down in the specifications. With all real-time systems, the performance must meet every time constraint listed in the specifications.

6.4.5   Correctness

Finally, a definition of **correctness** can be given. A product is correct if it satisfies its output specifications, independent of its use of computing resources, when operated under permitted conditions [Goodenough, 1979]. In other words, if input that satisfies the input specifications is provided and the product is given all the resources it needs, then the product is correct if the output satisfies the output specifications.

This definition of *correctness*, like the definition of *testing* itself, has worrisome implications. Suppose a product has been tested successfully against a broad variety of test data. Does this mean that the product is acceptable? Unfortunately, it does not. If a product is correct, all that means is that it satisfies its specifications. But what if the specifications themselves are incorrect? To illustrate this difficulty, consider the specification shown in Figure 6.1. The specifications state that the input to the sort is an array p of n integers, whereas the output is another array q sorted in nondecreasing order. Superficially, the specifications seem perfectly correct. But consider method trickSort shown in Figure 6.2. In that method, all n elements of array q are set to 0. The method satisfies the specifications of Figure 6.1 and is therefore correct.

What happened? Unfortunately, the specifications of Figure 6.1 are wrong. What has been omitted is a statement that the elements of q, the output array, are a permutation (rearrangement) of the elements of the input array p. An intrinsic aspect of sorting is that it is a rearrangement process. And the method of Figure 6.2 capitalizes on this specification fault. In other words, the method trickSort is correct, but the specifications of Figure 6.1 are wrong. Corrected specifications appear in Figure 6.3. From this example, it is clear that the consequences of specification faults are nontrivial. After all, the correctness of a product is meaningless if its specifications are incorrect.

The fact that a product is correct is not *sufficient*, because the specifications in terms of which it was shown to be correct may be wrong. But is it *necessary*? Consider the following example. A software organization has acquired a superb new C++ compiler. The new

Figure 6.1
Incorrect specifications for a sort.

Input specification:	p : array of n integers, n > 0.
Output specification:	q : array of n integers such that q[0] ≤ q[1] ≤ ⋯ ≤ q[n − 1]

Figure 6.2
Method trickSort, which satisfies the specifications of Figure 6.1.

```
void trickSort (int p[ ], int q[ ])
{
    int i;
    for (i = 0; i < n; i++)
        q[i] = 0;
}
```

Figure 6.3
Corrected
specifications
for the sort.

Input specification:	p : array of n integers, n > 0.
Output specification:	q : array of n integers such that $q[0] \leq q[1] \leq \cdots \leq q[n-1]$
	The elements of array q are a permutation of the elements of array p, which are unchanged.

compiler can translate twice as many lines of source code per second as the old compiler, the object code runs nearly 45 percent faster, and the size of the object code is about 20 percent smaller. In addition, the error messages are much clearer and the cost of postdelivery maintenance and updates is less than half of that of the old compiler. There is one problem, however; the first time that a **for** statement appears in any class, the compiler prints a spurious error message. The compiler therefore is not correct, because the specifications for a compiler implicitly or explicitly require that error messages be printed if, and only if, there is a fault in the source code. It is certainly possible to use the compiler—in fact, in every way but one the compiler is absolutely ideal. Furthermore, it is reasonable to expect that this minor fault will be corrected in the next release. In the meantime, the programmers learn to ignore the spurious error message. Not only can the organization live with the incorrect compiler, but if anyone were to suggest replacing it by the old correct compiler, there would be an outcry. Therefore, the correctness of a product is neither necessary nor sufficient.

Both preceding examples admittedly are somewhat artificial. But they do make the point that correctness simply means that the product is a correct implementation of its specifications. In other words, there is more to testing than just showing that the product is correct.

With all the difficulties associated with execution-based testing, computer scientists have tried to come up with other ways of ensuring that a product does what it is supposed to do. One such non-execution-based alternative that has received considerable attention for more than 40 years is correctness proving.

6.5   Testing versus Correctness Proofs

A ***correctness proof*** is a mathematical technique for showing that a product is correct, in other words, that it satisfies its specifications. The technique is sometimes termed *verification*. However, as previously pointed out, the term has another meaning within the testing context. In addition, *verification* is also often used to denote all non-execution-based techniques, not only correctness proving. For clarity, this mathematical procedure will be termed *correctness proving*, to remind the reader that it is a mathematical proof process.

6.5.1   Example of a Correctness Proof

To see how correctness is proven, consider the code fragment shown in Figure 6.4. The flowchart equivalent to the code is given in Figure 6.5. We now show that the code fragment is correct—after the code has been executed, the variable s will contain the sum of the n elements of the array y. In Figure 6.6, an *assertion* is placed before and after each

Figure 6.4
A code
fragment to be
proven correct.

```
int k, s;
int y[n];
k = 0;
s = 0;
while (k < n)
{
    s = s + y[k];
    k = k + 1;
}
```

Figure 6.5
The flowchart of
Figure 6.4.

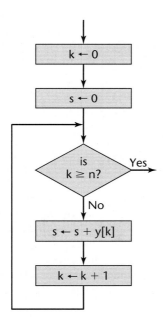

statement, at the places labeled with the letters *A* through *H*; that is, a claim has been made at each place that a certain mathematical property holds there. The correctness of each assertion is now proven.

The input specification, the condition that holds at *A* before the code is executed, is that the variable n is a positive integer; that is,

$$A: \quad n \in \{1, 2, 3, \ldots\} \tag{6.1}$$

An obvious output specification is that, if control reaches point *H*, the value of s contains the sum of the n values stored in array y, that is,

$$H: \quad s = y[0] + y[1] + \ldots + y[n - 1] \tag{6.2}$$

In fact, the code fragment can be proven correct with respect to a stronger output specification:

$$H: \quad k = n \text{ and } s = y[0] + y[1] + \ldots + y[n - 1] \tag{6.3}$$

Figure 6.6
Figure 6.5
with input
specification,
output
specification,
loop invariant,
and assertions
added.

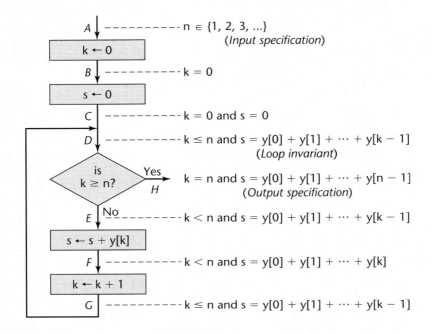

A --------- $n \in \{1, 2, 3, ...\}$
(Input specification)

$k \leftarrow 0$

B --------- $k = 0$

$s \leftarrow 0$

C --------- $k = 0$ and $s = 0$

D --------- $k \leq n$ and $s = y[0] + y[1] + \cdots + y[k - 1]$
(Loop invariant)

is $k \geq n$?   Yes $k = n$ and $s = y[0] + y[1] + \cdots + y[n - 1]$
H *(Output specification)*

E No --------- $k < n$ and $s = y[0] + y[1] + \cdots + y[k - 1]$

$s \leftarrow s + y[k]$

F --------- $k < n$ and $s = y[0] + y[1] + \cdots + y[k]$

$k \leftarrow k + 1$

G --------- $k \leq n$ and $s = y[0] + y[1] + \cdots + y[k - 1]$

A natural reaction to the last sentence is to ask, From where did output specification (6.3) come? By the end of the proof, we hope you have the answer to that question; also see Problems 6.10 and 6.11.

In addition to the input and output specifications, a third aspect of the proof process is to provide an invariant for the loop. That is, a mathematical expression must be provided that holds at point D irrespective of whether the loop has been executed 0, 1, or many times. The ***loop invariant*** that will be proven to hold is

$$D: \quad k \leq n \text{ and } s = y[0] + y[1] + \ldots + y[k - 1] \qquad (6.4)$$

Now it will be shown that if input specification (6.1) holds at point A, then output specification (6.3) will hold at point H; that is, the code fragment will be proven to be correct.

First, the assignment statement $k \leftarrow 0$ is executed. Control now is at point B, where the following assertion holds:

$$B: \quad k = 0 \qquad (6.5)$$

To be more precise, at point B, the assertion should read $k = 0$ and $n \in \{1, 2, 3, ...\}$. However, the input specification (6.1) holds at all points in the flowchart. For brevity, the and $n \in \{1, 2, 3, ...\}$ therefore is omitted from now on.

At point C, as a consequence of the second assignment statement, $s \leftarrow 0$, the following assertion is true:

$$C: \quad k = 0 \text{ and } s = 0 \qquad (6.6)$$

Now the loop is entered. It will be proven by induction that the loop invariant (6.4) indeed is correct. Just before the loop is executed for the first time, assertion (6.6) holds;

that is, $k = 0$ and $s = 0$. Now consider loop invariant (6.4). Because $k = 0$ by assertion (6.6) and $n \geq 1$ from input specification (6.1), it follows that $k \leq n$ as required. Furthermore, because $k = 0$, it follows that $k - 1 = -1$, so the sum in (6.4) is empty and $s = 0$ as required. Loop invariant (6.4) therefore is true just before the first time the loop is entered.

Next, the inductive hypothesis step is performed. Assume that, at some stage during the execution of the code fragment, the loop invariant holds. That is, for k equal to some value k_0, $0 \leq k_0 \leq n$, execution is at point D, and the assertion that holds is

$$D: \quad k_0 \leq n \text{ and } s = y[0] + y[1] + \ldots + y[k_0 - 1] \qquad (6.7)$$

Control now passes to the test box. If $k_0 \geq n$, then because $k_0 \leq n$ by hypothesis, it follows that $k_0 = n$. By inductive hypothesis (6.7), this implies that

$$H: \quad k_0 = n \text{ and } s = y[0] + y[1] + \ldots + y[n - 1] \qquad (6.8)$$

which is precisely the output specification (6.3).

On the other hand, if the test is $k_0 \geq n$? fails, then control passes from point D to point E. Because k_0 is not greater than or equal to n, $k_0 < n$ and (6.7) becomes

$$E: \quad k_0 < n \text{ and } s = y[0] + y[1] + \ldots + y[k_0 - 1] \qquad (6.9)$$

The statement $s \leftarrow s + y[k_0]$ now is executed, so from assertion (6.9), at point F, the following assertion must hold:

$$F: \quad k_0 < n \text{ and } s = y[0] + y[1] + \ldots + y[k_0 - 1] + y[k_0]$$

$$= y[0] + y[1] + \ldots + y[k_0] \qquad (6.10)$$

The next statement to be executed is $k_0 \leftarrow k_0 + 1$. To see the effect of this statement, suppose that the value of k_0 before executing this statement is 17. Then the last term in the sum in (6.10) is $y[17]$. Now the value of k_0 is increased by 1 to 18. The sum s is unchanged, so the last term in the sum still is $y[17]$, which is now $y[k_0 - 1]$. Also, at point F, $k_0 < n$. Increasing the value of k_0 by 1 means that if the inequality is to hold at point G, then $k_0 \leq n$. Therefore, the effect of increasing k_0 by 1 is that the following assertion holds at point G:

$$G: \quad k_0 \leq n \text{ and } s = y[0] + y[1] + \ldots + y[k_0 - 1] \qquad (6.11)$$

Assertion (6.11) that holds at point G is identical to assertion (6.7) that, by assumption, holds at point D. But point D is topologically identical to point G. In other words, if (6.7) holds at D for $k = k_0$, then it again will hold at D with $k = k_0 + 1$. It has been shown that the loop invariant holds for $k = 0$. By induction, it follows that loop invariant (6.4) holds for all values of k, $0 \leq k \leq n$.

All that remains is to prove that the loop terminates. Initially, by assertion (6.6), the value of k is equal to 0. Each iteration of the loop increases the value of k by 1 when the statement $k \leftarrow k + 1$ is executed. Eventually, k must reach the value n, at which time the loop is exited and the value of s is given by assertion (6.8), thereby satisfying output specification (6.3).

To review, given the input specification (6.1), it was proven that loop invariant (6.4) holds whether the loop has been executed 0, 1, or more times. Furthermore, it was proven that after n iterations the loop terminates; and when it does, the values of k and s satisfy the output specification (6.3). In other words, the code fragment of Figure 6.4 has been mathematically proven to be correct.

Mini Case Study

6.5.2 *Correctness Proof Mini Case Study*

An important aspect of correctness proofs is that they should be done in conjunction with design and coding. As Dijkstra put it, "The programmer should let the program proof and program grow hand in hand" [Dijkstra, 1972]. For example, when a loop is incorporated into the design, a loop invariant is put forward; and as the design is refined stepwise, so is the invariant. Developing a product in this way gives the programmer confidence that the product is correct and tends to reduce the number of faults. Quoting Dijkstra again, "The only effective way to raise the confidence level of a program significantly is to give a convincing proof of its correctness" [Dijkstra, 1972]. But even if a product is proven to be correct, it must be thoroughly tested as well. To illustrate the necessity for testing in conjunction with correctness proving, consider the following.

In 1969, Naur reported on a technique for constructing and proving a product correct [Naur, 1969]. The technique was illustrated by what Naur termed a *line-editing problem*; today this would be considered a text-processing problem. It may be stated as follows:

> Given a text consisting of words separated by blank characters or by newline (new line) characters, convert it to line-by-line form in accordance with the following rules:
>
> 1. Line breaks must be made only where the given text contains a blank or newline;
> 2. Each line is filled as far as possible, as long as
> 3. No line will contain more than maxpos characters

Naur constructed a procedure using his technique and informally proved its correctness. The procedure consisted of approximately 25 lines of code. The paper then was reviewed by Leavenworth in *Computing Reviews* [Leavenworth, 1970]. The reviewer pointed out that, in the output of Naur's procedure, the first word of the first line is preceded by a blank unless the first word is exactly maxpos characters long. Although this may seem a trivial fault, it is a fault that surely would have been detected had the procedure been tested, that is, executed with test data rather than only proven correct. But worse was to come. London [1971] detected three additional faults in Naur's procedure. One is that the procedure does not terminate unless a word longer than maxpos characters is encountered. Again, this fault is likely to have been detected if the procedure had been tested. London then presented a corrected version of the procedure and proved formally that the resulting procedure was correct; recall that Naur had used only informal proof techniques.

The next episode in this saga is that Goodenough and Gerhart [1975] found three faults that London had not detected, despite his formal "proof." These included the fact that the last word is not output unless it is followed by a blank or newline. Yet again, a reasonable choice of test data would have detected this fault without much difficulty. In fact, of the total of seven faults collectively detected by Leavenworth, London, and Goodenough and Gerhart, four could have been detected simply by running the procedure on test data, such as the illustrations given in Naur's original paper. The lesson from this saga is clear. Even if a product has been proven correct, it still must be tested thoroughly.

The example in Section 6.5.1 showed that proving the correctness of even a small code fragment can be a lengthy process. Furthermore, the mini case study of this section showed that it is a difficult, error-prone process, even for a 25-line procedure. The following issue therefore must be put forward: Is correctness proving just an interesting research idea or is it a powerful software engineering technique whose time has come? This is answered Section 6.5.3.

6.5.3   Correctness Proofs and Software Engineering

A number of software engineering practitioners have put forward reasons why correctness proving should not be viewed as a standard software engineering technique. First, it is claimed that software engineers lack adequate mathematical training. Second, it is suggested that proving is too expensive to be practical; and third, proving is too hard. Each of these reasons will be shown to be an oversimplification:

1. Although the proof given in Section 6.5.1 can be understood with hardly more than high school algebra, nontrivial proofs require that input specifications, output specifications, and loop invariants be expressed in first- or second-order predicate calculus or its equivalent. Not only does this make the proof process simpler for a mathematician, it allows correctness proving to be done by a computer. To complicate matters further, predicate calculus now is somewhat outdated. To prove the correctness of concurrent products, techniques using temporal or other modal logics are required [Manna and Pnueli, 1992]. There is no doubt that correctness proving requires training in mathematical logic. Fortunately, most computer science majors today either take courses in the requisite material or have the background to learn correctness-proving techniques on the job. Therefore, colleges now are turning out computer science graduates with sufficient mathematical skills for correctness proving. The claim that practicing software engineers lack the necessary mathematical training may have been true in the past, but it no longer applies in the light of the thousands of computer science majors joining the industry each year.

2. The claim that proving is too expensive for use in software development also is false. On the contrary, the economic viability of correctness proving can be determined on a project-by-project basis using cost–benefit analysis (Section 5.2). For example, consider the software for the international space station. Human lives are at stake, and if something goes wrong, a space shuttle rescue mission may not arrive in time. The cost of proving life-critical space station software correct is large. But the potential cost of a software fault that might be overlooked if correctness proving is not performed is even larger.

3. Despite the claim that correctness proving is too hard, many nontrivial products successfully have been proven correct, including operating system kernels, compilers, and communications systems [Landwehr, 1983; Berry and Wing, 1985]. Furthermore, many tools such as theorem provers assist in correctness proving. A theorem prover takes as input a product, its input and output specifications, and loop invariants. The theorem prover then attempts to prove mathematically that the product, when given input data satisfying the input specifications, produces output data satisfying the output specifications.

Figure 6.7
"Theorem
prover."

```
void theoremProver ( )
{
    print "This product is correct";
}
```

At the same time, there are some difficulties with correctness proving:

- For example, how can we be sure that a theorem prover is correct? If the theorem prover prints out This product is correct, can we believe it? To take an extreme case, consider the so-called theorem prover shown in Figure 6.7. No matter what code is submitted to this theorem prover, it will print out This product is correct. In other words, what reliability can be placed on the output of a theorem prover? One suggestion is to submit a theorem prover to itself and see whether it is correct. Apart from the philosophical implications, a simple way of seeing that this will not work is to consider what would happen if the theorem prover of Figure 6.7 were submitted to itself for proving. As always, it would print out This product is correct, thereby "proving" its own correctness.

- A further difficulty is finding the input and output specifications, and especially the loop invariants or their equivalents in other logics such as modal logic. Suppose a product is correct. Unless a suitable invariant for each loop can be found, there is no way of proving the product correct. Yes, tools do exist to assist in this task. But even with state-of-the-art tools, a software engineer simply may not be able to come up with a correctness proof. One solution to this problem is to develop the product and proof in parallel, as advocated in Section 6.5.2. When a loop is designed, an invariant for that loop is specified at the same time. With this approach, it is somewhat easier to prove that a code artifact is correct.

- Worse than not being able to find loop invariants, what if the specifications themselves are incorrect? An example of this is method trickSort (Figure 6.2). A good theorem prover, when given the incorrect specifications of Figure 6.1, undoubtedly will declare that the method shown in Figure 6.2 is correct.

Manna and Waldinger [1978] stated that, "We can never be sure that the specifications are correct" and "We can never be certain that a verification system is correct." These statements from two leading experts in the field encapsulate the various points made previously.

Does all this mean that there is no place for correctness proofs in software engineering? Quite the contrary. Proving products correct is an important, and sometimes vital, software engineering tool. Proofs are appropriate where human lives are at stake or where otherwise indicated by cost–benefit analysis. If the cost of proving software correct is less than the probable cost if the product fails, then the product should be proven. However, as the text-processing mini case study shows, proving alone is not enough. Instead, correctness proving should be viewed as an important component of the set of techniques that must be utilized together to check that a product is correct. Because the aim of software engineering is the production of quality software, correctness proving is indeed an important software engineering technique.

Even when a full formal proof is not justified, the quality of software can be markedly improved through the use of informal proofs. For example, a proof similar to that of

One feature of languages such as Java (but not C or C++) is bounds checking. An example of bounds checking is examining every array index during execution to ensure that it is within its declared range.

Hoare suggested that using bounds checking while developing a product but turning it off once the product is working correctly can be likened to learning to sail on dry land wearing a life jacket and then taking the life jacket off when actually at sea. In his Turing Award lecture, Hoare [1981] described a compiler he developed in 1961. When users later were offered the opportunity to turn off bounds checking after the final version of the compiler had been installed, they unanimously refused, because they had experienced so many incidents of values out of range during test runs of earlier versions of the compiler.

Bounds checking can be viewed as a special case of a more general concept, assertion checking. Hoare's life jacket analogy is equally applicable to turning off assertion checking once the final version has been installed.

Hoare's remarks were sadly prophetic. Today, a major technique used by hackers to penetrate computers is to send a long stream of data to an operating system to deliberately cause a buffer to overflow and overwrite a portion of the operating system with malicious executable code. This technique can work only if the programmers omitted to include bounds checking in the code for reading data into the buffer of an operating system written in C or C++, or turned off bounds checking.

Section 6.5.1 assists in checking that a loop is executed the correct number of times. A second way of improving software quality is to insert assertions such as those of Figure 6.6 into the code. Then, if at execution time an assertion does not hold, the product is halted and the software team can investigate whether the assertion that terminated execution is incorrect or whether indeed a fault in the code was detected by triggering the assertion. Languages such as Java (from version 1.4 onward) support assertions directly by means of an **assert** statement. Suppose that an informal proof requires that the value of variable xxx be positive at a particular point in the code. Even though the members of the design team may be convinced that there is no way for xxx to be negative, for additional reliability they may specify that the statement

$$\textbf{assert } (\text{xxx} > 0)$$

must appear at that point in the code. If xxx is less than or equal to 0, execution terminates, and the situation can be investigated by the software team. Unfortunately, *Assert* in C++ is a debugging statement; it is not part of the language itself. Ada 95 [ISO/IEC 8652, 1995] supports assertions via a **pragma**.

Once the users are confident that the product works correctly, they have the option of switching off assertion checking. This speeds up execution, but any fault that would have been detected by an assertion may not be found if assertion checking is switched off. Therefore, there is a trade-off between run-time efficiency and continuing assertion checking even after the product has been installed on the client's computer. (Just in Case You Wanted to Know Box 6.3 gives an interesting insight on this issue.)

A fundamental issue in execution-based testing is which members of the software development team should be responsible for carrying it out.

6.6 Who Should Perform Execution-Based Testing?

Suppose a programmer is asked to test a code artifact he or she has written. Testing has been described by Myers [1979] as the process of executing a product with the intention of finding faults. Testing therefore is a destructive process. On the other hand, the programmer doing the testing ordinarily does not wish to destroy his or her work. If the fundamental attitude of the programmer toward the code is the usual protective one, then the chances of that programmer using test data that will highlight faults is considerably lower than if the major motivation were truly destructive. A successful test finds faults. This, too, poses a difficulty. It means that, if the code artifact passes the test, then the test has failed. Conversely, if the code artifact does not perform according to specifications, then the test succeeds. A programmer who is asked to test a code artifact he or she has written is being asked to execute the code artifact in such a way that a failure (incorrect behavior) ensues. This goes against the creative instincts of programmers.

An inescapable conclusion is that programmers should not test their own code artifacts. After a programmer has been *con*structive and built a code artifact, testing that code artifact requires the creator to perform a *de*structive act and attempt to destroy that creation. A second reason why execution-based testing should be done by someone else is that the programmer may have misunderstood some aspect of the design or specifications. If testing is done by someone else, such faults may be discovered. Nevertheless, debugging (finding the cause of the failure and correcting the fault) is best done by the original programmer, the person most familiar with the code.

The statement that a programmer should not test his or her own code must not be taken too far. Consider the programming process. The programmer begins by reading the detailed design of the code artifact; this may be in the form of a flowchart or, more likely, pseudocode. But, whatever technique is used, the programmer must certainly **desk check** the code artifact before entering it into the computer. That is, the programmer must try out the flowchart or pseudocode with various test cases, tracing through the detailed design to check that each test case is executed correctly. Only when the programmer is satisfied that the detailed design is correct should the text editor be invoked to code the artifact.

Once the code artifact is in machine-readable form, it undergoes a series of tests. Test data are used to determine that the code artifact works successfully, probably the same test data used to desk check the detailed design. Next, if the code artifact executes correctly when correct test data are used, then the programmer tries out incorrect data to test the robustness of the code artifact. When the programmer is satisfied that the code artifact operates correctly, systematic testing commences. This **systematic testing** should not be performed by the programmer.

If the programmer is not to perform this systematic testing, who is to do it? As stated in Section 6.1.2, independent testing must be performed by the SQA group. The key word here is *independent*. Only if the SQA group truly is independent of the development team can its members fulfill their mission of ensuring that the product indeed satisfies its specifications, without software development managers applying pressures such as product deadlines that might hamper their work. SQA personnel must report to their own manager and thereby protect their independence.

How is systematic testing performed? An essential part of a test case is a statement of the expected output before the test is executed. It is a complete waste of time for the tester to sit at a terminal, execute the code artifact, enter haphazard test data, and then peer at the screen and say, "I guess that looks right." Equally futile is for the tester to plan test cases with great care and execute each test case in turn, look at the output, and say, "Yes, that certainly looks right." It is far too easy to be fooled by plausible results. If programmers are allowed to test their own code, then there always is the danger that the programmer will see what he or she wants to see. The same danger can occur even when the testing is done by someone else. The solution is for management to insist that, before a test is performed, both the test data and the expected results of that test be recorded. After the test has been performed, the actual results should be recorded and compared with the expected results.

Even in small organizations and with small products, it is important that this recording be done in machine-readable form, because test cases should never be thrown away. The reason for this is postdelivery maintenance. While the product is being maintained, *regression testing* must be performed. Stored test cases that the product has previously executed correctly must be rerun to ensure that the modifications made to add new functionality to the product have not destroyed the product's existing functionality. This is discussed further in Chapter 14.

6.7   When Testing Stops

After a product has been successfully maintained for many years, it eventually may lose its usefulness and be superseded by a totally different product, in much the same way that electronic valves were replaced by transistors. Alternatively, a product still may be useful, but the cost of porting it to new hardware or running it under a new operating system may be more than the cost of constructing a new product, using the old one as a prototype. So, finally, the software product is decommissioned and removed from service. Only at that point, when the software has been irrevocably discarded, is it time to stop testing.

Now that all the necessary background material has been covered, objects can be examined in greater detail. This is the subject of Chapter 7.

Chapter Review

A key theme of this chapter is that testing must be carried out in parallel with all activities of the software process. The chapter begins with a description of quality issues (Section 6.1). Next, non-execution-based testing is described (Section 6.2), with a careful discussion of walkthroughs and inspections. This is followed by a definition of execution-based testing (Sections 6.3 and 6.4) and a discussion of behavioral properties of a product that must be tested, including utility, reliability, robustness, performance, and correctness (Sections 6.4.1 through 6.4.5). In Section 6.5, correctness proving is introduced, and an example of such a proof is given in Section 6.5.1. The role of correctness proofs in software engineering then is analyzed (Sections 6.5.2 and 6.5.3). Another important issue is that systematic execution-based testing must be performed by the independent SQA group and not by the programmer (Section 6.6). Finally, the issue of when testing can finally stop is discussed in Section 6.7.

For Further Reading

The attitude of software producers to the testing process has changed over the years, from viewing testing as a means of showing that a product runs correctly to the modern attitude that testing should be used to prevent requirements, analysis, design, and implementation faults. This progression is described in [Gelperin and Hetzel, 1988]. The nature of software testing and the reasons why it is so hard are discussed in [Whittaker, 2000]. The pervasiveness of faults is described in [Lieberman and Fry, 2001]. Ways to reduce the number of faults appear in [Boehm and Basili, 2001].

Myths regarding software quality are discussed in [Voas, 1999]. Whittaker and Voas [2000] present an interesting theory of reliability.

[Baber, 1987] is a good introduction to proving programs correct. A standard technique of correctness proving uses the so-called Hoare logic, as described in [Hoare, 1969]. An alternative approach to ensuring that products satisfy their specifications is to construct the product stepwise, checking that each step preserves correctness. This is described in [Dijkstra, 1968] and [Wirth, 1971]. An important article regarding acceptance of correctness proofs by the software engineering community is [DeMillo, Lipton, and Perlis, 1979].

The IEEE *Standard for Software Reviews* [IEEE 1028, 1997] is an excellent source of information on non-execution-based testing. Experiments evaluating inspections of a large-scale software product are described in [Perry et al., 2002]. Vitharana and Ramamurthy [2003] suggest that inspections should be anonymous and computer mediated. The impact of group process support on inspections is presented in [Tyran and George, 2002]. The selection of inspection team members is discussed in [Miller and Yin, 2004]. A review of inspections is given in [Parnas and Lawford, 2003], and the state of the practice is described in [Ciolkowski, Laitenberger, and Biffl, 2003]. Object-oriented code inspections are discussed in [Dunsmore, Roper, and Wood, 2003].

The classic work on execution-based testing is [Myers, 1979], a work that has had a significant impact on the field of testing. [DeMillo, Lipton, and Sayward, 1978] remains an excellent source of information on the selection of test data. [Beizer, 1990] is a compendium on testing, a true handbook on the subject. A similar work is [Hetzel, 1988].

Turning specifically to the object-oriented paradigm, [Kung, Hsia, and Gao, 1998] is a book on object-oriented testing, and so is [Sykes and McGregor, 2000].

The proceedings of the International Symposium on Software Testing and Analysis cover a similar broad spectrum of testing issues. The February 2002 issue of *IEEE Transactions on Software Engineering* contains a variety of papers from the 2000 Symposium; [Elbaum, Malishevsky, and Rothermel, 2002] is of particular interest.

Key Terms

correctness 157	managerial independence 147	reliability 155
correctness proof 158	mean time between	review 153
defect 146	failures 155	rework 151
desk check 166	mean time to repair 155	robustness 156
error 146	mistake 146	simulator 155
execution-based testing 154	moderator 151	software quality assurance
failure 146	non-execution-	(SQA) 147
fault 146	based testing 148	systematic testing 166
fault density 153	overview 150	test workflow 146
fault detection efficiency 153	performance 156	testing 146
fault detection rate 153	preparation 150	utility 155
follow-up 151	quality 147	V & V 146
inspection 150	reader 151	validation 146
inspection rate 153	recorder 151	verification 146
loop invariant 160	regression testing 167	

Problems 6.1 How are the terms *correctness proving, verification,* and *validation* used in this book?

6.2 A software development organization currently employs 96 software professionals, including 19 managers, all of whom develop as well as test software. The latest figures show that 27 percent of their time is spent on testing activities. The average annual cost to the company of a manager is $144,000, whereas nonmanagerial professionals cost $107,000 a year on average; both figures include overhead. Use cost–benefit analysis to determine whether a separate SQA group should be set up within the organization.

6.3 Repeat the cost–benefit analysis of Problem 6.2 for a firm with only seven software professionals, including two managers. Assume that the other figures remain unchanged.

6.4 You have been testing a code artifact for 11 days and found two faults. What does this tell you about the existence of other faults?

6.5 What are the similarities between a walkthrough and an inspection? What are the differences?

6.6 You are a member of the SQA group at Ye Olde Fashioned Software. You suggest to your manager that inspections be introduced. He responds that he sees no reason why four people should waste their time looking for faults when one person can run test cases on the same piece of code. How do you respond?

6.7 You are the SQA manager at Hardy Hardware, a regional chain of 754 hardware stores. Your organization is considering buying a stock-control package for use throughout the organization. Before authorizing the purchase of the package, you decide to test it thoroughly. What properties of the package do you investigate?

6.8 All 754 stores in the Hardy Hardware organization are now to be connected by a communications network. A sales representative is offering you a 4-week free trial to experiment with the communications package he is trying to sell you. What sort of software tests would you perform and why?

6.9 You are a rear admiral in the Valorian Navy in charge of developing the software for controlling the ship-to-ship missile of Problem 1.4. The software has been delivered to you for acceptance testing. What properties of the software do you test?

6.10 What happens to the correctness proof of Section 6.5.1 if loop invariant

$$s = y[0] + y[1] + \ldots + y[k-1]$$

is used instead of (6.4)?

6.11 Assume that you have some experience with loop invariants and know that invariant (6.4) is the correct invariant for the loop of Figure 6.6. Show that output specification (6.3) is a natural consequence of the loop invariant.

6.12 Consider the following code fragment:

```
k = 0;
g = 1;
while (k < n)
{
    k = k + 1;
    g = g * k;
}
```

Prove that this code fragment correctly computes $g = n!$ if n is a positive integer.

6.13   Can correctness proving solve the problem that the product as delivered to the client may not be what the client really needs? Give reasons for your answer.

6.14   How should Dijkstra's statement (Section 6.3) be changed to apply to correctness proofs rather than testing? Bear in mind the mini case study of Section 6.5.2.

6.15   Design and implement a solution to the Naur text-processing problem (Section 6.5.2) using the language specified by your instructor. Execute it against test data and record the number of faults you find and the cause of each fault (e.g., logic fault, loop counter fault). Do not correct any of the faults you detect. Now exchange products with a fellow student and see how many faults each of you finds in the other's product and whether or not they are new faults. Again record the cause of each fault and compare the fault types found by each of you. Tabulate the results for the class as a whole.

6.16   Why is there a need to distinguish between a fault, a failure, and an error? Surely the use of the umbrella term *defect* simplifies matters?

6.17   (Term Project) Explain how you would test the utility, reliability, robustness, performance, and correctness of the Osric's Office Appliances and Decor product in Appendix A.

6.18   (Readings in Software Engineering) Your instructor will distribute copies of [Miller and Yin, 2004]. Would you use a cognitively based inspection team selection mechanism? Justify your answer.

References

[Ackerman, Buchwald, and Lewski, 1989] A. F. ACKERMAN, L. S. BUCHWALD, AND F. H. LEWSKI, "Software Inspections: An Effective Verification Process," *IEEE Software* **6** (May 1989), pp. 31–36.

[Baber, 1987] R. L. BABER, *The Spine of Software: Designing Provably Correct Software: Theory and Practice,* John Wiley and Sons, New York, 1987.

[Beizer, 1990] B. BEIZER, *Software Testing Techniques,* 2nd ed., Van Nostrand Reinhold, New York, 1990.

[Berry and Wing, 1985] D. M. BERRY AND J. M. WING, "Specifying and Prototyping: Some Thoughts on Why They Are Successful," in: *Formal Methods and Software Development, Proceedings of the International Joint Conference on Theory and Practice of Software Development,* Vol. 2, Springer-Verlag, Berlin, 1985, pp. 117–28.

[Boehm and Basili, 2001] B. BOEHM AND V. R. BASILI, "Software Defect Reduction Top Ten List," *IEEE Computer* **34** (January 2001), pp. 135–37.

[Bush, 1990] M. BUSH, "Improving Software Quality: The Use of Formal Inspections at the Jet Propulsion Laboratory," *Proceedings of the 12th International Conference on Software Engineering,* Nice, France, March 1990, pp. 196–99.

[Ciolkowski, Laitenberger, and Biffl, 2003] M. CIOLKOWSKI, O. LAITENBERGER, AND S. BIFFL, "Software Reviews, the State of the Practice," *IEEE Software* **20** (November/December 2003), pp. 46–51.

[DeMillo, Lipton, and Perlis, 1979] R. A. DEMILLO, R. J. LIPTON, AND A. J. PERLIS, "Social Processes and Proofs of Theorems and Programs," *Communications of the ACM* **22** (May 1979), pp. 271–80.

[DeMillo, Lipton, and Sayward, 1978] R. A. DEMILLO, R. J. LIPTON, AND F. G. SAYWARD, "Hints on Test Data Selection: Help for the Practicing Programmer," *IEEE Computer* **11** (April 1978), pp. 34–43.

[Dijkstra, 1968] E. W. DIJKSTRA, "A Constructive Approach to the Problem of Program Correctness," *BIT* **8** (No. 3, 1968), pp. 174–86.

[Dijkstra, 1972] E. W. DIJKSTRA, "The Humble Programmer," *Communications of the ACM* **15** (October 1972), pp. 859–66.

[Dunsmore, Roper, and Wood, 2003] A. DUNSMORE, M. ROPER, AND M. WOOD, "The Development and Evaluation of Three Diverse Techniques for Object-Oriented Code Inspection," *IEEE Transactions on Software Engineering* **29** (August 2003), pp. 677–86.

[Elbaum, Malishevsky, and Rothermel, 2002] A. ELBAUM, A. G. MALISHEVSKY, AND G. ROTHERMEL, "Test Case Prioritization: A Family of Empirical Studies," *IEEE Transactions on Software Engineering* **28** (2002), pp. 159–82.

[Fagan, 1976] M. E. FAGAN, "Design and Code Inspections to Reduce Errors in Program Development," *IBM Systems Journal* **15** (No. 3, 1976), pp. 182–211.

[Fagan, 1986] M. E. FAGAN, "Advances in Software Inspections," *IEEE Transactions on Software Engineering* **SE-12** (July 1986), pp. 744–51.

[Fowler, 1986] P. J. FOWLER, "In-Process Inspections of Workproducts at AT&T," *AT&T Technical Journal* **65** (March/April 1986), pp. 102–12.

[Gelperin and Hetzel, 1988] D. GELPERIN AND B. HETZEL, "The Growth of Software Testing," *Communications of the ACM* **31** (June 1988), pp. 687–95.

[Goodenough, 1979] J. B. GOODENOUGH, "A Survey of Program Testing Issues," in: *Research Directions in Software Technology*, P. Wegner (Editor), The MIT Press, Cambridge, MA, 1979, pp. 316–40.

[Goodenough and Gerhart, 1975] J. B. GOODENOUGH AND S. L. GERHART, "Toward a Theory of Test Data Selection," *Proceedings of the Third International Conference on Reliable Software*, Los Angeles, 1975, pp. 493–510; also published in *IEEE Transactions on Software Engineering* **SE-1** (June 1975), pp. 156–73. Revised version: J. B. Goodenough, and S. L. Gerhart, "Toward a Theory of Test Data Selection: Data Selection Criteria," in: *Current Trends in Programming Methodology*, Vol. 2, R. T. Yeh (Editor), Prentice Hall, Englewood Cliffs, NJ, 1977, pp. 44–79.

[Hetzel, 1988] W. HETZEL, *The Complete Guide to Software Testing,* 2nd ed., QED Information Systems, Wellesley, MA, 1988.

[Hoare, 1969] C. A. R. HOARE, "An Axiomatic Basis for Computer Programming," *Communications of the ACM* **12** (October 1969), pp. 576–83.

[Hoare, 1981] C. A. R. HOARE, "The Emperor's Old Clothes," *Communications of the ACM* **24** (February 1981), pp. 75–83.

[IEEE 610.12, 1990] *A Glossary of Software Engineering Terminology,* IEEE 610.12-1990, Institute of Electrical and Electronic Engineers, New York, 1990.

[IEEE 1028, 1997] *Standard for Software Reviews,* IEEE 1028, Institute of Electrical and Electronic Engineers, New York, 1997.

[ISO/IEC 8652, 1995] *Programming Language Ada: Language and Standard Libraries,* ISO/IEC 8652, International Organization for Standardization, International Electrotechnical Commission, Geneva, 1995.

[Jones, 1978] T. C. JONES, "Measuring Programming Quality and Productivity," *IBM Systems Journal* **17** (No. 1, 1978), pp. 39–63.

[Kelly, Sherif, and Hops, 1992] J. C. KELLY, J. S. SHERIF, AND J. HOPS, "An Analysis of Defect Densities Found during Software Inspections," *Journal of Systems and Software* **17** (January 1992), pp. 111–17.

[Kung, Hsia, and Gao, 1998] D. C. KUNG, P. HSIA, AND J. GAO, *Testing Object-Oriented Software,* IEEE Computer Society Press, Los Alamitos, CA, 1998.

[Landwehr, 1983] C. E. LANDWEHR, "The Best Available Technologies for Computer Security," *IEEE Computer* **16** (July 1983), pp. 86–100.

[Leavenworth, 1970] B. LEAVENWORTH, Review #19420, *Computing Reviews* **11** (July 1970), pp. 396–97.

[Lieberman and Fry, 2001] H. LIEBERMAN AND C. FRY, "Will Software Ever Work?" *Communications of the ACM* **44** (March 2001), pp. 122–24.

[London, 1971] R. L. LONDON, "Software Reliability through Proving Programs Correct," *Proceedings of the IEEE International Symposium on Fault-Tolerant Computing,* March 1971.

[Manna and Pnueli, 1992] Z. MANNA AND A. PNUELI, *The Temporal Logic of Reactive and Concurrent Systems,* Springer-Verlag, New York, 1992.

[Manna and Waldinger, 1978] Z. MANNA AND R. WALDINGER, "The Logic of Computer Programming," *IEEE Transactions on Software Engineering* **SE-4** (1978), pp. 199–229.

[Miller and Yin, 2004] J. MILLER AND Z. YIN, "A Cognitive-Based Mechanism for Constructing Software Inspection Teams," *IEEE Transactions on Software Engineering* **30** (November 30), pp. 811–25.

[Myers, 1979] G. J. MYERS, *The Art of Software Testing,* John Wiley and Sons, New York, 1979.

[Naur, 1969] P. NAUR, "Programming by Action Clusters," *BIT* **9** (No. 3, 1969), pp. 250–58.

[Parnas and Lawford, 2003] D. L. PARNAS AND M. LAWFORD, "The Role of Inspection in Software Quality Assurance," *IEEE Transactions on Software Engineering* **29** (August 2003), pp. 674–76.

[Perry et al., 2002] D. E. PERRY, A. PORTER, M. W. WADE, L. G. VOTTA, AND J. PERPICH, "Reducing Inspection Interval in Large-Scale Software Development," *IEEE Transactions on Software Engineering* **28** (July 2002), pp. 695–705.

[Sykes and McGregor, 2000] D. A. SYKES AND J. D. MCGREGOR, *Practical Guide to Testing Object-Oriented Software,* Addison-Wesley, Reading, MA, 2000.

[Tyran and George, 2002] C. K. TYRAN AND J. F. GEORGE, "Improving Software Inspections with Group Process Support," *Communications of the ACM* **45** (September 2002), pp. 87–92.

[Vitharana and Ramamurthy, 2003] P. VITHARANA AND K. RAMAMURTHY, "Computer-Mediated Group Support, Anonymity and the Software Inspection Process: An Empirical Investigation," *IEEE Transactions on Software Engineering* **29** (March 2003), pp. 167–80.

[Voas, 1999] J. VOAS, "Software Quality's Eight Greatest Myths," *IEEE Software* **16** (September/October 1999), pp. 118–20.

[Whittaker, 2000] J. A. WHITTAKER, "What Is Software Testing? And Why Is It So Hard?" *IEEE Software* **17** (January/February 2000), pp. 70–79.

[Whittaker and Voas, 2000] J. A. WHITTAKER AND J. VOAS, "Toward a More Reliable Theory of Software Reliability," *IEEE Computer* **33** (December 2000), pp. 36–42.

[Wirth, 1971] N. WIRTH, "Program Development by Stepwise Refinement," *Communications of the ACM* **14** (April 1971), pp. 221–27.

Chapter 7

From Modules to Objects

Learning Objectives

After studying this chapter, you should be able to

- Design classes with high cohesion and low coupling.
- Understand the need for information hiding.
- Describe the software engineering implications of inheritance, polymorphism, and dynamic binding.
- Distinguish between generalization, aggregation, and association.
- Discuss the object-oriented paradigm in greater depth than before.

Some of the more lurid computer magazines seem to suggest that the object-oriented paradigm was a sudden, dramatic new discovery of the mid-1980s, a revolutionary alternative to the then-popular classical paradigm. That is not the case. Instead, the theory of modularity underwent steady progress during the 1970s and the 1980s, and objects were simply an evolutionary development within the theory of modularity (but see Just in Case You Wanted to Know Box 7.1). This chapter describes objects within the context of modularity.

This approach is taken because it is extremely difficult to use objects correctly without understanding why the object-oriented paradigm is superior to the classical paradigm. And, to do that, it is necessary to appreciate that an object is merely the next logical step in the body of knowledge that begins with the concept of a module.

Object-oriented concepts were introduced as early as 1966 in the simulation language Simula 67 [Dahl and Nygaard, 1966]. However, at that time, the technology was too radical for practical use, so it lay dormant until the early 1980s, when it essentially was reinvented within the context of the theory of modularity.

This chapter includes other examples of the way leading-edge technology lies dormant until the world is ready for it. For example, information hiding (Section 7.6) was first proposed in 1971 within the software context by Parnas [1971], but the technology was not widely adopted until about 10 years later, when encapsulation and abstract data types had become part of software engineering.

We humans seem to adopt new ideas only when we are ready to use them, not necessarily when they are first presented.

7.1   What Is a Module?

When a large product consists of a single monolithic block of code, maintenance is a nightmare. Even for the author of such a monstrosity, attempting to debug the code is extremely difficult; for another programmer to understand it is virtually impossible. The solution is to break the product into smaller pieces, called *modules*. What is a module? Is the way a product is broken into modules important in itself or is it important only to break a large product into smaller pieces of code?

A ***module*** is a "lexically contiguous sequence of program statements, bounded by boundary elements, having an aggregate identifier" [Yourdon and Constantine, 1979]. Examples of boundary elements are {...} pairs in C++ or Java. In the object-oriented paradigm, an object is a module and so is a method within an object.

To understand the importance of modularization, consider the following somewhat fanciful example. John Fence is a highly incompetent computer architect. He still has not discovered that both NAND gates and NOR gates are complete; that is, every circuit can be built with only NAND gates or with only NOR gates. John therefore decides to build an arithmetic logic unit (ALU), shifter, and 16 registers using AND, OR, and NOT gates. The resulting computer is shown in Figure 7.1. The three components are connected in a simple fashion. Now, our architect friend decides that the circuit should be fabricated on three silicon chips, so he designs the three chips shown in Figure 7.2. One chip has all the gates of the ALU, a second contains the shifter, and the third is for the registers. At this point John vaguely recalls that someone in a bar told him that it is best to build chips so that they have only one kind of gate, so he redesigns his chips. On chip 1 he puts all the AND gates, on chip 2 all the OR gates, and all the NOT gates go onto chip 3. The resulting "work of art" is shown schematically in Figure 7.3.

Figures 7.2 and 7.3 are functionally equivalent; that is, they do exactly the same thing. But the two designs have markedly different properties:

1. Figure 7.3 is considerably harder to *understand* than Figure 7.2. Almost anyone with a knowledge of digital logic immediately knows that the chips in Figure 7.2 form an ALU, a shifter, and a set of registers. However, even a leading hardware expert would have trouble understanding the function of the various AND, OR, and NOT gates in Figure 7.3.

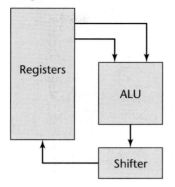

Figure 7.1 The design of a computer.

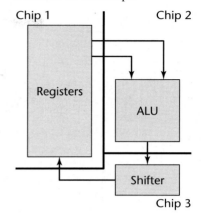

Figure 7.2 The computer of Figure 7.1 fabricated on three chips.

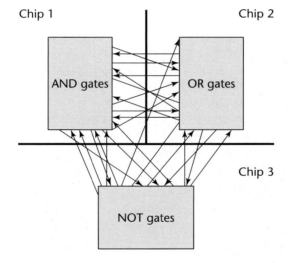

Figure 7.3 The computer of Figure 7.1 fabricated on three other chips.

2. *Corrective maintenance* of the circuits shown in Figure 7.3 is difficult. Should the computer have a design fault—and anyone capable of coming up with Figure 7.3 is undoubtedly going to make lots and lots of mistakes—it would be difficult to determine where the fault is located. On the other hand, if the design of the computer in Figure 7.2 has a fault, it can be localized by determining whether it appears to be in the way the ALU works, the way the shifter works, or the way the registers work. Similarly, if the computer of Figure 7.2 breaks down, it is relatively easy to determine which chip to replace; if the computer in Figure 7.3 breaks down, it is probably best to replace all three chips.

3. The computer of Figure 7.3 is difficult to *extend* or *enhance*. If a new type of ALU is needed or faster registers are required, it is back to the drawing board. But the

design of the computer of Figure 7.2 makes it easy to replace the appropriate chip. Perhaps worst of all, the chips of Figure 7.3 cannot be *reused* in any new product. There is no way that those three specific combinations of AND, OR, and NOT gates can be utilized for any product other than the one for which they were designed. In all probability, the three chips of Figure 7.2 can be reused in other products that require an ALU, a shifter, or registers.

The point here is that software products have to be designed to look like Figure 7.2, where there is a maximal relationship within each chip and a minimal relationship between chips. A module can be likened to a chip, in that it performs an operation or series of operations and is connected to other modules. The functionality of the product as a whole is fixed; what has to be determined is how to break the product into modules. Composite/structured design [Stevens, Myers, and Constantine, 1974] provides a rationale for breaking a product into modules as a way to reduce the cost of maintenance, the major component of the total software budget, as pointed out in Chapter 1. The maintenance effort, whether corrective, perfective, or adaptive, is reduced when there is maximal interaction within each module and minimal interaction between modules. In other words, the aim of composite/structured design (C/SD) is to ensure that the module decomposition of the product resembles Figure 7.2 rather than Figure 7.3.

Myers [1978b] quantified the ideas of module **cohesion**, the degree of interaction within a module, and module **coupling**, the degree of interaction between two modules. To be more precise, Myers used the term **strength** rather than *cohesion*. However, cohesion is preferable because modules can have high strength or low strength, and something is inherently contradictory in the expression *low strength*—something that is not strong is weak. To prevent terminological inexactitude, C/SD now uses the term *cohesion*. Some authors have used the term *binding* in place of *coupling*. Unfortunately, **binding** also is used in other contexts in computer science, such as binding values to variables. But *coupling* has none of these overtones and therefore is preferable.

It is necessary at this point to distinguish between the operation of a module, the logic of a module, and the context of a module. The **operation** of a module is what it does, that is, its behavior. For example, the operation of module m is to compute the square root of its argument. The **logic** of a module is how the module performs its operation; in the case of module m, the specific way of computing the square root is Newton's method [Gerald and Wheatley, 1999]. The **context** of a module is the specific use of that module. For example, module m is used to compute the square root of a double-precision integer. A key point in C/SD is that the name assigned to a module is its operation and not its logic or its context. Therefore, in C/SD, module m should be named computeSquareRoot; its logic and its context are irrelevant from the viewpoint of its name.

7.2 Cohesion

Myers [1978b] defined seven categories or levels of cohesion. In the light of modern theoretical computer science, Myers's first two levels need to be interchanged because, as will be shown, informational cohesion supports reuse more strongly than functional cohesion. The resulting ranking is shown in Figure 7.4. This is not a linear scale of any sort. It is merely a relative ranking, a way of determining which types of cohesion are high (good) and which are low (bad).

Figure 7.4
Levels of
cohesion.

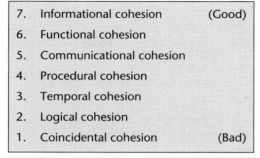

7.	Informational cohesion	(Good)
6.	Functional cohesion	
5.	Communicational cohesion	
4.	Procedural cohesion	
3.	Temporal cohesion	
2.	Logical cohesion	
1.	Coincidental cohesion	(Bad)

To understand what constitutes a module with high cohesion, it is necessary to start at the other end and consider the lower cohesion levels.

7.2.1   Coincidental Cohesion

A module has ***coincidental cohesion*** if it performs multiple, completely unrelated operations. An example of a module with coincidental cohesion is a module named printTheNextLine, reverseTheStringOfCharactersComprisingTheSecondArgument, add7ToTheFifthArgument, and convertTheFourthArgumentToFloatingPoint. An obvious question is, How can such modules possibly arise in practice? The most common cause is as a consequence of rigidly enforcing rules such as "every module shall consist of between 35 and 50 executable statements." If a software organization insists that modules must be neither too big nor too small, then two undesirable things happen. First, two or more otherwise ideal smaller modules are lumped together to create a larger module with coincidental cohesion. Second, pieces hacked from well-designed modules that management considers too large are combined, again resulting in modules with coincidental cohesion.

Why is coincidental cohesion so bad? Modules with coincidental cohesion suffer from two serious drawbacks. First, such modules degrade the maintainability of the product, both corrective maintenance and enhancement. From the viewpoint of trying to understand a product, modularization with coincidental cohesion is worse than no modularization at all [Shneiderman and Mayer, 1975]. Second, these modules are not reusable. It is extremely unlikely that the module with coincidental cohesion in the first paragraph of this section could be reused in any other product.

Lack of reusability is a serious drawback. The cost of building software is so great that it is essential to try to reuse modules wherever possible. Designing, coding, documenting, and above all, testing a module are time-consuming and hence costly processes. If an existing well-designed, thoroughly tested, and properly documented module can be used in another product, then management should insist that the existing module be reused. But there is no way that a module with coincidental cohesion can be reused, and the money spent to develop it can never be recouped. (Reuse is discussed in detail in Chapter 8.)

It is generally easy to rectify a module with coincidental cohesion—because it performs multiple operations, break the module into smaller modules that each perform one operation.

7.2.2   Logical Cohesion

A module has ***logical cohesion*** when it performs a series of related operations, one of which is selected by the calling module. All the following are examples of modules with logical cohesion.

Example 1   Method newOperation, which is invoked as follows:

functionCode = 7;
newOperation (functionCode, dummy1, dummy2, dummy3);
// dummy1, dummy2, *and* dummy3 *are dummy variables,*
// *not used if* functionCode *is equal to* 7

In this example, newOperation is called with four arguments, but as stated in the comment lines, three of them are not needed if functionCode is equal to 7. This degrades readability, with the usual implications for maintenance, both corrective and enhancement.

Example 2   An object that performs all input and output.

Example 3   An object that edits insertions, deletions, and modifications of master file records.

Example 4   A module with logical cohesion in an early version of OS/VS2 that performed 13 different operations; its interface contained 21 pieces of data [Myers, 1978b].

Two problems occur when a module has logical cohesion. First, the interface is difficult to understand (Example 1 is a case in point), and comprehensibility of the module as a whole may suffer as a result. Second, the code for more than one operation may be intertwined, leading to severe maintenance problems. For instance, an object that performs all input and output may be structured as shown in Figure 7.5. If a new tape unit is installed, it may be necessary to modify the sections numbered 1, 2, 3, 4, 6, 9, and 10. These changes may adversely affect other forms of input–output, such as laser printer output, because the laser printer is affected by changes to sections 1 and 3. This intertwined property is characteristic of modules with logical cohesion. A further consequence of intertwining is that it is difficult to reuse such a module in other products.

7.2.3   Temporal Cohesion

A module has ***temporal cohesion*** when it performs a series of operations related in time. An example of a module with temporal cohesion is an object named openOldMasterFile, newMasterFile, transactionFile, and printFile; initializeSalesRegionTable; readFirstTransactionRecordAndFirstOldMasterFileRecord. In the bad old days before C/SD, such an object would be called performInitialization.

The operations of this object are related weakly to one another but more strongly to operations in other objects. Consider, for example, the salesRegionTable. It is initialized in this object, but methods such as updateSalesRegionTable and printSalesRegionTable are located in other objects. Therefore, if the structure of the salesRegionTable is changed, perhaps because the organization is expanding into areas of the country where it previously had not done business, a number of objects have to be changed. Not only is there more chance of a regression fault (a fault caused by a change made to an apparently unrelated part of the product), but if the number of affected objects is large, one or two objects are

Figure 7.5
An object that
performs all
input and
output.

1. Code for all input and output
2. Code for input only
3. Code for output only
4. Code for disk and tape I/O
5. Code for disk I/O
6. Code for tape I/O
7. Code for disk input
8. Code for disk output
9.   Code for tape input
10. Code for tape output
⋮   ⋮   ⋮
37. Code for keyboard input

likely to be overlooked. It is much better to have all the operations on the salesRegionTable in one object, as described in Section 7.2.7. These methods then can be invoked, when needed, by other objects.

In addition, a module with temporal cohesion is unlikely to be reusable in a different product.

7.2.4   Procedural Cohesion

A module has ***procedural cohesion*** if it performs a series of operations related by the sequence of steps to be followed by the product. An example of a module with procedural cohesion is method readPartNumberFromDatabaseAndUpdateRepairRecordOnMaintenanceFile.

This clearly is better than temporal cohesion—at least the operations are related procedurally to one another. Even so, the operations are still weakly connected, and again the module is unlikely to be reusable in another product. The solution is to break a module with procedural cohesion into separate modules, each performing one operation.

7.2.5   Communicational Cohesion

A module has ***communicational cohesion*** if it performs a series of operations related by the sequence of steps to be followed by the product and if all the operations are performed on the same data. Two examples of modules with communicational cohesion are method updateRecordInDatabaseAndWrite*It*ToTheAuditTrail, and method calculateNewTrajectoryAndSend*It*ToThePrinter. This is better than procedural cohesion because the operations of the method are more closely connected, but it still has the same drawback as coincidental, logical, temporal, and procedural cohesion; namely, that the method cannot be reused. Again the solution is to break such a module into separate modules, each performing one operation.

In passing, it is interesting to note that Dan Berry [personal communication, 1978] uses the term ***flowchart cohesion*** to refer to temporal, procedural, and communicational cohesion, because the operations performed by such modules are adjacent in the product flowchart. The operations are adjacent in the case of temporal cohesion because they are performed at the same time. They are adjacent in procedural cohesion because the algorithm requires the operations to be performed in series. They are adjacent in communicational cohesion because, in addition to being performed in series, the operations are performed on the same data, and therefore it is natural that these operations should be adjacent in the flowchart.

7.2.6   Functional Cohesion

A module that performs exactly one operation or achieves a single goal has ***functional cohesion***. Examples of such modules are methods getTemperatureOfFurnace, computeOrbitalOfElectron, writeToHardDrive, and calculateSalesCommission.

A module with functional cohesion often can be reused because the one operation it performs frequently needs to be performed in other products. A properly designed, thoroughly tested, and well-documented module with functional cohesion is a valuable (economic and technical) asset to any software organization and should be reused as often as possible (but see Section 8.4).

Maintenance is easier to perform on a module with functional cohesion. First, functional cohesion leads to fault isolation. If it is clear that the temperature of the furnace is not being read correctly, then the fault almost certainly is in method getTemperatureOfFurnace. Similarly, if the orbital of an electron is computed incorrectly, then the first place to look is in method computeOrbitalOfElectron.

Once the fault has been localized to a single module, the next step is to make the required changes. Because a module with functional cohesion performs only one operation, such a module generally is easier to understand than a module with lower cohesion. This ease in understanding also simplifies the maintenance. Finally, when the change is made, the chance of that change affecting other modules is slight, especially if the coupling between modules is low (Section 7.3).

Functional cohesion also is valuable when a product has to be extended. For example, suppose that a personal computer has a 100-gigabyte hard drive but the manufacturer now wishes to market a more powerful model of the computer with a 300-gigabyte hard drive instead. Reading through the list of modules, the maintenance programmer finds a method named writeToHardDrive. The obvious thing to do is to replace that method with a new one called writeToLargerHardDrive.

In passing, it should be pointed out that the three "modules" of Figure 7.2 have functional cohesion, and the arguments made in Section 7.1 for favoring the design of Figure 7.2 over that of Figure 7.3 are precisely those made in the preceding discussion for favoring functional cohesion.

7.2.7   Informational Cohesion

A module has ***informational cohesion*** if it performs a number of operations, each with its own entry point, with independent code for each operation, all performed on the same data structure. An example is given in Figure 7.6. This does not violate the tenets of structured programming; each piece of code has exactly one entry point and one exit

Figure 7.6
A module with
informational
cohesion.

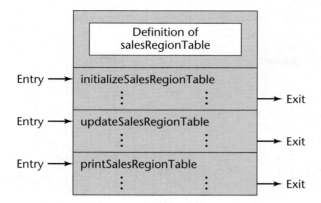

point. A major difference between logical cohesion and informational cohesion is that the various operations of a module with logical cohesion are intertwined, whereas in a module with informational cohesion the code for each operation is completely independent.

A module with informational cohesion essentially is an implementation of an abstract data type, as explained in Section 7.5, and all the advantages of using an abstract data type are gained when a module with informational cohesion is used. Because an object essentially is an instantiation (instance) of an abstract data type (Section 7.7), an object, too, is a module with informational cohesion.[1]

7.2.8   Cohesion Example

For further insight into cohesion, consider the example shown in Figure 7.7. Two methods in particular merit comment. It may seem somewhat surprising that the methods initializeSumsAndOpenFiles and closeFilesAndPrintAverageTemperatures have been labeled as having coincidental cohesion rather than temporal cohesion. First, consider method initializeSumsAndOpenFiles. It performs two operations related in time, in that both have to be done before any calculations can be performed, and therefore it seems that the method has temporal cohesion. Although the two operations of initializeSumsAndOpenFiles indeed are performed at the beginning of the calculation, another factor is involved. Initializing the sums is related to the problem, but opening files is a hardware issue that has nothing to do with the problem itself. The rule when two or more different levels of cohesion can be assigned to a module is to assign the lowest possible level. Consequently, because method initializeSumsAndOpenFiles could have either temporal or coincidental cohesion, the lower of the two levels of cohesion (coincidental) is assigned that method. That also is the reason why method closeFilesAndPrintAverageTemperatures has coincidental cohesion.

7.3   Coupling

Recall that cohesion is the degree of interaction within a module. Coupling is the degree of interaction between two modules. As before, a number of levels can be distinguished, as shown in Figure 7.8. To highlight good coupling, the various levels are described in order from the worst to the best.

---

[1] The discussion in this paragraph assumes that the abstract data type or object is well designed. If the methods of an object perform completely unrelated operations, then the object has coincidental cohesion.

Figure 7.7   A module interconnection diagram showing the cohesion of each module.

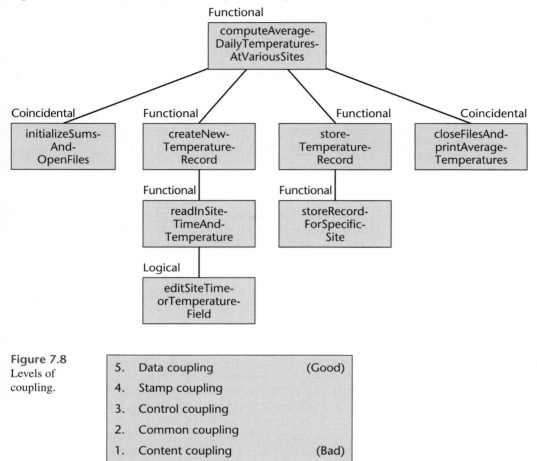

Figure 7.8
Levels of
coupling.

5.	Data coupling	(Good)
4.	Stamp coupling	
3.	Control coupling	
2.	Common coupling	
1.	Content coupling	(Bad)

7.3.1   Content Coupling

Two modules are ***content coupled*** if one directly references the contents of the other. All the following are examples of content coupling:

Example 1.   Module p modifies a statement of module q. This practice is not restricted to assembly language programming. The **alter** verb, now mercifully removed from COBOL, did precisely that: It modified another statement.

Example 2.   Module p refers to local data of module q in terms of some numerical displacement within q.

Example 3.   Module p branches to a local label of module q.

Suppose that module p and module q are content coupled. One of the many dangers is that almost any change to q, even recompiling q with a new compiler or assembler, requires a change to p. Furthermore, it is impossible to reuse module p in some new product without reusing module q as well. When two modules are content coupled, they are inextricably interlinked.

7.3.2   Common Coupling

Two modules are ***common coupled*** if both have access to the same global data. The situation is depicted in Figure 7.9. Instead of communicating with one another by passing arguments, modules cca and ccb can access and change the value of globalVariable. The most common situation in which this arises is when both cca and ccb have access to the same database and can read and write the same record. For common coupling, it is necessary that both modules can read *and* write to the database; if the database access mode is read-only, then this is not common coupling. But there are other ways of implementing common coupling, including use of the C++ or Java modifier **public**.

This form of coupling is undesirable for a number of reasons:

1. It contradicts the spirit of structured programming in that the resulting code is virtually unreadable. Consider the code fragment shown in Figure 7.10. If globalVariable is a global variable, then its value may be changed by method3, method4, or any method invoked by them. Determining under what conditions the loop terminates is a nontrivial question; if a run-time failure occurs, it may be difficult to reconstruct what happened, because any of a number of modules could have changed the value of globalVariable.

2. Consider the call record7.editThisTransaction (changedData). If there is common coupling, this call could change not just the value of record7 but any global variable that can be accessed by that method. In short, the entire method must be read to find out precisely what it does.

3. If a maintenance change is made in one module to the declaration of a global variable, then every module that can access that global variable has to be changed. Furthermore, all changes must be consistent.

4. Another problem is that a common-coupled module is difficult to reuse because the identical list of global variables has to be supplied each time the module is reused.

5. Common coupling possesses the unfortunate property that the number of instances of common coupling between a module p and the other modules in a product can change drastically, even if module p itself never changes; this is termed *clandestine common coupling* [Schach et al., 2003a]. For example, if both module p and module q can modify globalVariable, then there is one instance of common

Figure 7.9 An example of common coupling.

Figure 7.10 A code fragment reflecting common coupling.

```
while (globalVariable == 0)
{
   if (xyz.argument > 25)
      xyz.method3 ( );
   else
      xyz.method4 ( );
}
```

coupling between module p and the other modules in the software product. But if 10 new modules are designed and implemented, all of which can modify global-Variable, then the number of instances of common coupling between module p and the other modules increases to 11, even though module p itself has not been changed in any way. Clandestine common coupling can have surprising consequences. For example, between 1993 and 2000, there were nearly 400 releases of Linux; 5332 versions of the 17 Linux kernel modules were unchanged between successive releases. In more than half of the 5332 versions, the number of instances of common coupling between each of those kernel modules and the rest of Linux increased or decreased, even though the kernel module itself did not change. Considerably more modules exhibited clandestine common coupling in an upward direction (2482) than downward (379) [Schach et al., 2003a]. The number of lines of code in the Linux kernel grew linearly with version number, but the number of instances of common coupling grew exponentially [Schach et al., 2002]. It seems inevitable that, at some future date, the dependencies between modules induced by clandestine common coupling will render Linux extremely hard to maintain. It will then be exceedingly hard to change one part of Linux without inducing a regression fault (an apparently unrelated fault) elsewhere in the product.

6. This problem is potentially the most dangerous. As a consequence of common coupling, a module may be exposed to more data than it needs. This defeats any attempts to control data access and ultimately may lead to computer crime. Many types of computer crime need some form of collusion. Properly designed software should not allow any one programmer access to all the data and modules needed to commit a crime. For example, a programmer writing the check printing part of a payroll product needs to have access to employee records; but, in a well-designed product, such access is exclusively in read-only mode, preventing the programmer from making unauthorized changes to his or her monthly salary. To make such changes, the programmer has to find another dishonest employee, one with access to the relevant records in update mode. But if the product has been badly designed and every module can access the payroll database in update mode, then an unscrupulous programmer acting alone can make unauthorized changes to any record in the database.

Although we hope that these arguments will dissuade all but the most daring of readers from using common coupling, in some situations, common coupling might seem to be preferable to the alternatives. Consider, for example, a product that performs computer-aided design of petroleum storage tanks [Schach and Stevens-Guille, 1979]. A tank is specified by a large number of descriptors such as height, diameter, maximum wind speed to which the tank will be subjected, and insulation thickness. The descriptors have to be initialized but do not change in value thereafter, and most of the modules in the product need access to the values of the descriptors. Suppose that there are 55 tank descriptors. If all these descriptors are passed as arguments to every module, then the interface to each module will consist of at least 55 arguments and the potential for faults is huge. Even in an object-oriented language like Ada 95 [ISO/IEC 8652, 1995], which requires strict type checking of arguments, two arguments of the same type still can be interchanged, a fault that would not be detected by a type checker.

One solution is to put all the tank descriptors in a database and design the product in such a way that one module initializes the values of all the descriptors, whereas all the other modules access the database exclusively in read-only mode. However, if the database solution is impractical, perhaps because the specified implementation language cannot be interfaced with the available database management system, then an alternative is to use common coupling but in a controlled way. That is, the product should be designed so that the 55 descriptors are initialized by one module, but none of the other modules changes the value of a descriptor. This programming style has to be enforced by management, unlike the database solution, where enforcement is imposed by the software. Therefore, in situations where there is no good alternative to the use of common coupling, close supervision by management can reduce some of the risks. A better solution, however, is to obviate common coupling by using information hiding, as described in Section 7.6.

7.3.3   Control Coupling

Two modules are ***control coupled*** if one passes an element of control to the other module; that is, one module explicitly controls the logic of the other. For example, control is passed when a function code is passed to a module with logical cohesion (Section 7.2.2). Another example of control coupling is when a control switch is passed as an argument.

If module p calls module q and q passes back a flag to p that says, "I am unable to complete my task," then q is passing *data*. But if the flag means, "I am unable to complete my task; accordingly, display error message ABC123," then p and q are control coupled. In other words, if q passes information back to p and p decides what action to take as a consequence of receiving that information, then q is passing data. But, if q not only passes back information but also informs module p as to what action p must take, then control coupling is present.

The major difficulty that arises as a consequence of control coupling is that the two modules are not independent; module q, the called module, has to be aware of the internal structure and logic of module p. As a result, the possibility of reuse is reduced. In addition, control coupling generally is associated with modules that have logical cohesion and includes the difficulties associated with logical cohesion.

7.3.4   Stamp Coupling

In some programming languages, only simple variables, such as partNumber, satelliteAltitude, or degreeOfMultiprogramming, can be passed as arguments. But many languages also support passing data structures, such as records or arrays, as arguments. In such languages, valid arguments include partRecord, satelliteCoordinates, or segmentTable. Two modules are ***stamp coupled*** if a data structure is passed as an argument, but the called module operates on only some of the individual components of that data structure.

Consider, for example, the message employeeRecord.calculateWithholding ( ). It is not clear, without reading the entire calculateWithholding method, which fields of the employeeRecord the method accesses or changes. Passing the employee's salary obviously is essential for computing the withholding, but it is difficult to see how the employee's home telephone number is needed for this purpose. Instead, only those fields that it actually needs for computing the withholding should be passed to method calculateWithholding. Not only is the resulting method, and particularly its interface, easier to understand, it is likely to be reusable in a variety of other products that also need to compute withholding. (See Just in Case You Wanted to Know Box 7.2 for another perspective on this.)

Passing four or five different fields to a module may be slower than passing a complete record. This situation leads to a larger issue: What should be done when optimization issues (such as response time or space constraints) clash with what is generally considered to be good software engineering practice?

In my experience, this question frequently turns out to be irrelevant. The recommended approach may slow down the response time, but by only a millisecond or so, far too small to be detected by users. Therefore, in accordance with Knuth's [1974] First Law of Optimization: *Don't!*—rarely is there a need for optimization of any kind, including for performance reasons.

But what if optimization really is required? In this case, Knuth's Second Law of Optimization applies. The Second Law (labeled *for experts only*) is *Not yet!* In other words, first complete the entire product using appropriate software engineering techniques. Then, if optimization really is required, make only the necessary changes, meticulously documenting what is being changed and why. If at all possible, this optimization should be done by an experienced software engineer.

Perhaps even more important, because the call **employeeRecord.calculateWithholding ( )** passes more data than strictly necessary, the problems of uncontrolled data access, and conceivably computer crime, once again arise. This issue is discussed in Section 7.3.2.

Nothing is at all wrong with passing a data structure as an argument, provided all the components of the data structure are used by the called module. For example, calls like **invertMatrix (originalMatrix, invertedMatrix)** or **printInventoryRecord (warehouseRecord)** pass a data structure as an argument, but the called modules operate on all the components of that data structure. Stamp coupling is present when a data structure is passed as an argument but only some of the components are used by the called module.

A subtle form of stamp coupling can occur in languages like C++ when a pointer to a record is passed as an argument. Consider the call **checkAltitude (pointerToPositionRecord)**. At first sight, what is being passed is a simple variable. But the called module has access to all the fields in the **positionRecord** pointed to by **pointerToPositionRecord**. Because of the potential problems, it is a good idea to examine the coupling closely whenever a pointer is passed as an argument.

7.3.5   Data Coupling

Two modules are ***data coupled*** if all arguments are homogeneous data items. That is, every argument is either a simple argument or a data structure in which all elements are used by the called module. Examples include **displayTimeOfArrival (flightNumber)**, **computeProduct (firstNumber, secondNumber, result)**, and **determineJobWithHighestPriority (jobQueue)**.

Data coupling is a desirable goal. To put it in a negative way, if a product exhibits data coupling exclusively, then the difficulties of content, common, control, and stamp coupling are not present. From a more positive viewpoint, if two modules are data coupled, then maintenance is easier, because a change to one module is less likely to cause a regression fault in the other. The following example clarifies certain aspects of coupling.

7.3.6   Coupling Example

Consider the example shown in Figure 7.11. The numbers on the arcs represent interfaces that are defined in greater detail in Figure 7.12. For example, when module p calls module q (interface 1), it passes one argument, the type of the aircraft. When q returns control to p, it passes back a status flag. Using the information in Figures 7.11 and 7.12, the coupling between every pair of modules can be deduced. The results are shown in Figure 7.13.

Some of the entries in Figure 7.13 are obvious. For instance, the data coupling between p and q (interface 1 in Figure 7.11), between r and t (interface 5), and between s and u (interface 6) is a direct consequence of the fact that a simple variable is passed in each direction. The coupling between p and s (interface 2) is data coupling if all the elements of the list of parts passed from p to s are used or updated, but it is stamp coupling if s operates on only certain elements of the list. The coupling between q and s (interface 4) is similar. Because the information in Figures 7.11 and 7.12 does not completely describe the function of the various modules, there is no way of determining whether the coupling is data or stamp. The coupling between q and r (interface 3) is control coupling, because a function code is passed from q to r.

Perhaps somewhat surprising are the three entries marked common coupling in Figure 7.13. The three module pairs that are farthest apart in Figure 7.11—p and t, p and u, and t and u—at first appear not to be coupled in any way. After all, no interface connects them, so the very idea of coupling between them, let alone common coupling, requires some explanation. The answer lies in the annotation on the right-hand side of Figure 7.11,

Figure 7.11
The module interconnection diagram for a coupling example.

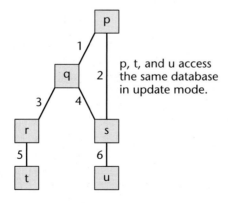

p, t, and u access
the same database
in update mode.

Figure 7.12
The interface description for Figure 7.11.

Number	In	Out
1	aircraftType	statusFlag
2	listOfAircraftParts	—
3	functionCode	—
4	listOfAircraftParts	—
5	partNumber	partManufacturer
6	partNumber	partName

Figure 7.13
Coupling
between pairs
of modules of
Figure 7.11.

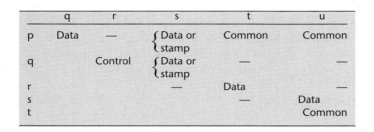

	q	r	s	t	u
p	Data	—	Data or stamp	Common	Common
q		Control	Data or stamp	—	—
r			—	Data	—
s				—	Data
t					Common

namely, that p, t, and u all access the same database in update mode. The result is that a number of global variables can be changed by all three modules, and hence they are pairwise common coupled.

7.3.7   The Importance of Coupling

Coupling is an important metric. If module p is tightly coupled to module q, then a change to module p may require a corresponding change to module q. If this change is made, as required, during integration or postdelivery maintenance, then the resulting product functions correctly; however, progress at that stage is slower than would have been the case had the coupling been looser. On the other hand, if the required change is not made to module q at that time, then the fault manifests itself later. In the best case, the compiler or linker informs the team right away that something is amiss or a failure will occur while testing the change to module p. What usually happens, however, is that the product fails either during subsequent integration testing or after the product has been installed on the client's computer. In both cases, the failure occurs after the change to module p has been completed. There no longer is any apparent link between the change to module p and the overlooked corresponding change to module q. The fault therefore may be hard to find.

It has been shown that the stronger (more undesirable) the coupling, the greater the fault-proneness [Briand, Daly, Porter, and Wüst, 1998]. A major reason underlying this phenomenon is that dependencies within the code lead to regression faults. Furthermore, if a module is fault prone, then it will have to undergo repeated maintenance, and these frequent changes are likely to compromise its maintainability. Furthermore, these frequent changes will not always be restricted to the fault-prone module itself; it is not uncommon to have to modify more than one module to fix a single fault. Consequently, the fault-proneness of one module can adversely affect the maintainability of a number of other modules. In other words, it is easy to believe that strong coupling can have a deleterious effect on maintainability [Yu, Schach, Chen, and Offutt, 2004].

Given that a design in which modules have high cohesion and low coupling is a good design, the obvious question is, How can such a design be achieved? Because this chapter is devoted to theoretical concepts surrounding design, the answer to the question is presented in Chapter 12. In the meantime, those qualities that identify a good design are examined further and refined. For convenience, the key definitions in this chapter appear in Figure 7.14, together with the section in which each definition appears.

Figure 7.14
Key definitions
of this chapter,
and the sections
in which they
appear.

Abstract data type: a data type together with the operations performed on instantiations of that data type (Section 7.5)

Abstraction: a means of achieving stepwise refinement by suppressing unnecessary details and accentuating relevant details (Section 7.4.1)

Class: an abstract data type that supports inheritance (Section 7.7)

Cohesion: the degree of interaction within a module (Section 7.1)

Coupling: the degree of interaction between two modules (Section 7.1)

Data encapsulation: a data structure together with the operations performed on that data structure (Section 7.4)

Encapsulation: the gathering together into one unit of all aspects of the real-world entity modeled by that unit (Section 7.4.1)

Information hiding: structuring the design so that the resulting implementation details are hidden from other modules (Section 7.6)

Object: an instantiation of a class (Section 7.7)

7.4   Data Encapsulation

Consider the problem of designing an operating system for a large mainframe computer. According to the specifications, any job submitted to the computer is classified as high priority, medium priority, or low priority. The task of the operating system is to decide which job to load into memory next, which of the jobs in memory gets the next time slice and how long that time slice should be, and which of the jobs that require disk access has highest priority. In performing this scheduling, the operating system must consider the priority of each job; the higher is the priority, the sooner that job should be assigned the resources of the computer. One way of achieving this is to maintain separate job queues for each job-priority level. The job queues have to be initialized, and facilities must exist for adding a job to a job queue when the job requires memory, CPU time, or disk access as well as for removing a job from a queue when the operating system decides to allocate the required resource to that job.

To simplify matters, consider the restricted problem of batch jobs queuing up for memory access. There are three queues for incoming batch jobs, one for each priority level. When submitted by a user, a job is added to the appropriate queue; and when the operating system decides that a job is ready to be run, it is removed from its queue and memory is allocated to it.

This portion of the product can be built in a number of different ways. One possible design, shown in Figure 7.15, depicts modules for manipulating one of the three job queues. The operations defined in modules m1, m2, and m3 are global methods (*static member functions* in C++, *static methods* or *class methods* in Java).

Consider Figure 7.15. Method initializeJobQueue in module m1 is responsible for the initialization of the job queue, and methods addJobToQueue and removeJobFrom-Queue in modules m2 and m3, respectively, are responsible for the addition and deletion of jobs. Module m123 contains invocations of all three methods in order to manipulate the job queue. To concentrate on data encapsulation, issues such as underflow (trying to remove a job from an empty queue) and overflow (trying to add a job to a full queue) have been suppressed here, as well as in the remainder of this chapter.

Figure 7.15
One possible
design of the job
queue portion
of the operating
system.

m1

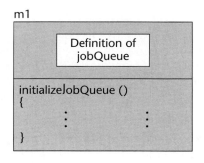

m2

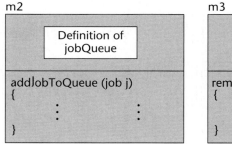

m3

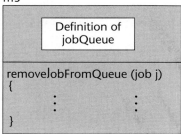

m123

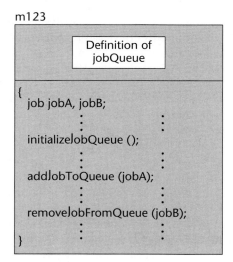

The modules of the design of Figure 7.15 have low cohesion, because operations on the job queue are spread all over the product. If a decision is made to change the way jobQueue is implemented (for example, as a linked list of records instead of as a linear list), then modules m1, m2, and m3 have to be drastically revised. Module m123 also has to be changed; at the very least, the data structure definition has to be changed.

Now suppose that the design of Figure 7.16 is chosen instead. The module on the right-hand side of the figure has informational cohesion (Section 7.2.7), in that it performs

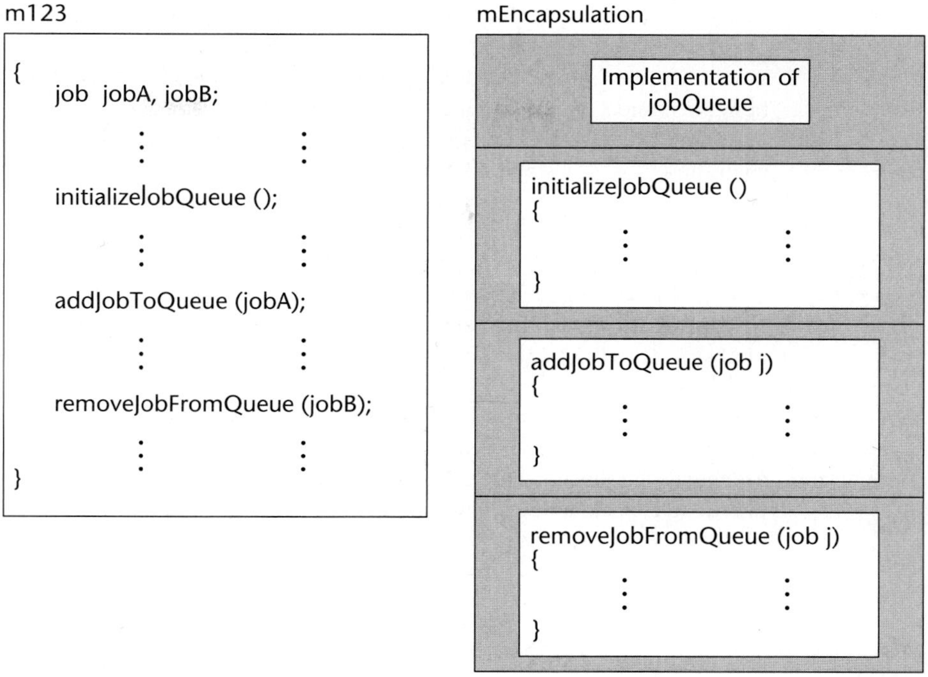

Figure 7.16
A design of
the job queue
portion of
the operating
system
using data
encapsulation.

m123

```
{
    job  jobA, jobB;
        ⋮           ⋮

    initializeJobQueue ();
        ⋮           ⋮

    addJobToQueue (jobA);
        ⋮           ⋮

    removeJobFromQueue (jobB);
        ⋮           ⋮
}
```

mEncapsulation

```
Implementation of
jobQueue
```

```
initializeJobQueue ()
{
        ⋮           ⋮
}
```

```
addJobToQueue (job j)
{
        ⋮           ⋮
}
```

```
removeJobFromQueue (job j)
{
        ⋮           ⋮
}
```

a number of operations on the same data structure. Each operation has its own entry point and exit point and independent code. Module mEncapsulation in Figure 7.16 is an implementation of ***data encapsulation***, that is, a data structure, in this case the job queue, together with the operations to be performed on that data structure.

An obvious question to ask at this point is, What is the advantage of designing a product using data encapsulation? This will be answered in two ways, from the viewpoint of development and from the viewpoint of maintenance.

7.4.1 Data Encapsulation and Development

Data encapsulation is an example of ***abstraction***. Returning to the job queue example, a data structure (the job queue) has been defined, together with three associated operations (initialize the job queue, add a job to the queue, and delete a job from the queue). The developer can conceptualize the problem at a higher level, the level of jobs and job queues, rather than at the lower level of records or arrays.

The basic theoretical concept behind abstraction, once again, is stepwise refinement. First, a design for the product is produced in terms of high-level concepts such as jobs, job queues, and the operations performed on job queues. At this stage, it is entirely irrelevant how the job queue is implemented. Once a complete high-level design has been obtained, the second step is to design the lower-level components in terms of which the data structure and operations on the data structure are implemented. In C++, for example, the data structure (the job queue) can be implemented in terms of records (structures) or arrays; the three operations (initialize the job queue, add a job to the queue, and remove a job from the queue) can be implemented as methods. The key point is that, while this lower level is being designed, the designer totally ignores the intended use of the jobs, job queue, and operations. Therefore, during the first step, the existence of the lower level is assumed, even though at this stage no thought has been given to that level; during the second step (the design of the lower level), the existence of the higher level is ignored. At the higher level, the concern is with the behavior of the data structure, the job queue; at the lower level, the implementation of that behavior is the primary concern. Of course, a larger product has many levels of abstraction.

Different types of abstraction exist. Consider Figure 7.16. That figure has two types of abstraction. Data encapsulation (that is, a data structure together with the operations to be performed on that data structure) is an example of **data abstraction**; the methods themselves are an example of **procedural abstraction**. *Abstraction*, to summarize, simply is a means of achieving stepwise refinement by suppressing unnecessary details and accentuating relevant details. **Encapsulation** now can be defined as the gathering into one unit of all aspects of the real-world entity modeled by that unit; this was termed *conceptual independence* in Section 1.9.

Data abstraction allows the designer to think at the level of the data structure and the operations performed on it and only later be concerned with the details of how the data structure and operations are implemented. Turning now to procedural abstraction, consider the result of defining a method, initializeJobQueue. The effect is to extend the language by supplying the developer with another method, one that is not part of the language as originally defined. The developer can use initializeJobQueue in the same way as sqrt or abs.

The implications of procedural abstraction for design are as powerful as those of data abstraction. The designer can conceptualize the product in terms of high-level operations. These operations can be defined in terms of lower-level operations, until the lowest level is reached. At this level, the operations are expressed in terms of the predefined constructs of the programming language. At each level, the designer is concerned only with expressing the product in terms of operations appropriate to that level. The designer can ignore the level below, which will be handled at the next level of abstraction, that is, the next refinement step. The designer also can ignore the level above, a level irrelevant from the viewpoint of designing the current level.

7.4.2   Data Encapsulation and Maintenance

Approaching data encapsulation from the viewpoint of maintenance, a basic issue is to identify the aspects of a product likely to change and design the product to minimize the effects of future changes. Data structures as such are unlikely to change; if a product includes job queues, for instance, then future versions are likely to incorporate them. At the same time, the specific way that job queues are implemented may well change, and data encapsulation provides a means of coping with that change.

Figure 7.17 depicts an implementation in C++ of the job queue data structure as a **JobQueueClass**; Figure 7.18 is the corresponding Java implementation. (Just in Case

Figure 7.17
A C++
implementation
of **JobQueue-
Class**.
(Problems
caused by
public
attributes will
be solved in
Section 7.7.)

```cpp
//
// Warning:
// This code has been written in such a way as to be accessible to readers
// who are not C++ experts, as opposed to using good C++ style. Also, vital
// features such as checks for overflow and underflow have been omitted for simplicity.
// See Just in Case You Wanted to Know Box 7.3 for details.
//
class JobQueueClass
{
    // attributes
    public:
        int queueLength;        // length of job queue
        int queue[25];          // queue can contain up to 25 jobs

    // methods
    public:
        void initializeJobQueue ()
        /*
         * an empty job queue has length 0
         */
        {
            queueLength = 0;
        }


        void addJobToQueue (int jobNumber)
        /*
         * add the job to the end of the job queue
         */
        {
            queue[queueLength] = jobNumber;
            queueLength = queueLength + 1;
        }


        int removeJobFromQueue ()
        /*
         * set jobNumber equal to the number of the job stored at the head of the queue,
         * remove the job at the head of the job queue, move up the remaining jobs,
         * and return jobNumber
         */
        {
            int jobNumber = queue[0];
            queueLength = queueLength - 1;
            for (int k = 0; k < queueLength; k++)
                queue[k] = queue[k + 1];
            return jobNumber;
        }
}// class JobQueueClass
```

Figure 7.18
A Java
implementation
of **JobQueue-
Class**.
(Problems
caused by
public
attributes will
be solved in
Section 7.7.)

```java
//
// Warning:
// This code has been written in such a way as to be accessible to readers
// who are not Java experts, as opposed to using good Java style.
// Also, vital features such as checks for overflow and underflow
// have been omitted for simplicity.
// See Just in Case You Wanted to Know Box 7.3 for details.
//
class JobQueueClass
{
    // attributes
    public int      queueLength;               // length of job queue
    public int      queue[ ] = new int[25];    // queue can contain up to 25 jobs

    // methods
    public void initializeJobQueue ()
    /*
     * an empty job queue has length 0
     */
    {
        queueLength = 0;
    }


    public void addJobToQueue (int jobNumber)
    /*
     * add the job to the end of the job queue
     */
    {
        queue[queueLength] = jobNumber;
        queueLength = queueLength + 1;
    }


    public int removeJobFromQueue ()
    /*
     * set jobNumber equal to the number of the job stored at the head of the queue,
     * remove the job at the head of the job queue, move up the remaining jobs,
     * and return jobNumber
     */
    {
        int jobNumber = queue[0];
        queueLength = queueLength - 1;
        for (int k = 0; k < queueLength; k++)
            queue[k] = queue[k + 1];
        return jobNumber;
    }
}// class JobQueueClass
```

I deliberately wrote the code examples of Figures 7.17 and 7.18 as well as the subsequent code examples in this chapter in such a way as to highlight data abstraction issues at the cost of good programming practice. For example, the number 25 in the definition of **JobQueueClass** in Figures 7.17 and 7.18 certainly should be coded as a parameter, that is, as a **const** in C++ or a **public static final** variable in Java. Also, for simplicity, I omitted checks for conditions such as underflow (trying to remove an item from an empty queue) or overflow (trying to add an item to a full queue). In any real product, it is absolutely essential to include such checks.

In addition, language-specific features have been minimized. For instance, a C++ programmer usually writes

queueLength++;

to increment the value of queueLength by 1, rather than

queueLength = queueLength + 1;

Similarly, use of constructors and destructors has been minimized.

In summary, I wrote the code in this chapter for pedagogic purposes only. It should not be utilized for any other purpose.

You Wanted to Know Box 7.3 has comments on the programming style in Figures 7.17 and 7.18, as well as in the subsequent code examples in this chapter.) In Figure 7.17 or Figure 7.18, the queue is implemented as an array of up to 25 job numbers; the first element is queue[0] and the 25th is queue[24]. Each job number is represented as an integer. The reserved word **public** allows queueLength and queue to be visible everywhere in the operating system. The resulting common coupling is extremely poor practice and is corrected in Section 7.6.

Because they are **public**, the methods in **JobQueueClass** may be invoked from anywhere in the operating system. In particular, Figure 7.19 shows how **JobQueueClass** may be used by method queueHandler using C++, and Figure 7.20 is the corresponding Java implementation. Method queueHandler invokes methods initializeJobQueue, addJobToQueue, and removeJobFromQueue of **JobQueueClass** without having any knowledge as to how the job queue is implemented; the only information needed to use **JobQueueClass** is interface information regarding the three methods.

Now suppose that the job queue currently is implemented as a linear list of job numbers, but a decision has been made to reimplement it as a two-way linked list of job records. Each job record will have three components: the job number as before, a pointer to the job record in front of it in the linked list, and a pointer to the job record behind it. This is specified in C++ as shown in Figure 7.21 and in Java as shown in Figure 7.22. What changes must be made to the software product as a whole as a consequence of this modification to the way the job queue is implemented? In fact, only **JobQueueClass** itself has to be changed. Figure 7.23 shows the outline of a C++ implementation of **JobQueueClass** using the two-way linked list of Figure 7.21. Implementation details have been suppressed to highlight that the interface between **JobQueueClass** and the rest of the product (including method queueHandler) has not changed (but see Problem 7.11). That is, the three methods initializeJobQueue, addJobToQueue, and removeJobFromQueue are invoked in exactly the same way as before. Specifically, when method addJobToQueue

Figure 7.19   A C++ implementation of queueHandler.

```
class SchedulerClass
{
  . . .
  public:
    void queueHandler ()
    {
      int              jobA, jobB;
      JobQueueClass    jobQueueJ;

          // various statements
      jobQueueJ.initializeJobQueue ();
          // more statements
      jobQueueJ.addJobToQueue (jobA);
          // still more statements
      jobB = jobQueueJ.removeJobFromQueue ();
          // further statements
    }// queueHandler
  . . .
}// class SchedulerClass
```

Figure 7.20   A Java implementation of queueHandler.

```
class SchedulerClass
{
  . . .
    public void queueHandler ()
    {
      int              jobA, jobB;
      JobQueueClass    jobQueueJ = new JobQueueClass ();

          // various statements
      jobQueueJ.initializeJobQueue ();
          // more statements
      jobQueueJ.addJobToQueue (jobA);
          // still more statements
      jobB = jobQueueJ.removeJobFromQueue ();
          // further statements
    }// queueHandler
  . . .
}// class SchedulerClass
```

is invoked, it still passes an integer value, and removeJobFromQueue still returns an integer value, even though the job queue itself has been implemented in an entirely different way. Consequently, the source code of method queueHandler (Figure 7.19) need not be changed at all. Accordingly, data encapsulation supports the implementation of data abstraction in a way that simplifies maintenance and reduces the chance of a regression fault.

Figure 7.21   A C++ implementation of a two-way linked **JobRecordClass**. (Problems caused by **public** attributes will be solved in Section 7.6.)

```
class JobRecordClass
{
  public:
    int              jobNo;        // number of the job (integer)
    JobRecordClass   *inFront;     // pointer to the job record in front
    JobRecordClass   *inRear;      // pointer to the job record behind
}// class JobRecordClass
```

Figure 7.22   A Java implementation of a two-way linked **JobRecordClass**. (Problems caused by **public** attributes will be solved in Section 7.6.)

```
class JobRecordClass
{
    public int              jobNo;     // number of the job (integer)
    public JobRecordClass   inFront;   // reference to the job record in front
    public JobRecordClass   inRear;    // reference to the job record behind
} // class JobRecordClass
```

Figure 7.23
Outline of a C++
implementation
of **JobQueue-
Class** using a
two-way linked
list.

```
class JobQueueClass
{
  public:
    JobRecordClass        *frontOfQueue;        // pointer to the front of the queue
    JobRecordClass        *rearOfQueue;         // pointer to the rear of the queue

    void initializeJobQueue ()
    {
      /*
       * initialize the job queue by setting frontOfQueue and rearOfQueue to NULL
       */
    }


    void addJobToQueue (int JobNumber)
    {
      /*
       * Create a new job record,
       * place jobNumber in its jobNo field,
       * set its inFront field to point to the current rearOfQueue
       * (thereby linking the new record to the rear of the queue),
       * and set its inRear field to NULL.
       * Set the inRear field of the record pointed to by the current rearOfQueue
       * to point to the new record (thereby setting up a two-way link), and
       * finally, set rearOfQueue to point to this new record.
       */
    }


    int removeJobFromQueue ()
    {
      /*
       * set jobNumber equal to the jobNo field of the record at the front of the queue,
       * update frontOfQueue to point to the next item in the queue,
       * set the inFront field of the record that is now the head of the queue to NULL,
       * and return jobNumber.
       */
    }
}// class JobQueueClass
```

Comparing Figures 7.17 and 7.18 and Figures 7.19 and 7.20, it is clear that, in these instances, the differences between the C++ and Java implementations essentially are syntactic. In the remainder of this chapter, we give only one implementation, together with a description of the syntactic differences in the other implementation. Specifically, the rest of the job queue code is in C++ and all the other code examples are in Java.

7.5   Abstract Data Types

Figure 7.17 (equivalently, Figure 7.18) is an implementation of a job queue **class**, that is, a data type together with the operations to be performed on instantiations of that data type. Such a construct is called an ***abstract data type***.

Figure 7.24 shows how this abstract data type may be utilized in C++ for the three job queues of the operating system. Three job queues are instantiated: highPriorityQueue, mediumPriorityQueue, and lowPriorityQueue. (The Java version differs only in the syntax of the data declarations of the three job queues.) The statement highPriorityQueue. initializeJobQueue () means "apply method initializeJobQueue to data structure high-PriorityQueue," and similarly for the other two statements.

Abstract data types are a widely applicable design tool. For example, suppose that a product is to be written in which a large number of operations have to be performed on rational numbers, that is, numbers that can be represented in the form n/d, where n and d are integers, d ≠ 0. Rational numbers can be represented in a variety of ways, such as two elements of a one-dimensional array of integers or two attributes of a class. To implement rational numbers in terms of an abstract data type, a suitable representation for the data structure is chosen. In Java, it could be defined as shown in Figure 7.25, together with the various operations that are performed on rational numbers, such as constructing a rational number from two integers, adding two rational numbers, or multiplying two rational numbers. (The problems induced by **public** attributes such as numerator and denominator in Figure 7.25 will be fixed in Section 7.6.) The corresponding C++ implementation differs in the placement of the reserved word **public**. Also, an ampersand is needed when an argument is passed by reference.

Abstract data types support both data abstraction and procedural abstraction (Section 7.4.1). In addition, when a product is modified, it is unlikely that the abstract data types will be changed; at worst, additional operations may have to be added to an abstract data type. Therefore, from both the development and the maintenance viewpoints, abstract data types are an attractive tool for software producers.

Figure 7.24
C++ method
queueHandler
implemented
using the
abstract data
type of
Figure 7.17.

```
class SchedulerClass
{
    . . .
    public:
      void queueHandler ()
      {
          int              job1, job2;
          JobQueueClass    highPriorityQueue;
          JobQueueClass    mediumPriorityQueue;
          JobQueueClass    lowPriorityQueue;

          // some statements
          highPriorityQueue.initializeJobQueue ();
          // some more statements
          mediumPriorityQueue.addJobToQueue (job1);
          // still more statements
          job2 = lowPriorityQueue.removeJobFromQueue ();
          // even more statements
      }// queueHandler
    . . .
}// class SchedulerClass
```

Figure 7.25
Java abstract data type implementation of a rational number. (Problems caused by **public** attributes will be solved in Section 7.6.)

```
class RationalClass
{
    public int          numerator;
    public int          denominator;

    public void sameDenominator (RationalClass r, RationalClass s)
    {
        // code to reduce r and s to the same denominator
    }

    public boolean equal (RationalClass t, RationalClass u)
    {
        RationalClass        v, w;
        v = t;
        w = u;
        sameDenominator (v, w);
        return (v.numerator == w.numerator);
    }

    // methods to add, subtract, multiply, and divide two rational numbers

}// class RationalClass
```

7.6   Information Hiding

The two types of abstraction discussed in Section 7.4.1 (data abstraction and procedural abstraction) are in turn instances of a more general design concept put forward by Parnas, **information hiding** [Parnas, 1971, 1972a, 1972b]. Parnas's ideas are directed toward future maintenance. Before a product is designed, a list should be made of implementation decisions likely to change in the future. Modules then should be designed so that the implementation details of the resulting design are hidden from other modules. As a result, each future change is localized to one specific module. Because the details of the original implementation decision are not visible to other modules, changing the design clearly cannot affect any other module. (See Just in Case You Wanted to Know Box 7.4 for a further insight into information hiding.)

To see how these ideas can be used in practice, consider Figure 7.24, which uses the abstract data type implementation of Figure 7.17. A primary reason for using an abstract data type is to ensure that the contents of a job queue can be changed only by invoking one of the three methods of Figure 7.17. Unfortunately, the nature of that implementation is such that job queues can be changed in other ways as well. Attributes queueLength and queue are both declared **public** in Figure 7.17 and therefore accessible inside queueHandler. As a result, in Figure 7.24, it is perfectly legal C++ (or Java) to use an assignment statement such as

$$\text{highPriorityQueue.queue}[7] = -5678;$$

anywhere in queueHandler to change highPriorityQueue. In other words, the contents of a job queue can be changed without using any of the three operations of the abstract data type. In addition to the implications this might have with regard to lowering cohesion and

Just in Case You Wanted to Know — Box 7.4

The term *information hiding* is somewhat of a misnomer. A more accurate description would be "details hiding," because what is hidden is not information but implementation details.

increasing coupling, management must recognize that the product may be vulnerable to computer crime as described in Section 7.3.2.

Fortunately, there is a way out. The designers of both C++ and Java provided for information hiding within a class specification. This is shown in Figure 7.26 for C++ (the Java syntactic differences are as before). Other than changing the visibility modifier for the attributes from **public** to **private**, Figure 7.26 is identical to Figure 7.17. Now the only information visible to other modules is that **JobQueueClass** is a class and that three operations with specified interfaces can operate on the resulting job queues. But the exact way job queues are implemented is **private**, that is, invisible to the outside. The diagram in Figure 7.27 shows how a class with **private** attributes enables a C++ or Java user to implement an abstract data type with full information hiding.

Information hiding techniques also can be used to obviate common coupling, as mentioned at the end of Section 7.3.2. Consider again the product described in that section, a computer-aided design tool for petroleum storage tanks specified by 55 descriptors. If the product is implemented with **private** operations for initializing a descriptor and **public** operations for obtaining the value of a descriptor, then there is no common

Figure 7.26 A C++ abstract data type implementation with information hiding, correcting the problem of Figures 7.17, 7.18, 7.21, 7.22, and 7.25.

```
class JobQueueClass
{
  // attributes
  private:
    int    queueLength;      // length of job queue
    int    queue[25];        // queue can contain up to 25 jobs


  // methods
  public:
    void initializeJobQueue ()
    {
      // body of method unchanged from Figure 7.17
    }


    void addJobToQueue (int jobNumber)
    {
      // body of method unchanged from Figure 7.17
    }


    int removeJobFromQueue ()
    {
      // body of method unchanged from Figure 7.17
    }
}// class JobQueueClass
```

Figure 7.27   Representation of an abstract data type with information hiding achieved via **private** attributes (Figure 7.26 with Figure 7.24).

SchedulerClass

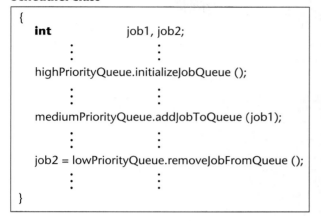

JobQueueClass

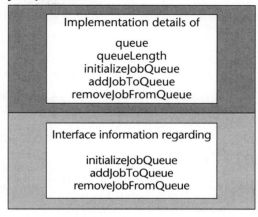

coupling. This type of solution is characteristic of the object-oriented paradigm, because as described in Section 7.7, objects support information hiding. This is another strength of object technology.

7.7   Objects

As stated at the beginning of this chapter, objects simply are the next step in the progression shown in Figure 7.28. Nothing is special about objects; they are as ordinary as abstract data types or modules with informational cohesion. The importance of objects is that they have all the properties possessed by their predecessors in Figure 7.28, as well as additional properties of their own.

An incomplete definition of an object is that an object is an instantiation (instance) of an abstract data type. That is, a product is designed in terms of abstract data types, and the variables (objects) of the product are instantiations of the abstract data types. But defining an object as an instantiation of an abstract data type is too simplistic. Something more is needed, namely, *inheritance*, a concept first introduced in Simula 67 [Dahl and Nygaard, 1966]. Inheritance is supported by all object-oriented programming languages, such as Smalltalk [Goldberg and Robson, 1989], C++ [Stroustrup, 2003], and Java [Flanagan, 2005]. The basic idea behind inheritance is that new data types can be defined as extensions of previously defined types, rather than having to be defined from scratch [Meyer, 1986].

In an object-oriented language, a *class* can be defined as an abstract data type that supports inheritance. An *object* then is an instantiation of a class. Consider the following example. Define **Human Being Class** to be a class and Joe to be an object, an

Figure 7.28
The major concepts of Chapter 7 and the section in which each is described.

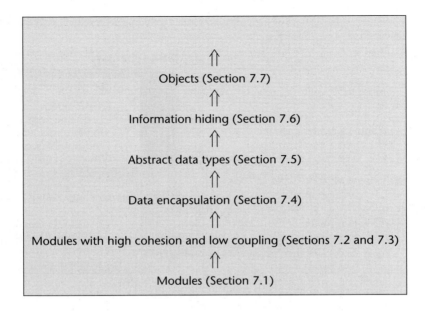

Objects (Section 7.7)

⇑

Information hiding (Section 7.6)

⇑

Abstract data types (Section 7.5)

⇑

Data encapsulation (Section 7.4)

⇑

Modules with high cohesion and low coupling (Sections 7.2 and 7.3)

⇑

Modules (Section 7.1)

instance of that class. Every instance of **Human Being Class** has certain attributes such as age and height, and values can be assigned to those attributes when describing the object Joe. Now suppose that **Parent Class** is defined to be a *subclass* (or derived class) of **Human Being Class**. This means that an instance of **Parent Class** has all the attributes of an instance of **Human Being Class** and, in addition, may have attributes of his or her own such as name of oldest child and number of children. This is depicted in Figure 7.29. In object-oriented terminology, a Parent *isA* Human Being. That is why the arrow in Figure 7.29 seems to be going in the wrong direction. In fact, the arrow depicts the *isA* relation and therefore points from the derived class to the base class. The use of the open arrowhead to denote inheritance is a UML convention; another is that class names appear in boldface with the first letter of each word capitalized. Finally, the open rectangle with the turned-over corner is a UML *note*. UML is discussed in more detail in Part 2, especially in Chapter 15.

Parent Class *inherits* all the attributes of **Human Being Class**, because **Parent Class** is a derived class (or subclass) of base class **Human Being Class**. If Fred is an object (instance) of **Parent Class**, then Fred has all the attributes of an instance of **Parent Class** and also inherits all the attributes of an instance of **Human Being Class**. A Java implementation is shown in Figure 7.30. The C++ version differs in the placement of the **private** and **public** modifiers. Also, the Java syntax **extends** is replaced in C++ by **: public** in this example.

The property of inheritance is an essential feature of all object-oriented programming languages. However, neither inheritance nor the concept of a class is supported by classical languages such as C or Lisp. Therefore, the object-oriented paradigm cannot be directly implemented in these languages.

In the terminology of the object-oriented paradigm, there are two other ways of looking at the relationship between **Parent Class** and **Human Being Class** in Figure 7.29.

Figure 7.29
UML diagram
showing derived
types and
inheritance.

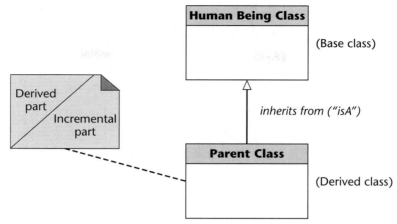

Figure 7.30
Java implemen-
tation of
Figure 7.29.

```
class HumanBeingClass
{
    private int       age;
    private float     height;

    // public declarations of operations on HumanBeingClass

}// class HumanBeingClass


class ParentClass extends HumanBeingClass
{
    private String    nameOfOldestChild;
    private int       numberOfChildren;

    // public declarations of operations on ParentClass

}// class ParentClass
```

We can say that **Parent Class** is a *specialization* of **Human Being Class** or that **Human Being Class** is a *generalization* of **Parent Class**. In addition to specialization and generalization, classes have two other basic relationships [Blaha, Premerlani, and Rumbaugh, 1988]: aggregation and association. **Aggregation** refers to the components of a class. For example, class **Personal Computer Class** might consist of components **CPU Class**, **Monitor Class**, **Keyboard Class**, and **Printer Class**. This is depicted in Figure 7.31; the use of a diamond to denote aggregation is another UML convention. Aggregation is used to group related items, resulting in a reusable class (Section 8.1).

   Association refers to a relationship of some kind between two apparently unrelated classes. For example, there seems to be no connection between a radiologist and a lawyer, but a radiologist may consult a lawyer for advice regarding a contract for leasing a new MRI machine. Association is depicted using UML in Figure 7.32. The nature of the association in this instance is indicated by the word consults. In addition, the solid triangle

Figure 7.31   UML aggregation example.

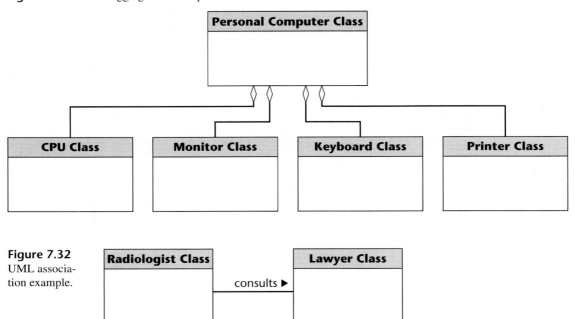

Figure 7.32
UML associa-
tion example.

(termed a ***navigation triangle*** in UML) indicates the direction of the association; after all, a lawyer with a broken ankle might consult a radiologist.

In passing, one aspect of Java and C++ notation, like that of other object-oriented languages, explicitly reflects the equivalence of operation and data. First, consider a classical language that supports records; C, for example. Suppose that record_1[2] is a **struct** (record) and field_2 is a field within the class. Then, the field is referred to as record_1.field_2. That is, the period . denotes membership within the record. If function_3 is a function within a C module, then function_3 ( ) denotes an invocation of that function.

In contrast, suppose that **AClass** is a **class**, with attribute attributeB and method methodC. Suppose further that ourObject is an instance of **AClass**. Then the field is referred to as ourObject.attributeB. Furthermore, ourObject.methodC ( ) denotes an invocation of the method. Hence, the period is used to denote membership within an object, whether the member is an attribute or a method.

The advantages of using objects (or, rather, classes) are precisely those of using abstract data types, including data abstraction and procedural abstraction. In addition, the inheritance aspects of classes provide a further layer of data abstraction, leading to easier and less fault-prone product development. Yet another strength follows from combining inheritance with polymorphism and dynamic binding, the subject of Section 7.8.

---

[2]In this book, the name of a variable in a classical software product is written using the classical convention of separating the parts of a variable name with underscores, for example, this_is_a_classical_variable (as opposed to the object-oriented convention of using an uppercase letter to mark the start of a new part of the name of a variable; for example, thisIsAnObjectOrientedVariable).

7.8   Inheritance, Polymorphism, and Dynamic Binding

Suppose that the operating system of a computer is called on to open a file. That file could be stored on a number of different media. For example, it could be a disk file, a tape file, or a diskette file. Using the classical paradigm, there would be three differently named functions, open_disk_file, open_tape_file, and open_diskette_file; this is shown in Figure 7.33(a). If my_file is declared to be a file, then at run time, it is necessary to test whether it is a disk file, a tape file, or a diskette file to determine which function to invoke. The corresponding classical code is shown in Figure 7.34(a).

In contrast, when the object-oriented paradigm is used, a class named **File Class** is defined, with three derived classes: **Disk File Class**, **Tape File Class**, and **Diskette File Class**. This is shown in Figure 7.33(b); recall that the UML open arrowhead denotes inheritance.

Now, suppose that method open were defined in parent class **File Class** and inherited by the three derived classes. Unfortunately, this would not work, because different operations need to be carried out to open the three different types of files.

The solution is as follows. In parent class **File Class**, a dummy method open is declared. In Java, such a method is declared to be **abstract**; in C++ , the reserved word **virtual** is used instead. A specific implementation of the method appears in each of the three derived classes and each method is given an identical name, that is, open, as shown in Figure 7.33(b). Again, suppose that myFile is declared to be a file. At run time, the message

myFile.open ( );

Figure 7.33   Operations needed to open a file. (a) Classical implementation. (b) Object-oriented file class hierarchy using UML notation.

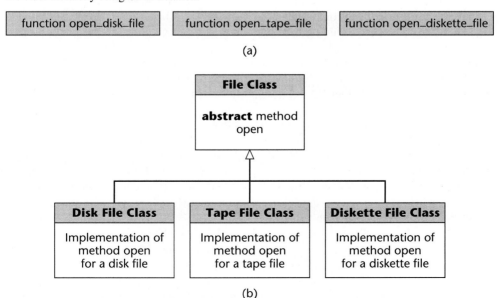

(a)

(b)

Figure 7.34
(a) Classical
code to
open a file,
corresponding to
Figure 7.33(a).
(b) Object-
oriented code
to open a file,
corresponding
to Figure 7.33(b).

```
switch (file_type)
{
    case 1:
        open_disk_file ( );          // file_type 1 corresponds to a disk file
        break;
    case 2:
        open_tape_file ( );          // file_type 2 corresponds to a tape file
        break;
    case 3:
        open_diskette_file ( );      // file_type 3 corresponds to a diskette file
        break;
}
```

(a)

```
myFile.open ( );
```

(b)

is sent. The object-oriented system now determines whether myFile is a disk file, a tape file, or a diskette file and invokes the appropriate version of open. That is, the system determines at run time whether object myFile is an instance of **Disk File Class**, **Tape File Class**, or **Diskette File Class** and automatically invokes the correct method. Because this has to be done at run time (dynamically) and not at compile time (statically), the act of connecting an object to the appropriate method is termed ***dynamic binding***. Furthermore, because the method open can be applied to objects of different classes, it is termed ***polymorphic***, which means "of many shapes." Just as carbon crystals come in many different shapes, including hard diamonds and soft graphite, so the method open comes in three different versions. In Java, these versions are denoted DiskFileClass.open, TapeFileClass.open, and DisketteFileClass.open. (In C++, the period is replaced by two colons, and the methods are denoted DiskFileClass::open, TapeFileClass::open, and DisketteFileClass::open.) However, because of dynamic binding, it is not necessary to determine which method to invoke to open a specific file. Instead, at run time, it is necessary to send only the message myFile.open ( ) and the system will determine the type (class) of myFile and invoke the correct method; this is shown in Figure 7.34(b).

These ideas are applicable to more than just **abstract (virtual)** methods. Consider a hierarchy of classes, as shown in Figure 7.35. All classes are derived by inheritance from the **Base** class. Suppose method checkOrder (b : **Base**) takes as an argument an instance of class **Base**. Then, as a consequence of inheritance, polymorphism, and dynamic binding, it is valid to invoke checkOrder with an argument not just of class **Base** but also of any subclass of class **Base**, that is, any class derived from **Base**. All that is needed is to invoke checkOrder and everything is taken care of at run time. This technique is extremely powerful, in that the software engineer need not be concerned about the precise type of an argument at the time that a message is sent.

However, polymorphism and dynamic binding also have major weaknesses.

Figure 7.35
A hierarchy
of classes

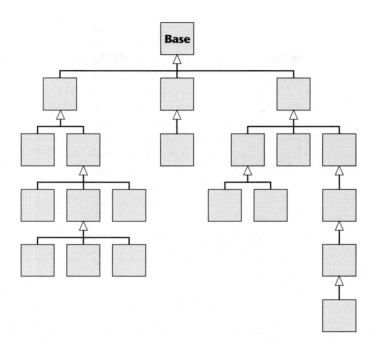

1. It generally is not possible to determine at compilation time which version of a specific polymorphic method will be invoked at run time. Accordingly, the cause of a failure can be extremely difficult to determine.

2. Polymorphism and dynamic binding can have a negative impact on maintenance. The first task of a maintenance programmer usually is to try to understand the product (as explained in Chapter 14, the maintainer rarely is the person who developed that code). However, this can be laborious if there are multiple possibilities for a specific method. The programmer has to consider all the possible methods that could be invoked dynamically at a specific place in the code, a time-consuming task.

In other words, polymorphism and dynamic binding add both strengths and weaknesses to the object-oriented paradigm.

We conclude this chapter with a discussion of the object-oriented paradigm.

7.9   The Object-Oriented Paradigm

There are two ways of looking at every software product. One way is to consider just the data, including local and global variables, arguments, dynamic data structures, and files. Another way of viewing a product is to consider just the operations performed on the data, that is, the procedures and the functions. In terms of this division of software into data and operations, the classical techniques essentially fall into two groups. Operation-oriented techniques primarily consider the operations of the product. The data are of secondary importance, considered only after the operations of the product have been analyzed in depth. Conversely, data-oriented techniques stress the data of the product; the operations are examined only within the framework of the data.

A fundamental weakness of both the data- and operation-oriented approaches is that data and operation are two sides of the same coin; a data item cannot change unless an operation is performed on it, and operations without associated data are equally meaningless. Therefore, techniques that give equal weight to data and operations are needed. It should not come as a surprise that the object-oriented techniques do this. After all, an object comprises both data and operations. Recall that an object is an instance of an abstract data type (more precisely, of a class). It therefore incorporates both data and the operations performed on those data, and the data and the operations are present in objects as equal partners. Similarly, in all the object-oriented techniques, data and operations are considered of the same importance; neither takes precedence over the other.

It is inaccurate to claim that data and operations are considered simultaneously in the techniques of the object-oriented paradigm. From the material on stepwise refinement (Section 5.1), it is clear that sometimes data have to be stressed and other times operations are more critical. Overall, however, data and operations are given equal importance during the workflows of the object-oriented paradigm.

Many reasons are given in Chapter 1 and this chapter as to why the object-oriented paradigm is superior to the classical paradigm. Underlying all these reasons is that a well-designed object, that is, an object with high cohesion and low coupling, models all the aspects of one physical entity. That is, there is a clear mapping between a real-world entity and the object that models it.

The details of how this is implemented are hidden; the only communication with an object is via messages sent to that object. As a result, objects essentially are independent units with a well-defined interface. Consequently, they can be maintained easily and safely; the chance of a regression fault is reduced. Furthermore, as will be explained in Chapter 8, objects are reusable, and this reusability is enhanced by the property of inheritance. Turning now to development using objects, it is safer to construct a large-scale product by combining these fundamental building blocks of software than to use the classical paradigm. Because objects essentially are independent components of a product, development of the product, as well as management of that development, is easier and hence less likely to induce faults.

All these aspects of the superiority of the object-oriented paradigm raise a question: If the classical paradigm is so inferior to the object-oriented paradigm, why has the classical paradigm had so much success? This can be explained by realizing that the classical paradigm was adopted at a time when software engineering was not widely practiced. Instead, software was simply "written." For managers, the most important thing was for programmers to churn out lines of code. Little more than lip service was paid to the requirements and analysis (*systems analysis*) of a product, and design was almost never performed. The code-and-fix model (Section 2.9.1) was typical of the techniques of the 1970s. Therefore, use of the classical paradigm exposed the majority of software developers to methodical techniques for the first time. Small wonder, then, that the so-called structured techniques of the classical paradigm led to major improvements in the software industry worldwide. However, as software products grew in size, inadequacies of the structured techniques started to become apparent, and the object-oriented paradigm was proposed as a better alternative.

This, in turn, leads to another question: How do we know for certain that the object-oriented paradigm is superior to all other present-day techniques? No data are available that prove beyond all doubt that object-oriented technology is better than anything else currently available, and it is hard to imagine how such data could be obtained. The best we can do is to rely on the experiences of organizations that have adopted the object-oriented paradigm. Although not all reports are favorable, the majority (if not the overwhelming majority) attest that using the object-oriented paradigm is a wise decision.

For example, IBM has reported on three totally different projects that were developed using object-oriented technology [Capper, Colgate, Hunter, and James, 1994]. In almost every respect, the object-oriented paradigm greatly outperformed the classical paradigm. Specifically, there were major decreases in the number of faults detected, far fewer change requests during both development and postdelivery maintenance that were not the result of unforeseeable business changes, and significant increases in both adaptive and perfective maintainability. Also improvement in usability was found, although not as large as the previous four improvements, and no meaningful difference in performance.

A survey of 150 experienced U.S. software developers was undertaken to determine their attitudes toward the object-oriented paradigm [Johnson, 2000]. The sample consisted of 96 developers who used the object-oriented paradigm and 54 who still used the classical paradigm to develop software. Both groups felt that the object-oriented paradigm is superior, although the positive attitude of the object-oriented group was significantly stronger. Both groups essentially discounted the various weaknesses of the object-oriented paradigm.

Notwithstanding the many strengths of the object-oriented paradigm, some difficulties and problems indeed have been reported. A frequently reported problem concerns development effort and size. The first time anything new is done, it takes longer than on subsequent occasions; this initial period is sometimes referred to as the ***learning curve***. But when the object-oriented paradigm is used for the first time by an organization, it often takes longer than anticipated, even allowing for the learning curve, because the size of the product is larger than when structured techniques are used. This is particularly noticeable when the product has a graphical user interface (GUI) (see Section 10.14). Thereafter, things improve greatly. First, postdelivery maintenance costs are lower, reducing the overall lifetime cost of the product. Second, the next time that a new product is developed, some of the classes from the previous project can often be reused, further reducing software costs. This has been especially significant when a GUI has been used for the first time; much of the effort that went into the GUI can be recouped in subsequent products.

Problems of inheritance are harder to solve.

1. A major reason for using inheritance is to create a new subclass that differs slightly from its parent class without affecting the parent class or any other ancestor class in the inheritance hierarchy. Conversely, however, once a product has been implemented, any change to an existing class directly affects all its descendants in the inheritance hierarchy; this often is referred to as the ***fragile base class problem***. At the very least, the affected units have to be recompiled. In some cases, the methods of the relevant objects (instantiations of the affected subclasses) have to be recoded; this can be a nontrivial task. To minimize this problem, it is important that all classes be meticulously designed during the

development process. This will reduce the ripple effect induced by a change to an existing class.

2. A second problem can result from a cavalier use of inheritance. Unless explicitly prevented, a subclass inherits all the attributes of its parent class(es). Usually, subclasses have additional attributes of their own. As a consequence, objects lower in the inheritance hierarchy quickly can get large, with resulting storage problems [Bruegge, Blythe, Jackson, and Shufelt, 1992]. One way to prevent this is to change the dictum "use inheritance wherever possible" to "use inheritance wherever appropriate." In addition, if a descendent class does not need an attribute of an ancestor, then that attribute should be explicitly excluded.

3. A third group of problems stem from polymorphism and dynamic binding. These were described in Section 7.8.

4. Fourth, it is possible to write bad code in any language. However, it is easier to write bad code in an object-oriented language than in a classical language because object-oriented languages support a variety of constructs that, when misused, add unnecessary complexity to a software product. Therefore, when using the object-oriented paradigm, extra care needs to be taken to ensure that the code is always of the highest quality.

One final question is this: Someday might there be something better than the object-oriented paradigm? That is, in the future will a new technology appear in the space above the topmost arrow in Figure 7.28? Even its strongest proponents do not claim that the object-oriented paradigm is the ultimate answer to all software engineering problems. Furthermore, today's software engineers are looking beyond objects to the next major breakthrough. After all, in few fields of human endeavor are the discoveries of the past superior to anything that is being put forward today. The object-oriented paradigm is sure to be superseded by the methodologies of the future. It has been suggested that **aspect-oriented programming (AOP)** may play a role [Murphy et al., 2001]. It remains to be seen whether AOP will indeed be the next major concept in future versions of Figure 7.28 or whether some other technology will be widely adopted as the successor to the object-oriented paradigm. The important lesson is that, based on today's knowledge, the object-oriented paradigm appears to be better than the alternatives.

Chapter Review

The chapter begins with a description of a module (Section 7.1); both objects and methods are modules. The next two sections analyze what constitutes a well-designed module in terms of module cohesion and module coupling (Sections 7.2 and 7.3). Specifically, a module should have high cohesion and low coupling. A description is given of the different types of cohesion and coupling. Various types of abstraction are presented in Sections 7.4 through 7.7. In data encapsulation (Section 7.4), a module comprises a data *structure* and the actions performed on that data structure. An abstract data type (Section 7.5) is a data *type*, together with the actions performed on instances of that type. Information hiding (Section 7.6) consists of designing a module in such a way that implementation details are hidden from other modules. The progression of increasing abstraction culminates in the description of a class, an abstract data type that supports inheritance (Section 7.7). An object is an instance of a class. Inheritance, polymorphism, and dynamic binding are the subjects of Section 7.8. The chapter concludes with a discussion of the object-oriented paradigm (Section 7.9).

For Further Reading

Objects were first described in [Dahl and Nygaard, 1966]. Many of the ideas in this chapter originally were put forward by Parnas [1971, 1972a, 1972b]. The use of abstract data types in software development was put forward in [Liskov and Zilles, 1974]; another important early paper is [Guttag, 1977].

The primary source on cohesion and coupling is [Stevens, Myers, and Constantine, 1974]. The ideas of composite/structured design have been extended to objects [Binkley and Schach, 1997].

Introductory material on objects can be found in [Meyer, 1997]. Different types of inheritance are described in [Meyer, 1996b]. A number of short articles on the object-oriented paradigm can be found in [El-Rewini et al., 1995]. The proceedings of the annual Conference on Object-Oriented Programming Systems, Languages, and Applications (OOPSLA) include a wide selection of research papers as well as reports describing successful object-oriented projects. The successful use of the object-oriented paradigm in three IBM projects is described in [Capper, Colgate, Hunter, and James, 1994]. A survey of attitudes toward the object-oriented paradigm appears in [Johnson, 2000]. Fayad, Tsai, and Fulghum [1996] describe how to make the transition to object-oriented technology; a number of recommendations for managers are included.

The October 1992 issue of *IEEE Computer* contains a number of important articles on objects, especially [Meyer, 1992], which describes "design by contract." A variety of articles on objects can be found in the January 1993 issue of *IEEE Software*; the paper by Snyder [1993] precisely defining key terms in the field is particularly useful. Possible drawbacks of polymorphism are described in [Ponder and Bush, 1994]. The October 1995 issue of the *Communications of the ACM* contains articles on object technology, as does issue no. 2, 2006, of the *IBM Systems Journal*.

Eleven articles on aspect-oriented programming appear in the October 2001 issue of the *Communications of the ACM*; [Elrad et al., 2001] and [Murphy et al., 2001] are of particular interest. Weaknesses of aspect-oriented programming are discussed in [R. Alexander, 2003].

An investigation of the impact of inheritance on fault densities appears in [Cartwright and Shepperd, 2000].

Key Terms

abstract data type 197	coupling 176	learning curve 209
abstraction 191	data abstraction 192	logic 176
aggregation 203	data coupling 186	logical cohesion 178
aspect-oriented programming (AOP) 210	data encapsulation 191	module 174
association 203	dynamic binding 206	navigation triangle 204
binding 176	encapsulation 192	note 202
class 201	flowchart cohesion 180	object 201
cohesion 176	fragile base class problem 209	operation 176
coincidental cohesion 177	functional cohesion 180	polymorphism 206
common coupling 183	generalization 203	procedural abstraction 192
communicational cohesion 179	information hiding 199	procedural cohesion 179
content coupling 182	informational cohesion 180	specialization 203
context 176	inheritance 201	stamp coupling 185
control coupling 185	*isA* 202	strength 176
		subclass 202
		temporal cohesion 178

Problems

7.1   Determine the cohesion of the following methods:

editProfitAndTaxRecord

editProfitRecordAndTaxRecord

readDeliveryRecordAndCheckSalaryPayments

computeTheOptimalCostUsingAksen'sAlgorithm

measureVaporPressureAndSoundAlarmIfNecessary

7.2   You are a software engineer involved in product development. Your manager asks you to investigate ways of ensuring that modules designed by your group will be as reusable as possible. What do you tell her?

7.3   Your manager now asks you to determine how existing modules can be reused. Your first suggestion is to break each module with coincidental cohesion into separate modules with functional cohesion. Your manager correctly points out that the separate modules have not been tested nor have they been documented. What do you say now?

7.4   What is the influence of cohesion on maintenance?

7.5   What is the influence of coupling on maintenance?

7.6   Distinguish between data encapsulation and abstract data types.

7.7   Distinguish between abstraction and information hiding.

7.8   Distinguish between polymorphism and dynamic binding.

7.9   What happens if we use polymorphism without dynamic binding?

7.10 What happens if we use dynamic binding without polymorphism?

7.11 Convert the comments in Figure 7.23 to C++ or Java, as specified by your instructor. Make sure that the resulting module executes correctly.

7.12 It has been suggested that C++ and Java support implementation of abstract data types but only at the cost of giving up information hiding. Discuss this claim.

7.13 As pointed out in Just in Case You Wanted to Know Box 7.1, objects first were put forward in 1966. Only after essentially being reinvented nearly 20 years later did objects begin to receive widespread acceptance. Can you explain this phenomenon?

7.14 Your instructor will distribute a software product. Analyze the modules (objects and methods) from the viewpoints of information hiding, levels of abstraction, coupling, and cohesion.

7.15 What are the strengths and weaknesses of inheritance?

7.16 (Term Project) Give examples of classes that you would expect to find in Osric's Office Appliances and Decor product of Appendix A.

7.17 (Readings in Software Engineering) Your instructor will distribute copies of [R. Alexander, 2003]. Do you think that aspect-oriented programming will be the next major concept in future versions of Figure 7.28? Justify your answer.

References

[R. Alexander, 2003] R. ALEXANDER, "The Real Costs of Aspect-Oriented Programming," *IEEE Software* **20** (November/December 2003), pp. 92–93.

[Binkley and Schach, 1997] A. B. BINKLEY AND S. R. SCHACH, "Toward a Unified Approach to Object-Oriented Coupling," *Proceedings of the 35th Annual ACM Southeast Conference*, Murfreesboro, TN, April 2–4, 1997, pp. 91–97.

[Blaha, Premerlani, and Rumbaugh, 1988] M. R. BLAHA, W. J. PREMERLANI, AND J. E. RUMBAUGH, "Relational Database Design Using an Object-Oriented Methodology," *Communications of the ACM* **31** (April 1988), pp. 414–27.

[Briand, Daly, Porter, and Wüst, 1998] L. C. BRIAND, J. DALY, V. PORTER, AND J. WÜST, "A Comprehensive Empirical Validation of Design Measures for Object-Oriented Systems," *Proceedings of the Fifth International Metrics Symposium*, Bethesda, MD, November 1998, pp. 246–57.

[Bruegge, Blythe, Jackson, and Shufelt, 1992] B. BRUEGGE, J. BLYTHE, J. JACKSON, AND J. SHUFELT, "Object-Oriented Modeling with OMT," Proceedings of the Conference on Object-Oriented Programming, Languages, and Systems, OOPSLA '92, *ACM SIGPLAN Notices* **27** (October 1992), pp. 359–76.

[Capper, Colgate, Hunter, and James, 1994] N. P. CAPPER, R. J. COLGATE, J. C. HUNTER, AND M. F. JAMES, "The Impact of Object-Oriented Technology on Software Quality: Three Case Histories," *IBM Systems Journal* **33** (No. 1, 1994), pp. 131–57.

[Cartwright and Shepperd, 2000] M. CARTWRIGHT AND M. SHEPPERD, "An Empirical Investigation of an Object-Oriented Software System," *IEEE Transactions on Software Engineering* **26** (August 2000), pp. 786–95.

[Dahl and Nygaard, 1966] O.-J. DAHL AND K. NYGAARD, "SIMULA—An ALGOL-Based Simulation Language," *Communications of the ACM* **9** (September 1966), pp. 671–78.

[Elrad et al., 2001] T. ELRAD, M. AKSIT, G. KICZALES, K. LIEBERHERR, AND H. OSSHER, "Discussing Aspects of AOP," *Communications of the ACM* **44** (October 2001), pp. 33–38.

[El-Rewini et al., 1995] H. EL-REWINI, S. HAMILTON, Y.-P. SHAN, R. EARLE, S. MCGAUGHEY, A. HELAL, R. BADRACHALAM, A. CHIEN, A. GRIMSHAW, B. LEE, A. WADE, D. MORSE, A. ELMAGRAMID, E. PITOURA, R. BINDER, AND P. WEGNER, "Object Technology," *IEEE Computer* **28** (October 1995), pp. 58–72.

[Fayad, Tsai, and Fulghum, 1996] M. E. FAYAD, W.-T. TSAI, AND M. L. FULGHUM, "Transition to Object-Oriented Software Development," *Communications of the ACM* **39** (February 1996), pp. 108–21.

[Flanagan, 2005] D. FLANAGAN, *Java in a Nutshell: A Desktop Quick Reference*, 5th ed., O'Reilly and Associates, Sebastopol, CA, 2005.

[Gerald and Wheatley, 1999] C. F. GERALD AND P. O. WHEATLEY, *Applied Numerical Analysis*, 6th ed., Addison-Wesley, Reading, MA, 1999.

[Goldberg and Robson, 1989] A. GOLDBERG AND D. ROBSON, *Smalltalk-80: The Language*, Addison-Wesley, Reading, MA, 1989.

[Guttag, 1977] J. GUTTAG, "Abstract Data Types and the Development of Data Structures," *Communications of the ACM* **20** (June 1977), pp. 396–404.

[ISO/IEC 8652, 1995] *Programming Language Ada: Language and Standard Libraries*, ISO/IEC 8652, International Organization for Standardization, International Electrotechnical Commission, Geneva, 1995.

[Johnson, 2000] R. A. JOHNSON, "The Ups and Downs of Object-Oriented System Development," *Communications of the ACM* **43** (October 2000), pp. 69–73.

[Knuth, 1974] D. E. KNUTH, "Structured Programming with **go to** Statements," *ACM Computing Surveys* **6** (December 1974), pp. 261–301.

[Liskov and Zilles, 1974] B. LISKOV AND S. ZILLES, "Programming with Abstract Data Types," *ACM SIGPLAN Notices* **9** (April 1974), pp. 50–59.

[Meyer, 1986] B. MEYER, "Genericity versus Inheritance," Proceedings of the Conference on Object-Oriented Programming Systems, Languages and Applications, *ACM SIGPLAN Notices* **21** (November 1986), pp. 391–405.

[Meyer, 1992] B. MEYER, "Applying 'Design by Contract'," *IEEE Computer* **25** (October 1992), pp. 40–51.

[Meyer, 1996b] B. MEYER, "The Many Faces of Inheritance: A Taxonomy of Taxonomy," *IEEE Computer* **29** (May 1996), pp. 105–8.

[Meyer, 1997] B. MEYER, *Object-Oriented Software Construction*, 2nd ed., Prentice Hall, Upper Saddle River, NJ, 1997.

[Murphy et al., 2001] G. C. MURPHY, R. J. WALKER, E. L. A. BANNIASSAD, M. P. ROBILLARD, A. LIA, AND M. A. KERSTEN, "Does Aspect-Oriented Programming Work?" *Communications of the ACM* **44** (October 2001), pp. 75–78.

[Myers, 1978b] G. J. MYERS, *Composite/Structured Design*, Van Nostrand Reinhold, New York, 1978.

[Parnas, 1971] D. L. PARNAS, "Information Distribution Aspects of Design Methodology," *Proceedings of the IFIP Congress*, Ljubljana, Yugoslavia, 1971, pp. 339–44.

[Parnas, 1972a] D. L. PARNAS, "A Technique for Software Module Specification with Examples," *Communications of the ACM* **15** (May 1972), pp. 330–36.

[Parnas, 1972b] D. L. PARNAS, "On the Criteria to Be Used in Decomposing Systems into Modules," *Communications of the ACM* **15** (December 1972), pp. 1053–58.

[Ponder and Bush, 1994] C. PONDER AND B. BUSH, "Polymorphism Considered Harmful," *ACM SIGSOFT Software Engineering Notes* **19** (April, 1994), pp. 35–38.

[Schach and Stevens-Guille, 1979] S. R. SCHACH AND P. D. STEVENS-GUILLE, "Two Aspects of Computer-Aided Design," *Transactions of the Royal Society of South Africa* **44** (Part 1, 1979), 123–26.

[Schach et al., 2002] S. R. SCHACH, B. JIN, D. R. WRIGHT, G. Z. HELLER, AND A. J. OFFUTT, "Maintainability of the Linux Kernel," *IEE Proceedings—Software* **149** (February 2002), pp. 18–23.

[Schach et al., 2003a] S. R. SCHACH, B. JIN, DAVID R. WRIGHT, G. Z. HELLER, AND J. OFFUTT, "Quality Impacts of Clandestine Common Coupling," *Software Quality Journal* **11** (July 2003), pp. 211–18.

[Shneiderman and Mayer, 1975] B. SHNEIDERMAN AND R. MAYER, "Towards a Cognitive Model of Programmer Behavior," Technical Report TR-37, Indiana University, Bloomington, 1975.

[Snyder, 1993] A. SNYDER, "The Essence of Objects: Concepts and Terms," *IEEE Software* **10** (January 1993), pp. 31–42.

[Stevens, Myers, and Constantine, 1974] W. P. STEVENS, G. J. MYERS, AND L. L. CONSTANTINE, "Structured Design," *IBM Systems Journal* **13** (No. 2, 1974), pp. 115–39.

[Stroustrup, 2003] B. STROUSTRUP, *The C++ Standard: Incorporating Technical Corrigendum No. 1*, 2nd ed., John Wiley and Sons, New York, 2003.

[Yourdon and Constantine, 1979] E. YOURDON AND L. L. CONSTANTINE, *Structured Design: Fundamentals of a Discipline of Computer Program and Systems Design*, Prentice Hall, Englewood Cliffs, NJ, 1979.

[Yu, Schach, Chen, and Offutt, 2004] L. YU, S. R. SCHACH, K. CHEN, AND J. OFFUTT, "Categorization of Common Coupling and its Application to the Maintainability of the Linux Kernel," *IEEE Transactions on Software Engineering* **30** (October 2004), pp. 694–706.

Chapter

8

Reusability and Portability

Learning Objectives

After studying this chapter, you should be able to

- Explain why reuse is so important.
- Appreciate the obstacles to reuse.
- Describe techniques for achieving reuse during the various workflows.
- Appreciate the importance of design patterns.
- Discuss the impact of reuse on maintainability.
- Explain why portability is essential.
- Understand the obstacles to achieving portability.
- Develop portable software.

If reinventing the wheel were a criminal offense, many software professionals would today be languishing in jail. For example, there are tens of thousands (if not hundreds of thousands) of different COBOL payroll programs, all doing essentially the same thing. Surely, the world needs just one payroll program that can run on a variety of hardware and be tailored, if necessary, to cater to the specific needs of an individual organization. However, instead of utilizing previously developed payroll programs, myriad organizations all over the world have built their own payroll program from scratch. In this chapter, we investigate why software engineers delight in continually reinventing the wheel, and what can be done to achieve portable software built using reusable components. We begin by distinguishing between portability and reusability.

As explained in the Preface, the material of this chapter may be taught in parallel with that of Part 2

Reuse is not restricted to software. For example, lawyers nowadays rarely draft wills from scratch. Instead, they use a word processor to store wills they have previously drafted, and then make appropriate changes to an existing will. Other legal documents, like contracts, are usually drafted in the same way from existing documents.

Classical composers frequently reused their own music. For example, in 1823 Franz Schubert wrote an entr'acte for Helmina von Chezy's play, *Rosamunde, Fürstin von Zypern (Rosamunde, Princess of Cyprus)* and the following year he reused that material in the slow movement of his String Quartet No. 13. Ludwig van Beethoven's Opus 66, "Variations for Cello on Mozart's *Ein Mädchen oder Weibchen*," is a good example of one great composer reusing the music of another great composer; Beethoven simply took the aria "A Girlfriend or Little Wife" from Scene 22 of Wolfgang Amadeus Mozart's opera *Der Zauberflöte (The Magic Flute)* and wrote a series of seven variations on that aria for the cello with piano accompaniment.

In my opinion, the greatest reuser of all time was William Shakespeare. His genius lay in reusing the plots of others—I cannot think of a single story line he made up himself. For example, his historical plays heavily reused parts of Raphael Holinshed's 1577 work, *Chronicles of England, Scotland and Ireland*. Then, Shakespeare's *Romeo and Juliet* (1594) is borrowed, on an almost line-for-line basis, from Arthur Brooke's lengthy poem *The Tragicall Historye of Romeus and Iuliet* published in 1562, two years before Shakespeare was born.

But this reuse saga didn't begin there. In fact, the earliest known version appeared around 200 CE in *Ephesiaka (Ephesian Tale)* by the Greek novelist Xenophon of Ephesus. In 1476, Tommaso Guardati (more commonly known as Masuccio Salernitano) reused Xenophon's tale in novella 33 in his collection of 50 novellas, *Il Novellino*. In 1530, Luigi da Porto reused that story in *Historia Novellamente Ritrovata di Due Nobili Amanti (A Newly Found Story of Two Noble Lovers)*, for the first time setting it in Verona, Italy. Brooke's poem reuses parts of *Giulietta e Romeo* (1554) by Matteo Bandello, a reuse of da Porto's version.

And this reuse saga didn't end with *Romeo and Juliet*, either. In 1957, *West Side Story* opened on Broadway. The musical, with book by Arthur Laurents, lyrics by Stephen Sondheim, and score by Leonard Bernstein, reused Shakespeare's version of the story. The Broadway musical was then reused in a Hollywood movie, which won 10 Academy Awards in 1961.

8.1   Reuse Concepts

A product is **portable** if it is significantly easier to modify the product as a whole to run it on another compiler–hardware–operating system configuration than to recode it from scratch. In contrast, **reuse** refers to using components of one product to facilitate the development of a different product with a different functionality. A reusable component need not necessarily be a module or a code fragment—it could be a design, a part of a manual, a set of test data, or a duration and cost estimate. (For a different view on reuse, see Just in Case You Wanted to Know Box 8.1.)

There are two types of reuse, opportunistic reuse and deliberate reuse. If the developers of a new product realize that a component of a previously developed product can be reused in the new product, then this is **opportunistic reuse**, sometimes referred to as **accidental reuse**. On the other hand, utilization of software components constructed specifically for possible future reuse is **systematic reuse** or **deliberate reuse**. A potential advantage of systematic reuse over opportunistic reuse is that artifacts specially constructed for use in future products are more likely to be easy and safe to reuse; such artifacts generally are robust, well documented, and thoroughly tested. In addition, they usually display a uniformity of style that makes maintenance easier. The other side of the coin is that implementing systematic reuse within a company can be expensive. It takes time to specify, design, implement, test, and document a software artifact. However, there can be no guarantee that such an artifact will be reused and thereby recoup the money invested in developing the potentially reusable artifact.

When computers were first constructed, nothing was reused. Every time a product was developed, items such as multiplication routines, input–output routines, or routines for computing sines and cosines were constructed from scratch. Quite soon, however, it was realized that this was a considerable waste of effort, and subroutine libraries were constructed. Programmers then simply could invoke square root or sine functions whenever they wished. These subroutine libraries have become more and more sophisticated and developed into run-time support routines. Therefore, when a programmer calls a C++ or Java method, there is no need to write code to manage the stack or pass the arguments explicitly; it is handled automatically by calling the appropriate run-time support routines. The concept of subroutine libraries has been extended to large-scale statistical libraries such as SPSS [Norušis, 2005] and numerical analysis libraries like NAG [2003]. Class libraries also play a major role in assisting users of object-oriented languages. For example, the success of Smalltalk is due at least partly to the wide variety of items in the Smalltalk library together with the presence of a browser, a CASE tool that assists the user to scan a class library. With regard to C++, a large number of different libraries are available, many in the public domain. One example is the C++ Standard Template Library (STL) [Musser and Saini, 1996].

An application programming interface (API) generally is a set of operating system calls that facilitate programming. For example, Win32 is an API for Microsoft operating systems such as Windows XP; and Cocoa is an API for Mac OS X, a Macintosh operating system. Although an API usually is implemented as a set of operating system calls, to the programmer the routines constituting the API can be viewed as a subroutine library. For example, the Java Application Programming Interface consists of a number of packages (libraries).

No matter how high the quality of a software product may be, it will not sell if it takes 2 years to get it onto the market when a competitive product can be delivered in only 1 year. The length of the development process is critical in a market economy. All other criteria as to what constitutes a "good" product are irrelevant if the product cannot compete timewise. For a corporation that has repeatedly failed to get a product to market first, software reuse offers a tempting technique. After all, if an existing component is reused, then there is no need to specify, design, implement, test, and document that component. The key point is that, on average, only about 15 percent of any software product serves a truly original purpose [Jones, 1984]. The other 85 percent of the product in theory could be standardized and reused in future products.

The figure of 85 percent is essentially a theoretical upper limit for the reuse rate; nevertheless, reuse rates on the order of 40 percent can be achieved in practice. This leads to an obvious question: If such reuse rates are attainable in practice and reuse is by no means a new idea, why do so few organizations employ reuse to shorten the development process?

8.2 Impediments to Reuse

There are a number of impediments to reuse:

- All too many software professionals would rather rewrite a component from scratch than reuse a component written by someone else, the implication being that a component cannot be any good unless they wrote it themselves, otherwise known as the ***not invented here (NIH) syndrome*** [Griss, 1993]. NIH is a management issue, and, if management is aware of the problem, it can be solved, usually by offering financial incentives to promote reuse.

- Many developers would be willing to reuse a component provided they could be sure that the component in question would not introduce faults into the product. This attitude toward software quality is perfectly easy to understand. After all, every software professional has seen faulty software written by others. The solution here is to subject potentially reusable components to exhaustive testing before making them available for reuse.

- A large organization may have hundreds of thousands of potentially useful components. How should these components be stored for effective later retrieval? For example, a reusable components database might consist of 20,000 items, 125 of which are sort routines. The database must be organized so that the designer of a new product can quickly determine which (if any) of those 125 sort routines is appropriate for the new product. Solving the storage/retrieval problem is a technical issue for which a wide variety of solutions have been proposed (e.g., [Meyer, 1987] or [Prieto-Díaz, 1991]).

- Reuse can be expensive. Tracz [1994] has stated that three costs are involved: the cost of making a component reusable, the cost of reusing a component, and the cost of defining and implementing a reuse process. He estimates that just making a component reusable increases its cost by at least 60 percent. Some organizations have reported cost increases of 200 percent and even up to 480 percent, whereas the cost of making a component reusable was only 11 percent in one Hewlett-Packard reuse project [Lim, 1994].

- Legal issues can arise with contract software. In terms of the type of contract usually drawn up between a client and a software development organization, the software product belongs to the client. Therefore, if the software developer reuses a component of one client's product in a new product for a different client, this essentially constitutes a violation of the first client's copyright. For internal software, that is, when the developers and client are members of the same organization, this problem does not arise.

- Another impediment arises when commercial off-the-shelf (COTS) components are reused. Rarely are developers given the source code of a COTS component, so software that reuses COTS components has limited extensibility and modifiability.

The first four impediments can be overcome, at least in principle. So, other than certain legal issues and problems with COTS components, essentially no major impediments prevent implementing reuse within a software organization (but see Just in Case You Wanted to Know Box 8.2).

The World Wide Web is a great source of "urban myths," that is, apparently true stories that somehow just do not stand up under scrutiny when they are investigated closely. One such urban myth concerns code reuse.

The story is told that the Australian Air Force set up a virtual reality training simulator for helicopter combat training. To make the scenarios as realistic as possible, programmers included detailed landscapes and (in the Northern Territory) herds of kangaroos. After all, the dust from a herd disturbed by a helicopter might reveal the position of that helicopter to the enemy.

The programmers were instructed to model both the movements of the kangaroos and their reaction to helicopters. To save time, the programmers reused code originally used to simulate the reaction of infantry to attack by a helicopter. Only two changes were made: They changed the icon from a soldier to a kangaroo, and they increased the speed of movement of the figures.

One fine day, a group of Australian pilots wanted to demonstrate their prowess with the flight simulator to some visiting American pilots. They "buzzed" (flew extremely low over) the virtual kangaroos. As expected, the kangaroos scattered, and then reappeared from behind a hill and launched Stinger missiles at the helicopter. The programmers had forgotten to remove that part of the code when they reused the virtual infantry implementation.

However, as reported in *The Risks Digest*, it appears that the story is not totally an urban myth—much of it actually happened [Green, 2000]. Dr. Anne-Marie Grisogono, head of the Simulation Land Operations Division at the Australian Defence Science and Technology Organisation, told the story at a meeting in Canberra, Australia, on May 6, 1999. Although the simulator was designed to be as realistic as possible (it even included over 2 million virtual trees, as indicated on aerial photographs), the kangaroos were included for fun. The programmers indeed reused Stinger missile detachments so that the kangaroos could detect the arrival of helicopters, but the behavior of the kangaroos was set to "retreat" so that the kangaroos, correctly, would flee if a helicopter approached. However, when the software team tested their simulator in their laboratory (not in front of visitors), they discovered that they had forgotten to remove both the weapons and "fire" behavior. Also, they had not specified what weapons were to be used by the simulated figures, so when the kangaroos fired on the helicopters, they fired the default weapon, which happened to be large multicolored beachballs.

Grisogono confirmed that the kangaroos were immediately disarmed and therefore it is now safe to fly over Australia. But notwithstanding this happy ending, software professionals still must take care when reusing code not to reuse too much of it.

8.3   Reuse Case Studies

Many published case studies show how reuse has been successfully achieved in practice; reuse case studies that have had a major impact include [Matsumoto, 1984, 1987; Selby, 1989; Prieto-Díaz, 1991; and Lim, 1994]. Here, we analyze two case studies. The first, which describes a reuse project that took place between 1976 and 1982, is important because the reuse mechanism used then for COBOL designs is the same as the reuse mechanism used today in object-oriented application frameworks (Section 8.5.2). This case study therefore serves to clarify modern reuse practices.

8.3.1   Raytheon Missile Systems Division

In 1976, a study was undertaken at Raytheon's Missile Systems Division to determine whether systematic reuse of designs and code was feasible [Lanergan and Grasso, 1984]. Over 5000 COBOL products in use were analyzed and classified. The researchers determined that only six basic operations are performed in a business application product. As a result, between 40 and 60 percent of business application designs and modules could be standardized and reused. The basic operations were found to be sort data, edit or manipulate data, combine data, explode data, update data, and report on data. For the next 6 years, a concerted attempt was made to reuse both design and code wherever possible.

The Raytheon approach employed reuse in two ways, what the researchers termed *functional modules* and *COBOL program logic structures*. In Raytheon's terminology a **functional module** is a COBOL code fragment designed and coded for a specific purpose, such as an edit routine, database procedure division call, tax computation routine, or date aging routine for accounts receivable. Use of the 3200 reusable modules resulted in applications that, on average, consisted of 60 percent reused code. Functional modules were carefully designed, tested, and documented. Products that used these functional modules were found to be more reliable, and less testing of the product as a whole was needed.

The modules were stored in a standard copy library and obtained with the **copy** verb. That is, the code was not physically present within the application product but was included by the COBOL compiler at compilation time, a mechanism similar to #**include** in C++. The resulting source code therefore was shorter than if the copied code were physically present. As a consequence, maintenance was easier.

The Raytheon researchers also used what they termed a **COBOL program logic structure**. This is a framework that has to be fleshed out into a complete product. One example of a logic structure is the update logic structure. This is used to perform a sequential update, such as the mini case study in Section 5.1.1. Error handling is built in, as is sequence checking. The logic structure is 22 paragraphs (units of a COBOL program) in length. Many of the paragraphs can be filled in by using functional modules such as get-transaction, print-page-headings, and print-control-totals. Figure 8.1 is a symbolic depiction of the framework of a COBOL program logic structure with the paragraphs filled in by functional modules.

Figure 8.1
A symbolic representation of the Raytheon Missile Systems Division reuse mechanism.

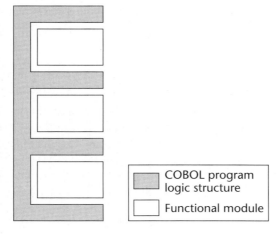

COBOL program logic structure

Functional module

The use of such templates has many advantages. It makes the design and coding of a product quicker and easier, because the framework of the product already is present; all that is needed is to fill in the details. Fault-prone areas such as end-of-file conditions already have been tested. In fact, testing as a whole is easier. But Raytheon believed that the major advantage would occur when the users requested modifications or enhancements. Once a maintenance programmer was familiar with the relevant logic structure, it was almost as if he or she had been a member of the original development team.

By 1983, logic structures had been used over 5500 times in developing new products. About 60 percent of the code consisted of functional modules, that is, reusable code. This meant that design, coding, module testing, and documentation time also was reduced by 60 percent, leading to an estimated 50 percent increase in productivity in software product development. But, for Raytheon, the real benefit of the technique lay in the hope that the readability and understandability resulting from the consistent style would reduce the cost of maintenance by between 60 and 80 percent. Unfortunately, Raytheon closed the division before the necessary maintenance data could be obtained.

The second reuse case study is a cautionary tale, rather than a success story.

8.3.2   European Space Agency

On June 4, 1996, the European Space Agency launched the Ariane 5 rocket for the first time. As a consequence of a software fault, the rocket crashed about 37 seconds after liftoff. The cost of the rocket and payload was about \$500 million [Jézéquel and Meyer, 1997].

The primary cause of the failure was an attempt to convert a 64-bit integer into a 16-bit unsigned integer. The number being converted was larger than 2^{16}, so an Ada **exception** (run-time failure) occurred. Unfortunately, there was no explicit exception handler in the code to deal with this exception, so the software crashed. This caused the onboard computers to crash which, in turn, caused the Ariane 5 rocket to crash.

Ironically, the conversion that caused the failure was unnecessary. Certain computations are performed before liftoff to align the inertial reference system. These computations should stop 9 seconds before liftoff. However, if there is a subsequent hold in the countdown, resetting the inertial reference system after the countdown has recommenced can take several hours. To prevent that happening, the computations continue for 50 seconds after the start of flight mode, that is, well into the flight (notwithstanding that, once liftoff has occurred, there is no way to align the inertial reference system). This futile continuation of the alignment process caused the failure.

The European Space Agency uses a careful software development process that incorporates an effective software quality assurance component. Then, why was there no exception handler in the Ada code to handle the possibility of such an overflow? To prevent overloading the computer, conversions that could not possibly result in overflow were left unprotected. The code in question was 10 years old. It had been reused, unchanged and without any further testing, from the software controlling the Ariane 4 rocket (the precursor of the Ariane 5). Mathematical analysis had proven that the computation in question was totally safe for the Ariane 4. However, the analysis was performed on the basis of certain assumptions that were true for the Ariane 4 but not for the Ariane 5. Therefore, the analysis no longer was valid, and the code needed the protection of an exception handler to cater to the possibility of an overflow. Were it not for the performance constraint, there surely would have been exception handlers throughout the Ariane 5 Ada code. Alternatively, the use of the **assert pragma** both during testing and after the product had been installed (Section 6.5.3) could have prevented the Ariane 5 crash if the relevant module had included an assertion that the number to be converted was smaller than 2^{16} [Jézéquel and Meyer, 1997].

The major lesson of this reuse experience is that software developed in one context must be retested when reused in another context. That is, a reused software module does not need to be retested by itself, but it must be retested after it has been integrated into the product in which it is reused. Another lesson is that it is unwise to rely exclusively on the results of mathematical proofs, as discussed in Section 6.5.2.

We now examine the impact of the object-oriented paradigm on reuse.

8.4 Objects and Reuse

When the theory of composite/structured design first was put forward about 30 years ago, the claim was made that an ideal module has functional cohesion (Section 7.2.6). That is, if a module performed only one operation, it was thought to be an exemplary candidate for reuse, and maintenance of such a module was expected to be easy. The flaw in this reasoning is that a module with functional cohesion is not self-contained and independent. Instead, it has to operate on data. If such a module is reused, then the data on which it is to operate must be reused, too. If the data in the new product are not identical to those in the original, then either the data have to be changed or the module with functional cohesion has to be changed. Therefore, contrary to what we used to believe, functional cohesion is not ideal for reuse.

According to C/SD as originally put forward in 1974, the next best type of module is one with informational cohesion (Section 7.2.7). Nowadays, we appreciate that such a module essentially is an object, that is, an instance of a class. A well-designed object is the fundamental building block of software because it models all aspects of a particular real-world entity (conceptual independence, or encapsulation) but conceals the implementation of both its data and the operations that operate on the data (physical independence, or information hiding). Therefore, when the object-oriented paradigm is utilized correctly, the resulting modules (objects) have informational cohesion, and this promotes reuse.

8.5 Reuse during Design and Implementation

Dramatically different types of reuse are possible during design. The reused material can vary from just one or two artifacts to the architecture of the complete software product. We now examine various types of design reuse, some of which carry over into implementation.

8.5.1 Design Reuse

When designing a product, a member of the design team may realize that a class from an earlier design can be reused in the current project, with or without minor modifications. This type of reuse is particularly common in an organization that develops software in one specific application domain, such as banking or air traffic control systems. The organization can

Figure 8.2   A symbolic representation of four types of design reuse. Shading denotes design reuse within (a) a library or a toolkit, (b) a framework, (c) a design pattern, and (d) a software architecture comprising a framework, a toolkit, and three design patterns.

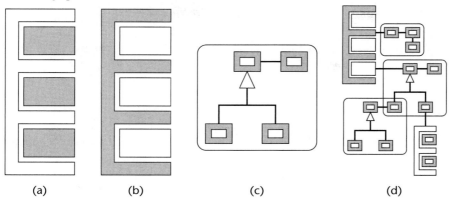

(a)   (b)   (c)   (d)

promote this type of reuse by setting up a repository of design components likely to be reused in the future and encouraging designers to reuse them, perhaps by a cash bonus for each such reuse. This type of reuse, limited though it may be, has two advantages. First, tested designs are incorporated into the product. The overall design therefore can be produced more quickly and is likely to have a higher quality than when the entire design is produced from scratch. Second, if the design of a class can be reused, then it is likely that the implementation of that class also can be reused, if not the actual code then at least conceptually.

This approach can be extended to library reuse, depicted in Figure 8.2(a). A library is a set of related reusable routines. For example, developers of scientific software rarely write the methods to perform such common tasks as matrix inversion or finding eigenvalues. Instead, a scientific class library such as LAPACK++ [2000] is purchased. Then, whenever possible, the classes in the scientific library are utilized in future software.

Another example is a library for a graphical user interface. Instead of writing the GUI methods from scratch, it is far more convenient to use a GUI class library or **toolkit**, that is, a set of classes that can handle every aspect of the GUI. Many GUI toolkits of this kind are available, including the Java Abstract Windowing Toolkit [Flanagan, 2005].

A problem with library reuse is that libraries frequently are presented in the format of a set of reusable code artifacts rather than reusable designs. Toolkits, too, generally promote code reuse rather than design reuse. This problem can be alleviated with the help of a browser, that is, a CASE tool for displaying the inheritance tree. The designer then can traverse the inheritance tree of the library, examine the fields of the various classes, and determine which class is applicable to the current design.

A key aspect of library and toolkit reuse is that, as depicted in Figure 8.2(a), the designer is responsible for the control logic of the product as a whole. The library or toolkit contributes to the software development process by supplying parts of the design that incorporate the specific operations of the product.

On the other hand, an application framework is the converse of a library or toolkit in that it supplies the control logic; the developers are responsible for the design of the specific operations. This is described in Section 8.5.2.

8.5.2   Application Frameworks

As shown in Figure 8.2(b), an ***application framework*** incorporates the control logic of a design. When a framework is reused, the developers have to design the application-specific operations of the product being built. The places where the application-specific operations are inserted frequently are referred to as ***hot spots***.

The term ***framework*** nowadays usually refers to an object-oriented application framework. For example, in [Gamma, Helm, Johnson, and Vlissides, 1995], a *framework* is defined as a "set of cooperating classes that make up a reusable design for a specific class of software." However, consider the Raytheon Missiles Systems Division case study of Section 8.3.1. Figure 8.1 is identical to Figure 8.2(b). In other words, the Raytheon COBOL program logic structure of the 1970s is a classical precursor of today's object-oriented application framework.

An example of an application framework is a set of classes for the design of a compiler. The design team merely has to provide classes specific to the language and desired target machine. These classes then are inserted into the framework, as depicted by the white boxes in Figure 8.2(b). Another example of a framework is a set of classes for the software controlling an ATM. Here, the designers need to provide the classes for the specific banking services offered by the ATMs of that banking network.

Reusing a framework results in faster product development than reusing a toolkit, for two reasons. First, more of the design is reused with a framework, so there is less to design from scratch. Second, the portion of the design that is reused with a framework (the control logic) generally is harder to design than the operations, so the quality of the resulting design also is likely to be higher than when a toolkit is reused. As with library or toolkit reuse, often the implementation of the framework can be reused as well. The developers probably have to use the names and calling conventions of the framework, but that is a small price to pay. Also, the resulting product is likely to be maintained easily because the control logic has been tested in other products that reuse the application framework and the maintainer previously may have maintained another product that reused that same framework.

IBM's WebSphere (formerly known as *e-Components*, and originally as *San Francisco*) is a framework for building online information systems in Java. It utilizes Enterprise Java-Beans, that is, classes that provide services for clients distributed throughout a network.

In addition to application frameworks, many code frameworks are available. One of the first commercially successful code frameworks was MacApp, a framework for writing application software on the Macintosh. Borland's Visual Component Library (VCL) is an object-oriented set of frameworks for building GUIs in Windows-based applications. VCL applications can perform standard windowing operations, such as moving and resizing windows, processing input via dialog boxes, and handling events like mouse clicks or menu selections.

We now consider design patterns.

8.5.3   Design Patterns

Christopher Alexander (see Just in Case You Wanted to Know Box 8.3) said, "Each pattern describes a problem which occurs over and over again in our environment, and then describes the core of the solution to that problem, in such a way that you can use this solution a million times over, without ever doing it the same way twice" [Alexander et al., 1977]. Although he was writing within the context of patterns in buildings and other architectural objects, his remarks are equally applicable to design patterns.

One of the most influential individuals in the field of object-oriented software engineering is Christopher Alexander, a world-famous architect who freely admits to knowing little or nothing about objects or software engineering. In his books, and especially in [Alexander et al., 1977], he describes a pattern language for architecture, that is, for describing towns, buildings, rooms, gardens, and so on. His ideas were adopted and adapted by object-oriented software engineers, especially the so-called Gang of Four (Erich Gamma, Richard Helm, Ralph Johnson, and John Vlissides). Their best-selling book on design patterns [Gamma, Helm, Johnson, and Vlissides, 1995] resulted in Alexander's ideas being widely accepted by the object-oriented community.

Patterns occur in other contexts as well. For example, when approaching an airport, pilots have to know the appropriate landing pattern, that is, the sequence of directions, altitudes, and turns needed to land the plane on the correct runway. Also, a dressmaking pattern is a series of shapes that can be used repeatedly to create a particular dress. The concept of a pattern itself is by no means novel. What is new is the application of patterns to software development and especially design.

A design pattern is a solution to a general design problem in the form of a set of interacting classes that have to be customized to create a specific design. This is depicted in Figure 8.2(c). The shaded boxes connected by lines denote the interacting classes. The white boxes inside the shaded boxes denote that these classes must be customized for a specific design.

To understand how patterns can assist with software development, consider the following example. Suppose that a software engineer wishes to reuse two existing classes, **P** and **Q**, say, but that their interfaces are incompatible. For example, when **P** sends a message to **Q**, it passes four parameters, but **Q**'s interface is such that it expects only three parameters. Changing the interface of **P** or **Q** would create a whole host of incompatibility problems in all the applications that currently incorporate **P** or **Q**. Instead, a class **A** needs to be constructed that accepts a message from **P** with four parameters, and sends a message to **Q** with only three parameters. (A class of this kind is sometimes called a ***wrapper***.)

What we have described is a specific solution to a more general problem, namely, enabling any two incompatible classes to work together. Instead of designing this one solution, we need a design pattern, the *Adapter* pattern. Just as an instance of a class is an object, an instance of the *Adapter* pattern is a solution to the incompatibility problem tailored to the two classes involved. This pattern is described in more detail in Section 8.6.

Patterns can interact with other patterns. This is represented symbolically in Figure 8.2(d) where the bottom-left block of the middle pattern again is a pattern. A case study of a document editor in [Gamma, Helm, Johnson, and Vlissides, 1995] contains eight interacting patterns. That is what happens in practice; it is unusual for the design of a product to contain only one pattern.

As with toolkits and frameworks, if a design pattern is reused, then an implementation of that pattern probably also can be reused. In addition, analysis patterns can assist with the analysis workflow [Fowler, 1997]. Finally, in addition to patterns, there are antipatterns; these are described in Just in Case You Wanted to Know Box 8.4.

Because of the importance of design patterns, we return to this topic in Section 8.6, after we have concluded our overview of reuse in design and implementation.

An antipattern is a practice that can cause a project to fail, such as "analysis paralysis" (spending far too much time and effort on the analysis workflow) or designing an object-oriented product in which just one object does almost all the work. A major motivation for writing the first antipattern book was that nearly one-third of all software projects are canceled, two-thirds of all software projects encounter cost overruns in excess of 200 percent, and over 80 percent of all software projects are deemed failures [Brown et al., 1998].

8.5.4   Software Architecture

The architecture of a cathedral might be described as Romanesque, Gothic, or Baroque. Similarly, the architecture of a software product might be described as object-oriented, pipes and filters (UNIX components), or client–server (with a central server providing file storage and computing facilities for a network of client computers). Figure 8.2(d) symbolically depicts an architecture composed of a toolkit, a framework, and three design patterns.

Because it applies to the design of a product as a whole, the field of **software architecture** encompasses a variety of design issues, including the organization of the product in terms of its components; product-level control structures; issues of communication and synchronization; databases and data access; the physical distribution of the components; performance; and choice of design alternatives [Shaw and Garlan, 1996]. Accordingly, software architecture is a considerably more wide-ranging concept than design patterns.

In fact, Shaw and Garlan [1996] state, "Abstractly, software architecture involves the description of elements from which systems are built, interactions among those elements, *patterns that guide their composition, and constraints on those patterns*" [emphasis added]. Consequently, in addition to the many items listed in the previous paragraph, software architecture includes patterns as a subfield. This is one reason why Figure 8.2(d) shows three design patterns as components of a software architecture.

The many strengths of design reuse are even greater when a software architecture is reused. One way that reuse of architectures is achieved in practice is with **software product lines** [Lai, Weiss, and Parnas, 1999; Jazayeri, Ran, and van der Linden, 2000]. The idea is to develop a software architecture common to a number of software products and instantiate this architecture when developing a new product. For example, Hewlett-Packard manufactures a broad variety of printers, and new models constantly are being developed. Hewlett-Packard now has a firmware architecture that is instantiated for each new printer model. The results have been impressive. For example, between 1995 and 1998, the number of person-hours to develop the firmware for a new printer model decreased by a factor of 4 and the time to develop the firmware decreased by a factor of 3. Also, reuse has increased. For more recent printers, over 70 percent of the components of the firmware are reused, almost unchanged, from earlier products [Toft, Coleman, and Ohta, 2000].

Architecture patterns are another way of achieving architectural reuse. One popular architecture pattern is the **model-view-controller (MVC) architecture pattern**. As shown in Section 5.1, a traditional way of designing software is to decompose it into three pieces: input, processing, and output. The MVC pattern can be viewed as an extension of the input–processing–output architecture to the GUI domain. The

Figure 8.3 The correspondence between the components of the MVC model and the input–processing–output model.

MVC component	Description	Corresponds to
Model	Core functionality, data	Processing
View	Displays information	Output
Controller	Handles user input	Input

correspondence is shown in Figure 8.3. The view(s) and the controller provide the GUI. The decomposition of the architecture into model, view, and controller allows each of the components to be changed independently of the other two, thereby enhancing the reusability.

Another popular architectural pattern is the three-tier architecture. The **presentation logic tier** accepts user input and generates user output—this tier corresponds to the GUI. The **business logic tier** incorporates the processing of the business rules. The **data access logic tier** communicates with the underlying database. Again, this architectural pattern permits each of the three components to be changed independently of the other two. This independence is a major reason why the three-tier architecture promotes reuse.

8.5.5   Component-Based Software Engineering

The goal of **component-based software engineering** is to construct a standard collection of reusable components. Then, instead of reinventing the wheel each time, in the future all software will be constructed by choosing a standard architecture and standard reusable frameworks and inserting standard reusable code artifacts into the hot spots of the frameworks. That is, software products will be built by composing reusable components. Ideally, this will be done using an automated tool.

In this chapter, we describe the many advantages that accrue through the reuse of code artifacts, design patterns, and software architectures. Hence, achieving component-based software engineering would solve numerous problems in software development. In particular, it would lead to order-of-magnitude increases in software productivity and quality and decreases in time to market and maintenance effort.

Unfortunately, the state of the art with regard to reuse is currently far from this ambitious target. In addition, component-based software construction has many challenges, including the definition, standardization, and retrieval of components. However, researchers in many centers are actively engaged in trying to achieve the goal of component-based software engineering [Heineman and Councill, 2001].

8.6   More on Design Patterns

Because of the importance of design patterns in object-oriented software engineering, we now examine design patterns in greater detail. We begin with a mini case study that illustrates the *Adapter* design pattern (Section 8.5.3).

Mini Case Study

8.6.1 *FLIC Mini Case Study*

Until recently, premiums at Flintstock Life Insurance Company (FLIC) depended on both the age and the gender of the person applying for insurance. FLIC has recently decided that certain policies will now be gender-neutral; that is, the premium for those policies will depend solely on the age of the applicant.

Up to now, premiums have been computed by sending a message to method computePremium of class **Applicant**, passing the age and gender of the applicant. Now, however, a different computation has to be made, based solely on the applicant's age. A new class is written, **Neutral Applicant**, and premiums are computed by sending a message to method computeNeutralPremium in that class. However, there has not been enough time to change the whole system. The situation is therefore as shown in Figure 8.4.

There are serious interfacing problems. First, an **Insurance** object passes a message to an object of type **Applicant**, instead of **Neutral Applicant**. Second, the message is sent to method computePremium instead of method computeNeutralPremium. Third, parameters age and gender are passed, instead of just age. The three question marks on the lower arrow in Figure 8.4 represent these three interfacing problems.

To solve these problems, we need to interpose class **Wrapper**, as shown in Figure 8.5. An object of class **Insurance** sends the same message computePremium passing the same two parameters (age and gender), but now the message is sent to an object of type **Wrapper**. This object then sends message computeNeutralPremium to an object of class **NeutralApplicant**, passing only age as the parameter. The three interfacing problems have been solved.

Figure 8.4
A UML diagram showing interfacing problems between classes.

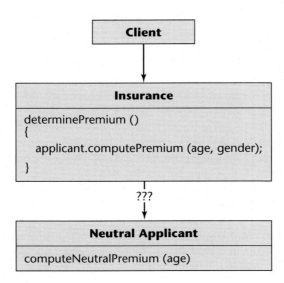

Figure 8.5 Wrapper solution to the interfacing problems of Figure 8.4.

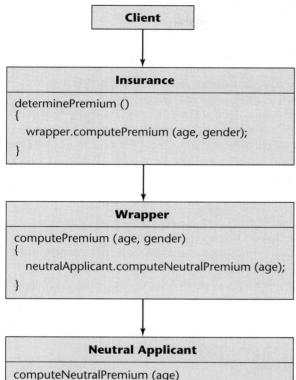

Figure 8.6 The *Adapter* design pattern.

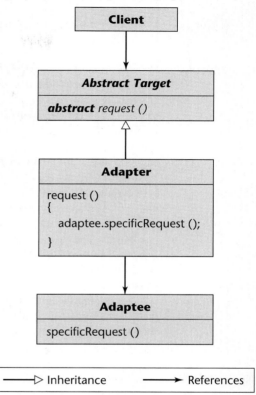

8.6.2   *Adapter* Design Pattern

Generalizing the solution of Figure 8.5 leads to the **Adapter design pattern** shown in Figure 8.6 [Gamma, Helm, Johnson, and Vlissides, 1995]. In this figure, the names of abstract classes and their abstract (virtual) methods are in *sans serif italics*. (An **abstract class** is a class that cannot be instantiated, although it can be used as a base class. An abstract class usually contains at least one **abstract method**, that is, a method with an interface but without an implementation.) Method *request* is defined as an abstract method of class **Abstract Target**. It is then implemented in (concrete) class **Adapter** to send message specificRequest to an object of class **Adaptee**. This solves the implementation incompatibilities. Class **Adapter** is a concrete subclass of abstract class **Abstract Target**, as reflected by the open arrow denoting inheritance in Figure 8.6.

Figure 8.6 depicts a general solution to the problem of permitting communication between two objects with incompatible interfaces. In fact, the *Adapter* design pattern is even more powerful than that. It provides a way for an object to permit access to its internal implementation in such a way that clients are not coupled to the structure of that internal implementation. That is, it provides all the advantages of information hiding (Section 7.6) without having to actually hide the implementation details.

We now turn to the *Bridge* design pattern.

8.6.3   *Bridge* Design Pattern

The aim of the **Bridge design pattern** is to decouple an abstraction from its implementation so that the two can be changed independently of one another. The *Bridge* pattern is sometimes called a **driver** (for example, a printer driver or video driver).

Suppose that part of a design is hardware-dependent, but the rest is not. The design then consists of two pieces. Those parts of the design that are hardware-dependent are put on one side of the bridge, the hardware-independent pieces on the other side. In this way, the abstract operations are uncoupled from the hardware-dependent parts; there is a "bridge" between the two parts. Now, if the hardware changes, the modifications to the design and the code are localized to only one side of the bridge. The *Bridge* design pattern can therefore be viewed as a way of achieving information hiding via encapsulation.

This is shown in Figure 8.7. The implementation-independent piece is in classes **Abstract Conceptualization** and **Refined Conceptualization**, and the implementation-dependent piece is in classes **Abstract Implementation** and **Concrete Implementation**.

The *Bridge* design pattern is also useful for decoupling operating system–dependent pieces or compiler-dependent pieces, thereby supporting multiple implementations. This is shown in Figure 8.8.

Figure 8.7   The *Bridge* design pattern.

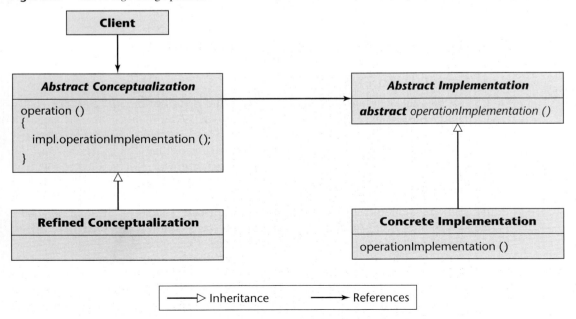

Figure 8.8 Using the *Bridge* design pattern to support multiple implementations.

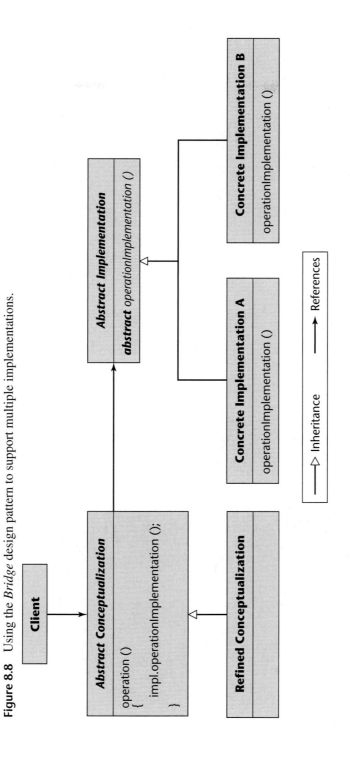

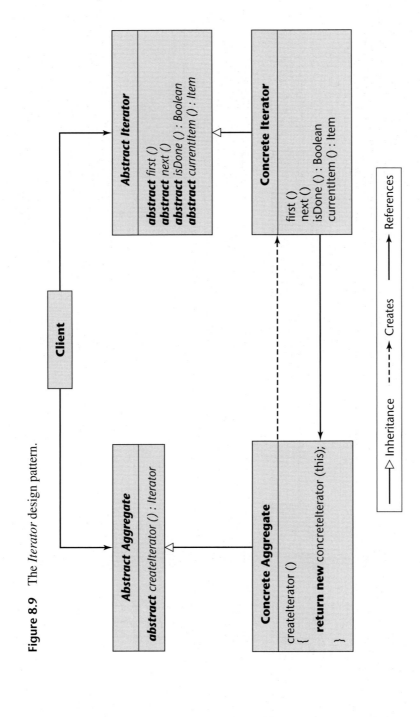

Figure 8.9 The *Iterator* design pattern.

8.6.4   *Iterator* Design Pattern

An **aggregate** object (or **container** or **collection**) is an object that contains other objects grouped together as a unit. Examples include a linked list and a hash table. An **iterator** is a programming construct that allows a programmer to traverse the elements of an aggregate object without exposing the implementation of that aggregate. An iterator is frequently referred to as a **cursor**, especially within a database context.

An iterator may be viewed as a pointer with two main operations: **element access**, or referencing a specific element in the collection; and **element traversal**, or modifying itself so it points to the next element in the collection.

A well-known example of an iterator is a television remote control. Every remote control has a key (often labeled Up or ▲) that increases the channel number by 1 and a key (often labeled Down or ▼) that decreases the channel number by 1. The remote control increases or decreases the channel number without the viewer having to specify (or even having to know) the current channel number, let alone the program that is being carried on that channel. That is, the device implements element traversal without exposing the implementation of the aggregate.

The **Iterator design pattern** is shown in Figure 8.9. A Client object deals with only the **Abstract Aggregate** and **Abstract Iterator** (essentially an interface). The Client object asks the **Abstract Aggregate** object to create an iterator for the **Concrete Aggregate** object and then utilizes the returned **Concrete Iterator** to traverse the contents of the aggregate. The **Abstract Aggregate** object has to have an abstract method, *createIterator*, as a way of returning an iterator to the Client object within the application program, whereas the **Abstract Iterator** interface needs to define only the basic four traversal operations, abstract methods *first*, *next*, *isDone*, and *currentItem*. Implementation of these five methods is achieved at the next level of abstraction, in **Concrete Aggregate** (createIterator) and **Concrete Iterator** (first, next, isDone, and currentItem).

The key aspect of the *Iterator* design pattern is that implementation details of the elements are hidden from the iterator itself. Accordingly, we can use an iterator to process every element in a collection, independently of the implementation of the container of the elements.

Furthermore, the pattern allows different traversal methods. It even allows multiple traversals to be in progress concurrently, and these traversals can be achieved without having the specific operations listed in the interface. Instead, we have one uniform interface, namely, the four abstract operations *first*, *next*, *isDone*, and *currentItem* in **Abstract Iterator**, with the specific traversal method(s) implemented in **Concrete Iterator**.

8.6.5   *Abstract Factory* Design Pattern

Suppose that a software organization wishes to build a widget generator, a tool that assists developers in constructing a graphical user interface. Instead of having to develop the various **widgets** (such as windows, buttons, menus, sliders, and scroll bars) from scratch, a developer can use the set of classes created by the widget generator that define the widgets to be utilized within the application program.

The problem is that the application program (and, therefore, the widgets) may have to run under many different operating systems, including Linux, Mac OS, and Windows. The widget generator is to support all three operating systems. However, if the widget generator hard-codes routines that run under one specific system into an application program, it will be difficult to modify that application program in the future, replacing the generated routines with different routines that run under a different operating system. For example, suppose that the application program is to run under Linux. Then, every time a menu is to be generated, message create Linux menu is sent. However, if that application program now needs to run under Mac OS, every instance of create Linux menu must be replaced by create Mac OS menu. For a large application program, such a conversion from Linux to Mac OS is laborious and fault prone.

The solution is to design the widget generator in such a way that the application program is uncoupled from the specific operating system. This can be achieved using the **_Abstract Factory design pattern_** [Gamma, Helm, Johnson, and Vlissides, 1995]. Figure 8.10 shows the resulting design of the graphical user interface toolkit. Again, the names of abstract classes and their abstract (virtual) methods are in _sans serif italics_. At the top of Figure 8.10 is abstract class **_Abstract Widget Factory_**. This abstract class contains numerous abstract methods; for simplicity, only two are shown here: _create menu_ and _create window_. Moving down in the figure, **Linux Widget Factory**, **Mac OS Widget Factory**, and **Windows Widget Factory** are concrete subclasses of **_Abstract Widget Factory_**. Each class contains the specific methods for creating widgets that run under a given operating system. For example, create menu within **Linux Widget Factory** causes a menu object to be created that will run under Linux.

There are also abstract classes for each widget. Two are shown here, **_Abstract Menu_** and **_Abstract Window_**. Each has concrete subclasses, one for each of the three operating systems. For example, **Linux Menu** is one concrete subclass of **_Abstract Menu_**. Method create menu within concrete subclass **Linux Widget Factory** causes an object of type **Linux Menu** to be created.

To create a window, a **Client** object within the application program need only send a message to abstract method _create window_ of **_Abstract Widget Factory_** and polymorphism ensures that the correct widget is created. Suppose that the application program has to run under Linux. First, an object Widget Factory of type (class) **Linux Widget Factory** is created. Then a message to virtual (abstract) method _create window_ of **_Abstract Widget Factory_** passing Linux as a parameter is interpreted as a message to method create window within concrete subclass **Linux Widget Factory**. Method create window in turn sends a message to create a **Linux Window**; this is indicated by the leftmost vertical dashed line in Figure 8.10.

The critical aspect of this figure is that the three interfaces between the **Client** within the application program and the widget generator, classes **_Abstract Widget Factory_**, **_Abstract Menu_**, and **_Abstract Window_**, all are abstract classes. None of these interfaces is specific to any one operating system because the methods of the abstract classes are **abstract** (**virtual** in C++). Consequently, the design of Figure 8.10 indeed has uncoupled the application program from the operating system.

The design of Figure 8.10 is an instance of the _Abstract Factory_ design pattern shown in Figure 8.11. To use this pattern, specific classes replace the generic names like **Concrete Factory 2** and **Product B3**. That is why Figure 8.2(c), the symbolic representation of a design pattern, contains white rectangles within the shaded rectangles; the white rectangles represent the details that have to be supplied to reuse this pattern in a design.

Figure 8.10
Design of
graphical user
interface toolkit.
The names of
abstract classes
and their virtual
functions are
italicized.

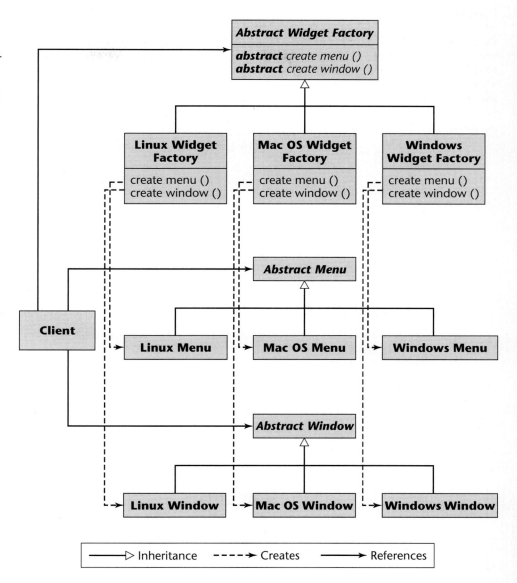

8.7   Categories of Design Patterns

The definitive list of 23 design patterns given in [Gamma, Helm, Johnson, and Vlissides, 1995] is presented in Figure 8.12. The patterns are divided into three categories: creational patterns, structural patterns, and behavioral patterns. **Creational design patterns** solve design problems by creating objects; the *Abstract Factory* pattern (Section 8.6.5) is an example. **Structural design patterns** solve design problems by identifying a simple

Figure 8.11
Abstract Factory design pattern. The names of abstract classes and their virtual functions are italicized.

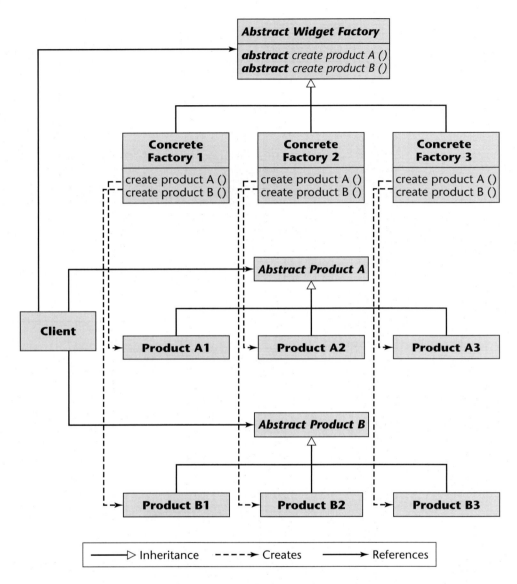

way to realize relationships between entities. Examples include the *Adapter* pattern (Section 8.6.2) and the *Bridge* pattern (Section 8.6.3). Finally, **behavioral design patterns** solve design problems by identifying common communication patterns between objects. An example of this type of design pattern is the *Iterator* pattern (Section 8.6.4).

Many other lists of design patterns, organized into a variety of different categories, have been put forward. These categories are either for design patterns in general, or for specific domains, such as design patterns for Web pages or computer games. However, these alternative lists of patterns have not been widely accepted.

Figure 8.12
The 23 design patterns listed in [Gamma, Helm, Johnson, and Vlissides, 1995].

Creational patterns

Abstract factory	Creates an instance of several families of classes (Section 8.6.5)
Builder	Allows the same construction process to create different representations
Factory method	Creates an instance of several possible derived classes
Prototype	A class to be cloned
Singleton	Restricts instantiation of a class to a single instance

Structural patterns

Adapter	Matches interfaces of different classes (Section 8.6.2)
Bridge	Decouples an abstaction from its implementation (Section 8.6.3)
Composite	A class that is a composition of similar classes
Decorator	Allows additional behavior to be dynamically added to a class
Façade	A single class that provides a simplified interface
Flyweight	Uses sharing to support large numbers of fine-grained classes efficiently
Proxy	A class functioning as an interface

Behavioral patterns

Chain-of-responsibility	A way of processing a request by a chain of classes
Command	Encapsulates an action within a class
Interpreter	A way to implement specialized language elements
Iterator	Sequentially accesses the elements of a collection (Section 8.6.4)
Mediator	Provides a unified interface to a set of interfaces
Memento	Captures and restores an object's internal state
Observer	Allows the observation of the state of an object at run time
State	Allows an object to partially change its type at run time
Strategy	Allows an algorithm to be dynamically selected at run time
Template method	Defers implementations of an algorithm to its subclasses
Visitor	Adds new operations to a class without changing it

8.8   Strengths and Weaknesses of Design Patterns

Design patterns have many strengths:

1. As pointed out in Section 8.5.3, design patterns promote reuse by solving a general design problem. The reusability of a design pattern can be enhanced by careful incorporation of features that can be used to further enhance reuse, such as inheritance.

2. A design pattern provides high-level documentation of the design, because patterns specify design abstractions.

3. Implementations of many design patterns exist. In such cases, there is no need to code or document those parts of a program that implement design patterns. (Testing of those parts of the program is still essential, of course.)

4. If a maintenance programmer is familiar with design patterns, it will be easier to comprehend a program that incorporates design patterns, even if he or she has never seen that specific program before.

However, design patterns have a number of weaknesses, too:

1. The use of the 23 standard design patterns in [Gamma, Helm, Johnson, and Vlissides, 1995] in a software product may be an indication that the language we are using is not powerful enough. Norwig [1996] examined the C++ implementations of those patterns and found that 16 out of the 23 have simpler implementations in Lisp or Dylan than in C++, for at least some uses of each pattern.

2. A major problem is that there is as yet no systematic way to determine when and how to apply design patterns. Design patterns are still described informally, using natural language text. Accordingly, we have to decide manually when to apply a pattern; a CASE tool (Chapter 5) cannot be used.

3. To obtain maximal benefit from design patterns, multiple interacting patterns are employed. For example, as stated in Section 8.5.3, a case study of a document editor in [Gamma, Helm, Johnson, and Vlissides, 1995] contains eight interacting patterns. As already pointed out, we do not yet have a systematic way of knowing when and how to use one pattern, let alone multiple interacting patterns.

4. When performing maintenance on a software product built using the classical paradigm, it is essentially impossible to retrofit classes and objects. It is similarly all but impossible to retrofit patterns to an existing software product, whether classical or object-oriented.

However, the weaknesses of design patterns are outweighed by their strengths. Furthermore, once current research efforts to formalize and hence automate design patterns have succeeded, patterns will be much easier to use than at present.

8.9   Reuse and Postdelivery Maintenance

The traditional reason for promoting reuse is that it can shorten the development process. For example, a number of major software organizations are trying to halve the time needed to develop a new product, and reuse is a primary strategy in these endeavors. However, as reflected in Figure 1.3, for every $1 spent on developing a product, $2 or more are spent on maintaining that product. Therefore, a second important reason for reuse is to reduce the time and cost of maintaining a product. In fact, reuse has a greater impact on postdelivery maintenance than on development.

Suppose now that 40 percent of a product consists of components reused from earlier products and this reuse is evenly distributed across the entire product. That is, 40 percent of the specification artifacts consist of reused components, 40 percent of the design artifacts, 40 percent of the code artifacts, 40 percent of the manuals, and so on. Unfortunately, this does not mean that the time to develop the product as a whole will be 40 percent less than it would have been without reuse. First, some of the components have to be tailored to the new product. Suppose that one-quarter of the reused components are changed. If a component has to be changed, then the documentation for that component also has to be changed. Furthermore, the changed component has to be tested. Second, if a code artifact is reused unchanged, then unit testing of that code artifact is not required. However, integration testing of that code artifact still is needed. So, even if 30 percent of a product consists of components reused unchanged and a further 10 percent are reused changed, the time needed to develop the complete product at best is only about 27 percent less [Schach, 1992]. Suppose that, as in Figure 1.3(a), 33 percent of a software budget is devoted to development. Then, if reuse reduces development costs by 27 percent, the overall cost of that product over its 12- to 15-year lifetime is reduced by only about 9 percent as a consequence of reuse; this is reflected in Figure 8.13.

Similar but lengthier arguments can be applied to the postdelivery maintenance component of the software process [Schach, 1994]. Under the assumptions of the previous paragraph, the effect of reuse on postdelivery maintenance is an overall cost saving of about

Figure 8.13 Average percentage cost savings under the assumption that 40 percent of a new product consists of reused components, three-quarters of which are reused unchanged.

Activity	Percentage of Total Cost over Product Lifetime	Percentage Savings over Product Lifetime due to Reuse
Development	33%	9.3%
Postdelivery maintenance	67	17.9

18 percent, as shown in Figure 8.13. Clearly, the major impact of reuse is on postdelivery maintenance rather than development. The underlying reason is that reused components generally are well designed, thoroughly tested, and comprehensively documented, thereby simplifying all three types of postdelivery maintenance.

If the actual reuse rates in a given product are lower (or higher) than assumed in this section, then the benefits of reuse are different. But the overall result is still the same: Reuse affects postdelivery maintenance more than it does development.

We turn now to portability.

8.10   Portability

The ever-rising cost of software makes it imperative that some means be found to contain costs. One way is to ensure that the product as a whole can be adapted easily to run on a variety of different hardware–operating system combinations. Some of the cost of writing the product may then be recouped by selling versions that run on other computers. But the most important reason for writing software that can be implemented easily on other computers is that, every 4 years or so, the client organization purchases new hardware, and all its software then must be converted to run on the new hardware. A product is considered portable if it is significantly less expensive to adapt the product to run on the new computer than to write a new product from scratch [Mooney, 1990].

More precisely, *portability* may be defined as follows: Suppose a product *P* is compiled by compiler *C* and then runs on the **source computer**, namely, hardware configuration *H* under operating system *O*. A product *P'* is needed that functionally is equivalent to *P* but must be compiled by compiler *C'* and run on the **target computer**, namely, hardware configuration *H'* under operating system *O'*. If the cost of converting *P* into *P'* is significantly less than the cost of coding *P'* from scratch, then *P* is said to be *portable*.

Overall, the problem of porting software is nontrivial because of incompatibilities among different hardware configurations, operating systems, and compilers. Each of these aspects is examined in turn.

8.10.1   Hardware Incompatibilities

Product *P* currently running on hardware configuration *H* is to be installed on hardware configuration *H'*. Superficially, this is simple; copy *P* from the hard drive of *H* onto DAT tape and transfer it to *H'*. However, this will not work if *H'* uses a Zip drive for backup; DAT tape cannot be read on a Zip drive.

Suppose now that the problem of physically copying the source code of product P to computer H' has been solved. There is no guarantee that H' can interpret the bit patterns created by H. A number of different character codes exist, the most popular of which are Extended Binary Coded Decimal Interchange Code (EBCDIC) and American Standard Code for Information Interchange (ASCII), the American version of the 7-bit ISO code [Mackenzie, 1980]. If H uses EBCDIC but H' uses ASCII, then H' will treat P as so much garbage.

Although the original reason for these differences is historical (that is, researchers working independently for different manufacturers developed different ways of doing the same thing), there are definite economic reasons for perpetuating them. To see this, consider the following imaginary situation. MCM Computer Manufacturers has sold thousands of its MCM-1 computer. MCM now wishes to design, manufacture, and market a new computer, the MCM-2, which is more powerful in every way than the MCM-1 but costs considerably less. Suppose further that the MCM-1 uses ASCII code and has 36-bit words consisting of four 9-bit bytes. Now, the chief computer architect of MCM decides that the MCM-2 should employ EBCDIC and have 16-bit words consisting of two 8-bit bytes. The sales force then has to tell current MCM-1 owners that the MCM-2 is going to cost them $35,000 less than any competitor's equivalent machine but will cost them up to $200,000 to convert existing software and data from MCM-1 format to MCM-2 format. No matter how good the scientific reasons for redesigning the MCM-2, marketing considerations will ensure that the new computer is compatible with the old one. A salesperson then can point out to an existing MCM-1 owner that, not only is the MCM-2 computer $35,000 less expensive than any competitor's machine, but any customer ill-advised enough to buy from a different manufacturer will be spending $35,000 too much and also will have to pay some $200,000 to convert existing software and data to the format of the non-MCM machine.

Moving from the preceding imaginary situation to the real world, the most successful line of computers to date has been the IBM System/360–370 series [Gifford and Spector, 1987]. The success of this line of computers is due largely to full compatibility between machines; a product that runs on an IBM System/360 Model 30 built in 1964 runs unchanged on an IBM eServer zSeries 990 built in 2007. However, the product that runs on the IBM System/360 Model 30 under OS/360 may require considerable modification before it can run on a totally different 2007 machine, such as a Sun Fire E25K server under Solaris. Part of the difficulty may be due to hardware incompatibilities. But part may be caused by operating system incompatibilities.

8.10.2   Operating System Incompatibilities

The job control languages (JCLs) of any two computers usually are vastly different. Some of the difference is syntactic—the command for executing an executable load image might be @xeq on one computer, //xqt on another, and .exc on a third. When porting a product to a different operating system, syntactic differences are relatively straightforward to handle by simply translating commands from the one JCL into the other. But other differences can be more serious. For example, some operating systems support virtual memory. Suppose that a certain operating system allows products to be up to 1024 MB in size, but the actual area of main memory allocated to a particular product may be only 64 MB. What happens is that the user's product is partitioned into pages 2048 KB in size, and only 32 of these pages can be in main memory at any one time. The rest of the pages are stored on disk and swapped in and out as needed by the virtual memory operating system. As a result, products can be written with no effective constraints as to size. But, if a product that has been successfully implemented under a virtual memory operating system is to be ported to an operating system with physical constraints on product size, the entire product may have to be rewritten and then linked using overlay techniques to ensure that the size limit is not exceeded.

8.10.3   Numerical Software Incompatibilities

When a product is ported from one machine to another or even compiled using a different compiler, the results of performing arithmetic may differ. On a 16-bit machine, that is, a computer with a word size of 16 bits, an integer ordinarily is represented by one word (16 bits) and a double-precision integer by two adjacent words (32 bits). Unfortunately, some language implementations do not include double-precision integers. For example, standard Pascal does not include double-precision integers. Therefore, a product that functions perfectly on a compiler–hardware–operating system configuration in which Pascal integers are represented using 32 bits may fail to run correctly when ported to a computer in which integers are represented by only 16 bits. The obvious solution—representing integers larger than 2^{16} by floating-point numbers (type **real**)—does not work because integers are represented exactly whereas floating-point numbers in general are only approximated using a mantissa (fraction) and exponent.

This problem can be solved in Java, because each of the eight primitive data types has been carefully specified. For example, type **int** always is implemented as a signed 32-bit two's complement integer, and type **float** always occupies 32 bits and satisfies ANSI/IEEE (Standard) 754 [1985] for floating-point numbers. The problem of ensuring that a numerical computation is performed correctly on every target hardware–operating system therefore cannot arise in Java. (For more insights into the design of Java, see Just in Case You Wanted to Know Box 8.5.) However, where a numerical computation is performed in a language other than Java, it is important, but often difficult, to ensure that numerical computations are performed correctly on the target hardware–operating system.

8.10.4   Compiler Incompatibilities

Portability is difficult to achieve if a product is implemented in a language for which few compilers exist. If the product has been implemented in a specialized language such as CLU [Liskov, Snyder, Atkinson, and Schaffert, 1977], it may be necessary to rewrite it in a different language if the target computer has no compiler for that language. On the other hand, if a product is implemented in a popular object-oriented language such as C++ or Java, the chances are good that a compiler or interpreter for that language can be found for a target computer.

Suppose that a product is written in an object-oriented language such as standard Fortran, Fortran 2003 (see Just in Case You Wanted to Know Box 8.6 for more on the name "Fortran 2003"). In theory, there should be no problem in porting the product from one machine to another—after all, standard Fortran is standard Fortran. Regrettably, that is not the case; in practice, there is no such thing as standard Fortran. Even though there is an ISO/

In 1991, James Gosling of Sun Microsystems developed Java. While developing the language, he frequently stared out the window at a large oak tree outside his office. In fact, he did this so often that he decided to name his new language *Oak*. However, his choice of name was unacceptable to Sun because it could not be trademarked, and without a trademark Sun would lose control of the language.

After an intensive search for a name that could be trademarked and was easy to remember, Gosling's group came up with *Java*. During the 18th century, much of the coffee imported into England was grown in Java, the most populous island in the Dutch East Indies (now Indonesia). As a result, *Java* now is a slang word for coffee, the third most popular beverage among software engineers. Unfortunately, the names of the Big Two carbonated cola beverages are already trademarked.

To understand why Gosling designed Java, it is necessary to appreciate the source of the weaknesses he perceived in C++. And, to do that, we have to go back to C, the parent language of C++.

In 1972, the programming language C was developed by Dennis Ritchie at AT&T Bell Laboratories (now Lucent Technologies) for use in systems software. The language was designed to be extremely flexible. For example, it permits arithmetic on pointer variables, that is, on variables used to store memory addresses. From the viewpoint of the average programmer, this poses a distinct danger; the resulting programs can be extremely insecure because control can be passed to anywhere in the computer. Also, C does not embody arrays as such. Instead, a pointer to the address of the beginning of the array is used. As a result, the concept of an out-of-range array subscript is not intrinsic to C. This is a further source of possible insecurity.

These and other insecurities were no problem at Bell Labs. After all, C was designed by an experienced software engineer for use by other experienced software engineers at Bell Labs. These professionals could be relied on to use the powerful and flexible features of C in a secure way. A basic philosophy in the design of C was that the person using C knows exactly what he or she is doing. Software failures that occurred when C is used by less competent or inexperienced programmers should not be blamed on Bell Labs; there never was any intent that C should be widely employed as a general-purpose programming language, as it is today.

IEC standard for Fortran 2003 [ISO/IEC 1539–1, 2004], there is no reason for a compiler writer to adhere to it. For example, a decision may be taken to support additional features not usually found in Fortran 2003 so that the marketing division can tout a "new, extended Fortran compiler." Conversely, a compiler for a small embedded microprocessor may not be a full Fortran implementation. Also, with a deadline to produce a compiler, management may decide to bring out a less-than-complete implementation, intending to support the full standard in a later revision. Suppose that the compiler on the source computer supports a superset of Fortran 2003. Suppose further that the compiler on the target computer is an implementation of standard Fortran 2003. When a product implemented on that source computer is ported to the target, any portions of the product that use nonstandard Fortran 2003 constructs from the superset have to be recoded. Therefore, to ensure portability, programmers should use only standard Fortran language features.

Early COBOL standards were developed by the COnference on DAta SYstems Languages (CODASYL), a committee of American computer manufacturers and government and private users. Joint Technical Committee 1 of Subcommittee 22 of the International Organization for Standardization (ISO) and the International Electrotechnical

With the rise of the object-oriented paradigm, a number of object-oriented programming languages based on C were developed, including Object C, Objective C, and C++. The idea behind these languages was to embed object-oriented constructs within C, which by then was a popular programming language. It was argued that it would be easier for programmers to learn a language based on a familiar language than to learn a totally new syntax. However, only one of the many C-based object-oriented languages became widely accepted, C++, developed by Bjarne Stroustrup, also of AT&T Bell Laboratories.

It has been suggested that the reason behind the success of C++ was the enormous financial clout of AT&T (now part of SBC Communications). However, if corporate size and financial strength were relevant features in promoting a programming language, today we would all be using PL/I, a language developed and strongly promoted by IBM. The reality is that PL/I, notwithstanding the prestige of IBM, has retreated into obscurity. The real reason for the success of C++ is that it is a true superset of C. That is, unlike any of the other C-based object-oriented programming languages, virtually any C program is also valid C++. Therefore, organizations realized that they could switch from C to C++ without changing any of their existing C software. They could advance from the classical paradigm to the object-oriented paradigm without disruption. A remark frequently encountered in the Java literature is, "Java is what C++ should have been." The implication is that, if only Stroustrup had been as smart as Gosling, C++ would have turned out to be Java. On the contrary, if C++ had not been a true superset of C, it would have gone the way of all other C-based object-oriented programming languages; that is, it essentially would have disappeared. Only after C++ had taken hold as a popular language was Java designed in reaction to perceived weaknesses in C++. Java is not a superset of C; for example, Java has no pointer variables. Therefore, it would be more accurate to say that "Java is what C++ could not possibly have been."

Finally, it is important to realize that Java, like every other programming language, has weaknesses of its own. In addition, in some areas (such as access rules), C++ is superior to Java [Schach, 1997]. It will be interesting to see, in the coming years, whether C++ continues to be the predominant object-oriented programming language or whether it is supplanted by Java or some other language.

Commission (IEC) now are responsible for COBOL standards [Schricker, 2000]. Unfortunately, COBOL standards do not promote portability. A COBOL standard has an official life of 5 years, but each successive standard is not necessarily a superset of its predecessor. Equally worrisome is that many features are left to the individual implementer, subsets may be termed *standard COBOL*, and there is no restriction on extending the language to form a superset. OO-COBOL [ISO/IEC 1989, 2002], the language of the current COBOL standard, is object oriented, as is Fortran 2003 [ISO/IEC 1539–1, 2004].

The standard for C++ [ISO/IEC 14882, 1998] was unanimously approved by the various national standards committees (including ANSI) in November 1997. The standard received final ratification in 1998.

The only truly successful language standard so far has been the Ada 83 standard, embodied in the Ada Reference Manual [ANSI/MIL-STD-1815A, 1983]. (For background information on Ada, see Just in Case You Wanted to Know Box 8.6.) Until the end of 1987, the name Ada was a registered trademark of the U.S. government, Ada Joint Program Office (AJPO). As owner of the trademark, the AJPO stipulated that the name Ada legally could be used only for language implementations that complied exactly with the standard; subsets and supersets

Names of programming languages are spelled in uppercase when the name is an acronym. Examples include ALGOL (ALGOrithmic Language), COBOL (COmmon Business Oriented Language), and FORTRAN (FORmula TRANslator). Conversely, all other programming languages begin with an uppercase letter and the remaining letters in the name (if any) are in lowercase. Examples include Ada, C, C++, Java, and Pascal. *Ada* is not an acronym; the language was named after Ada, Countess of Lovelace (1815–1852). Daughter of the poet Lord Alfred Byron, Ada was the world's first programmer by virtue of her work on Charles Babbage's difference engine. *Pascal* is not an acronym either—this language was named after the French mathematician and philosopher, Blaise Pascal (1623–1662). And I am sure that you have read all about the name *Java* in Just in Case You Wanted to Know Box 8.5.

There is one exception: Fortran. The FORTRAN Standards Committee decided that, effective with the 1990 version, the name of the language would thenceforth be written *Fortran*.

were expressly forbidden. A mechanism was set up for validating Ada compilers, and only a compiler that successfully passed the validation process could be called an Ada compiler. Consequently, the trademark was used as a means of enforcing standards and hence portability.

Now that the name Ada no longer is a trademark, enforcement of the standard is being achieved via a different mechanism. There is little or no market for an Ada compiler that has not been validated. Therefore, strong economic forces encourage Ada compiler developers to have their compilers validated and hence certified as conforming to the Ada standard. This has applied to compilers for both Ada 83 [ANSI/MIL-STD-1815A, 1983] and Ada 95 [ISO/IEC 8652, now 1995]; the latter is object oriented.

For Java to be a totally portable language, it is essential for the language to be standardized and to ensure that the standard is strictly obeyed. Sun Microsystems, like the Ada Joint Program Office, uses the legal system to achieve standardization. As mentioned in Just in Case You Wanted to Know Box 8.5, Sun chose a name for its new language that could be copyrighted so that Sun could enforce its copyright and bring legal action against alleged violators (which happened when Microsoft developed nonstandard Java classes). After all, portability is one of the most powerful features of Java. If multiple versions of Java are permitted, the portability of Java suffers; Java can be truly portable only if every Java program is handled identically by every Java compiler. To try to influence public opinion, in 1997 Sun ran a "Pure Java" advertising campaign.

Version 1.0 of Java was released early in 1997. A series of revised versions followed in response to comments and criticisms. The latest version at the time of writing is Java J2SE (Java 2 Platform, Standard Edition), version 5.0. This process of stepwise refinement of Java will continue. When the language eventually stabilizes, it is likely that a standards organization such as ANSI or ISO will publish a draft standard and elicit comments from all over the world. These comments will be used to put together the official Java standard.

8.11   Why Portability?

In the light of the many barriers to porting software, the reader might well wonder if it is worthwhile to port software at all. An argument in favor of portability stated in Section 8.10 is that the cost of software may be partially recouped by porting the product to a different hardware–operating system configuration. However, selling multiple variants of the software may not be possible. The application may be highly specialized, and no other client may need the software. For instance, a management information system written for one major car rental corporation may simply be inapplicable to the operations of other car rental corporations. Alternatively, the software itself may give the client a competitive advantage, and selling copies of the product would be tantamount to economic suicide. In the light of all this, is it not a waste of time and money to engineer portability into a product when it is designed?

The answer to this question is an emphatic *No*. The major reason why portability is essential is that the life of a software product generally is longer than the life of the hardware for which it was first written. Good software products can have a life of 15 years or more, whereas hardware frequently is changed every 4 years. Therefore, good software can be implemented, over its lifetime, on three or more different hardware configurations.

One way to solve this problem is to buy upwardly compatible hardware. The only expense is the cost of the hardware; the software need not be changed. Nevertheless, in some cases it may be economically more sound to port the product to different hardware entirely. For example, the first version of a product may have been implemented 7 years ago on a mainframe. Although it may be possible to buy a new mainframe on which the product can run with no changes, it may be considerably less expensive to implement multiple copies of the product on a network of personal computers, one on the desk of each user. In this instance, if the software has been written in a way that would promote portability, then porting the product to the personal computer network makes good financial sense.

But there are other kinds of software. For example, many organizations that write software for personal computers make their money by selling multiple copies of COTS software. For instance, the profit on a spreadsheet package is small and cannot possibly cover the cost of development. To make a profit, 50,000 (or even 500,000) copies may have to be sold. After this point, additional sales are pure profit. So, if the product can be ported to additional types of hardware with ease, even more money can be made.

Of course, as with all software, the product is not just the code but also the documentation, including the manuals. Porting the spreadsheet package to other hardware means changing the documentation as well. Therefore, portability also means being able to change the documentation easily to reflect the target configuration, instead of having to write new documentation from scratch. Considerably less training is needed if a familiar, existing product is ported to a new computer than if a completely new product were to be written. For this reason, too, portability is to be encouraged.

Techniques to facilitate portability now are described.

8.12   Techniques for Achieving Portability

One way to try to achieve portability is to forbid programmers to use constructs that might cause problems when ported to another computer. For example, an obvious principle would seem to be this: Write all software in a standard version of a high-level programming language. But how is a portable operating system to be written? After all, it is inconceivable that an operating system could be written without at least some assembler code. Similarly, a compiler has to generate object code for a specific computer. Here, too, it is impossible to avoid all implementation-dependent components.

8.12.1   Portable System Software

Instead of forbidding all implementation-dependent aspects, which would prevent almost all system software from being written, a better technique is to isolate any necessary implementation-dependent pieces. An example of this technique is the way the original UNIX operating system was constructed [Johnson and Ritchie, 1978]. About 9000 lines of the operating system were written in C. The remaining 1000 lines constituted the kernel. The kernel was written in assembler and had to be rewritten for each implementation. About 1000 lines of the C code consisted of device drivers; this code, too, had to be rewritten each time. However, the remaining 8000 lines of C code remained largely unchanged from implementation to implementation.

Another useful technique for increasing the portability of system software is to use levels of abstraction (Section 7.4.1). Consider, for example, graphical display routines for a workstation. A user inserts a command such as drawLine into his or her source code. The source code is compiled and then linked with graphical display routines. At run time, drawLine causes the workstation to draw a line on the screen as specified by the user. This can be implemented using two levels of abstraction. The upper level, written in a high-level language, interprets the user's command and calls the appropriate lower-level code artifact to execute that command. If the graphical display routines are ported to a new type of workstation, then no changes need be made to the user's code or the upper level of the graphical display routines. However, the lower-level code artifacts of the routines have to be rewritten, because they interface with the actual hardware, and the hardware of the new workstation is different from that of the workstation on which the package was previously implemented. This technique also has been used successfully for porting communications software that conforms to the seven levels of abstraction of the ISO-OSI model [Tanenbaum, 2002].

8.12.2   Portable Application Software

With regard to application software, rather than system software such as operating systems and compilers, it generally is possible to write the product in a high-level language. Section 13.1 points out that frequently no choice can be made with regard to implementation language, but that when it is possible to select a language, the choice should be made on the basis of cost–benefit analysis (Section 5.2). One factor that must enter into the cost–benefit analysis is the impact on portability.

At every stage in the development of a product, decisions can be made that result in a more portable product. For example, some compilers distinguish between uppercase and lowercase letters. For such a compiler, thisIsAName and thisisaname are different variables. But other compilers treat the two names the same. A product that relies on differences between uppercase letters and lowercase letters can lead to hard-to-discover faults when the product is ported.

Just as frequently no choice can be made of programming language, no choice may be allowed in the operating system. However, if at all possible, the operating system under which the product runs should be a popular one. This is an argument in favor of the UNIX operating system. UNIX has been implemented on a wide range of hardware. In addition, UNIX, or more precisely, UNIX-like operating systems, have been implemented on top of many mainframe operating systems. For personal computers, it remains to be seen whether

Linux will overtake Windows as the most widely used operating system. Just as use of a widely implemented programming language promotes portability, so too does use of a widely implemented operating system.

To facilitate the moving of software from one UNIX-based system to another, the Portable Operating System Interface for Computer Environments (POSIX) was developed [NIST 151, 1988]. POSIX standardizes the interface between an application program and a UNIX operating system. POSIX has been implemented on a number of non-UNIX operating systems as well, broadening the number of computers to which application software can be ported with little or no problem.

Language standards can play their part in achieving portability. If the coding standards of a development organization stipulate that only standard constructs may be used, then the resulting product is more likely to be portable. To this end, programmers must be provided a list of nonstandard features supported by the compiler but whose use is forbidden without prior managerial approval. Like other sensible coding standards, this one can be checked by machine.

Graphical user interfaces similarly are becoming portable via the introduction of standard GUI languages. Examples of these include Motif and X11. The standardization of GUI languages is in reaction to the growing importance of GUIs, and the resulting need for portability of human–computer interfaces.

It is also necessary to plan for potential lack of compatibility between the operating system under which the product is being constructed and any future operating systems to which the product may be ported. If at all possible, operating system calls should be localized to one or two code artifacts. In any event, every operating system call must be carefully documented. The documentation standard for operating system calls should assume that the next programmer to read the code will have no familiarity with the current operating system, often a reasonable assumption.

Documentation in the form of an installation manual should be provided to assist with future porting. That manual points out what parts of the product have to be changed when porting the product and what parts may have to be changed. In both instances, a careful explanation must be provided of what has to be done and how to do it. Finally, lists of changes that have to be made in other manuals, such as the user manual or the operator manual, also must appear in the installation manual.

8.12.3 Portable Data

The problem of portability of data can be vexing. Problems of hardware incompatibilities were pointed out in Section 8.10.1. But even after such problems have been solved, software incompatibilities remain. For instance, the format of an indexed-sequential file is determined by the operating system; a different operating system generally implies a different format. Many files require headers containing information such as the format of the data in that file. The format of a header almost always is unique to the specific compiler and operating system under which that file was created. The situation can be even worse when database management systems are used.

The safest way of porting data is to construct an unstructured (sequential) file, which can then be ported with minimal difficulty to the target machine. From this unstructured file, the desired structured file can be reconstructed. Two special conversion routines have to be written, one running on the source machine to convert the original structured file into sequential form and one running on the target machine to reconstruct the structured file from the ported sequential file. Although this solution seems simple enough, the two routines are nontrivial when conversions between complex database models have to be performed.

8.12.4   Web-Based Applications

One of the greatest strengths of the World Wide Web is that Web-based applications can achieve an extremely high level of portability. First, Web-based applications can be made portable by utilizing a language like HTML (Hypertext Markup Language) [HTML, 2006] or XML (Extensible Markup Language) [XML, 2003] that can be read by any Web browser, and by employing Java applets, which can be run on virtually every client. A further degree of portability can be achieved by separating the HTML or XML interface from the rest of the program (especially the application logic). The resulting application program will then run on a server, but can be accessed via virtually any client with a Web browser, including a personal digital assistant (PDA) or cell phone. Furthermore, such an application program can be ported to a new server without changing the clients that access it.

At the time of writing, not all applications can be run with every Web browser. For example, some applications that run under Internet Explorer will not work with Firefox because Firefox conforms to the World Wide Web Consortium (W3C) standards [W3C, 2006], but Internet Explorer does not [Computer Gripes, 2004]. However, as Web technology evolves in the future, it is likely that the highest levels of portability will be attained.

We conclude this chapter with a summary of the strengths of and impediments to reuse and portability (Figure 8.14); the section in which each item is discussed is stated.

Figure 8.14
Strengths of and impediments to reuse and portability, and the section in which the topic is discussed.

Strengths	Impediments
Reuse	
Shorter development time (Section 8.1)	NIH syndrome (Section 8.2)
Lower development cost (Section 8.1)	Potential quality issues (Section 8.2)
Higher-quality software (Section 8.1)	Retrieval issues (Section 8.2)
Shorter maintenance time (Section 8.6)	Cost of making a component reusable
Lower maintenance cost (Section 8.6)	(opportunistic reuse) (Section 8.2)
	Cost of making a component for future
	reuse (systematic reuse) (Section 8.2)
	Legal issues (contract software only)
	(Section 8.2)
	Lack of source code for COTS
	components (Section 8.2)
Portability	
Software has to be ported to new	Potential incompatibilities:
hardware every 4 years or so	Hardware (Section 8.7.1)
(Section 8.11)	Operating systems (Section 8.7.2)
More copies of COTS software can be	Numerical software (Section 8.7.3)
sold (Section 8.11)	Compilers (Section 8.7.4)
	Data formats (Section 8.9.3)

Chapter Review

Reuse is described in Section 8.1. Various impediments to reuse are described in Section 8.2. Two reuse case studies are presented in Section 8.3. The impact of the object-oriented paradigm on reuse is analyzed in Section 8.4. Reuse during design and implementation is the subject of Section 8.5; the topics covered include frameworks, patterns, software architecture, and component-based software engineering. Design patterns are discussed in greater detail in Section 8.6; after a mini case study (Section 8.6.1), the *Adapter*, *Bridge*, *Iterator*, and *Abstract Factory* design patterns are described in Sections 8.6.2, 8.6.3, 8.6.4, and 8.6.5, respectively. Categories of design patterns are discussed in Section 8.7. Section 8.8 contains a discussion of strengths and weaknesses of design patterns. The impact of reuse on postdelivery maintenance is discussed in Section 8.9.

Portability is discussed in Section 8.10. Portability can be hampered by incompatibilities caused by hardware (Section 8.10.1), operating systems (Section 8.10.2), numerical software (Section 8.10.3), or compilers (Section 8.10.4). Nevertheless, it is extremely important to try to make all products as portable as possible (Section 8.11). Ways of facilitating portability include using popular high-level languages, isolating the nonportable pieces of a product (Section 8.12.1), adhering to language standards (Section 8.12.2), and the use of unstructured data (Section 8.12.3). The chapter concludes with a discussion of Web-based applications (8.12.4).

For Further Reading

A variety of reuse case studies can be found in [Lanergan and Grasso, 1984; Matsumoto, 1984, 1987; Selby, 1989; Prieto-Díaz, 1991; Lim, 1994; Jézéquel and Meyer, 1997; and Toft, Coleman, and Ohta, 2000]. Successful reuse experiences at four European companies are described in [Morisio, Tully, and Ezran, 2000]. The management of reuse is described in [Lim, 1998]. A search scheme for object retrieval and reuse is described in [Isakowitz and Kauffman, 1996]. The cost-effectiveness of reuse is described in [Barnes and Bollinger, 1991] and ways of identifying components for future reuse in [Caldiera and Basili, 1991]. Meyer [1996a] analyzes the claim that the object-oriented paradigm promotes reuse; four case studies in reuse and object technology appear in [Fichman and Kemerer, 1997]. Reuse metrics are discussed in [Poulin, 1997]. Factors that affect the success of reuse programs are presented in [Morisio, Ezran, and Tully, 2002]. Reuse strategies are discussed in [Ravichandran and Rothenberger, 2003]. A comprehensive model for evaluating software reuse alternatives is presented in [Tomer et al., 2004]. Further papers on reuse are to be found in the May 2000 issue of *IEEE Transactions on Software Engineering*.

A good source of information on frameworks is [Lewis et al., 1995]. D'Souza and Wills [1999] present a development methodology based on object-oriented frameworks and components. A series of articles on frameworks can be found in [Fayad and Johnson, 1999; Fayad and Schmidt, 1999; and Fayad, Schmidt, and Johnson, 1999]. The October 2000 issue of *Communications of the ACM* includes articles on component-based frameworks, including [Fingar, 2000] and [Kobryn, 2000], which describes how to model components and frameworks using UML. Achieving reuse via frameworks and patterns is described in [Fach, 2001].

Design patterns were put forward by Alexander within the context of architecture, as described in [Alexander et al., 1977]. A first-hand account of the origins of pattern theory appears in [Alexander, 1999]. The primary work on software design patterns is [Gamma, Helm, Johnson, and Vlissides, 1995]; a newer book is [Vlissides, 1998]. Analysis patterns are described in [Fowler, 1997], and requirements patterns in [Hagge and Lappe, 2005].

Experiments to assess the impact of design pattern documentation on maintenance are described in [Prechelt, Unger-Lamprecht, Philippsen, and Tichy, 2002]. Antipatterns are described in [Brown et al., 1998]. Patterns for designing embedded systems are discussed in [Pont and Banner, 2004]. Vokac [2004] describes the impact of patterns on fault rates in a 500-KLOC product.

The primary source of information on software architectures is [Shaw and Garlan, 1996]. Newer works on software architectures include [Bosch, 2000] and [Bass, Clements, and Kazman, 2003]. Software product lines are described in [Jazayeri, Ran, and van der Linden, 2000; Knauber,

Muthig, Schmid, and Widen, 2000; Donohoe, 2000; and Clements and Northrop, 2002]. The state of the practice of software product lines is discussed in [Birk et al. 2003]. Cost–benefit analysis of software product lines is presented in [Bockle et al., 2004]. The July/August 2002 issue of *IEEE Software* contains a variety of articles on product lines.

Papers on component-based software engineering can be found in the September/October 1998 issue of *IEEE Software*, including [Weyuker, 1998], which discusses the testing of component-based software. Brereton and Budgen [2000] discuss the key issues in component-based software products. Articles on experiences with component-based software engineering include [Sparling, 2000] and [Baster, Konana, and Scott, 2001]. Strengths and weaknesses of component-based software engineering are discussed in [Vitharana, 2003]. [Heineman and Councill, 2001] is a highly recommended compendium of articles on component-based software engineering.

Strategies for achieving portability can be found in [Mooney, 1990]. Portability of UNIX is discussed in [Johnson and Ritchie, 1978].

Key Terms

abstract class 229	container 233	not invented here (NIH)
Abstract Factory design	creational design	syndrome 218
pattern 234	patterns 235	opportunistic reuse 216
abstract method 229	cursor 233	portable 216
accidental reuse 216	data access logic tier 227	presentation logic tier 227
Adapter design pattern 229	deliberate reuse 216	reuse 216
aggregate 233	driver 230	software architecture 226
application framework 224	element access 233	software product line 226
architecture pattern 226	element traversal 233	source computer 239
Bridge design pattern 230	framework 224	structural design
behavioral design	functional module 220	patterns 235
patterns 236	hot spot 224	systematic reuse 216
business logic tier 227	iterator 233	target computer 239
COBOL program logic	*Iterator* design pattern 233	toolkit 223
structure 220	model-view-controller	widget 233
collection 233	(MVC) architecture	wrapper 225
component-based software	pattern 226	
engineering 227		

Problems

8.1 Explain in detail the differences between reusability and portability.

8.2 A code artifact is reused, unchanged, in a new product. In what ways does this reuse reduce the overall cost of the product? In what ways is the cost unchanged?

8.3 Suppose that a code artifact is reused with one change, an addition operation is changed to a subtraction. What impact does this minor change have on the savings of Problem 8.2?

8.4 What is the influence of cohesion on reusability?

8.5 What is the influence of coupling on reusability?

8.6 You have just joined a large organization that manufactures a variety of pollution control products. The organization has hundreds of software products consisting of some 8000 different Fortran 2003 classes. You have been hired to come up with a plan for reusing as many of these classes as possible in future products. What is your proposal?

8.7   Consider an automated library circulation system. Every book has a bar code, and every borrower has a card bearing a bar code. When a borrower wishes to check out a book, the librarian scans the bar codes on the book and the borrower's card, and enters C at the computer terminal. Similarly, when a book is returned, it is again scanned and the librarian enters R. Librarians can add books (+) to the library collection or remove them (−). Borrowers can go to a terminal and determine all the books in the library by a particular author (the borrower enters A= followed by the author's name), all the books with a specific title (T= followed by the title), or all the books in a particular subject area (S= followed by the subject area). Finally, if a borrower wants a book currently checked out, the librarian can place a hold on the book so that, when it is returned, it will be held for the borrower who requested it (H= followed by the number of the book). Explain how you would ensure a high percentage of reusable code artifacts.

8.8   You are required to build a product for determining whether a bank statement is correct. The data needed include the balance at the beginning of the month; the number, date, and amount of each check; the date and amount of each deposit; and the balance at the end of the month. Explain how you would ensure that as many code artifacts as possible of the product can be reused in future products.

8.9   Consider an automated teller machine (ATM). The user puts a card into a slot and enters a four-digit personal identification number (PIN). If the PIN is incorrect, the card is ejected. Otherwise, the user may perform the following operations on up to four different bank accounts:

(i)   Deposit any amount. A receipt is printed showing the date, amount deposited, and account number.

(ii)   Withdraw up to $200 in units of $20 (the account may not be overdrawn). In addition to the money, the user is given a receipt showing the date, amount withdrawn, account number, and account balance after the withdrawal.

(iii) Determine the account balance. This is displayed on the screen.

(iv)   Transfer funds between two accounts. Again, the account from which the funds are transferred must not be overdrawn. The user is given a receipt showing the date, amount transferred, and the two account numbers.

(v)   Quit. The card is ejected.

Explain how you would ensure that as many code artifacts as possible of the product can be reused in future products.

8.10   How early in the software life cycle could the developers have caught the fault in the Ariane 5 software (Section 8.3.2)?

8.11   Section 8.5.2 states that "the Raytheon COBOL program logic structure of the 1970s is a classical precursor of today's object-oriented application framework." What are the implications of this for technology transfer?

8.12   Explain the role played by abstract classes in the design pattern of Figure 8.10.

8.13   Explain how you would ensure that the automated library circulation system (Problem 8.7) is as portable as possible.

8.14   Explain how you would ensure that the product that checks whether a bank statement is correct (Problem 8.8) is as portable as possible.

8.15   Explain how you would ensure that the software for the automated teller machine (ATM) of Problem 8.9 is as portable as possible.

8.16   Your organization is developing a real-time control system for a new type of laser that will be used in cancer therapy. You are in charge of writing two assembler modules. How will you instruct your team to ensure that the resulting code will be as portable as possible?

8.17   You are responsible for porting a 750,000-line OO-COBOL product to your company's new computer. You copy the source code to the new machine but discover when you try to compile it that every one of the over 15,000 input–output statements has been written in a nonstandard OO-COBOL syntax that the new compiler rejects. What do you do now?

8.18   In what ways does the object-oriented paradigm promote portability and reusability?

8.19   (Term Project) Suppose that the Osric's Office Appliances and Decor product of Appendix A has been developed using the object-oriented paradigm. What parts of the product could be reused in future products?

8.20   (Readings in Software Engineering) Your instructor will distribute copies of [Tomer et al., 2004]. What data would you need to accumulate in order to use the model?

References   [Alexander, 1999] C. Alexander, "The Origins of Pattern Theory," *IEEE Software* **16** (September/ October 1999), pp. 71–82.
[Alexander et al., 1977] C. Alexander, S. Ishikawa, M. Silverstein, M. Jacobson, I. Fiksdahl-King, and S. Angel, *A Pattern Language*, Oxford University Press, New York, 1977.
[ANSI/IEEE 754, 1985] *Standard for Binary Floating Point Arithmetic*, ANSI/IEEE 754, American National Standards Institute, Institute of Electrical and Electronic Engineers, New York, 1985.
[ANSI/MIL-STD-1815A, 1983] *Reference Manual for the Ada Programming Language*, ANSI/ MIL-STD-1815A, American National Standards Institute, United States Department of Defense, Washington, DC, 1983.
[Barnes and Bollinger, 1991] B. H. Barnes and T. B. Bollinger, "Making Reuse Cost-Effective," *IEEE Software* **8** (January 1991), pp. 13–24.
[Bass, Clements, and Kazman, 2003] L. Bass, P. Clements, and R. Kazman, *Software Architecture in Practice*, 2nd ed., Addison-Wesley, Reading, MA, 2003.
[Baster, Konana, and Scott, 2001] G. Baster, P. Konana, and J. E. Scott, "Business Components: A Case Study of Bankers Trust Australia Limited," *Communications of the ACM* **44** (May 2001), pp. 92–98.
[Birk et al. 2003] A. Birk, G. Heller, I. John, K. Schmid, T. von der Massen, and K. Muller, "Product Line Engineering, the State of the Practice," *IEEE Software* **20** (November/December 2003), pp. 52–60.
[Bockle et al., 2004] G. Bockle, P. Clements, J. D. McGregor, D. Muthig, and K. Schmid, "Calculating ROI for Software Product Lines," *IEEE Software* **21** (May/June 2004), pp. 23–31.
[Bosch, 2000] J. Bosch, *Design and Use of Software Architectures*, Addison-Wesley, Reading, MA, 2000.
[Brereton and Budgen, 2000] P. Brereton and D. Budgen, "Component-Based Systems: A Classification of Issues," *IEEE Computer* **33** (November 2000), pp. 54–62.
[Brown et al., 1998] W. J. Brown, R. C. Malveau, W. H. Brown, H. W. McCormick, III, and T. J. Mowbray, *AntiPatterns: Refactoring Software, Architectures, and Projects in Crisis,* John Wiley and Sons, New York, 1998.
[Caldiera and Basili, 1991] G. Caldiera and V. R. Basili, "Identifying and Qualifying Reusable Software Components," *IEEE Computer* **24** (February 1991), pp. 61–70.
[Clements and Northrop, 2002] P. Clements and L. Northrop, *Software Product Lines: Practices and Patterns*, Addison-Wesley, Reading, MA, 2002.
[Computer Gripes, 2004] "Gripes about Web Sites That Don't Work Well with Firefox," at: www. computergripes.com/firefoxsites.html, 2004.
[Donohoe, 2000] P. Donohoe (Editor), *Software Product Lines: Experience and Research Directions*, Kluwer Academic Publishers, Boston, 2000.

[D'Souza and Wills, 1999] D. D'SOUZA AND A. WILLS, *Objects, Components, and Frameworks with UML: The Catalysis Approach*, Addison-Wesley, Reading, MA, 1999.

[Fach, 2001] P. W. FACH, "Design Reuse through Frameworks and Patterns," *IEEE Software* **18** (September/October 2001), pp. 71–76.

[Fayad and Johnson, 1999] M. FAYAD AND R. JOHNSON, *Domain-Specific Application Frameworks: Frameworks Experience by Industry,* John Wiley and Sons, New York, 1999.

[Fayad and Schmidt, 1999] M. FAYAD AND D. C. SCHMIDT, *Building Application Frameworks: Object-Oriented Foundations of Framework Design,* John Wiley and Sons, New York, 1999.

[Fayad, Schmidt, and Johnson, 1999] M. FAYAD, D. C. SCHMIDT, AND R. JOHNSON, *Implementing Application Frameworks: Object-Oriented Frameworks at Work,* John Wiley and Sons, New York, 1999.

[Fichman and Kemerer, 1997] R. G. FICHMAN AND C. F. KEMERER, "Object Technology and Reuse: Lessons from Early Adopters," *IEEE Computer* **30** (July 1997), pp. 47–57.

[Fingar, 2000] P. FINGAR, "Component-Based Frameworks for e-Commerce," *Communications of the ACM* **43** (October 2000), pp. 61–66.

[Flanagan, 2005] D. FLANAGAN, *Java in a Nutshell: A Desktop Quick Reference*, 5th ed., O'Reilly and Associates, Sebastopol, CA, 2005.

[Fowler, 1997] M. FOWLER, *Analysis Patterns: Reusable Object Models*, Addison-Wesley, Reading, MA, 1997.

[Gamma, Helm, Johnson, and Vlissides, 1995] E. GAMMA, R. HELM, R. JOHNSON, AND J. VLISSIDES, *Design Patterns: Elements of Reusable Object-Oriented Software*, Addison-Wesley, Reading, MA, 1995.

[Gifford and Spector, 1987] D. GIFFORD AND A. SPECTOR, "Case Study: IBM's System/360–370 Architecture," *Communications of the ACM* **30** (April 1987), pp. 292–307.

[Green, 2000] P. GREEN, "FW: Here's an Update to the Simulated Kangaroo Story," *The Risks Digest* 20 (January 23, 2000), catless.ncl.ac.uk/Risks/20.76.html.

[Griss, 1993] M. L. GRISS, "Software Reuse: From Library to Factory," *IBM Systems Journal* **32** (No. 4, 1993), pp. 548–66.

[Hagge and Lappe, 2005] L. HAGGE AND K. LAPPE, "Sharing Requirements Engineering Experience Using Patterns," *IEEE Software* **22** (January/February 2005), pp. 24–31.

[Heineman and Councill, 2001] G. T. HEINEMAN AND W. T. COUNCILL, *Component-Based Software Engineering: Putting the Pieces Together*, Addison-Wesley, Reading, MA, 2001.

[HTML, 2006] "W3C HTML Homepage," at www.w3.org/MarkUp, 2006.

[Isakowitz and Kauffman, 1996] T. ISAKOWITZ AND R. J. KAUFFMAN, "Supporting Search for Reusable Software Objects," *IEEE Transactions on Software Engineering* **22** (June 1996), pp. 407–23.

[ISO/IEC 1539–1, 2004] *Information Technology—Programming Languages—Fortran—Part 1: Base Language*, ISO/IEC 1539–1, International Organization for Standardization, International Electrotechnical Commission, Geneva, 2004.

[ISO/IEC 1989, 2002] *Information Technology—Programming Language COBOL*, ISO 1989:2002, International Organization for Standardization, International Electrotechnical Commission, Geneva, 2002.

[ISO/IEC 8652, 1995] *Programming Language Ada: Language and Standard Libraries*, ISO/IEC 8652, International Organization for Standardization, International Electrotechnical Commission, Geneva, 1995.

[ISO/IEC 14882, 1998] *Programming Language C++*, ISO/IEC 14882, International Organization for Standardization, International Electrotechnical Commission, Geneva, 1998.

[Jazayeri, Ran, and van der Linden, 2000] M. JAZAYERI, A. RAN, AND F. VAN DER LINDEN, *Software Architecture for Product Families: Principles and Practice,* Addison-Wesley, Reading, MA, 2000.

[Jézéquel and Meyer, 1997] J.-M. JÉZÉQUEL AND B. MEYER, "Put It in the Contract: The Lessons of Ariane," *IEEE Computer* **30** (January 1997), pp. 129–30.

[Johnson and Ritchie, 1978] S. C. JOHNSON AND D. M. RITCHIE, "Portability of C Programs and the UNIX System," *Bell System Technical Journal* **57** (No. 6, Part 2, 1978), pp. 2021–48.

[Jones, 1984] T. C. JONES, "Reusability in Programming: A Survey of the State of the Art," *IEEE Transactions on Software Engineering* **SE-10** (September 1984), pp. 488–94.

[Knauber, Muthig, Schmid, and Widen, 2000] P. KNAUBER, D. MUTHIG, K. SCHMID, AND T. WIDEN, "Applying Product Line Concepts in Small and Medium-Sized Companies," *IEEE Software* **17** (September/October 2000), pp. 88–95.

[Kobryn, 2000] C. KOBRYN, "Modeling Components and Frameworks with UML," *Communications of the ACM* **43** (October 2000), pp. 31–38.

[Lai, Weiss, and Parnas, 1999] C. T. R. LAI, D. M. WEISS, AND D. L. PARNAS, *Software Product-Line Engineering: A Family-Based Software Development Process,* Addison-Wesley, Reading, MA, 1999.

[Lanergan and Grasso, 1984] R. G. LANERGAN AND C. A. GRASSO, "Software Engineering with Reusable Designs and Code," *IEEE Transactions on Software Engineering* **SE-10** (September 1984), pp. 498–501.

[LAPACK++, 2000] "LAPACK++: Linear Algebra Package in C++," at math.nist.gov/lapack++, 2000.

[Lewis et al., 1995] T. LEWIS, L. ROSENSTEIN, W. PREE, A. WEINAND, E. GAMMA, P. CALDER, G. ANDERT, J. VLISSIDES, AND K. SCHMUCKER, *Object-Oriented Application Frameworks*, Manning, Greenwich, CT, 1995.

[Lim, 1994] W. C. LIM, "Effects of Reuse on Quality, Productivity, and Economics," *IEEE Software* **11** (September 1994), pp. 23–30.

[Lim, 1998] W. C. LIM, *Managing Software Reuse*, Prentice Hall, Upper Saddle River, NJ, 1998.

[Liskov, Snyder, Atkinson, and Schaffert, 1977] B. LISKOV, A. SNYDER, R. ATKINSON, AND C. SCHAFFERT, "Abstraction Mechanisms in CLU," *Communications of the ACM* **20** (August 1977), pp. 564–76.

[Mackenzie, 1980] C. E. MACKENZIE, *Coded Character Sets: History and Development*, Addison-Wesley, Reading, MA, 1980.

[Matsumoto, 1984] Y. MATSUMOTO, "Management of Industrial Software Production," *IEEE Computer* **17** (February 1984), pp. 59–72.

[Matsumoto, 1987] Y. MATSUMOTO, "A Software Factory: An Overall Approach to Software Production," in: *Tutorial: Software Reusability*, P. Freeman (Editor), Computer Society Press, Washington, DC, 1987, pp. 155–78.

[Meyer, 1987] B. MEYER, "Reusability: The Case for Object-Oriented Design," *IEEE Software* **4** (March 1987), pp. 50–64.

[Meyer, 1996a] B. MEYER, "The Reusability Challenge," *IEEE Computer* **29** (February 1996), pp. 76–78.

[Mooney, 1990] J. D. MOONEY, "Strategies for Supporting Application Portability," *IEEE Computer* **23** (November 1990), pp. 59–70.

[Morisio, Ezran, and Tully, 2002] M. MORISIO, M. EZRAN, AND C. TULLY, "Success and Failure Factors in Software Reuse," *IEEE Transactions on Software Engineering* **28** (April 2002), pp. 340–57.

[Morisio, Tully, and Ezran, 2000] M. MORISIO, C. TULLY, AND M. EZRAN, "Diversity in Reuse Processes," *IEEE Software* **17** (July/August 2000), pp. 56–63.

[Musser and Saini, 1996] D. R. MUSSER AND A. SAINI, *STL Tutorial and Reference Guide: C++ Programming with the Standard Template Library*, Addison-Wesley, Reading, MA, 1996.

[NAG, 2003] "NAG The Numerical Algorithms Group Ltd," at www.nag.co.uk, 2003.

[NIST 151, 1988] "POSIX: Portable Operating System Interface for Computer Environments," Federal Information Processing Standard 151, National Institute of Standards and Technology, Washington, DC, 1988.

[Norušis, 2005] M. J. NORUŠIS, *SPSS 13.0 Guide to Data Analysis,* Prentice Hall, Upper Saddle Valley River, NJ, 2005.

[Norwig, 1996] P. NORWIG, "Design Patterns in Dynamic Programming," norvig.com/design-patterns/ppframe.htm/, 1996.

[Pont and Banner, 2004] M. J. PONT AND M. P. BANNER, "Designing Embedded Systems Using Patterns: A Case Study," *Journal of Systems and Software* **71** (May 2004), pp. 201–13.

[Poulin, 1997] J. S. POULIN, *Measuring Software Reuse: Principles, Practice, and Economic Models*, Addison-Wesley, Reading, MA, 1997.

[Prechelt, Unger-Lamprecht, Philippsen, and Tichy, 2002] L. PRECHELT, B. UNGER-LAMPRECHT, M. PHILIPPSEN, AND W. F. TICHY, "Two Controlled Experiments in Assessing the Usefulness of Design Pattern Documentation in Program Maintenance," *IEEE Transactions on Software Engineering* **28** (June 2002), pp. 595–606.

[Prieto-Díaz, 1991] R. PRIETO-DÍAZ, "Implementing Faceted Classification for Software Reuse," *Communications of the ACM* **34** (May 1991), pp. 88–97.

[Ravichandran and Rothenberger, 2003] T. RAVICHANDRAN AND M. A. ROTHENBERGER, "Software Reuse Strategies and Component Markets," *Communications of the ACM* **46** (August 2003), pp. 109–14

[Schach, 1992] S. R. SCHACH, *Software Reuse: Past, Present, and Future*, videotape, 150 min, US-VHS format, IEEE Computer Society Press, Los Alamitos, CA, November 1992.

[Schach, 1994] S. R. SCHACH, "The Economic Impact of Software Reuse on Maintenance," *Journal of Software Maintenance—Research and Practice* **6** (July/August 1994), pp. 185–96.

[Schach, 1997] S. R. SCHACH, *Software Engineering with Java*, Richard D. Irwin, Chicago, 1997.

[Schricker, 2000] D. SCHRICKER, "Cobol for the Next Millennium," *IEEE Software* **17** (March/April 2000), pp. 48–52.

[Selby, 1989] R. W. SELBY, "Quantitative Studies of Software Reuse," in: *Software Reusability*, Vol. 2, *Applications and Experience*, T. J. Biggerstaff and A. J. Perlis (Editors), ACM Press, New York, 1989, pp. 213–33.

[Shaw and Garlan, 1996] M. SHAW AND D. GARLAN, *Software Architecture: Perspectives on an Emerging Discipline*, Prentice Hall, Upper Saddle River, NJ, 1996.

[Sparling, 2000] M. SPARLING, "Lessons Learned through Six Years of Component-Based Development," *Communications of the ACM* **43** (October 2000), pp. 47–53.

[Tanenbaum, 2002] A. S. TANENBAUM, *Computer Networks,* 4th ed., Prentice Hall, Upper Saddle River, NJ, 2002.

[Toft, Coleman, and Ohta, 2000] P. TOFT, D. COLEMAN, AND J. OHTA, "A Cooperative Model for Cross-Divisional Product Development for a Software Product Line," in: *Software Product Lines: Experience and Research Directions*, P. Donohoe (Editor), Kluwer Academic Publishers, Boston, 2000, pp. 111–32.

[Tomer et al., 2004] A. TOMER, L. GOLDIN, T. KUFLIK, E. KIMCHI, AND S. R. SCHACH, "Evaluating Software Reuse Alternatives: A Model and Its Application to an Industrial Case Study," *IEEE Transactions on Software Engineering* **30** (September 2004), pp. 601–12.

[Tracz, 1994] W. TRACZ, "Software Reuse Myths Revisited," *Proceedings of the 16th International Conference on Software Engineering*, Sorrento, Italy, May 1994, pp. 271–72.

[Vitharana, 2003] P. VITHARANA, "Risks and Challenges of Component-Based Software Development," *Communications of the ACM* **46** (August 2003), pp. 67–72.

[Vlissides, 1998] J. VLISSIDES, *Pattern Hatching: Design Patterns Applied,* Addison-Wesley, Reading, MA, 1998.

[Vokac, 2004] M. VOKAC, "Defect Frequency and Design Patterns: An Empirical Study of Industrial Code," *IEEE Transactions on Software Engineering* **30** (December 2004), pp. 904–17.

[Weyuker, 1998] E. J. WEYUKER, "Testing Component-Based Software: A Cautionary Tale," *IEEE Software* **15** (September/October 1998), pp. 54–59.

[XML, 2003] "Extensible Markup Language (XML)," at www.w3.org/XML/, 2003.

Chapter

9

Planning and Estimating

Learning Objectives

After studying this chapter, you should be able to

- Explain the importance of planning.
- Estimate the size and cost of building a software product.
- Appreciate the importance of updating and tracking estimates.
- Draw up a project management plan that conforms to the IEEE standard.

The challenges of constructing a software product have no easy solution. To put together a large software product takes time and resources. And, like any other large construction project, careful planning at the beginning of the project perhaps is the single most important factor that distinguishes success from failure. This initial planning, however, by no means is enough. Planning, like testing, must continue throughout the software development and maintenance process. Notwithstanding the need for continual planning, these activities reach a peak after the specifications have been drawn up but before design activities commence. At this point in the process, meaningful duration and cost estimates are computed and a detailed plan for completing the project produced.

In this chapter, we distinguish these two types of *planning*, the planning that proceeds throughout the project and the intense planning that must be carried out once the specifications are complete.

As explained in the Preface, the material of this chapter may be taught in parallel with Part 2. The material of Chapter 9 is required for the software project management plan for the MSG Foundation case study (Section 11.20; Problems 11.26 and 11.27) and for the Osric's Office Appliances and Decor term project (Problem 11.23).

9.1   Planning and the Software Process

Ideally, we would like to plan the entire software project at the very beginning of the process, and then follow that plan until the target software finally has been delivered to the client. This is impossible, however, because we lack enough information during the initial workflows to be able to draw up a meaningful plan for the complete project. For example, during the requirements workflow, any sort of planning (other than just for the requirements workflow itself) is futile.

There is a world of difference between the information at the developers' disposal at the end of the requirements workflow and at the end of the analysis workflow, analogous to the difference between a rough sketch and a detailed blueprint. By the end of the requirements workflow, the developers at best have an informal understanding of what the client needs. In contrast, by the end of the analysis workflow, at which time the client signs a document stating precisely what is going to be built, the developers have a detailed appreciation of most (but usually still not all) aspects of the target product. This is the earliest point in the process at which accurate duration and cost estimates can be determined.

Nevertheless, in some situations, an organization may be required to produce duration and cost estimates before the specifications can be drawn up. In the worst case, a client may insist on a bid on the basis of an hour or two of preliminary discussion. Figure 9.1 shows how problematic this can be. Based on a model in [Boehm et al., 2000], it depicts the relative range of cost estimates for the various workflows of the life cycle. For example, suppose that, when a product passes its acceptance test at the end of the implementation workflow and is delivered to the client, its cost is found to be $1 million. If a cost estimate had been made midway through the requirements workflow, it is likely that it would have been somewhere in the range ($0.25 million, $4 million), as shown in Figure 9.2. Similarly, if the cost estimate had been made midway through the analysis workflow, the range of

Figure 9.1
A model for estimating the relative range of a cost estimate for each life-cycle workflow.

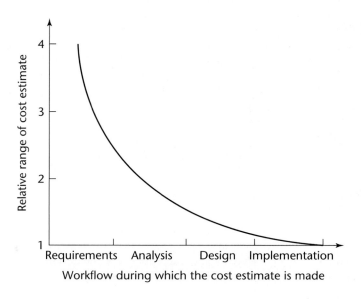

Figure 9.2
The range of cost estimates for a software product that cost $1 million to build.

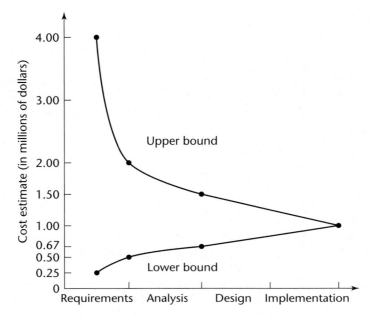

likely estimates would have shrunk to ($0.5 million, $2 million). Furthermore, if the cost estimate had been made at the end of the analysis workflow, that is, at the appropriate time, the result probably would have been in the still relatively wide range of ($0.67 million, $1.5 million). All four points are marked on the upper and lower bound lines in Figure 9.2, which has a logarithmic scale on the vertical axis. This model is called the **cone of uncertainty**. It is clear from Figures 9.1 and 9.2 that cost estimation is not an exact science; reasons for this are given in Section 9.2.

The data on which the cone of uncertainty model is based are old, including five proposals submitted to the U.S. Air Force Electronic Systems Division [Devenny, 1976], and estimation techniques have improved since that time. Nevertheless, the overall shape of the curve in Figure 9.1 probably has not changed overmuch. Consequently, a premature duration or cost estimate, that is, an estimate made before the specifications have been signed off on by the client, is likely to be considerably less accurate than an estimate made when sufficient data have accumulated.

We now examine techniques for estimating duration and cost. The assumption throughout the remainder of this chapter is that the analysis workflow has been completed; that is, meaningful estimating and planning now can be carried out.

9.2 Estimating Duration and Cost

The budget is an integral part of any software project management plan. Before design commences, the client needs to know how much he or she will have to pay for the product. If the development team underestimates the actual cost, the development organization can lose money on the project. On the other hand, if the development team overestimates, then the client may decide that, on the basis of cost–benefit analysis or return on investment, there is no point in having the product built. Alternatively, the client may give the job to another development organization whose estimate is more reasonable. Either way, it is clear that accurate cost estimation is critical.

In fact, two types of costs are associated with software development. The first is the **internal cost**, the **cost** to the developers; the second is the **external cost**, the **price** that the client will pay. The internal cost includes the salaries of the development teams, managers, and support personnel involved in the project; the cost of the hardware and software for developing the product; and the cost of overhead such as rent, utilities, and salaries of senior management. Although the price generally is based on the cost plus a profit margin, in some cases economic and psychological factors are important. For example, developers who desperately need the work may be prepared to charge the client at cost. A different situation arises when a contract is to be awarded on the basis of bids. The client may reject a bid that is significantly lower than all the other bids on the grounds that the quality of the resulting product probably also would be significantly lower. A development team therefore may try to come up with a bid that will be slightly, but not significantly, lower than what it believes will be the competitors' bids.

Another important part of any plan is estimating the duration of the project. The client certainly wants to know when the finished product will be delivered. If the development organization is unable to keep to its schedule, then at best the organization loses credibility, at worst penalty clauses are invoked. In all cases, the managers responsible for the software project management plan have a lot of explaining to do. Conversely, if the development organization overestimates the time needed to build the product, then there is a good chance that the client will go elsewhere.

Unfortunately, it is by no means easy to estimate cost and duration requirements accurately. Too many variables are involved to be able to get an accurate handle on either cost or duration. One big difficulty is the human factor. Over 35 years ago, Sackman and coworkers observed differences of up to 28 to 1 between pairs of programmers [Sackman, Erikson, and Grant, 1968]. It is easy to try to brush off their results by saying that experienced programmers always outperform beginners, but Sackman and his colleagues compared matched pairs of programmers. They observed, for example, two programmers with 10 years of experience on similar types of projects and measured the time it took them to perform tasks like coding and debugging. Then they observed, say, two beginners who had been in the profession for the same short length of time and had similar educational backgrounds. Comparing worst and best performances, they observed differences of 6 to 1 in product size, 8 to 1 in product execution time, 9 to 1 in development time, 18 to 1 in coding time, and 28 to 1 in debugging time. A particularly alarming observation is that the best and worst performances on one product were by two programmers, each of whom had 11 years of experience. Even when the best and worst cases were removed from Sackman et al.'s sample, observed differences were still on the order of 5 to 1. On the basis of these results, clearly, we cannot hope to estimate software cost or duration with any degree of accuracy (unless we have detailed information regarding all the skills of all the employees, which would be most unusual). It has been argued that, on a large project, differences among individuals tend to cancel out, but this perhaps is wishful thinking; the presence of one or two exceedingly good (or exceedingly bad) team members can cause marked deviations from schedules and significantly affect the budget.

Another human factor that can affect estimation is that, in a free country, there is no way of ensuring that a critical staff member will not resign during the project. Time and money then are spent attempting to fill the vacated position and integrate the replacement into the team, or in reorganizing the remaining team members to compensate for the loss. Either way, schedules slip and estimates come unstuck.

Underlying the cost estimation problem is another issue: How is the size of a product to be measured?

9.2.1   Metrics for the Size of a Product

The most common metric for the size of a product is the number of lines of code. Two units commonly are used: *lines of code (LOC)* and *thousand delivered source instructions (KDSI)*. Many problems are associated with the use of lines of code [van der Poel and Schach, 1983].

- Creation of source code is only a small part of the total software development effort. It seems somewhat far-fetched that the time required for the requirements, analysis, design, implementation, and testing workflows (which include planning and documentation activities) can be expressed solely as a function of the number of lines of code of the final product.

- Implementing the same product in two different languages results in versions with different numbers of lines of code. Also, with languages such as Lisp or with many nonprocedural languages the concept of a line of code is not defined.

- It often is unclear exactly how to count lines of code. Should only executable lines of code be counted or data definitions as well? And should comments be counted? If not, there is a danger that programmers will be reluctant to spend time on what they perceive to be "nonproductive" comments, but if comments are counted, then the opposite danger is that programmers will write reams of comments in an attempt to boost their apparent productivity. Also, what about counting job control language statements? Another problem is how changed lines or deleted lines are counted—in the course of enhancing a product to improve its performance, sometimes the number of lines of code is decreased. Reuse of code (Section 8.1) also complicates line counting: If reused code is modified, how is it counted? And, what if code is inherited from a parent class (Section 7.8)? In short, the apparently straightforward metric of lines of code is anything but straightforward to count.

- Not all the code written is delivered to the client. It is not uncommon for half the code to consist of tools needed to support the development effort.

- Suppose that a software developer uses a code generator, such as a report generator, a screen generator, or a graphical user interface (GUI) generator. After a few minutes of design activity on the part of the developer, the tool may generate many thousands of lines of code.

- The number of lines of code in the final product can be determined only when the product is completely finished. Therefore, basing cost estimation on lines of code is doubly dangerous. To start the estimation process, the number of lines of code in the finished product must be estimated. Then, this estimate is used to estimate the cost of the product. Not only is there uncertainty in every costing technique, but if the input to an uncertain cost estimator itself is uncertain (that is, the number of lines of code in a product that has not yet been built), then the reliability of the resulting cost estimate is unlikely to be terribly high.

Because the number of lines of code is so unreliable, other metrics must be considered. An alternative approach to estimating the size of a product is the use of metrics based on measurable quantities that can be determined early in the software process. For example, van der Poel and Schach [1983] put forward the **FFP metric** for cost estimation of medium-scale data-processing products. The three basic structural elements of a data-processing product are its files, flows, and processes; the name FFP is an acronym formed from the initial letters of those elements. A *file* is defined as a collection of logically or physically related records permanently resident in the product; transaction and temporary files are excluded. A *flow* is a data interface between the product and the environment, such as a screen or a report. A *process* is a functionally defined logical or arithmetic manipulation of data; examples include sorting, validating, or updating. Given the number of files, *Fi*; flows, *Fl*; and processes, *Pr*, in a product, its size *S* and cost *C* are given by

$$S = Fi + Fl + Pr \qquad\qquad (9.1)$$

$$C = d \times S \qquad\qquad (9.2)$$

where *d* is a constant that varies from organization to organization. Constant *d* is a measure of the **efficiency (productivity)** of the software development process within that organization. The size of a product simply is the sum of the number of files, flows, and processes, a quantity that can be determined at the end of the analysis workflow. The cost then is proportional to the size, the constant of proportionality *d* being determined by a least-squares fit to cost data relating to products previously developed by that organization. Unlike metrics based on the number of lines of code, the cost can be estimated before coding begins.

The validity and reliability of the FFP metric were demonstrated using a purposive sample that covered a range of medium-scale data-processing applications. Unfortunately, the metric was never extended to include databases, an essential component of many data-processing products.

A similar, but independently developed, metric for the size of a product was developed by Albrecht [1979] based on function points; Albrecht's metric is based on the number of input items, *Inp*; output items, *Out*; inquiries, *Inq*; master files, *Maf*; and interfaces, *Inf*. In its simplest form the number of function points, *FP*, is given by the equation

$$FP = 4 \times Inp + 5 \times Out + 4 \times Inq + 10 \times Maf + 7 \times Inf \quad (9.3)$$

Because this is a measure of the product's size, it can be used for cost estimation and productivity estimation.

Equation (9.3) is an oversimplification of a three-step calculation. First, the unadjusted function points are computed:

1. Each of the components of a product—*Inp*, *Out*, *Inq*, *Maf*, and *Inf*—must be classified as simple, average, or complex (see Figure 9.3).
2. Each component is assigned a number of function points depending on its level. For example, an average input is assigned 4 function points, as reflected in equation (9.3), but a simple input is assigned only 3, whereas a complex input is assigned 6 function points. The data needed for this step appear in Figure 9.3.
3. The function points assigned to each component are then summed, yielding the **unadjusted function pointS (UFP)**.

Figure 9.3
Table of function point values.

Component	Level of Complexity		
	Simple	Average	Complex
Input item	3	4	6
Output item	4	5	7
Inquiry	3	4	6
Master file	7	10	15
Interface	5	7	10

Figure 9.4
Technical factors for function point computation.

1. Data communications

2. Distributed data processing

3. Performance criteria

4. Heavily utilized hardware

5. High transaction rates

6. Online data entry

7. End-user efficiency

8. Online updating

9. Complex computations

10. Reusability

11. Ease of installation

12. Ease of operation

13. Portability

14. Maintainability

Second, the ***technical complexity factoR (TCF)*** is computed. This is a measure of the effect of 14 technical factors, such as high transaction rates, performance criteria (for example, throughput or response time), and online updating; the complete set of factors is shown in Figure 9.4. Each of these 14 factors is assigned a value from 0 ("not present or no influence") to 5 ("strong influence throughout"). The resulting 14 numbers are summed, yielding the total degree of influence (DI). The TCF is then given by

$$TCF = 0.65 + 0.01 \times DI \qquad (9.4)$$

Because DI can vary from 0 to 70, TCF varies from 0.65 to 1.35.

Third, FP, the number of ***function points***, is given by

$$FP = UFP \times TCF \qquad (9.5)$$

Experiments to measure software productivity rates have shown a better fit using function points than using KDSI. For example, Jones [1987] has stated that he observed errors in excess of 800 percent counting KDSI, but *only* [emphasis added] 200 percent in counting function points, a most revealing remark.

Figure 9.5
A comparison
of assembler
and Ada
products.

Source: [Jones, 1987].
(© 1987 IEEE.)

	Assembler Version	Ada Version
Source code size	70 KDSI	25 KDSI
Development costs	$1,043,000	$590,000
KDSI per person-month	0.335	0.211
Cost per source statement	$14.90	$23.60
Function points per person-month	1.65	2.92
Cost per function point	$3,023	$1,170

To show the superiority of function points over lines of code, Jones [1987] cites the example shown in Figure 9.5. The same product was coded both in assembler and in Ada and the results compared. First, consider KDSI per person-month. This metric tells us that coding in assembler is apparently 60 percent more efficient than coding in Ada, which is patently false. Third-generation languages like Ada have superseded assembler simply because it is much more efficient to code in a third-generation language. Now consider the second metric, cost per source statement. Note that one Ada statement in this product is equivalent to 2.8 assembler statements. Use of cost per source statement as a measure of efficiency again implies that again it is more efficient to code in assembler than in Ada. However, when function points per person-month is taken as the metric of programming efficiency, the superiority of Ada over assembler is reflected clearly.

On the other hand, both function points and the FFP metric of equations (9.1) and (9.2) suffer from the same weakness: Product maintenance often is inaccurately measured. When a product is maintained, major changes to the product can be made without changing the number of files, flows, and processes or the number of inputs, outputs, inquiries, master files, and interfaces. Lines of code is no better in this respect. To take an extreme case, it is possible to replace every line of a product by a completely different line without changing the total number of lines of code.

At least 40 variants of and extensions to Albrecht's function points have been proposed [Maxwell and Forselius, 2000]. Mk II function points were put forward by Symons [1991] to provide a more accurate way of computing the unadjusted function points (*UFP*). The software is decomposed into a set of component transactions, each consisting of an input, a process, and an output. The value of *UFP* then is computed from these inputs, processes, and outputs. Mk II function points are widely used all over the world [Boehm, 1997].

9.2.2   Techniques of Cost Estimation

Notwithstanding the difficulties with estimating size, it is essential that software developers simply do the best they can to obtain accurate estimates of both project duration and project cost, while taking into account as many as possible of the factors that can affect their estimates. These include the skill levels of the personnel, the complexity of the project, the size of the project (cost increases with size but much more than linearly), familiarity of the development team with the application area, the hardware on which the product is to be run, and availability of CASE tools. Another factor is the deadline effect. If a project has to be completed by a certain time, the effort in person-months is greater than if no constraint is placed on completion time; hence, the greater the cost. This shows that duration and cost are not independent; the shorter is the deadline, the greater the effort and, hence, the greater the cost.

From the preceding list, which is by no means comprehensive, clearly estimation is a difficult problem. A number of approaches have been used, with greater or lesser success.

1. Expert Judgment by Analogy

In the **expert judgment by analogy** technique, a number of experts are consulted. An expert arrives at an estimate by comparing the target product to completed products with which the expert was actively involved and noting the similarities and differences. For example, an expert may compare the target product to a similar product developed 2 years ago for which the data were entered in batch mode, whereas the target product is to have online data capture. Because the organization is familiar with the type of product to be developed, the expert reduces development time and effort by 15 percent. However, the graphical user interface is somewhat complex; this increases time and effort by 25 percent. Finally, the target product has to be developed in a language with which most of the team members are unfamiliar, consequently increasing time by 15 percent and effort by 20 percent. Combining these three figures, the expert decides that the target product will take 25 percent more time and 30 percent more effort than the previous one. Because the previous product took 12 months to complete and required 100 person-months, the target product is estimated to take 15 months and consume 130 person-months.

Two other experts within the organization compare the same two products. One concludes that the target product will take 13.5 months and 140 person-months. The other comes up with the figures of 16 months and 95 person-months. How can the predictions of these three experts be reconciled? One technique is the **Delphi technique**: It allows experts to arrive at a consensus without having group meetings, which can have the undesirable side effect of one persuasive member swaying the group. In this technique, the experts work independently. Each produces an estimate and a rationale for that estimate. These estimates and rationales then are distributed to all the experts, who now produce a second estimate. This process of estimation and distribution continues until the experts can agree within an accepted tolerance. No group meetings take place during the iteration process.

Valuation of real estate frequently is done on the basis of expert judgment by analogy. An appraiser arrives at a valuation by comparing a house with similar houses that have been sold recently. Suppose that house A is to be valued, house B next door has just been sold for $205,000, and house C on the next street was sold 3 months ago for $218,000. The appraiser may reason as follows: House A has one more bathroom than house B, and the yard is 5000 square feet larger. House C is approximately the same size as house A, but its roof is in poor condition. On the other hand, House C has a Jacuzzi. After careful thought, the appraiser may arrive at a figure of $215,000 for house A.

In the case of software products, expert judgment by analogy is less accurate than real estate valuation. Recall that our first software expert claimed that using an unfamiliar language would increase time by 15 percent and effort by 20 percent. Unless the expert has some validated data from which the effect of each difference can be determined (a highly unlikely possibility), errors induced by what can be described only as guesses will result in hopelessly incorrect cost estimates. In addition, unless the experts are blessed with total recall (or have kept detailed records), their recollections of completed products may be sufficiently inaccurate as to invalidate their predictions. Finally, experts are human and, therefore, have biases that may affect their predictions. At the same time, the results of estimation by a group of experts should reflect their collective experience; if this is broad enough, the result well may be accurate.

2. Bottom-up Approach

One way of trying to reduce the errors resulting from evaluating a product as a whole is to break the product into smaller components. Estimates of duration and cost are made for each component separately and combined to provide an overall figure. This **bottom-up approach** has the advantage that estimating costs for several smaller components generally is quicker and more accurate than for one large one. In addition, the estimation process is likely to be more detailed than with one large, monolithic product. The weakness of this approach is that a product is more than the sum of its components.

The independence of classes helps the bottom-up approach. However, interactions among the various objects in the product complicate the estimation process.

3. Algorithmic Cost Estimation Models

In this approach, a metric, such as function points or the FFP metric, is used as input to a model for determining product cost. The estimator computes the value of the metric; duration and cost estimates then can be computed using the model. On the surface, an **algorithmic cost estimation model** is superior to expert opinion, because a human expert, as pointed out previously, is subject to biases and may overlook certain aspects of both the completed and target products. In contrast, an algorithmic cost estimation model is unbiased; every product is treated the same way. The danger with such a model is that its estimates are only as good as the underlying assumptions. For example, underlying the function point model is the assumption that every aspect of a product is embodied in the five quantities on the right-hand side of equation (9.3) and the 14 technical factors. A further problem is that a significant amount of subjective judgment often is needed in deciding what values to assign to the parameters of the model. For example, frequently it is unclear whether a specific technical factor of the function point model should be rated a 3 or a 4.

Many algorithmic cost estimation models have been proposed. Some are based on mathematical theories as to how software is developed. Other models are statistically based; large numbers of projects are studied and empirical rules determined from the data. Hybrid models incorporate mathematical equations, statistical modeling, and expert judgment. The most important hybrid model is Boehm's COCOMO, which is described in detail in Section 9.2.3. (See Just in Case You Wanted to Know Box 9.1 for a discussion of the acronym COCOMO.)

9.2.3   Intermediate COCOMO

COCOMO actually is a series of three models, ranging from a macroestimation model that treats the product as a whole to a microestimation model that treats the product in detail. In this section, a description is given of intermediate COCOMO, which has a middle level of complexity and detail. COCOMO is described in detail in [Boehm, 1981]; an overview is presented in [Boehm, 1984].

Computing development time using intermediate COCOMO is done in two stages. First, a rough estimate of the development effort is provided. Two parameters have to be estimated: the length of the product in KDSI and the product's development mode, a measure of the intrinsic level of difficulty of developing that product. There are three modes: *organic* (small and straightforward), *semidetached* (medium sized), and *embedded* (complex).

COCOMO is an acronym formed from the first two letters of each word in COnstructive COst MOdel. Any connection with Kokomo, Indiana, is purely coincidental.

The *MO* in COCOMO stands for "model," so the phrase *COCOMO model* should not be used. That phrase falls into the same category as "ATM machine" and "PIN number," both of which were dreamed up by the Department of Redundant Information Department.

From these two parameters, the **nominal effort** can be computed. For example, if the project is judged essentially straightforward (organic), then the nominal effort (in person-months) is given by the equation

$$\text{Nominal effort} = 3.2 \times (\text{KDSI})^{1.05} \text{ person-months} \qquad (9.6)$$

The constants 3.2 and 1.05 are the values that best fitted the data on the organic mode products used by Boehm to develop intermediate COCOMO.

For example, if the product to be built is organic and estimated to be 12,000 delivered source statements (12 KDSI), then the nominal effort is

$$3.2 \times (12)^{1.05} = 43 \text{ person-months}$$

(but read Just in Case You Wanted to Know Box 9.2 for a comment on this value).

Next, this nominal value must be multiplied by 15 **software development effort multipliers**. These multipliers and their values are given in Figure 9.6. Each multiplier can have up to six values. For example, the product complexity multiplier is assigned the values 0.70, 0.85, 1.00, 1.15, 1.30, or 1.65, according to whether the developers rate the project complexity as very low, low, nominal (average), high, very high, or extra high. As can be seen from Figure 9.6, all 15 multipliers take on the value 1.00 when the corresponding parameter is nominal.

Boehm provides guidelines to help the developer determine whether the parameter should indeed be rated nominal or whether the rating is lower or higher. For example, consider again the module complexity multiplier. If the control operations of the module essentially consist of a sequence of the constructs of structured programming (such as **if-then-else, do-while, case**), then the complexity is rated *very low*. If these operators are nested, then the rating is *low*. Adding intermodule control and decision tables increases the rating to *nominal*. If the operators are highly nested, with compound predicates, and queues and stacks, then the rating is *high*. The presence of reentrant and recursive coding and fixed-priority interrupt handling pushes the rating to *very high*. Finally, multiple resource scheduling with dynamically changing priorities and microcode-level control ensures that the rating is *extra high*. These ratings apply to control operations. A module also has to be evaluated from the viewpoint of computational operations, device-dependent operations, and data management operations. For details on the criteria for computing each of the 15 multipliers, refer to [Boehm, 1981].

To see how this works, Boehm [1984] gives the example of microprocessor-based communications processing software for a highly reliable new electronic funds transfer network, with performance, development schedule, and interface requirements. This product fits the description of embedded mode and is estimated to be 10,000 delivered source instructions (10 KDSI) in length, so the nominal development effort is given by

$$\text{Nominal effort} = 2.8 \times (\text{KDSI})^{1.20} \qquad (9.7)$$

One reaction to the value of the nominal effort might be, "If 43 person-months of effort are needed to produce 12,000 delivered source instructions, then on average each programmer is turning out fewer than 300 lines of code a month—I have written more than that in one night!"

A 300-line product usually is just that: 300 lines of code. In contrast, a maintainable 12,000-line product has to go through all the workflows of the life cycle. In other words, the total effort of 43 person-months is shared among many activities, including coding.

Figure 9.6 Intermediate COCOMO software development effort multipliers.

Source: [Boehm, 1984]. (© 1984 IEEE.)

				Rating		
Cost Drivers	Very Low	Low	Nominal	High	Very High	Extra High
Product Attributes						
Required software reliability	0.75	0.88	1.00	1.15	1.40	
Database size		0.94	1.00	1.08	1.16	
Product complexity	0.70	0.85	1.00	1.15	1.30	1.65
Computer Attributes						
Execution time constraint			1.00	1.11	1.30	1.66
Main storage constraint			1.00	1.06	1.21	1.56
Virtual machine volatility*		0.87	1.00	1.15	1.30	
Computer turnaround time		0.87	1.00	1.07	1.15	
Personnel Attributes						
Analyst capabilities	1.46	1.19	1.00	0.86	0.71	
Applications experience	1.29	1.13	1.00	0.91	0.82	
Programmer capability	1.42	1.17	1.00	0.86	0.70	
Virtual machine experience*	1.21	1.10	1.00	0.90		
Programming language experience	1.14	1.07	1.00	0.95		
Project Attributes						
Use of modern programming practices	1.24	1.10	1.00	0.91	0.82	
Use of software tools	1.24	1.10	1.00	0.91	0.83	
Required development schedule	1.23	1.08	1.00	1.04	1.10	

*For a given software product, the underlying virtual machine is the complex of hardware and software (operating system, database management system) it calls on to accomplish its task.

(Again, the constants 2.8 and 1.20 are the values that best fitted the data on embedded products.) Because the project is estimated to be 10 KDSI in length, the nominal effort is

$$2.8 \times (10)^{1.20} = 44 \text{ person-months}$$

The estimated development effort is obtained by multiplying the nominal effort by the 15 software development effort multipliers. The ratings of these multipliers and their values are given in Figure 9.7. Using these values, the product of the multipliers is found to be 1.35, so the estimated effort for the project is

$$1.35 \times 44 = 59 \text{ person-months}$$

This number is then used in additional formulas to determine dollar costs, development schedules, phase and activity distributions, computer costs, annual maintenance costs, and other related items; for details, see [Boehm, 1981]. Intermediate COCOMO is a complete algorithmic cost estimation model, giving the user virtually every conceivable assistance in project planning.

Intermediate COCOMO has been validated with respect to a broad sample of 63 projects covering a wide variety of application areas. The results of applying intermediate COCOMO to this sample are that the actual values come within 20 percent of the predicted values about 68 percent of the time. Attempts to improve on this accuracy make little sense because in most organizations, the input data for intermediate COCOMO generally are accurate to within only about 20 percent. Nevertheless, the accuracy obtained by experienced estimators placed intermediate COCOMO at the cutting edge of cost estimation research during the 1980s; no other technique was consistently as accurate.

The major problem with intermediate COCOMO is that its most important input is the number of lines of code in the target product. If this estimate is incorrect, then every single prediction of the model may be incorrect. Because of the possibility that the predictions of intermediate COCOMO or any other estimation technique may be inaccurate, management must monitor all predictions throughout software development.

Figure 9.7
Intermediate COCOMO effort multiplier ratings for microprocessor communications software.

Source: [Boehm, 1984]. (© 1984 IEEE.)

Cost Drivers	Situation	Rating	Effort Multiplier
Required software reliability	Serious financial consequences of software fault	High	1.15
Database size	20,000 bytes	Low	0.94
Product complexity	Communications processing	Very high	1.30
Execution time constraint	Will use 70% of available time	High	1.11
Main storage constraint	45K of 64K store (70%)	High	1.06
Virtual machine volatility	Based on commercial microprocessor hardware	Nominal	1.00
Computer turnaround time	2-hour average turnaround time	Nominal	1.00
Analyst capabilities	Good senior analysts	High	0.86
Applications experience	3 years	Nominal	1.00
Programmer capability	Good senior programmers	High	0.86
Virtual machine experience	6 months	Low	1.10
Programming language experience	12 months	Nominal	1.00
Use of modern programming practices	Most techniques in use over 1 year	High	0.91
Use of software tools	At basic minicomputer tool level	Low	1.10
Required development schedule	9 months	Nominal	1.00

9.2.4   COCOMO II

COCOMO was put forward in 1981. At that time, the only life-cycle model in use was the waterfall model. Most software was run on mainframes. Technologies such as client–server and object orientation essentially were unknown. Accordingly, COCOMO did not incorporate any of these factors. However, as newer technologies began to become accepted software engineering practice, COCOMO started to become less accurate.

COCOMO II [Boehm et al., 2000] is a major revision of the 1981 COCOMO. COCOMO II can handle a wide variety of modern software engineering techniques, including object-orientation, the various life-cycle models described in Chapter 2, rapid prototyping (Section 10.13), reuse (Section 8.1), and COTS software (Section 1.10). COCOMO II is both flexible and sophisticated. Unfortunately, to achieve this goal, COCOMO II is considerably more complex than the original COCOMO. Accordingly, the reader who wishes to utilize COCOMO II should study [Boehm et al., 2000] in detail; only an overview of the major differences between COCOMO II and intermediate COCOMO is given here.

First, intermediate COCOMO consists of one overall model based on lines of code (KDSI). On the other hand, COCOMO II consists of three different models. The *application composition model*, based on object points (similar to function points), is applied at the earliest workflows, when minimal knowledge is available regarding the product to be built. Then, as more knowledge becomes available, the *early design model* is used; this model is based on function points. Finally, when the developers have maximal information, the *postarchitecture model* is used. This model uses function points or lines of code (KDSI). The output from intermediate COCOMO is a cost and size estimate; the output from each of the three models of COCOMO II is a range of cost and size estimates. Accordingly, if the most likely estimate of the effort is E, then the application composition model returns the range $(0.50E, 2.0E)$, and the postarchitecture model returns the range $(0.80E, 1.25E)$. This reflects the increasing accuracy of the progression of models of COCOMO II.

A second difference lies in the effort model underlying COCOMO:

$$\text{effort} = a \times (\text{size})^b \qquad (9.8)$$

where a and b are constants. In intermediate COCOMO, the exponent b takes on three different values, depending on whether the mode of the product to be built is organic ($b = 1.05$), semidetached ($b = 1.12$), or embedded ($b = 1.20$). In COCOMO II, the value of b varies between 1.01 and 1.26, depending on a variety of parameters of the model. These include familiarity with products of that type, process maturity level (Section 3.13), extent of risk resolution (Section 2.7), and degree of team cooperation (Section 4.1).

A third difference is the assumption regarding reuse. Intermediate COCOMO assumes that the savings due to reuse are directly proportional to the amount of reuse. COCOMO II takes into account that small changes to reused software incur disproportionately large costs (because the code has to be understood in detail for even a small change and the cost of testing a modified module is relatively large).

Fourth, there now are 17 multiplicative cost drivers, instead of 15 in intermediate COCOMO. Seven of the cost drivers are new, such as required reusability in future products, annual personnel turnover, and whether the product is being developed at multiple sites.

COCOMO II has been calibrated using 83 projects from a variety of different domains. The model still is too new for there to be many results regarding its accuracy and, in particular, the extent to which it is an improvement over its predecessor, the original (1981) COCOMO.

9.2.5   Tracking Duration and Cost Estimates

While the product is being developed, the actual development effort constantly must be compared against predictions. For example, suppose that the estimation metric used by the software developers predicted that the ***duration*** of the analysis workflow would last 3 months and require 7 person-months of effort. However, 4 months have gone by and 10 person-months of effort have been expended, yet the specifications are by no means complete. Deviations of this kind can serve as an early warning that something has gone wrong and corrective action must be taken. The problem could be that the size of the product was seriously underestimated or the development team is not as competent as it was thought to be. Whatever the reason, there are going to be serious duration and cost overruns, and management must take appropriate action to minimize the effects.

Careful tracking of predictions must be done throughout the development process, irrespective of the techniques by which the predictions were made. Deviations could be due to metrics that are poor predictors, inefficient software development, a combination of both, or some other reason. The important thing is to detect deviations early and take immediate corrective action. In addition, it is essential to continually update predictions in the light of additional information as it becomes available.

9.3   Estimation Issues

Use of the object-oriented paradigm results in a product consisting of a number of relatively independent smaller components, namely, the classes. This makes planning considerably easier, in that cost and duration estimates can be computed more easily and more accurately for smaller units. Of course, the estimates must take into account that a product is more than just the sum of its parts. The separate components are not totally independent; they can invoke one another, and these effects must not be overlooked.

Are the techniques for estimating cost and duration described in Section 9.2 applicable to the object-oriented paradigm? COCOMO II (Section 9.2.4) was designed to handle modern software technology, including object orientation, but what about earlier metrics such as function points (Section 9.2.1) and intermediate COCOMO (Section 9.2.3)? In the case of intermediate COCOMO, minor changes to some of the cost multipliers are required [Pittman, 1993]. Other than that, the estimation tools of Section 9.2 appear to work reasonably well on object-oriented projects—provided that there is no reuse. Reuse enters the object-oriented paradigm in two ways: reuse of existing components during development and the deliberate production (during the current project) of components to be reused in future products. Both forms of reuse affect the estimating process. Reuse during development clearly reduces the cost and duration. Formulas have been published showing the savings as a function of this reuse [Schach, 1994], but these results relate to the classical paradigm. At present, no information is available as to how the cost and duration change when reuse is utilized in the development of an object-oriented product.

We turn now to the goal of reusing parts of the current project. It can take about three times as long to design, implement, test, and document a reusable component as a similar nonreusable component [Pittman, 1993]. Cost and duration estimates must be modified to incorporate this additional labor, and the software project management plan as a whole must be adjusted to incorporate the effect of the reuse endeavor. Therefore, the two reuse activities work in opposite directions. Reuse of existing components reduces the overall effort in developing an object-oriented product, whereas designing components for reuse in future products increases the effort. It is expected that, in the long term, the savings due to reuse of classes will outweigh the costs of the original developments, and already some evidence supports this [Lim, 1994].

Now that metrics for estimating duration and cost have been discussed, the components of the software project management plan are described.

9.4   Components of a Software Project Management Plan

A software project management plan (SPMP) has three main components: the work to be done, the resources with which to do it, and the money to pay for it all. In this section, these three ingredients of the plan are discussed. The terminology is taken from [IEEE 1058, 1998], which is discussed in greater detail in Section 9.5.

Software development requires resources. The major **_resources_** required are the people who will develop the software, the hardware on which the software is run, and the support software such as operating systems, text editors, and version control software (Section 5.7).

Use of resources such as personnel varies with time. Norden [1958] has shown that for large projects, the **_Rayleigh distribution_** is a good approximation of the way that resource consumption, R_c, varies with time, t, that is,

$$R_c = \frac{t}{k^2}e^{-t^2/2k^2} \quad 0 \le t < \infty \tag{9.9}$$

Parameter k is a constant, the time at which consumption is at its peak, and e = 2.71828..., the base of Naperian (natural) logarithms. A typical Rayleigh curve is shown in Figure 9.8. Resource consumption starts small, climbs rapidly to a peak, and then decreases at a slower rate. Putnam [1978] investigated the applicability of Norden's results

Figure 9.8
Rayleigh curve showing how resource consumption varies with time.

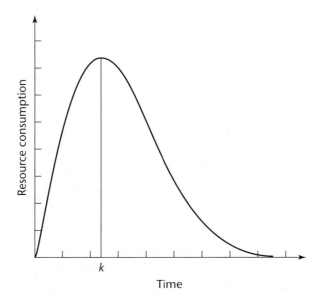

to software development and found that personnel and other resource consumption was modeled with some degree of accuracy by the Rayleigh distribution.

It therefore is insufficient in a software plan merely to state that three senior programmers with at least 5 years of experience are required. What is needed is something like the following:

> Three senior programmers with at least 5 years of experience in real-time programming are needed, two to start 3 months after the project commences, the third to start 6 months after that. Two will be phased out when product testing commences, the third when postdelivery maintenance begins.

The fact that resource needs depend on time applies not only to personnel but also to computer time, support software, computer hardware, office facilities, and even travel. Consequently, the software project management plan is a function of time.

The work to be done falls into two categories. First is work that continues throughout the project and does not relate to any specific workflow of software development. Such work is termed a **project function**. Examples are project management and quality control. Second is work that relates to a specific workflow in the development of the product; such work is termed an *activity* or a *task*. An **activity** is a major unit of work that has precise beginning and ending dates; consumes resources, such as computer time or person-days; and results in **work products**, such as a budget, design documents, schedules, source code, or a user's manual. An activity, in turn, comprises a set of tasks, a **task** being the smallest unit of work subject to management accountability. There are therefore three kinds of work in a software project management plan: project functions carried on throughout the project, activities (major units of work), and tasks (minor units of work).

A critical aspect of the plan concerns completion of work products. The date on which a work product is deemed completed is termed a **milestone**. To determine whether a work product indeed has reached a milestone, it must first pass a series of **reviews** performed by fellow team members, management, or the client. A typical milestone is the date on which the design is completed and passes review. Once a work product has been reviewed and agreed on, it becomes a **baseline** and can be changed only through formal procedures, as described in Section 5.8.2.

In reality, there is more to a work product than merely the product itself. A **work package** defines not just the work product but also the staffing requirements, duration, resources, name of the responsible individual, and acceptance criteria for the work product. **Money** of course is a vital component of the plan. A detailed budget must be worked out and the money allocated, as a function of time, to the project functions and activities.

The issue of how to draw up a plan for software production is addressed next.

9.5   Software Project Management Plan Framework

There are many ways of drawing up a project management plan. One of the best is IEEE Standard 1058 [1998]. The components of the plan are shown in Figure 9.9.

- The standard was drawn up by representatives of numerous major organizations involved in software development. Input came from both industry and universities, and the members of the working group and reviewing teams had many years of experience in drawing up project management plans. The standard incorporates this experience.

Figure 9.9
The IEEE project management plan framework.

1. Overview
   1.1 Project summary
       1.1.1 Purpose, scope, and objectives
       1.1.2 Assumptions and constraints
       1.1.3 Project deliverables
       1.1.4 Schedule and budget summary
   1.2 Evolution of the project management plan
2. Reference materials
3. Definitions and acronyms
4. Project organization
   4.1 External interfaces
   4.2 Internal structure
   4.3 Roles and responsibilities
5. Managerial process plans
   5.1 Start-up plan
       5.1.1 Estimation plan
       5.1.2 Staffing plan
       5.1.3 Resource acquisition plan
       5.1.4 Project staff training plan
   5.2 Work plan
       5.2.1 Work activities
       5.2.2 Schedule allocation
       5.2.3 Resource allocation
       5.2.4 Budget allocation
   5.3 Control plan
       5.3.1 Requirements control plan
       5.3.2 Schedule control plan
       5.3.3 Budget control plan
       5.3.4 Quality control plan
       5.3.5 Reporting plan
       5.3.6 Metrics collection plan
   5.4 Risk management plan
   5.5 Project close-out plan
6. Technical process plans
   6.1 Process model
   6.2 Methods, tools, and techniques
   6.3 Infrastructure plan
   6.4 Product acceptance plan
7. Supporting process plan
   7.1 Configuration management plan
   7.2 Testing plan
   7.3 Documentation plan
   7.4 Quality assurance plan
   7.5 Reviews and audits plan
   7.6 Problem resolution plan
   7.7 Subcontractor management plan
   7.8 Process improvement plan
8. Additional plans

- The IEEE project management plan is designed for use with all types of software products. It does not impose a specific life-cycle model or prescribe a specific methodology. The plan essentially is a framework, the contents of which are tailored by each organization for a particular domain, development team, or technique.

- The IEEE project management plan framework supports process improvement. For example, many of the sections of the framework reflect CMM key process areas (Section 3.13) such as configuration management and metrics.

- The IEEE project management plan framework is ideal for the Unified Process. For instance, one section of the plan is devoted to requirements control and another to risk management, both central aspects of the Unified Process.

On the other hand, although the claim is made in IEEE Standard 1058 [1998] that the IEEE project management plan is applicable to software projects of all sizes, some of the sections are not relevant to small-scale software. For example, Section 7.7 of the plan framework is headed "Subcontractor Management Plan," but it is all but unheard of for subcontractors to be used in small-scale projects.

Accordingly, we now present the plan framework in two different ways. First, the full framework is described in Section 9.6. Second, a slightly abbreviated version of the framework is used in Appendix E for a management plan for a small-scale project, the MSG Foundation case study (Section 10.6).

9.6   IEEE Software Project Management Plan

The **IEEE software project management plan** (SPMP) framework itself now is described in detail. The numbers and headings in the text correspond to the entries in Figure 9.9. The various terms used have been defined in Section 9.4.

1 Overview.

1.1 Project summary.

1.1.1 Purpose, scope, and objectives. A brief description is given of the purpose and scope of the software product to be delivered, as well as project objectives. Business needs are included in this subsection.

1.1.2 Assumptions and constraints. Any assumptions underlying the project are stated here, together with constraints, such as the delivery date, budget, resources, and artifacts to be reused.

1.1.3 Project deliverables. All the items to be delivered to the client are listed here, together with the delivery dates.

1.1.4 Schedule and budget summary. The overall schedule is presented here, together with the overall budget.

1.2 Evolution of the project management plan. No plan can be cast in concrete. The project management plan, like any other plan, requires continual updating in the light of experience and change within both the client organization and the software development organization. In this section, the formal procedures and mechanisms for changing the plan are described, including the mechanism for placing the project management plan itself under configuration control.

2 Reference materials. All documents referenced in the project management plan are listed here.

3 Definitions and acronyms. This information ensures that the project management plan will be understood the same way by everyone.

4 Project organization.

4.1 External interfaces. No project is constructed in a vacuum. The project members have to interact with the client organization and other members of their own organization. In addition, subcontractors may be involved in a large project. Administrative and managerial boundaries between the project and these other entities must be laid down.

4.2 Internal structure. In this section, the structure of the development organization itself is described. For example, many software development organizations are divided into two types of groups: development groups that work on a single project and support groups that provide support functions, such as configuration management and quality assurance, on an organization-wide basis. Administrative and managerial boundaries between the project group and the support groups also must be defined clearly.

4.3 Roles and responsibilities. For each project function, such as quality assurance, and for each activity, such as product testing, the individual responsible must be identified.

5 Managerial process plans.

5.1 Start-up plan.

5.1.1 Estimation plan. The techniques used to estimate project duration and cost are listed here, as well as the way these estimates are tracked and, if necessary, modified while the project is in progress.

5.1.2 Staffing plan. The numbers and types of personnel required are listed, together with the durations for which they are needed.

5.1.3 Resource acquisition plan. The way of acquiring the necessary resources, including hardware, software, service contracts, and administrative services, is given here.

5.1.4 Project staff training plan. All training needed for successful completion of the project is listed in this subsection.

5.2 Work plan.

5.2.1 Work activities. In this subsection, the work activities are specified, down to the task level if appropriate.

5.2.2 Schedule allocation. In general, the work packages are interdependent and further dependent on external events. For example, the implementation workflow follows the design workflow and precedes product testing. In this subsection, the relevant dependencies are specified.

5.2.3 Resource allocation. The various resources previously listed are allocated to the appropriate project functions, activities, and tasks.

5.2.4 Budget allocation. In this subsection, the overall budget is broken down at the project function, activity, and task levels.

5.3 Control plan.

5.3.1 Requirements control plan. As described in Chapter 2 of this book, while a software product is being developed, the requirements frequently change. The mechanisms used to monitor and control the changes to the requirements are given in this section.

5.3.2 Schedule control plan. In this subsection, mechanisms for measuring progress are listed, together with a description of the actions to be taken if actual progress lags behind planned progress.

5.3.3 Budget control plan. It is important that spending should not exceed the budgeted amount. Control mechanisms for monitoring when actual cost exceeds budgeted cost, as well as the actions to be taken should this happen, are described in this subsection.

5.3.4 Quality control plan. The ways in which quality is measured and controlled are described in this subsection.

5.3.5 Reporting plan. To monitor the requirements, schedule, budget, and quality, reporting mechanisms need to be in place. These mechanisms are described in this subsection.

5.3.6 Metrics collection plan. As explained in Section 5.3, it is not possible to manage the development process without measuring relevant metrics. The metrics to be collected are listed in this subsection.

5.4 Risk management plan. Risks have to be identified, prioritized, mitigated, and tracked. All aspects of risk management are described in this section.

5.5 Project close-out plan. The actions to be taken once the project is completed, including reassignment of staff and archiving of artifacts, are presented here.

6 Technical process plans.

6.1 Process model. In this section, a detailed description is given of the life-cycle model to be used.

6.2 Methods, tools, and techniques. The development methodologies and programming languages to be used are described here.

6.3 Infrastructure plan. Technical aspects of hardware and software are described in detail in this section. Items that should be covered include the computing systems (hardware, operating systems, network, and software) to be used for developing the software product, as well as the target computing systems on which the software product will be run and CASE tools to be employed.

6.4 Product acceptance plan. To ensure that the completed software product passes its acceptance test, acceptance criteria must be drawn up, the client must agree to the criteria in writing, and the developers must then ensure that these criteria are indeed met. The way that these three stages of the acceptance process will be carried out is described in this section.

7 Supporting process plans.

7.1 Configuration management plan. In this section, a detailed description is given of the means by which all artifacts are put under configuration management.

7.2 Testing plan. Testing, like all other aspects of software development, needs careful planning.

7.3 Documentation plan. A description of documentation of all kinds, whether or not to be delivered to the client at the end of the project, is included in this section.

7.4 Quality assurance plan. All aspects of quality assurance, including testing, standards, and reviews, are encompassed by this section.

7.5 Reviews and audits plan. Details as to how reviews are conducted are presented in this section.

7.6 Problem resolution plan. In the course of developing a software product, problems are all but certain to arise. For example, a design review may bring to light a critical fault in the analysis workflow that requires major changes to almost all the artifacts already completed. In this section, the way such problems are handled is described.

7.7 Subcontractor management plan. This section is applicable when subcontractors are to supply certain work products. The approach to selecting and managing subcontractors then appears here.

7.8 Process improvement plan. Process improvement strategies are included in this section.

8 Additional plans. For certain projects, additional components may need to appear in the plan. In terms of the IEEE framework, they appear at the end of the plan. Additional components may include security plans, safety plans, data conversion plans, installation plans, and the software project postdelivery maintenance plan.

9.7 Planning Testing

One component of the SPMP frequently overlooked is **test planning**. Like every other activity of software development, testing must be planned. The SPMP must include resources for testing, and the detailed schedule must explicitly indicate the testing to be done during each workflow.

Without a test plan, a project can go awry in a number of ways. For example, during product testing (Section 3.7.4), the SQA group must check that every aspect of the specification document, as signed off on by the client, has been implemented in the completed product. A good way of assisting the SQA group in this task is to require that the development be traceable (Section 3.7). That is, it must be possible to connect each statement in the specification document to a part of the design, and each part of the design must be reflected explicitly in the code. One technique for achieving this is to number each statement in the specification document and ensure that these numbers are reflected in both the design and the resulting code. However, if the test plan does not specify that this is to be done, it is highly unlikely that the analysis, design, and code artifacts will be labeled appropriately. Consequently, when the product testing finally is performed, it will be extremely difficult for the SQA group to determine that the product is a complete implementation of the specifications. In fact, traceability should start with the requirements; each statement in the requirements artifacts must be connected to part of the analysis artifacts.

One powerful aspect of inspections is the detailed list of faults detected during an inspection. Suppose that a team is inspecting the specifications of a product. As explained in Section 6.2.3, the list of faults is used in two ways. First, the fault statistics from this inspection must be compared with the accumulated averages of fault statistics from previous specification inspections. Deviations from previous norms indicate problems within the project. Second, the fault statistics from the current specification inspection must be carried forward to the design and code inspections of the product. After all, if there are a large number of faults of a particular type, it is possible that not all of them were detected during the inspection of the specifications, and the design and code inspections provide an additional opportunity for locating any remaining faults of this type. However, unless the test plan states that details of all faults have to be carefully recorded, it is unlikely that this task will be done.

An important way of testing code modules is so-called black-box testing (Section 13.10) in which the code is executed with test cases based on the specifications. Members of the SQA group read through the specifications and draw up test cases to check whether the code obeys the specification document. The best time to draw up black-box test cases is at the end of the analysis workflow, when the details of the specification document still are fresh in the minds of the members of the SQA group that inspected it. However, unless the test plan explicitly states that the black-box test cases are to be selected at this time, in all probability only a few black-box test cases will hurriedly be thrown together later. That is, a limited number of test cases will be rapidly assembled only when pressure starts mounting from the programming team for the SQA group to approve its modules so that they can be integrated into the product as a whole. As a result, the quality of the product as a whole suffers.

Therefore, every test plan must specify what testing is to be performed, when it is to be performed, and how it is to be performed. Such a test plan is an essential part of Section 7.2 of the SPMP. Without it, the quality of the overall product undoubtedly will suffer.

9.8   Training Requirements

When the subject of **_training_** is raised in discussions with the client, a common response is, "We don't need to worry about training until the product is finished, and then we can train the users." This is a somewhat unfortunate remark, implying as it does that only users require training. In fact, training also may be needed by members of the development team, starting with training in software planning and estimating. When new software development techniques, such as new design techniques or testing procedures, are used, training must be provided to every member of the team using the new technique.

Introduction of the object-oriented paradigm has major training consequences. The introduction of hardware or software tools such as workstations or an integrated environment (see Section 13.23.2) also requires training. Programmers may need training in the operating system of the machine to be used for product development as well as in the implementation language. Documentation preparation training frequently is overlooked, as evidenced by the poor quality of so much documentation. Computer operators certainly require some sort of training to be able to run the new product; they also may require additional training if new hardware is utilized.

The required training can be obtained in a number of ways. The easiest and least disruptive is in-house training, by either fellow employees or consultants. Many companies offer a variety of training courses, and colleges often offer training courses in the evenings. World Wide Web-based courses are another alternative.

Once the training needs have been determined and the training plan drawn up, the plan must be incorporated into the SPMP.

9.9   Documentation Standards

The development of a software product is accompanied by a wide variety of **documentation**. Jones found that 28 pages of documentation were generated per 1000 instructions (KDSI) for an IBM internal commercial product around 50 KDSI in size, and about 66 pages per KDSI for a commercial software product of the same size. Operating system IMS/360 Version 2.3 was about 166 KDSI in size, and 157 pages of documentation per KDSI were produced. The documentation was of various types, including planning, control, financial, and technical [Jones, 1986a]. In addition to these types of documentation, the source code itself is a form of documentation; comments within the code constitute further documentation.

A considerable portion of the software development effort is absorbed by documentation. A survey of 63 development projects and 25 postdelivery maintenance projects showed that, for every 100 hours spent on activities related to code, 150 hours were spent on activities related to documentation [Boehm, 1981]. For large TRW products, the proportion of time devoted to documentation-related activities rose to 200 hours per 100 code-related hours [Boehm et al., 1984].

Standards are needed for every type of documentation. For instance, uniformity in design documentation reduces misunderstandings between team members and aids the SQA group. Although new employees have to be trained in the documentation standards, no further training is needed when existing employees move from project to project within the organization. From the viewpoint of postdelivery maintenance, uniform coding standards assist maintenance programmers in understanding source code. Standardization is even more important for user manuals, because these have to be read by a wide of variety of individuals, few of whom are computer experts. The IEEE has developed a standard for user manuals (IEEE Standard 1063 for Software User Documentation).

As part of the planning process, standards must be established for all documentation to be produced during software production. These standards are incorporated in the SPMP.

Where an existing standard is to be used, such as the ANSI/IEEE Standard for Software Test Documentation [ANSI/IEEE 829, 1991], the standard is listed in Section 2 of the SPMP (reference materials). If a standard is specially written for the development effort, then it appears in Section 6.2 (methods, tools, and techniques).

Documentation is an essential aspect of the software production effort. In a very real sense, the product *is* the documentation, because without documentation the product cannot be maintained. Planning the documentation effort in every detail, and then ensuring that the plan is adhered to, is a critical component of successful software production.

9.10   CASE Tools for Planning and Estimating

A number of tools are available that automate intermediate COCOMO and COCOMO II. For speed of computation when the value of a parameter is modified, several implementations of intermediate COCOMO have been written in spreadsheet languages such as Lotus 1-2-3 or Excel. For developing and updating the plan itself, a word processor is essential.

Management information tools also are useful for planning. For example, suppose that a large software organization has 150 programmers. A scheduling tool can help planners keep track of which programmers already are assigned to specific tasks and which are available for the current project.

More general types of management information also are needed. A number of commercially available management tools can be used both to assist with the planning and estimating process and monitor the development process as a whole. These include MacProject and Microsoft Project.

Turning to documentation, Javadoc is a widely used tool for documenting Java classes. It generates documentation in HTML format from comments in Java source code. Doxygen is a more powerful open-source tool of this type; it generates documentation for a variety of languages and runs on a number of different platforms.

9.11   Testing the Software Project Management Plan

As pointed out at the beginning of this chapter, a fault in the software project management plan can have serious financial implications for the developers. It is critical that the development organization neither overestimate nor underestimate the cost of the project or its duration. For this reason, the entire SPMP must be checked by the SQA group before estimates are given to the client. The best way to test the plan is by a plan inspection.

The plan inspection team must review the SPMP in detail, paying particular attention to the cost and duration estimates. To reduce risks even further, irrespective of the metrics used, the duration and cost estimates should be computed independently by a member of the SQA group as soon as the members of the planning team have determined their estimates.

Chapter Review

The main theme of this chapter is the importance of planning in the software process (Section 9.1). A vital component of any software project management plan is estimating the duration and the cost (Section 9.2). Several metrics are put forward for estimating the size of a product, including function points (Section 9.2.1). Next, various metrics for cost estimation are described, especially intermediate COCOMO (Section 9.2.3) and COCOMO II (Section 9.2.4). As described in Section 9.2.5, it is essential to track all estimates. Estimation issues are discussed in Section 9.3. The three major components of a software project management plan—the work to be done, the resources with which to do it, and the money to pay for it—are explained in Section 9.4. One particular SPMP, the IEEE standard, is outlined in Section 9.5 and described in detail in Section 9.6. Next follow sections on planning testing (Section 9.7) and training requirements and documentation standards and their implications for the planning process (Sections 9.8 and 9.9). CASE tools for planning and estimating are described in Section 9.10. The chapter concludes with material on testing the software project management plan (Section 9.11).

For Further Reading

Weinberg's four-volume work [Weinberg, 1992; 1993; 1994; 1997] provides detailed information on many aspects of software management, as do [Bennatan, 2000] and [Reifer, 2000]. Metrics for managing software projects are discussed in [Weller, 1994].

For management of the object-oriented paradigm, [Pittman, 1993] and [Nesi, 1998] should be consulted. For further information on IEEE Standard 1058 for Software Project Management Plans, the standard itself should be read carefully [IEEE 1058, 1998]. The need for careful planning is described in [McConnell, 2001].

Sackman's classic work is described in [Sackman, Erikson, and Grant, 1968]. A more detailed source is [Sackman, 1970].

Useful information on function points can be found in [Low and Jeffrey, 1990]. A careful analysis of function points, as well as suggested improvements, appears in [Symons, 1991]. Criticisms of function points appear in [Kitchenham, 1997].

The reliability of function points is discussed in [Kemerer and Porter, 1992] and [Kemerer, 1993]. Strengths and weaknesses of function points are presented in [Furey and Kitchenham, 1997]. A comprehensive source of information on all aspects of function points is [Boehm, 1997].

The theoretical justification for intermediate COCOMO, together with full details for implementing it, appears in [Boehm, 1981]; a shorter version is found in [Boehm, 1984]. COCOMO II is described in [Boehm et al., 2000]. Ways of enhancing COCOMO predictions are presented in [Smith, Hale, and Parrish, 2001].

Briand and Wüst [2001] describe how to estimate the development effort for object-oriented products. Estimating both the size and defects of object-oriented software products is described in [Cartwright and Shepperd, 2000]. Class points, an extension of function points to classes, are introduced in [Costagliola, Ferrucci, Tortora, and Vitiello, 2005].

Errors in estimating software effort are analyzed in [Jorgensen and Molokken-Ostvold, 2004]. Software productivity data for a variety of business data-processing products are presented in [Maxwell and Forselius, 2000]; the unit of productivity utilized is function points per hour. Other measures of productivity are discussed in [Kitchenham and Mendes, 2004]. Size estimation for software written in a fourth-generation language is presented in [Dolado, 2000]. A variety of articles on estimation appear in the November/December 2000 issue of *IEEE Software*.

Key Terms

activity 272
algorithmic cost estimation model 265
application composition model 269
baseline 272
bottom-up approach 265
COCOMO 265
COCOMO II 269
cone of uncertainty 258
cost 259
Delphi technique 264
documentation 279
duration 270
early design model 269
efficiency 261
expert judgment by analogy 264

external cost 259
FFP metric 261
function point 262
IEEE software project management plan (SPMP) 274
internal cost 259
lines of code (LOC) 260
milestone 272
money 272
nominal effort 266
planning 256
postarchitecture model 269
price 259
productivity 261
project function 272
Rayleigh distribution 271
resources 271
review 272

software development effort multipliers 266
task 272
technical complexity factor (TCF) 262
test planning 277
thousand delivered source instructions (KDSI) 260
training 278
unadjusted function points (UFP) 261
work package 272
work product 272

Problems   9.1   Why do you think that some cynical software organizations refer to *milestones* as *millstones*? (Hint: Look up the figurative meaning of *millstone* in a dictionary.)

9.2   You are a software engineer at Bronkhorstspruit Software Developers. A year ago, your manager announced that your next product would comprise 9 files, 49 flows, and 92 processes.

(i)   Using the FFP metric, determine its size.

(ii)   For Bronkhorstspruit Software Developers, the constant d in equation (9.2) has been determined to be $1003. What cost estimate did the FFP metric predict?

(iii)   The product recently was completed at a cost of $132,800. What does this tell you about the productivity of your development team?

9.3   A target product has 7 simple inputs, 2 average inputs, and 10 complex inputs. There are 56 average outputs, 8 simple inquiries, 12 average master files, and 17 complex interfaces. Determine the number of unadjusted function points (*UFP*).

9.4   If the total degree of influence for the product of Problem 9.3 is 49, determine the number of function points.

9.5   Why do you think that, despite its drawbacks, lines of code (LOC or KDSI) is so widely used as a metric of product size?

9.6   You are in charge of developing a 67-KDSI embedded product that is nominal except that the database size is rated very high and the use of software tools is low. Using intermediate COCOMO, what is the estimated effort in person-months?

9.7   You are in charge of developing two 33-KDSI organic-mode products. Both are nominal in every respect except that product P1 has extra-high complexity and product P2 has extra-low complexity. To develop the product, you have two teams at your disposal. Team A has very high analyst capability, applications experience, and programmer capability. Team A also has high virtual machine experience and programming language experience. Team B is rated very low on all five attributes.

(i)   What is the total effort (in person-months) if team A develops product P1 and team B develops product P2?

(ii)   What is the total effort (in person-months) if team B develops product P1 and team A develops product P2?

(iii)   Which of the two preceding staffing assignments makes more sense? Is your intuition backed by the predictions of intermediate COCOMO?

9.8   You are in charge of developing a 49-KDSI organic-mode product that is nominal in every respect.

(i)   Assuming a cost of $9900 per person-month, how much is the project estimated to cost?

(ii)   Your entire development team resigns at the start of the project. You are fortunate enough to be able to replace the nominal team with a very highly experienced and capable team, but the cost per person-month will rise to $12,900. How much money do you expect to gain (or lose) as a result of the personnel change?

9.9   You are in charge of developing the software for a product that uses a set of newly developed algorithms to compute the most cost-effective routes for a large trucking company. Using intermediate COCOMO, you determine that the cost of the product will be $470,000. However, as a check, you ask a member of your team to estimate the effort using function points. She reports that the function point metric predicts a cost of $985,000, more than twice as large as your COCOMO prediction. What do you do now?

9.10   Show that the Rayleigh distribution (equation (9.9)) attains its maximum value when $t = k$. Find the corresponding resource consumption.

9.11   A product postdelivery maintenance plan is considered an "additional component" of an IEEE software project management plan. Bearing in mind that every nontrivial product is maintained and that the cost of postdelivery maintenance, on average, is about twice or three times the cost of developing the product, how can this be justified?

9.12   Why do software development projects generate so much documentation?

9.13   (Term project) Consider the Osric's Office Appliances and Decor project described in Appendix A. Why is it not possible to estimate the cost and duration purely on the basis of the information in Appendix A?

9.14   (Readings in Software Engineering) Your instructor will distribute copies of [Costagliola, Ferrucci, Tortora, and Vitiello, 2005]. Are you convinced by the empirical validation of class points?

References   [Albrecht, 1979] A. J. ALBRECHT, "Measuring Application Development Productivity," *Proceedings of the IBM SHARE/GUIDE Applications Development Symposium,* Monterey, CA, October 1979, pp. 83–92.

[ANSI/IEEE 829, 1991] *Software Test Documentation,* ANSI/IEEE 829-1991, American National Standards Institute, Institute of Electrical and Electronic Engineers, New York, 1991.

[Bennatan, 2000] E. M. BENNATAN, *On Time within Budget: Software Project Management Practices and Techniques,* 3rd ed., John Wiley and Sons, New York, 2000.

[Boehm, 1981] B. W. BOEHM, *Software Engineering Economics,* Prentice Hall, Englewood Cliffs, NJ, 1981.

[Boehm, 1984] B. W. BOEHM, "Software Engineering Economics," *IEEE Transactions on Software Engineering* **SE-10** (January 1984), pp. 4–21.

[Boehm, 1997] R. BOEHM (EDITOR), "Function Point FAQ," at ourworld.compuserve.com/homepages/softcomp/fpfaq.htm, June 25, 1997.

[Boehm et al., 1984] B. W. BOEHM, M. H. PENEDO, E. D. STUCKLE, R. D. WILLIAMS, AND A. B. PYSTER, "A Software Development Environment for Improving Productivity," *IEEE Computer* **17** (June 1984), pp. 30–44.

[Boehm et al., 2000] B. W. BOEHM, C. ABTS, A. W. BROWN, S. CHULANI, B. K. CLARK, E. HOROWITZ, R. MADACHY, D. REIFER, AND B. STEECE, *Software Cost Estimation with COCOMO II,* Prentice Hall, Upper Saddle River, NJ, 2000.

[Briand and Wüst, 2001] L. C. BRIAND AND J. WÜST, "Modeling Development Effort in Object-Oriented Systems Using Design Properties," *IEEE Transactions on Software Engineering* **27** (November 2001), pp. 963–86.

[Cartwright and Shepperd, 2000] M. CARTWRIGHT AND M. SHEPPERD, "An Empirical Investigation of an Object-Oriented Software System," *IEEE Transactions on Software Engineering* **26** (August 2000), pp. 786–95.

[Costagliola, Ferrucci, Tortora, and Vitiello, 2005] G. COSTAGLIOLA, F. FERRUCCI, G. TORTORA, AND G. VITIELLO, "Class Point: An Approach for the Size Estimation of Object-Oriented Systems," *IEEE Transactions on Software Engineering* **31** (January 2005), pp. 52–74.

[Devenny, 1976] T. DEVENNY, "An Exploratory Study of Software Cost Estimating at the Electronic Systems Division," Thesis No. GSM/SM/765–4, Air Force Institute of Technology, Dayton, OH, 1976.

[Dolado, 2000] J. J. DOLADO, "A Validation of the Component-Based Method for Software Size Estimation," *IEEE Transactions on Software Engineering* **26** (October 2000), pp. 1006–21.

[Furey and Kitchenham, 1997] S. FUREY AND B. KITCHENHAM, "Function Points," *IEEE Software* **14** (March/April 1997), pp. 28–32.

[IEEE 1058, 1998] "IEEE Standard for Software Project Management Plans," IEEE Std. 1058–1998, Institute of Electrical and Electronic Engineers, New York, 1998.

[Jones, 1986a] C. JONES, *Programming Productivity,* McGraw-Hill, New York, 1986.

[Jones, 1987] C. JONES, Letter to the Editor, *IEEE Computer* **20** (December 1987), p. 4.

[Jorgensen and Molokken-Ostvold, 2004] M. JORGENSEN AND K. MOLOKKEN-OSTVOLD, "Reasons for Software Effort Estimation Error: Impact of Respondent Role, Information Collection Approach, and Data Analysis Method," *IEEE Transactions on Software Engineering* **30** (December 2004), pp. 993–1007.

[Kemerer, 1993] C. F. KEMERER, "Reliability of Function Points Measurement: A Field Experiment," *Communications of the ACM* **36** (February 1993), pp. 85–97.

[Kemerer and Porter, 1992] C. F. KEMERER AND B. S. PORTER, "Improving the Reliability of Function Point Measurement: An Empirical Study," *IEEE Transactions on Software Engineering* **18** (November 1992), pp. 1011–24.

[Kitchenham, 1997] B. KITCHENHAM, "The Problem with Function Points," *IEEE Software* **14** (March/April 1997), pp. 29, 31.

[Kitchenham and Mendes, 2004] B. KITCHENHAM AND E. MENDES, "Software Productivity Measurement Using Multiple Size Measures," *IEEE Transactions on Software Engineering* **30** (December 2004), pp. 1023–35.

[Lim, 1994] W. C. LIM, "Effects of Reuse on Quality, Productivity, and Economics," *IEEE Software* **11** (September 1994), pp. 23–30.

[Low and Jeffrey, 1990] G. C. LOW AND D. R. JEFFREY, "Function Points in the Estimation and Evaluation of the Software Process," *IEEE Transactions on Software Engineering* **16** (January 1990), pp. 64–71.

[Maxwell and Forselius, 2000] K. D. MAXWELL AND P. FORSELIUS, "Benchmarking Software Development Productivity," *IEEE Software* **17** (January/February 2000), pp. 80–88.

[McConnell, 2001] S. MCCONNELL, "The Nine Deadly Sins of Project Planning," *IEEE Software* **18** (November/December 2001), pp. 5–7.

[Nesi, 1998] P. NESI, "Managing OO Projects Better," *IEEE Software* **15** (July/August 1998), pp. 50–60.

[Norden, 1958] P. V. NORDEN, "Curve Fitting for a Model of Applied Research and Development Scheduling," *IBM Journal of Research and Development* **2** (July 1958), pp. 232–48.

[Pittman, 1993] M. PITTMAN, "Lessons Learned in Managing Object-Oriented Development," *IEEE Software* **10** (January 1993), pp. 43–53.

[Putnam, 1978] L. H. PUTNAM, "A General Empirical Solution to the Macro Software Sizing and Estimating Problem," *IEEE Transactions on Software Engineering* **SE-4** (July 1978), pp. 345–61.

[Reifer, 2000] D. J. REIFER, "Software Management: The Good, the Bad, and the Ugly," *IEEE Software* **17** (March/April 2000), pp. 73–75.

[Sackman, 1970] H. SACKMAN, *Man–Computer Problem Solving: Experimental Evaluation of Time-Sharing and Batch Processing,* Auerbach, Princeton, NJ, 1970.

[Sackman, Erikson, and Grant, 1968] H. SACKMAN, W. J. ERIKSON, AND E. E. GRANT, "Exploratory Experimental Studies Comparing Online and Offline Programming Performance," *Communications of the ACM* **11** (January 1968), pp. 3–11.

[Schach, 1994] S. R. SCHACH, "The Economic Impact of Software Reuse on Maintenance," *Journal of Software Maintenance: Research and Practice* **6** (July/August 1994), pp. 185–96.

[Smith, Hale, and Parrish, 2001] R. K. SMITH, J. E. HALE, AND A. S. PARRISH, "An Empirical Study Using Task Assignment Patterns to Improve the Accuracy of Software Effort Estimation," *IEEE Transactions on Software Engineering* **27** (March 2001), pp. 264–71.

[Symons, 1991] C. R. SYMONS, *Software Sizing and Estimating:* Mk II FPA, John Wiley and Sons, Chichester, UK, 1991.

[van der Poel and Schach, 1983] K. G. VAN DER POEL AND S. R. SCHACH, "A Software Metric for Cost Estimation and Efficiency Measurement in Data Processing System Development," *Journal of Systems and Software* **3** (September 1983), pp. 187–91.

[Weinberg, 1992] G. M. WEINBERG, *Quality Software Management: Systems Thinking,* Vol. 1, Dorset House, New York, 1992.

[Weinberg, 1993] G. M. WEINBERG, *Quality Software Management: First-Order Measurement,* Vol. 2, Dorset House, New York, 1993.

[Weinberg, 1994] G. M. WEINBERG, *Quality Software Management: Congruent Action,* Vol. 3, Dorset House, New York, 1994.

[Weinberg, 1997] G. M. WEINBERG, *Quality Software Management: Anticipating Change,* Vol. 4, Dorset House, New York, 1997.

[Weller, 1994] E. F. WELLER, "Using Metrics to Manage Software Projects," *IEEE Computer* **27** (September 1994), pp. 27–34.

The Workflows of the Software Life Cycle

Part 2

In Part 2, the workflows of the software life cycle are described in depth. For each workflow, the activities, CASE tools, metrics, and testing techniques appropriate to that workflow are presented, as well as the challenges of that workflow.

Chapter 10, "The Requirements Workflow," examines requirements. The aim of this workflow is to determine the client's real needs. Various requirements analysis techniques are presented.

Once the requirements have been determined, the next step is to draw up the specifications, as described in Chapter 11, "The Analysis Workflow." Object-oriented analysis is utilized here.

Object-oriented design is the primary topic of Chapter 12, "The Design Workflow."

Implementation is discussed in Chapter 13, "The Implementation Workflow." Areas covered include implementation, integration, good programming practice, and programming standards.

Chapter 14 is entitled "Postdelivery maintenance." Topics covered in this chapter include the importance and challenges of postdelivery maintenance. The management of postdelivery maintenance is considered in some detail.

In Chapter 15, "More on UML," additional information is provided about the Unified Modeling Language.

By the end of Part 2, you should have a clear understanding of all the workflows of the software process, the challenges associated with each workflow, and how to meet those challenges.

Chapter 10

The Requirements Workflow

Learning Objectives

After studying this chapter, you should be able to

- Perform the requirements workflow.
- Draw up the initial business model.
- Draw up the requirements.

The chances of a product being developed on time and within budget are somewhat slim unless the members of the software development team agree on what the software product is to do. The first step in achieving this unanimity is to analyze the client's current situation as precisely as possible. For example, it is inadequate to say, "The client needs a computer-aided design system because they claim their manual design system is lousy." Unless the development team knows exactly what is wrong with the current manual system, there is a high probability that aspects of the new computerized system will be equally "lousy." Similarly, if a personal computer manufacturer is contemplating development of a new operating system, the first step is to evaluate the firm's current operating system and analyze carefully exactly why it is unsatisfactory. To take an extreme example, it is vital to know whether the problem exists only in the mind of the sales manager who blames the operating system for poor sales, or whether users of the operating system are thoroughly disenchanted with its functionality and reliability. Only after a clear picture of the present situation has been gained can the team attempt to answer the critical question, What must the new product be able to do? The process of answering this question is the primary objective of the requirements workflow.

S. I. Hayakawa (1906–1992), U.S. Senator from California, once told a group of reporters, "I know you believe you understood what you think I said, but I am not sure you realize that what you heard is not what I meant." This excuse applies equally well to the issue of requirements analysis. The software engineers hear their client's requests, but what they hear is not what the client should be saying.

That quotation has been wrongly attributed to former U.S. presidential candidate George Romney (1907–1995) who once announced at a press conference, "I didn't say that I didn't say it. I said that I didn't say I said it. I want to make that very clear." Romney's "clarification" highlights another challenge of requirements analysis—it is easy to misunderstand what the client says.

10.1   Determining What the Client Needs

A commonly held misconception is that, during the requirements workflow, the developers must determine what software the client *wants*. On the contrary, the real objective of the requirements workflow is to determine what software the client *needs*. One problem is that many clients do not know what they need. Furthermore, even a client who has a good idea of what is needed may have difficulty in accurately conveying these ideas to the developers, because most clients are less computer literate than the members of the development team. (For more insight into this issue, see Just in Case You Wanted to Know Box 10.1.)

Another problem is that the client may not appreciate what is going on in his or her own organization. For example, it is no use for a client to ask for a faster software product when the real reason why the current software product has such a long response time is that the database is badly designed. What needs to be done is to reorganize and improve the way that data are stored in the current software product. A new software product will be just as slow. Or, if the client operates an unprofitable chain of retail stores, the client may ask for a financial management information system that reflects such items as sales, salaries, accounts payable, and accounts receivable. Such an information system will be of little use if the real reason for the losses is shrinkage (shoplifting and theft by employees). If that is the case, then a stock control system rather than a financial management information system is required.

At first sight, determining what the client needs is straightforward—the members of the development team simply ask him or her. However, there are two reasons why this direct approach usually does not work too well.

First, as has just been stated, the client may not appreciate what is going on in his or her own organization. But the major reason why a client so often asks for the wrong software product is that software is complex. It is difficult enough for a software engineer to visualize a software product and its functionality—the problem is far worse for the client, who usually is not an expert in software engineering.

Without the assistance of a skilled software development team, the client may be a poor source of information regarding what needs to be developed. On the other hand, unless there is face-to-face communication with the client, there is no way of finding out what really is needed.

The object-oriented approach is to obtain initial information from the client and future users of the target product and to use this initial information as an input to the requirements workflow of the Unified Process [Jacobson, Booch, and Rumbaugh, 1999]. This is described in Section 10.2.

10.2   Overview of the Requirements Workflow

The first step in the **requirements workflow** is to gain an understanding of the **application domain** (or **domain**, for short), that is, the specific environment in which the target product is to operate. The domain could be banking, space exploration, automobile manufacturing, or telemetry. Once the members of the development team understand the domain to a sufficient depth, they can build a business model, that is, use UML diagrams to describe the client's business processes. The business model is used to determine what the client's initial requirements are. Then iteration is applied.

In other words, the starting point is an initial understanding of the domain. This information is used to build the initial business model. The initial business model is utilized to draw up an initial set of the client's requirements. Then, in the light of what has been learned about the client's requirements, a deeper understanding of the domain is gained; and this knowledge is utilized in turn to refine the business model and hence the client's requirements. This iteration continues until the team is satisfied with the set of requirements. At this point, the iteration stops.

The process of discovering the client's requirements is termed **requirements elicitation** (or **requirements capture**). Once the initial set of requirements has been drawn up, the process of refining and extending them is termed **requirements analysis**.

We now examine each of these steps in detail.

10.3   Understanding the Domain

To elicit the client's needs, the members of the requirements team must be familiar with the application domain, that is, the general area in which the target product is to be used. For example, it is not easy to ask meaningful questions of a banker or a neurosurgeon without first acquiring some familiarity with banking or neurosurgery. Therefore, an initial task of each member of the requirements analysis team is to acquire familiarity with the application domain, unless he or she already has experience in that general area. It is particularly important to use correct terminology when communicating with the client and potential users of the target software. After all, it is hard to be taken seriously by a person working in a specific domain unless the interviewer uses the nomenclature appropriate for that domain. More important, use of an inappropriate word may lead to a misunderstanding, eventually resulting in a faulty product being delivered. The same problem can arise if the members of the requirements team do not understand the subtleties of the terminology of the domain. For example, to a layperson words like *brace*, *beam*, *girder*, and *strut* may appear to be synonyms, but to a civil engineer they are distinct terms. If a developer does not appreciate that a civil engineer is using these four terms in a precise way and if the civil engineer assumes that the developer is familiar with the distinctions among the terms, the developer may treat the four terms as equivalent; the resulting computer-aided bridge design software may contain faults that result in a bridge collapsing. Computer professionals hope that the output of every program will be scrutinized carefully by a human before decisions are made based on that program, but the growing popular faith in computers means that it is distinctly unwise to rely on the likelihood of such a check being made. So, it is by no means far-fetched that a misunderstanding in terminology could lead to the software developers being sued for negligence.

One way to address the problem with terminology is to construct a **_glossary_**, a list of technical words used in the domain, together with their meanings. The initial entries are inserted into the glossary while the team members are busy learning as much as they can about the application domain. Then, the glossary is updated whenever the members of the requirements team encounter new terminology. Every so often, the glossary can be printed out and distributed to team members or downloaded to a PDA (such as a Palm Pilot). Not only does such a glossary reduce confusion between client and developers, it also is useful in lessening misunderstandings between the members of the development team.

Once the requirements team has acquired familiarity with the domain, the next step is to build the business model.

10.4   The Business Model

A **_business model_** is a description of the business processes of an organization. For example, some of the business processes of a bank include accepting deposits from clients, loaning money to clients, and making investments.

The reason for building a business model first is that the business model provides an understanding of the client's business as a whole. With this knowledge, the developers can advise the client as to which portions of the client's business to computerize. Alternatively, if the task is to extend an existing software product, the developers have to understand the existing business as a whole to determine how to incorporate the extension and to learn what parts, if any, of the existing product need to be modified to add the new piece.

To build a business model, a developer needs to obtain a detailed understanding of the various business processes. These processes are now _refined_, that is, analyzed in greater detail. A number of different techniques can be used to obtain the information needed to build the business model, primarily interviewing.

10.4.1   Interviewing

The members of the requirements team meet with members of the client organization until they are convinced that they have elicited all relevant information from the client and future users of the target software product.

There are two basic types of question. A closed-ended question requires a specific answer. For example, the client might be asked how many salespeople the company employs or how fast a response time is required. Open-ended questions are asked to encourage the person being interviewed to speak out. For instance, asking the client, "Why is your current software product unsatisfactory?" may explain many aspects of the client's approach to business. Some of these facts might not come to light if the question were closed ended.

Similarly, there are two basic types of interview, structured and unstructured. In a **_structured interview_**, specific preplanned questions are asked, frequently closed ended. In an **_unstructured interview_**, the interviewer may start with one or two prepared closed-ended questions, but subsequent questions are posed in response to the answers he or she receives from the person being interviewed. Many of these subsequent questions are likely to be open ended in nature to provide the interviewer with wide-ranging information.

At the same time, it is not a good idea if the interview is too unstructured. Saying to the client, "Tell me about your business" is unlikely to yield much relevant knowledge. In other words, questions should be posed in such a way as to encourage the person being interviewed to give wide-ranging answers but always within the context of the specific information needed by the interviewer.

Conducting a good interview is not always easy. First, the interviewer must be fully familiar with the application domain. Second, there is no point in interviewing a member of the client organization if the interviewer has already made up his or her mind regarding the client's needs. No matter what the interviewer has previously been told or what he or she has learned by other means, the interviewer must approach every interview with the intention of listening carefully to what the person being interviewed has to say, while firmly suppressing any preconceived notions regarding the client company or the needs of the clients and the potential users of the target product to be developed.

After the interview is concluded, the interviewer must prepare a written report outlining the results of the interview. It is strongly advisable to give a copy of the report to the person who was interviewed; he or she may want to clarify certain statements or add overlooked items.

10.4.2   Other Techniques

Interviewing is the primary technique for obtaining information for the business model. This section describes some other techniques that may be used in conjunction with interviewing.

One way of gaining knowledge about the activities of the client organization is to send a **questionnaire** to the relevant members of the client organization. This technique is useful when the opinions of, say, hundreds of individuals need to be determined. Furthermore, a carefully thought-out written answer from an employee of the client organization may be more accurate than an immediate verbal response to a question posed by an interviewer. However, an unstructured interview conducted by a methodical interviewer who listens carefully and poses questions that elicit amplifications of initial responses usually yields far better information than a thoughtfully worded questionnaire. Because questionnaires are preplanned, there is no way that a question can be posed in response to an answer.

A different way of eliciting requirements is to examine the various **forms** used by the business. For example, a form in a printing works might reflect press number, paper roll size, humidity, ink temperature, paper tension, and so on. The various fields in this form shed light on the flow of print jobs and the relative importance of the steps in the printing process. Other documents, such as operating procedures and job descriptions, also can be powerful tools for finding out exactly what is done and how. If a software product is being used, the user manuals should also be carefully studied. A comprehensive set of different types of data regarding how the client currently does business can be extraordinarily helpful in determining the client's needs. Therefore, a good software professional carefully studies client documentation, treating it as a valuable potential source of information that can lead to an accurate assessment of the client's needs.

Another way of obtaining such information is by **direct observation** of the users, that is, by members of the requirements team observing and writing down the actions of the employees while they perform their duties. A modern version of this technique is to set up **videotape cameras** within the workplace to record (with the prior written permission of those being observed) exactly what is being done. One difficulty of this technique is that it can take a long time to analyze the tapes. In general, one or more members of the requirements team has to spend an hour playing back the tape for every hour that the cameras record. This time is in addition to what is needed to assess what was observed. More seriously, this technique has been known to backfire badly because employees may view the cameras as an unwarranted invasion of privacy. It is important that the requirements team have the full cooperation of all employees; it can be extremely difficult to obtain the necessary information if people feel threatened or harassed. The possible risks should be considered carefully before introducing cameras or, for that matter, taking any other action that has the potential to annoy or even anger employees.

10.4.3   Use Cases

As stated in Section 3.2, a ***model*** is a set of UML diagrams that represent one or more aspects of the software product to be developed (recall that the *ML* in UML stands for "modeling language"). A primary UML diagram used in business modeling is the use case.

A ***use case*** models an interaction between the software product itself and the users of that software product (***actors***). For example, Figure 10.1 depicts a use case from a banking software product. There are two actors, represented by the UML stick figures, the **Customer** and the **Teller**. The label inside the oval describes the business activity represented by the use case, in this instance `Withdraw Money`.

Another way of looking at a use case is that it shows the interaction between the software product and the environment in which the software product operates. That is, an actor is a member of the world outside the software product, whereas the rectangle in the use case represents the software product itself.

It is usually easy to identify an actor.

- An actor is frequently a user of the software product. In the case of a banking software product, the users of that software product are the customers of the bank and the staff of the bank, including tellers and managers.
- In general, an actor plays a role with regard to the software product. This role may be as a user of the software product. However, an initiator of a use case or someone who plays a critical part in a use case is also playing a role and is therefore regarded as an actor, irrespective of whether that person is also a user of the software product. An example of this is given in Section 10.7.

A user of the system can play more than one role. For example, a customer of the bank can be a **Borrower** (when he or she takes out a loan) or a **Lender** (when he or she deposits money in the bank—a bank makes much of its profits by investing the money deposited by customers). Conversely, one actor can participate in multiple use cases. For example,

Figure 10.1
The `Withdraw Money` use case of the banking software product.

Customer   **Banking Software Product**   **Teller**

Withdraw Money

Figure 10.2
Generalization
of medical staff.

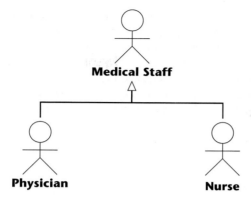

a **Borrower** may be an actor in the `Borrow Money` use case, the `Pay Interest on Loan` use case, and the `Repay Loan Principal` use case. Also, the actor **Borrower** may stand for many thousands of bank customers.

An actor need not be a human. Recall that an actor is a user of a software product, and in many cases another software product can be a user. For example, an e-commerce information system that allows purchasers to pay with credit cards has to interact with the credit card company information system. That is, the credit card company information system is an actor from the viewpoint of the e-commerce company information system. Similarly, the e-commerce information system is an actor from the viewpoint of the credit card company information system.

As previously stated, identification of actors is easy. Generally, the only difficulty that arises in this part of the paradigm is that an overzealous software professional sometimes identifies overlapping actors. For example, in a hospital software product, having a use case with actor **Nurse** and a different use case with actor **Medical Staff** is not a good idea, because all nurses are medical staff, but some medical staff (such as physicians) are not nurses. It would be better to have actors **Physician** and **Nurse**. Alternatively, actor **Medical Staff** can be defined with two specializations, **Physician** and **Nurse**. This is depicted in Figure 10.2. In Section 7.7, it was pointed out that inheritance is a special case of generalization. Generalization was applied to classes in Section 7.7. Figure 10.2 shows how generalization can be applied to actors, too.

10.5   Initial Requirements

To determine the client's requirements, initial requirements are drawn up based on the initial business model. Then, as the understanding of the domain and the business model is refined on the basis of further discussions with the client, the requirements are refined.

The requirements are dynamic. That is, there are frequent changes not just to the requirements themselves but also to the attitudes of the development team, client, and future users toward each requirement. For example, a particular requirement may first appear to the development team to be optional. After further analysis, that requirement may now seem to be critically important. However, after discussion with the client, the requirement is rejected. A good way to handle these frequent changes is to maintain a list of likely requirements, together with use cases of the requirements that have been agreed to by the members of the development team and approved by the client.

It is important to bear in mind that the object-oriented paradigm is iterative and the glossary, the business model, or the requirements therefore may have to be modified at any time. In particular, additions to the requirements list, modifications to items already on the list, and removal of items from the list can be triggered by a wide variety of events, ranging from a casual remark made by a user to a suggestion from the client at a formal meeting of the systems analysts on the requirements team. Any such change may trigger corresponding changes to the business model.

Requirements fall into two categories, functional and nonfunctional. A **functional requirement** specifies an action that the target product must be able to perform. Functional requirements are often expressed in terms of inputs and outputs: Given a specific input, the functional requirement stipulates what the output must be. Conversely, a **nonfunctional requirement** specifies properties of the target product itself, such as **platform constraints** ("The software product shall run under Linux"), **response times** ("On average, queries of Type 3B shall be answered within 2.5 seconds"), or **reliability** ("The software product shall run 99.5 percent of the time").

Functional requirements are handled while the requirements and analysis workflows are being performed, whereas some nonfunctional requirements may have to wait until the design workflow. The reason is that, to be able to handle certain nonfunctional requirements, detailed knowledge about the target software product may be needed, and this knowledge is usually not available until the requirements and analysis workflows have been completed (see Problems 10.1 and 10.2). However, wherever possible, nonfunctional requirements should also be handled during the requirements and analysis workflows.

The requirements workflow is now illustrated by a running case study.

Case Study

10.6   Initial Understanding of the Domain: The MSG Foundation Case Study

When Martha Stockton Greengage died at the age of 87, she left her entire $2.3 billion fortune to charity. Specifically, her will set up the Martha Stockton Greengage (MSG) Foundation to assist young couples in purchasing their own homes by providing low-cost loans.

In order to reduce operating expenses, the trustees of the MSG Foundation are investigating computerization. Because none of the trustees has any experience with computers, they decide to commission a small software development organization to implement a pilot project, namely, a software product that will perform the calculations needed to determine how much money is available each week to purchase homes.

The first step, as always, is to understand the application domain, home mortgages in this instance. Not many people can afford to pay cash to buy a home. Instead, they pay a small percentage of the purchase price out of their own savings and borrow the rest of the money. This type of loan, where real estate is pledged as security for the loan, is termed a **mortgage** (see Just in Case You Wanted to Know Box 10.2).

Have you ever wondered why the word *mortgage* is pronounced "more gidge" with the accent on the first syllable? The word, which was first used in Middle English in the 14th century, comes from the Old French word *mort* meaning "dead" and the Germanic word *gage* meaning "a pledge," that is, a promise to forfeit property if the debt is not paid. Strangely enough, a mortgage is a "dead pledge" in two different senses. If the loan is not repaid, the property is forfeited, or "dead" to the borrower, forever. And if the loan is repaid, then the promise to repay is dead. This two-way explanation was first given by the English judge Sir Edward Coke (1552–1634).

And the strange pronunciation? The final letter in a French word like *mort* is silent—hence the "more." And the suffix *-age* is frequently pronounced "idge" in English. Examples include the words carriage, marriage, disparage, and encourage.

For example, suppose that someone wishes to buy a house for $100,000. (Many houses nowadays cost much more than that, particularly in the larger cities, but the round number makes the arithmetic easier.) The person buying the house pays a **deposit** of (say) 10 percent, or $10,000, and borrows the remaining $90,000 from a financial institution such as a bank or a savings and loan company in the form of a mortgage for that amount. As a result, the **principal** (or **capital**) borrowed is $90,000.

Suppose that the terms of the mortgage are that the loan is to be repaid in monthly installments over 30 years at an interest rate of 7.5 percent per annum (or 0.625 percent per month). Each month, the borrower pays the finance company $629.30. Part of this amount is the interest on the outstanding balance; the rest is used to reduce the principal. This monthly payment is therefore often referred to as **P & I** (principal and **interest**). For example, in the first month the outstanding balance is $90,000. Monthly interest at 0.625 percent on $90,000 is $562.50. The remainder of the P & I payment of $629.30, namely $66.80, is used to reduce the principal. Consequently, at the end of the first month, after the first payment has been made, only $89,933.20 is owed to the finance company.

The interest for the second month is 0.625 percent of $89,933.20, or $562.08. The P & I payment is $629.30, as before, and the balance of the P & I payment (now $67.22) again is used to reduce the principal, this time to $89,865.98.

After 15 years (180 months), the monthly P & I payment is still $629.30, but now the principal has been reduced to $67,881.61. The monthly interest on $67,881.61 is $424.26, so the remaining $205.04 of the P & I payment is used to reduce the principal. After 30 years (360 months), the entire loan will have been repaid.

The finance company wants to be certain that it will be repaid the $90,000 it is owed, plus interest. It ensures this in a number of different ways.

- First, the borrower signs a legal document (the mortgage deed) that states that, if the monthly payments are not made, the finance company may sell the house and use the proceeds to pay off the outstanding balance of the loan.

- Second, the finance company requires the borrower to insure the house, so that if (say) the house burns down, the insurance company will cover the loss and the check from the insurance company will then be used to repay the loan. The insurance premium is usually paid once a year by the finance company.

Figure 10.3 The initial glossary of the MSG Foundation case study.

Balance: the amount of the loan still owing

Capital: synonym for principal

Closing costs: other costs involved in buying a house, such as legal costs and various taxes

Deposit: an initial installment toward the total cost of the house

Escrow account: a savings account managed by the finance company into which the weekly installments toward the annual insurance premium and annual real-estate tax payment are deposited, and from which the annual insurance premium and the annual real estate tax payment are paid

Interest: a cost of borrowing money, computed as a fraction of the amount owing

Mortgage: a loan in which real estate is pledged as security for the loan

P & I: abbreviation for "principal and interest"

Points: a cost of borrowing money, computed as a fraction of the total amount borrowed

Principal: the lump sum borrowed

Principal and interest: an installment payment consisting of the interest plus the fraction of the principal for that installment

To obtain the money for the premium from the borrower, the finance company requires the borrower to pay monthly insurance installments. It deposits the installments in an ***escrow account***, essentially a savings account managed by the finance company. When the annual insurance premium is due, the money is taken from the escrow account. Real-estate taxes paid on a home are treated the same way; that is, monthly installments are deposited in the escrow account and the annual real-estate tax payment is made from that account.

- Third, the finance company wants to be sure that the borrower can afford to pay for the mortgage. Typically, a mortgage will not be granted if the total monthly payment (P & I plus insurance plus real-estate taxes) exceeds 28 percent of the borrower's total income.

In addition to the monthly payments, the finance company almost always wants to be paid a lump sum up front in return for lending the money to the borrower. Typically, the finance company will want 2 percent of the principal ("2 ***points***"). In the case of the $90,000 loan, this amounts to $1800.

Finally, there are other costs involved in buying a house, such as legal costs and various taxes. Consequently, when the contract to buy the $100,000 house is signed (when the deal is "closed"), the ***closing costs*** (legal costs, taxes, and so on) plus the points can easily amount to $7000.

The initial glossary of the MSG Foundation domain is shown in Figure 10.3.

The initial business model of the MSG Foundation case study is now constructed.

*C*ase Study

10.7 Initial Business Model: The MSG Foundation Case Study

Members of the development organization interview various managers and staff members of the MSG Foundation and discover the way the Foundation operates. At the start of each week, the MSG Foundation estimates how much money will be available that week to fund mortgages. Couples whose income is too low to afford a standard mortgage to buy a home can apply at any time to the MSG Foundation for a mortgage. An MSG Foundation staff member first determines whether the couple qualifies for an MSG mortgage and then determines whether the MSG Foundation still has sufficient funds on hand that week to purchase the home. If so, the mortgage is granted and the weekly mortgage repayment is computed according to the MSG Foundation's rules. This repayment amount may vary from week to week, depending on the couple's current income.

The corresponding part of the business model consists of three use cases: `Estimate Funds Available for Week`, `Apply for an MSG Mortgage`, and `Compute Weekly Repayment Amount`. These use cases are shown in Figures 10.4, 10.5, and 10.6, and the corresponding initial **use-case descriptions** appear in Figures 10.7, 10.8, and 10.9, respectively.

Consider the use case `Apply for an MSG Mortgage` (Figure 10.5). The actor on the right is **Applicants**. But is **Applicants** really an actor? Recall from Section 10.4.3 that an actor is a user of a software product. However, applicants do not use the software product. They fill in a form. Their answers are then entered into the software product by an MSG staff member. In addition, they may ask questions of the staff member or answer questions put to them by the staff member. But regardless of their interactions with MSG staff members, applicants never interact with the software product.[1]

However,

- The **Applicants** initiate the use case. That is, if a couple does not apply for a mortgage, this use case never occurs.

Figure 10.4
The `Estimate Funds Available for Week` use case of the initial business model of the MSG Foundation case study.

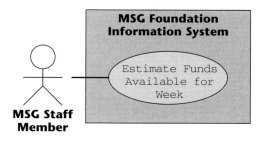

---

[1] This will change if the MSG Foundation ever decides to accept applications over the Web. Specifically, **Applicants** will then become the only actor in Figure 10.6; **MSG Staff Member** will no longer play a role.

Figure 10.5 The `Apply for an MSG Mortgage` use case of the initial business model of the MSG Foundation case study.

Figure 10.6 The `Compute Weekly Repayment Amount` use case of the initial business model of the MSG Foundation case study.

Figure 10.7 The description of the `Estimate Funds Available for Week` use case of the initial business model of the MSG Foundation case study.

Brief Description
The `Estimate Funds Available for Week` use case enables an MSG Foundation staff member to estimate how much money the Foundation has available that week to fund mortgages.
Step-by-Step Description
Not applicable at this initial stage.

- Second, the information that the **MSG Staff Member** gives to the software product is provided by **Applicants**.
- Third, in a sense, the real actor is **Applicants**; the **MSG Staff Member** is merely an agent of the **Applicants**.

For all these reasons, **Applicants** is indeed an actor.

Now consider Figure 10.6, which depicts the use case `Compute Weekly Repayment Amount`. The actor on the right is now **Borrowers**. Once an application has been granted, the couple who applied for the mortgage (the **Applicants**) become **Borrowers**. But even as borrowers they do not interact with the software product. As before, only MSG staff members can enter information into the software product. Nevertheless, again the use case is initiated by actor

Figure 10.8   The description of the `Apply for an MSG Mortgage` use case of the initial business model of the MSG Foundation case study.

Brief Description
When a couple applies for a mortgage, the `Apply for an MSG Mortgage` use case enables an MSG Foundation staff member to determine whether they qualify for an MSG mortgage and, if so, whether funds are currently available for the mortgage.
Step-by-Step Description
Not applicable at this initial stage.

Figure 10.9   The description of the `Compute Weekly Repayment Amount` use case of the initial business model of the MSG Foundation case study.

Brief Description
The `Compute Weekly Repayment Amount` use case enables an MSG Foundation staff member to compute how much borrowers have to repay each-week.
Step-by-Step Description
Not applicable at this initial stage.

Figure 10.10   The `Manage an Investment` use case of the initial business model of the MSG Foundation case study.

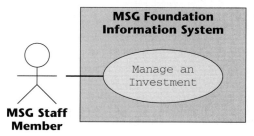

Borrowers and again the information entered by the **MSG Staff Member** is supplied by **Borrowers**. Accordingly, **Borrowers** is indeed an actor in the use case shown in Figure 10.6.

Another aspect of the MSG Foundation business model concerns the investments of the MSG Foundation. At this initial stage details are not yet known regarding the buying and selling of investments or how investment income becomes available for mortgages, but it is certainly clear that the use case `Manage an Investment` shown in Figure 10.10 is an essential part of the initial business model. The initial description appears in Figure 10.11; in a future iteration, details of how investments are handled will be inserted.

For conciseness, the four use cases of Figures 10.4, 10.5, 10.6, and 10.10 are combined into the ***use-case diagram*** of Figure 10.12.

Now the initial requirements have to be drawn up.

Figure 10.11   The description of the `Manage an Investment` use case of the initial business model of the MSG Foundation case study.

Brief Description

The `Manage an Investment` use case enables an MSG Foundation staff member to buy and sell investments and manage the investment portfolio.

Step-by-Step Description

Not applicable at this initial stage.

Figure 10.12   The use-case diagram of the initial business model of the MSG Foundation case study.

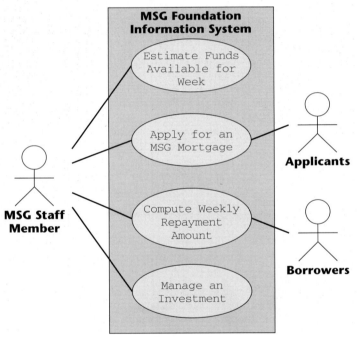

10.8   Initial Requirements: The MSG Foundation Case study

The four use cases of Figure 10.12 comprise the business model of the MSG Foundation. However, it is not immediately obvious whether they are all requirements of the MSG Foundation software product that is to be developed. Recall that what the client *wants* is "a pilot project, namely, a software product that will perform the calculations needed to determine how much money is available each week to purchase homes." As always, the task of the developers is to determine, with the aid of the client, what the client *needs*. At this early stage, however, there is not enough information at the analysts' disposal to be able to decide whether just this "pilot project" will be what is needed. In situations like this, the best way to proceed is to draw up the initial requirements on the basis of what the client wants, and then iterate.

Accordingly, each of the use cases of Figure 10.12 in turn is considered. Use case Estimate Funds Available for Week is obviously part of the initial requirements. On the other hand, Apply for an MSG Mortgage does not seem to have anything to do with the pilot project, so it is excluded from the initial requirements. At first sight, the third use case, Compute Weekly Repayment Amount, seems equally irrelevant to the pilot project. However, the pilot project deals with the "money that is available each week to purchase homes." Part of that money surely comes from the weekly repayment of existing mortgages, so the third use case is indeed part of the initial requirements. The fourth use case, Manage an Investment, is also part of the initial requirements for a similar reason—income from investments also must be used to fund new mortgages.

The initial requirements then consist of three use cases and their descriptions, namely, Estimate Funds Available for Week (Figures 10.4 and 10.7), Compute Weekly Repayment Amount (Figures 10.6 and 10.9), and Manage an Investment (Figures 10.10 and 10.11). These three use cases appear in Figure 10.13.

The next step is to iterate the requirements workflow; that is, the steps are performed again in order to obtain a better model of the client's needs.

Figure 10.13   The use-case diagram of the initial requirement of the MSG Foundation case study.

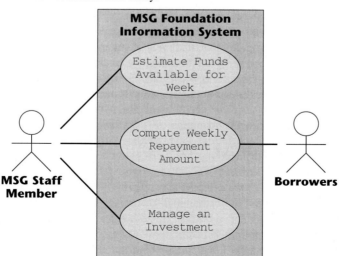

Case Study

10.9 Continuing the Requirements Workflow: The MSG Foundation Case Study

Armed with domain knowledge and familiarity with the initial business model, members of the development team now interview the MSG Foundation managers and staff in greater depth. They discover the following information.

The MSG Foundation grants a 100 percent mortgage to buy a home under the following conditions:

- The couple has been married for at least 1 year but not more than 10 years.
- Both husband and wife are gainfully employed. Specifically, proof must be provided that both were employed full time for at least 48 weeks of the preceding year.
- The price of the home must be below the published median price for homes in that area for the past 12 months.
- The installments on a fixed-rate, 30-year, 90 percent mortgage would exceed 28 percent of their combined gross income and/or they do not have sufficient savings to pay 10 percent of the cost of the home plus $7,000. (The $7,000 is an estimate of the additional costs involved, including closing costs and points.)
- The Foundation has sufficient funds to purchase the home; this is described later in more detail.

If the application is approved, then the amount that the couple should pay the MSG Foundation every week for the next 30 years is the total of the principal and interest payment, which never changes over the life of the mortgage, and the escrow payment, which is $\frac{1}{52}$nd of the sum of the annual real-estate tax and the annual homeowner's insurance premium. If this total is greater than 28 percent of the couple's gross weekly income, then the MSG Foundation will pay the difference in the form of a grant. As a result, the mortgage is paid in full each week, but the couple will never have to pay more than 28 percent of their combined gross income.

The couple must provide a copy of their income tax return each year so that the MSG Foundation has proof of their previous year's income. In addition, the couple may file copies of pay slips as proof of current gross income. The amount the couple has to pay for their mortgage may therefore vary from week to week.

The MSG Foundation uses the following algorithm to determine whether it has the funds to approve a mortgage application:

1. At the beginning of each week, the estimated annual income from its investments is computed and divided by 52.
2. The estimated annual MSG Foundation operating expenses are divided by 52.
3. The total of the estimated mortgage payments for that week is computed.
4. The total of the estimated grants for that week is computed.
5. The amount available at the beginning of the week is then (Item 1) – (Item 2) + (Item 3) – (Item 4).

6. During the week, if the cost of the home is no more than the amount available for mortgages, then the MSG Foundation deems that it has the funds needed to purchase the home; the amount available for mortgages that week is reduced by the cost of that home.

7. At the end of each week, any unspent funds are invested by the MSG Foundation investment advisors.

To keep the cost of the pilot project as low as possible, the developers are told that only those data items needed for the weekly funds computation should be incorporated into the software product. The rest can be added later if the MSG Foundation decides to computerize all aspects of its operation. Therefore, only three types of data are needed, namely, investment data, operating expenses data, and mortgage data.

With regard to investments, the following data are required:

Item number.
Item name.
Estimated annual return. (This figure is updated whenever new information becomes available. On average, this occurs about four times a year.)
Date estimated annual return was last updated.

With regard to operating expenses, the following data are required:

Estimated annual operating expenses. (This figure is currently determined four times a year.)
Date estimated annual operating expenses were last updated.

For each mortgage, the following data are required:

Account number.
Last name of mortgagees.
Original purchase price of home.
Date mortgage was issued.
Weekly principal and interest payment.
Current combined gross weekly income.
Date combined gross weekly income was last updated.
Annual real-estate tax.
Date annual real-estate tax was last updated.
Annual homeowner's insurance premium.
Date annual homeowner's insurance premium was last updated.

In the course of further discussions with MSG managers, the developers learn that three types of reports are needed:

The results of the funds computation for the week.
A listing of all investments (to be printed on request).
A listing of all mortgages (to be printed on request).

ase Study

10.10 Revising the Requirements: The MSG Foundation Case Study

Recall that the initial requirements model (Section 10.8) includes three use cases, namely, Estimate Funds Available for Week, Compute Weekly Repayment Amount, and Manage an Investment. These use cases are shown in Figure 10.13. Now, in the light of the additional information that has been received, the initial requirements can be revised.

The formula given in Section 10.9 for determining how much money is available at the beginning of a week is as follows:

1. The estimated annual income from investments is computed and divided by 52.
2. The estimated annual MSG Foundation operating expenses are divided by 52.
3. The total of the estimated mortgage payments for that week is computed.
4. The total of the estimated grants for that week is computed.
5. The amount available is then (Item 1) − (Item 2) + (Item 3) − (Item 4).

Consider each of these items in turn.

1. *Estimated annual income from investments.* For each investment in turn, sum the estimated annual return on each investment, and divide the result by 52. To do this, an additional use case is needed, namely, Estimate Investment Income for Week. (Use case Manage an Investment is still needed for adding, deleting, and modifying investments.) This new use case is depicted in Figure 10.14 and described in Figure 10.15. In Figure 10.14, the dashed line with the open arrowhead labeled «include» denotes that use case Estimate Investment Income for Week is part of use case Estimate Funds Available for Week. The resulting first iteration of the revised use-case diagram is shown in Figure 10.16 with the new use case shaded.

Figure 10.14   The Estimate Investment Income for Week use case of the revised requirements of the MSG Foundation case study.

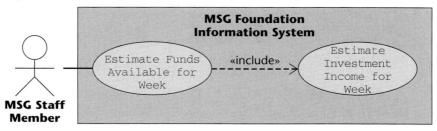

Figure 10.15   The description of the `Estimate Investment Income for Week` use case of the revised requirements of the MSG Foundation case study.

Brief Description
The `Estimate Investment Income for Week` use case enables the `Estimate Funds Available for Week` use case to estimate how much investment income is available for this week.
Step-by-Step Description
1. For each investment, extract the estimated annual return on that investment. 2. Sum the values extracted in Step 1 and divide the result by 52.

Figure 10.16   The first iteration of the use-case diagram of the revised requirements of the MSG Foundation case study. The new use case is shaded.

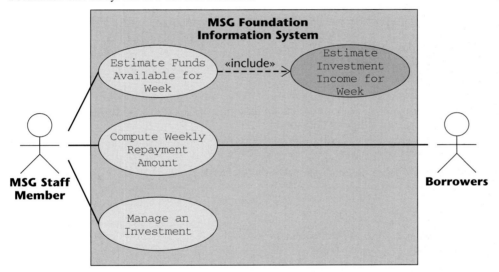

2. *Estimated annual operating expenses.* Up to now, the estimated annual operating expenses have not been considered. To incorporate these expenses, two additional use cases are needed. Use case `Update Estimated Annual Operating Expenses` models adjustments to the value of the estimated annual operating expenses, and use case `Estimate Operating Expenses for Week` provides the estimate of the operating expenses that is required. The use cases are shown in Figures 10.17 through 10.20. In Figure 10.19, use case `Estimate Operating Expenses for Week` is similarly part of use case `Estimate Funds Available for Week`, as indicated by the dashed line with the open arrowhead labeled «include». The resulting second iteration of the revised use-case diagram is shown in Figure 10.21. The two new use cases, `Estimate Operating Expenses for Week` and `Update Estimated Annual Operating Expenses`, are shaded.

3. *Total estimated mortgage payments for the week.*   See item 4.

Figure 10.17 The Update `Estimated Annual Operating Expenses` use case of the revised requirements of the MSG Foundation case study.

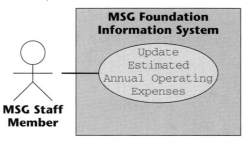

Figure 10.18 The description of the `Update Estimated Annual Operating Expenses` use case of the revised requirements of the MSG Foundation case study.

Brief Description
The `Update Estimated Annual Operating Expenses` use case enables an MSG Foundation staff member to update the estimated annual operating expenses.
Step-by-Step Description
1. Update the estimated annual operating expenses.

Figure 10.19 The Estimate `Operating Expenses for Week` use case of the revised requirements of the MSG Foundation case study.

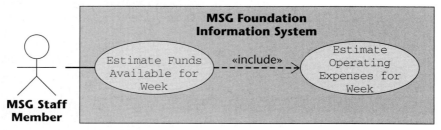

4. *Total estimated grant payments for the week.* The weekly repayment amount from use case `Compute Weekly Repayment Amount` is the total estimated mortgage payment less the estimated total grant payment. In other words, use case `Compute Weekly Repayment Amount` models the computation of both the estimated mortgage payment and the estimated grant payment for each mortgage separately. Summing these separate quantities will yield the total estimated mortgage payments for the week as well as the total estimated grant

Figure 10.20   The description of the `Estimate Operating Expenses for Week` use case of the revised requirements of the MSG Foundation case study.

Brief Description

The `Estimate Operating Expenses for Week` use case enables the `Estimate Funds Available for Week` use case to estimate the operating expenses for the week.

Step-by-Step Description

1. Divide the estimated annual operating expenses by 52.

Figure 10.21   The second iteration of the use-case diagram of the revised requirements of the MSG Foundation case study. The two new use cases, `Estimate Operating Expenses for Week` and `Update Estimated Annual Operating Expenses`, are shaded.

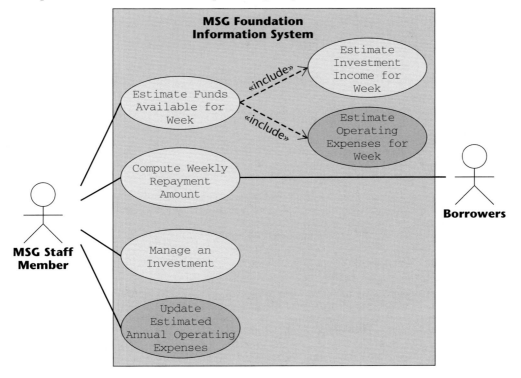

payments for the week. However, `Compute Weekly Repayment Amount` also models the borrowers changing the amount of their weekly income. Accordingly, `Compute Weekly Repayment Amount` needs to be split into two separate use cases, namely, `Estimate Payments and Grants for Week` and `Update Borrowers' Weekly Income`. The two new use cases are described in Figures 10.22 through 10.25. Once more, one of the new use cases, namely, `Estimate Payments and Grants for Week`, is part of use case `Estimate Funds Available for Week`, as indicated by the dashed line with the open arrowhead labeled «include» in Figure 10.22. The resulting third iteration of the revised use-case diagram is shown in Figure 10.26 with the two use cases derived from use case `Compute Weekly Repayment Amount` shaded.

Consider Figure 10.26 again. Use case `Estimate Funds Available for Week` models the computation that uses the data obtained from three other use

Figure 10.22 The `Estimate Payments and Grants for Week` use case of the revised requirements of the MSG Foundation case study.

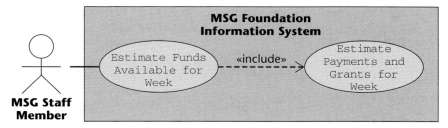

Figure 10.23 The description of the `Estimate Payments and Grants for Week` use case of the revised requirements of the MSG Foundation case study.

Brief Description

The `Estimate Payments and Grants for Week` use case enables the `Estimate Funds Available for Week` use case to estimate the total estimated mortgage payments paid by borrowers to the MSG Foundation for this week and the total estimated grants paid by the MSG Foundation for this week.

Step-by-Step Description

1. For each mortgage:
    1.1 The amount to be paid this week is the total of the principal and interest payment and $\frac{1}{52}$nd of the sum of the annual real-estate tax and the annual homeowner's insurance premium.
    1.2 Compute 28 percent of the couple's current gross weekly income.
    1.3 If the result of Step 1.1 is greater than the result of Step 1.2, then the mortgage payment for this week is the result of Step 1.2, and the amount of the grant for-this week is the difference between the result of Step 1.1 and the result of Step 1.2.
    1.4 Otherwise, the mortgage payment for this week is the result of Step 1.1 and there is no grant this week.
2. Summing the mortgage payments of Steps 1.3 and 1.4 yields the estimated mortgage payments for the week.
3. Summing the grant payments of Step 1.3 yields the estimated grant payments for the week.

Figure 10.24 The `Update Borrowers' Weekly Income` use case of the revised requirements of the MSG Foundation case study.

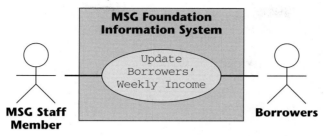

Figure 10.25 The description of the `Update Borrowers' Weekly Income` use case of the revised requirements of the MSG Foundation case study.

Brief Description

The `Update Borrowers' Weekly Income` use case enables an MSG Foundation staff member to update the weekly income of a couple who have borrowed money from the Foundation.

Step-by-Step Description

1. Update the borrower's weekly income.

---

cases, namely, `Estimate Investment Income for Week`, `Estimate Operating Expenses for Week`, and `Estimate Payments and Grants for Week`. This is shown in Figure 10.27, which shows the second iteration of the use case Estimate Funds Available for Week; this figure has been extracted from the use-case diagram of Figure 10.26. Figure 10.28 is the corresponding description of the use case.

Why is it so important to indicate the ***«include» relationship*** in UML diagrams? For example, Figure 10.29 shows two versions of Figure 10.26, the correct version on top and an incorrect version below. The top diagram correctly models use case `Estimate Funds Available for Week` as part of use case `Estimate Payments and Grants for Week`. The bottom diagram of Figure 10.29 models use cases `Estimate Funds Available for Week` and `Estimate Payments and Grants for Week` as two independent use cases. However, as stated in Section 10.4.3, a use case models an interaction between the software product itself and users of the software product (actors). This is fine for use case `Estimate Funds Available for Week`. However, use case `Estimate Payments and Grants for Week` does not interact with an actor and, therefore, cannot be a use case in its own right. Instead, it is a portion of use case `Estimate Funds Available for Week`, as reflected in the top diagram of Figure 10.29.

Figure 10.26 The third iteration of the use-case diagram of the revised requirements of the MSG Foundation case study. The two use cases derived from use case `Compute Weekly Repayment Amount` are shaded.

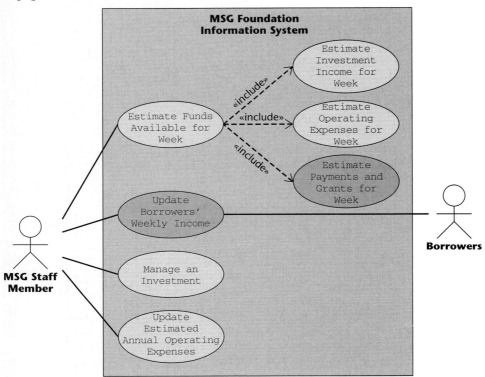

Figure 10.27 The second iteration of the `Estimate Funds Available for Week` use case of the revised requirements of the MSG Foundation case study.

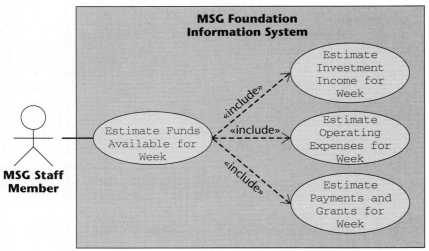

FIGURE 10.28 The second iteration of the description of the `Estimate Funds Available for Week` use case of the revised requirements of the MSG Foundation case study.

Brief Description

The `Estimate Funds Available for Week` use case enables an MSG Foundation staff member to estimate how much money the Foundation has available that week to fund mortgages.

Step-by-Step Description

1. Determine the estimated income from investments for the week utilizing use case `Estimate Investment Income for Week`.
2. Determine the operating expenses for the week utilizing use case `Estimate Operating Expenses for Week`.
3. Determine the total estimated mortgage payments for the week utilizing use case `Estimate Payments and Grants for Week`.
4. Determine the total estimated grants for the week utilizing use case `Estimate Payments and Grants for Week`.
5. Add the results of Steps 1 and 3 and subtract the results of Steps 2 and 4. This is the total amount available for mortgages for the current week.

Figure 10.29 Correct (top) and incorrect (bottom) versions of Figure 10.22.

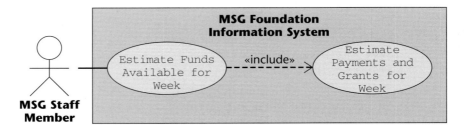

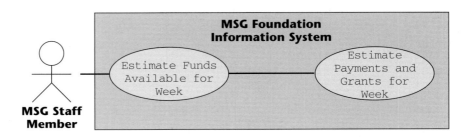

ase Study

10.11 The Test Workflow: The MSG Foundation Case Study

A common side effect of the iterative and incremental life-cycle model is that details that correctly have been postponed somehow get forgotten. That is one of the many reasons why continual testing is essential. In this instance, the details of the use case Manage an Investment have been overlooked. This is remedied in Figures 10.30 and 10.31.

Further review brings to light the omission of use case Manage a Mortgage to model the addition of a new mortgage, the modification of an existing mortgage, or the removal of an existing mortgage, analogous to use case Manage an Investment. Figures 10.32 and 10.33 correct this omission, and the fourth iteration of the revised use-case diagram is shown in Figure 10.34 with the new use case, Manage a Mortgage, shaded.

Figure 10.30   The Manage an Investment use case of the revised requirements of the MSG Foundation case study.

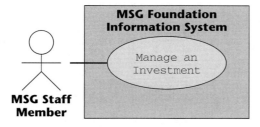

Figure 10.31   The description of the Manage an Investment use case of the revised requirements of the MSG Foundation case study.

Brief Description
The Manage an Investment use case enables an MSG Foundation staff member to add and delete investments and manage the investment portfolio.
Step-by-Step Description
1. Add, modify, or delete an investment.

Figure 10.32   The `Manage a Mortgage` use case of the revised requirements of the MSG Foundation case study.

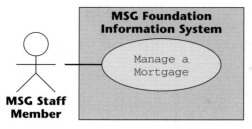

Figure 10.33   The description of the `Manage a Mortgage` use case of the revised requirements of the MSG Foundation case study.

Brief Description
The `Manage a Mortgage` use case enables an MSG Foundation staff member to add and delete mortgages and manage the mortgage portfolio.
Step-by-Step Description
1. Add, modify, or delete a mortgage.

Furthermore, the use case for printing the various reports has also been overlooked. Accordingly, use case `Produce a Report`, which models the printing of the three reports, is added. The details of the use case appear in Figures 10.35 and 10.36. The fifth iteration of the revised use-case diagram is shown in Figure 10.37 with the new use case, `Produce a Report`, shaded.

The revised requirements are checked yet again, and two new problems are uncovered. First, a use case has been partially duplicated. Second, two of the use cases need to be reorganized.

The first change to be made is to remove the partially duplicated use case. Consider the use case `Manage a Mortgage` (Figures 10.32 and 10.33). As stated in Figure 10.33, one of the actions of this use case is to modify a mortgage. Now consider the use case `Update Borrowers' Weekly Income` (Figures 10.24 and 10.25). The only purpose of this use case (Figure 10.25) is to update the borrowers' weekly income. But the borrowers' weekly income is an attribute of the mortgage. That is, use case `Manage a Mortgage` already includes the use case `Update Borrowers' Weekly Income`. Accordingly, use case `Update Borrowers' Weekly Income` is superfluous and should be deleted. The result is shown in Figure 10.38, the sixth iteration of the revised use-case diagram. The modified use case, `Manage a Mortgage`, is shaded.

This is the first iteration that has resulted in a decrement rather than an increment. That is, this is the first time in this book that the result of an iteration has been

Figure 10.34   The fourth iteration of the use-case diagram of the revised requirements of the MSG Foundation case study. The new use case, `Manage a Mortgage`, is shaded.

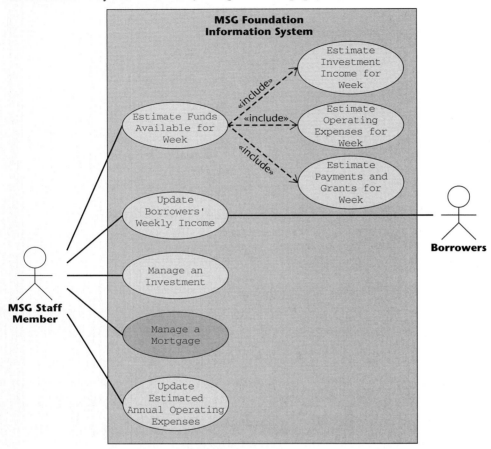

Figure 10.35   The `Produce a Report` use case of the revised requirements of the MSG Foundation case study.

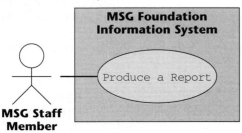

Figure 10.36   The description of the `Produce a Report` use case of the revised requirements of the MSG Foundation case study.

Brief Description

The `Produce a Report` use case enables an MSG Foundation staff member to print the results of the weekly computation of funds available for new mortgages or to print a listing of all investments or all mortgages.

Step-by-Step Description

1. The following reports must be generated:
1.1 Investments report—printed on demand:
> The information system prints a list of all investments. For each investment, the following attributes are printed:
>> Item number
>> Item name
>> Estimated annual return
>> Date estimated annual return was last updated
1.2 Mortgages report—printed on demand:
> The information system prints a list of all mortgages. For each mortgage, the following attributes are printed:
>> Account number
>> Name of mortgagee
>> Original price of home
>> Date mortgage was issued
>> Principal and interest payment
>> Current combined gross weekly income
>> Date current combined gross weekly income was last updated
>> Annual real-estate tax
>> Date annual real-estate tax was last updated
>> Annual homeowner's insurance premium
>> Date annual homeowner's insurance premium was last updated
1.3 Results of the weekly computation—printed each week:
> The information system prints the total amount available for new mortgages during the current week

---

to delete an artifact (the `Update Borrowers' Weekly Income` use case). In fact, deletion occurs all too often, namely, whenever a mistake is made. Sometimes an incorrect artifact can be fixed, but frequently an artifact has to be deleted. The key point is that, when a fault is discovered, there is no need to abandon everything done to date and start the whole requirements process from scratch. Instead, an attempt is made to fix the current iteration, as was done in this case study. If this strategy fails (because the mistake really is serious), we backtrack to the previous iteration and try to find a better way to go forward from there.

The second change that must be made to improve the requirements is to reorganize two use cases. Consider the descriptions of the use cases `Estimate Funds Available for Week` (Figure 10.28) and `Produce a Report` (Figure 10.36). Suppose that an MSG staff member wants to determine the funds available for the current week. Use case `Estimate Funds Available for Week` performs the calculation, and Step 1.3 of use case `Produce a Report` prints out the result

FIGURE 10.37   The fifth iteration of the use-case diagram of the revised requirements of the MSG Foundation case study. The new use case, `Produce a Report`, is shaded.

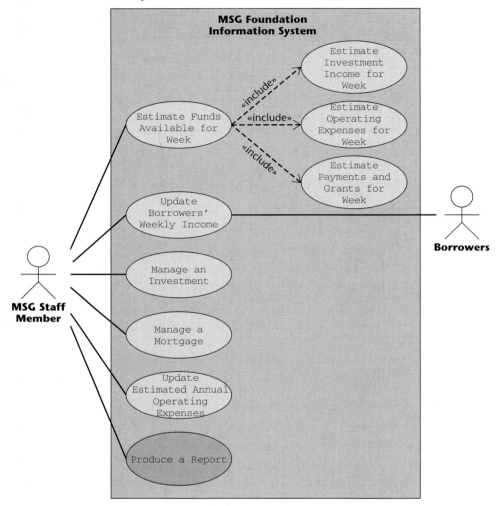

of the computation. This is ridiculous. After all, there is no point in estimating the funds available unless the results are printed out.

In other words, Step 1.3 of `Produce a Report` needs to be moved from the description of that use case to the end of the description of use case `Estimate Funds Available for Week`. This does not change the use cases themselves (Figures 10.27 and 10.35) or the current use-case diagram (Figure 10.38), but the descriptions of the two use cases (Figures 10.28 and 10.36) have to be modified. The resulting modified descriptions are shown in Figures 10.39 and 10.40.

FIGURE 10.38   The sixth iteration of the use-case diagram of the revised requirements of the MSG Foundation case study. The modified use case, `Manage a Mortgage`, is shaded.

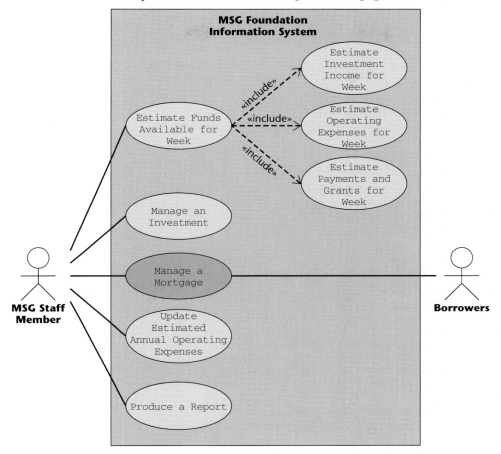

Now the use-case diagram can be improved still further. Consider the top four use cases in Figure 10.38. The three use cases on the right, namely, `Estimate Investment Income for Week`, `Estimate Operating Expenses for Week`, and `Estimate Payments and Grants for Week`, are part of the use case `Estimate Funds Available for Week`. The usual reason for an «include» relationship is where one use case is part of two or more other use cases. For example, Figure 10.41 shows that use case `Print Tax Form` is part of use cases `Prepare Form 1040`, `Prepare Form 1040A`, and `Prepare Form 1040EZ`, the three primary U.S. tax forms for individuals. In this situation, it makes sense to retain `Print Tax Form` as an independent use case. Incorporating the operations of `Print Tax Form` into the other three use cases would mean triplicating that use case.

With regard to Figure 10.38, however, all the included use cases are part of only one use case, namely, `Estimate Funds Available for Week`—there is

FIGURE 10.39   The second iteration of the description of the `Produce a Report` use case of the revised requirements of the MSG Foundation case study.

Brief Description

The `Produce a Report` use case enables an MSG Foundation staff member to print a listing of all investments or all mortgages.

Step-by-Step Description

1. The following reports must be generated:
    1.1 Investments report—printed on demand:
        The information system prints a list of all investments. For each investment, the following attributes are printed:
            Item number
            Item name
            Estimated annual return
            Date estimated annual return was last updated
    1.2 Mortgages report—printed on demand:
        The information system prints a list of all mortgages. For each mortgage, the following attributes are printed:
            Account number
            Name of mortgagee
            Original price of home
            Date mortgage was issued
            Principal and interest payment
            Current combined gross weekly income
            Date current combined gross weekly income was last updated
            Annual real-estate tax
            Date annual real-estate tax was last updated
            Annual homeowner's insurance premium
            Date annual homeowner's insurance premium was last updated

---

FIGURE 10.40   The third iteration of the description of the `Estimate Funds Available for Week` use case of the revised requirements of the MSG Foundation case study.

Brief Description

The `Estimate Funds Available for Week` use case enables an MSG Foundation staff member to estimate how much money the Foundation has available that week to fund mortgages.

Step-by-Step Description

1. Determine the estimated income from investments for the week utilizing use case `Estimate Investment Income for Week`.
2. Determine the operating expenses for the week utilizing use case `Estimate Operating Expenses for Week`.
3. Determine the total estimated mortgage payments for the week utilizing use case `Estimate Payments and Grants for Week`.
4. Determine the total estimated grants for the week utilizing use case `Estimate Payments and Grants for Week`.
5. Add the results of Steps 1 and 3 and subtract the results of Steps 2 and 4. This is the total amount available for mortgages for the current week.
6. Print the total amount available for new mortgages during the current week.

FIGURE 10.41   Use case `Print Tax Form` is part of three other use cases.

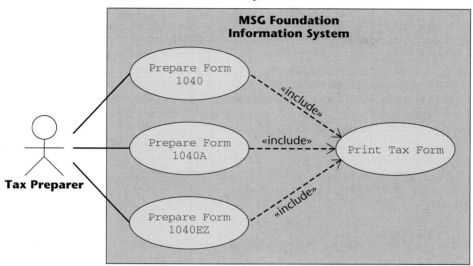

FIGURE 10.42
The seventh
iteration of
the use-case
diagram of
the revised
requirements
of the MSG
Foundation
case study.
The modified
use case,
`Estimate
Funds
Available
for Week`, is
shaded.

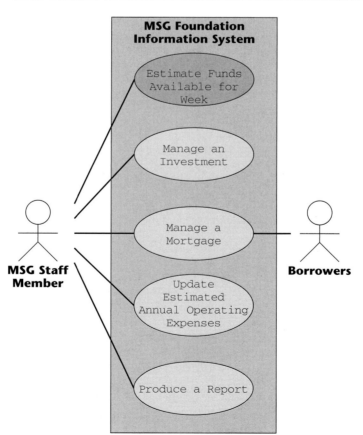

FIGURE 10.43 The fourth iteration of the description of the use case `Estimate Funds Available for Week` of the revised requirements of the MSG Foundation case study.

Brief Description

The `Estimate Funds Available for Week` use case enables an MSG Foundation staff member to estimate how much money the Foundation has available that week to fund mortgages.

Step-by-Step Description

1. For each investment, extract the estimated annual return on that investment. Summing the separate returns and dividing the result by 52 yields the estimated investment income for the week.
2. Determine the estimated MSG Foundation operating expenses for the week by extracting the estimated annual MSG Foundation operating expenses and dividing by 52.
3. For each mortgage:
   3.1 The amount to be paid this week is the total of the principal and interest payment and $\frac{1}{52}$nd of the sum of the annual real-estate tax and the annual homeowner's insurance premium.
   3.2 Compute 28 percent of the couple's current gross weekly income.
   3.3 If the result of Step 3.1 is greater than the result of Step 3.2, then the mortgage payment for this week is the result of Step 3.2, and the amount of the grant for this week is the difference between the result of Step 3.1 and the result of Step 3.2.
   3.4 Otherwise, the mortgage payment for this week is the result of Step 3.1, and there is no grant this week.
4. Summing the mortgage payments of Steps 3.3 and 3.4 yields the estimated total mortgage payments for the week.
5. Summing the grant payments of Step 3.3 yields the estimated total grant payments for the week.
6. Add the results of Steps 1 and 4 and subtract the results of Steps 2 and 5. This is the total amount available for mortgages for the current week.
7. Print the total amount available for new mortgages during the current week.

---

no duplication. Accordingly, it makes sense to incorporate those three «include» use cases into `Estimate Funds Available for Week`, as shown in Figure 10.42, the seventh iteration of the use-case diagram. The resulting fourth iteration of the description of the `Estimate Funds Available for Week` use case is shown in Figure 10.43.

Now the requirements appear to be correct.

- First, they correspond to what the client has requested.
- Second, there do not seem to be any faults.
- Third, at this stage it would seem that what the client wants coincides with what the client needs.

Accordingly, the requirements workflow appears to be complete, for now. Nevertheless, it is certainly possible that, during subsequent workflows, additional requirements may surface. Also, it may be necessary to split one or more of the five use cases into additional use cases. For example, in a future iteration the `Produce a Report` use case described in Figure 10.36 may be split into two separate use cases, one for the investments report, the other for the mortgages report. But for now, everything seems to be satisfactory,

This concludes the description of the requirements workflow for the MSG Foundation case study.

10.12 What Are Object-Oriented Requirements?

On the one hand, there is no such thing as "object-oriented requirements," nor should there be such a thing. The aim of the requirements workflow is to determine the client's needs, that is, what the functionality of the target system should be. The requirements workflow has nothing to do with how the product is to be built. From this viewpoint, it makes no sense to refer to the object-oriented paradigm within the context of the requirements workflow, any more than one can refer to an object-oriented user manual. After all, the user manual describes the steps to be followed by the user when running the software product and has nothing to do with how the product was built. In the same way, the requirements workflow results in a statement of what the product is to do; the way that the product will be built does not enter into it.

On the other hand, the entire approach of Sections 10.2 through 10.11 is object oriented in nature in that it is model oriented. The use cases, together with their descriptions, form the basis of the requirements workflow. As is shown throughout Part 2 of this book, modeling is the essence of the object-oriented paradigm.

Building a rapid prototype for the product as a whole is not part of the object-oriented paradigm, for the reasons given in Section 11.22. However, when using the object-oriented paradigm, it is strongly advisable to build a rapid prototype of the user interface, as will be described.

10.13 Rapid Prototyping

A **_rapid prototype_** is hastily built software that exhibits the key functionality of the target product. For example, a product that helps to manage an apartment complex must incorporate an input screen that allows the user to enter details of a new tenant and print an occupancy report for each month. These aspects are incorporated into the rapid prototype. However, error-checking capabilities, file-updating routines, and complex tax computations probably are not included. The key point is that a rapid prototype reflects the functionality

The idea of constructing models to show key aspects of a product goes back a long time. For example, a 1618 painting by Domenico Cresti (known as "Il Passignano" because he was born in the town of Passignano in the Chianti region of Italy) shows Michelangelo presenting a wooden model of his design for St. Peter's (in Rome) to Pope Paul IV. Such architectural models could be huge; a model of an earlier design proposal for St. Peter's by the architect Bramante is more than 20 feet long on each side.

Architectural models were used for a number of different purposes. First, as depicted in the Cresti painting (now hanging in Casa Buonarroti in Florence), models were used to try to interest a client in funding a project. This is analogous to the use of a rapid prototype to determine the client's real needs, as is done in the classical paradigm. Second, in an age before architectural drawings, the model showed the builder the structure of the building and indicated to the stonemasons how the building was to be decorated. This is similar to the way we now build a rapid prototype of the user interface, as described in Section 10.14.

the client sees, such as input screens and reports, but omits "hidden" aspects such as file updating. (For a different way of looking at rapid prototypes, see Just in Case You Wanted to Know Box 10.3.)

The client and intended users of the product now experiment with the rapid prototype, while members of the development team watch and take notes. Based on their hands-on experience, users tell the developers how the rapid prototype satisfies their needs and, more important, identify the areas that need improvement. The developers change the rapid prototype until both sides are convinced that the needs of the client are accurately encapsulated in the rapid prototype.

In the classical paradigm, the rapid prototype of the key aspects of the product is then used as the basis for drawing up the specifications. Within the context of the object-oriented paradigm, rapid prototyping is an essential component within the development of the user interface to a product, as discussed in Section 10.14.

10.14 Human Factors

It is important that both the client and the future users of the product interact with the rapid prototype of the user interface. Encouraging users to experiment with the human–computer interface (HCI) greatly reduces the risk that the finished product will have to be altered. In particular, this experimentation helps achieve user-friendliness, a vital objective for all software products.

The term **user friendliness** refers to the ease with which human beings can communicate with the software product. If users have difficulty in learning how to use a product or find the screens confusing or irritating, then they will either not use the product or use it incorrectly. To try to eliminate this problem, menu-driven products were introduced. Instead of having to enter a command such as Perform computation or Print service rate report, the user merely has to select from a set of possible responses, such as

1. Perform computation
2. Print service rate report
3. Select view to be graphed

In this example, the user enters 1, 2, or 3 to invoke the corresponding command.

Nowadays, instead of simply displaying lines of text, HCIs employ graphics. Windows, icons, and pull-down menus are components of a ***graphical user interface (GUI)***. Because of the plethora of windowing systems, standards such as X Window have evolved. Also, ***point-and-click*** selection is now the norm. The user moves a mouse (that is, a handheld pointing device) to move the screen cursor to the desired response ("point"), and pushes a mouse button ("click") to select that response.

However, even when the target product employs modern technology, the designers must never forget that the product is to be used by human beings. In other words, the HCI designers must consider ***human factors*** such as size of letters, capitalization, color, line length, and the number of lines on the screen.

Another example of human factors applies to the preceding menu. If the user chooses option 3. Select view to be graphed, then another menu appears with another list of choices. Unless a menu-driven system is thoughtfully designed, there is the danger that users will encounter a lengthy sequence of menus to achieve even a relatively simple operation. This delay can anger users, sometimes causing them to make inappropriate menu selections. Also, the HCI must allow the user to change a previous selection without having to return to the top-level menu and start again. This problem can exist even when a GUI is used because many graphical user interfaces are essentially a series of menus displayed in an attractive screen format.

Sometimes it is impossible for a single user interface to cater to all users. For example, if a product is to be used by both computer professionals and high-school dropouts with no previous computer experience, then it is preferable that two different sets of HCIs be designed, each carefully tailored to the skill level and psychological profile of its intended users. This technique can be extended by incorporating sets of user interfaces requiring varied levels of sophistication. If the product deduces that the user would be more comfortable with a less sophisticated user interface, perhaps because the user is making frequent mistakes or is continually invoking help facilities, then the user is automatically shown screens that are more appropriate to his or her current skill level. But, as the user becomes more familiar with the product, streamlined screens that provide less information are displayed, leading to speedier completion. This automated approach reduces user frustration and leads to increased productivity [Schach and Wood, 1986].

Many benefits can accrue when human factors are taken into account during the design of an HCI, including reduced learning times and lower error rates. Although help facilities must always be provided, they are utilized less with a carefully designed HCI. This, too, increases productivity. Uniformity of HCI appearance across a product or group of products can result in users intuitively knowing how to use a screen that they have never seen before because it is similar to other screens with which they are familiar. Designers of Macintosh software have taken this principle into account; this is one of the many reasons that software for the Macintosh is generally so user-friendly.

It has been suggested that simple common sense is all that is needed to design a user-friendly HCI. Whether or not this charge is true, it is essential that a rapid prototype of the HCI of every product be constructed. Intended users of the product can experiment with the rapid prototype of the HCI and inform the designers whether the target product indeed is user-friendly, that is, whether the designers have taken the necessary human factors into account.

In Section 10.15, reuse is discussed within the context of rapid prototyping.

10.15 Reusing the Rapid Prototype

After the rapid prototype has been built to test the user interface, it is discarded early in the software process. An alternate, but generally unwise, way of proceeding is to develop and refine the rapid prototype until it becomes the complete product. In theory, this approach should lead to fast software development; after all, instead of throwing away the code constituting the rapid prototype, along with the knowledge built into it, the rapid prototype is converted into the final product. However, in practice, the process is extremely similar to the code-and-fix approach of Figure 2.8. So, as with the code-and-fix model, the first problem with this form of the rapid prototyping model follows from the fact that, in the course of refining the rapid prototype, changes have to be made to a working product. This is an expensive way to proceed, as shown in Figure 1.5. A second problem is that a primary objective when constructing a rapid prototype is speed of building. A rapid prototype is (correctly) hurriedly put together, rather than carefully specified, designed, and implemented. In the absence of specification and design documents, the resulting code is difficult and expensive to maintain. It might seem wasteful to construct a rapid prototype and then throw it away and design the user interface from scratch, but it is far cheaper in both the short term and the long term to do this rather than try to convert a rapid prototype into production-quality software [Brooks, 1975].

Nevertheless, there is one instance when it is permissible to refine a rapid prototype or, more specifically, portions of the rapid prototype. When portions of the rapid prototype of the user interface are computer generated, those portions may be used in the final product. CASE tools such as screen generators and report generators (Section 5.5) are frequently utilized to generate the user interfaces, and those portions of the rapid prototype may indeed be used as part of production-quality software.

10.16 CASE Tools for the Requirements Workflow

The many UML diagrams in this chapter reflect the importance of having a graphical tool to assist with the requirements workflow. That is, what is needed is a drawing tool that enables the user to draw the relevant UML diagrams with ease. Such a tool has two major strengths. First, while iterating it is generally far easier to change a diagram stored in such a tool than to redraw the diagram by hand. Second, when a CASE tool of this kind is used, the details of the product are stored in the CASE tool itself. Therefore, the documentation is always available and up to date.

One weakness of such CASE tools is that they are not always user-friendly. A powerful graphical workbench or environment has so much functionality that it generally has a steep learning curve, and even experienced users sometimes have difficulty remembering how to achieve a particular outcome. A second weakness is that it is almost impossible to program a computer to draw UML diagrams that are as aesthetically pleasing as diagrams drawn by hand by humans. One alternative is to spend a considerable amount of time "tweaking" a diagram created by a tool. However, this approach is sometimes as slow as drawing the diagrams by hand. Worse, the constraints of many graphical CASE tools are such that, no matter how much time and effort are put into a diagram, it can never look as polished as a hand-drawn diagram. A third problem is that many CASE tools are expensive. It is not unusual to have to pay $5000 or more per user for a comprehensive CASE tool. On the other hand, a number of open-source CASE tools of this type can be downloaded at no cost. Overall, the two strengths of CASE tools given in the first paragraph of this section outweigh these weaknesses.

Many of the classical graphical CASE workbenches and environments, such as System Architect and Software through Pictures, have been extended to support UML diagrams and, hence, the object-oriented paradigm. In addition, there are object-oriented CASE workbenches and environments, such as IBM Rational Rose and Together. There are also open-source CASE tools of this type, including ArgoUML.

10.17 Metrics for the Requirements Workflow

A key feature of the requirements workflow is how rapidly the requirements team determines the client's real needs. So, a useful metric during this workflow is a measure of requirements volatility. Keeping a record of how frequently the requirements change during the requirements workflow gives management a way of determining the rate at which the requirements team converges on the actual requirements of the product. This metric has the further advantage that it can be applied to any requirements elicitation technique, such as interviewing or forms analysis.

Another measure of how well the requirements team is doing its job is the number of requirements that change during the rest of the software development process. For each such change in requirements, it should be recorded whether that change was initiated by the client or the developers. If a large number of changes in requirements are initiated by the developers during the analysis, design, and subsequent workflows, then it is clear that the process used by the team to carry out the requirements workflow should be thoroughly reviewed. Conversely, if the client makes repeated changes to the requirements during subsequent workflows, then this metric can be used to warn the client that the moving-target problem can adversely affect the project, and future changes should be held to a minimum.

10.18 Challenges of the Requirements Workflow

Like every other workflow of the software development process, potential problems and pitfalls are associated with the requirements workflow. First, it is essential to have the wholehearted cooperation of the potential users of the target product from the beginning of the process. Individuals often feel threatened by computerization, fearing that the computer will take their jobs. There is some truth to that fear. Over the past 30 years or so, the impact of computerization has been to reduce the need for unskilled workers but also to generate jobs for skilled workers. Overall, the number of well-paying employment opportunities created as a direct consequence of computerization has far exceeded the number of relatively unskilled jobs made redundant, as evidenced by both decreased unemployment rates and increased average compensation. But the unparalleled economic growth of so many countries worldwide as a direct or indirect consequence of the so-called Computer Age in no way can compensate for the negative impact on those individuals who lose their jobs as a result of computerization.

It is essential that every member of the requirements team be aware at all times that the members of the client organization with whom they interact in all probability are deeply concerned about the potential impact of the target software product on their jobs. In the worst case, employees may deliberately give misleading or wrong information to try to ensure that the product does not meet the client's needs and, hence, protect those employees' jobs. But, even with no sabotage of this kind, some members of the client organization may be less than helpful simply because they have a vague feeling of being threatened by computerization.

Another challenge of the requirements workflow is the ability to ***negotiate***. For example, it is often essential to scale down what the client wants. Not surprisingly, almost every client would love to have a software product that can do everything that might conceivably be needed. Such a product would take an unacceptably long time to build and cost far more than the client considers reasonable. Therefore, it often is necessary to persuade the client to accept less (sometimes far less) than he or she wants. Computing the costs and benefits (see Section 5.2) of each requirement in dispute can help in this regard.

Another example of the negotiating skill needed is the ability to arrive at a compromise among managers regarding the functionality of the target product. For example, a cunning manager may attempt to extend his or her power by including a requirement that can be implemented only by incorporating into his or her areas of responsibility certain business functions currently the responsibility of another manager. Not surprisingly, the other manager will object strongly on discovering what is going on. The requirements team must sit down with both managers and resolve the issue.

A third challenge of the requirements workflow is that, in many organizations, the individuals who possess information the requirements team needs to elicit, simply lack the time to meet for in-depth discussions. When this happens, the team must inform the client, who then must decide which is more important, the individuals' current job responsibilities or the software product to be constructed. And, if the client fails to insist that the software product comes first, the developers may have no alternative but to withdraw from a project all but doomed to failure.

Finally, flexibility and objectivity are essential for requirements elicitation. It is vital that the members of the requirements team approach each interview with no preconceived ideas. In particular, an interviewer must never make assumptions about the requirements as a result of earlier interviews and then conduct subsequent interviews within the framework of those assumptions. Instead, an interviewer must consciously suppress any information gleaned at previous interviews and conduct each interview in an impartial way. Making premature assumptions regarding the requirements is dangerous; making any assumptions during the requirements workflow regarding the software product to be built can be disastrous.

How to Perform the Requirements Workflow	**Box 10.1**

- **Iterate**

    Obtain an understanding of the domain.
    Draw up the business model.
    Draw up the requirements.

- **Until** the requirements are satisfactory.

Chapter Review

The chapter concludes with How to Perform Box 10.1, which summarizes the steps of the requirements workflow.

The chapter begins with a description of the importance of determining the client's needs (Section 10.1), followed by an overview of the requirements workflow (Section 10.2). In Section 10.3, the need to understand the domain is described. How to draw up the business model is described in Section 10.4. Interviewing and other techniques of requirements extraction are discussed in Sections 10.4.1 and 10.4.2. The business model is modeled using use cases, which are introduced in Section 10.4.3. Drawing up the initial requirements is described in Section 10.5. The requirements workflow of the MSG Foundation case study is presented in the next six sections. Obtaining an initial understanding of the domain is described in Section 10.6; the initial business model and the initial requirements are presented in Sections 10.7 and 10.8, respectively. The requirements are then refined in Sections 10.9 and 10.10. Finally, the test workflow for the MSG Foundation case study is described (Section 10.11). In Section 10.12, the object orientation of the requirements workflow of the Unified Process is discussed. Rapid prototyping is then presented in greater detail in Sections 10.13 and 10.14; in the latter section, the importance of constructing a rapid prototype for the user interface is stressed. In Section 10.15, a warning is given regarding reuse of the rapid prototype. CASE tools for the requirements workflow (Section 10.16) and metrics for the requirements workflow (Section 10.17) are then discussed. The chapter concludes with a description of challenges of the requirements phase (Section 10.18).

For Further Reading

[Jackson, 1995] is an excellent introduction to requirements analysis. [Thayer and Dorfman, 1999] is a collection of papers on requirements analysis. Berry [2004] suggests that the ripple effect of the inevitable changes to the requirements is the reason why there cannot be a software engineering silver bullet (Just in Case You Wanted to Know Box 3.5). The use of cost–benefit analysis in setting priorities among requirements is described in [Karlsson and Ryan, 1997]. Nonfunctional requirements are discussed in [Cysneiros and do Prado Leite, 2004]. A variety of articles on requirements appear in the January/February 2005 issue of *IEEE Software*.

The requirements workflow of the Unified Process is described in detail in Chapters 6 and 7 of [Jacobson, Booch, and Rumbaugh, 1999]. Misuse cases (use cases that model interactions that the software should prevent) are described in [I. Alexander, 2003].

For an introduction to rapid prototyping, suggested books include [Connell and Shafer, 1989] and [Gane, 1989]. The rapid prototyping model is one version of rapid application development (RAD); a variety of articles on RAD are in the September 1995 issue of *IEEE Software*. The importance of prototyping is described in [Schrage, 2004].

The standard work on user interface design is [Shneiderman, 2003]. Methods for achieving good user interfaces are described in [Holzinger, 2005]. Articles on user interfaces can be found in the March 2002 issue of *IEEE Computer* and the March 2003 issue of *Communications of the ACM*. The proceedings of the Annual Conference on Human Factors in Computer Systems (sponsored by ACM SIGCHI) are a valuable source of information on wide-ranging aspects of human factors.

Key Terms

actor 292	form 291	human factors 323
application domain 289	functional requirement 294	«include» relationship 309
business model 290	glossary 290	model 292
direct observation 291	graphical user	negotiation 326
domain 289	interface (GUI) 323	nonfunctional requirement 294

platform constraint 294
point and click 323
questionnaire 291
rapid prototype 321
reliability 294
requirements analysis 289

requirements capture 289
requirements elicitation 289
requirements workflow 289
response time 294
structured interview 290
unstructured interview 290

use case 292
use-case description 297
use-case diagram 299
user-friendly 322
videotape camera 291

Case Study Key Terms

capital 295
closing costs 296
deposit 295

escrow account 296
interest 295
mortgage 294

P & I 295
points 296
principal 295

Problems

10.1 Give a nonfunctional requirement that can be handled without having detailed knowledge about the target software product.

10.2 Now, give a nonfunctional requirement that can be handled only after the requirements workflow has been completed.

10.3 Distinguish between a use *case* and a *use-case* diagram.

10.4 Distinguish between a *user* and an *actor*.

10.5 Draw a flowchart representing the requirements workflow.

10.6 Why does the same couple appear as two different actors (**Applicants** and **Borrowers**) in the use-case diagram of Figure 10.12?

10.7 Noting that only MSG Foundation staff members can use the software product, why do **Applicants** and **Borrowers** appear as actors in the use-case diagram of Figure 10.12?

10.8 Use a spreadsheet to show that, at the end of 30 years, monthly installments of $629.30 will pay off a loan for $90,000 with interest compounded monthly at an annual rate of 7.5 percent.

10.9 Suppose that the MSG Foundation decides that it wants its software product to include the mortgage application process. Give the description of the `Apply for an MSG Mortgage use case`. Give as many details as you can.

10.10 Sections 10.9 and 10.10 describe the restructuring of the use cases of the MSG Foundation. How would this restructuring change if, as in Problem 10.9, the `Apply for an MSG Mortgage` use case had been included in the requirements model?

10.11 You have just joined Angel & Iguassu Software as a software manager. Angel & Iguassu has been developing accounting software for small businesses for many years using the waterfall model, usually with some success. On the basis of your experience, you think that the Unified Process is a far superior way of developing software. Write a report addressed to the vice-president for software development explaining why you believe the organization should switch to the Unified Process. Remember that vice-presidents do not like reports that are more than half a page in length.

10.12 You are the vice-president for software development of Angel & Iguassu. Reply to the report of Problem 10.11.

10.13 What is the result if a rapid prototype is not constructed rapidly?

10.14   (Analysis and Design Project) Perform the requirements workflow for the automated library circulation system of Problem 8.7.

10.15   (Analysis and Design Project) Perform the requirements workflow for the product for determining whether a bank statement is correct of Problem 8.8.

10.16   (Analysis and Design Project) Perform the requirements workflow for the automated teller machine (ATM) of Problem 8.9.

10.17   (Term Project) Perform the requirements workflow for the Osric's Office Appliances and Decor project in Appendix A.

10.18   (Case Study) The trustees of the MSG Foundation have decided to expand their activities by providing scholarships for higher education to children of current borrowers with a sufficiently high grade-point average. Draw the use case `Apply for an MSG Scholarship`. Give the description of the use case, providing as much detail as you can.

10.19   (Case Study) A report of all scholarships awarded during the past year (Problem 10.18) has to be generated. Modify Figures 10.35 and 10.36 appropriately to incorporate this additional report.

10.20   (Case Study) Construct a rapid prototype for the user interface of the MSG Foundation case study. Use the software and hardware specified by your instructor.

10.21   (Readings in Software Engineering) Your instructor will distribute copies of [Cysneiros and do Prado Leite, 2004]. In what ways did reading this article change your views on the importance of nonfunctional requirements?

References   [I. Alexander, 2003] I. ALEXANDER, "Misuse Cases: Use Cases with Hostile Intent," *IEEE Software* **20** (January/February 2003), pp. 58–66.

[Berry, 2004] D. M. BERRY, "The Inevitable Pain of Software Development: Why There Is No Silver Bullet," in: *Radical Innovations of Software and Systems Engineering in the Future*, Lecture Notes in Computer Science, Vol. 2941, Springer-Verlag, Berlin, 2004, pp. 50–74.

[Brooks, 1975] F. P. BROOKS, JR., *The Mythical Man-Month: Essays on Software Engineering*, Addison-Wesley, Reading, MA, 1975; Twentieth Anniversary Edition, Addison-Wesley, Reading, MA, 1995.

[Connell and Shafer, 1989] J. L. CONNELL AND L. SHAFER, *Structured Rapid Prototyping: An Evolutionary Approach to Software Development*, Yourdon Press, Englewood Cliffs, NJ, 1989.

[Cysneiros and do Prado Leite, 2004] L. M. CYSNEIROS AND J. C. S. DO PRADO LEITE, "Nonfunctional Requirements: From Elicitation to Conceptual Models," *IEEE Transactions on Software Engineering* **30** (May 2004), pp. 328–50.

[Gane, 1989] C. GANE, *Rapid System Development: Using Structured Techniques and Relational Technology*, Prentice Hall, Englewood Cliffs, NJ, 1989.

[Holzinger, 2005] A. HOLZINGER, "Usability Engineering Methods for Software Developers," *Communications of the ACM* **48** (January 2005), pp. 71–74.

[Jackson, 1995] M. JACKSON, *Software Requirements and Specifications: A Lexicon of Practice, Principles and Prejudices*, Addison-Wesley Longman, Reading, MA, 1995.

[Jacobson, Booch, and Rumbaugh, 1999] I. JACOBSON, G. BOOCH, AND J. RUMBAUGH, The Unified Software Development Process, Addison-Wesley, Reading, MA, 1999.

[Karlsson and Ryan, 1997] J. KARLSSON AND K. RYAN, "A Cost-Value Approach for Prioritizing Requirements," *IEEE Software* **14** (September/October 1997), pp. 67–74.

[Schach and Wood, 1986] S. R. SCHACH AND P. T. WOOD, "An Almost Path-Free Very High-Level Interactive Data Manipulation Language for a Microcomputer-Based Database System," *Software—Practice and Experience* **16** (March 1986), pp. 243–68.

[Schrage, 2004] M. SCHRAGE, "Never Go to a Client Meeting without a Prototype," *IEEE Software* **21** (2004), pp. 42–45.

[Shneiderman, 2003] B. SHNEIDERMAN, *Designing the User Interface: Strategies for Effective Human-Computer Interaction*, 4th ed., Addison-Wesley Longman, Reading, MA, 2003.

[Thayer and Dorfman, 1999] R. H. THAYER AND M. DORFMAN, *Software Requirements Engineering*, revised 2nd ed., IEEE Computer Society Press, Los Alamitos, CA, 1999.

Chapter 11

The Analysis Workflow

Learning Objectives

After studying this chapter, you should be able to

- Perform the analysis workflow.
- Extract the boundary, control, and entity classes.
- Perform functional modeling.
- Perform class modeling.
- Perform dynamic modeling.
- Perform use-case realization.

A specification document must satisfy two mutually contradictory requirements. On the one hand, this document must be clear and intelligible to the client, who probably is not a computer specialist. After all, the client is paying for the product, and unless the client believes that he or she really understands what the new product will be like, there is a good chance that the client will either decide not to authorize the development of the product or will ask some other software organization to build it.

On the other hand, the specification document must be complete and detailed, because this is virtually the sole source of information available for drawing up the design. Even if the client agrees that all needs have been determined accurately during the requirements, if the specification document contains faults such as omissions, contradictions, or ambiguities, the inevitable result will be faults in the design that are carried over into the implementation. What is needed, therefore, are techniques for representing the target product in a format sufficiently nontechnical to be intelligible to the client yet precise enough to result in a fault-free product being delivered to the client at the end of the development cycle. These analysis (specification) techniques are the subject of this chapter.

11.1 The Specification Document

The **specification document** is a contract between client and developer. It specifies precisely what the product must do and the constraints on the product. Virtually every specification document incorporates constraints that the product has to satisfy. Almost always, a deadline is specified for delivering the product. Another common stipulation is, "The product shall be installed in such a way that it can run in parallel with the existing product," until the client is satisfied that the new product indeed satisfies every aspect of the specification document. Other constraints might include portability: The product shall be constructed to run on other hardware under the same operating system or perhaps run under a variety of different operating systems. Reliability may be another constraint. If the product has to monitor patients in an intensive care unit, then it is of paramount importance that it be fully operational 24 hours a day. Rapid response time may be a requirement; a typical constraint in this category might be "95 percent of all queries of Type 4 shall be answered within 0.25 seconds." Many response-time constraints have to be expressed in probabilistic terms because the response time depends on the current load on the computer. In contrast, so-called hard real-time constraints are expressed in absolute terms. For instance, it is useless to develop software that informs a warplane pilot of an incoming missile within 0.25 seconds only 95 percent of the time—the product must meet the constraint 100 percent of the time.

A vital component of the specification document is the set of acceptance criteria. It is important from the viewpoint of both the client and the developers to spell out a series of tests that can be used to prove to the client that the product indeed satisfies its specifications and that the developer's job is done. Some of the acceptance criteria may be restatements of the constraints, whereas others address different issues. For example, the client might supply the developer with a description of the data that the product will handle. An appropriate acceptance criterion then would be that the product correctly processes data of this type and filters out nonconforming (that is, erroneous) data. Once the development team fully understands the problem, possible solution strategies can be suggested. A **solution strategy** is a general approach to building the product. For example, one possible solution strategy for a product would be to use an online database; another would be to use conventional flat files and extract the required information using overnight batch runs. When determining solution strategies, it often is a good idea to come up with strategies without worrying about the constraints in the specification document. Then, the various solution strategies can be evaluated in the light of the constraints and necessary modifications can be made. There are a number of ways of determining whether a specific solution strategy will satisfy the client's constraints. An obvious one is to construct a proof-of-concept prototype, which can be a good technique for resolving issues relating to user interfaces and timing constraints, as previously discussed in Section 2.9.7. Other techniques for determining whether constraints will be satisfied include simulation [Banks, Carson, Nelson, and Nichol, 2001] and analytic network modeling [Kleinrock, and Gail, 1996].

During this process, a number of solution strategies are put forward and then discarded. It is important that a written record be kept of all discarded strategies and the reasons they were rejected. This will assist the development team if it ever is called on to justify the chosen strategy. But, more important, there is an ever-present danger during postdelivery maintenance that the process of enhancement will be accompanied by an attempt to come up with a new and unwise solution strategy. Having a record of why certain strategies were rejected during development can be extremely helpful during postdelivery maintenance.

By this point in the life cycle, the development team will have determined one or more possible solution strategies that satisfy the constraints. A two-stage decision now has to be made. First, whether the client should be advised to computerize and, if so, which of the viable solution strategies should be adopted. The answer to the first question can best be decided on the basis of cost–benefit analysis (Section 5.2). Second, if the client decides to proceed with the project, then the client must inform the development team as to the optimization criterion to be used, such as minimizing the total cost to the client or maximizing the return on investment. The developers then advise the client as to which of the viable solution strategies best satisfies the optimization criterion.

11.2   Informal Specifications

In many development projects, the specification document consists of page after page of English, or some other **natural language** such as French or Xhosa. A typical paragraph of such an **informal specification** reads:

> BV.4.2.5. If the sales for the current month are below the target sales, then a report is to be printed, unless the difference between target sales and actual sales is less than half of the difference between target sales and actual sales in the previous month or if the difference between target sales and actual sales for the current month is under 5 percent.

The background leading up to that paragraph is as follows. The management of a retail chain sets a target sales figure for each shop for each month; and if a shop does not meet this target, a report is to be printed. Consider the following scenario: Suppose that the January sales target for one particular shop is $100,000, but actual sales are only $64,000, that is, 36 percent below target. In this case, a report must be printed. Now suppose further that the February target figure is $120,000 and that actual sales are only $100,000, 16.7 percent below target. Although sales are below the target figure, the percentage difference for February, 16.7 percent, is less than half of the previous month's percentage difference, 36 percent; management believes that an improvement has been made, and no report is to be printed. Next suppose that, in March, the target is again $100,000 but the shop makes $98,000, only 2 percent below target. Because the percentage difference is small, less than 5 percent, no report should be printed.

Careful rereading of the preceding specification paragraph shows some divergence from what the retail chain's management actually requested. Paragraph BV.4.2.5 speaks of the "difference between target sales and actual sales"; percentage difference is not mentioned. The difference in January was $36,000 and in February it was $20,000. The percentage difference, which is what management wanted, dropped from 36 percent in January to 16.7 percent in February, less than half of the January percentage difference. However, the actual difference dropped from $36,000 to $20,000, which is greater than half of $36,000. So if the development team had faithfully implemented the specification document, the report would have been printed, which is not what management wanted. Then the last clause speaks of a "difference ... [of] 5 percent." What is meant, of course, is a percentage difference of 5 percent, only the word *percentage* does not occur anywhere in the paragraph.

Therefore, the specification document contains a number of faults. First, the wishes of the client have been ignored. Second, there is ambiguity —should the last clause read "percentage difference ... [of] 5 percent," or "difference ... [of] $5000," or something else entirely? In addition, the style is poor. What the paragraph says is, "If something happens, print a report. However, if something else happens, don't print it. And if a third thing happens, don't print it either." It would have been much clearer if the specifications had simply stated when the report is to be printed. All in all, paragraph BV.4.2.5 is not a terribly good example of how to write a specification document.

Paragraph BV.4.2.5 is fictitious but, unfortunately, typical of too many specification documents. You may think that the example is unfair and this sort of problem cannot arise if specifications are written with care by professional specification writers. To refute this charge, the mini case study of Chapter 6 resumes here.

11.3 Correctness Proof Mini Case Study Redux

Recall from Section 6.5.2 that in 1969 Naur wrote a paper on correctness proving Naur, 1969]. He illustrated his technique by means of a text-processing problem. Using his technique, Naur constructed an ALGOL 60 procedure to solve the problem and informally proved the correctness of his procedure. A reviewer of Naur's paper [Leavenworth, 1970] pointed out one fault in the procedure. London [1971] then detected three additional faults in Naur's procedure, presented a corrected version of the procedure, and proved its correctness formally. Goodenough and Gerhart [1975] found three further faults that London had not detected. Of the total of seven faults collectively detected by the reviewer, London, and Goodenough and Gerhart, two can be considered analysis faults. For example, Naur's specifications do not state what happens if the input includes two successive adjacent breaks (blank or newline characters). For this reason, Goodenough and Gerhart produced a new set of specifications. Their specifications were about four times longer than Naur's, which are given in Section 6.5.2.

In 1985, Meyer wrote an article on formal specification techniques [Meyer, 1985]. The main thrust of his article is that a specification document written in a natural language such as English tends to have contradictions, ambiguities, and omissions. He recommended using mathematical terminology to express specifications formally. Meyer detected some 12 faults in Goodenough and Gerhart's specifications and developed a set of mathematical specifications to correct all the problems. Meyer then paraphrased his mathematical specifications and constructed English specifications. In my opinion, Meyer's English specifications contain a fault. Meyer points out in his paper that, if the maximum number of characters per line is, say, 10, and the input is, for instance, WHO WHAT WHEN, then, in terms of both Naur's and Goodenough and Gerhart's specifications, there are two equally valid outputs: WHO WHAT on the first line and WHEN on the second or WHO on the first line and WHAT WHEN on the second. In fact, Meyer's paraphrased English specifications also contain this ambiguity.

The key point is that Goodenough and Gerhart's specifications were constructed with the greatest of care. After all, they were constructed to correct Naur's specifications. Furthermore, Goodenough and Gerhart's paper went through two versions, the first of which was published in the proceedings of a refereed conference and the second in a refereed journal [Goodenough and Gerhart, 1975]. Finally, both Goodenough and Gerhart are experts in software engineering in general and specifications in particular. Therefore, if two experts with as much time as they needed carefully produced specifications in which Meyer detected 12 faults, what chance does an ordinary computer professional working under time pressure have of producing a fault-free specification document? Worse still, the text-processing problem can be coded in 25 or 30 lines, whereas real-world products can consist of hundreds of thousands or even millions of lines of source code.

In this chapter, a better alternative is described. ***Object-oriented analysis (OOA)*** is a graphical technique for the object-oriented paradigm. Well over 60 different techniques have been put forward for OOA; all the techniques are largely equivalent. The For Further Reading section of this chapter includes references to a wide variety of techniques, as well as to published comparisons of different techniques. However, as explained in Section 3.1, today the Unified Process [Jacobson, Booch, and Rumbaugh, 1999] is almost always the methodology of choice for object-oriented software production. For this reason, the first and last parts of this chapter are devoted to the analysis workflow of the Unified Process.

The analysis workflow is a key component of the object-oriented paradigm; during this workflow, the classes are extracted. The use cases and the classes are the basis of the software product to be developed. (For more insight into the object-oriented paradigm, see Just in Case You Wanted to Know Box 11.1.)

11.4   The Analysis Workflow

The ***analysis workflow*** of the Unified Process [Jacobson, Booch, and Rumbaugh 1999] has two aims. From the viewpoint of the requirements workflow (the preceding workflow), the aim of the analysis workflow is to obtain a deeper understanding of the requirements. Conversely, from the viewpoint of the design and implementation workflows (the workflows that follow the analysis workflow), the aim of the analysis workflow is to describe those requirements in such a way that the resulting design and implementation are easy to maintain.

The Unified Process is use-case driven. During the analysis workflow, the use cases are described in terms of the classes of the software product. The Unified Process has three types of classes: entity classes, boundary classes, and control classes. An ***entity class*** models information that is long lived. In the case of a banking software product, **Account Class** is an entity class because information on accounts has to stay in the software product. For the MSG Foundation software product, **Investment Class** is an entity class; again, information on investments has to be long lived.

A ***boundary class*** models the interaction between the software product and its actors. Boundary classes are generally associated with input and output. For example, in the MSG Foundation software product, reports have to be printed listing the investments of the Foundation, as well as all the mortgages currently held. This means that boundary classes **Investments Report Class** and **Mortgages Report Class** are needed.

Most of the major advances in the object-oriented paradigm were made between 1990 and 1995. Because it usually takes some 15 years for new technology to become accepted, widespread adoption of the object-oriented paradigm should have started no sooner than 2005. However, the ***millennium bug*** or ***Y2K problem*** changed the expected timetable.

In the 1960s, when computers first started to be used for business on a widespread basis, hardware was far more expensive than it is today. As a result, the vast majority of software products of that vintage represented a date using only the last two digits for a year; the leading 19 was understood. The problem with this scheme is that the year 00 is then interpreted as 1900, not 2000.

When hardware became cheaper in the 1970s and 1980s, few managers saw any point in spending large sums of money rewriting existing software products with four-digit dates. After all, by the time the year 2000 arrived, it would be someone else's problem. As a result, ***legacy systems*** remained year-2000 noncompliant. However, as the deadline of January 1, 2000, neared, software organizations were forced to work against the clock to fix their software products; there was no way to postpone the arrival of Y2K.

Problems facing the maintenance programmers included a lack of documentation for many legacy software products, as well as software products written in programming languages that were now obsolete. When modifying an existing software product was impossible, the only alternative was to start again from scratch. Some companies decided to use COTS technology (Section 1.10). Others decided that new custom software products were needed. For obvious reasons, managers wanted these software products to be developed using modern technology that had already been shown to be cost effective, and that meant using the object-oriented paradigm. The Y2K problem was therefore a significant catalyst for the widespread acceptance of the object-oriented paradigm.

A ***control class*** models complex computations and algorithms. In the case of the MSG Foundation software product, the algorithm for estimating the funds available for the week is a control class, namely, **Estimate Funds for Week Class**.

The UML notation for these three types of classes is shown in Figure 11.1. These are ***stereotypes***, that is, extensions of UML. A strength of UML is that it allows additional constructs to be defined that are not part of UML but may be needed to model a specific system accurately.

As stated at the beginning of this section, during the analysis workflow, the use cases are described in terms of the classes of the software product. The Unified Process itself does not describe how classes are to be extracted, because users of the Unified Process are expected to have a background in object-oriented analysis and design.

Figure 11.1   UML stereotypes (extensions of UML) for representing an entity class, a boundary class, and a control class.

Entity Class   Boundary Class   Control Class

The elevator problem truly is a classic problem of software engineering. It first appeared in print in 1968 in the first volume of Don Knuth's landmark book, *The Art of Computer Programming* [Knuth 1968]. It is based on the single elevator in the mathematics building at the California Institute of Technology. The example was used to illustrate coroutines in the mythical programming language MIX.

By the mid-1980s, the elevator problem had been generalized to n elevators; in addition, specific properties of the solution had to be proven, for example, that an elevator eventually would arrive within a finite time. It was now *the* problem for researchers working in the area of formal (mathematically based) specification languages, and any proposed formal specification language had to work for the elevator problem.

The problem attained broader prominence in 1986 when it was published in *ACM SIGSOFT Software Engineering Notes* in the Call for Papers for the Fourth International Workshop on Software Specification and Design [IWSSD, 1986]. The elevator problem was one of five problems to be used as examples by researchers in their submissions to the conference, held in Monterey, California, in May 1987. In the form in which it appeared in the Call for Papers, it was termed the *lift problem* and attributed to N. [Neil] Davis of STC-IDEC (a division of Standard Telecommunications and Cable, in Stevenage, United Kingdom).

Since then, the problem has attained even wider prominence and been used to demonstrate an extensive variety of techniques within software engineering in general, not just formal specification languages. It is used in this book to illustrate every technique because, as you soon will discover, the problem is by no means as simple as it looks.

Accordingly, this discussion of the Unified Process is temporarily suspended so that an explanation can be given of how classes are extracted; we return to the Unified Process in Section 11.18.

Entity classes, that is, classes that model long-lived information, are considered first.

11.5 Extracting the Entity Classes

Entity class extraction consists of three steps that are carried out iteratively and incrementally:

1. **Functional modeling**. Present scenarios of all the use cases (a **scenario** is an instance of a use case).
2. **Entity class modeling**. Determine the entity classes and their attributes. Then, determine the interrelationships and interactions between the entity classes. Present this information in the form of a class diagram.
3. **Dynamic modeling**. Determine the operations performed by or to each entity class or subclass. Present this information in the form of a statechart.

However, as with all iterative and incremental processes, the three steps are not necessarily always performed in this order; a change in one model frequently triggers corresponding revisions of the other two models.

To show how this is done, we will extract the entity classes of a modified version of the so-called elevator problem; see Just in Case You Wanted to Know Box 11.2 for background information on the elevator problem.

ase Study

11.6   The Elevator Problem

The problem concerns the logic required to move n elevators between m floors according to the following constraints:

1. Each ***elevator*** has a set of m ***buttons***, one for each floor. These illuminate when pressed and cause the elevator to visit the corresponding floor. The illumination is canceled when the corresponding floor is visited by the elevator.

2. Each floor, except the first floor and the top floor, has two buttons, one to request an up-elevator and one to request a down-elevator. These buttons illuminate when pressed. The illumination is canceled when an elevator visits the floor and then moves in the desired direction.

3. When an elevator has no requests, it remains at its current floor with its doors closed.

There are two sets of buttons in the problem. In each of the n elevators, there is a set of m buttons, one for each floor. Because these n × m buttons are inside the elevators, we refer to them as ***elevator buttons***. Then, on each floor there are two buttons, one to request an up-elevator, one to request a down-elevator. These are referred to as ***floor buttons***. Each button can be in one of two states: on (***illuminated***) or off. Finally, we assume that, after the ***elevator doors*** open, they close again after a ***timeout***.

The first step in OOA is to model the use cases.

ase Study

11.7   Functional Modeling: The Elevator Problem Case Study

A ***use case*** describes the interaction between the product to be constructed and the ***actors***, that is, the external users of that product. The only interactions possible between a user and an elevator are the user pressing an elevator button to summon an elevator or the user pressing a floor button to request the elevator to stop at a specific floor, hence, the two use cases, `Press an Elevator Button` and `Press a Floor Button`. The two use cases are shown in the use-case diagram (Section 10.7) of Figure 11.2.

Figure 11.2
Use-case diagram for the elevator problem case study.

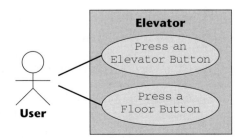

A use case provides a generic description of the overall functionality; a scenario is a specific instantiation of a use case, just as an object is an instantiation of a class. In general, there are a large number of scenarios, each representing one specific set of interactions. In this section, we consider the scenario of Figure 11.3, which incorporates instantiations of both use cases.

Figure 11.3 depicts a ***normal scenario***, that is, a set of interactions between users and elevators that corresponds to the way we understand elevators should be used. Figure 11.3 was constructed after carefully observing different users interacting with elevators (or, more precisely, with elevator buttons and floor buttons). The 15 numbered events describe in detail the two interactions between User A and the buttons of the elevator system (event 1 and event 6) and the operations performed by the components of the elevator system (events 2 through 5 and 7 through 15). Two items, User A enters the elevator and User A exits from the elevator, are unnumbered. Such items essentially are comments; User A does not interact with the components of the elevator when entering or leaving an elevator.

In contrast, Figure 11.4 is an ***exception scenario***. It depicts what happens when a user presses the Up button at floor 3 but actually wants to go down to floor 1. This scenario, too, was constructed by observing the actions of many users in elevators; it is unlikely that someone who has never used an elevator would realize that users sometimes press the wrong button.

The scenarios of Figures 11.3 and 11.4, plus innumerable others, are specific instances of the use cases shown in Figure 11.2. Sufficient scenarios should be studied

Figure 11.3   The first iteration of a normal scenario.

1. User A presses the Up floor button at floor 3 to request an elevator. User A wishes to go to floor 7.
2. The Up floor button is turned on.
3. An elevator arrives at floor 3. It contains User B, who has entered the elevator at floor 1 and pressed the elevator button for floor 9.
4. The elevator doors open.
5. The timer starts.
   User A enters the elevator.
6. User A presses the elevator button for floor 7.
7. The elevator button for floor 7 is turned on.
8. The elevator doors close after a timeout.
9. The Up floor button is turned off.
10. The elevator travels to floor 7.
11. The elevator button for floor 7 is turned off.
12. The elevator doors open to allow User A to exit from the elevator.
13. The timer starts.
    User A exits from the elevator.
14. The elevator doors close after a timeout.
15. The elevator proceeds to floor 9 with User B.

Figure 11.4   An exception scenario.

1. User A presses the Up floor button at floor 3 to request an elevator. User A wishes to go to floor 1.
2. The Up floor button is turned on.
3. An elevator arrives at floor 3. It contains User B, who has entered the elevator at floor 1 and pressed the elevator button for floor 9.
4. The elevator doors open.
5. The timer starts.
   User A enters the elevator.
6. User A presses the elevator button for floor 1.
7. The elevator button for floor 1 is turned on.
8. The elevator doors close after a timeout.
9. The Up floor button is turned off.
10. The elevator travels to floor 9.
11. The elevator button for floor 9 is turned off.
12. The elevator doors open to allow User B to exit from the elevator.
13. The timer starts.
    User B exits from the elevator.
14. The elevator doors close after a timeout.
15. The elevator proceeds to floor 1 with User A.

to give the OOA team a comprehensive insight into the behavior of the system being modeled. This information is used in the next step, entity class modeling, to determine the entity classes.

Case Study

11.8 Entity Class Modeling: The Elevator Problem Case Study

In this step, the entity classes and their attributes are extracted and represented in a UML class diagram. Only the attributes of an entity class are determined at this time, not the methods; the latter are assigned to the classes during the design workflow.

A characteristic of the whole object-oriented paradigm is that the various steps rarely are easy to carry out. Fortunately, the benefits of using objects make the effort worthwhile. So it should not come as a surprise that the first part of the analysis workflow, extracting entity classes and their attributes, usually is difficult to get right the first time.

One method of determining the entity classes is to deduce them from the use cases. That is, the developers carefully study all the scenarios, both normal and exception, and identify the components that play a role in the use cases. From just the scenarios of Figures 11.3 and 11.4, candidate entity classes are elevator buttons, floor buttons, elevators, doors, and timers. As we will see, these candidate entity classes are close to the actual classes extracted during entity class modeling. In general, however, there are many scenarios and, consequently, a large number of potential classes. An inexperienced developer may be tempted to infer too many candidate entity classes from the scenarios. This has a deleterious effect on the entity class modeling, because it is easier to add a new entity class than to remove a candidate entity class that should not have been included.

Another approach to determining the entity classes, which is effective when the developers have domain expertise, is CRC cards (Section 11.8.2). However, if the developers have little or no experience in the application domain, then it is advisable to use noun extraction, described in Section 11.8.1.

11.8.1 Noun Extraction

For developers with no domain expertise, a good way to proceed is to use the following two-stage ***noun-extraction method*** to extract candidate entity classes and then to refine the solution:

Stage 1. Describe the Software Product in a Single Paragraph

One possible way to do this for the elevator problem case study is as follows:

> Buttons in elevators and on the floors control the movement of n elevators in a building with m floors. Buttons illuminate when pressed to request the elevator to stop at a specific floor; the illumination is canceled when the request has been satisfied. When an elevator has no requests, it remains at its current floor with its doors closed.

Stage 2. Identify the Nouns

Identify the nouns in the informal strategy (excluding those that lie outside the problem boundary), and then use these nouns as candidate entity classes. The informal strategy is now reproduced, but this time with the identified nouns printed in a sans serif type.

> Buttons in elevators and on the floors control the movement of n elevators in a building with m floors. Buttons illuminate when pressed to request an elevator to stop at a specific floor; the illumination is canceled when the request has been satisfied. When an elevator has no requests, it remains at its current floor with its doors closed.

There are eight different nouns: button, elevator, floor, movement, building, illumination, request, and door. Three of these nouns—floor, building, and door—lie outside the problem boundary and therefore may be ignored. Three of the remaining nouns—movement, illumination, and request—are ***abstract nouns***; that is, they identify things that have no physical existence. A useful rule of thumb is that abstract nouns rarely end up corresponding to classes. Instead, they frequently are attributes of classes. For example, illumination is an ***attribute*** of button. This

Figure 11.5
The first
iteration of the
class diagram
for the elevator
problem case
study.

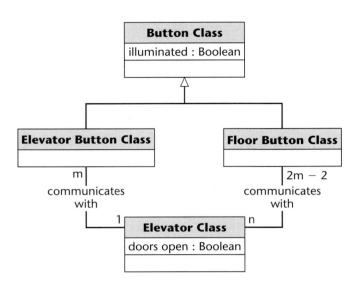

leaves two nouns and, therefore, two candidate entity classes: **Elevator Class** and **Button Class**. (The UML convention is to use boldface for class names and capitalize the initial letter of each word in a class name.)

The resulting *class diagram* is shown in Figure 11.5. **Button Class** has the Boolean attribute illuminated to model events 2, 7, 9, and 11 of the scenarios of Figures 11.3 and 11.4. The problem specifies two types of button, so two subclasses of **Button Class** are defined: **Elevator Button Class** and **Floor Button Class** (the open triangle denotes inheritance in UML). Each instance of **Elevator Button Class** and **Floor Button** communicates with the instance of **Elevator Class**. The latter class has the Boolean attribute doors open to model events 4, 8, 12, and 14 of the two scenarios.

Unfortunately, this is not a good beginning. In a real elevator, the buttons do not directly communicate with the elevators; some sort of *elevator controller* is needed, if only to decide which elevator to dispatch in response to a particular request. However, the problem statement makes no mention of a controller, so it was not selected as an entity class during the noun-extraction process. In other words, the technique of this section for finding candidate entity classes provides a starting point but certainly should not be relied on to do more than that.

Adding the **Elevator Controller Class** to Figure 11.5 yields Figure 11.6. This certainly makes more sense. Furthermore, there are now one-to-many relationships in Figure 11.6, as opposed to the hard to model many-to-many relationship of Figure 11.5. It therefore seems reasonable to go on to stage 3 at this point, bearing in mind that it is possible to return to entity class modeling at any time, even as late as the implementation workflow. However, before proceeding with the dynamic modeling, a different technique for entity class modeling is considered.

Figure 11.6
The second
iteration of the
class diagram
for the elevator
problem case
study.

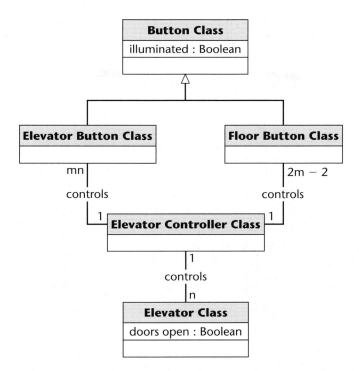

11.8.2   CRC Cards

For a number of years, *class–responsibility–collaboration (CRC) cards* have been utilized during the analysis workflow [Wirfs-Brock, Wilkerson, and Wiener, 1990]. For each class, the software development team fills in a card showing the name of the class, its functionality (responsibility), and a list of the other classes it invokes to achieve that functionality (collaboration).

This approach subsequently has been extended. First, a CRC card often explicitly contains the attributes and methods of the class, rather than just its "responsibility" expressed in some natural language. Second, the technology has changed. Instead of using cards, some organizations put the names of the classes on Post-it Notes, which they move around on a white board; lines are drawn between the Post-it Notes to denote collaboration. Nowadays the whole process can be automated; CASE tools like System Architect include components for creating and updating CRC "cards" on the screen.

The strength of CRC cards is that, when utilized by a team, the interaction among the members can highlight missing or incorrect fields in a class, whether attributes or methods. Also, the relationships between classes are clarified when CRC cards are used. One especially powerful technique is to distribute the cards among the team members, who then act out the responsibilities of their classes. Accordingly, someone might say, "I am the **Date Class**, and my responsibility is to create new date objects." Another team member might then interject that he or she needs additional functionality from the **Date Class**, such as converting a date from the conventional format to an integer, the number of days from January 1, 1900, so that finding the number of days between any two dates can be computed

How do we find the number of days between February 21, 1999, and August 16, 2007? Such subtractions are needed in many financial computations, such as calculating an interest payment or determining the present value of a future cash flow. The usual way this is done is to convert each date into an integer, the number of days since a specified starting date. The problem is that we cannot agree what starting date to use.

Astronomers use Julian days, the number of days since noon GMT on January 1, 4713, B.C.E. This system was invented in 1582 by Joseph Scaliger, who named it for his father, Julius Caesar Scaliger. (If you really, really have to know why January 1, 4713 B.C.E., was chosen, consult [USNO, 2000].)

A Lilian date is the number of days since October 15, 1582, the first day of the Gregorian calendar, introduced by Pope Gregory XIII. Lilian dates are named for Luigi Lilio, a leading proponent of the Gregorian calendar reform. Lilio was responsible for deriving many of the algorithms of the Gregorian calendar, including the rule for leap years.

Turning to software, COBOL intrinsic functions use January 1, 1600, as the starting date for integer dates. Almost all spreadsheets, however, use January 1, 1900, following the lead of Lotus 1-2-3.

---

easily by subtracting the corresponding two integers (see Just in Case You Wanted to Know Box 11.3). Consequently, acting out the responsibilities of CRC cards is an effective means of verifying that the class diagram is complete and correct.

As previously mentioned, a weakness of CRC cards is that this approach generally is not a good way of identifying entity classes unless the team members have considerable experience in the relevant application domain. On the other hand, once the developers have determined many of the classes and have a good idea of their responsibilities and collaborations, CRC cards can be an excellent way of completing the process and making sure that everything is correct. This is described in Section 11.10.

Case Study

11.9 Dynamic Modeling: The Elevator Problem Case Study

The aim of dynamic modeling is to produce a **statechart** for each class, a description of the dynamic behavior of the target product. First, consider **Elevator Controller Class**. For simplicity, only one elevator is considered. The relevant statechart for **Elevator Controller Class** is shown in Figure 11.7.

Statecharts embody states, events, and predicates. The key concept here is the notion of **state**. The attributes of a class sometimes are termed **state variables**. The reason for this terminology is that, in most object-oriented implementations, the state of the product is determined by the values of the attributes of the various component objects. An **event** is an occurence that can cause the product to go into some other state. Finally, a **predicate** is something that is true or false.

States, events, and predicates are distributed over a statechart. For example, the state **Going Into Wait State** in Figure 11.7 is entered if the present state is

Figure 11.7   The first iteration of the statechart for **Elevator Controller Class**.

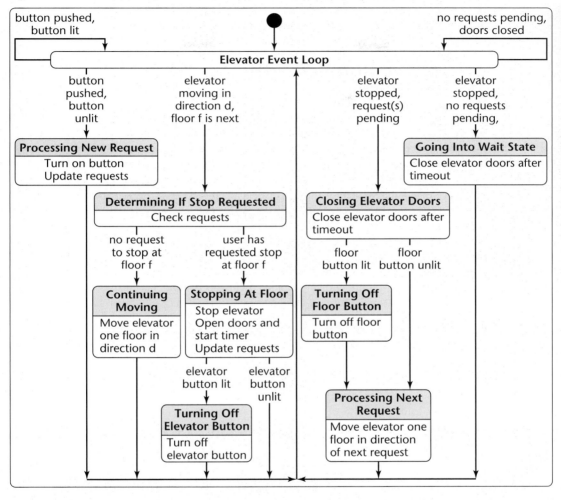

Elevator Event Loop and the event elevator stopped, no requests pending is true. When the state **Going Into Wait State** has been entered, operation Close elevator doors after timeout is to be carried out.

Consider the first part of the scenario of Figure 11.3. Event 1 is User A presses the Up floor button at floor 3. Now consider the statechart of Figure 11.7. The solid circle denotes the initial state, which takes the system into state **Elevator Event Loop**. Following the leftmost vertical line, if the button is unlit when pushed, the system enters state **Processing New Request** of Figure 11.7, and the button is turned on. The following state is **Elevator Event Loop**.

Event 3 in the scenario of Figure 11.3 is that the elevator arrives at floor 3. Returning to the statechart of Figure 11.7, consider what happens when the elevator nears floor 3. Because the elevator is in motion, the next state entered is **Determining**

If Stop Requested. The requests are checked and, because User A has requested the elevator to stop there, the next state is **Stopping At Floor**. The elevator stops at floor 3, the doors open, and the timer starts. The elevator button for floor 3 has not been pressed, so state **Elevator Event Loop** is next.

User A enters and presses the elevator button for floor 7. Therefore, the next state is again **Processing New Request**, followed again by **Elevator Event Loop**. The elevator has stopped and two requests are pending, so state **Closing Elevator Doors** is next and the doors close after a timeout. The floor button at floor 3 was pressed by User A, so **Turning Off Floor Button** is the following state, and the floor button is turned off. State **Processing Next Request** is next, and the elevator starts to move toward floor 4.

From the preceding discussion, it should come as no surprise to learn that Figure 11.7 was constructed from the scenarios. More precisely, the specific events of the scenarios were generalized. For example, consider the first event of the scenario of Figure 11.3, User A presses the Up floor button at floor 3. This specific event is generalized to an arbitrary button (floor button or elevator button) being pushed. Then, there are two possibilities. Either the button already is lit (in which case nothing happens) or the button is unlit (in which case action must be taken to process the user's request).

To model this event, the **Elevator Event Loop** state is drawn in Figure 11.7. The case of an already lit button is modeled by the do-nothing loop with event button pushed, button lit in the top left-hand corner of Figure 11.7. The other case, an unlit button, is modeled by the arrow labeled with the event button pushed, button unlit leading to state **Processing New Request**. From event 2 of the scenario it is clear that the operation Turn on button is needed in this state. Furthermore, the purpose of the user's action of pressing an arbitrary button is to request an elevator (floor button) or request an elevator to move to a specific floor (elevator button), so operation Update requests also must be carried out in the state **Processing New Request**.

Now consider event 3 of the scenario: An elevator arrives at floor 3. This was generalized to the concept of an arbitrary elevator moving between floors. The motion of the elevator is modeled by the event elevator moving in direction d, floor f is next and the state **Determining If Stop Requested**. But there again are two possibilities: either a request to stop at floor f or no such request. In the former case, corresponding to event no request to stop at floor f, the elevator simply must be in the state of **Continuing Moving** one more floor in direction d. In the latter case (corresponding to event user has requested stop at floor f), from the scenario of Figure 11.3 it is clear that it is necessary to Stop elevator (from event 3), and then Open doors and start timer (from events 4 and 5); state **Stopping At Floor** is needed to perform these actions. Also, similar to the **Processing New Request** state, it becomes apparent that it is necessary also to Update requests in state **Stopping At Floor**. In addition, generalizing event 9 of the scenario leads to the realization that the floor button has to be turned off if it is lit. This is modeled by state **Turning Off Floor Button**, together with the two events above the box representing that state. Similarly, generalizing event 11 of the scenario similarly implies that the elevator button has to be turned off if it is lit. This is modeled by state **Turning Off Elevator Button**, together with the two events above the box representing that state.

Generalizing event 8 of the scenario of Figure 11.3 yields state **Closing Elevator Doors**; generalizing event 10 yields state Processing Next Request. However, the need for the state **Going Into Wait State** and the event no requests pending, doors closed is deduced by generalizing an event of a different scenario, one in which the user exits from the elevator but no buttons remain lit.

The statecharts for the other classes are relatively straightforward and therefore left as an exercise (Problem 11.6).

11.10 The Test Workflow: The Elevator Problem Case Study

At this point, the functional, entity class, and dynamic models appear to be complete and the *test workflow* resumes. The next step is to review the analysis workflow to date. One component of this review, as suggested in Section 11.8.2, is to use CRC cards.

Accordingly, CRC cards are filled in for each of the entity classes, **Button Class**, **Elevator Button Class**, **Floor Button Class**, **Elevator Class**, and **Elevator Controller Class**. The CRC card for **Elevator Controller Class**, shown in Figure 11.8, is deduced from the class diagram of Figure 11.5 and the statechart of Figure 11.6. In more detail, the RESPONSIBILITY of **Elevator Controller Class** is obtained by listing all the operations in the statechart for **Elevator Controller Class** (Figure 11.7). The COLLABORATION of the **Elevator Controller Class** is determined by examining the class diagram of Figure 11.6 and noting that classes **Elevator Button Class**, **Floor Button Class**, and **Elevator Class** interact with the **Elevator Controller Class**.

This CRC card highlights two major problems with the first iteration of the object-oriented analysis.

1. Consider responsibility 1. Turn on elevator button. This command is totally out of place in the object-oriented paradigm. From the viewpoint of responsibility-driven design (Section 1.9), objects (instances) of **Elevator Button Class** are responsible for turning themselves on or off. Also, from the viewpoint of information hiding (Section 7.6), the **Elevator Controller Class** should not have the knowledge of the internals of **Elevator Button Class** needed to turn on a button. The correct responsibility is this: Send a message to **Elevator Button Class** to turn itself on. Similar changes are needed for responsibilities 2 through 6 in Figure 11.8. These six corrections are reflected in Figure 11.9, the second iteration of the CRC card for the **Elevator Controller Class**.

2. A class has been overlooked. Returning to Figure 11.8, consider responsibility 7. Open elevator doors and start timer. The concept of state can be used to help determine whether a component should be modeled as a class. If the component in question possesses a state that is changed during execution of the implementation, then it probably should be modeled as a class. Clearly, the doors of the elevator possess a state (open or closed), and **Elevator Doors Class** therefore should be a class.

Figure 11.8
The first
iteration of
the CRC card
for **Elevator
Controller
Class**.

CLASS
Elevator Controller Class
RESPONSIBILITY
1. Turn on elevator button
2. Turn off elevator button
3. Turn on floor button
4. Turn off floor button
5. Move elevator up one floor
6. Move elevator down one floor
7. Open elevator doors and start timer
8. Close elevator doors after timeout
9. Check requests
10. Update requests
COLLABORATION
1. **Elevator Button Class**
2. **Floor Button Class**
3. **Elevator Class**

Figure 11.9
The second
iteration of the
CRC card for
the **Elevator
Controller
Class**.

CLASS
Elevator Controller Class
RESPONSIBILITY
1. Send message to **Elevator Button Class** to turn on button
2. Send message to **Elevator Button Class** to turn off button
3. Send message to **Floor Button Class** to turn on button
4. Send message to **Floor Button Class** to turn off button
5. Send message to **Elevator Class** to move up one floor
6. Send message to **Elevator Class** to move down one floor
7. Send message to **Elevator Doors Class** to open
8. Start timer
9. Send message to **Elevator Doors Class** to close after timeout
10. Check requests
11. Update requests
COLLABORATION
1. **Elevator Button Class** (subclass)
2. **Floor Button Class** (subclass)
3. **Elevator Doors Class**
4. **Elevator Class**

There is another reason why **Elevator Doors Class** should be a class. The object-oriented paradigm allows the state to be hidden within an object and hence protected from unauthorized change. If there is an **Elevator Doors Class** object, the only way that the doors of the elevator can be opened or shut is by sending a message to that **Elevator Doors Class** object. Serious accidents can be caused by

Some years ago, I was on the 10th floor of a building, waiting impatiently for an elevator. The doors opened, I started to step forward — only no elevator was there. What saved my life was the total blackness I saw as I was about to step into the elevator shaft, and I instinctively realized that something was wrong.

Perhaps, if that elevator control system had been developed using the object-oriented paradigm, the inappropriate opening of the doors on the 10th floor might have been avoided.

Figure 11.10
The third iteration of the class diagram for the elevator problem case study.

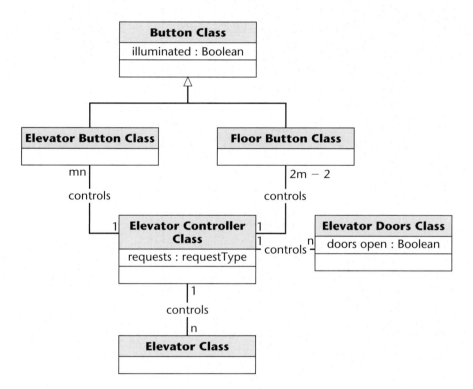

opening or closing the doors of an elevator at the wrong time; see Just in Case You Wanted to Know Box 11.4. Therefore, for certain types of products, safety considerations should be added to the other strengths of objects listed in Chapters 7 and 8.

Adding **Elevator Doors Class** means that responsibilities 7 and 8 in Figure 11.8 need to be changed analogously to responsibilities 1 through 6. That is, messages should be sent to instances of the **Elevator Doors Class** to open and close themselves. But there is an additional complication. Responsibility 7 is Open elevator doors and start timer.

This must be split into two separate responsibilities. A message indeed must be sent to **Elevator Doors Class** to open. However, the timer is part of the **Elevator Controller Class**, and starting the timer therefore is the responsibility of the **Elevator Controller Class** itself. The second iteration of the CRC card for

Figure 11.11   The second iteration of a normal scenario for the elevator problem case study.

1. User A presses the Up floor button at floor 3 to request an elevator. User A wishes to go to floor 7.
2. The floor button informs the elevator controller that the floor button has been pushed.
3. The elevator controller sends a message to the Up floor button to turn itself on.
4. The elevator controller sends a series of messages to the elevator to move itself up to floor 3. The elevator contains User B, who has entered the elevator at floor 1 and pressed the elevator button for floor 9.
5. The elevator controller sends a message to the elevator doors to open themselves.
6. The elevator controller starts the timer.
   User A enters the elevator.
7. User A presses elevator button for floor 7.
8. The elevator button informs the elevator controller that the elevator button has been pushed.
9. The elevator controller sends a message to the elevator button for floor 7 to turn itself on.
10. The elevator controller sends a message to the elevator doors to close themselves after a timeout.
11. The elevator controller sends a message to the Up floor button to turn itself off.
12. The elevator controller sends a series of messages to the elevator to move itself up to floor 7.
13. The elevator controller sends a message to the elevator button for floor 7 to turn itself off.
14. The elevator controller sends a message to the elevator doors to open themselves to allow User A to exit from the elevator.
15. The elevator controller starts the timer.
    User A exits from the elevator.
16. The elevator controller sends a message to the elevator doors to close themselves after a timeout.
17. The elevator controller sends a series of messages to the elevator to move itself up to floor 9 with User B.

Elevator Controller Class (Figure 11.9) shows that this separation of responsibilities has been achieved satisfactorily.

In addition to the two major problems highlighted by the CRC card of Figure 11.8, responsibilities Check requests and Update requests of **Elevator Controller Class** require the attribute requests be added to **Elevator Controller Class**. At this stage, requests are defined simply to be of type requestType; a data structure for requests will be chosen during the design workflow.

The corrected class diagram is shown in Figure 11.10. Having modified the class diagram, the use-case diagram and statecharts must be reexamined to see if they, too, need further refinement. The use-case diagram clearly still is adequate. However, the operations in the statechart of Figure 11.7 must be modified to reflect the responsibilities of Figure 11.9 (the second iteration of the CRC card) and not Figure 11.8 (the first iteration).

Also, the set of statecharts must be extended to include the additional class. The scenarios need to be updated to reflect these changes; Figure 11.11 shows the second iteration of the scenario of Figure 11.3. Even after all these changes have been made and checked (including the modified CRC cards), it still may be necessary during the design workflow to return to the analysis workflow and revise one or more of the analysis artifacts. However, at this stage it appears that the entity classes for the elevator problem case study have been correctly extracted.

11.11 Extracting the Boundary and Control Classes

Unlike entity classes, boundary classes are usually easy to extract. In general, each input screen, output screen, and printed report is modeled by its own boundary class. Recall that a class incorporates attributes (data) and **operations**. The boundary class modeling (say) a printed report incorporates all the various data items that can be included in the report and the various operations performed to print the report.

Control classes are usually as easy to extract as boundary classes. In general, each nontrivial computation is modeled by a control class.

We now illustrate entity, boundary, and control class extraction by extracting the classes of the MSG Foundation case study. The starting point is the use-case diagram of Figure 10.42, reproduced here as Figure 11.12.

Figure 11.12
The seventh iteration of the use-case diagram of the MSG Foundation case study.

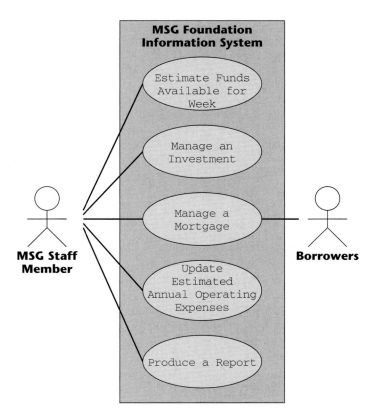

ase Study

11.12 The Initial Functional Model: The MSG Foundation Case Study

As described in Section 11.2, functional modeling consists of finding the scenarios of the use cases. Recall that a scenario is an instance of a use case. Consider the use case `Manage a Mortgage` (Figures 10.32 and 10.33). One possible scenario is shown in Figure 11.13. There is a change in the annual real-estate tax to be paid on a home for which the MSG Foundation has provided a mortgage. Because the borrowers pay this tax in equal weekly payments, any change in the real-estate tax must be entered in the relevant mortgage record so that the total weekly installment (and perhaps the grant) can be adjusted accordingly. The normal portion of the extended scenario models an MSG staff member accessing the relevant mortgage record and changing the annual real-estate tax. Sometimes, however, the staff member may not be able to locate the correct mortgage stored in the software product because he or she has entered the mortgage number incorrectly. This possibility is modeled by the exception portion of the scenario.

Figure 11.13   An extended scenario of managing a mortgage.

An MSG Foundation staff member wants to update the annual real-estate tax on a home for which the Foundation has provided a mortgage.
1. The staff member enters the new value of the annual real-estate tax.
2. The software product updates the date on which the annual real-estate tax was last changed.

Possible alternatives:

A. The staff member enters the mortgage number incorrectly.

Figure 11.14   Another extended scenario of managing a mortgage.

There is a change in the weekly income of a couple who have borrowed money from the MSG Foundation. They wish to have their weekly income updated in the Foundation records by an MSG staff member so that their mortgage payments will be correctly computed.
1. The staff member enters the new value of the weekly income.
2. The software product updates the date on which the weekly income was last changed.

Possible alternatives:

A. The staff member enters the mortgage number incorrectly.
B. The borrowers do not bring documentation regarding their new income.

A second scenario corresponding to the `Manage a Mortgage` use case (Figures 10.32 and 10.33) is shown in Figure 11.14. Here the borrowers' weekly income has changed. They would like this information to be reflected in the MSG Foundation records so that their weekly installment can be correctly computed. The normal portion of this extended scenario shows this operation proceeding as expected. The abnormal portion of this scenario shows two possibilities. First, as in the previous scenario, the staff member may enter the mortgage number incorrectly. Second, the borrowers may not bring with them adequate documentation to support their claim regarding their income, in which case the requested change is not implemented.

A third scenario (Figure 11.15) is an instance of use case `Estimate Funds Available for Week` (Figure 10.42). This scenario is directly derived from the description of the use case (Figure 10.43).

The scenarios of Figures 11.16 and 11.17 are instances of use case `Produce a Report`. Again, these scenarios are directly derived from the corresponding description of the use case (Figure 10.39). The remaining scenarios are equally straightforward and are therefore left as an exercise (Problems 11.12 and 11.13).

Figure 11.15   A scenario of the `Estimate Funds Available for Week` use case.

An MSG Foundation staff member wishes to determine the funds available for mortgages this week.

1. For each investment, the software product extracts the estimated annual return on that investment. It sums the separate returns and divides the result by 52 to yield the estimated investment income for the week.
2. The software product then extracts the estimated annual MSG Foundation operating expenses and divides the result by 52.
3. For each mortgage:
   3.1 The software product computes the amount to be paid this week by adding the principal and interest payment to $\frac{1}{52}$nd of the sum of the annual real-estate tax and the annual homeowner's insurance premium.
   3.2 It then computes 28 percent of the couple's current gross weekly income.
   3.3 If the result of Step 3.1 is greater than the result of Step 3.2, then it determines the mortgage payment for the week as the result of Step 3.2, and the amount of the grant for this week as the difference between the result of Step 3.1 and the result of Step 3.2.
   3.4 Otherwise, it takes the mortgage payment for this week as the result of Step 3.1, and there is no grant for the week.
4. The software product sums the mortgage payments of Steps 3.3 and 3.4 to yield the estimated total mortgage payments for the week.
5. It sums the grant payments of Step 3.3 to yield the estimated total grant payments for the week.
6. The software product adds the results of Steps 1 and 4 and subtracts the results of Steps 2 and 5. This is the total amount available for mortgages for the current week.
7. Finally, the software product prints the total amount available for new mortgages during the current week.

Figure 11.16 A scenario of the `Produce a Report` use case.

> An MSG staff member wishes to print a list of all mortgages.
> 1. The staff member requests a report listing all mortgages.

Figure 11.17 Another scenario of the `Produce a Report` use case.

> An MSG staff member wishes to print a list of all investments.
> 1. The staff member requests a report listing all investments.

Case Study

11.13 The Initial Class Diagram: The MSG Foundation Case Study

The second step is class modeling. The aim of this step is to extract the entity classes, determine their interrelationships, and find their attributes. The best way to start this step is usually to use the two-stage noun extraction method (Section 11.8.1).

In stage 1 we describe the software product in a single paragraph. In the case of the MSG Foundation case study, a way to do this is:

> Weekly reports are to be printed showing how much money is available for mortgages. In addition, lists of investments and mortgages must be printed on demand.

In Stage 2 we identify the nouns in this paragraph. For clarity, the nouns are printed in sans serif type.

> Weekly reports are to be printed showing how much money is available for mortgages. In addition, lists of investments and mortgages must be printed on demand.

The nouns are report, money, mortgage, list, and investment. Nouns report and list are not long lived, so they are unlikely to be entity classes (report will surely turn out to be a boundary class), and money is an abstract noun. This leaves two candidate entity classes, namely, **Mortgage Class** and **Investment Class**, as shown in Figure 11.18, the first iteration of the initial class diagram.

Now we consider interactions between these two entity classes. Looking at the descriptions of use cases `Manage an Investment` and `Manage a Mortgage` (Figures 10.31 and 10.33, respectively) it appears that the operations performed on the two entity classes are likely to be extremely similar, namely, insertions,

Figure 11.18 The first iteration of the initial class diagram of the MSG Foundation case study.

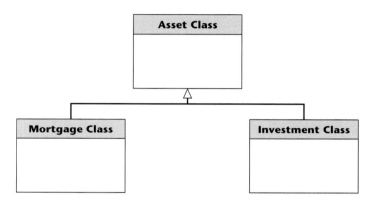

Figure 11.19 The second iteration of the initial class diagram of the MSG Foundation case study.

deletions, and modifications. Also, the second iteration of the description of use case `Produce a Report` (Figure 10.39) shows all the members of both entity classes have to be printed on demand. In other words, **Mortgage Class** and **Investment Class** should probably be subclasses of some superclass. We will call that superclass **Asset Class**, because mortgages and investments are both assets of the MSG Foundation. The resulting second iteration of the initial class diagram is shown in Figure 11.19.

A useful side effect of constructing this superclass is that we can once again reduce the number of use cases. As shown in Figure 11.12, we currently have five use cases, including `Manage a Mortgage` and `Manage an Investment`. However, if we consider a mortgage or an investment to be a special case of an asset, we can combine the two use cases into a single use case, `Manage an Asset`. The eighth iteration of the use-case diagram is shown in Figure 11.20. The new use case is shaded. Now the attributes are added, as shown in Figure 11.21.

The phrase "iteration and *in*crementation" also includes the possibility of the need for a *de*crementation in what has been developed to date. There are two reasons for such a decrease. First, if a mistake is made, the best way to correct it may be to **backtrack** to an earlier version of the software product and find a better way of performing the step that was incorrectly carried out. When backtracking, everything that was added in the course of the incorrect step now has to be removed. Second, as a consequence of reorganizing the models to date, one or more

Figure 11.20
The eighth
iteration of
the use-case
diagram of
the MSG
Foundation
case study.
The new use
case, Manage
an Asset, is
shaded.

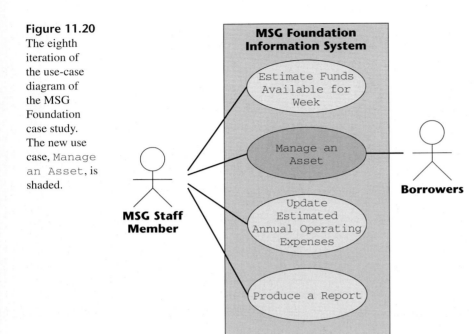

Figure 11.21 Attributes added to the second iteration of the initial class diagram of the MSG
Foundation case study.

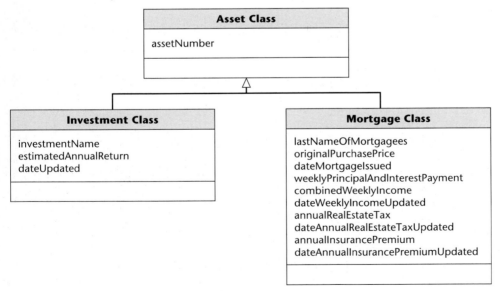

artifacts may have become superfluous. Developing a software product is hard. It
is therefore important to remove superfluous use cases or other artifacts as soon
as possible.

ase Study

11.14 The Initial Dynamic Model: The MSG Foundation Case Study

The third step in object-oriented analysis is dynamic modeling. In this step, a statechart is drawn that reflects all the operations performed by or to that system, indicating the events that cause the transition from state to state. The major source of information regarding the relevant operations is the scenarios.

The statechart of Figure 11.22 reflects the operations of the complete MSG Foundation case study. The solid circle on the top left represents the initial state, the starting point of the statechart. The arrow from the initial state leads us to the state labeled **MSG Foundation Event Loop**; states other than the initial and final states are represented by rectangles with rounded corners. In state **MSG Foundation Event Loop**, one of five events can occur. In more detail, an MSG staff member can issue one of five commands: estimate funds for the week, manage an asset, update estimated annual operating expenses, produce a report, or quit. These possibilities are indicated by the five events estimate funds for the week selected, manage an asset selected, update estimated annual operating expenses selected, produce a report selected, and quit selected. (An event causes a ***transition*** between states.)

Figure 11.22   The initial statechart of the MSG Foundation case study.

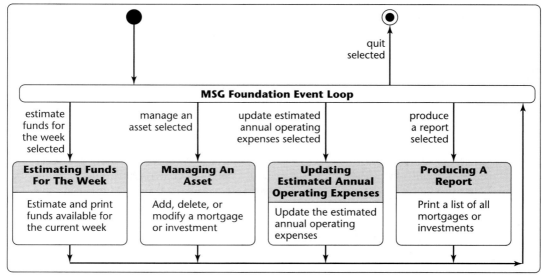

Figure 11.23   Menu in the target MSG Foundation case study.

Figure 11.24   Textual version of the menu of Figure 11.23.

> MAIN MENU
> Martha Stockton Greengage Foundation
> 1. Estimate funds available for week
> 2. Manage an asset
> 3. Update estimated annual operating expenses
> 4. Produce a report
> 5. Quit
> Type your choice and press <ENTER>:

When the system is in state **MSG Foundation Event Loop**, any one of the five events may occur, depending on which option the MSG staff member selects from the menu, shown in Figure 11.23, that will be incorporated in the target software product. (The C++ and Java implementations of the MSG Foundation case study given in Appendices G and H, respectively, use a textual interface rather than a graphical user interface (GUI). That is, instead of clicking on a box, as shown in Figure 11.23, the user types in a choice, as shown in Figure 11.24. For example, the user types 1 to Estimate funds available for week, 2 to Manage an asset, and so on. The reason the implementations in Appendices G and H use a textual interface, such as Figure 11.24, is that a textual interface can be run on all computers; a GUI generally needs special software.)

Suppose that the MSG staff member clicks on the choice *Manage an asset* in the menu of Figure 11.23. The event manage an asset selected (second from the left below the **MSG Foundation Event Loop** box in Figure 11.22) has now occurred, so the system moves from its current state, **MSG Foundation Event Loop**, to the state **Managing An Asset**. The operations that the MSG staff member can perform in this state, namely, Add, delete, or modify a mortgage or investment, appear below the line in the box with rounded corners.

Once the operation has been performed, the system returns to the state **MSG Foundation Event Loop**, as shown by the arrows. The behavior of the rest of the statechart is equally straightforward.

In summary, the software product moves from state to state. In each state, the MSG staff member can perform the operations supported by that state, as listed below the line in the box with rounded corners that represents the state. This continues until the MSG staff member clicks on menu choice *Quit* when the software product is in the state **MSG Foundation Event Loop**. At this time the software product enters the final state (represented by the white circle containing the small black circle). When this state is entered, execution of the statechart terminates; recall that the statechart is a model of the execution of the target software product.

ase Study

11.15 Revising the Entity Classes:
The MSG Foundation Case Study

The initial functional model, the initial class diagram, and the initial dynamic model have now been completed. However, a check of all three models reveals that something has been overlooked.

Look at the initial statechart of Figure 11.22 and consider state **Updating Estimated Annual Operating Expenses** with operation Update the estimated annual operating expenses. This operation has to be performed on data, namely, the current value of the estimated annual operating expenses. But where

Figure 11.25   The third iteration of the initial class diagram of the MSG Foundation case study.

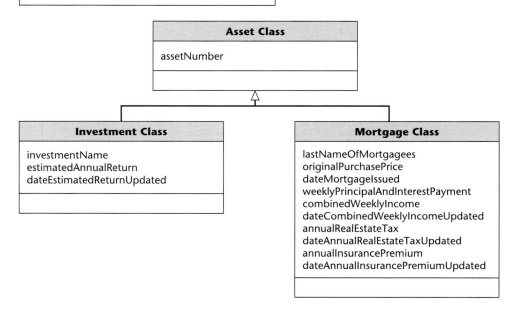

Figure 11.26
Figure 11.25
redrawn to show
the stereotypes.

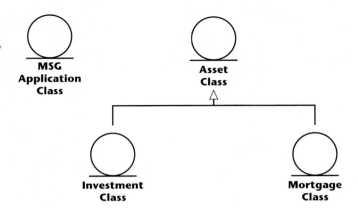

is the value of the estimated annual operating expenses to be found? Looking at Figure 11.21, it would have been a serious error to have it as an attribute of **Asset Class** or either of its subclasses. On the other hand, currently there is only one class (**Asset Class**) and its two subclasses. This means that the only way a value can be stored on a long-term basis is as an attribute of an instance of that class or its subclasses.

The solution is obvious: Another entity class is needed in which the value of the estimated annual operating expenses can be stored. In fact, other values need to be stored as well; the result is shown in Figure 11.25. A new class, **MSG Application Class**, has been introduced in which the various static attributes shown in the top box in the figure can be stored. In addition, the **MSG Application Class** will be assigned the task of starting the execution of the rest of the software product.

Now the class diagram of Figure 11.25 is redrawn to reflect the stereotypes. This is shown in Figure 11.26. All four classes are entity classes. The entity classes seem to be correct, at least for now. The next step is to determine the boundary classes and control classes.

Case Study

11.16 Extracting the Boundary Classes: The MSG Foundation Case Study

Extracting entity classes is usually considerably harder than extracting boundary classes. After all, entity classes generally have interrelationships, whereas each input screen, output screen, and printed report is usually modeled by an (independent) boundary class, as pointed out in Section 11.11.

In view of the fact that the target MSG Foundation software product appears to be relatively straightforward (at least at this early stage of the Unified Process), it is reasonable to try to have just one screen that the MSG staff member

Figure 11.27
The initial
boundary classes
of the MSG
Foundation case
study.

User Interface Class
Estimated Funds Report Class
Mortgages Report Class
Investments Report Class

can use for all four use cases: Estimate Funds Available for Week, Manage an Asset, Update Estimated Annual Operating Expenses, and Produce a Report. As more is learned about the MSG Foundation, it is certainly possible that this one screen may have to be refined into two or more screens. But the initial class extraction has just the one screen class, **User Interface Class**.

There are three reports that have to be printed, the estimated funds for the week report and the two asset reports, namely, the complete listing of all mortgages or of all investments. Each of these has to be modeled by a separate boundary class because the content of each report is different. The four corresponding initial boundary classes are then **User Interface Class**, **Estimated Funds Report Class**, **Mortgages Report Class**, and **Investments Report Class**. These four classes are displayed in Figure 11.27.

ase Study

11.17 Extracting the Control Classes: The MSG Foundation Case Study

Control classes are generally as easy to extract as boundary classes because each nontrivial computation is almost always modeled by a control class, as stated in Section 11.11. For the MSG Foundation case study, there is just one computation, namely, estimating the funds available for the week. This yields the initial control class **Estimate Funds for Week Class** shown in Figure 11.28.

The next step is to check all three sets of classes: entity classes, boundary classes, and control classes. Careful examination of the classes yields no obvious discrepancies.

This concludes the material on class extraction starting at Section 11.5; we therefore now return to the Unified Process.

Figure 11.28   The initial control class
of the MSG Foundation case study.

Estimate Funds for Week Class

*C*ase Study

11.18 Use-Case Realization: The MSG Foundation Case Study

A use case is a description of an interaction between an actor and the software product. Use cases are first utilized at the beginning of the software life cycle, that is, in the requirements workflow. During the analysis and design workflows, more details are added to each use case, including a description of the classes involved in carrying out the use case. This process of extending and refining use cases is called **use-case realization**. Finally, during the implementation workflow, the use cases are implemented in code.

This terminology is somewhat confusing, because the verb *realize* can be used in at least three different senses:

- Understand ("Harvey slowly began to realize that he was in the wrong classroom").
- Receive ("Ingrid will realize a profit of $45,000 on the stock transaction").
- Accomplish ("Janet hopes to realize her dream of starting a software development organization").

In the phrase *realize a use* case, the word **realize** is used in this last sense, that is, it means to accomplish (or *achieve*) the use case.

An **interaction diagram** (**sequence diagram** or **communication diagram**) depicts the realization of a specific scenario of the use case. We first consider the use case Estimate Funds Available for Week.

11.18.1 Estimate Funds Available for Week Use Case

The use-case diagram of Figure 11.20 shows all the use cases. These include Estimate Funds Available for Week, which is shown separately in Figure 11.29. The description of that use case was given in Figure 10.43, which is reproduced here as Figure 11.30 for convenience. From the description we deduce that, as reflected in the class diagram of Figure 11.31, the classes that enter into this use case are **User Interface Class**, which models the user interface;

Figure 11.29
The Estimate Funds Available for Week use case.

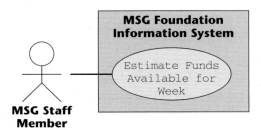

Figure 11.30   The description of the `Estimate Funds Available for Week` use case.

Brief Description

The `Estimate Funds Available for Week` use case enables an MSG Foundation staff member to estimate how much money the Foundation has available that week to fund mortgages.

Step-by-Step Description

1. For each investment, extract the estimated annual return on that investment. Summing the separate returns and dividing the result by 52 yields the estimated investment income for the week.
2. Determine the estimated MSG Foundation operating expenses for the week by extracting the estimated annual MSG Foundation operating expenses and dividing by 52.
3. For each mortgage:
   3.1 The amount to be paid this week is the total of the principal and interest payment and $\frac{1}{52}$nd of the sum of the annual real-estate tax and the annual homeowner's insurance premium.
   3.2 Compute 28 percent of the couple's current gross weekly income.
   3.3 If the result of Step 3.1 is greater than the result of Step 3.2, then the mortgage payment for this week is the result of Step 3.2, and the amount of the grant for this week is the difference between the result of Step 3.1 and the result of Step 3.2.
   3.4 Otherwise, the mortgage payment for this week is the result of Step 3.1, and there is no grant this week.
4. Summing the mortgage payments of Steps 3.3 and 3.4 yields the estimated total mortgage payments for the week.
5. Summing the grant payments of Step 3.3 yields the estimated total grant payments for the week.
6. Add the results of Steps 1 and 4 and subtract the results of Steps 2 and 5. This is the total amount available for mortgages for the current week.
7. Print the total amount available for new mortgages during the current week.

Estimate Funds for Week Class, the control class that models the computation of the estimate of the funds that are available to fund mortgages during that week; **Mortgage Class**, which models the estimated grants and payments for the week; **Investment Class**, which models the estimated return on investments for the week; **MSG Application Class**, which models the estimated operating expenses for the week; and **Estimated Funds Report Class**, which models the printing of the report.

Figure 11.31 is a class diagram. That is, it shows the classes that participate in the realization of the use case and their relationships. A working software product, on the other hand, uses objects rather than classes. For example, a specific mortgage cannot be represented by **Mortgage Class** but rather by an object, a specific instance of **Mortgage Class**, denoted by **: Mortgage Class**. Also, the class diagram of Figure 11.31 shows the participating classes in the use case and their relationships; it does not show the sequence of events as they occur. Something more is needed to model a specific scenario such as the scenario of Figure 11.18, reproduced here as Figure 11.32.

Figure 11.31
Class diagram
showing the
classes that
realize the
Estimate
Funds
Available
for Week use
case of the MSG
Foundation case
study.

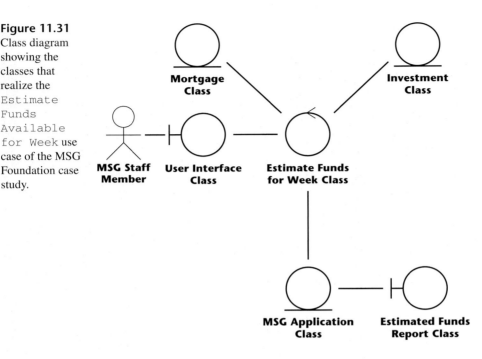

Figure 11.32 A scenario of the Estimate Funds Available for Week use case.

An MSG Foundation staff member wishes to determine the funds available for mortgages this week.
1. For each investment, the software product extracts the estimated annual return on that invest-
    ment. It sums the separate returns and divides the result by 52 to yield the estimated investment
    income for the week.
2. The software product then extracts the estimated annual MSG Foundation operating expenses
    and divides the result by 52.
3. For each mortgage:
    3.1 The software product computes the amount to be paid this week by adding the princi-
         pal and interest payment to $\frac{1}{52}$nd of the sum of the annual real-estate tax and the annual
         homeowner's insurance premium.
    3.2 It then computes 28 percent of the couple's current gross weekly income.
    3.3 If the result of Step 3.1 is greater than the result of Step 3.2, then it determines the mort-
         gage payment for the week as the result of Step 3.2, and the amount of the grant for this
         week as the difference between the result of Step 3.1 and the result of Step 3.2.
    3.4 Otherwise, it takes the mortgage payment for this week as the result of Step 3.1, and there is
         no grant for the week.
4. The software product sums the mortgage payments of Steps 3.3 and 3.4 to yield the estimated
    total mortgage payments for the week.
5. It sums the grant payments of Step 3.3 to yield the estimated total grant payments for the week.
6. The software product adds the results of Steps 1 and 4 and subtracts the results of Steps 2 and 5.
    This is the total amount available for mortgages for the current week.
7. Finally, the software product prints the total amount available for new mortgages during the
    current week.

Figure 11.33 A communication diagram of the realization of the scenario of Figure 11.32 of the `Estimate Funds Available for Week` use case of the MSG Foundation case study.

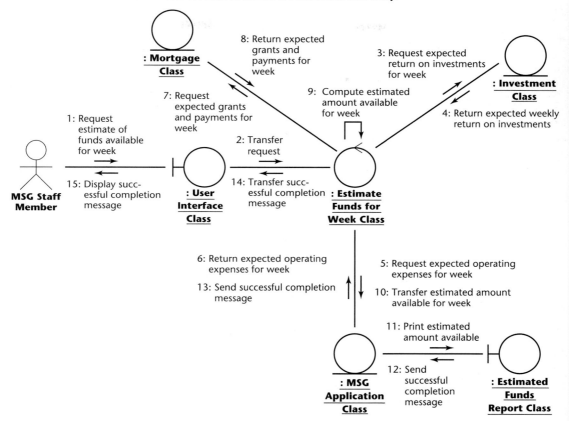

Now consider Figure 11.33. This figure is a communication diagram ("collaboration diagram" in older versions of UML). It therefore shows the objects that interact as well as the messages that are sent, numbered in the order in which they are sent. A communication diagram depicts a realization of a specific scenario of a use case. In this case, Figure 11.33 depicts the scenario of Figure 11.32. In more detail, in the scenario the staff member wants to compute the funds available for the week. This is represented by message 1: Request estimate of funds available for week from **MSG Staff Member** to **: User Interface Class**, an instance of **User Interface Class**.

Next, this request is passed on to **: Estimate Funds for Week Class**, an instance of the control class that actually performs the calculation. This is represented by message 2: Transfer request.

Four separate financial estimates are now determined by **: Estimate Funds for Week Class**. In Step 1 of the scenario (Figure 11.32), the estimated annual return on investments is summed for each investment and the result divided by 52. This extraction of the estimated weekly return is modeled in Figure 11.33 by message 3: Request estimated return on investments for week from **: Estimate Funds for Week Class** to **: Investment Class** followed by message 4: Return estimated weekly return on investments in the reverse direction, that is, back to the object that is controlling the computation.

In Step 2 of the scenario (Figure 11.32), the weekly operating expenses are estimated by taking the estimated annual operating expenses and dividing by 52. This extraction of the weekly return is modeled in Figure 11.33 by message 5: Request estimated operating expenses for week from **: Estimate Funds for Week Class** to **: MSG Application Class** followed by message 6: Return estimated operating expenses for week in the other direction.

In Steps 3, 4, and 5 of the scenario (Figure 11.32), two estimates are determined, namely the estimated grants for the week and the estimated payments for the week. This is modeled in Figure 11.33 by message 7: Request estimated grants and payments for week from **: Estimate Funds for Week Class** to **: Mortgage Class** and by message 8: Return estimated grants and payments for week in the reverse direction.

Now the arithmetic computation of Step 6 of the scenario is performed. This is modeled in Figure 11.33 by message 9: Compute estimated amount available for week. This is a self-call, that is, **: Estimate Funds for Week Class** tells itself to perform the calculation. The result of the computation is stored in **: MSG Application Class** by message 10: Transfer estimated amount available for week.

Next, the result is printed in Step 7 of the scenario (Figure 11.32). This is modeled in Figure 11.33 by message 11: Print estimated amount available from **: MSG Application Class** to **: Estimated Funds Report Class**.

Finally, an acknowledgment is sent to the MSG staff member that the task has been successfully completed. This is modeled in Figure 11.33 by messages 12: Send successful completion message, 13: Send successful completion message, 14: Transfer successful completion message, and 15: Display successful completion message.

No client is going to approve the specification document unless he or she understands precisely what the proposed software product will do. For this reason, a written description of the communication diagram is essential. This is shown in Figure 11.34,

Figure 11.34   The flow of events of the communication diagram of Figure 11.33 of the realization of the scenario of Figure 11.32 of the `Estimate Funds Available for Week` use case of the MSG Application case study.

An MSG staff member requests an estimate of the funds available for mortgages for the week (1, 2). The software product estimates the return on investments for the week (3, 4), the operating expenses for the week (5, 6), and the grants and payments for the week (7, 8). Then it estimates (9), stores (10), and prints out (11–15) the funds available for the week.

the *flow of events*. Finally, the equivalent sequence diagram of the realization of the scenario is shown in Figure 11.35. When constructing a software product, either a communication diagram or a sequence diagram may prove to give better insight of a realization of a use case. In some situations, both are needed to get a full understanding of a specific realization of a given use case. That is why, in this chapter, every communication diagram is followed by the equivalent sequence diagram. The sequence diagram of Figure 11.35 is fully equivalent to the communication diagram of Figure 11.33, so its flow of events is also shown in Figure 11.34.

The strength of a sequence diagram is that it shows the flow of messages unambiguously. The order of the messages is particularly clear, as are the sender and receiver of each individual message. So, when the transfer of information is the focus of attention (which is the case for much of the time when performing the analysis workflow), a sequence diagram is superior to a communication diagram. On the other hand, the similarity between a class diagram (such as Figure 11.31) and the communication diagram that realizes the relevant scenario (such as Figure 11.33) is strong. Accordingly, on those occasions when the developers are concentrating on the classes, a communication diagram is generally more useful than the equivalent sequence diagram.

Summarizing, Figures 11.29 through 11.35 do not depict a random collection of UML artifacts. On the contrary, these figures depict a use case and artifacts derived from that use case. In more detail:

- Figure 11.29 depicts the use case `Estimate Funds Available for Week`. That is, Figure 11.29 models all possible sets of interactions, between the actor **MSG Staff Member** (an entity that is external to the software product) and the MSG Foundation software product itself, that relate to the action of estimating funds available for the week.

- Figure 11.30 is the description of that use case; that is, it provides a written account of the details of the `Estimate Funds Available for Week` use case of Figure 11.29.

- Figure 11.31 is a class diagram showing the classes that realize the `Estimate Funds Available for Week` use case. The class diagram depicts the classes that are needed to model all possible scenarios of the use case, together with their interactions.

- Figure 11.32 is a scenario, that is, one specific instance of the use case of Figure 11.29.

- Figure 11.33 is a communication diagram of the realization of the scenario of Figure 11.32; that is, it depicts the objects and the messages sent between them in the realization of that one specific scenario.

- Figure 11.34 is the flow of events of the communication diagram of the realization of the scenario of Figure 11.32. That is, just as Figure 11.30 is a written description of the `Estimate Funds Available for Week` use case of Figure 11.29, Figure 11.34 is a written description of the realization of the scenario of Figure 11.32.

Figure 11.35 A sequence diagram of the realization of the scenario of Figure 11.32 of the `Estimate Funds Available for Week` use case of the MSG Foundation case study. This sequence diagram is fully equivalent to the communication diagram of Figure 11.33, so its flow of events is also shown in Figure 11.34.

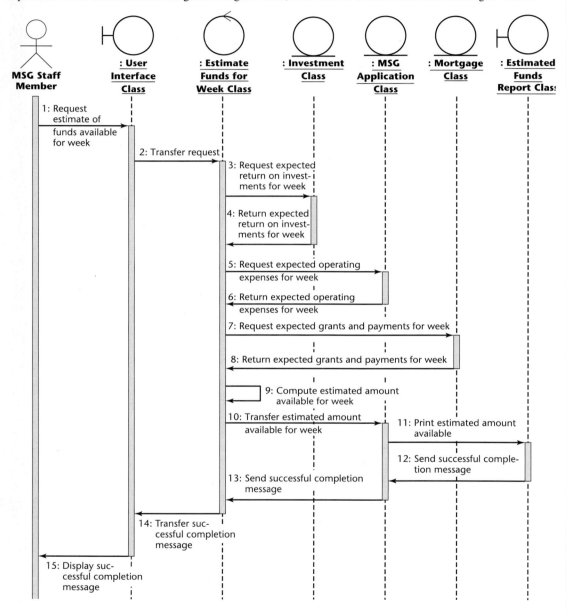

- Figure 11.35 is the sequence diagram that is fully equivalent to the communication diagram of Figure 11.33. That is, the sequence diagram depicts the objects and the messages sent between them in the realization of the scenario of Figure 11.32. Its flow of events is therefore also shown in Figure 11.34.

It has been stated many times in this book that the Unified Process is use-case driven. These bulleted items explicitly state the precise relationship between each of the artifacts of Figures 11.30 through 11.35 and the use case of Figure 11.29 that underlies each of them.

11.18.2 `Manage an Asset` **Use Case**

The `Manage an Asset` use case is shown in Figure 11.36 and its description in Figure 11.37. A class diagram showing the classes that realize the `Manage an Asset` use case is shown in Figure 11.38. Initially it was assumed that only one control class is needed (see Figure 11.28). However, Figure 11.38 shows that a second control class, **Manage an Asset Class**, is required; additional control classes may have to be added in subsequent iterations.

The normal part of the extended scenario of Figure 11.13 of the use case `Manage a Mortgage` (and hence of `Manage an Asset`) is reproduced

Figure 11.36
The `Manage an Asset` use case.

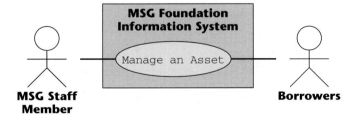

MSG Staff Member

Borrowers

Figure 11.37
Description of the `Manage an Asset` use case.

Brief Description

The `Manage an Asset` use case enables an MSG Foundation staff member to add and delete assets and manage the portfolio of assets (investments and mortgages). Managing a mortgage includes updating the weekly income of a couple who have borrowed money from the Foundation.

Step-by-Step Description

1. Add, modify, or delete an investment or mortgage, or update the borrower's weekly income.

Figure 11.38
A class diagram showing the classes that realize the `Manage an Asset` use case of the MSG Foundation case study.

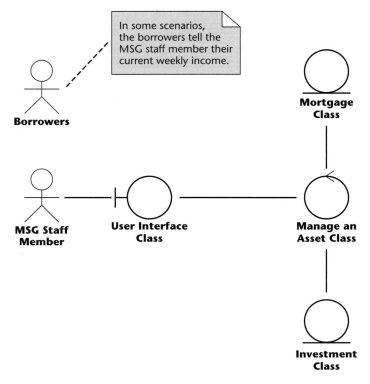

Figure 11.39
A scenario of the `Manage an Asset` use case.

An MSG Foundation staff member wants to update the annual real-estate tax on a home for which the Foundation has provided a mortgage.
1. The staff member enters the new value of the annual real-estate tax.
2. The information system updates the date on which the annual real-estate tax was last changed.

as Figure 11.39. In this scenario, an MSG staff member updates the annual real-estate tax on a mortgaged home and the software product updates the date on which the tax was last changed. Figure 11.40 is the communication diagram of this scenario. Notice that object **: Investment Class** does not play an active role in this communication diagram because the scenario of Figure 11.39 does not involve an investment, only a mortgage. Also, the **Borrowers** do not play a role in this scenario either. The flow of events is left as an exercise (Problem 11.14). The sequence diagram equivalent to the communication diagram of Figure 11.40 is shown in Figure 11.41.

Figure 11.40   A communication diagram of the realization of the scenario of Figure 11.39 of the `Manage an Asset` use case of the MSG Foundation case study.

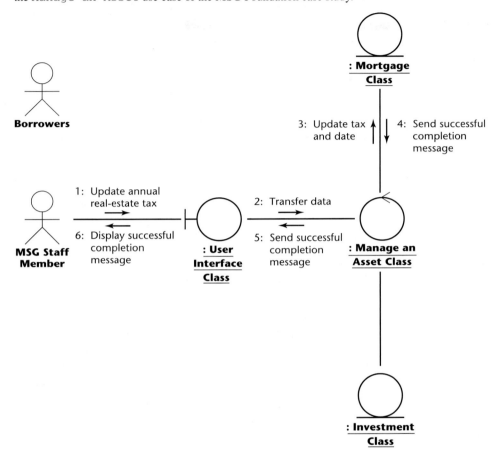

Now consider a different scenario of the use case `Manage an Asset` (Figure 11.36), namely, the extended scenario of Figure 11.14, the normal part of which is reproduced here as Figure 11.42. In this scenario, at the request of the borrowers, the MSG staff member updates the weekly income of a couple who have an MSG mortgage. As explained in Section 10.7, the scenario is initiated by the **Borrowers**, and their data are entered into the software product by the **MSG Staff Member**, as stated in the note in the communication diagram of Figure 11.43. The flow of events is again left as an exercise (Problem 11.15). The equivalent sequence diagram is shown in Figure 11.44.

Comparing the communication diagrams of Figures 11.40 and 11.43 (or, equivalently, the sequence diagrams of Figures 11.41 and 11.44), we see that, other than the actors involved, the only other difference between the two diagrams is that messages

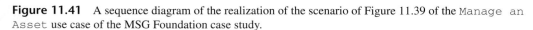

Figure 11.41   A sequence diagram of the realization of the scenario of Figure 11.39 of the `Manage an Asset` use case of the MSG Foundation case study.

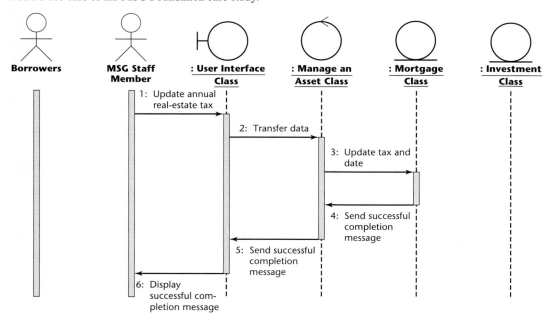

Figure 11.42   A second scenario of the `Manage an Asset` use case.

> There is a change in the weekly income of a couple who have borrowed money from the MSG Foundation. They wish to have their weekly income updated in the Foundation records by an MSG staff member so that their mortgage payments will be correctly computed.
> 1. The staff member enters the new value of the weekly income.
> 2. The information system updates the date on which the weekly income was last changed.

1, 2, and 3 involve annual real-estate tax in the case of Figure 11.40 (or Figure 11.41) and weekly income in the case of Figure 11.43 (or Figure 11.44). This example highlights the difference between a use case, scenarios (instances of the use case), and communication or sequence diagrams of the realization of different scenarios of that use case.

Boundary class **User Interface Class** appears in all the realizations considered so far. In fact, the same screen will be used for all commands of the software product. An MSG staff member clicks on the appropriate operation in the revised menu of

Figure 11.43   A communication diagram of the realization of the scenario of Figure 11.42 of the `Manage an Asset` use case of the MSG Foundation case study.

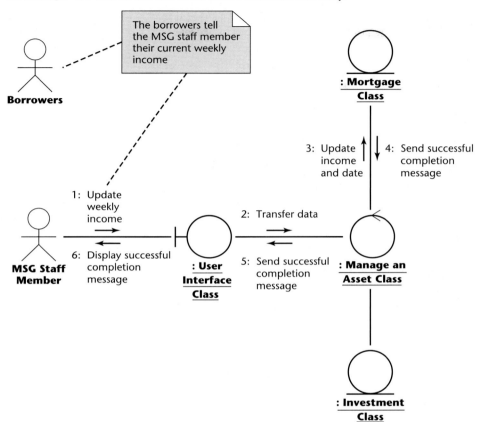

Figure 11.45. (The corresponding textual interface, as implemented in Appendices G and H, is given in Figure 11.46.)

11.18.3 `Update Estimated Annual Operating Expenses` **Use Case**

The use case `Update Estimated Annual Operating Expenses` is shown in Figure 10.17 with a description in Figure 10.18. A class diagram showing the classes that realize the `Update Estimated Annual Operating Expenses` use case appears in Figure 11.47, and a communication diagram of a realization of a scenario of the use case in Figure 11.48. The equivalent sequence diagram is shown in Figure 11.49. Details of the scenario and the flow of events are left as an exercise (Problems 11.16 and 11.17).

Figure 11.44   A sequence diagram of the realization of the scenario of Figure 11.42 of the `Manage an Asset` use case of the MSG Foundation case study.

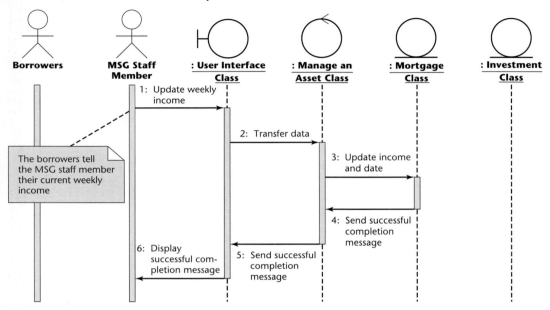

Figure 11.45   Revised menu of the target MSG Foundation case study.

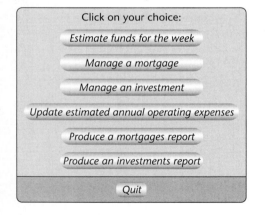

Figure 11.46   Textual version of the revised menu of Figure 11.45.

MAIN MENU
MARTHA STOCKTON GREENGAGE FOUNDATION
1. Estimate funds available for week
2. Manage a mortgage
3. Manage an investment
4. Update estimated annual operating expenses
5. Produce a mortgages report
6. Produce an investments report
7. Quit
Type your choice and press <ENTER>:

Figure 11.47   A class diagram showing the classes that realize the `Update Estimated Annual Operating Expenses` use case of the MSG Foundation case study.

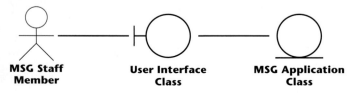

Figure 11.48 A communication diagram of the realization of a scenario of the `Update Estimated Annual Operating Expenses` use case of the MSG Foundation case study.

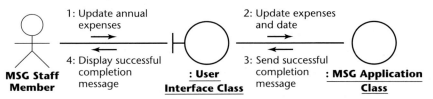

Figure 11.49
A sequence diagram of the realization of a scenario of the `Update Estimated Annual Operating Expenses` use case of the MSG Foundation case study.

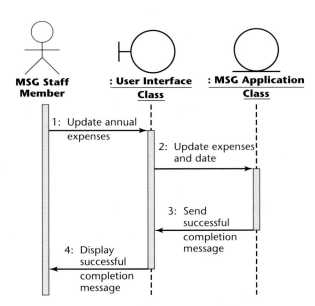

Figure 11.50
The `Produce a Report` use case.

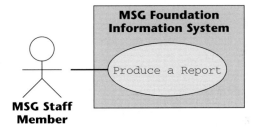

11.18.4 `Produce a Report` **Use Case**

Use case `Produce a Report` is shown in Figure 11.50. The description of use case `Produce a Report` of Figure 10.39 is reproduced here as Figure 11.51. A class diagram showing the classes that realize the `Produce a Report` use case is shown in Figure 11.52.

Figure 11.51
Description of
the `Produce`
`a Report`
use case.

Brief Description
The `Produce a Report` use case enables an MSG Foundation staff member to print a listing of all investments or all mortgages.

Step-by-Step Description
1.   The following reports must be generated
    1.1   Investments report—printed on demand:
           The software product prints a list of all investments. For each investment, the following attributes are printed:
                Item number
                Item name
                Estimated annual return
                Date estimated annual return was last updated
    1.2   Mortgages report—printed on demand:
           The software product prints a list of all mortgages. For each mortgage, the following attributes are printed:
                Account number
                Name of mortgagee
                Original price of home
                Date mortgage was issued
                Principal and interest payment
                Current combined gross weekly income
                Date current combined gross weekly income was last updated
                Annual real-estate tax
                Date annual real-estate tax was last updated
                Annual homeowner's insurance premium
                Date annual homeowner's insurance premium was last updated

Figure 11.52
A class diagram
showing the
classes that
realize the
`Produce a`
`Report` use
case of the MSG
Foundation case
study.

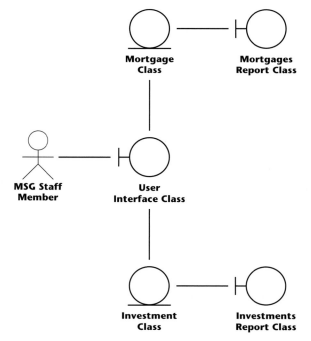

First consider the scenario of Figure 11.16 for listing all mortgages, reproduced here as Figure 11.53. A communication diagram of the realization of this scenario is shown in Figure 11.54. This realization models the listing of all mortgages.

Figure 11.53   A scenario of the `Produce a Report` use case.

An MSG staff member wishes to print a list of all mortgages.

1.   The staff member requests a report listing all the mortgages.

Figure 11.54   A communication diagram of the realization of the scenario of Figure 11.53 of the `Produce a Report` use case of the MSG Foundation case study.

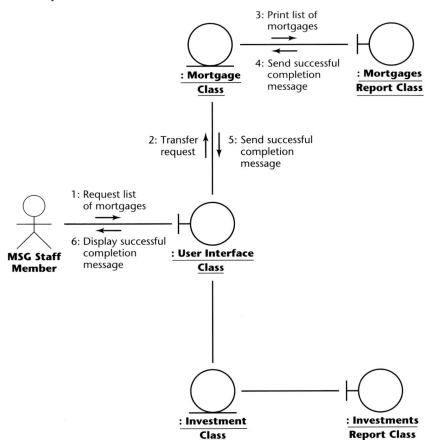

Figure 11.55 A sequence diagram of the realization of the scenario of Figure 11.53 of the `Produce a Report` use case of the MSG Foundation case study.

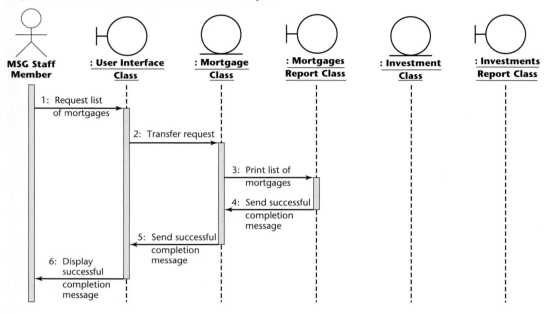

Figure 11.56 Another scenario of the `Produce a Report` use case.

An MSG staff member wishes to print a list of all investments.

1. The staff member requests a report listing all the investments.

Accordingly, object **: Investment Class**, an instance of the other subclass of **Asset Class**, plays no role in this realization, and neither does **: Investments Report Class**. The flow of events is left as an exercise (Problem 11.14). The equivalent sequence diagram is shown in Figure 11.55.

Now consider the scenario of Figure 11.17 for listing all investments, reproduced here as Figure 11.56. A communication diagram of the realization of this scenario is shown in Figure 11.57. As opposed to the previous realization, Figure 11.57 models the listing of the investments; mortgages are ignored here. The equivalent sequence diagram is shown in Figure 11.58.

This concludes the realization of the four use cases of Figure 11.20, the eighth iteration of the use-case diagram of the MSG Foundation case study.

Figure 11.57
A communication diagram of the realization of the scenario of Figure 11.56 of the Produce a Report use case of the MSG Foundation case study.

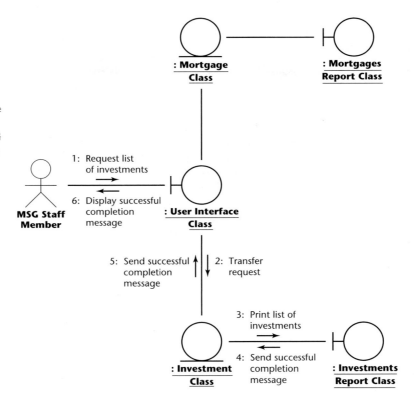

Figure 11.58   A sequence diagram of the realization of the scenario of Figure 11.56 of the Produce a Report use case of the MSG Foundation case study.

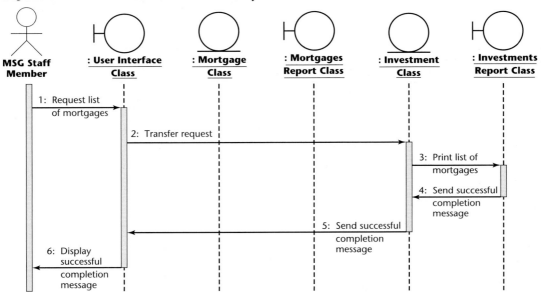

Case Study

11.19 Incrementing the Class Diagram: The MSG Foundation Case Study

The entity classes were extracted in Sections 11.12 through 11.15, yielding Figure 11.26, which shows four entity classes. The boundary classes were extracted in Section 11.16 and the control classes in Sections 11.14 and 11.18.2. In the course of realizing the various use cases in Section 11.18, interrelationships between many of the classes became apparent; these interrelationships are reflected in the class diagrams of Figures 11.31, 11.38, 11.47, and 11.52. Figure 11.59 combines these class diagrams.

Figure 11.59
Class diagram combining the class diagrams of 11.31, 11.38, 11.47, and 11.52.

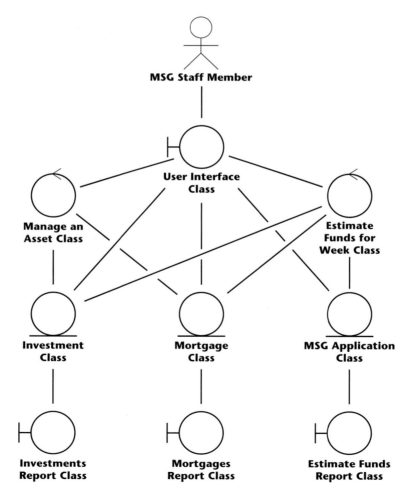

Figure 11.60   The fourth iteration of the class diagram of the MSG Foundation case study, obtained by combining the class diagrams of Figures 11.26 and 11.59.

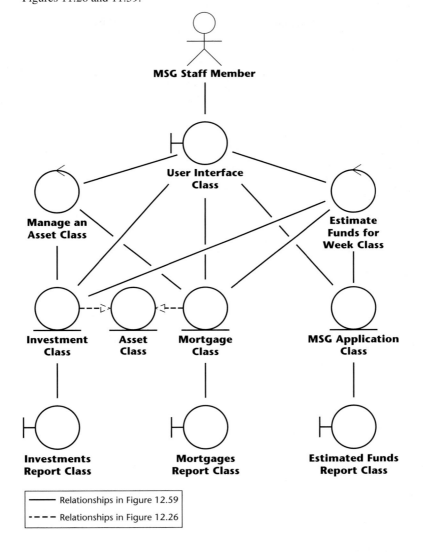

Now the class diagrams of Figures 11.26 and 11.59 are combined to yield the fourth iteration of the class diagram of the MSG Foundation case study, shown in Figure 11.60. More specifically, starting with Figure 11.59, **Asset Class** of Figure 11.26 is added. Then the two inheritance (generalization) relationships in Figure 11.26 are drawn in; they are shown with dashed lines to distinguish them. The result, Figure 11.60, the fourth iteration of the class diagram, is the class diagram at the end of the analysis workflow.

ase Study

11.20 The Software Project Management Plan: The MSG Foundation Case Study

The last step of the analysis workflow of the MSG Foundation case study is to draw up the software project management plan (this is done during the elaboration phase; see Section 3.10.2). Appendix E contains a software project management plan for the development of the MSG Foundation product by a small (three-person) software organization. This plan fits the IEEE SPMP format (Section 9.6).

ase Study

11.21 The Test Workflow: The MSG Foundation Case Study

The analysis workflow of the MSG Foundation case study is checked in two ways. First the entity classes are checked using CRC cards, as described in Section 11.10. Then all the artifacts of the analysis workflow are inspected (Section 6.2.3).

This concludes the analysis workflow of the MSG Foundation case study.

11.22 The Specification Document in the Unified Process

A primary goal of the analysis workflow is to produce the specification document, but at the end of Section 11.21 it was claimed that the analysis workflow is now complete. The obvious question is, Where is the specification document?

The short answer is, The Unified Process is use-case driven. In more detail, the use cases and the artifacts derived from them contain all the information that, in the traditional paradigm, appears in the specification document in text form, and more.

For example, consider the use case `Estimate Funds Available for Week`. When the requirements workflow is performed, the `Estimate Funds Available for Week` use case (Figure 10.27) and its description (Figure 10.40) are shown to the client, the trustees of the MSG Foundation. The developers must be meticulous in ensuring that the trustees fully understand these two artifacts and agree that these artifacts accurately model the software product the Foundation needs. Then, during the analysis workflow, the trustees are shown the use case `Estimate Funds Available for Week` (Figure 11.29), its description (Figure 11.30), the class diagram showing the classes that realize the use case (Figure 11.31), a scenario of the use case (Figure 11.32), the interaction diagrams of the realization of a scenario of the use case (Figures 11.33 and 11.35), and the flow of events of these interaction diagrams (Figure 11.34).

The set of artifacts just listed all appertain to only the use case `Estimate Funds Available for Week`. As shown in Figure 11.20, there are four use cases altogether. The same set of artifacts are produced for each of the scenarios of each of the use cases. The resulting collection of artifacts, some diagrammatic and some textual, convey to the client more information more accurately than the purely textual specification document of the traditional paradigm possibly could.

The traditional specification document usually plays a contractual role. That is, once it has been signed by both the developers and the client, it essentially constitutes a legal document. If the developers build a software product that satisfies the specification document, the client is obligated to pay for the software product, and conversely, if the product does not conform to its specification document, the developers are required to fix it if they want to get paid. In the case of the Unified Process, the collection of artifacts of all the scenarios of all the use cases similarly constitutes a contract. Therefore, as claimed at the end of Section 11.21 the analysis workflow of the MSG Foundation case study is indeed complete.

As stated before, the Unified Process is use-case driven. When using the Unified Process, instead of constructing a rapid prototype, the use cases, or more precisely, interaction diagrams reflecting the classes that realize the scenarios of the use cases, are shown to the client. The client can understand how the target software product will behave just as well from the interaction diagrams and their written flow of events as from a rapid prototype. After all, a scenario is a particular execution sequence of the proposed software product, as is each execution of a rapid prototype. The difference is that a rapid prototype is generally discarded, whereas the use cases are successively refined, with more information added each time.

However, there is one area where a rapid prototype is superior to a scenario, the user interface (Section 10.14). This does not mean that a rapid prototype should be built just so that specimen screens and reports can be examined by the client and users. But specimen screens and reports need to be constructed, as described in Section 10.14, preferably with the aid of CASE tools such as screen generators and report generators (Section 5.5).

In Section 11.23, methods for determining actors and use cases are provided.

11.23 More on Actors and Use Cases

As stated in Section 10.4.3, a use case depicts an interaction between the software product itself and the actors (the users of that software product). Now that a number of examples of actors and use cases have been presented, it is appropriate to describe how to find actors and use cases.

To find the actors, we have to consider every *role* in which an individual can interact with the software product. For example, consider a couple who wish to obtain a mortgage from the MSG Foundation. When they apply for the mortgage, they are **Applicants**, whereas after their application has been approved and money to buy their home loaned

How to Perform the Analysis Workflow	Box 11.1

- **Iterate**

  Perform functional modeling.

  Perform entity class modeling.

  Perform dynamic modeling.

- **Until** the entity classes have been satisfactorily extracted.

- Extract the boundary classes and control classes.

- Refine the use cases.

- Perform use-case realization.

to them, they become **Borrowers**. In other words, actors are not so much individuals as roles played by those individuals. In our example, the actors are not the couple, but rather first the couple playing the role of **Applicants** and then the couple playing the role of **Borrowers**. This means that merely listing all the individuals who will use the software product is not a satisfactory way of finding the actors. Instead, we need to find all the roles played by each user (or group of users). From the list of roles we can extract the actors.

In the terminology of the Unified Process, the term ***worker*** is used to denote a particular role played by an individual. This is a somewhat unfortunate term, because the word *worker* usually refers to an employee. In the terminology of the Unified Process, in the case of a couple with a mortgage, **Applicants** and **Borrowers** are two different workers. In this book, in the interests of clarity the word *role* is used in place of *worker*.

Within a business context, the task of finding the roles is generally straightforward. The use-case business model usually displays all the roles played by the individuals who interact with the business, thereby highlighting the business actors. We then find the subset of the use-case business model that corresponds to the use-case model of the requirements. In more detail,

1. Construct the use-case business model by finding all the roles played by the individuals who interact with the business.
2. Find the subset of the use-case diagram of the business model that models the software product we wish to develop. That is, consider only those parts of the business model that correspond to the proposed software product.
3. The actors in this subset are the actors we seek.

Once the actors have been determined, finding the use cases is generally straightforward. For each role, there are one or more use cases. So, the starting point in finding the use cases of the requirements is finding the actors, as described in this section.

How to Perform Box 11.1 summarizes the analysis workflow.

11.24 CASE Tools for the Analysis Workflow

Bearing in mind the role played by diagrams in the analysis workflow, it is not surprising that a number of CASE tools have been developed to support the analysis workflow. In its basic form, such a tool is essentially a drawing tool that makes it easy to perform each of the modeling steps. More important, it is far simpler to modify a diagram constructed with a drawing tool than to attempt to change a hand-drawn figure. Consequently, a CASE tool of this type supports the graphical aspects of the analysis workflow. In addition, some tools of this type not only draw all the relevant diagrams but CRC cards as well. A strength of these tools is that a change to the underlying model is reflected automatically in all the affected diagrams; after all, the various diagrams are merely different views of the underlying model.

On the other hand, some CASE tools support not just the analysis workflow but a considerable portion of the rest of the object-oriented life cycle as well. Nowadays virtually all these tools support UML [Rumbaugh, Jacobson, and Booch, 1999]. Examples of such tools include IBM Rational Rose and Together. ArgoUML is a typical open-source CASE tool of this type.

11.25 Challenges of the Analysis Workflow

A challenge of analysis is that the boundary line between analysis (what) and design (how) is all too easy to cross. The specification document should describe what the product must do; it must never say how the product is to do it. For example, suppose that the client requires a response time of no more than 0.05 seconds whenever a certain network routing computation is performed. The specification document should state exactly this—and nothing more. In particular, the specification document should *not* state which algorithm must be used to achieve this response time. That is, a specification document has to list all constraints, but it must never state how those constraints are to be achieved.

Similarly, the specification document has to describe the operations of the target process. It must never specify how those operations are to be implemented, and certainly not the class to which each is assigned. The design team's task is to study the specifications as a whole and decide on a design that will result in an optimal implementation of those specifications; this is described in Chapter 12.

The presence of classes from early in the OOA workflow means that the temptation to carry the OOA too far can be extremely strong. For example, consider the issue of allocation of methods to classes. During the analysis workflow, we determine the classes and their interactions; the result is depicted in the class diagram. Therefore, there is no apparent reason why we should wait until the design workflow before allocating methods to classes.

Nevertheless, it is important to remember that the analysis workflow is an iterative process. In the course of refining the various models, frequently large portions of the class diagram have to be reorganized. Reallocating the methods then results in unnecessary additional rework.

At each step of the OOA process it is a good idea to minimize the information that would have to be reorganized during iteration. Therefore, allocation of methods to classes should wait until the design workflow, no matter how tempting it may be to go just a little further during the analysis workflow.

**Chapter
Review**

Specifications (Section 11.1) can be expressed informally in a natural language (Section 11.2), but this can lead to problems (Section 11.3). The analysis workflow is now introduced (Section 11.4). Extracting entity classes is described in Section 11.5. The technique is then applied to the elevator problem case study (Section 11.6); functional modeling, entity class modeling, and dynamic modeling are performed in Sections 11.7, 11.8, and 11.9, respectively. Next, analysis aspects of the test workflow are covered in Section 11.10. Extraction of boundary and control classes is the subject of Section 11.11. The analysis workflow of the MSG Foundation case study is described in Section 11.12 (the initial functional model), Section 11.13 (the initial class diagram), Section 11.14 (the initial dynamic model), Section 11.15 (revision of the entity classes), Section 11.16 (extraction of the boundary classes), and Section 11.17 (extraction of the control classes). Application of the Unified Process to the MSG Foundation case study resumes in Section 11.18 (realization of the use cases), Section 11.19 (class diagram incrementation), and Section 11.20 (software project management plan). The test workflow is described in Section 11.21. The specification document for the Unified Process is discussed in Section 11.22. Additional information regarding actors and use cases appears in Section 11.23. CASE tools for the analysis workflow are described in Section 11.24. The chapter concludes with a discussion of the challenges of the analysis workflow (Section 11.25).

**For
Further
Reading**

Early books describing different versions of object-oriented analysis include [Coad and Yourdon, 1991a; Rumbaugh et al., 1991; Shlaer and Mellor, 1992; and Booch, 1994]. As mentioned in the chapter, these techniques (and others not listed here) are basically similar.

In addition to object-oriented analysis techniques of this type, Fusion [Coleman et al., 1994] is a second-generation OOA technique, a combination (or fusion) of a number of first-generation techniques, including OMT [Rumbaugh et al., 1991] and Objectory [Jacobson, Christerson, Jonsson, and Overgaard, 1992]. The Unified Software Development Process unifies the work of Jacobson, Booch, and Rumbaugh [1999]. Catalysis is another important object-oriented methodology [D'Souza and Wills, 1999].

ROOM is an object-oriented methodology for real-time software [Selic, Gullekson, and Ward, 1995]. Further information on real-time object-oriented technologies can be found in [Awad, Kuusela, and Ziegler, 1996].

Full details regarding UML can be found in [Booch, Rumbaugh, and Jacobson, 1999] and [Rumbaugh, Jacobson, and Booch, 1999]. The October 1999 issue of *Communications of the ACM* contains a broad variety of papers on the use of UML. UML is now under the control of the Object Management Group; the latest version of UML will be found at the OMG Web site, www.omg.org.

The noun-extraction technique used in this chapter to extract candidate classes is formalized in [Juristo, Moreno, and López, 2000]. CRC cards were first put forward in [Beck and Cunningham, 1989]. Wirfs-Brock, Wilkerson, and Wiener [1990] are a good source of information on CRC cards.

A number of comparisons of object-oriented analysis techniques have been published, including [de Champeaux and Faure, 1992; Monarchi and Puhr, 1992; and Embley, Jackson, and Woodfield, 1995]. A comparison of both object-oriented and classical analysis techniques appears in [Fichman and Kemerer, 1992].

Management of iteration in object-oriented projects is described in [Williams, 1996]. Statecharts are described in [Harel and Gery, 1997]. The reuse of specifications in the object-oriented paradigm is described in [Bellinzona, Fugini, and Pernici, 1995].

A variety of papers on formal techniques for object-oriented software appear in the July 2000 issue of *IEEE Transactions on Software Engineering*.

Key Terms

abstract noun 341
actor 338
analysis workflow 335
attribute 341
backtrack 355
boundary class 335
class diagram 342
class–responsibility–
    collaboration cards
    (CRC) 343
communication diagram 362
control class 336
dynamic modeling 337
entity class 335
entity class modeling 337
event 344

exception scenario 339
flow of events 367
functional modeling 337
informal specification 333
interaction diagram 362
legacy system 336
millennium bug 336
natural language 333
normal scenario 339
noun-extraction method 341
object-oriented analysis
    (00A) 335
operations 351
predicate 344
realize (in the Unified
    Theory context) 362

role 383
scenario 337
sequence diagram 362
solution strategy 332
specification document 332
state 344
state variable 344
statechart 344
stereotype 336
test workflow 347
transition 357
use case 338
use-case realization 362
worker 384
Y2K problem 336

**Case Study
Key Terms**

button 338
elevator 338
elevator button 338

elevator controller 342
elevator door 338
floor button 338

illumination 338
timeout 338

Problems

11.1   Why should the following constraints not appear in a specification document:

(i)   The product must reduce significantly transportation expenses that arise from distributing our beer in central Queensland.

(ii)   The credit card database must be set up at a reasonable cost.

11.2   Consider the following recipe for grilled pockwester.

Ingredients: 1 large onion

1 can of frozen orange juice

Freshly squeezed juice of 1 lemon

1 cup bread crumbs

Flour

Milk

3 medium-sized shallots

2 medium-sized eggplants

1 fresh pockwester

1/2 cup Pouilly Fuissé

1 garlic

Parmesan cheese

4 free-range eggs

The night before, take one lemon, squeeze it, strain the juice, and freeze it. Take one large onion and three shallots, dice them, and grill them in a skillet. When clouds of black smoke start to come off, add 2 cups of fresh orange juice. Stir vigorously. Slice the lemon into paper-thin slices and add to the mixture. In the meantime, coat the mushrooms in flour, dip them in milk, and then shake them in a paper bag with the bread crumbs. In a saucepan, heat 1/2 cup of Pouilly Fuissé. When it reaches 170°, add the sugar and continue to heat. When the sugar has caramelized, add the mushrooms. Blend the mixture for 10 minutes or until all lumps have been removed. Add the eggs. Now take the pockwester, and kill it by sprinkling it with frobs. Skin the pockwester, break it into bite-sized chunks, and add it to the mixture. Bring to a boil and simmer, uncovered. The eggs previously should have been vigorously stirred with a wire whisk for 5 minutes. When the pockwester is soft to the touch, place it on a serving platter, sprinkle with Parmesan cheese, and broil for not more than 4 minutes.

Determine the ambiguities, omissions, and contradictions in the preceding specification. (For the record, a pockwester is an imaginary sort of fish and *frobs* is slang for generic hors d'oeuvres.)

11.3 Correct the specification paragraph of Section 11.2 to reflect the client's wishes more accurately.

11.4 Use mathematical formulas to represent the specification paragraph of Section 11.2. Compare your answer with your answer to Problem 11.3.

11.5 Write a precise English specification for the product to determine whether a bank statement is correct (Problem 8.8).

11.6 Complete the elevator problem case study by developing statecharts for the other classes shown in Figure 11.10.

11.7 What is the latest point in the analysis workflow in which classes can be introduced without adversely affecting the project?

11.8 What is the earliest point in the Unified Process in which classes can meaningfully be introduced?

11.9 Is it possible to represent the dynamic model using a formalism other than the statechart described in this chapter? Explain your answer.

11.10 Why are the attributes of the classes but not the methods determined during the analysis workflow?

11.11 A noun-extraction process is described in Section 11.8.1. Why do we not also extract the verbs? And what about the other six parts of speech (adjectives, adverbs, conjunctions, interjections, prepositions, and pronouns)?

11.12 Give an extended scenario of the use case **Manage an Investment** of Figures 10.30 and 10.31.

11.13 Give an extended scenario of the use case **Update Estimated Annual Operating Expenses** of Figures 10.17 and 10.18.

11.14 Give the flow of events of the interaction diagrams of Figures 11.40 and 11.41.

11.15 Give the flow of events of the interaction diagrams of Figures 11.43 and 11.44.

11.16 Check that your answer to Problem 11.13 is a possible scenario for the interaction diagrams of Figures 11.48 and 11.49. If not, modify your scenario.

11.17   Give the flow of events of the interaction diagrams of Figures 11.48 and 11.49.

11.18   Give the flow of events of the interaction diagrams of Figures 11.54 and 11.55.

11.19   (Analysis and Design Project) Perform the analysis workflow of the library software product of Problem 8.7.

11.20   (Analysis and Design Project) Perform the analysis workflow of the product for determining whether a bank statement is correct of Problem 8.8.

11.21   (Analysis and Design Project) Perform the analysis workflow of the automated teller machine of Problem 8.9. There is no need to consider the details of the constituent hardware components such as the card reader, printer, and cash dispenser. Instead, simply assume that, when the ATM sends commands to those components, they are correctly executed.

11.22   (Term Project) Perform the analysis workflow of the Osric's Office Appliances and Decor product described in Appendix A.

11.23   (Term Project) Draw up a software project management plan for developing the Osric's Office Appliances and Decor product described in Appendix A.

11.24   (Case Study) Add **Report Class** to the analysis workflow of the MSG Foundation case study (Sections 11.12 through 11.19). Is this an improvement or an unnecessary complication?

11.25   (Case Study) Determine what happens when the analysis workflow starts with dynamic modeling. Start with the statechart of Figure 11.22, and complete the analysis workflow process for the MSG Foundation case study.

11.26   (Case Study) The software project management plan of Section 11.20 is for a small software engineering organization consisting of three software engineers. Modify the plan so that it is appropriate for a medium-sized organization with over 1000 software engineers.

11.27   (Case Study) In what way would the software project management plan of Section 11.20 have to be modified if the MSG Foundation product had to be completed in only 8 weeks?

11.28   (Readings in Software Engineering) Your instructor will distribute copies of [Juristo, Moreno, and López, 2000]. What is your opinion of their approach to object-oriented analysis?

References   [Awad, Kuusela, and Ziegler, 1996] M. AWAD, J. KUUSELA, AND J. ZIEGLER, *Object-Oriented Technology for Real-Time Systems: A Practical Approach Using OMT and Fusion,* Prentice Hall, Upper Saddle River, NJ, 1996.

[Banks, Carson, Nelson, and Nichol, 2001] J. BANKS, J. S. CARSON, B. L. NELSON, AND D. M. NICHOL, *Discrete-Event System Simulation,* 3rd ed., Prentice Hall, Upper Saddle River, NJ, 2001.

[Beck and Cunningham, 1989] K. BECK AND W. CUNNINGHAM, "A Laboratory for Teaching Object-Oriented Thinking," Proceedings of OOPSLA '89, *ACM SIGPLAN Notices* **24** (October 1989), pp. 1–6.

[Bellinzona, Fugini, and Pernici, 1995] R. BELLINZONA, M. G. FUGINI, AND B. PERNICI, "Reusing Specifications in OO Applications," *IEEE Software* **12** (March 1995), pp. 656–75.

[Booch, 1994] G. BOOCH, *Object-Oriented Analysis and Design with Applications,* 2nd ed., Benjamin/Cummings, Redwood City, CA, 1994.

[Booch, Rumbaugh, and Jacobson, 1999] G. BOOCH, J. RUMBAUGH, AND I. JACOBSON, *The UML Users Guide*, Addison-Wesley, Reading, MA, 1999.

[Coad and Yourdon, 1991a] P. COAD AND E. YOURDON, *Object-Oriented Analysis,* 2nd ed., Yourdon Press, Englewood Cliffs, NJ, 1991.

[Coleman et al., 1994] D. COLEMAN, P. ARNOLD, S. BODOFF, C. DOLLIN, H. GILCHRIST, F. HAYES, AND P. JEREMAES, *Object-Oriented Development: The Fusion Method*, Prentice Hall, Englewood Cliffs, NJ, 1994.

[D'Souza and Wills, 1999] D. D'SOUZA AND H. WILLS, *Objects, Components, and Frameworks with UML: The Catalysis Approach*, Addison-Wesley, Reading, MA, 1999.

[de Champeaux and Faure, 1992] D. DE CHAMPEAUX AND P. FAURE, "A Comparative Study of Object-Oriented Analysis Methods," *Journal of Object-Oriented Programming* **5** (March/April 1992), pp. 21–33.

[Embley, Jackson, and Woodfield, 1995] D. W. EMBLEY, R. B. JACKSON, AND S. N. WOODFIELD, "OO Systems Analysis: Is It or Isn't It?" *IEEE Software* **12** (July 1995), pp. 18–33.

[Fichman and Kemerer, 1992] R. G. FICHMAN AND C. F. KEMERER, "Object-Oriented and Conventional Analysis and Design Methodologies: Comparison and Critique," *IEEE Computer* **25** (October 1992), pp. 22–39.

[Goodenough and Gerhart, 1975] J. B. GOODENOUGH AND S. L. GERHART, "Toward a Theory of Test Data Selection," *Proceedings of the Third International Conference on Reliable Software*, Los Angeles, 1975, pp. 493–510; also published in: *IEEE Transactions on Software Engineering* **SE-1** (June 1975), pp. 156–73. Revised version: J. B. Goodenough, and S. L. Gerhart, "Toward a Theory of Test Data Selection: Data Selection Criteria," in: *Current Trends in Programming Methodology,* Vol. 2, R. T. Yeh (Editor), Prentice Hall, Englewood Cliffs, NJ, 1977, pp. 44–79.

[Harel and Gery, 1997] D. HAREL AND E. GERY, "Executable Object Modeling with Statecharts," *IEEE Computer* **30** (July 1997), pp. 31–42.

[IWSSD, 1986] Call for Papers, Fourth International Workshop on Software Specification and Design, *ACM SIGSOFT Software Engineering Notes* **11** (April 1986), pp. 94–96.

[Jacobson, Booch, and Rumbaugh, 1999] G. BOOCH, I. JACOBSON, AND J. RUMBAUGH, *The Unified Software Development Process*, Addison-Wesley, Reading, MA, 1999.

[Jacobson, Christerson, Jonsson, and Overgaard, 1992] I. JACOBSON, M. CHRISTERSON, P. JONSSON, AND G. OVERGAARD, *Object-Oriented Software Engineering: A Use Case Driven Approach*, ACM Press, New York, 1992.

[Juristo, Moreno, and López, 2000] N. JURISTO, A. M. MORENO, AND M. LÓPEZ, "How to Use Linguistic Instruments for Object-Oriented Analysis," *IEEE Software* **17** (May/June 2000), pp. 80–89.

[Kleinrock and Gail, 1996] L. KLEINROCK AND R. GAIL, *Queuing Systems: Problems and Solutions*, John Wiley and Sons, New York, 1996.

[Knuth, 1968] D. E. KNUTH, *The Art of Computer Programming,* Vol. I, *Fundamental Algorithms*, Addison-Wesley, Reading, MA, 1968.

[Leavenworth, 1970] B. LEAVENWORTH, Review #19420, *Computing Reviews* **11** (July 1970), pp. 396–97.

[London, 1971] R. L. LONDON, "Software Reliability through Proving Programs Correct," *Proceedings of the IEEE International Symposium on Fault-Tolerant Computing,* Pasadena, CA, March 1971.

[Meyer, 1985] B. MEYER, "On Formalism in Specifications," *IEEE Software* **2** (January 1985), pp. 6–26.

[Monarchi and Puhr, 1992] D. E. MONARCHI AND G. I. PUHR, "A Research Typology for Object-Oriented Analysis and Design," *Communications of the ACM* **35** (September 1992), pp. 35–47.

[Naur, 1969] P. NAUR, "Programming by Action Clusters," *BIT* **9** (No. 3, 1969), pp. 250–58.

[Rumbaugh et al., 1991] J. RUMBAUGH, M. BLAHA, W. PREMERLANI, F. EDDY, AND W. LORENSEN, *Object-Oriented Modeling and Design*, Prentice Hall, Englewood Cliffs, NJ, 1991.

[Rumbaugh, Jacobson, and Booch, 1999] J. RUMBAUGH, I. JACOBSON, AND G. BOOCH, *The Unified Modeling Language Reference Manual,* Addison-Wesley, Reading, MA, 1999.

[Selic, Gullekson, and Ward, 1995] B. SELIC, G. GULLEKSON, AND P. T. WARD, *Real-Time Object-Oriented Modeling*, John Wiley and Sons, New York, 1995.

[Shlaer and Mellor, 1992] S. SHLAER AND S. MELLOR, *Object Lifecycles: Modeling the World in States,* Yourdon Press, Englewood Cliffs, NJ, 1992.

[USNO, 2000] "The 21st Century and the Third Millennium—When Will They Begin?" U.S. Naval Observatory, Astronomical Applications Department, at **aa.usno.navy.mil/AA/faq/docs/millennium.html**, February 22, 2000.

[Williams, 1996] J. D. WILLIAMS, "Managing Iteration in OO Projects," *IEEE Computer* **29** (September 1996), pp. 39–43.

[Wirfs-Brock, Wilkerson, and Wiener, 1990] R. WIRFS-BROCK, B. WILKERSON, AND L. WIENER, *Designing Object-Oriented Software*, Prentice Hall, Englewood Cliffs, NJ, 1990.

Chapter 12

The Design Workflow

Learning Objectives

After studying this chapter, you should be able to

- Perform the design workflow.
- Perform object-oriented design.

The past 40 or so years, hundreds of design techniques have been put forward. Some are variations on existing techniques, others are radically different from anything previously proposed. A few design techniques have been used by tens of thousands of software engineers; many have been used by only their authors. Some design strategies, particularly those developed by academics, have a firm theoretical basis. Others, including many drawn up by academics, are more pragmatic in nature; they were put forward because their authors found that they worked well in practice. Most design techniques are manual, but automation increasingly is becoming an important aspect of design, if only to assist in the management of documentation.

Notwithstanding this plethora of design techniques, a certain underlying pattern emerges. As previously discussed, two essential aspects of a product are its operations and the data on which the operations act. Therefore, the two basic ways of designing a product are operation-oriented design and data-oriented design. In **operation-oriented design**, the emphasis is on the operations. An example is data flow analysis [Yourdon and Constantine, 1979], where the objective is to design modules with high cohesion (Section 7.2). In **data-oriented design**, the data are considered first. For example, in Michael Jackson's technique [Jackson, 1975], the structure of the data is determined first and then the procedures are designed to conform to the structure of the data.

A weakness of operation-oriented design techniques is that they concentrate on the operations; the data are of only secondary importance. Data-oriented design techniques similarly emphasize the data, to the detriment of the operations. The solution is to use object-oriented techniques, which give equal weight to operations and data. In this chapter, object-oriented design is presented in detail within the context of the design paradigm.

12.1   Object-Oriented Design

The Unified Process assumes previous knowledge of **object-oriented design (OOD)**. Accordingly, we now describe OOD and then discuss the design workflow of the Unified Process in Section 12.4.

The aim of OOD is to design the product in terms of objects, that is, instantiations of the classes and subclasses extracted during the analysis workflow. Classical languages, such as C, and older (pre-2000) versions of COBOL and Fortran do not support objects as such. This might seem to imply that OOD is accessible only to users of object-oriented languages like Smalltalk [Goldberg and Robson, 1989], C++ [Stroustrup, 2003], Ada 95 [ISO/IEC 8652, 1995], and Java [Flanagan, 2005].

That is not the case. Although OOD as such is not supported by classical languages, a large subset of OOD can be used. As explained in Section 7.7, a class is an abstract data type with inheritance and an object is an instance of a class. When using an implementation language that does not support inheritance, the solution is to utilize those aspects of OOD that can be achieved in the programming language used in the project, that is, to use **abstract data type design**. Abstract data types can be implemented in virtually any language that supports **type** statements. Even in a classical language that does not support type statements as such, and hence cannot support abstract data types, it still may be possible to implement data encapsulation. Figure 7.28 depicts a hierarchy of design concepts starting with modules and ending with objects. In those cases where full OOD is not possible, the developers should endeavor to ensure that their design uses the highest possible concept in the hierarchy of Figure 7.28 that their implementation language supports.

The two key steps of OOD are to complete the class diagram and perform the detailed design. With regard to the first step, completing the **class diagram**, the formats of the attributes need to be determined, and the methods need to be assigned to the relevant classes. The formats of the attributes can generally be deduced directly from the analysis artifacts. For example, in the United States the specifications may state that a date such as December 3, 1947, is represented as 12/03/1947 (mm/dd/yyyy format) or in Europe as 03/12/1947 (dd/mm/yyyy format). But, irrespective of which date convention is used, a total of 10 characters is needed.

The information for determining the formats is obtained during the analysis workflow, so the formats could certainly be added to the class diagram at that time. However, the object-oriented paradigm is iterative. Each iteration results in a change to what has already been completed. For practical reasons, then, information should be added to UML models as late as possible. Consider, for example, Figures 11.18, 11.19, 11.25 and 11.60, which show the first four iterations of the class diagram of the MSG Foundation case study. None of those four iterations show the attributes of the classes. If the attributes had been determined earlier, they would probably have had to be modified, as well as possibly moved from class to class, until the analysis team was satisfied with the class diagram. Instead, all that had to be modified was the classes themselves. In general, it makes little sense to add an item to a class diagram (or any other UML diagram) before it is absolutely essential to do so, because adding the item will make the next iteration unnecessarily burdensome. In particular, it makes little sense to specify formats before they are strictly needed.

The other major component of the first step of OOD is to assign methods (implementations of operations) to classes. Determination of all the operations of the product is performed by examining the interaction diagrams of every scenario. This is straightforward. The hard part is to determine how to decide which methods should be associated with each class.

A method can be assigned to either a class or to a client that sends a message to an object of that class. (A client of an object is a program unit that sends a message to that object.) One principle that can be employed to assist in deciding how to assign an operation is information hiding (Section 7.6). That is, the state variables of a class should be declared **private** (accessible only within an object of that class) or **protected** (accessible only within an object of that class or a subclass of that class). Accordingly, operations performed on state variables must be local to that class.

A second principle is that, if a particular operation is invoked by a number of different clients of an object, it makes sense to have a single copy of that operation implemented as a method of the object, rather than have a copy in each client of that object.

A third principle that can be employed to assist in deciding where to locate a method is to use responsibility-driven design. As explained in Section 1.9, *responsibility-driven design* is a key aspect of the object-oriented paradigm. If a client sends a message to an object, then that object is responsible for every aspect of carrying out the request of the client. The client does not know how the request will be carried out and is not permitted to know. Once the request has been carried out, control returns to the client. At that point, all the client knows is that the request has been carried out; it still has no idea how this was achieved.

The second step of the object-oriented design is to perform the *detailed design*, during which each class is designed in detail. For example, specific algorithms are selected and data structures are chosen. One way of representing a detailed design is shown in Figure 12.1, which shows method find of class **Mortgage** of the MSG Foundation case study.

Figure 12.1   Detailed design of method find of class **Mortgage**.

Class name	**Mortgage**
Method name	find
Return type	**boolean**
Input argument(s)	String findMortgageID
Output argument(s)	None
Error messages	If file not found, prints message ***** Error: Mortgage.find () *****
Files accessed	mortgage.dat
Files changed	None
Methods invoked	None
Narrative	Method find locates a given mortgage record if it exists. It returns true if the mortgage is located, otherwise false.

A different way of representing a detailed design is shown in Figures 12.2 and 12.3. Figure 12.2 shows the detailed design of method computeEstimatedFunds of class **EstimateFundsForWeek** of the MSG Foundation case study. This method invokes method totalWeeklyNetPayments of class **Mortgage**, shown in Figure 12.3.

Figures 12.2 and 12.3 are written in a ***program description language (PDL)*** with the flavor of Java. (***Pseudocode*** is an earlier name for PDL.) PDL essentially consists of comments connected by the control statements of the chosen implementation language. A PDL has the advantage that it generally is clear and concise, and the implementation step usually consists merely of translating the comments into the relevant programming language. The weakness is that sometimes there is a tendency for the designers to go into too much detail and produce a complete code implementation of a class rather than a PDL detailed design.

Figure 12.2
The detailed design of method compute-Estimated-Funds of class **Estimate-FundsFor-Week** of the MSG Foundation case study.

```
public static void computeEstimatedFunds( )
```
This method computes the estimated funds available for the week.
```
{
    float expectedWeeklyInvestmentReturn;              (expected weekly investment return)
    float expectedTotalWeeklyNetPayments = (float) 0.0;

                                                       (expected total mortgage payments
                                                        less total weekly grants)
    float estimatedFunds = (float) 0.0;                (total estimated funds for week)
```
Create an instance of an investment record.
```
    Investment inv = new Investment ( );
```
Create an instance of a mortgage record.
```
    Mortgage mort = new Mortgage ( );
```
Invoke method totalWeeklyReturnOnInvestment.
```
    expectedWeeklyInvestmentReturn = inv.totalWeeklyReturnOnInvestment ( );
```
Invoke method expectedTotalWeeklyNetPayments   *(see Figure 12.3)*
```
    expectedTotalWeeklyNetPayments = mort.totalWeeklyNetPayments ( );
```
Now compute the estimated funds for the week.
```
    estimatedFunds = (expectedWeeklyInvestmentReturn

        – (MSGApplication.getAnnualOperatingExpenses ( ) / (float) 52.0)

        + expectedTotalWeeklyNetPayments);
```
Store this value in the appropriate location.
```
    MSGApplication.setEstimatedFundsForWeek (estimatedFunds);
} // computeEstimatedFunds
```

Figure 12.3
The detailed design of method totalWeekly-NetPayments of class **Mortgage** of the MSG Foundation case study.

public float totalWeeklyNetPayments ( )

This method computes the net total weekly payments made by the mortgagees, that is, the expected total weekly mortgage amount less the expected total weekly grants.

{

```
File mortgageFile = new File ("mortgage.dat");          (file of mortgage records)

float expectedTotalWeeklyMortgages = (float) 0.0;       (expected total weekly mortgage payments)

float expectedTotalWeeklyGrants = (float) 0.0;          (expected total weekly grants)

float capitalRepayment;                                 (capital repayment)

float interestPayment;                                  (interest payment)

float escrowPayment;                                    (escrow payment)

float tempMortgage;                                     (temporary value)

float maximumPermittedMortgagePayment;                  (maximum amount the couple may pay)
```

Open the file of mortgages, name it inFile, *and read each element in turn.*

```
    {
        read (inFile);
```

Compute the capital repayment, interest payment, and escrow payment for this mortgage.

```
        capitalRepayment = price / NUMBER_OF_MORTGAGE_PAYMENTS;
        interestPayment = mortgageBalance * INTEREST_RATE / WEEKS_IN_YEAR ;
        escrowPayment = (annualPropertyTax + annualInsurancePremium) / WEEKS_IN_YEAR;
```

First assume that the couple can pay the mortgage in full, without a grant.

```
        tempMortgage = capitalRepayment + interestPayment + escrowPayment;
```

Add this amount to the running total of mortgage payments.

```
        expectedTotalWeeklyMortgages += tempMortgage;
```

Now determine how much the couple can actually pay.

```
        maximumPermittedMortgagePayment = currentWeeklyIncome *
                MAXIMUM_PERC_OF_INCOME;
```

If a grant is needed, add the grant amount to the running total of grants.

```
        if (tempMortgage > maximumPermittedMortgagePayment)
            expectedTotalWeeklyGrants += tempMortgage − maximumPermittedMortgagePayment;
    }
```

Close the file of mortgages. Return the total expected net payments for the week.

```
    return (expectedTotalWeeklyMortgages − expectedTotalWeeklyGrants);
} // totalWeeklyNetPayments
```

To see how these principles are utilized, we now illustrate OOD by means of two examples. As before, the elevator problem case study is presented, with just one elevator for simplicity. Then, we return to the MSG Foundation case study.

Case Study

12.2 Object-Oriented Design: The Elevator Problem Case Study

Step 1. Complete the Class Diagram

A design workflow class diagram (Figure 12.4) is obtained by adding the operations (methods) to the class diagram of Figure 11.10. (In the case of a Java implementation,

Figure 12.4   The detailed class diagram for the elevator problem case study.

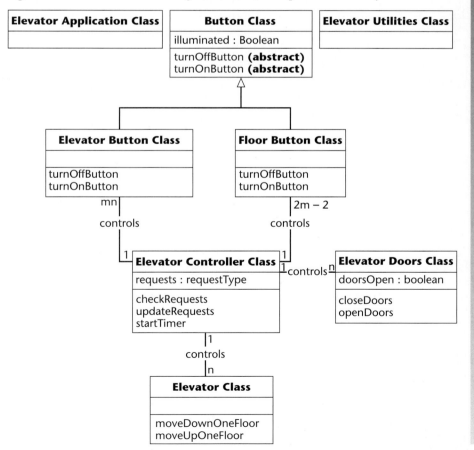

two additional classes are needed. **Elevator Application Class** corresponds to the C++ main function, and **Elevator Utilities Class** contains the Java routines that correspond to the C++ functions declared external to the C++ classes.)

Consider the second iteration of the CRC card for the elevator controller (Figure 11.9). The responsibilities fall into two groups. Three responsibilities—8. Start timer, 10. Check requests, and 11. Update requests—are assigned to the elevator controller on the basis of responsibility-driven design; those tasks are carried out by the elevator controller itself.

On the other hand, the remaining eight responsibilities (events 1 through 7 and event 9) have the form "Send a message to another class to tell it to do something." This implies the principle that should be used in assigning the relevant method to classes again should be responsibility-driven design. In addition, because of safety concerns, the principle of information hiding is equally applicable in all eight cases.

For these two reasons, methods closeDoors and openDoors are assigned to **Elevator Doors Class**. That is, a client of **Elevator Doors Class** (in this case, an object of **Elevator Controller Class**) sends a message to an object of **Elevator Doors Class** to close or open the doors of the elevator, and that request is then carried out by the relevant method. Every aspect of those two methods is encapsulated within **Elevator Doors Class**. In addition, information hiding results in a truly independent **Elevator Doors Class**, instances of which can undergo detailed design and implementation independently and be reused later in other products.

The same two design principles are applied to methods moveDownOneFloor and moveUpOneFloor, and they are assigned to **Elevator Class**. There is no need for an explicit instruction to cause an elevator to stop. If neither of its two methods is invoked, an elevator cannot move; there is no way to change the state of an elevator other than by invoking one of its two methods.

Finally, methods turnOffButton and turnOnButton are assigned to both **Elevator Button Class** and **Floor Button Class**. The reasoning here is the same as for the methods assigned to **Elevator Doors Class** and **Elevator Class**. First, the principle of responsibility-driven design requires that the buttons have full control over whether they are on or off. Second, the principle of information hiding requires the internal state of a button to be hidden. The methods that turn an elevator button on or off therefore must be local to **Elevator Button Class**, and similarly for **Floor Button Class**. To make use of polymorphism and dynamic binding, methods turnOffButton and turnOnButton are declared **abstract** (**virtual**) in the base class **Button Class** for the reasons stated in Section 7.8. At run time, the correct version of method turnOffButton or turnOnButton will then be invoked.

Step 2. Perform the Detailed Design

A detailed design now is developed for all the classes. Any suitable technique may be used, such as the stepwise refinement described in Chapter 5. The detailed design of method elevatorEventLoop is shown in Figure 12.5. The design is presented in a PDL based on C++.

Figure 12.5 is constructed from the statechart of Figure 11.7. For example, the event button pushed, button unlit is implemented by the two nested **if** statements at the beginning of Figure 12.5. The two operations of the state **Process Requests** then follow. The **else-if** condition corresponds to the next event leading from state **Elevator Event Loop**, elevator moving in direction d, floor f is next. The remainder of the detailed design is equally straightforward.

Now we consider the object-oriented design of the MSG Foundation case study.

Figure 12.5   The detailed design of method elevatorEventLoop.

```
void elevatorEventLoop (void)
{
  while (TRUE)
  {
    if (a button has been pressed)
      if (button is not on)
      {
        updateRequests;
        button::turnOnButton;
      }
    else if (elevator is moving up)
    {
      if (there is no request to stop at floor f)
        elevator::moveUpOneFloor;
      else
      {
        stop elevator by not sending a message to move;
        elevatorDoors::openDoors;
        startTimer;
        if (elevatorButton is on)
          elevatorButton::turnOffButton;
        updateRequests;
      }
    }
    else if (elevator is moving down)
      [similar to up case]
    else if (elevator is stopped and request is pending)
    {
      elevatorDoors::closeDoors;
      determine direction of next request;
      if (appropriate floorButton is on)
        floorButton::turnOffButton;
      elevator::moveUp/DownOneFloor;
    }
    else if (elevator is at rest and not (request is pending))
      elevatorDoors::closeDoors;
    else
      there are no requests, elevator is stopped with elevatorDoors closed, so do nothing;
  }
}
```

ase Study

Object-Oriented Design:
The MSG Foundation Case Study

As described in Section 12.1, object-oriented design consists of two steps.

Step 1. Complete the Class Diagram
The final class diagram for the MSG Foundation case study is shown in Figure 12.6.
The user-defined **Date Class** is drawn dashed to denote that it is needed for only

Figure 12.6
The overall
class diagram
for the MSG
Foundation
case study.

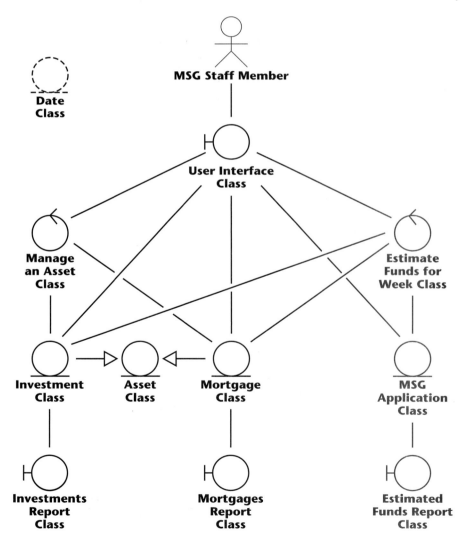

a C++ implementation; Java has built-in classes for handling dates, including **java. text.Dateformat** and **java.util.Calendar**.

The formats for the attributes of the classes were deduced from discussions with the client and users during the analysis workflow; examination of forms (Section 10.4.2) can also be extremely useful in this regard. A portion of the result is shown in Figure 12.7.

The methods of the product are found in the various interaction diagrams. The task of the designer is to decide to which class each method should be assigned. For example, the convention in an object-oriented software product is that associated with each attribute of a class are ***mutator*** method setAttribute, used to assign a specific value to that attribute, and ***accessor*** method getAttribute, which returns the current value of that attribute.

For example, consider method setAssetNumber, used to assign a number to an asset (investment or mortgage). In the classical paradigm, we would need separate functions set_investment_number and set_mortgage_number. However, the object-oriented paradigm supports inheritance. Therefore, method setAssetNumber should be assigned to **Asset Class**. Then, as reflected in Figure 12.8, the method can then be applied not only to instances of **Asset Class** but also, as a consequence

Figure 12.7   Part of the overall class diagram for the MSG Foundation case study with the attribute formats added.

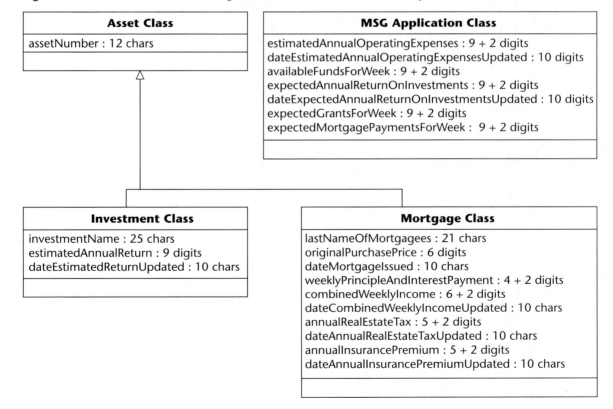

Figure 12.8 Part of the class diagram for the MSG Foundation case study with methods setAssetNumber and getAssetNumber assigned to **Asset Class**.

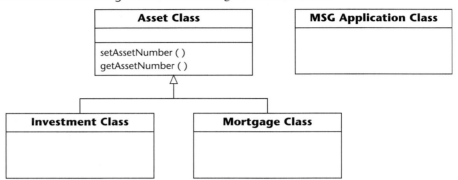

of inheritance, to instances of every subclass of **Asset Class**, that is, to instances of **Investment Class** and **Mortgage Class**. Similarly, method getAssetNumber should also be allocated to the superclass **Asset Class**.

Assigning the other methods to the appropriate classes is equally straightforward. The resulting design is shown in Appendix F.

Step 2. Perform the Detailed Design

Next, the detailed design is built by taking each method and determining what it does. The detailed designs of three methods have been presented in Section 12.1. The tabular-format detailed design of method findMortgageID of class **Mortgage** appears in Figure 12.1. Figure 12.2 shows the detailed design (in a PDL for Java) of a method computeEstimatedFunds of class **EstimateFundsForWeek** of the MSG Foundation case study. This method invokes method totalWeeklyNetPayments of class **Mortgage** shown in Figure 12.3.

The steps of object-oriented design are summarized in How to Perform Box 12.1.

12.4   The Design Workflow

The input to the **design workflow** is the analysis workflow artifacts (Chapter 11). During the design workflow, these artifacts are iterated and incremented until they are in a format that can be utilized by the programmers.

One aspect of this iteration and incrementation is the identification of methods and their allocation to the appropriate classes. Another aspect is performing the detailed design. These two steps constitute the object-oriented design component of the design workflow.

In addition to performing the object-oriented design, many decisions have to be made as part of the design workflow. One such decision is the selection of the programming

How to Perform Object-Oriented Design	**Box 12.1**
• Complete the class diagram.	
• Perform the detailed design.	

language in which the software product will be implemented. This process is described in detail in Chapter 13. Another decision is how much of existing software products to reuse in the new software product to be developed. Reuse is described in Chapter 8. Portability is another important design decision; this topic, too, is described in Chapter 8. Also, large software products are often implemented on a network of computers; yet another design decision is the allocation of each software component to the hardware component on which it is to run.

The major motivation behind the development of the Unified Process was to present a methodology that could be used to develop large-scale software products, typically, 500,000 lines of code or more. On the other hand, the implementations of the MSG Foundation case study in Appendices G and H are less than 5000 lines of C++ and Java, respectively. In other words, the Unified Process is intended primarily for software products at least 100 times larger than the MSG Foundation case study presented in this book. Accordingly, many aspects of the Unified Process are inapplicable to this case study. For instance, an important part of the analysis workflow is to partition the software product into analysis packages. Each *package* consists of a set of related classes, usually of relevance to a small subset of the actors, that can be implemented as a single unit. For example, accounts payable, accounts receivable, and general ledger are typical analysis packages. The concept underlying analysis packages is that it is much easier to develop smaller software products than larger software products. Accordingly, a large software product is easier to develop if it can be decomposed into relatively independent packages.

This idea of decomposing a large workflow into relatively independent smaller workflows is carried forward to the design workflow. Here, the objective is to break up the upcoming implementation workflow into manageable pieces, termed *subsystems*. Again, it does not make sense to break up the MSG Foundation case study into subsystems; the case study is just too small.

There are two reasons why larger workflows are broken into subsystems:

1. As previously explained, it is easier to implement a number of smaller subsystems than one large system.

2. If the subsystems to be implemented are indeed relatively independent, then they can be implemented by programming teams working in parallel. This results in the software product as a whole being delivered sooner.

Recall from Section 8.5.4 that the *architecture* of a software product includes the various components and how they fit together. The allocation of components to subsystems is a major part of the architectural task. Deciding on the architecture of a software product is by no means easy and, in all but the smallest software products, is performed by a specialist, the software *architect*.

In addition to being a technical expert, an architect needs to know how to make *trade-offs*. A software product has to satisfy the functional requirements, that is, the use cases. It also needs to satisfy the nonfunctional requirements, including portability (Chapter 8), reliability (Section 6.4.2), robustness (Section 6.4.3), maintainability, and security. But it needs to do all these things within budget and time constraints. It is almost never possible to develop a software product that satisfies all its requirements, both functional and nonfunctional, and finish the project within the cost and time constraints; compromises almost always have to be made. The client has to relax some of the requirements, increase the budget, or move the delivery deadline, or do more than one of these. The architect must assist the client's decision making by clearly mapping out the trade-offs.

In some cases the trade-offs are obvious. For example, the architect may point out that a set of security requirements that conform to a new high-security standard are going to take a further 3 months and $350,000 to incorporate in the software product. If the product is an international banking network, the issue is moot—there is no way that the client could possibly agree to compromise on security in any way. However, in other instances, the client needs to make critical determinations regarding trade-offs and has to rely on the technical expertise of the architect to assist in coming to the right business decision. For example, the architect might point out that deferring a particular requirement until the software product has been delivered and is being maintained may save $150,000 now but will cost $300,000 to incorporate later (see Figure 1.5). The decision as to whether or not to defer a requirement can be made by only the client, but he or she needs the technical expertise of the architect to assist in coming to the correct decision.

The architecture of a software product is a vital factor as to whether the delivered product is a success or a failure. And, the critical decisions regarding the architecture have to be made while performing the design workflow. If the requirements workflow is badly performed, it is still possible to have a successful project, provided additional time and money are spent on the analysis workflow. Similarly, if the analysis workflow is inadequate, it is possible to recover by making an extra effort as part of the design workflow. But, if the architecture is suboptimal, there is no way to recover; the architecture must immediately be redesigned. It is therefore essential that the development team include an architect with the necessary technical expertise and people skills.

12.5 The Test Workflow: Design

The goal of testing the design is to verify that the specifications have been accurately and completely incorporated into the design as well as to ensure the correctness of the design itself. For example, the design must have no logic faults and all interfaces must be correctly defined. It is important that any faults in the design be detected before coding commences; otherwise, the cost of fixing the faults will be considerably higher, as reflected in Figure 1.5. Design faults can be detected by means of design inspections as well as design walkthroughs. Design inspections are discussed in the remainder of this section, but the remarks apply equally to design walkthroughs.

A ***transaction*** is an operation from the viewpoint of a user of the product, such as "process a request" or "print a list of today's orders." When the product is transaction oriented, the design inspection should reflect this [Beizer, 1990]. Inspections that include all possible transaction types should be scheduled. The reviewer should relate each transaction in the design to the specifications, showing how the transaction arises from the specification document. For example, if the application is an automated teller machine, a transaction corresponds to each operation the customer can perform, such as deposit to or withdraw from a credit card account. In other instances, the correspondence between specifications and transactions is not necessarily one to one. In a traffic-light control system, for example, if an automobile driving over a sensor pad results in the system deciding to change a particular light from red to green in 15 seconds, then further impulses from that sensor pad may be ignored. Conversely, to speed traffic flow, a single impulse may cause a whole series of lights to be changed from red to green.

Restricting reviews to ***transaction-driven inspections*** does not detect cases where the designers have overlooked instances of transactions required by the specifications. To take an extreme example, the specifications for the traffic-light controller may stipulate that between 11:00 P.M. and 6:00 A.M. all lights are to flash yellow in one direction and red in the other direction. If the designers overlooked this stipulation, then clock-generated transactions at 11:00 P.M. and 6:00 A.M. would not be included in the design; and if these transactions were overlooked, they could not be tested in a design inspection based on transactions. Therefore, it is not adequate to schedule design inspections that are just transaction driven; specification-driven inspections also are essential to ensure that no statement in the specification document has been either overlooked or misinterpreted.

Case Study

12.6   The Test Workflow: The MSG Foundation Case Study

Now that the design is apparently complete, all aspects of the design of the MSG Foundation case study must be checked by means of a design inspection (Section 6.2.3). In particular, each design artifact must be examined. Even if no faults are found, it is possible that the design will change again, perhaps radically, when the MSG Foundation case study is implemented.

12.7   Formal Techniques for Detailed Design

One technique for detailed design has already been presented. In Section 5.1, a description of stepwise refinement was given. It then was applied to detailed design using flowcharts. In addition to stepwise refinement, formal techniques can be used to advantage in detailed design. Chapter 6 suggests that implementing a complete product and then proving it correct could be counterproductive. However, developing the proof and the detailed design in parallel and carefully testing the code as well is quite a different matter. Formal techniques applied to detailed design can greatly assist in three ways:

1. The state of the art in proving correctness is such that, although it generally cannot be applied to a product as a whole, it can be applied to module-sized pieces of a product.

2. Developing a proof together with the detailed design should lead to a design with fewer faults than if correctness proofs were not used.

3. If the same programmer is responsible for both the detailed design and the implementation, then that programmer will feel confident that the detailed design is correct. This positive attitude toward the design should lead to fewer faults in the code.

12.8   Real-Time Design Techniques

As explained in Section 6.4.4, ***real-time software*** is characterized by hard time constraints, that is, time constraints of such a nature that, if a constraint is not met, information is lost. In particular, each input must be processed before the next input arrives. An example of such a system is a computer-controlled nuclear reactor. Inputs such as the temperature of the core and the level of the water in the reactor chamber continually are being sent to the computer that reads the value of each input and performs the necessary processing before the next input arrives. Another example is a computer-controlled intensive care unit. There are two types of patient data: routine information such as heart rate, temperature, and blood pressure of each patient, and emergency information, when the system deduces that the condition of a patient has become critical. When such emergencies occur, the software must process both the routine inputs and the emergency-related inputs from one or more patients.

A characteristic of many real-time systems is that they are implemented on distributed hardware. For example, software controlling a fighter aircraft may be implemented on five computers: one to handle navigation, another the weapons system, a third for electronic countermeasures, a fourth to control the flight hardware such as wing flaps and engines, and the fifth to propose tactics in combat. Because hardware is not totally reliable, there may be additional backup computers that automatically replace a malfunctioning unit. Not only does the design of such a system have major communications implications, but timing issues, over and above those of the type just described, arise as a consequence of the distributed nature of the system. For example, under combat conditions, the tactical computer might suggest that the pilot should climb, whereas the weapons computer recommends that the pilot go into a dive so that a particular weapon may be launched under optimal conditions. However, the human pilot decides to move the stick to the right, thereby sending a signal to the flight hardware computer to make the necessary adjustments so that the plane banks in the indicated direction. All this information must be managed carefully in such a way that the actual motion of the plane takes precedence in every way over suggested maneuvers. Furthermore, the actual motion must be relayed to the tactical and weapons computers so that new suggestions can be formulated in the light of actual, rather than suggested, conditions.

A further difficulty with real-time systems is the problem of synchronization. Suppose that a real-time system is to be implemented on distributed hardware. Situations such as deadlock (or deadly embrace) can arise when two operations each have exclusive use of a data item and each requests exclusive use of the other's data item in addition. Of course, deadlock does not occur only in real-time systems, implemented on distributed hardware. But it is particularly troublesome in real-time systems where there is no control over the order or timing of the inputs, and the situation can be complicated by the distributed nature of the hardware. In addition to deadlock, other synchronization problems are possible, including race conditions; for details, the reader may refer to [Silberschatz, Galvin, and Gagne, 2002] or other operating systems textbooks.

From these examples it is clear that the major difficulty with regard to the design of real-time systems is ensuring that the timing constraints are met by the design. That is, the design technique should provide a mechanism for checking that, when implemented, the design is able to read and process incoming data at the required rate. Furthermore, it should be possible to show that synchronization issues in the design also have been addressed correctly.

Since the beginning of the computer age, advances in hardware technology have outstripped, in almost every respect, advances in software technology. Therefore, although the hardware exists to handle every aspect of the real-time systems described previously, software design technology has lagged behind considerably. In some areas of real-time software engineering, major progress has been made. For instance, the analysis technique of Chapter 11 has been extended to specify real-time systems. Unfortunately, software design has not yet reached the same level of sophistication. Great strides indeed are being made, but the state of the art is not yet comparable to what has been achieved with regard to analysis. Because almost any design technique for real-time systems is preferable to no technique at all, a number of real-time design techniques are used in practice. But, there still is a long way to go before it will be possible to design real-time systems such as those described previously and be certain that, before the system has been implemented, every real-time constraint will be met and synchronization problems cannot arise.

Older real-time design techniques, such as structured development for real-time systems (SDRTS) [Ward and Mellor, 1985], are extensions of non-real-time techniques to the real-time domain. Newer techniques are described in [Liu, 2000] and [Gomaa, 2000].

As stated previously, it is unfortunate that the state of the art of real-time design is not as advanced as one would wish. Nevertheless, efforts are under way to improve the situation.

12.9   CASE Tools for Design

As stated in Section 12.5, a critical aspect of design is testing that the design artifacts accurately incorporate all aspects of the analysis. What therefore is needed is a CASE tool that can be used both for the analysis artifacts and the design artifacts, a so-called front-end or upperCASE tool (as opposed to a back-end or lowerCASE tool, which assists with the implementation artifacts).

A number of upperCASE tools are on the market. They generally are built around a data dictionary; typical data dictionary entries are shown in Figure 12.9. The CASE tool incorporates a consistency checker that can determine whether every item in the dictionary is mentioned somewhere in the design artifacts or whether every item in the design artifacts is reflected in the analysis artifacts. Furthermore, many upperCASE tools incorporate screen and report generators. That is, the client can specify what items are to appear in a report or on an input screen and where and how each item is to appear. Because full details regarding every item are in the data dictionary, the CASE tool easily can generate the code for printing the report or displaying the input screen according to the client's wishes. Some upperCASE products also incorporate management tools for estimating and planning.

With regard to the design workflow, Together and IBM Rational Rose are examples of CASE tools that provide support for this workflow within the context of the complete object-oriented life cycle. Open-source CASE tools of this type include ArgoUML.

Figure 12.9
Data dictionary
entries for class
Asset of
the MSG
Foundation
case study.

Name	Access Specifier	Description	Narrative
Asset	**package private** (default)	Abstract class Attribute: assetNumber Accessors/mutators: getAssetNumber setAssetNumber Virtual methods: read print write find obtainNewData performDeletion Methods: add delete	Abstract superclass of **Investment** and **Mortgage** classes. Comprises the attributes and methods that enable a user to add or delete an asset.
assetNumber	**protected**	12-digit integer	Unique number returned by method getAssetNumber. The first 10 digits contain the asset number itself, the last 2 digits are check digits.
delete	**public**	Method Return type: **void** Input parameter: None Output parameter: None	This method invokes methods obtainNewData, save, and UserInterface. pressEnter to add a new asset (investment or mortgage).

12.10 Metrics for Design

A variety of metrics can be used to describe aspects of the design. For example, the number of methods and classes is a crude measure of the size of the target product. Cohesion and coupling are measures of the quality of the design, as are fault statistics. As with all other types of inspection, it is vital to keep a record of the number and type of design faults detected during a design inspection. This information is used during code inspections of the product and in design inspections of subsequent products.

The **cyclomatic complexity** M of a detailed design is the number of binary decisions (predicates) plus 1 [McCabe, 1976] or, equivalently, the number of branches in the code artifact. It has been suggested that cyclomatic complexity is a metric of design quality; the lower the value of M, the better. A strength of this metric is that it is easy to compute. However, it has an inherent problem. Cyclomatic complexity is a measure purely of the control complexity; the data complexity is ignored. That is, M does not measure the complexity of a code artifact that is data driven, such as by the values in a table. For example, suppose a designer is unaware of the C++ library function toascii and designs a code artifact from scratch that reads a character input by the user and returns the corresponding ASCII code (an integer between 0 and 127). One way of designing this is by means of a 128-way branch implemented by means of a **switch** statement. A second way is to have an array containing the 128 characters in ASCII code order and utilize a loop to compare the character input by the user with each element of the array of characters; the loop is exited when a match is obtained. The current value of the loop variable then is the corresponding ASCII code. The two designs are equivalent in functionality but have cyclomatic complexities of 128 and 1, respectively.

An additional complication is that the cyclomatic complexity of a class usually is low, because many classes typically include a large number of small, straightforward methods. Furthermore, as previously pointed out, cyclomatic complexity ignores data complexity. Because data and operations are equal partners within the object-oriented paradigm, cyclomatic complexity overlooks a major component that could contribute to the complexity of an object. Therefore, metrics for classes that incorporate cyclomatic complexity generally are of little use.

A related class of metrics for the design workflow is based on representing the design as a directed graph with the classes represented by nodes and the flows between classes (messages sent to methods) represented by arcs. The **fan-in** of a class can be defined as the number of flows into the class plus the number of global data structures accessed by the class. The **fan-out** similarly is the number of flows out of the class plus the number of global data structures updated by the class. A measure of complexity of the class then is given by $length \times (fan\text{-}in \times fan\text{-}out)^2$ [Henry and Kafura, 1981], where **length** is a measure of the size of the class (Section 9.2.1). Because the definitions of *fan-in* and *fan-out* incorporate global data, this metric has a data-dependent component. Nevertheless, experiments have shown that this metric is no better a measure of complexity than simpler metrics, such as cyclomatic complexity [Kitchenham, Pickard, and Linkman, 1990; Shepperd, 1990].

A number of object-oriented design metrics have been put forward, for example, in [Chidamber and Kemerer, 1994]. These and other metrics have been questioned on both theoretical and experimental grounds [Binkley and Schach, 1996; 1997; 1998].

12.11 Challenges of the Design Workflow

As pointed out in Section 11.25, it is important not to do too much in the analysis workflow; that is, the analysis team must not prematurely start parts of the design workflow. In the design workflow, the design team can go wrong in two ways: by doing too much and by doing too little.

Consider the PDL (pseudocode) detailed designs of Figures 12.2, 12.3, and 12.5. The temptation is strong for a designer who enjoys programming to write the detailed design in C++ or Java, rather than PDL. That is, instead of sketching the detailed design in pseudocode, the designer may all but code the class. This takes longer to write than just outlining the class and longer to fix if a fault is detected in the design (see Figure 1.5). Like the analysis team, the members of the design team must firmly resist the urge to do more than what is required of them.

In addition, there is a much more significant challenge. In "No Silver Bullet" (see Just in Case You Wanted to Know Box 3.5), Brooks [1986] decries the lack of what he terms *great designers*, that is, designers who are significantly more outstanding than the other members of the design team. In Brooks's opinion, the success of a software project depends critically on whether the design team is led by a great designer. Good design can be taught; great design is produced only by great designers, and they are "very rare."

The challenge, then, is to grow great designers. They should be identified as early as possible (the best designers are not necessarily the most experienced), assigned a mentor, provided a formal education as well as apprenticeships to great designers, and allowed to interact with other designers. A specific career path should be available for these designers, and the rewards they receive should be commensurate with the contribution that only a great designer can make to a software development project.

Chapter Review

The design workflow is introduced in Section 12.1. Object-oriented design is applied to the elevator problem case study in Section 12.2 and to the MSG Foundation case study in Section 12.3. The design workflow is presented in Section 12.4. The design aspects of the test workflow are described in Section 12.5 and applied to the MSG Foundation case study in Section 12.6. Formal techniques for detailed design are discussed in Section 12.7. Real-time system design is described in Section 12.8. CASE tools and metrics for the design workflow are presented in Sections 12.9 and 12.10, respectively. The chapter concludes with a discussion of the challenges of the design workflow (Section 12.11).

For Further Reading

Information about object-oriented design can be obtained from [Wirfs-Brock, Wilkerson, and Wiener, 1990; Coad and Yourdon, 1991b; Shlaer and Mellor, 1992; and Jacobson, Booch, and Rumbaugh, 1999]. Comparisons of a variety of techniques for object-oriented design appear in [Monarchi and Puhr, 1992] and [Walker, 1992]. Briand, Bunse, and Daly [2001] discuss the maintainability of object-oriented designs. A comparison of both object-oriented and classical design techniques appears in [Fichman and Kemerer, 1992]. The redesign of an air traffic control system is described in [Jackson and Chapin, 2000]. Design techniques for high-performance, reliable systems are given in [Stolper, 1999].

Formal design techniques are described in [Hoare, 1987].

With regard to reviews during the design process, the original paper on design inspections is [Fagan, 1976]; detailed information can be obtained from that paper. Later advances in review techniques are described in [Fagan, 1986]. The use of walkthroughs to test user interface design is described in [Bias, 1991]. Architecture reviews are discussed in [Maranzano et al., 2005].

Turning to real-time design, specific techniques are to be found in [Liu, 2000] and [Gomaa, 2000]. A comparison of four real-time design techniques is found in [Kelly and Sherif, 1992]. A documentation-driven approach to the design of complex real-time systems is described in [Luqi, Zhang, Berzins, and Qiao, 2004]. The design of concurrent systems is described in [Magee and Kramer, 1999]. The March/April 2005 issue of *IEEE Software* contains a number of papers on design.

Metrics for design are described in [Henry and Kafura, 1981] and [Zage and Zage, 1993]. Metrics for object-oriented design are discussed in [Chidamber and Kemerer, 1994] and in [Binkley and Schach, 1996]. A model for object-oriented quality is presented in [Bansiya and Davis, 2002].

The proceedings of the International Workshops on Software Specification and Design are a comprehensive source for information on design techniques.

Key Terms

abstract data type
    design 393
accessor 401
architect 403
class diagram 393
cyclomatic complexity 409
data-oriented design 392
design workflow 402
detailed design 394
fan-in 409

fan-out 409
length 409
mutator 401
object-oriented design
    (OOD) 393
operation-oriented
    design 392
package 403
program description
    language (PDL) 395

pseudocode 395
real-time software 406
responsibility-driven
    design 394
subsystem 403
trade-off 403
transaction 404
transaction-driven
    inspections 405

Problems

12.1   Represent the tabular detailed design of Figure 12.1 using program description language (PDL).

12.2   Represent the PDL detailed design of Figure 12.2 using tabular format.

12.3   Represent the PDL detailed design of Figure 12.3 using tabular format.

12.4   Why are methods assigned to classes during the design workflow and not the analysis workflow?

12.5   Why are attributes assigned to classes during the analysis workflow and not the design workflow?

12.6   Why has the validity of the cyclomatic complexity metric been questioned?

12.7   (Analysis and Design Project) Starting with the artifacts of your analysis workflow for the automated library circulation system (Problem 11.19), perform the design workflow.

12.8   (Analysis and Design Project) Starting with the artifacts of your analysis workflow for the product for determining whether a bank statement is correct (Problem 11.20), perform the design workflow.

12.9   (Analysis and Design Project) Starting with the artifacts of your analysis workflow for the ATM software (Problem 11.21), perform the design workflow.

12.10   (Term Project) Starting with the artifacts of your analysis workflow for Problem 11.22, perform the design workflow for the Osric's Office Appliances and Decor product (Appendix A).

12.11 (Case Study) Redesign the MSG Foundation product using a method specified by your instructor.

12.12 (Readings in Software Engineering) Your instructor will distribute copies of [Luqi, Zhang, Berzins, and Qiao, 2004]. Would you use this approach for developing real-time systems? Give reasons for your answer.

References

[Bansiya and Davis, 2002] J. BANSIYA AND C. G. DAVIS, "A Hierarchical Model for Object-Oriented Design Quality Assessment," *IEEE Transactions on Software Engineering* **28** (January 2002), pp. 4–17.

[Beizer, 1990] B. BEIZER, *Software Testing Techniques*, 2nd ed., Van Nostrand Reinhold, New York, 1990.

[Bias, 1991] R. BIAS, "Walkthroughs: Efficient Collaborative Testing," *IEEE Software* **8** (September 1991), pp. 94–95.

[Binkley and Schach, 1996] A. B. BINKLEY AND S. R. SCHACH, "A Comparison of Sixteen Quality Metrics for Object-Oriented Design," *Information Processing Letters* **57** (No. 6, June 1996), pp. 271–75.

[Binkley and Schach, 1997] A. B. BINKLEY AND S. R. SCHACH, "Toward a Unified Approach to Object-Oriented Coupling," *Proceedings of the 35th Annual ACM Southeast Conference*, Murfreesboro, TN, April 2–4, 1997, pp. 91–97.

[Binkley and Schach, 1998] A. B. BINKLEY AND S. R. SCHACH, "Validation of the Coupling Dependency Metric as a Predictor of Run-Time Failures and Maintenance Measures," *Proceedings of the 20th International Conference on Software Engineering,* Kyoto, Japan, April 1988, pp. 542–55.

[Briand, Bunse, and Daly, 2001] L. C. BRIAND, C. BUNSE, AND J. W. DALY, "A Controlled Experiment for Evaluating Quality Guidelines on the Maintainability of Object-Oriented Designs," *IEEE Transactions on Software Engineering* **27** (June 2001), pp. 513–30.

[Brooks, 1986] F. P. BROOKS, Jr., "No Silver Bullet," in: *Information Processing '86*, H.-J. Kugler (Editor), Elsevier North-Holland, New York, 1986; reprinted in: *IEEE Computer* **20** (April 1987), pp. 10–19.

[Chidamber and Kemerer, 1994] S. R. CHIDAMBER AND C. F. KEMERER, "A Metrics Suite for Object Oriented Design," *IEEE Transactions on Software Engineering* **20** (June 1994), pp. 476–93.

[Coad and Yourdon, 1991b] P. COAD AND E. YOURDON, *Object-Oriented Design*, Yourdon Press, Englewood CliffsNJ, 1991.

[Fagan, 1976] M. E. FAGAN, "Design and Code Inspections to Reduce Errors in Program Development," *IBM Systems Journal* **15** (No. 3, 1976), pp. 182–211.

[Fagan, 1986] M. E. FAGAN, "Advances in Software Inspections," *IEEE Transactions on Software Engineering* **SE-12** (July 1986), pp. 744–51.

[Fichman and Kemerer, 1992] R. G. FICHMAN AND C. F. KEMERER, "Object-Oriented and Conventional Analysis and Design Methodologies: Comparison and Critique," *IEEE Computer* **25** (October 1992), pp. 22–39.

[Flanagan, 2005] D. FLANAGAN, *Java in a Nutshell*: *A Desktop Quick Reference*, 5th ed., O'Reilly and Associates, Sebastopol, CA, 2005.

[Goldberg and Robson, 1989] A. GOLDBERG AND D. ROBSON, *Smalltalk-80: The Language*, Addison-Wesley, Reading, MA, 1989.

[Gomaa, 2000] H. GOMAA, *Designing Concurrent, Distributed, and Real-Time Applications with UML*, Addison-Wesley, Reading, MA, 2000.

[Henry and Kafura, 1981] S. M. HENRY AND D. KAFURA, "Software Structure Metrics Based on Information Flow," *IEEE Transactions on Software Engineering* **SE-7** (September 1981), pp. 510–18.

[Hoare, 1987] C. A. R. HOARE, "An Overview of Some Formal Methods for Program Design," *IEEE Computer* **20** (September 1987), pp. 85–91.

[ISO/IEC 8652, 1995] *Programming Language Ada: Language and Standard Libraries*, ISO/IEC 8652, International Organization for Standardization, International Electrotechnical Commission, Geneva, Switzerland, 1995.

[Jackson, 1975] M. A. JACKSON, *Principles of Program Design*, Academic Press, New York, 1975.

[Jackson and Chapin, 2000] D. JACKSON AND J. CHAPIN, "Redesigning Air Traffic Control: An Exercise in Software Design," *IEEE Software* **17** (May/June 2000), pp. 63–70.

[Jacobson, Booch, and Rumbaugh, 1999] I. JACOBSON, G. BOOCH, AND J. RUMBAUGH, *The Unified Software Development Process*, Addison-Wesley, Reading, MA, 1999.

[Kelly and Sherif, 1992] J. C. KELLY AND J. S. SHERIF, "A Comparison of Four Design Methods for Real-Time Software Development," *Information and Software Technology* **34** (February 1992), pp. 74–82.

[Kitchenham, Pickard, and Linkman, 1990] B. A. KITCHENHAM, L. M. PICKARD, AND S. J. LINKMAN, "An Evaluation of Some Design Metrics," *Software Engineering Journal* **5** (January 1990), pp. 50–58.

[Liu, 2000] J. W. S. LIU, *Real Time Systems,* Prentice Hall, Upper Saddle River, NJ, 2000.

[Luqi, Zhang, Berzins, and Qiao, 2004] LUQI, L. ZHANG, V. BERZINS, AND Y. QIAO, "Documentation Driven Development for Complex Real-Time Systems," *IEEE Transactions on Software Engineering* **30** (December 2004), pp. 936–52.

[Magee and Kramer, 1999] J. MAGEE AND J. KRAMER, *Concurrency: State Models & Java Programs*, John Wiley and Sons, New York, 1999.

[Maranzano et al., 2005] J. F. MARANZANO, S. A. ROZSYPAL, G. H. ZIMMERMAN, G. W. WARNKEN, P. E. WIRTH, AND D. M. WEISS, "Architecture Reviews: Practice and Experience," *IEEE Software* **22** (March/April 2005), pp. 34–43.

[McCabe, 1976] T. J. MCCABE, "A Complexity Measure," *IEEE Transactions on Software Engineering* **SE-2** (December 1976), pp. 308–20.

[Monarchi and Puhr, 1992] D. E. MONARCHI AND G. I. PUHR, "A Research Typology for Object-Oriented Analysis and Design," *Communications of the ACM* **35** (September 1992), pp. 35–47.

[Shepperd, 1990] M. SHEPPERD, "Design Metrics: An Empirical Analysis," *Software Engineering Journal* **5** (January 1990), pp. 3–10.

[Shlaer and Mellor, 1992] S. SHLAER AND S. MELLOR, *Object Lifecycles: Modeling the World in States*, Yourdon Press, Englewood Cliffs, NJ, 1992.

[Silberschatz, Galvin, and Gagne, 2002] A. SILBERSCHATZ, P. B. GALVIN, AND G. GAGNE, *Operating System Concepts*, 6th ed., Addison-Wesley, Reading, MA, 2002.

[Stolper, 1999] S. A. STOLPER, "Streamlined Design Approach Lands Mars Pathfinder," *IEEE Software* **16** (September/October 1999), pp. 52–62.

[Stroustrup, 2003] B. STROUSTRUP, *The C++ Standard: Incorporating Technical Corrigendum No. 1*, 2nd ed., John Wiley and Sons, New York, 2003.

[Walker, 1992] I. J. WALKER, "Requirements of an Object-Oriented Design Method," *Software Engineering Journal* **7** (March 1992), pp. 102–13.

[Ward and Mellor, 1985] P. T. WARD AND S. MELLOR, *Structured Development for Real-Time Systems*. Vols. 1, 2, and 3, Yourdon Press, New York, 1985.

[Wirfs-Brock, Wilkerson, and Wiener, 1990] R. WIRFS-BROCK, B. WILKERSON, AND L. WIENER, *Designing Object-Oriented Software*, Prentice Hall, Englewood Cliffs, NJ, 1990.

[Yourdon and Constantine, 1979] E. YOURDON AND L. L. CONSTANTINE, *Structured Design: Fundamentals of a Discipline of Computer Program and Systems Design*, Prentice Hall, Englewood Cliffs, NJ, 1979.

[Zage and Zage, 1993] W. M. ZAGE AND D. M. ZAGE, "Evaluating Design Metrics on Large-Scale Software," *IEEE Software* **10** (July 1993), pp. 75–81.

Chapter 13

The Implementation Workflow

Learning Objectives

After studying this chapter, you should be able to

- Perform the implementation workflow.
- Perform black-box, glass-box, and non-execution-based unit testing.
- Perform integration testing, product testing, and acceptance testing.
- Appreciate the need for good programming practices and programming standards.

Implementation is the process of translating the detailed design into code. When this is done by a single individual, the process is relatively well understood. But, most real-life products today are too large to be implemented by one programmer within the given time constraints. Instead, the product is implemented by a team, working at the same time on different components of the product; this is termed **programming-in-the-many**. Issues associated with programming-in-the-many are examined in this chapter.

13.1 Choice of Programming Language

In most cases, the issue of which programming language to choose for the implementation simply does not arise. Suppose the client wants a product to be written in, say, Smalltalk. Perhaps, in the opinion of the development team, Smalltalk is entirely unsuitable for the product. Such an opinion is irrelevant to the client. Management of the development organization has only two choices: Implement the product in Smalltalk or turn down the job.

Similarly, if the product has to be implemented on a specific computer and the only language available on that computer is assembler, then again there is no choice. If no other language is available, either because no compiler has yet been written for any high-level language on that computer or management is not prepared to pay for a new C++ compiler for the stipulated computer, then again clearly the issue of choice of programming language is not relevant.

A more interesting situation is this: A contract specifies that the product is to be implemented in "the most-suitable" programming language. What language should be chosen? To answer this question, consider the following scenario. QQQ Corporation has been writing COBOL products for over 30 years. The entire 200-member software staff of QQQ, from the most junior programmer to the vice-president for software, has COBOL expertise. Why on earth should the most suitable programming language be anything but COBOL? The introduction of a new language, Java, for example, would mean having to hire new programmers, or, at the very least, existing staff would have to be intensively retrained. Having invested all that money and effort in Java training, management might well decide that future products also should be written in Java. Nevertheless, all the existing COBOL products would have to be maintained. There then would be two classes of programmers, COBOL maintenance programmers and Java programmers writing the new applications. Quite undeservedly, maintenance almost always is considered inferior to developing new applications, so there would be distinct unhappiness among the ranks of the COBOL programmers. This unhappiness would be compounded by the fact that Java programmers usually are paid more than COBOL programmers because Java programmers are in short supply. Although QQQ has excellent development tools for COBOL, a Java compiler would have to be purchased, as well as appropriate Java CASE tools. Additional hardware may have to be purchased or leased to run this new software. Perhaps most serious of all, QQQ has accumulated hundreds of person-years of COBOL expertise, the kind of expertise that can be gained only through hands-on experience, such as what to do when a certain cryptic error message appears on the screen or how to handle the quirks of the compiler. In brief, it would seem that "the most suitable" programming language could be only COBOL—any other choice would be financial suicide, either from the viewpoint of the cost involved or as a consequence of plummeting staff morale leading to poor-quality code.

And yet, the most suitable programming language for QQQ Corporation's latest project may indeed be some language other than COBOL. Notwithstanding its position as the world's most widely used programming language (see Just in Case You Wanted to Know Box 13.1), COBOL is suited for only one class of software products, data processing applications. If QQQ Corporation has software needs outside this class, then COBOL rapidly loses its attractiveness. For example, if QQQ wishes to construct a knowledge-based product using artificial intelligence (AI) techniques, then an AI language such as Lisp could be used; COBOL is totally unsuitable for AI applications. If large-scale communications software is to be built, perhaps because QQQ requires satellite links to hundreds of branch offices all over the world, then a language such as Java would prove far more suitable than COBOL. If QQQ is to go into the business of writing systems software, such as operating systems, compilers, and linkers, then COBOL very definitely is unsuitable. And, if QQQ Corporation decides to go into defense contracting, management will soon discover that COBOL simply cannot be used for real-time embedded software.

The issue of which programming language to use often can be decided by using cost–benefit analysis (Section 5.2). That is, management must compute the dollar cost of an implementation in COBOL as well as the dollar benefits, present and future, of using COBOL. This

Far more code has been written in COBOL than in all other programming languages put together. COBOL is the most widely used language primarily because COBOL is a product of the U.S. Department of Defense (DoD). COBOL was approved by the DoD in 1960. Thereafter, the DoD would not buy hardware for running data-processing applications unless that hardware had a COBOL compiler [Sammet, 1978]. The DoD was, and still is, the world's largest purchaser of computer hardware; and in the 1960s, a considerable proportion of DoD software was written for data processing. As a result, COBOL compilers were written as a matter of urgency for virtually every computer. This widespread availability of COBOL, at a time when the only alternative language usually was assembler, resulted in COBOL becoming the world's most popular programming language.

Languages such as C++ and Java undoubtedly are growing in popularity for new applications. Nevertheless, postdelivery maintenance still is the major software activity, and this maintenance is being performed on existing COBOL software. In short, the DoD put its stamp onto the world's software via its first major programming language, COBOL.

Another reason for the popularity of COBOL is that COBOL frequently is the best language for implementing a data-processing product. In particular, COBOL generally is the language of choice when money is involved. Financial books have to balance, so rounding errors cannot be allowed to creep in. Therefore, all computations have to be performed using integer arithmetic. COBOL supports integer arithmetic on very large numbers (that is, billions of dollars). In addition, COBOL can handle very small numbers, such as fractions of a cent. Banking regulations require interest computations to be calculated to at least four decimal places of a cent, and COBOL can do this arithmetic with ease as well. Finally, COBOL probably has the best formatting, sorting, and report generation facilities of any third-generation language (or high-level language). All these reasons have made COBOL an excellent choice for implementing a data-processing product.

As mentioned in Section 8.10.4, the current COBOL language standard is for an object-oriented language. This OO-COBOL standard surely will further boost the popularity of COBOL.

computation must be repeated for every language under consideration. The language with the largest expected gain (that is, the difference between estimated benefits and estimated costs) is then the appropriate implementation language. Another way of deciding which programming language to select is to use risk analysis. For each language under consideration, a list is made of the potential risks and ways of resolving them. The language for which the overall risk is the smallest then is selected.

Software organizations are under pressure to develop new software in an object-oriented language—any object-oriented language. The question that arises is this: Which is the appropriate object-oriented language? Twenty years ago, there really was only one choice, Smalltalk. Today, however, the most widely used object-oriented programming language is C++ [Borland, 2002], with Java in second place. There are a number of reasons for the popularity of C++. One is the widespread availability of C++ compilers. In fact, some C++ compilers simply translate the source code from C++ into C, and then invoke the C compiler. Therefore, any computer with a C compiler essentially can handle C++.

But the real explanation for the popularity of C++ is its apparent similarity to C. This is unfortunate, in that a number of managers view C++ as a superset of C and, therefore, conclude that any programmer who knows C can quickly pick up the additional pieces. Indeed, from just a syntactical viewpoint, C++ essentially is a superset of C. After all, virtually any C program can be compiled using a C++ compiler. Conceptually, however, C++ is totally different from C. C is a product of the classical paradigm, whereas C++ is for the object-oriented paradigm. Using C++ makes sense only if object-oriented techniques have been used and if the product is organized around objects and classes, not functions.

Therefore, before an organization adopts C++, it is essential that the relevant software professionals be trained in the object-oriented paradigm. It is particularly important that the information of Chapter 7 be taught. Unless it is clear to all involved, and particularly to management, that the object-oriented paradigm is a different way of developing software and what the precise differences are, the classical paradigm just will continue to be used but with the code written in C++ rather than C. When organizations are disappointed with the results of switching from C to C++, a major contributory factor is a lack of education in the object-oriented paradigm.

Suppose that an organization decides to adopt Java. In that case it is not possible to move gradually from the classical paradigm to the object-oriented paradigm. Java is a pure object-oriented programming language; it does not support the functions and procedures of the classical paradigm. Unlike a hybrid object-oriented language such as C++, Java programmers have to use the object-oriented paradigm (and only the object-oriented paradigm) from the very beginning. Because of the necessity of an abrupt transition from the one paradigm to the other, education and training is even more important when adopting Java (or other pure object-oriented language, such as Smalltalk) than if the organization were to switch to a hybrid object-oriented language like C++ or OO-COBOL.

Having decided on the implementation language, the next issue is how software engineering principles can lead to better-quality code.

13.2   Good Programming Practice

Many recommendations on good coding style are language specific. For example, suggestions regarding use of COBOL 88-level entries or parentheses in Lisp are of little interest to programmers implementing a product in Java. Accordingly, recommendations regarding language independent *good programming practice* for object-oriented programming languages like Java and C++ are now given.

13.2.1   Use of Consistent and Meaningful Variable Names

As stated in Chapter 1, on average at least two-thirds of a software budget is devoted to postdelivery maintenance. This implies that the programmer developing a code artifact is merely the first of many who will work on that code artifact. It is counterproductive for a programmer to give names to variables that are meaningful to only that programmer; within the context of software engineering, the term *meaningful variable names* means "meaningful from the viewpoint of future maintenance programmers." This point is amplified in Just in Case You Wanted to Know Box 13.2.

In addition to the use of meaningful variable names, it is equally essential that *consistent variable names* be chosen. For example, the following four variables are declared in a code artifact: averageFreq, frequencyMaximum, minFr, and frqncyTotl. A maintenance programmer who is trying to understand the code has to know if freq, frequency, fr, and frqncy all refer to the same thing. If yes, then the identical word should be used, preferably

In the late 1970s, a small software organization in Johannesburg, South Africa, consisted of two programming teams. Team A was made up of émigrés from Mozambique. They were of Portuguese extraction, and their native language was Portuguese. Their code was well written. Variable names were meaningful but unfortunately only to a speaker of Portuguese. Team B comprised Israeli immigrants whose native language was Hebrew. Their code was equally well written, and the names they chose for their variables were equally meaningful—but only to a speaker of Hebrew.

One day, team A resigned en masse, together with its team leader. Team B was totally unable to maintain any of the excellent code that team A had written, because they spoke no Portuguese. The variable names, meaningful as they were to Portuguese speakers, were incomprehensible to the Israelis, whose linguistic abilities were restricted to Hebrew and English. The owner of the software organization was unable to hire enough Portuguese-speaking programmers to replace team A, and the company soon went into bankruptcy, under the weight of numerous lawsuits from disgruntled customers whose code was now essentially unmaintainable.

The situation could have been avoided easily. The head of the company should have insisted from the start that all variable names be in English, the language understood by every South African computer professional. Variable names then would have been meaningful to any maintenance programmer.

---

frequency, although freq or frqncy is marginally acceptable; fr is not. But if one or more variable names refer to a different quantity, then a totally different name, such as rate, should be used. Conversely, do not use two different names to denote the identical concept; for example, both average and mean should not be used in the same program.

A second aspect of consistency is the ordering of the components of variable names. For example, if one variable is named frequencyMaximum, then the name minimumFrequency would be confusing; it should be frequencyMinimum. To make the code clear and unambiguous for future maintenance programmers, the four variables listed previously should be named frequencyAverage, frequencyMaximum, frequencyMinimum, and frequencyTotal, respectively. Alternatively, the frequency component can appear at the end of all four variable names, yielding the variable names averageFrequency, maximumFrequency, minimumFrequency, and totalFrequency. It clearly does not matter which of the two sets is chosen; what is important is that all the names be from one set or the other.

A number of different naming conventions have been put forward that are intended to make it easier to understand the code. The idea is that the name of a variable should incorporate type information. For example, ptrChTmp might denote a temporary variable (Tmp) of type pointer (ptr) to a character (Ch). The best known of such schemes are the Hungarian Naming Conventions [Klunder, 1988]. (If you want to know why they are called Hungarian, see Just in Case You Wanted to Know Box 13.3.) One drawback of many of such schemes is that the effectiveness of code inspections (Section 13.13) can be reduced when participants are unable to pronounce the names of variables. It is extremely frustrating to have to spell out variable names, letter by letter.

13.2.2 The Issue of Self-Documenting Code

When asked why their code contains no comments whatsoever, programmers often proudly reply, "I write *self-documenting code*." The implication is that their variable

There are two explanations for the term **Hungarian Naming Conventions**. First, these conventions were invented by Charles Simonyi, who was born in Hungary. Second, it generally is agreed that, to the uninitiated, programs with variable names conforming to the conventions are about as easy to read as Hungarian. Nevertheless, organizations (such as Microsoft) that use them claim that they enhance code readability for those with experience in the Hungarian Naming Conventions.

names are chosen so carefully and their code crafted so exquisitely that there is no need for comments. Self-documenting code does exist, but it is exceedingly rare. Instead, the usual scenario is that the programmer appreciates every nuance of the code at the time the code artifact is written. It is conceivable that the programmer uses the same style for every code artifact and that in 5 years' time the code still is crystal clear in every respect to the original programmer. Unfortunately, this is irrelevant. The important point is whether the code artifact can be understood easily and unambiguously by all the other programmers who have to read it, starting with the software quality assurance group and including a number of different postdelivery maintenance programmers. The problem becomes more acute in the light of the unfortunate practice of assigning postdelivery maintenance tasks to inexperienced programmers and not supervising them closely. The undocumented code of the artifact may be only partially comprehensible to an experienced programmer. How much worse, then, is the situation when the maintenance programmer is inexperienced.

To see the sort of problems that can arise, consider the variable xCoordinateOfPositionOfRobotArm. Such a variable name undoubtedly is self-documenting in every sense of the word, but few programmers are prepared to use a 31-character variable name, especially if that name is used frequently. Instead, a shorter name is used, xCoord, for example. The reasoning behind this is that if the entire code artifact deals with the movement of the arm of a robot, xCoord can refer only to the x coordinate of the position of the arm of the robot. Although that argument holds water within the context of the development process, it is not necessarily true for postdelivery maintenance. The maintenance programmer may not have sufficient knowledge of the product as a whole to realize that, within this code artifact, xCoord refers to the arm of the robot or may not have the necessary documentation to understand the workings of the code artifact. The way to avoid this sort of problem is to insist that every variable name be explained at the beginning of the code artifact, in the **prologue comments**. If this rule is followed, the maintenance programmer quickly will understand that variable xCoord is used for the x-coordinate of the position of the robot arm.

Prologue comments are mandatory in every code artifact. The minimum information that must be provided at the top of every code artifact is listed in Figure 13.1.

Even if a code artifact is clearly written, it is unreasonable to expect someone to have to read every line to understand what the code artifact does and how it does it. Prologue comments make it easy for others to understand the key points. Only a member of the SQA group or a maintenance programmer modifying a specific code artifact should be expected to have to read every line of that code artifact.

In addition to prologue comments, inline comments should be inserted into the code to assist maintenance programmers in understanding that code. It has been suggested that inline comments should be used only when the code is written in a nonobvious way or uses

Figure 13.1
Minimal
prologue
comments for a
code artifact.

The name of the code artifact
A brief description of what the code artifact does
The programmer's name
The date the code artifact was coded
The date the code artifact was approved
The name of the person who approved the code artifact
The arguments of the code artifact
A list of the name of each variable of the code artifact, preferably in alphabetical order, and a brief description of its use
The names of any files accessed by this code artifact
The names of any files changed by this code artifact
Input–output, if any
Error-handling capabilities
The name of the file containing test data (to be used later for regression testing)
A list of each modification made to the code artifact, the date the modification was made, and who approved the modification
Any known faults

some subtle aspect of the language. On the contrary, confusing code should be rewritten in a clearer way. Inline comments are a means of helping maintenance programmers and should not be used to promote or excuse poor programming practice.

13.2.3   Use of Parameters

There are very few genuine constants, that is, variables whose values *never* change. For instance, satellite photographs have caused changes to be made in submarine navigation systems incorporating the latitude and longitude of Pearl Harbor, Hawaii, to reflect more accurate geographic data regarding the exact location of Pearl Harbor. To take another example, sales tax is not a genuine constant; legislators tend to change the sales tax rate from time to time. Suppose that the sales tax rate currently is **6.0** percent. If the value **6.0** has been hard coded in a number of code artifacts of a product, then changing the product is a major exercise, with the likely outcome of one or two instances of the "constant" **6.0** being overlooked and, perhaps, changing an unrelated **6.0** by mistake. A better solution is a C++ declaration such as

const float SALES_TAX_RATE = 6.0;

or, in Java,

public static final float SALES_TAX_RATE = (**float**) 6.0;

Then, wherever the value of the sales tax rate is needed, the constant SALES_TAX_RATE should be used and not the number **6.0**. If the sales tax rate changes, then only the line containing the value of SALES_TAX_RATE need be altered using an editor. Better still, the value of the sales tax rate should be read in from a parameter file at the beginning of the run. All such apparent constants should be treated as parameters. If a value should change for any reason, this change can be implemented quickly and effectively.

13.2.4   Code Layout for Increased Readability

It is relatively simple to make a code artifact easy to read. For example, no more than one statement should appear on a line, even though many programming languages permit more than one. Indentation is perhaps the most important technique for increasing readability. Just imagine how difficult it would be to read the code examples in Chapter 7 if indentation had not been used to assist in understanding the code. In C++ or Java, indentation can be used to connect corresponding { … } pairs. Indentation also shows which statements belong in a given block. In fact, correct indentation is too important to be left to humans. Instead, as described in Section 5.6, CASE tools should be used to ensure that indentation is done correctly.

Another useful aid is blank lines. Methods should be separated by blank lines; in addition, it often is helpful to break up large blocks of code with blank lines. The extra "white space" makes the code easier to read and, hence, comprehend.

13.2.5   Nested **if** Statements

Consider the following example. A map consists of two squares, as shown in Figure 13.2. It is required to write code to determine whether a point on the Earth's surface lies in mapSquare1, mapSquare2, or not on the map at all. The solution of Figure 13.3 is so badly formatted that it is incomprehensible. A properly formatted version appears in Figure 13.4. Notwithstanding this, the combination of **if-if** and **if-else-if** constructs is so complex that it is difficult to check whether the code fragment is correct. This is fixed in Figure 13.5.

Figure 13.2
Coordinates
for a map.

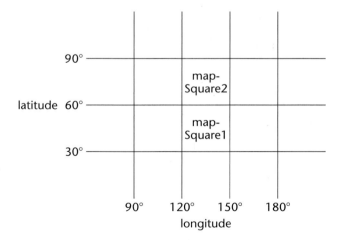

Figure 13.3
Badly formatted
nested **if**
statements.

if (latitude > 30 && longitude > 120) {**if** (latitude <= 60 && longitude <= 150) mapSquareNo = 1; **else if** (latitude <= 90 && longitude <= 150) mapSquareNo = 2 **else** *print* "Not on the map";} **else** *print* "Not on the map";

Figure 13.4
Well-formatted
but badly
constructed
nested **if**
statements.

```
if (latitude > 30 && longitude > 120)
{
  if (latitude <= 60 && longitude <= 150)
    mapSquareNo = 1;
  else
    if (latitude <= 90 && longitude <= 150)
      mapSquareNo = 2;
    else
      print "Not on the map";
}
else
  print "Not on the map";
```

Figure 13.5
Acceptably
nested **if**
statements.

```
if (longitude > 120 && longitude <= 150 && latitude > 30 && latitude <= 60)
  mapSquareNo = 1;
else
  if (longitude > 120 && longitude <= 150 && latitude > 60 && latitude <= 90)
    mapSquareNo = 2;
  else
    print "Not on the map";
```

When faced with complex code containing the **if-if** construct, one way to simplify it is to use the fact that the **if-if** combination

$$\textbf{if} <condition\ 1>$$

$$\textbf{if} <condition\ 2>$$

is equivalent to the single condition

$$\textbf{if} <condition\ 1> \textbf{ and } <condition\ 2>$$

provided that *<condition 2>* is defined even if *<condition 1>* does not hold. For example, *<condition 1>* might check that a pointer is not null and, if so, then *<condition 2>* can use that pointer. (This problem does not arise in Java or C++. The && operator is defined such that if *<condition 1>* is false, then *<condition 2>* is not evaluated.)

Another problem with the **if-if** construct is that nesting **if** statements too deeply leads to code that can be difficult to read. As a rule of thumb, **if** statements nested to a depth greater than three is poor programming practice and should be avoided.

13.3 Coding Standards

Coding standards can be both a blessing and a curse. Section 7.2.1 pointed out that modules with coincidental cohesion generally arise as a consequence of rules such as, "Every module will consist of between 35 and 50 executable statements." Instead of stating a rule in such a dogmatic fashion, a better formulation is, "Programmers should consult their managers before constructing a module with fewer than 35 or more than 50 executable statements." The point is that no coding standard can be applicable under all possible circumstances.

Coding standards imposed from above tend to be ignored. As mentioned previously, a useful rule of thumb is that **if** statements should not be nested to a depth greater than three. If programmers are shown examples of unreadable code resulting from nesting **if** statements too deeply, then it is likely that they will conform to such a regulation. But they are unlikely to adhere to a list of coding rules imposed on them with no discussion or explanation. Furthermore, such standards are likely to lead to friction between programmers and their managers.

In addition, unless a coding standard can be checked by machine, it is going to either waste a lot of the SQA group's time or simply be ignored by the programmers and SQA group alike. On the other hand, consider the following rules:

- Nesting of **if** statements should not exceed a depth of three, except with prior approval from the team leader.
- Modules should consist of between 35 and 50 statements, except with prior approval from the team leader.
- The use of **goto** statements should be avoided. However, with prior approval from the team leader, a forward **goto** may be used for error handling.

Such rules may be checked by machine, provided some mechanism is set up for capturing the data relating to permission to deviate from the standard.

The aim of coding standards is to make maintenance easier. However, if the effect of a standard is to make the life of software developers difficult, then such a standard should be modified, even in the middle of a project. Overly restrictive coding standards are counterproductive, in that the quality of software production inevitably must suffer if programmers have to develop software within such a framework. On the other hand, standards such as those just listed regarding nesting of **if** statements, module size, and goto statements, coupled with a mechanism for deviating from those standards, can lead to improved software quality, which, after all, is a major goal of software engineering.

13.4   Code Reuse

Reuse was presented in detail in Chapter 8. In fact, the material on reuse could have appeared virtually anywhere in this book, because artifacts from all workflows of the software process are reused, including portions of specifications, contracts, plans, designs, and code artifacts. That is why the material on reuse was put into the first part of the book, rather than tying it to one or another specific workflow. In particular, it was important that the material on reuse not be presented in this chapter to underline the fact that, even though reuse of code is by far the most common form of reuse, more than just code can be reused.

13.5   Integration

Consider the product depicted in Figure 13.6. One approach to ***integration*** of the product is to code and test each code artifact separately, link together all 13 code artifacts, and test the product as a whole. There are two difficulties with this approach. First, consider artifact a. It cannot be tested on its own, because it calls artifacts b, c, and d. Therefore, to unit test artifact a, artifacts b, c, and d must be coded as ***stubs***. In its simplest form, a stub is an empty artifact. A more effective stub prints a message such as artifact

Figure 13.6
A typical
interconnection
diagram.

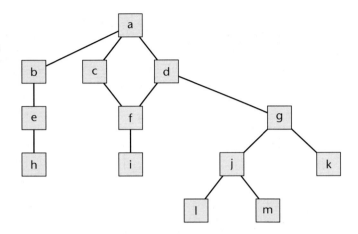

displayRadarPattern called. Best of all, a stub should return values corresponding to preplanned test cases.

Now consider artifact h. To test it on its own requires a ***driver***, a code artifact that calls it one or more times, if possible checking the values returned by the artifact under test. Similarly, testing artifact d requires a driver and two stubs. Therefore, one problem that arises with separate implementation and integration is that effort has to be put into constructing stubs and drivers, all of which are thrown away after unit testing is completed.

The second, and much more important, difficulty that arises when implementation is completed before integration starts is lack of fault isolation. If the product as a whole is tested against a specific test case and the product fails, then the fault could lie in any of the 13 code artifacts or 13 interfaces. In a large product with, say, 103 code artifacts and 108 interfaces, the fault might lie in no fewer than 211 places.

The solution to both difficulties is to combine unit and integration testing.

13.5.1   Top-down Integration

In ***top-down integration***, if code artifact mAbove sends a message to artifact mBelow, then mAbove is implemented and integrated before mBelow. Suppose that the product shown in Figure 13.6 is implemented and integrated top down. One possible top-down ordering is a, b, c, d, e, f, g, h, i, j, k, l, and m. First, artifact a is coded and tested with b, c, and d implemented as stubs. Next stub b is expanded into artifact b, linked to artifact a, and tested with artifact e implemented as a stub. Implementation and integration proceed in this way until all the artifacts have been integrated into the product. Another possible top-down ordering is a, b, e, h, c, d, f, i, g, j, k, l, and m. With this ordering, portions of the integration can proceed in parallel in the following way. After a has been coded and tested, one programmer can use artifact a to implement and integrate b, e, and h, while another programmer can use a to work in parallel on c, d, f, and i. Once d and f are completed, a third programmer can start work on g, j, k, l, and m.

Suppose that artifact a by itself executes correctly on a specific test case. However, when the same test data are submitted after b has been coded and integrated into the product, now consisting of artifacts a and b linked together, the test fails. The fault can be in one of two places, in artifact b or the interface between artifacts a and b. In general, whenever a code artifact mNew is added to what has been tested so far and a previously successful test case fails, the fault almost certainly lies either in mNew or in the interface(s) between mNew and the rest of the product. In this way, top-down integration supports fault isolation.

Another strength of top-down integration is that major design flaws show up early. The artifacts of a product can be divided into two groups, logic artifacts and operational artifacts. **Logic artifacts** essentially incorporate the decision-making flow of control aspects of the product. The logic artifacts generally are those situated close to the root in the interconnection diagram. For example, in Figure 13.6, it is reasonable to expect artifacts a, b, c, d, and perhaps g and j to be logic artifacts. The **operational artifacts**, on the other hand, perform the actual operations of the product. For example, an operational artifact may be named getLineFromTerminal or measureTemperatureOfReactorCore. The operational artifacts generally are found in the lower levels, close to the leaves, of the interconnection diagram. In Figure 13.6, artifacts e, f, h, i, k, l, and m are operational artifacts.

It always is important to code and test the logic artifacts before coding and testing the operational artifacts. This ensures that any major design faults show up early. Suppose the whole product is completed before a major fault is detected. Large parts of the product have to be rewritten, especially the logic artifacts that embody the flow of control. Many of the operational artifacts probably are reusable in the rebuilt product; for example, an artifact like getLineFromTerminal or measureTemperatureOfReactorCore is needed no matter how the product is restructured. However, the way the operational artifacts are connected to the other artifacts in the product may have to be changed, resulting in unnecessary work. Therefore, the earlier a design fault is detected, the quicker and less costly it is to correct the product and get back on the development schedule. The order in which artifacts are implemented and integrated using the top-down strategy essentially ensures that logic artifacts indeed are implemented and integrated before operational artifacts, because logic artifacts almost always are the ancestors of operational artifacts in the interconnection diagram. This is a major strength of top-down integration.

Nevertheless, top-down integration has a weakness: Potentially reusable code artifacts may not be adequately tested, as will be explained. Reuse of an artifact that is thought, incorrectly, to have been thoroughly tested is likely to be less cost-effective than writing that artifact from scratch, because the assumption that an artifact is correct can lead to wrong conclusions when the product fails. Instead of suspecting the insufficiently tested, reused artifact, the tester may think that the fault lies elsewhere, resulting in a waste of effort.

Logic artifacts are likely to be somewhat problem specific and hence unusable in another context. However, operational artifacts, particularly if they have informational cohesion (Section 7.2.7), probably are reusable in future products and, therefore, require thorough testing. Unfortunately, the operational artifacts generally are the lower-level code artifacts in the interconnection diagram and hence are not tested as frequently as the upper-level artifacts. For example, if there are 184 artifacts, the root artifact is tested 184 times, whereas the last artifact to be integrated into the product is tested only once. Top-down integration makes reuse a risky undertaking as a consequence of inadequate testing of operational artifacts.

The situation is exacerbated if the product is well designed; in fact, the better the design, the less thoroughly the artifacts are likely to be tested. To see this, consider an artifact computeSquareRoot. This artifact takes two arguments, a floating-point number x whose square root is to be determined and an errorFlag that is set to true if x is negative. Suppose further that computeSquareRoot is invoked by artifact a3 and that a3 contains the statement

if (x >= 0)

y = computeSquareRoot (x, errorFlag);

In other words, computeSquareRoot is never invoked unless the value of x is nonnegative; therefore, the artifact can never be tested with negative values of x to see if it behaves correctly. The type of design where the calling artifact includes a safety check of this kind is referred to as ***defensive programming***. As a result of defensive programming, subordinate operational artifacts are unlikely to be thoroughly tested if integrated top down. An alternative to defensive programming is the use of responsibility-driven design (Section 1.9). Here, the necessary safety checks are built into the invoked artifact, rather than the invoker. Another approach is the use of assertions in the invoked artifact (Section 6.5.3).

13.5.2   Bottom-up Integration

In ***bottom-up integration***, if artifact mAbove sends a message to artifact mBelow, then mBelow is implemented and integrated before mAbove. In Figure 13.6, one possible bottom-up ordering is l, m, h, i, j, k, e, f, g, b, c, d, and a. To have the product coded by a team, a better bottom-up ordering is as follows: h, e, and b are given to one programmer and i, f, and c to another. The third programmer starts with l, m, j, k, and g, and then implements d and integrates his or her work with the work of the second programmer. Finally, when b, c, and d have been successfully integrated, a can be implemented and integrated.

The operational artifacts consequently are tested thoroughly when a bottom-up strategy is used. In addition, the testing is done with the aid of drivers, rather than by fault-shielding, defensively programmed artifacts. Although bottom-up integration solves the major difficulty of top-down integration and shares with top-down integration the advantage of fault isolation, it unfortunately has a difficulty of its own. Specifically, major design faults are detected late in the implementation workflow. The logic artifacts are integrated last; hence, if there is a major design fault, it will be picked up at the end of the implementation workflow with the resulting huge cost of redesigning and recoding large portions of the product.

Therefore, both top-down and bottom-up integration have their strengths and weaknesses. The solution for product development is to combine the two strategies in such a way as to use their strengths and minimize their weaknesses. This leads to the idea of sandwich integration.

13.5.3   Sandwich Integration

Consider the interconnection diagram shown in Figure 13.7. Six of the code artifacts—a, b, c, d, g, and j—are logic artifacts and therefore should be integrated top down. Seven are operational artifacts—e, f, h, i, k, l, and m—and should be integrated bottom up. Because neither top-down nor bottom-up integration is suitable for all the artifacts, the solution is to partition them. The six logic artifacts are integrated top down, and any major design faults can be caught early. The seven operational artifacts are integrated bottom up. They

The term *sandwich integration* [Myers, 1979] comes from viewing the logic artifacts and the operational artifacts as the top and the bottom of a sandwich, and the interfaces that connect them as the sandwich filling. This can be seen (sort of) in Figure 13.7.

Figure 13.7
The product of Figure 13.6 developed using sandwich integration.

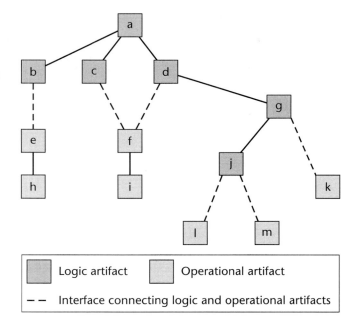

therefore receive a thorough testing, unshielded by defensively programmed artifacts that invoke them, and therefore can be reused with confidence in other products. When all artifacts have been appropriately integrated, the interfaces between the two groups of artifacts are tested, one by one. There is fault isolation at all times during this process, called ***sandwich integration*** (see Just in Case You Wanted to Know Box 13.4).

Figure 13.8 summarizes the strengths and weaknesses of sandwich integration, as well as the other integration techniques previously discussed in this chapter.

Sandwich integration is summarized in How to Perform Box 13.1.

How to Perform Sandwich Integration   Box 13.1

- **In parallel,**
    Implement and integrate the logic artifacts top down.
    Implement and integrate the operational artifacts bottom up.
- Test the interfaces between the logic artifacts and the operational artifacts.

Figure 13.8
A summary of
the integration
approaches
presented in
this chapter and
the section in
which each is
described.

Approach	Strengths	Weaknesses
Implementation then integration (Section 13.5)	—	No fault isolation Major design faults show up late Potentially reusable code artifacts are not adequately tested
Top-down integration (Section 13.5.1)	Fault isolation Major design faults show up early	Potentially reusable code artifacts are not adequately tested
Bottom-up integration (Section 13.5.2)	Fault isolation Potentially reusable code artifacts are adequately tested	Major design faults show up late
Sandwich integration (Section 13.5.3)	Fault isolation Major design faults show up early Potentially reusable code artifacts are adequately tested	—

13.5.4   Integration Techniques

Objects can be integrated either bottom up or top down. If top-down integration is chosen, stubs are used for each method.

If bottom-up integration is used, the objects that do not send messages to other objects are implemented and integrated first. Then, the objects that send messages to those objects are implemented and integrated, and so on, until all the objects in the product have been implemented and integrated. (This process must be modified if there is recursion.)

Because both top-down and bottom-up integration are supported, sandwich integration also can be used. If the product is implemented in a hybrid object-oriented language like C++, the classes generally are operational artifacts and therefore integrated bottom up. Many of the artifacts that are not classes are logic artifacts. These are implemented and integrated in a top-down manner. The other artifacts are operational, so they are implemented and integrated bottom up. Finally, all the nonobject artifacts are integrated with the objects.

Even when the product is implemented using a pure object-oriented language like Java, class methods (sometimes referred to as ***static methods***) such as main and utility methods usually are similar in structure to logic modules. Therefore, class methods are also implemented top down and then integrated with the other objects. In other words, when implementing and integrating an object-oriented product, variants of sandwich integration are used.

13.5.5   Management of Integration

A problem for management is discovering, at integration time, that the code artifacts simply do not fit together. For example, suppose that programmer 1 coded object o1, and programmer 2 coded object o2. In the version of the design documentation used by programmer 1, object o1 sends a message to object o2 passing four arguments, but the version of the design documentation used by programmer 2 states clearly that only three arguments are passed to o2. A problem like this can arise when a change is made to only one copy of the design document, without informing all the members of the development group. Both programmers know that they are in the right; neither is prepared to compromise, because the programmer who gives in must recode large portions of the product.

To solve these and similar problems of incompatibility, the entire integration process should be run by the SQA group. Furthermore, as with testing during other workflows, the SQA group has the most to lose if the integration testing is performed improperly. The SQA group therefore is the most likely to ensure that the testing is performed thoroughly. Hence, the manager of the SQA group should have responsibility for all aspects of integration testing. He or she must decide which artifacts are implemented and integrated top down and which bottom up and assign integration-testing tasks to the appropriate individuals. The SQA group, which will have drawn up the integration test plan in the software project management plan, is responsible for implementing that plan.

At the end of the integration process, all the code artifacts will have been tested and combined into a single product.

13.6   The Implementation Workflow

The aim of the ***implementation workflow*** is to implement the target software product in the selected implementation language. More precisely, as explained in Section 12.4, a large software product is partitioned into smaller subsystems, which are then implemented in parallel by coding teams. The subsystems, in turn, consist of **code artifacts**.

As soon as a code artifact has been coded, the programmer tests it; this is termed **unit testing**. Once the programmer is satisfied that the code artifact is correct, it is passed onto the quality assurance group for further testing. This testing by the quality assurance group is part of the test workflow, described in Sections 13.19 through 13.21.

ase Study

13.7   The Implementation Workflow: The MSG Foundation Case Study

Complete implementations of the MSG Foundation product in both C++ and Java can be downloaded from www.mhhe.com/schach. The programmers included a variety of comments to aid the postdelivery maintenance programmers.

Testing during the implementation workflow is examined next.

13.8   The Test Workflow: Implementation

A number of different types of testing have to be performed during the implementation workflow, including unit testing, integration testing, product testing, and acceptance testing. These types of testing are discussed in the following sections.

It is reasonable to ask why so many different names are given for the same testing concept. As so often happens in software engineering, the same concept was discovered, independently, by a number of different researchers, each of whom invented his or her own term. By the time the software engineering community realized that these were different names for the identical concept, it was too late—the diverse names had crept into the software engineering vocabulary.

In this book, I use the terms *black-box testing* and *glass-box testing*. These terms are particularly descriptive. When we test to specifications, we treat the code as a totally opaque black box. Conversely, when we test to code, we need to be able to see inside the box; hence the term *glass-box testing*. I avoid the term *white-box testing* because it is somewhat confusing. After all, a box painted white is just as opaque as one painted black.

As pointed out in Section 6.6, code artifacts undergo two types of testing: informal unit testing performed by the programmer while developing the code artifact and methodical unit testing carried out by the SQA group after the programmer is satisfied that the artifact appears to function correctly. This methodical testing is described in Sections 13.9 through 13.13. In turn, there are two basic types of methodical testing, **non-execution-based testing**, in which the artifact is reviewed by a team, and **execution-based testing** in which the artifact is run against test cases. Techniques for selecting test cases now are described.

13.9   Test Case Selection

The worst way to test a code artifact is to use haphazard test data. The tester sits in front of the keyboard, and whenever the artifact requests input, the tester responds with arbitrary data. As will be shown, there is never time to test more than the tiniest fraction of all possible test cases, which easily can number many more than 10^{100}. The few test cases that can be run, perhaps, on the order of 1000, are too valuable to waste on haphazard data. Worse, there is a tendency when the machine solicits input to respond more than once with the same data, wasting even more test cases. It is clear that **test case selection** must be performed systematically.

13.9.1   Testing to Specifications versus Testing to Code

Test data for unit testing can be constructed systematically in two basic ways. The first is to **test to specifications**. This technique also is called **black-box**, **behavioral**, **data-driven**, **functional**, and **input/output-driven testing**. In this approach, the code itself is ignored; the only information used in drawing up test cases is the specification document. The other extreme is to **test to code** and to ignore the specification document when selecting test cases. Other names for this technique are **glass-box**, **white-box**, **structural**, **logic-driven**, and **path-oriented testing** (for an explanation of why there are so many different terms, see Just in Case You Wanted to Know Box 13.5).

We now consider the feasibility of each of these two techniques, starting with testing to specifications.

13.9.2   Feasibility of Testing to Specifications

Consider the following example. Suppose that the specifications for a certain data-processing product state that five types of commission and seven types of discount must be incorporated. Testing every possible combination of just commission and discount requires 35 test cases. It is no use saying that commission and discount are computed in two entirely separate code artifacts and hence may be tested independently—in black-box testing, the product is treated as a black box, and its internal structure therefore is completely irrelevant.

This example contains only two factors, commission and discount, taking on five and seven different values, respectively. Any realistic product has hundreds, if not thousands, of different factors. Even if there are only 20 factors, each taking on only four different values, a total of 4^{20} or 1.1×10^{12} different test cases must be examined.

To see the implications of over a trillion test cases, consider how long it would take to test them all. If a team of programmers could be found that could generate, run, and examine test cases at an average rate of one every 30 seconds, then it would take more than a million years to test the product exhaustively.

Therefore, exhaustive testing to specifications is impossible in practice because of the combinatorial explosion. There simply are too many test cases to consider. Testing to code now is examined.

13.9.3   Feasibility of Testing to Code

The most common form of testing to code requires that each path through the code artifact be executed at least once.

- To see the infeasibility of this, consider the code fragment of Figure 13.9. The corresponding flowchart is shown in Figure 13.10. Even though the flowchart appears to be almost trivial, it has over 10^{12} different paths. There are five possible paths through the central group of six shaded boxes, and the total number of possible paths through the flowchart therefore is

$$5^1 + 5^2 + 5^3 + \cdots + 5^{18} = \frac{5 \times (5^{18} - 1)}{(5-1)} = 4.77 \times 10^{12}$$

Figure 13.9
A code fragment.

```
read (kmax)                    // kmax is an integer between 1 and 18
for (k = 0; k < kmax; k++) do
{
    read (myChar)              // myChar is the character A, B, or C
    switch (myChar)
    {
      case 'A':
        blockA;
        if (cond1) blockC;
        break;
      case 'B':
        blockB;
        if (cond2) blockC;
        break;
      case 'C':
        blockC;
        break;
    }
    blockD;
}
```

Figure 13.10
A flowchart
with over 10^{12}
possible paths.

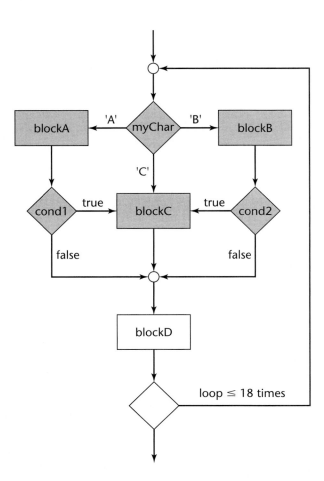

- If there can be this many paths through a simple flowchart containing a single loop, it is not difficult to imagine the total number of different paths in a code artifact of reasonable size and complexity, let alone a large artifact with many loops. In short, the huge number of possible paths renders exhaustive testing to code as infeasible as exhaustive testing to specifications.

- Furthermore, testing to code requires the tester to exercise every path. It is possible to exercise every path without detecting every fault in the product; that is, testing to code is not reliable. To see this, consider the code fragment shown in Figure 13.11 [Myers, 1976]. The fragment was written to test the equality of three integers, x, y, and z, using the totally fallacious assumption that if the average of three numbers is equal to the first number, then the three numbers are equal. Two test cases are shown in Figure 13.11. In the first test case the value of the average of the three numbers is $\frac{6}{3}$ or 2, which is not equal to 1. The product therefore correctly informs the tester that x, y, and z are unequal. The integers x, y, and z all equal 2 in the second test case, so the product computes their average as 2, which is equal to the value of x, and the product correctly concludes that the three numbers are equal. Accordingly, both paths through

Figure 13.11
An incorrect
code fragment
for determining
if three integers
are equal,
together with
two test cases.

if ((x + y + z)/3 == x)
   print "x, y, z are equal in value";
else
   print "x, y, z are unequal";

Test case 1:   x = 1, y = 2, z = 3
Test case 2:   x = y = z = 2

Figure 13.12
Two code
fragments for
computing a
quotient.

if (d == 0)
   zeroDivisionRoutine ();
else
   x = n/d;
          (a)

x = n/d;
     (b)

the product have been exercised without the fault being detected. Of course, the fault would come to light if test data such as x = 2, y = 1, z = 3 are used.

- A third difficulty with path testing is that a path can be tested only if it is present. Consider the code fragment shown in Figure 13.12(a). Clearly, two paths are to be tested, corresponding to the cases d = 0 and d ≠ 0. Next, consider the single statement of Figure 13.12(b). Now there is only one path, and this path can be tested without the fault being detected. In fact, a programmer who omits checking whether d = 0 in his or her code is likely to be unaware of the potential danger, and the case d = 0 will not be included in the programmer's test data. This problem is an additional argument for having an independent software quality assurance group whose job includes detecting faults of this type.

These examples show conclusively that the criterion "exercise all paths in the product" is not **reliable**, as products exist for which some data exercising a given path detect a fault and different data exercising the same path do not. However, path-oriented testing is **valid**, because it does not inherently preclude selecting test data that might reveal the fault.

Because of the combinatorial explosion, neither exhaustive testing to specifications nor exhaustive testing to code is feasible. A compromise is needed, using techniques that highlight as many faults as possible, while accepting that there is no way to guarantee that all faults have been detected. A reasonable way to proceed is to use black-box test cases first (testing to specifications) and then develop additional test cases using glass-box techniques (testing to code).

13.10 Black-Box Unit-Testing Techniques

Exhaustive black-box testing generally requires billions and billions of test cases. The art of testing is to devise a small, manageable set of test cases to maximize the chances of detecting a fault while minimizing the chances of wasting a test case by having the same fault detected by more than one test case. Every test case must be chosen to detect a previously undetected fault. One such black-box technique is equivalence testing combined with boundary value analysis.

13.10.1 Equivalence Testing and Boundary Value Analysis

Suppose the specifications for a database product state that the product must be able to handle any number of records from 1 through 16,383 ($2^{14} - 1$). If the product can handle 34 records and 14,870 records, then the chances are good that it will work fine for, say, 8252 records. In fact, the chances of detecting a fault, if present, are likely to be equally good if any test case from 1 through 16,383 records is selected. Conversely, if the product works correctly for any one test case in the range from 1 through 16,383, then it probably will work for any other test case in the range. The range from 1 through 16,383 constitutes an **equivalence class**, that is, a set of test cases such that any one member of the class is as good a test case as any other. To be more precise, the specified range of numbers of records that the product must be able to handle defines three equivalence classes:

Equivalence class 1. Less than 1 record.

Equivalence class 2. From 1 through 16,383 records.

Equivalence class 3. More than 16,383 records.

Testing the database product using the technique of equivalence classes then requires that one test case from each equivalence class be selected. The test case from equivalence class 2 should be handled correctly, whereas error messages should be printed for the test cases from class 1 and class 3.

A successful test case detects a previously undetected fault. To maximize the chances of finding such a fault, a high-payoff technique is **boundary value analysis**.

Experience has shown that, when a test case on or just to one side of the boundary of an equivalence class is selected, the probability of detecting a fault increases. Therefore, when testing the database product, seven test cases should be selected:

Test case 1.   0 records: Member of equivalence class 1 and adjacent to boundary value.

Test case 2.   1 record: Boundary value.

Test case 3.   2 records: Adjacent to boundary value.

Test case 4.   723 records: Member of equivalence class 2.

Test case 5.   16,382 records: Adjacent to boundary value.

Test case 6.   16,383 records: Boundary value.

Test case 7.   16,384 records: Member of equivalence class 3 and adjacent to boundary value.

This example applies to the input specifications. An equally powerful technique is to examine the output specifications. For example, in 2006, the minimum Social Security deduction or, more precisely, the minimum Old-Age, Survivors, and Disability Insurance (OASDI) deduction from any one paycheck permitted by the U.S. tax code was $0 and the maximum was $5840.40, the latter corresponding to gross earnings of $94,200. Therefore, when testing a payroll product, the test cases for the Social Security deduction from

| How to Perform Sandwich Integration | Box 13.2 |

- **For** both the input and output specifications
    For each range (*L, U*)
        Select five test cases: less than *L*, equal to *L*, greater than *L* but less than *U*, equal to *U*, and greater than *U*.
    For each set *S*
        Select two test cases: a member of *S* and a nonmember of *S*.
    For each precise value *P*
        Select two cases: *P* and anything else.

paychecks should include input data that are expected to result in deductions of exactly $0 and $5840.40. In addition, test data should be set up that might result in deductions of less than $0 or more than $5840.40.

In general, for each range (R_1, R_2) listed in either the input or the output specifications, five test cases should be selected, corresponding to values less than R_1, equal to R_1, greater than R_1 but less than R_2, equal to R_2, and greater than R_2. Where it is specified that an item has to be a member of a certain set (for example, the input must be a letter), two equivalence classes must be tested, a member of the specified set and a nonmember of the set. Where the specifications lay down a precise value (for example, the response must be followed by a # sign), then again there are two equivalence classes, the specified value and anything else.

The use of equivalence classes, together with boundary value analysis, to test both the input specifications and the output specifications is a valuable technique for generating a relatively small set of test data with the potential of uncovering a number of faults that might well remain hidden if less powerful techniques for test data selection were used.

The process of equivalence testing is summarized in How to Perform Box 13.2.

13.10.2 Functional Testing

An alternative form of black-box testing is to base the test data on the functionality of the code artifact under test. In **functional testing** [Howden, 1987], the methods implemented in the code artifact under test are identified, and test data are devised to test each method separately. Now, the functional testing is taken a step further. If the code artifact consists of a hierarchy of items of lower-level functionality, connected by the control structures of structured programming, then functional testing proceeds recursively. For example, if the higher-level functionality is of the form

<higher-level functionality> ::= **if** <conditional expression>
                        <lower-level functionality 1>;
                    else
                        <lower-level functionality 2>;

then, because <conditional expression>, <lower-level functionality 1>, and <lower-level functionality 2> have been subjected to functional testing, <higher-level functionality>

can be tested using branch coverage, a glass-box technique described in Section 13.12.1. This form of structural testing is a hybrid technique—the lower-level functionalities are tested using a black-box technique, but the higher-level functionalities are tested using a glass-box technique.

In practice, however, higher-level functionalities are not constructed in such a structured fashion from lower-level functionalities. Instead, the lower-level functionalities usually are intertwined in some way. To determine faults in this situation, **functional analysis** is required, a somewhat complex procedure; for details, see [Howden, 1987]. A further complicating factor is that functionality frequently does not coincide with code artifact boundaries. Therefore, the distinction between unit testing and integration testing becomes blurred; one code artifact cannot be tested without, at the same time, testing the other code artifacts whose functionality it uses. This problem also arises when a method of one object sends a message to (invokes) a method of a different object.

The random interrelationships between code artifacts from the viewpoint of functional testing may have unacceptable consequences for management. For example, milestones and deadlines can become somewhat ill defined, making it difficult to determine the status of the product with respect to the software project management plan.

13.11 Black-Box Test Cases: The MSG Foundation Case Study

Figures 13.13 and 13.14 contain black-box test cases for the MSG Foundation case study. First consider test cases derived from equivalence classes and boundary value analysis. The first test case in Figure 13.13 tests whether the product detects an error if the itemName of an investment does not begin with an alphabetic character. The next set of five test cases checks that an itemName consists of between 1 and 25 characters. Similar test cases check other statements in the specifications, as reflected in Figure 13.13.

Turning now to functional testing, 10 functions are listed in the specification document, as shown in Figure 13.14. An additional 11 test cases correspond to misuses of these functions.

It is important to be aware that these test cases could have been developed as soon as the analysis workflow was complete; the only reason that they appear here is that test case selection is a topic of this chapter, rather than an earlier chapter. A major component of every test plan should be a stipulation that black-box test cases be drawn up as soon as the analysis artifacts have been approved, for use by the SQA group during the implementation workflow.

13.12 Glass-Box Unit-Testing Techniques

In glass-box techniques, test cases are selected on the basis of examination of the code rather than the specifications. There are a number of different forms of glass-box testing, including statement, branch, and path coverage.

Figure 13.13
Black-box
test cases
for the MSG
Foundation
case study
derived from
equivalence
classes and
boundary value
analysis.

Investment data:

Equivalence classes for itemName.

1.	First character not alphabetic	Error
2.	< 1 character	Error
3.	1 character	Acceptable
4.	Between 1 and 25 characters	Acceptable
5.	25 characters	Acceptable
6.	> 25 characters	Error (name too long)

Equivalence classes for itemNumber.

1.	Character instead of digit	Error (not a number)
2.	< 12 digits	Acceptable
3.	12 digits	Acceptable
4.	> 12 digits	Error (too many digits)

Equivalence classes for estimatedAnnualReturn and expectedAnnualOperatingExpenses.

1.	< $0.00	Error
2.	$0.00	Acceptable
3.	$0.01	Acceptable
4.	Between $0.01 and $999,999,999.97	Acceptable
5.	$999,999,999.98	Acceptable
6.	$999,999,999.99	Acceptable
7.	$1,000,000,000.00	Error
8.	> $1,000,000,000.00	Error
9.	Character instead of digit	Error (not a number)

Mortgage information:

Equivalence classes for accountNumber are same as for itemNumber above.

Equivalence classes for last name of mortgagees

1.	First character not alphabetic	Error
2.	< 1 character	Error
3.	1 character	Acceptable
4.	Between 1 and 21 characters	Acceptable
5.	21 characters	Acceptable
6.	> 21 characters	Acceptable (truncated to 21 characters)

Equivalence classes for original price of home, current family income, and mortgage balance.

1.	< $0.00	Error
2.	$0.00	Acceptable
3.	$0.01	Acceptable
4.	Between $0.01 and $999,999.98	Acceptable
5.	$999,999.98	Acceptable
6.	$999,999.99	Acceptable
7.	$1,000,000.00	Error
8.	> $1,000,000.00	Error
9.	Character instead of digit	Error (not a number)

Figure 13.13
(*continued*)

Equivalence classes for annual property tax and annual home-owner's premium.

1. < $0.00	Error
2. $0.00	Acceptable
3. $0.01	Acceptable
4. Between $0.01 and $99,999.98	Acceptable
5. $99,999.98	Acceptable
6. $99,999.99	Acceptable
7. $100,000.00	Error
8. > $100,000.00	Error
9. Character instead of digit	Error (not a number)

Figure 13.14
Functional
analysis test
cases for
the MSG
Foundation
case study.

The functions outlined in the specifications document are used to create test cases:

1. Add a mortgage.
2. Add an investment
3. Modify a mortgage.
4. Modify an investment.
5. Delete a mortgage.
6. Delete an investment.
7. Update operating expenses.
8. Compute funds to purchase houses.
9. Print list of mortgages.
10. Print list of investments.

In addition to these direct tests, it is necessary to perform the following additional tests:

11. Attempt to add a mortgage that is already on file.
12. Attempt to add an investment that is already on file.
13. Attempt to delete a mortgage that is not on file.
14. Attempt to delete an investment that is not on file.
15. Attempt to modify a mortgage that is not on file.
16. Attempt to modify an investment that is not on file.
17. Attempt to delete twice a mortgage that is already on file.
18. Attempt to delete twice an investment that is already on file.
19. Attempt to update each field of a mortgage twice and check that the second version is stored.
20. Attempt to update each field of an investment twice and check that the second version is stored.
21. Attempt to update operating expenses twice and check that second version is stored.

13.12.1 Structural Testing: Statement, Branch, and Path Coverage

The simplest form of glass-box unit testing is **statement coverage**, that is, running a series of test cases during which every statement is executed at least once. To keep track of which statements are still to be executed, a CASE tool keeps a record of how many times each statement has been executed over the series of tests; PureCoverage is an example of such a tool.

A weakness of this approach is that there is no guarantee that all outcomes of branches are properly tested. To see this, consider the code fragment of Figure 13.15. The programmer made a mistake; the compound conditional $s > 1$ && $t == 0$ should read $s > 1$ || $t == 0$.

Figure 13.15
Code fragment
with test data.

```
if (s > 1 && t == 0)
    x = 9;
```

Test case: s = 2, t = 0.

The test data shown in the figure allow the statement x = 9 to be executed without the fault being highlighted.

An improvement over statement coverage is **branch coverage**, that is, running a series of tests to ensure that all branches are tested at least once. Again, a tool usually is needed to help the tester keep track of which branches have or have not been tested. Techniques such as statement or branch coverage are termed **structural tests**.

The most powerful form of structural testing is **path coverage**, that is, testing all paths. As shown previously, in a product with loops, the number of paths can be very large indeed. As a result, researchers have been investigating ways of reducing the number of paths to be examined while uncovering more faults than would be possible using branch coverage. One criterion for selecting paths is to restrict test cases to **linear code sequences** [Woodward, Hedley, and Hennell, 1980]. To do this, first identify the set of points L from which control flow may jump. The set L includes entry and exit points and branch statements such as an **if** or **goto** statement. The linear code sequences are those paths that begin at an element of L and end at an element of L. The technique has been successful in that it has uncovered many faults without having to test every path.

Another way of reducing the number of paths to test is **all-definition-use-path coverage** [Rapps and Weyuker, 1985]. In this technique, each occurrence of a variable pqr, say, in the source code is labeled either as a *definition* of the variable, such as pqr = 1 or read (pqr), or a *use* of the variable, such as y = pqr + 3 or **if** (pqr < 9) errorB (). All paths between the definition of a variable and the use of that definition are identified, nowadays by means of an automatic tool. Finally, a test case is set up for each such path. All-definition-use-path coverage is an excellent test technique in that large numbers of faults frequently are detected by relatively few test cases. However, all-definition-use-path coverage has the weakness that the upper bound on the number of paths is 2^d, where d is the number of decision statements (branches) in the product. Examples can be constructed exhibiting the upper bound. However, it has been shown that, for real products as opposed to artificial examples, this upper bound is not reached, and the actual number of paths is proportional to d [Weyuker, 1988a]. In other words, the number of test cases needed for all-definition-use-path coverage generally is much smaller than the theoretical upper bound. Therefore, all-definition-use-path coverage is a practical test case selection technique.

When using structural testing, the tester simply might not come up with a test case that exercises a specific statement, branch, or path. What may have happened is that an infeasible path ("dead code") is in the code artifact, that is, a path that cannot possibly be executed for any input data. Figure 13.16 shows two examples of infeasible paths. In Figure 13.16(a) the programmer omitted a minus sign. If k is less than 2, then k cannot possibly be greater than 3, so the statement x = x * k cannot be reached. Similarly, in Figure 13.16(b), j is never less than 0, so the statement total = total + value[j] can never be reached; the programmer had intended the test to be j < 10, but made a typing mistake. A tester using statement coverage would soon realize that neither statement could be reached, and the faults would be found.

Figure 13.16
Two examples
of infeasible
paths.

```
if (k < 2)
{
    if (k > 3)              [should be: k > −3]
         ↑
       x = x * k;
}
                        (a)
```

```
for (j = 0; j < 0; j++)  [should be: j < 10]
              ↑
    total = total + value[j];
                  (b)
```

13.12.2 Complexity Metrics

The quality assurance viewpoint provides another approach to glass-box unit testing. Suppose a manager is told that code artifact m1 is more complex than code artifact m2. Irrespective of the precise way in which the term *complex* is defined, the manager intuitively believes that m1 is likely to have more faults than m2. Following this idea, computer scientists have developed a number of metrics of software **complexity** as an aid in determining which code artifacts are most likely to have faults. If the complexity of a code artifact is found to be unreasonably high, a manager may direct that the artifact be redesigned and reimplemented on the grounds that it probably is less costly and faster to start from scratch than to attempt to debug a fault-prone code artifact.

A simple metric for predicting numbers of faults is lines of code. The underlying assumption is that there is a constant probability, p, that a line of code contains a fault. If a tester believes that, on average, a line of code has a 2 percent chance of containing a fault, and the artifact under test is 100 lines long, then this implies that the artifact is expected to contain two faults; and an artifact that is twice as long is likely to have four faults. Basili and Hutchens [1983] as well as Takahashi and Kamayachi [1985] showed that the number of faults indeed is related to the size of the product as a whole.

Attempts have been made to find more sophisticated predictors of faults based on measures of product complexity. A typical contender is McCabe's [1976] measure of **cyclomatic complexity**, the number of binary decisions (predicates) plus 1. As described in Section 12.10, the cyclomatic complexity essentially is the number of branches in the code artifact. Accordingly, cyclomatic complexity can be used as a metric for the number of test cases needed for branch coverage of a code artifact. This is the basis for so-called **structured testing** [Watson and McCabe, 1996].

McCabe's metric can be computed almost as easily as lines of code. In some cases, it has been shown to be a good metric for predicting faults; the higher the value of M, the greater is the chance that a code artifact contains a fault. For example, Walsh [1979] analyzed 276 modules in the Aegis system, a shipboard combat system. Measuring the cyclomatic complexity, M, he found that 23 percent of the modules with M greater than or equal to 10 had 53 percent of the faults detected. In addition, the modules with M greater than or equal to 10 had 21 percent more faults per line of code than the modules with smaller M values. However, the validity of McCabe's metric has been questioned seriously on both theoretical grounds and the basis of the many different experiments cited in [Shepperd, 1988b] and [Shepperd and Ince, 1994].

Musa, Iannino, and Okumoto [1987] analyzed the data available on fault densities. They concluded that most complexity metrics, including McCabe's, show a high correlation with the number of lines of code or, more precisely, the number of deliverable, executable source instructions. In other words, when researchers measure what they believe to be the complexity of a code artifact or a product, the result they obtain largely may be a reflection of the number of lines of code, a measure that correlates strongly with the number of faults. In addition, complexity metrics provide little improvement over lines of code for predicting fault rates. Other problems with complexity are discussed in [Shepperd and Ince, 1994].

13.13 Code Walkthroughs and Inspections

Section 6.2 made a strong case for the use of walkthroughs and inspections in general. The same arguments hold for code walkthroughs and inspections. In brief, the fault-detecting power of these two non-execution-based techniques leads to rapid, thorough, and early fault detection. The additional time required for code walkthroughs or inspections is more than repaid by increased productivity due to the presence of fewer faults when integration is performed. Furthermore, code inspections have led to a reduction of up to 95 percent in corrective maintenance costs [Crossman, 1982].

Another reason why code inspections should be performed is that the alternative, execution-based testing (test cases), can be extremely expensive in two ways. First, it is time consuming. Second, inspections lead to detection and correction of faults earlier in the life cycle than with execution-based testing. As reflected in Figure 1.5, the earlier a fault is detected and corrected, the less it costs. An extreme case of the high cost of running test cases is that 80 percent of the budget for the software of the NASA Apollo Program was consumed by testing [Dunn, 1984].

Further arguments in favor of walkthroughs and inspections are given in Section 13.14.

13.14 Comparison of Unit-Testing Techniques

A number of studies have compared strategies for unit testing. Myers [1978a] compared black-box testing, a combination of black-box and glass-box testing, and three-person code walkthroughs. The experiment was performed using 59 highly experienced programmers testing the same product. All three techniques were equally effective in finding faults, but code walkthroughs proved to be less cost effective than the other two techniques. Hwang [1981] compared black-box testing, glass-box testing, and code reading by one person. All three techniques were found to be equally effective, with each technique having its own strengths and weaknesses. A major experiment was conducted by Basili and Selby [1987]. The techniques compared were the same as in Hwang's experiment: black-box testing, glass-box testing, and one-person code reading. The subjects were 32 professional programmers and 42 advanced students. Each tested three products, using each testing technique once. Fractional factorial design [Basili and Weiss, 1984] was used to compensate for the different ways the products were tested by different participants; no participant tested the same product in more than one way. Different results were obtained from the two groups of participants. The professional programmers detected more faults with code reading than with the other two techniques, and the fault detection rate was faster. Two groups of advanced students participated. In one group, no significant difference was found among the three techniques; in the other, code reading and black-box testing were equally good and both outperformed glass-box testing. However, the rate at which students detected faults was the same for all techniques. Overall, code reading led to the detection of more interface faults than the other two techniques, whereas black-box testing was most successful at finding control faults. The main conclusion that can be drawn from this experiment is that code inspection is at least as successful at detecting faults as glass-box and black-box testing.

A development technique that makes good use of this conclusion is the Cleanroom software development technique.

13.15 Cleanroom

The **Cleanroom** technique [Linger, 1994] is a combination of a number of different software development techniques, including an incremental life-cycle model, formal techniques for analysis and design, and non-execution-based unit-testing techniques, such as code reading [Mills, Dyer, and Linger, 1987] and code walkthroughs and inspections (Section 13.13). A critical aspect of Cleanroom is that a code artifact is not compiled until it has passed inspection. That is, a code artifact should be compiled only after non-execution-based testing has been successfully completed.

The technique has had a number of great successes. For example, a prototype automated documentation system was developed for the U.S. Naval Underwater Systems Center using Cleanroom [Trammel, Binder, and Snyder, 1992]. Altogether 18 faults were detected while the design underwent "functional verification," a review process in which correctness-proving techniques are employed (Section 6.5). Informal proofs such as the one presented in Section 6.5.1 were used as much as possible; full mathematical proofs were developed only when participants were unsure of the correctness of the portion of the design being inspected. Another 19 faults were detected during walkthroughs of the 1820 lines of FoxBASE code; when the code was then compiled, there were no compilation errors. Furthermore, there were no failures at execution time. This is an additional indication of the power of non-execution-based testing techniques.

This certainly is an impressive result. But, as has been pointed out, results that apply to small-scale software products cannot necessarily be scaled up to large-scale software. In the case of Cleanroom, however, results for larger products also are impressive. The relevant metric is the **testing fault rate**, that is, the total number of faults detected per KLOC (thousand lines of code), a relatively common metric in the software industry. Yet, there is a critical difference in the way this metric is computed when Cleanroom is used as opposed to traditional development techniques.

As pointed out in Section 6.6, when traditional development techniques are used, a code artifact is tested informally by its programmer while it is being developed and thereafter it is tested methodically by the SQA group. Faults detected by the programmer while developing the code are not recorded. However, from the time the artifact leaves the private workspace of the programmer and is handed over to the SQA group for execution-based and non-execution-based testing, a tally is kept of the number of faults detected. In contrast, when Cleanroom is used, "testing faults" are counted from the time of compilation. Fault counting then continues through execution-based testing. In other words, when traditional development techniques are used, faults detected informally by the programmer do not count toward the testing fault rate. When Cleanroom is used, faults detected during the inspections and other non-execution-based testing procedures that precede compilation are recorded, but they do not count toward the testing fault rate.

A report on 17 Cleanroom products appears in [Linger, 1994]. For example, Cleanroom was used to develop the 350,000-line Ericsson Telecom OS32 operating system. The product was developed in 18 months by a team of 70. The testing fault rate was only 1.0 fault per KLOC. Another product was the prototype automated documentation system described previously; the testing fault rate was 0.0 faults per KLOC for the 1820-line program. The 17 products together total nearly 1 million lines of code. The weighted average testing fault rate was 2.3 faults per KLOC, which Linger describes as a remarkable quality achievement. That praise certainly is no exaggeration.

13.16 Testing Issues

One of the many reasons put forward for using the object-oriented paradigm is that it reduces the need for testing. Reuse via inheritance is a major strength of the paradigm; once a class has been tested, the argument goes, there is no need to retest it. Furthermore, new methods defined within a subclass of such a tested class have to be tested, but inherited methods need no further testing.

In fact, both claims are only partially true. In addition, the testing of objects poses certain problems that are specific to object orientation. These issues are discussed here.

To begin, it is necessary to clarify an issue regarding the testing of classes and of objects. As explained in Section 7.7, a class is an abstract data type that supports inheritance, and an object is an instance of a class. That is, a class has no concrete realization, whereas an object is a physical piece of code executing within a specific environment. Therefore, it is impossible to perform execution-based testing on a class; only non-execution-based testing, such as an inspection, can be done.

Information hiding and the fact that many methods consist of relatively few lines of code can have a significant impact on testing. First, consider a product developed using the classical paradigm. Nowadays, such a product generally consists of modules of roughly 50 executable instructions. The interface between a module and the rest of the product is the argument list. Arguments are of two kinds, input arguments supplied to the module when it is invoked and output arguments returned by the module when it returns control to the calling module. Testing a module consists of supplying values to the input arguments and invoking the module and then comparing the values of the output arguments to the predicted results of the test.

In contrast, a "typical" object contains perhaps 30 methods, many of which are relatively small, frequently just two or three executable statements [Wilde, Matthews, and Huitt, 1993]. These methods do not return a value to the caller but rather change the state of the object. That is, these methods modify attributes (state variables) of the object. The difficulty here is that, to test that the change of state has been performed correctly, it is necessary to send additional messages to the object. For example, consider the bank account object described in Section 1.9. The effect of method deposit is to increase the value of state variable accountBalance. However, as a consequence of information hiding, the only way to test whether a particular deposit method has been executed correctly is to invoke method determineBalance both before and after invoking method deposit and see how the bank balance changes.

The situation is worse if the object does not include methods that can be invoked to determine the values of all the state variables. One alternative is to include additional methods for this purpose and then use conditional compilation to ensure that they are unavailable except for testing purposes (in C++, this can be implemented using #ifdef). The test plan (Section 9.7) should stipulate that the value of every state variable be accessible during testing. To satisfy this requirement, additional methods that return the values of the state variables may have to be added to the relevant classes during the design workflow. As a result, it is possible to test the effect of invoking a specific method of an object by querying the value of the applicable state variable.

Surprisingly enough, an inherited method still may have to be tested. That is, even if a method has been adequately tested, it may require thorough testing when inherited, unchanged, by a subclass. To see this latter point, consider the class hierarchy shown in Figure 13.17. Two methods, namely, displayNodeContents and printRoutine, are

Figure 13.17
A Java implementation of a tree hierarchy.

```
class RootedTreeClass
{
   ...
   void displayNodeContents (Node a);
   void printRoutine (Node b);
//
// method displayNodeContents uses method printRoutine
//
   ...
}

class BinaryTreeClass extends RootedTreeClass
{
   ...
   void displayNodeContents (Node a);
//
// method displayNodeContents defined in this class uses
// method printRoutine inherited from RootedTreeClass
//
   ...
}

class BalancedBinaryTreeClass extends BinaryTreeClass
{
   ...
   void printRoutine (Node b);
//
// method displayNodeContents (inherited from BinaryTreeClass) uses this
// local version of printRoutine within class BalancedBinaryTreeClass
//
   ...
}
```

defined in the base class **RootedTreeClass**, where method displayNodeContents uses method printRoutine.

Next consider subclass **BinaryTreeClass**. This subclass inherits method printRoutine from its base class **RootedTreeClass**. In addition, a new method, displayNodeContents, is defined that overrides the method defined in **RootedTreeClass**. This new method still uses printRoutine. In Java notation, BinaryTreeClass.displayNodeContents uses RootedTreeClass.printRoutine.

Now consider the subclass **BalancedBinaryTreeClass**. This subclass inherits method displayNodeContents from its superclass **BinaryTreeClass**. However, a new method printRoutine is defined that overrides the one defined in **RootedTreeClass**. When displayNodeContents uses printRoutine within the context of **Balanced-BinaryTreeClass**, the scope rules of C++ and Java specify that the local version of printRoutine is to be used. In Java notation, when method BinaryTreeClass.display NodeContents is invoked within the lexical scope of **BalancedBinaryTreeClass**, it uses method BalancedBinaryTreeClass.printRoutine.

Therefore, the actual code (method printRoutine) executed when displayNodeContents is invoked within instantiations of **BinaryTreeClass** is different from what is executed when displayNodeContents is invoked within instantiations of **BalancedBinaryTreeClass**. This holds notwithstanding that the method displayNodeContents itself is inherited, unchanged, by **BalancedBinaryTreeClass** from **BinaryTreeClass**. Therefore, even if method displayNodeContents has been thoroughly tested within a **BinaryTreeClass** object, it has to be retested from scratch when reused within a **BalancedBinaryTreeClass** environment. To make matters even more complex, there are theoretical reasons why it needs to be retested with different test cases [Perry and Kaiser, 1990].

It must be pointed out immediately that these complications are no reason to abandon the object-oriented paradigm. First, they arise only through the interaction of methods (displayNodeContents and printRoutine in the example). Second, it is possible to determine when this retesting is needed [Harrold, McGregor, and Fitzpatrick, 1992].

Suppose an instantiation of a class has been thoroughly tested. Any new or redefined methods of a subclass then need to be tested, together with methods flagged for retesting because of their interaction with other methods. In short, then, the claim that use of the object-oriented paradigm reduces the need for testing largely is true.

Some management implications of unit testing now are considered.

13.17 Management Aspects of Unit Testing

An important decision that must be made during the development of every code artifact is how much time, and therefore money, to spend on testing of that artifact. As with so many other economic issues in software engineering, cost–benefit analysis (Section 5.2) can play a useful role. For example, the decision as to whether the cost of correctness proving exceeds the benefit of the assurance that a specific product satisfies its specifications can be decided on the basis of cost–benefit analysis. Cost–benefit analysis also can be used to compare the cost of running additional test cases against the cost of failure of the delivered product caused by inadequate testing.

There is another approach for determining whether testing of a specific code artifact should continue or it is likely that virtually all the faults have been removed. The techniques of reliability analysis can be used to provide statistical estimates of how many faults remain. A variety of different techniques have been proposed for determining statistical estimates of the number of remaining faults. The basic idea underlying these techniques is the following. Suppose a code artifact is tested for 1 week. On Monday, 23 faults are found and 7 more on Tuesday. On Wednesday, five more faults are found, two on Thursday, and none on Friday. Because the rate of fault detection decreases steadily from 23 faults per day to none, it seems likely that most faults have been found, and testing that code artifact could be halted. Determining the probability that there are no more faults in the code requires a level of mathematical statistics beyond that required for readers of this book. Details therefore are not given here; the reader interested in reliability analysis should consult Grady [1992].

13.18 When to Rewrite Rather than Debug a Code Artifact

When a member of the SQA group detects a failure (erroneous output), as stated previously, the code artifact must be returned to the original programmer for ***debugging***, that is, detection of the fault and correction of the code. On some occasions, it is preferable for the code artifact to be thrown away and redesigned and recoded from scratch, either by the original programmer or by another, possibly more senior, member of the development team.

To see why this may be necessary, consider Figure 13.18. The graph shows the counterintuitive concept that the probability of the existence of more faults in a code artifact is proportional to the number of faults already found in that code artifact [Myers, 1979]. To see why this should be so, consider two code artifacts, a1 and a2. Suppose that both code artifacts are approximately the same length and both have been tested for the same number of hours. Suppose further that only 2 faults were detected in a1, but 48 faults were detected in a2. It is likely that more faults remain to be rooted out of a2 than out of a1. Furthermore, additional testing and debugging of a2 is likely to be a lengthy process, and the suspicion that a2 is still not perfect will remain. In both the short run and the long run, it is preferable to discard a2, redesign it, and then recode it.

The distribution of faults in modules certainly is not uniform. Myers [1979] cites the example of faults found by users in OS/370. It was found that 47 percent of the faults were associated with only 4 percent of the modules. An earlier study by Endres [1975] regarding

Figure 13.18
Graph showing that the probability that faults are still to be found is proportional to the number of faults already detected.

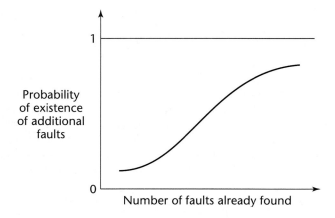

Probability of existence of additional faults

Number of faults already found

The discussion regarding the maximum permitted number of faults detected during development of a code artifact means precisely that: the maximum number permitted *during development*. The maximum permitted number of faults detected after the product has been delivered to the client should be *zero* for all code artifacts of all products. That is, it should be the aim of every software engineer to deliver fault-free code to the client.

internal tests of DOS/VS (Release 28) at IBM Laboratories, Böblingen, Germany, showed similar nonuniformity. Of the total of 512 faults detected in 202 modules, only 1 fault was detected in each of 112 of the modules. On the other hand, some modules were found to have 14, 15, 19, and 28 faults, respectively. Endres points out that the latter three modules were three of the largest modules in the product, each comprising over 3000 lines of DOS macro assembler language. However, the module with 14 faults was a relatively small module previously known to be extremely unstable. This type of module is a prime candidate for being discarded and recoded.

The way for management to cope with this sort of situation is to predetermine the maximum number of faults permitted during development of a given code artifact; when that maximum is reached, the code artifact must be thrown away, and then redesigned and recoded, preferably by an experienced software professional. This maximum varies from application domain to application domain and from code artifact to code artifact. After all, the maximum permitted number of faults detected in a code artifact that reads a record from a database and checks the validity of the part number should be far smaller than the number of faults in a complex code artifact from a tank weapons control system that must coordinate data from a variety of sensors and direct the aim of the main gun toward the intended target. One way to decide on the maximum fault figure for a specific code artifact is to examine fault data on similar code artifacts that have required corrective maintenance. But, whatever estimation technique is used, management must ensure that the code artifact is scrapped if that figure is exceeded (but see Just in Case You Wanted to Know Box 13.6.)

13.19 Integration Testing

Each new code artifact must be tested when it is added to what has already been integrated; this is termed **integration testing**. The key point here is first to test the new code artifact as described in Sections 13.9 through 13.13 (unit testing) and then to check that the rest of the partial product continues to behave as it did before the new code artifact was integrated into it.

When the product has a graphical user interface, special issues can arise with regard to integration testing. In general, testing a product usually can be simplified by storing the input data for a test case in a file. The product then is executed, and the relevant data submitted to it. With the aid of a CASE tool, the whole process can be automated; that is, a set of test cases is set up, together with the expected outcome of each case. The CASE tool runs each test case, compares the actual results with the expected results, and reports to the user on each case. The test cases then are stored, for use in regression testing whenever the product is modified. SilkTest is an example of a tool of this kind.

However, when a product incorporates a graphical user interface, this approach does not work. Specifically, test data for pulling down a menu or clicking on a mouse button cannot be stored in a file in the same way as conventional test data. At the same time, it is time consuming and boring to test a GUI manually. The solution to this problem is to use a special CASE tool that keeps a record of mouse clicks, key presses, and so on. The GUI is tested once manually so that the CASE tool can set up the test file. Thereafter, this file is used in subsequent tests. A number of CASE tools support testing GUIs, including QARun and XRunner.

When the integration process is complete, the product as a whole is tested; this is termed **product testing**. When the developers are confident about the correctness of every aspect of the product, it is handed over to the client for **acceptance testing**. These two forms of testing are now described in more detail.

13.20 Product Testing

The fact that the last code artifact has been integrated successfully into the product does not mean that the task of the developers is complete. The SQA group still must perform a number of testing tasks to ascertain that the product will be successful. There are two main types of software, commercial off-the-shelf (COTS) software (Section 1.10) and custom software. The aim of COTS product testing is to ensure that the product as a whole is free of faults. When the product testing is complete, the product undergoes alpha and beta testing, as described in Section 3.7.4. That is, preliminary versions are shipped to selected prospective buyers of the product to get feedback, particularly regarding residual faults overlooked by the SQA team.

Custom software, on the other hand, undergoes somewhat different product testing. The SQA group performs a number of testing tasks to be certain that the product will not fail its acceptance test, the final hurdle that the custom software development team must overcome. The failure of a product to pass its acceptance test almost always is a poor reflection on the management capabilities of the development organization. The client may conclude that the developers are incompetent, which all but guarantees that the client will do everything to avoid employing those developers again. Worse, the client may believe that the developers are dishonest and deliberately handed over substandard software to finish the contract and be paid as quickly as possible. If the client genuinely believes this and tells other potential clients, then the developers face a major public relations problem. It is up to the SQA group to make sure the product passes the acceptance test with flying colors.

To ensure a successful acceptance test, the SQA group must test the product using tests that the SQA group believes closely approximate the forthcoming acceptance tests:

- Black-box test cases for the product as a whole must be run. Up to now, test cases have been set up on an artifact-by-artifact or class-by-class basis, ensuring that each code artifact or class individually satisfies its specifications.

- The robustness of the product as a whole must be tested. Again, the robustness of individual code artifacts and classes was tested during integration; now productwide robustness is the issue for which test cases must be set up and run. In addition, the product must be subjected to **stress testing**, that is, making sure that it behaves correctly when operating under a peak load, such as all terminals trying to log on at the same time or customers operating all the automated teller machines simultaneously. The product also must be subjected to **volume testing**, for example, making sure that it can handle large input files.

- The SQA group must check that the product satisfies all its constraints. For example, if the specifications state that the response time for 95 percent of queries when the product is working under full load must be under 3 seconds, then it is the responsibility of the SQA group to verify that this indeed is the case. There is no question that the client will check constraints during acceptance testing; and if the product fails to meet a major constraint, then the development organization will lose a considerable amount of credibility. Similarly, storage constraints and security constraints must be checked.

- The SQA group must review all documentation to be handed over to the client together with the code. The SQA group must check that the documentation conforms to the standards laid down in the SPMP. In addition, the documentation must be checked against the product. For instance, the SQA group has to determine that the user manual indeed reflects the correct way of using the product and that the product functions as specified in the user manual.

Once the SQA group assures management that the product can handle anything the acceptance testers can throw at it, the product (that is, the code plus all the documentation) is handed to the client organization for acceptance testing.

13.21 Acceptance Testing

The purpose of acceptance testing is for the client to determine whether the product indeed satisfies its specifications as claimed by the developer. Acceptance testing is done by either the client organization, the SQA group in the presence of client representatives, or an independent SQA group hired by the client for this purpose. Acceptance testing naturally includes correctness testing, but in addition, it is necessary to test performance and robustness. The four major components of acceptance testing—testing correctness, robustness, performance, and documentation—are exactly what is done by the developer during product testing; this is not surprising, because product testing is a comprehensive rehearsal for the acceptance test.

A key aspect of acceptance testing is that it must be performed on actual data rather than on test data. No matter how well test cases are set up, by their very nature, they are artificial. More important, test data should be a true reflection of the corresponding actual data, but in practice, this is not always the case. For example, the member of the specification team responsible for characterizing the actual data may perform this task incorrectly. Alternatively, even if the data are specified correctly, the SQA group member who uses that data specification may misunderstand or misinterpret it. The resulting test cases are not a true reflection of the actual data, leading to an inadequately tested product. For these reasons, acceptance testing must be performed on actual data. Furthermore, because the development team endeavors to ensure that the product testing duplicates every aspect of the acceptance testing, as much of the product testing as possible should also be performed on actual data.

When a new product is to replace an existing one, the specification document almost always includes a clause to the effect that the new product must be installed to run in parallel with the existing product. The reason is that there is a very real possibility that the new product may be faulty in some way. The existing product works correctly but is inadequate in some respects. If the existing product is replaced by a new product that works incorrectly, then the client is in trouble. Therefore, both products must run in parallel until the client is satisfied that the new product can take over the functions of the existing product. Successful parallel running concludes acceptance testing, and the existing product can be retired.

When the product has passed its acceptance test, the task of the developers is complete. Any changes now made to that product constitute postdelivery maintenance.

Case Study

13.22 The Test Workflow: The MSG Foundation Case Study

The C++ and Java implementations of the MSG Foundation product (available for download at **www.mhhe.com/schach**) were tested against the black-box test cases of Figures 13.13 and 13.14, as well as the glass-box test cases of Problems 13.30 through 13.34.

13.23 CASE Tools for Implementation

CASE tools to support implementation of code artifacts were described in some detail in Chapter 5. For integration, version-control tools, build tools, and configuration management tools are needed (Chapter 5). The reason is that code artifacts under test change continually as a consequence of faults being detected and corrected, and these CASE tools are essential to ensure that the appropriate version of each artifact is compiled and linked. Commercially available configuration-control workbenches include PVCS and SourceSafe. A popular open-source configuration-control tool is CVS.

In each chapter so far, CASE tools and workbenches specific to that workflow have been described. Now that all workflows of the development process have been described, it is appropriate to consider CASE tools for the process as a whole.

13.23.1 CASE Tools for the Complete Software Process

There is a natural progression within CASE. As described in Section 5.5, the simplest CASE device is a single *tool*, such as an online interface checker or a build tool. Next, tools can be combined, leading to a *workbench* that supports one or two activities within the software process, such as configuration control or coding. However, such a workbench might not provide management information even for the limited portion of the software process to which it is applicable, let alone for the project as a whole. Finally, an *environment* provides computer aided support for most, if not all, of the process.

Ideally, every software development organization should utilize an environment. But the cost of an environment can be large—not just the package itself but the hardware on which to run it. For a smaller organization, a workbench, or perhaps just a set of tools, may suffice. But, if at all possible, an *integrated environment* should be utilized to support the development and maintenance effort.

13.23.2 Integrated Development Environments

The most common meaning of the word *integrated* within the CASE context is in terms of **user interface integration**. That is, all the tools in the environment share a common user interface. The idea behind this is that, if all the tools have the same visual appearance, the user of one tool should have little difficulty in learning and using another tool in the environment. This has been successfully achieved on the Macintosh, where most applications have a similar "look and feel." Although this is the usual meaning, there are other types of integration as well.

The term **tool integration** means that all the tools communicate via the same data format. For example, in the UNIX Programmer's Workbench, the UNIX pipe formalism assumes that all data are in the form of an ASCII stream. It therefore is easy to combine two tools by directing the output stream from one tool to the input stream of the other tool. Eclipse is an open-source environment for tool integration.

Process integration refers to an environment that supports one specific software process. A subset of this class of environment is the **technique-based environment** (but see Just in Case You Wanted to Know Box 13.7). An environment of this type supports only a specific technique for developing software, rather than a complete process. The majority of these environments provide graphical support for analysis and design and incorporate a data dictionary. Some consistency checking usually is provided. Support for managing the development process frequently is incorporated into the environment. Many environments of this type are commercially available, including Rhapsody, which supports statecharts [Harel et al., 1990], and IBM Rational Rose, which supports the Unified Process [Jacobson, Booch, and Rumbaugh, 1999]. In addition, some older environments have been extended to support the object-oriented paradigm; Software through Pictures is an example of this type.

The emphasis in most technique-based environments is on the support and formalization of the manual operations for software development laid down by the technique. That is, these environments force users to utilize the technique step by step in the way intended by its author, while assisting the user by providing graphical tools, a data dictionary, and consistency checking. This computerized framework is a strength of technique-based environments in that users are forced to use a specific technique and use it correctly. But it can be a weakness as well. Unless the software process of the organization incorporates this specific technique, use of a technique-based environment can be counterproductive.

13.23.3 Environments for Business Applications

An important class of environments is used for building business-oriented products. The emphasis is on ease of use, achieved in a number of ways. In particular, the environment incorporates a number of standard screens, and these can be modified endlessly via a user-friendly GUI generator. One popular feature of such environments is a code generator. The lowest level of abstraction of a product then is the detailed design. The detailed design is the input to a code generator that automatically generates code in a language such as C++ or Java. This automatically generated code is compiled; no "programming" of any kind is performed on it.

Languages for specifying the detailed design could well be the programming languages of the future. The level of abstraction of programming languages rose from the physical machine level of first-generation languages (machine code) and second-generation languages (assemblers) to the abstract machine level of third-generation (high-level) and fourth-generation languages. Today, the level of abstraction of environments of this type is the detailed design level, a portable level. The use of code generators can result in quicker development and easier postdelivery maintenance; the programmer has to provide fewer details to a code generator than to an interpreter or compiler. Therefore, it is expected that use of business-oriented environments that support code generators will increase productivity.

A number of environments of this type are currently available, including Oracle Developer Suite. Bearing in mind the size of the market for business-oriented CASE environments, it is likely that many more environments of this type will be developed in future years.

13.23.4 Public Tool Infrastructures

The European Strategic Programme for Research in Information Technology (ESPRIT) developed an infrastructure for supporting CASE tools. Despite its name, the ***portable common tool environment (PCTE)*** [Long and Morris, 1993] is *not* an environment. Instead, it is an infrastructure that provides the services needed by CASE tools, in much the same way that UNIX provides the operating system services needed by user products. (The word *common* in PCTE is in the sense of "public" or "not copyrighted.")

PCTE has gained widespread acceptance. For example, PCTE and the C and Ada interfaces to PCTE were adopted as ISO/IEC Standard 13719 in 1995. Implementations of PCTE include those of Emeraude and IBM.

The hope is that, in the future, many more CASE tools will conform to the PCTE standard and that PCTE itself will be implemented on a wider variety of computers. A tool that conforms to PCTE would run on any computer that supports PCTE. Accordingly, this should result in the widespread availability of a broad range of CASE tools. This, in turn, should lead to better software processes and better-quality software.

13.23.5 Potential Problems with Environments

No one environment is ideal for all products and all organizations, any more than one programming language can be considered "the best." Every environment has its strengths and its weaknesses, and choosing an inappropriate environment can be worse than using no environment at all. For example, as explained in Section 13.23.2, a technique-based environment essentially automates a manual process. If an organization chooses to use an environment that enforces a technique inappropriate for it as a whole or for a current software product under development, then use of that CASE environment is counterproductive.

A worse situation occurs when an organization chooses to ignore the advice of Section 5.10, that the use of a CASE environment should be firmly avoided until the organization has attained CMM level 3. Of course, every organization should use CASE tools, and there generally is little harm in using a workbench. However, an environment imposes an automated software process on an organization that uses it. If a good process is being used, that is, the organization is at level 3 or higher, then use of the environment assists in all aspects of software production by automating that process. But, if the organization is at the crisis-driven level 1 or even at level 2, then no process as such is in place. Automation of this nonexistent process, that is, the introduction of a CASE environment (as opposed to a CASE tool or CASE workbench), can lead only to chaos.

13.24 CASE Tools for the Test Workflow

Numerous CASE tools are available to support the different types of testing that are performed during the implementation workflow. First consider unit testing. The XUnit testing frameworks, including JUnit for Java and CppUnit for C++, are a set of open-source automated tools for unit testing; that is, they are utilized to test each class in turn. A set of test cases is prepared, and the tool checks that each of the messages sent to the class results in the expected answer being returned. Commercial tools of this type are produced by many vendors, including Parasoft.

We now turn to integration testing. Examples of commercial tools that support automated integration testing (as well as unit testing) include SilkTest and IBM Rational Functional Tester. It is common for tools of this kind to pool the unit-testing test cases and utilize the resulting set of test cases for integration testing and regression testing.

During the test workflow, it is essential for management to know the status of all defects. In particular, it is vital to know which defects have been detected but have not yet been corrected. The best-known defect-tracking tool is Bugzilla, an open-source product.

Returning to Figure 1.5 yet again, it is vital to detect coding faults as soon as possible. One way to achieve this is to use a CASE tool to analyze the code, looking for common syntactic and semantic faults, or constructs that could lead to problems later. Examples of such tools include IBM Rational Purify, Sun's Jackpot Source Code Metrics, and three Microsoft tools: PREfix, PREfast, and SLAM.

The Hyades project (otherwise known as the Eclipse test and performance tools project) is an open-source integrated test, trace, and monitoring environment that currently can be used with Java and C++. It has facilities for a variety of different testing tools. As more and more tool vendors adapt their tools to work under Eclipse, users will be able to select from a wider choice of testing tools, all of which will work in conjunction with one another.

13.25 Metrics for the Implementation Workflow

A number of different complexity metrics for the implementation workflow are discussed in Section 13.12.2, including lines of code and McCabe's cyclomatic complexity.

From a testing viewpoint, the relevant metrics include the total number of test cases and the number of test cases that resulted in a failure. The usual fault statistics must be maintained for code inspections. The total number of faults is important, because if the number of faults detected in a code artifact exceeds a predetermined maximum, then that code artifact must be redesigned and recoded, as discussed in Section 13.19. In addition, detailed statistics need to be kept regarding the types of faults detected. Typical fault types include misunderstanding the design, lack of initialization, and inconsistent use of variables. The fault data can be incorporated into the checklists to be used during code inspections of future products.

A number of metrics specific to the object-oriented paradigm have been put forward, for example, the height of the inheritance tree [Chidamber and Kemerer, 1994]. Many of these metrics have been questioned on both theoretical and experimental grounds [Binkley and Schach, 1996; 1997]. Furthermore, Alshayeb and Li [2003] have shown that, whereas object-oriented metrics can relatively accurately predict the number of lines of code added, changed, and deleted in agile processes, they are of little use in predicting the same measures in a framework-based process (see Section 8.5.2). It remains to be shown that there is a need for specifically object-oriented metrics, as opposed to classical metrics that can be applied equally to object-oriented software.

13.26 Challenges of the Implementation Workflow

Paradoxically, a major challenge of the implementation workflow has to be met in the workflows that precede it. As explained in Chapter 8, code reuse is an effective way of reducing software development cost and delivery time. However, it is hard to achieve code reuse if it is attempted as late as the implementation workflow.

For example, suppose the decision is made to implement a product in language L. Now, after half the code artifacts have been implemented and tested, management decides to utilize package P for the graphical user interfaces of the software product. No matter how powerful the routines of P may be, if they are written in a language that is hard to interface with L, then they cannot be reused in the software product.

Even if language interoperability is not an issue, there is little point in trying to reuse an existing code artifact unless the item to be reused fits the design exactly. More work may be needed to modify the existing code artifact than to create a new code artifact from scratch.

Code reuse therefore has to be built into a software product from the very beginning. Reuse has to be a user requirement as well as a constraint of the specification document. The software project management plan (Section 9.6) must incorporate reuse. Also, the design document must state which code artifacts are to be implemented and which are to be reused.

So, as stated at the beginning of this section, even though code reuse is an important challenge of implementation, code reuse has to be incorporated into the requirements, analysis, and design workflows.

From a purely technical viewpoint, the implementation workflow is relatively straightforward. If the requirements, analysis, and design workflows were carried out satisfactorily, the task of implementation should pose few problems to competent programmers. However, management of integration is of critical importance; the challenges of the implementation workflow are to be found in this area.

Typical make-or-break issues include use of the appropriate CASE tools (Section 13.23), test planning once the specifications have been signed off on by the client (Section 9.7), ensuring that changes to the design are communicated to all relevant personnel (Section 13.5.5), and deciding when to stop testing and deliver the product to the client (Section 6.1.2).

Chapter Review

This chapter presents various issues relating to the implementation of a product by a team. These include choice of programming language (Section 13.1). Good programming practice is described in Section 13.2, and the need for practical coding standards is presented in Section 13.3. Then, comments are made regarding code reuse (Section 13.4). Implementation and integration activities must be carried out in parallel (Section 13.5). Top-down, bottom-up, and sandwich integration are described and compared (Sections 13.5.1 through 13.5.3). Integration techniques are discussed in Section 13.5.4, and management of integration in Section 13.5.5. The implementation workflow is presented in Section 13.6 and applied to the MSG Foundation case study in Section 13.7. Next, implementation aspects of the test workflow are presented (Section 13.8). Test cases must be selected systematically (Section 13.9). Various black-box, glass-box, and non-execution-based unit-testing techniques are described (Sections 13.10, 13.12, and 13.13, respectively) and then compared (Section 13.14). Black-box testing of the MSG Foundation case study is presented in Section 13.11. The Cleanroom technique is described in Section 13.15. Testing objects is discussed in Section 13.16, followed by a discussion of the managerial implications of unit testing (Section 13.17). Another problem is when to rewrite rather than debug a code artifact (Section 13.18). Integration testing is described in Section 13.19, product testing in Section 13.20, and acceptance testing in Section 13.21. The test workflow for the MSG Foundation case study is outlined in Section 13.22. CASE tools for the implementation workflow are described in Section 13.23. In more detail, CASE tools for the complete process are discussed in Section 13.23.1 and integrated development environments in Section 13.23.2. Environments for business applications are presented in Section 13.23.3. Section 13.23.4 is devoted to public tool infrastructures. Next, potential problems with environments are discussed (Section 13.23.5). Now CASE tools for the test workflow are described (Section 13.24). Metrics for the implementation workflow are discussed in Section 13.25. The chapter concludes with an analysis of the challenges of the implementation workflow (Section 13.26).

For Further Reading

Excellent books on good programming practice include [Kernighan and Plauger, 1974] and [McConnell, 1993].

Probably the most important early work on execution-based testing is [Myers, 1979]. A comprehensive source of information on testing in general is [Beizer, 1990]. Functional testing is described in [Howden, 1987]; structural techniques are compared in [Clarke, Podgurski, Richardson, and Zeil, 1989]. Black-box testing is described in detail in [Beizer, 1995]. The design of black-box test cases is presented in [Yamaura, 1998]. The relationship between the various coverage measures of structural testing and software quality is discussed in [Horgan, London, and Lyu, 1994]. A formal approach to glass-box testing is described in [Stocks and Carrington, 1996]. Elbaum, Malishevsky, and Rothermel [2002] discuss setting test case priorities.

Cleanroom is described in [Linger, 1994]. The use of Cleanroom during postdelivery maintenance is presented in [Sherer, Kouchakdjian, and Arnold, 1996]. A criticism of Cleanroom is given in [Beizer, 1997].

A good introduction to software reliability is [Musa and Everett, 1990]. In addition, the proceedings of the annual International Symposium on Software Reliability Engineering contain a wide variety of articles on software reliability.

The proceedings of the International Symposia on Software Testing and Analysis cover a particularly broad range of testing issues; selected papers for the 2000 International Symposium appear in the February 2002 issue of *IEEE Transactions on Software Engineering*.

A survey of different approaches to the testing of objects can be found in [Turner, 1994]. Two important papers on the subject are [Perry and Kaiser, 1990] and [Harrold, McGregor, and Fitzpatrick, 1992]. Jorgensen and Erickson [1994] describe the integration testing of object-oriented software.

With regard to metrics for implementation, McCabe's cyclomatic complexity was first presented in [McCabe, 1976]. Extensions of the metric to design appear in [McCabe and Butler, 1989]. Articles questioning the validity of cyclomatic complexity include [Shepperd, 1988; Weyuker, 1988b; and Shepperd and Ince, 1994]. Metrics for managing code inspections are described in [Barnard and Price, 1994]. The validity of object-oriented metrics is discussed in [Alshayeb and Li, 2003].

Selection of test data for integration testing appears in [Harrold and Soffa, 1991]. The generation of test cases for testing GUIs is described in [Memon, Pollack, and Soffa, 2001].

Every 2 or 3 years, ACM SIGSOFT and SIGPLAN sponsor a Symposium on Practical Software Development Environments. The proceedings provide information on a broad spectrum of toolkits and environments. Also useful are the proceedings of the annual International Workshops on Computer-Aided Software Engineering.

With regard to PCTE, [Long and Morris, 1993] contains a number of information sources on that topic.

Key Terms

aacceptance testing 448
all-definition-use-path
    coverage 439
behavioral testing 430
black-box testing 430
bottom-up integration 426
boundary value
    analysis 434
branch coverage 439
Cleanroom 442
code artifact 429
coding standards 422
complexity 440
consistent variable names 417
cyclomatic complexity 440
data-driven testing 430
debugging 446
defensive programming 426
driver 424
end-user programming 000
environment 450
equivalence class 434
execution-based testing 430
functional analysis 436
functional testing 000
glass-box testing 430
good programming
    practice 417

Hungarian Naming
    Conventions 419
implementation workflow 429
input/output-driven
    testing 430
integrated environment 450
integration 423
integration testing 447
linear code sequences 439
logic artifact 425
logic-driven testing 430
meaningful variable
    names 417
method-based
    environment 451
non-execution-based
    testing 430
operational artifact 425
path coverage 439
path-oriented testing 430
portable common tool
    environment (PCTE) 452
process integration 451
product testing 448
programming-
    in-the-many 414
prologue comments 419
reliable 433

sandwich integration 427
self-documenting code 418
statement coverage 438
static method 428
stress testing 448
structural test 439
structural testing 430
structured testing 440
stub 423
technique-based
    environment 451
test case selection 430
testing fault rate 442
testing to code 430
testing to specifications 430
tool 450
tool integration 451
top-down integration 424
unit testing 429
user interface integration 451
valid 433
volume testing 449
white-box testing 430
workbench 450

Problems   13.1   Your instructor has asked you to implement the Osric's Office Appliances and Decor product (Appendix A). Which language would you choose for implementing the product, and why? Of the various languages available to you, list their benefits and their costs. Do not attempt to attach dollar values to your answers.

13.2   Repeat Problem 13.1 for the elevator problem (Section 11.6).

13.3   Repeat Problem 13.1 for the automated library circulation system (Problem 8.7).

13.4   Repeat Problem 13.1 for the product that determines whether a bank statement is correct (Problem 8.8).

13.5   Repeat Problem 13.1 for the automated teller machine (Problem 8.9).

13.6   Add prologue comments to a code artifact that you have recently written.

13.7   How do coding standards for a one-person software production company differ from those in organizations with 300 software professionals?

13.8   How do coding standards for a software company that develops and maintains software for intensive-care units differ from those in an organization that develops and maintains accounting products?

13.9   Set up black-box test cases for Naur's text-processing problem (Section 6.5.2). For each test case, state what is being tested and the expected outcome of that test case.

13.10   Using your solution to Problem 6.15 (or code distributed by your instructor), set up statement coverage test cases. For each test case, state what is being tested and the expected outcome of that test case.

13.11   Repeat Problem 13.10 for branch coverage.

13.12   Repeat Problem 13.10 for all-definition-use-path coverage.

13.13   Repeat Problem 13.10 for path coverage.

13.14   Repeat Problem 13.10 for linear code sequences.

13.15   Draw a flowchart of your solution to Problem 6.15 (or code distributed by your instructor). Determine its cyclomatic complexity. If you are unable to determine the number of branches, consider the flowchart as a directed graph. Determine the number of edges e, nodes n, and connected components c. (Each method constitutes a connected component.) The cyclomatic complexity V is then given by the formula [McCabe, 1976]

$$V = e - n + 2c$$

13.16   You are the owner and sole employee of One-Person Software Company. You bought the programming workbench described in Section 5.6. List its five capabilities in order of importance to you, giving reasons.

13.17   You are now the vice-president for software technology of Very Big Software Company; there are 17,500 employees in your organization. How do you rank the capabilities of the programming workbench described in Section 5.6? Explain any differences between your answer to this problem and that of Problem 13.16.

13.18   As SQA manager for a software development organization, you are responsible for determining the maximum number of faults that may be found in a given code artifact during testing. If this maximum is exceeded, then the code artifact must be redesigned and recoded. What criteria would you use to determine the maximum for a given code artifact?

13.19   Explain the difference between logic artifacts and operational artifacts.

13.20   Defensive programming is good software engineering practice. At the same time, it can prevent operational artifacts from being tested thoroughly enough for reuse purposes. How can this apparent contradiction be resolved?

13.21   What are the similarities between product testing and acceptance testing? What are the major differences?

13.22   What is the role of the SQA group during implementation?

13.23   You are the owner and sole employee of One-Person Software Company. You decide that to be competitive you must buy CASE tools. You therefore apply for a bank loan for $15,000. Your bank manager asks you for a statement no more than one page in length (preferably shorter) explaining in lay terms why you need CASE tools. Write the statement.

13.24   The newly appointed vice-president for software development of Ye Olde Fashioned Software Corporation has hired you to help her change the way the company develops software. There are 650 employees, all writing COBOL code without the assistance of any CASE tools. Write a memo to the vice-president stating what sort of CASE equipment the company should purchase. Justify your choice.

13.25   You and a friend decide to start Personal Computer Software Programs 'R Us, developing software for personal computers on personal computers. Then a distant cousin dies, leaving you $1 million on the condition that you spend the money on a business-oriented environment and the hardware needed to run it and that you keep the environment for at least 5 years. What do you do, and why?

13.26   You are a computer science professor at an excellent small liberal arts college. Programming assignments for computer science courses are done on a network of 35 personal computers. Your dean asks you whether to use the limited software budget to buy CASE tools, bearing in mind that, unless some sort of site license can be obtained, 35 copies of every CASE tool have to be purchased. What do you advise?

13.27   You have just been elected mayor of a major city. You discover that no CASE tools are being used to develop software for the city. What do you do?

13.28   (Term Project) Draw up black-box test cases for the product you specified in Problem 11.22. For each test case, state what is being tested and the expected outcome of that test case.

13.29   (Term Project) Implement and integrate the Osric's Office Appliances and Decor product (Appendix A). Use the programming language specified by your instructor. Your instructor will tell you whether to build a Web-based user interface, a graphical user interface, or a text-based user interface. Remember to utilize the black-box test cases you developed in Problem 13.28 for testing your code.

13.30   (Case Study) Download a copy of the implementation of the MSG Foundation product described in Section 13.7. Draw up statement coverage test cases for the product. For each test case, state what is being tested and the expected outcome of that test case.

13.31   (Case Study) Repeat Problem 13.30 for branch coverage.

13.32   (Case Study) Repeat Problem 13.30 for all-definition-use-path coverage.

13.33   (Case Study) Repeat Problem 13.30 for path coverage.

13.34   (Case Study) Repeat Problem 13.30 for linear code sequences.

13.35   (Case Study) Starting with the detailed design of Appendix F, code the MSG Foundation case study in an object-oriented language other than C++ or Java.

13.36   (Case Study) Recode the MSG Foundation case study (Section 13.7) in pure C, with no C++ features. Although C does not support inheritance, object-based concepts such as encapsulation and information hiding can be achieved relatively easily. How would you implement polymorphism and dynamic binding?

13.37   (Case Study) To what extent is the documentation of the code of the implementation of Section 13.7 inadequate? Make any necessary additions.

13.38   (Readings in Software Engineering) Your instructor will distribute copies of [Alshayeb and Li, 2003]. Does this paper give you confidence in the validity of object-oriented metrics?

References   [Alshayeb and Li, 2003] M. ALSHAYEB, AND W. LI, "An Empirical Validation of Object-Oriented Metrics in Two Different Iterative Software Processes," *IEEE Transactions on Software Engineering* **29** (November 2003), pp. 1043–49.

[Barnard and Price, 1994] J. BARNARD AND A. PRICE, "Managing Code Inspection Information," *IEEE Software* **11** (March 1994), pp. 59–69.

[Basili and Hutchens, 1983] V. R. BASILI AND D. H. HUTCHENS, "An Empirical Study of a Syntactic Complexity Family," *IEEE Transactions on Software Engineering* **SE-9** (November 1983), pp. 664–72.

[Basili and Selby, 1987] V. R. BASILI AND R. W. SELBY, "Comparing the Effectiveness of Software Testing Strategies," *IEEE Transactions on Software Engineering* **SE-13** (December 1987), pp. 1278–96.

[Basili and Weiss, 1984] V. R. BASILI AND D. M. WEISS, "A Methodology for Collecting Valid Software Engineering Data," *IEEE Transactions on Software Engineering* **SE-10** (November 1984), pp. 728–38.

[Beizer, 1990] B. BEIZER, *Software Testing Techniques*, 2nd ed., Van Nostrand Reinhold, New York, 1990.

[Beizer, 1995] B. BEIZER, *Black-Box Testing: Techniques for Functional Testing of Software and Systems*, John Wiley and Sons, New York, 1995.

[Beizer, 1997] B. BEIZER, "Cleanroom Process Model: A Critical Examination," *IEEE Software* **14** (March/April 1997), pp. 14–16.

[Binkley and Schach, 1996] A. B. BINKLEY AND S. R. SCHACH, "A Comparison of Sixteen Quality Metrics for Object-Oriented Design," *Information Processing Letters* **57** (No. 6, June 1996), pp. 271–75.

[Binkley and Schach, 1997] A. B. BINKLEY AND S. R. SCHACH, "Toward a Unified Approach to Object-Oriented Coupling," Proceedings of the 35th Annual ACM Southeast Conference, Murfreesboro, TN, April 2–4, 1997, pp. 91–97.

[Borland, 2002] BORLAND, "Press Release: Borland Unveils C++ Application Development Strategy for 2002," www.borland.com/news/press_releases/2002/01_28_02_cpp.strategy.html, January 28, 2002.

[Chidamber and Kemerer, 1994] S. R. CHIDAMBER AND C. F. KEMERER, "A Metrics Suite for Object Oriented Design," *IEEE Transactions on Software Engineering* **20** (June 1994), pp. 476–93.

[Clarke, Podgurski, Richardson, and Zeil, 1989] L. A. CLARKE, A. PODGURSKI, D. J. RICHARDSON, AND S. J. ZEIL, "A Formal Evaluation of Data Flow Path Selection Criteria," *IEEE Transactions on Software Engineering* **15** (November 1989), pp. 1318–32.

[Crossman, 1982] T. D. CROSSMAN, "Inspection Teams, Are They Worth It?" *Proceedings of the Second National Symposium on EDP Quality Assurance*, Chicago, November 1982.

[Date, 2003] C. J. DATE, *An Introduction to Database Systems*, 8th ed., Addison-Wesley, Reading, MA, 2003.

[Dunn, 1984] R. H. DUNN, *Software Defect Removal*, McGraw-Hill, New York, 1984.

[Elbaum, Malishevsky, and Rothermel, 2002] S. ELBAUM, A. G. MALISHEVSKY, AND G. ROTHERMEL, "Test Case Prioritization: A Family of Empirical Studies," *IEEE Transactions on Software Engineering* **28** (February 2002), pp. 159–82.

[Endres, 1975] A. Endres, "An Analysis of Errors and their Causes in System Programs," *IEEE Transactions on Software Engineering* **SE-1** (June 1975), pp. 140–49.

[Grady, 1992] R. B. Grady, *Practical Software Metrics for Project Management and Process Improvement*, Prentice Hall, Englewood Cliffs, NJ, 1992.

[Harel et al., 1990] D. Harel, H. Lachover, A. Naamad, A. Pnueli, M. Politi, R. Sherman, A. Shtull-Trauring, and M. Trakhtenbrot, "STATEMATE: A Working Environment for the Development of Complex Reactive Systems," *IEEE Transactions on Software Engineering* **16** (April 1990), pp. 403–14.

[Harrold and Soffa, 1991] M. J. Harrold and M. L. Soffa, "Selecting and Using Data for Integration Testing," *IEEE Software* **8** (1991), pp. 58–65

[Harrold, McGregor, and Fitzpatrick, 1992] M. J. Harrold, J. D. McGregor, and K. J. Fitzpatrick, "Incremental Testing of Object-Oriented Class Structures," *Proceedings of the 14th International Conference on Software Engineering*, Melbourne, Australia, May 1992, pp. 68–80.

[Horgan, London, and Lyu, 1994] J. R. Horgan, S. London, and M. R. Lyu, "Achieving Software Quality with Testing Coverage Measures," *IEEE Computer* **27** (1994), pp. 60–69.

[Howden, 1987] W. E. Howden, *Functional Program Testing and Analysis*, McGraw-Hill, New York, 1987.

[Hwang, 1981] S.-S. V. Hwang, "An Empirical Study in Functional Testing, Structural Testing, and Code Reading Inspection," Scholarly Paper 362, Department of Computer Science, University of Maryland, College Park, 1981.

[Jacobson, Booch, and Rumbaugh, 1999] I. Jacobson, G. Booch, and J. Rumbaugh, *The Unified Software Development Process*, Addison-Wesley, Reading, MA, 1999.

[Jorgensen and Erickson, 1994] P. C. Jorgensen and C. Erickson, "Object-Oriented Integration Testing," *Communications of the ACM* **37** (September 1994), pp. 30–38.

[Kernighan and Plauger, 1974] B. W. Kernighan and P. J. Plauger, *The Elements of Programming Style*, McGraw-Hill, New York, 1974.

[Klunder, 1988] D. Klunder, "Hungarian Naming Conventions," Technical Report, Microsoft Corporation, Redmond, WA, January 1988.

[Linger, 1994] R. C. Linger, "Cleanroom Process Model," *IEEE Software* **11** (March 1994), pp. 50–58.

[Long and Morris, 1993] F. Long and E. Morris, "An Overview of PCTE: A Basis for a Portable Common Tool Environment," Technical Report CMU/SEI–93–TR–1, Software Engineering Institute, Carnegie Mellon University, Pittsburgh, January 1993.

[McCabe, 1976] T. J. McCabe, "A Complexity Measure," *IEEE Transactions on Software Engineering* **SE-2** (December 1976), pp. 308–20.

[McCabe and Butler, 1989] T. J. McCabe and C. W. Butler, "Design Complexity Measurement and Testing," *Communications of the ACM* **32** (December 1989), pp. 1415–25.

[McConnell, 1993] S. McConnell, *Code Complete: A Practical Handbook of Software Construction*, Microsoft Press, Redmond, WA, 1993.

[Memon, Pollack, and Soffa, 2001] A. M. Memon, M. E. Pollack, and M. L. Soffa, "Hierarchical GUI Test Case Generation Using Automated Planning," *IEEE Transactions on Software Engineering* **27** (February 2001), pp. 144–55.

[Mills, Dyer, and Linger, 1987] H. D. Mills, M. Dyer, and R. C. Linger, "Cleanroom Software Engineering," *IEEE Software* **4** (September 1987), pp. 19–25.

[Musa and Everett, 1990] J. D. Musa and W. W. Everett, "Software-Reliability Engineering: Technology for the 1990s," *IEEE Software* **7** (November 1990), pp. 36–43.

[Musa, Iannino, and Okumoto, 1987] J. D. Musa, A. Iannino, and K. Okumoto, *Software Reliability: Measurement, Prediction, Application*, McGraw-Hill, New York, 1987.

[Myers, 1976] G. J. Myers, *Software Reliability: Principles and Practices*, Wiley-Interscience, New York, 1976.

[Myers, 1978a] G. J. MYERS, "A Controlled Experiment in Program Testing and Code Walkthroughs/ Inspections," *Communications of the ACM* **21** (September 1978), pp. 760–68.

[Myers, 1979] G. J. MYERS, *The Art of Software Testing*, John Wiley and Sons, New York, 1979.

[Perry and Kaiser, 1990] D. E. PERRY AND G. E. KAISER, "Adequate Testing and Object-Oriented Programming," *Journal of Object-Oriented Programming* **2** (January/February 1990), pp. 13–19.

[Rapps and Weyuker, 1985] S. RAPPS AND E. J. WEYUKER, "Selecting Software Test Data Using Data Flow Information," *IEEE Transactions on Software Engineering* **SE-11** (April 1985), pp. 367–75.

[Sammet, 1978] J. E. SAMMET, "The Early History of COBOL," *Proceedings of the History of Programming Languages Conference*, Los Angeles, 1978, pp. 199–276.

[Shepperd, 1988] M. SHEPPERD, "A Critique of Cyclomatic Complexity as a Software Metric," *Software Engineering Journal* **3** (March 1988), pp. 30–36.

[Shepperd and Ince, 1994] M. SHEPPERD AND D. C. INCE, "A Critique of Three Metrics," *Journal of Systems and Software* **26** (September 1994), pp. 197–210.

[Sherer, Kouchakdjian, and Arnold, 1996] S. W. SHERER, A. KOUCHAKDJIAN, AND P. G. ARNOLD, "Experience Using Cleanroom Software Engineering," *IEEE Software* **13** (May 1996), pp. 69–76.

[Stocks and Carrington, 1996] P. STOCKS AND D. CARRINGTON, "A Framework for Specification-Based Testing," *IEEE Transactions on Software Engineering* **22** (November 1996), pp. 777–93.

[Takahashi and Kamayachi, 1985] M. TAKAHASHI AND Y. KAMAYACHI, "An Empirical Study of a Model for Program Error Prediction," *Proceedings of the Eighth International Conference on Software Engineering*, London, 1985, pp. 330–36.

[Trammel, Binder, and Snyder, 1992] C. J. TRAMMEL, L. H. BINDER, AND C. E. SNYDER, "The Automated Production Control Documentation System: A Case Study in Cleanroom Software Engineering," *ACM Transactions on Software Engineering and Methodology* **1** (January 1992), pp. 81–94.

[Turner, 1994] C. D. TURNER, "State-Based Testing: A New Method for the Testing of Object-Oriented Programs," Ph.D. thesis, Computer Science Division, University of Durham, Durham, UK, November, 1994.

[Walsh, 1979] T. J. WALSH, "A Software Reliability Study Using a Complexity Measure," *Proceedings of the AFIPS National Computer Conference*, New York, 1979, pp. 761–68.

[Watson and McCabe, 1996] A. H. WATSON AND T. J. MCCABE, "Structured Testing: A Testing Methodology Using the Cyclomatic Complexity Metric," NIST Special Publication 500–235, Computer Systems Laboratory, National Institute of Standards and Technology, Gaithersburg, MD, 1996.

[Weyuker, 1988a] E. J. WEYUKER, "An Empirical Study of the Complexity of Data Flow Testing," *Proceedings of the Second Workshop on Software Testing, Verification, and Analysis*, Banff, Canada, July 1988, pp. 188–95.

[Weyuker, 1988b] E. WEYUKER, "Evaluating Software Complexity Measures," *IEEE Transactions on Software Engineering* **14** (September 1988), pp. 1357–65.

[Wilde, Matthews, and Huitt, 1993] N. WILDE, P. MATTHEWS, AND R. HUITT, "Maintaining Object-Oriented Software," *IEEE Software* **10** (January 1993), pp. 75–80.

[Woodward, Hedley, and Hennell, 1980] M. R. WOODWARD, D. HEDLEY, AND M. A. HENNELL, "Experience with Path Analysis and Testing of Programs," *IEEE Transactions on Software Engineering* **SE-6** (May 1980), pp. 278–86.

[Yamaura, 1998] T. YAMAURA, "How to Design Practical Test Cases," *IEEE Software* **15** (November/ December 1998), pp. 30–36.

[Yourdon, 1989] E. YOURDON, *Modern Structured Analysis*, Yourdon Press, Englewood Cliffs, NJ, 1989.

Chapter

14

Postdelivery Maintenance

Learning Objectives

After studying this chapter, you should be able to

- Perform postdelivery maintenance.
- Appreciate the importance of postdelivery maintenance.
- Describe the challenges of postdelivery maintenance.
- Describe the maintenance implications of the object-oriented paradigm.
- Describe the skills needed for maintenance.

A major theme of this book is the vital importance of postdelivery maintenance. Therefore, it is somewhat surprising that this is a relatively short chapter. The reason is that maintainability has to be built into a product from the very beginning and must not be compromised at any time during the development process. Accordingly, in a very real sense, all the previous chapters have been devoted to the subject of postdelivery maintenance. What is described in this chapter is how to ensure that maintainability is not compromised during postdelivery maintenance itself.

14.1 Development and Maintenance

Once the product has passed its acceptance test, it is handed over to the client. The product is installed and used for the purpose for which it was constructed. Any useful product, however, is almost certain to undergo **postdelivery maintenance**, either to fix faults (corrective maintenance) or extend the functionality of the product (enhancement).

Because a product consists of more than just the source code, any changes to the documentation, manuals, or any other component of the product after it has been delivered to the client are examples of postdelivery maintenance. Some computer scientists prefer to use the term **evolution** rather than maintenance to indicate that a product evolves over time. In fact, some view the entire software life cycle, from beginning to end, as an evolutionary process.

This is how maintenance is viewed by the Unified Process. In fact, the word *maintenance* hardly occurs anywhere in Jacobson, Booch, and Rumbaugh [1999]. Instead, maintenance is implicitly treated merely as another increment of the software product. However, there is a basic difference between development and maintenance, a difference that will be illustrated by means of the following example.

Suppose that a woman has her portrait painted when she is 18. The oil painting depicts just her head and shoulders. Twenty years later she marries and now wants the portrait to be modified so that it depicts both her new husband and herself. There are four difficulties that would arise if the portrait were to be changed in this way.

- The canvas is not large enough for her husband's head to be added.
- The original portrait was hung where sunlight fell on it much of the day, so the colors have faded somewhat. In addition, the brand of oil paint that was used for the original painting is no longer manufactured. For both these reasons, it will be hard to achieve consistency of color.
- The original artist has retired, so it will be hard to achieve consistency of style.
- The woman's face has aged 20 years since the original portrait was painted, so considerable work will have to be done to ensure that the modified painting is an accurate likeness.

For all these reasons, it would be laughable even to think about modifying the original portrait. Instead, a new artist will paint a new portrait of the couple from scratch (but see Just in Case You Wanted to Know Box 14.1).

Now consider the maintenance of a software product that originally cost $2 million to develop. There are four difficulties that have to be solved:

- Unfortunately, the disk on which the database is stored is all but full—the current disk is not large enough for more data to be added.
- The company that manufactured the original disk is no longer in business, so a larger disk will have to be bought from a different manufacturer. However, there are hardware incompatibilities between the new disk and the existing software product (Section 8.10.1), and it will cost about $100,000 to make all the changes needed to use the new disk.
- The original developers left the company some years ago, so the changes to the software product will have to be made by a team of maintainers who have never seen the software product before.
- The original software product was developed using the classical paradigm. Nowadays, the object-oriented paradigm (and specifically the Unified Process) is commonly used.

There is a clear correspondence between each portrait bullet point and the corresponding software product bullet point. The inescapable conclusion regarding the oil painting is to paint a new portrait from scratch. Does that mean that, instead of performing a $100,000 maintenance task, we should develop a totally new software product at a cost of $2 million?

The National Gallery in London contains a masterpiece that was ruined when an additional head was added to a portrait. In 1515, the artist Lorenzo Lotto (ca. 1480–after 1556) painted a picture of Giovanni Agostino della Torre, a physician who lived in Bergamo, then in the State of Venice, Italy. Download the picture [Lotto, 1515] and examine it. It certainly appears as if the artist added della Torre's son, Niccolò, after the original portrait had been completed, thereby irreparably marring the painting.

Another spoiled masterpiece is in the Hagia Sophia Museum in Istanbul. A 12th century mosaic on a wall in the southern gallery depicts Empress Zoe of the Byzantine Empire (ca. 978–1050). Opposite Zoe is her third husband, Emperor Constantine IX Monomachos. As you can see [Magnus, 2005], he appears to have a rather short neck. The reason is that the mosaic originally depicted Zoe with her first husband, Emperor Romanus III Argyrus. The mosaic panel was updated after her third marriage, but the artist made Constantine's head slightly too large, so the lower part of his head covers most of Romanus's neck.

The answer is that analogies should never be taken too far. Just as it is obvious that a new portrait should be painted, it is equally obvious that the existing software product should undergo maintenance at 5 percent of the cost of a new software product.

Nevertheless, there is an important lesson to be learned from this otherwise poor analogy. Whether we are dealing with portraits or software products, it is easier to create a new version than to modify an existing version. In the case of the portrait, not only was it all but impossible to modify the existing portrait, but the cost of doing so would surely have been more than the cost of painting a new portrait from scratch. In the case of the software product, not only were the changes feasible, but the cost of doing them would be a fraction of the cost of developing a new software product from scratch. In other words, even though it is harder to make changes to existing artifacts than to construct new artifacts from scratch, economic considerations make maintenance far preferable to redevelopment.

14.2   Why Postdelivery Maintenance Is Necessary

There are three main reasons for making changes to a product:

1. A fault needs correcting, whether an analysis fault, design fault, coding fault, documentation fault, or any other type of fault. This is termed **corrective maintenance**.

2. In **perfective maintenance**, a change is made to the code to improve the effectiveness of the product. For instance, the client may wish additional functionality or request that the product be modified so that it runs faster. Improving the maintainability of a product is another example of perfective maintenance.

3. In **adaptive maintenance**, a change is made to the product to react to a change in the environment in which the product operates. For example, a product almost certainly has to be modified if it is ported to a new compiler, operating system, or hardware. With each change to the tax code, a product that prepares tax returns has to be modified accordingly. When the U.S. Postal Service introduced nine-digit ZIP codes in 1981, products that had allowed for only five-digit ZIP codes had to be changed. Adaptive maintenance is not requested by a client; instead, it is externally imposed on the client.

14.3   What Is Required of Postdelivery Maintenance Programmers?

During the software life cycle, more time is spent on postdelivery maintenance than on any other activity. In fact, on average, at least 67 percent of the total cost of a product can be attributed to postdelivery maintenance, as shown in Figure 1.3. But many organizations, even today, assign the task of postdelivery maintenance to beginners and less competent programmers, leaving the "glamorous" job of product development to better or more experienced programmers.

In fact, postdelivery maintenance is the most difficult of all aspects of software production. A major reason is that postdelivery maintenance incorporates aspects of all the other workflows of the software process. Consider what happens when a defect report is handed to a maintenance programmer (recall from Section 1.10 that a **defect** is a generic term for a fault, failure, or error). A defect report is filed if, in the opinion of the user, the product is not working as specified in the user manual. A number of causes are possible. First, nothing at all could be wrong; perhaps the user has misunderstood the user manual or is using the product incorrectly. Alternatively, if there is a fault in the product, it simply might be that the user manual has been badly worded and nothing is wrong with the code itself. Usually, however, there is a fault in the code. But, before making any changes, the maintenance programmer has to determine exactly where the fault lies, using the defect report filed by the user, the source code—and often nothing else. Therefore, the maintenance programmer needs to have far above average debugging skills, because the fault could lie anywhere within the product. And the original cause of the defect might lie in the by now nonexistent analysis or design artifacts.

Suppose that the maintenance programmer has located a fault and must fix it without inadvertently introducing another fault elsewhere in the product, that is, a **regression fault**. If regression faults are to be minimized, detailed documentation for the product as a whole and each individual code artifact must be available. However, software professionals are notorious for their dislike of paperwork of all kinds, especially documentation; and it is quite common for the documentation to be incomplete, erroneous, or totally missing. In these cases, the maintenance programmer has to deduce from the source code itself, the only valid form of documentation available, all the information needed to avoid introducing a regression fault.

Having determined the probable fault and tried to correct it, the maintenance programmer now must test that the modification works correctly and no regression faults have been introduced. To check the modification itself, the maintenance programmer must construct special test cases; checking for regression faults is done using the set of test data stored precisely for performing **regression testing** (Section 3.8). Then the test cases constructed for checking the modification must be added to the set of stored test cases to be used for future regression testing of the modified product. In addition, if changes to the analysis or design had to be made to correct the fault, then these changes also must be checked. Expertise in testing therefore is an additional prerequisite for postdelivery maintenance. Finally, it is essential that the maintenance programmer document every change. The preceding discussion relates to corrective maintenance. For that task, the maintenance programmer primarily must be a superb diagnostician to determine if there is a fault and, if so, an expert technician to fix it.

The other major maintenance tasks are adaptive and perfective maintenance. To perform these, the maintenance programmer must perform the requirements, analysis, design, and implementation workflows, taking the existing product as the starting point. For some types of changes, additional code artifacts have to be designed and implemented. In other cases, changes to the design and implementation of existing code artifacts are needed. Therefore, whereas specifications frequently are produced by analysis experts, designs by design experts, and code by programming experts, a maintenance programmer has to be an expert in all three areas. Perfective and adaptive maintenance are adversely affected by a lack of adequate documentation, just like corrective maintenance. Furthermore, the ability to design suitable test cases and write good documentation is needed for perfective and adaptive maintenance, just as in corrective maintenance. Therefore, none of the forms of maintenance is a task for a less experienced programmer unless a top-rank computer professional supervises the process.

From the preceding discussion, it is clear that maintenance programmers have to possess almost every technical skill that a software professional could have. But what does he or she get in return?

- Postdelivery maintenance is a thankless task in every way. Maintainers deal with dissatisfied users; if the user were happy with the product, it would not need maintenance.
- The user's problems have frequently been caused by the individuals who developed the product, not the maintainer.
- The code itself may be badly written, adding to the frustrations of the maintainer.
- Postdelivery maintenance is looked down on by many software developers, who consider development to be a glamorous job and maintenance to be drudge work fit only for junior programmers or incompetents.

Postdelivery maintenance can be likened to after-sales service. The product has been delivered to the client. But the client is dissatisfied, because the product does not work correctly, it does not do everything that the client currently wants, or the circumstances for which the product was built have changed in some way. Unless the software organization provides good maintenance service, the client will take all future product development business elsewhere. When the client and software group are part of the same organization, and hence inextricably tied from the viewpoint of future work, a dissatisfied client may use every means, fair or foul, to discredit the software group. This, in turn, leads to an erosion of confidence, from both outside and inside the software group, and resignations and dismissals. It is important for every software organization to keep its clients happy by providing excellent postdelivery maintenance service. So, for product after product, postdelivery maintenance is the most challenging aspect of software production—and frequently the most thankless.

How can this situation be changed? Managers must restrict postdelivery maintenance tasks to programmers with all the skills needed to perform maintenance. They must make it known that only top computer professionals merit maintenance assignments in their organization and pay them accordingly. If management believes that postdelivery maintenance is a challenge and good maintenance is critical for the success of the organization, attitudes toward postdelivery maintenance will slowly improve (but see Just in Case You Wanted to Know Box 14.2).

Some of the problems that maintenance programmers face are now highlighted in a mini case study.

In *Practical Software Maintenance*, Tom Pigoski [1996] describes how he set up a U.S. Navy postdelivery maintenance organization in Pensacola, Florida. His idea was that, if prospective employees were told in advance that they were to work as maintainers, they would have a positive attitude toward postdelivery maintenance. In addition, he tried to keep morale high by ensuring that all employees received plenty of training and had the opportunity to travel all over the world in the course of their work. The beautiful nearby beaches certainly helped, as did the brand-new building they occupied.

Nevertheless, within 6 months of starting work at the postdelivery maintenance organization, every employee asked when he or she could do some development work. It seems that it is extremely hard to change the attitudes of individuals toward postdelivery maintenance.

Mini Case Study

14.4 *Postdelivery Maintenance Mini Case Study*

In countries with centralized economies, the government controls the distribution and marketing of agricultural products. In one such country, temperate fruits, such as peaches, apples, and pears, were the responsibility of the Temperate Fruit Committee (TFC). One day, the chairman of the TFC asked a government computer consultant to computerize the operations of the TFC. The chairman informed the consultant that there are exactly seven temperate fruits: apples, apricots, cherries, nectarines, peaches, pears, and plums. The database was to be designed for those seven fruits, no more and no less. After all, that was the way that the world was, and the consultant was not to waste time and money allowing for any sort of expandability.

The product was duly delivered to the TFC. About a year later, the chairman summoned the maintenance programmer responsible for the product. "What do you know about kiwi fruit?" asked the chairman. "Nothing," replied the mystified programmer. "Well," said the chairman, "it seems that kiwi fruit is a temperate fruit that has just started to be grown in our country, and the TFC is responsible for it. Please change the product accordingly."

The maintenance programmer discovered that the consultant fortunately had not carried out the chairman's original instructions to the letter. The good practice of allowing for some sort of future expansion was too ingrained, and the consultant had provided a number of unused fields in the relevant database records. By slightly rearranging certain items, the maintenance programmer was able to incorporate kiwi fruit, the eighth temperate fruit, into the product.

Another year went by, and the product functioned well. Then the maintenance programmer again was called to the chairman's office. The chairman was in a good mood. He jovially informed the programmer that the government had reorganized the distribution and marketing of agricultural products. His committee was now responsible for all fruit produced in that country, not just temperate fruit, and so the product now had to be modified to incorporate the 26 additional kinds of fruit on the list he handed to the maintenance programmer. The programmer protested, pointing out that this change would take almost as long as rewriting the product from scratch. "Nonsense," replied the chairman. "You had no trouble adding kiwi fruit. Just do the same thing another 26 times!"

A number of important lessons are to be learned from this:

- The problem with the product, no provision for expansion, was caused by the developer, not the maintainer. The developer made the mistake of obeying the chairman's instruction regarding future expandability of the product, but the maintenance programmer suffered the consequences. In fact, unless she reads this book, the consultant who developed the original product may never realize that her product was anything but a success. One of the more annoying aspects of postdelivery maintenance is that the maintainer is responsible for fixing other people's mistakes. The person who caused the problem either has other duties or has left the organization, but the maintenance programmer is left holding the baby.

- The client frequently does not understand that postdelivery maintenance can be difficult or, in some instances, all but impossible. The problem is exacerbated when the maintenance programmer has successfully carried out previous perfective and adaptive maintenance tasks but suddenly protests that a new assignment cannot be done, even though superficially it seems no different from what has been done before with little difficulty.

- All software development must be carried out with an eye on future postdelivery maintenance. If the consultant had designed the product for an arbitrary number of different kinds of fruit, there would have been no difficulty in incorporating first the kiwi fruit and then the 26 other kinds of fruit.

As stated many times, postdelivery maintenance is a vital aspect of software production, and the one that consumes the most resources. During product development, it is essential that the development team never forget the maintenance programmer, who will be responsible for the product once it has been installed.

14.5   Management of Postdelivery Maintenance

Issues regarding management of postdelivery maintenance are now considered.

14.5.1   Defect Reports

The first thing needed when maintaining a product is a mechanism for changing the product. With regard to corrective maintenance, that is, removing residual faults, if the product appears to be functioning incorrectly, then a ***defect report*** should be filed by the user. This must include enough information to enable the maintenance programmer to re-create the problem, which usually is some sort of software failure. In addition, the maintenance programmer must indicate the severity of the defect; typical severity categories include critical, major, normal, minor, and trivial.

Ideally, every defect reported by a user should be fixed immediately. In practice, programming organizations usually are understaffed, with a backlog of work, both development and maintenance. If the defect is critical, such as if a payroll product crashes the day before payday or overpays or underpays employees, immediate corrective action must be taken. Otherwise, each defect report must at least receive an immediate preliminary investigation.

The maintenance programmer should first consult the defect report file. This contains all reported defects that have not yet been fixed, together with suggestions for working around them, that is, ways for the user to bypass the portion of the product that apparently is responsible for the failure, until such time as the defect can be fixed. If the defect has been reported previously, any information in the defect report file should be given to the user. But, if what the user reports appears to be a new defect, then the maintenance programmer should study the problem and attempt to find the cause and a way to fix it. In addition, an attempt should be made to find a way to work around the problem, because it may take 6 or 9 months before someone can be assigned to make the necessary changes to the software. In the light of the serious shortage of programmers and in particular programmers good enough to perform maintenance, suggesting a way to live with the defect until it can be solved often is the only way to deal with defect reports that are not true emergencies.

The maintenance programmer's conclusions should be added to the defect report file, together with any supporting documentation, such as listings, designs, and manuals used to arrive at those conclusions. The manager in charge of postdelivery maintenance should consult the file regularly, setting priorities for the various fixes. The file also should contain the client's requests for perfective and adaptive maintenance. The next modification made to the product then will be the one with the highest priority.

When copies of a product have been distributed to a variety of sites, copies of defect reports must be circulated to all users of the product, together with an estimate of when each defect can be fixed. Then, if the same failure occurs at another site, the user can consult the relevant defect report to determine if it is possible to work around the defect and when it will be fixed. It would be preferable to fix every defect immediately and distribute a new version of the product to all sites, of course. Given the current worldwide shortage of good programmers and the realities of postdelivery software maintenance, distributing defect reports probably is the best that can be done.

There is another reason why defects usually are not fixed immediately. It almost always is cheaper to make a number of changes, test them all, change the documentation, and install the new version than it is to perform each change separately, test it, document it, install the new version, and then repeat the entire cycle for the next change. This is particularly true if every new version has to be installed on a significant number of computers (such as a large number of clients in a client–server network) or when the software is running at different sites. As a result, organizations prefer to accumulate noncritical maintenance tasks and then implement the changes as a group.

14.5.2   Authorizing Changes to the Product

Once a decision has been made to perform corrective maintenance, a maintenance programmer is assigned the task of determining the fault that caused the failure and repairing it. After the code has been changed, the repair must be tested, as must the product as a whole (regression testing). Then, the documentation must be updated to reflect the changes. In particular, a detailed description of what was changed, why it was changed, by whom, and when must be added to the prologue comments of any changed code artifact (Figure 13.1). If necessary, analysis or design artifacts also are changed. A similar set of steps is followed when performing perfective or adaptive maintenance; the only real difference is that perfective and adaptive maintenance are initiated by a change in requirements rather than by a defect report.

At this point all that would seem to be needed would be to distribute the new version to the users. But, what if the maintenance programmer has not tested the repair adequately? Before the product is distributed, it must be subjected to software quality assurance performed by an independent group, that is, the members of the maintenance SQA group must not report to the same manager as the maintenance programmer. It is important that the SQA group remain managerially independent (Section 6.1.2).

Reasons were given previously as to why postdelivery maintenance is difficult. For those same reasons, maintenance also is fault prone. Testing during postdelivery maintenance is difficult and time consuming, and the SQA group should not underestimate the implications of software maintenance with regard to testing. Once the new version has been approved by the SQA group, it can be distributed.

Another area in which management must ensure that procedures are followed carefully is when the technique of baselines and private copies (Section 5.8.2) is used. Suppose a programmer wishes to change **Tax Provision Class**. The programmer makes copies of **Tax Provision Class** and all the other code artifacts needed to perform the required maintenance task; often this includes all the other classes in the product. The programmer makes the necessary changes to **Tax Provision Class** and tests them. Now, the previous version of **Tax Provision Class** is frozen, and the **Tax Provision Class** incorporating the changes is installed in the baseline. But, when the modified product is delivered to the user, it immediately crashes. What went wrong is that the maintenance programmer tested the **Tax Provision Class** using his or her private workspace copies, that is, the copies of the other code artifacts that were in the baseline at the time that maintenance of **Tax Provision Class** was started. In the meantime, certain other code artifacts were updated by other maintenance programmers working on the same product. The lesson is clear: Before installing a code artifact, it must be tested using the current baseline versions of all the other code artifacts and not the programmer's private versions. This is a further reason for stipulating an independent SQA group—members of the SQA group simply have no access to programmers' private workspaces. A third reason is that it has been estimated that the initial correction of a fault is itself incorrect some 70 percent of the time [Parnas, 1999].

14.5.3   Ensuring Maintainability

Postdelivery maintenance is not a one-time effort. A well-written product goes through a series of versions over its lifetime. As a result, it is necessary to plan for postdelivery maintenance during the entire software process. During the design workflow, for example, information-hiding techniques (Section 7.6) should be employed; during implementation, variable names should be selected that will be meaningful to future maintenance programmers (Section 13.2.1). Documentation should be complete, correct, and reflect the current version of every component code artifact of the product.

During postdelivery maintenance, it is important not to compromise the maintainability that has been built into the product from the very beginning. In other words, just as software development personnel always should be conscious of the inevitable postdelivery maintenance, so software maintenance personnel always should be conscious of the equally inevitable further future postdelivery maintenance. The principles established for maintainability during development apply equally to postdelivery maintenance.

14.5.4   Problem of Repeated Maintenance

One of the more frustrating difficulties of software development is the ***moving-target problem*** (Section 2.4). As fast as the developer constructs the product, the client can change the requirements. Not only is this frustrating to the development team, frequent changes can result in a poorly constructed product. In addition, such changes add to the cost of the product.

The problem is exacerbated during postdelivery maintenance. The more a completed product is changed, the more it deviates from its original design, and the more difficult further changes become. Under repeated maintenance, the documentation is likely to become even less reliable than usual, and the regression testing files may not be up to date. If still more maintenance is done, the product as a whole may first have to be completely rewritten.

The problem of the moving target clearly is a management problem. In theory, if management is sufficiently firm with the client and explains the problem at the beginning of the project, then the requirements can be frozen from the time the specifications are signed off on until the product is delivered. Again, after each request for perfective maintenance, the requirements can be frozen for, say, 3 months or 1 year. In practice, it does not work that way. For example, if the client happens to be the president of the corporation and the development organization is the software division of that corporation, then the president can order changes every Monday and Thursday and they will be implemented. The old proverb, "He who pays the piper calls the tune," unfortunately is all too relevant in this situation. Perhaps, the best that the vice-president for software can do is to try to explain to the president the effect on the product of repeated maintenance, and then simply have the complete product rewritten whenever further maintenance would be hazardous to the integrity of the product.

Trying to discourage additional maintenance by ensuring that the requested changes are implemented slowly may mean that the relevant personnel are replaced by others prepared to do the job faster. In short, if the person who requests repeated changes has sufficient clout, there is no solution to the problem of the moving target.

14.6   Maintenance Issues

One reason put forward for using the object-oriented paradigm is that it promotes maintainability. After all, an object is an independent unit of a program. More specifically, a well-designed object exhibits conceptual independence, otherwise known as ***encapsulation*** (Section 7.4). Every aspect of the product that relates to the portion of the real world modeled by that object is localized to the object itself. In addition, objects exhibit physical independence; information hiding is employed to ensure that implementation details are not visible outside that object (Section 7.6). The only form of communication permitted is sending a message to the object to invoke a specific method.

As a consequence, the argument goes, it is easy to maintain an object for two reasons. First, conceptual independence means it is easy to determine which part of a product must be changed to achieve a specific maintenance goal, be it enhancement or corrective maintenance. Second, information hiding ensures that a change made to an object has no impact outside that object, and hence the number of regression faults is reduced greatly.

In practice, however, the situation is not quite this idyllic. In fact, three obstacles are specific to the maintenance of object-oriented software. One of the problems can be solved through use of appropriate CASE tools, but the others are less tractable:

1. Consider the C++ class hierarchy shown in Figure 14.1. Method displayNode is defined in **UndirectedTreeClass**, inherited by **DirectedTreeClass**, and then redefined in **RootedTreeClass**. This redefined version is inherited by **BinaryTreeClass** and **BalancedBinaryTreeClass** and utilized in **BalancedBinaryTreeClass**. Therefore, a maintenance programmer has to study the complete inheritance hierarchy to understand **BalancedBinaryTreeClass**. Worse, the hierarchy may not be displayed in the linear fashion of Figure 14.1 but generally is spread over the entire product. So, to understand what displayNode does in **BalancedBinaryTreeClass**, the maintenance programmer may have to peruse a major proportion of the product. This is a far cry from the "independent" object described at the beginning of this section. The solution to this problem is straightforward: use the appropriate CASE tool. Just as a C++ compiler can resolve precisely the version of displayNode within instances of the class **BalancedBinaryTreeClass**, so a programming workbench can provide a "flattened" version of a class, that is, a definition of the class with all features inherited directly or indirectly appearing explicitly, with any renaming or redefinition incorporated. The flattened form of **BalancedBinaryTreeClass** of Figure 14.1 includes the definition of displayNode from **RootedTreeClass**.

Figure 14.1
C++ implementation of a class hierarchy.

```
class UndirectedTreeClass
{
    ...
    void displayNode (Node a);
    ...
}// class UndirectedTreeClass

class DirectedTreeClass : public UndirectedTreeClass
{
    ...
}// class DirectedTreeClass

class RootedTreeClass : public DirectedTreeClass
{
    ...
    void displayNode (Node a);
    ...
}// class RootedTreeClass

class BinaryTreeClass : public RootedTreeClass
{
    ...
}// class BinaryTreeClass

class BalancedBinaryTreeClass : public BinaryTreeClass
{
    Node        hhh;
    displayNode (hhh);
}// class BalancedBinaryTreeClass
```

Figure 14.2
Definition of base class **File Class** with derived classes **Disk File Class**, **Tape File Class**, and **Diskette File Class**.

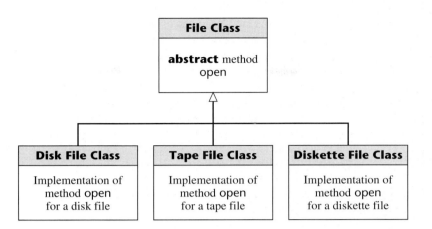

2. Another obstacle to the maintenance of a product implemented using an object-oriented language is less easy to solve. It arises as a consequence of polymorphism and dynamic binding, concepts explained in Section 7.8. An example was given in that section, a base class named **File Class**, together with three subclasses: **Disk File Class**, **Tape File Class**, and **Diskette File Class**. This is shown in Figure 7.33(b), reproduced here for convenience as Figure 14.2. In base class **File Class**, a dummy (**abstract** or **virtual**) method open is declared. Then, a specific implementation of the method appears in each of the three subclasses; each method is given the identical name, open, as shown in Figure 14.2. Suppose that myFile is declared to be an object, an instance of **File Class**, and the code to be maintained contains the message myFile.open (). As a consequence of polymorphism and dynamic binding, at run time, myFile could be a member of any of the three derived classes of **File Class**, that is, a disk file, a tape file, or a diskette file. Once the run-time system has determined in which derived class it is, the appropriate version of open is invoked. This can have adverse consequences for maintenance. If a maintenance programmer encounters the call myFile.open () in the code, then, to understand that part of the product, he or she has to consider what would happen if myFile were an instance of each of the three subclasses. A CASE tool cannot help here, because, in general, there is no way to resolve dynamic binding issues using static methods. The only way to determine which of a number of dynamic bindings actually occurs in a particular set of circumstances is to trace through the code, either by running it on a computer or tracing through it manually. Polymorphism and dynamic binding indeed are extremely powerful aspects of object-oriented technology that promote the development of an object-oriented product. However, they can have a deleterious impact on maintenance, by forcing the maintenance programmer to investigate a wide variety of possible bindings that might occur at run time and hence determine which of a number of different methods could be invoked at that point in the code.

3. The final problem arises as a consequence of *inheritance*. Suppose a particular base class does most, but not all, of what is required for the design of a new product. A derived class now is defined, that is, a class identical to the base class

in many ways, but new features may be added and existing features renamed, reimplemented, suppressed, or changed in other ways. Furthermore, these changes may be made without having an effect on the base class or any other derived classes. However, suppose now that the base class itself is changed. If this happens, all derived classes are changed in the same way. In other words, the strength of inheritance is that new leaves can be added to the inheritance tree (or graph, if the implementation language supports multiple inheritance, as C++ does) without altering any other class in the tree. But, if an interior node of the tree is changed in any way, then this change is propagated to all its descendants (the **fragile base class problem**).

Accordingly, inheritance is another feature of object-oriented technology that can have a major positive influence on development but a negative impact on maintenance.

14.7   Postdelivery Maintenance Skills versus Development Skills

Earlier in this chapter, much was said about the skills needed for postdelivery maintenance.

- For corrective maintenance, the ability to determine the cause of a failure of a large product was deemed essential. But this skill is not needed exclusively for postdelivery maintenance. It is used throughout integration and product testing.
- Another vital skill is the ability to function effectively without adequate documentation. Again, the documentation rarely is complete while integration and product testing are under way.
- Also stressed was that skills with regard to analysis, design, implementation, and testing are essential for adaptive and perfective maintenance. These activities also are carried out during the development process, and each requires specialized skills if it is to be performed correctly.

In other words, the skills a postdelivery maintenance programmer needs are in no way different from those needed by software professionals specializing in other aspects of software production. The key point is that a maintenance programmer must not be merely skilled in a broad variety of areas but highly skilled in all those areas. Although the average software developer can specialize in one area of software development, such as design or testing, the software maintainer must be a specialist in virtually every area of software production. After all, postdelivery maintenance is the same as development, only more so.

14.8   Reverse Engineering

As has been pointed out, sometimes the only documentation available for postdelivery maintenance is the source code itself. (This happens all too frequently when maintaining **legacy systems**, that is, software in current use but developed some 15 or 20 years ago, if not earlier.) Under these circumstances, maintaining the code can be extremely difficult. One way of handling this problem is to start with the source code and attempt to re-create the design documents or even the specifications. This process is called **reverse engineering**.

CASE tools can assist with this process. One of the simplest is a pretty printer (Section 5.6), which may help display the code more clearly. Other tools construct diagrams, such as flowcharts or UML diagrams, directly from the source code; these visual aids can help in the process of design recovery.

Once the maintenance team has reconstructed the design, there are two possibilities. One alternative is to attempt to reconstruct the specifications, modify the reconstructed specifications to reflect the necessary changes, and reimplement the product the usual way. (Within the context of reverse engineering, the usual development process that proceeds from analysis through design to implementation is called **forward engineering**. The process of reverse engineering followed by forward engineering sometimes is called **reengineering**.) In practice, reconstruction of the specifications is an extremely hard task. More frequently, the reconstructed design is modified and the modified design then is forward engineered.

A related activity often performed during maintenance is restructuring. Reverse engineering takes the product from a lower level of abstraction to a higher level of abstraction, for example, from code to design. Forward engineering takes the product from a higher level of abstraction to a lower level. **Restructuring**, however, takes place at the same level. It is the process of improving the product without changing its functionality. Pretty printing is one form of restructuring, and so is converting code from unstructured to structured form. In general, restructuring is performed to make the source code (or design or even the database) easier to maintain. When an agile process (Section 2.9.5) is used, the design modification known as **refactoring** is another example of restructuring.

A worse situation occurs if the source code is lost and the executable version of the product is all that is available. At first sight, it might seem that the only possible way to re-create the source code is to use a disassembler to create assembler code and then to build a tool (that might be termed a *reverse compiler*) to try to re-create the original high-level language code. A number of virtually insurmountable problems accompany this approach:

- The names of the variables will have been lost as a consequence of the original compilation.
- Many compilers optimize the code in some way, making it extremely difficult to attempt to re-create the source code.
- A construct such as a loop in the assembler could correspond to a number of different possible constructs in the source code.

In practice, therefore, the existing product is treated as a black box and reverse engineering is used to deduce the specifications from the behavior of the current product. The reconstructed specifications are modified as required, and a new version of the product is forward engineered from those specifications.

14.9   Testing during Postdelivery Maintenance

While the product is being developed, many members of the development team have a broad overview of the product as a whole, but as a result of the rapid personnel turnover in the computer industry, it is unlikely that members of the postdelivery maintenance team have been involved in the original development. Therefore, the maintainer tends to see the product as a set of loosely related components and generally is not aware that a change to one code artifact may seriously affect one or more other artifacts and hence the product as a whole. Even if the maintainer wished to understand every aspect of the product, the pressures to fix or to extend the product generally are such that no time is allowed for the detailed study needed to achieve this. Furthermore, in many cases, little or no documentation is available to assist in gaining that understanding. One way of trying to minimize this difficulty is to use regression testing, that is, testing the changed product against previous test cases to ensure that it still works correctly.

For this reason, it is vital to store all test cases, together with their expected outcomes, in machine-readable form. As a result of changes made to the product, certain stored test cases may have to be modified. For example, if salary withholding percentages change as a consequence of tax legislation, then the correct output from a payroll product for each test case involving withholding changes, too. Similarly, if satellite observations lead to corrections in the latitude and longitude of an island, then the correct output from a product that calculates the position of an aircraft using the coordinates of the island must correspondingly change. Depending on the maintenance performed, some valid test cases become invalid. But the computations that need to be made to correct the stored test cases are essentially the same as would have to be made to set up new test data for checking that the maintenance has been correctly performed. No additional work therefore is involved in maintaining the file of test cases and their expected outcomes.

It can be argued that regression testing is a waste of time because regression testing requires the complete product to be retested against a host of test cases, most of which apparently have nothing to do with the code artifacts modified in the course of product maintenance. The word *apparently* in the previous sentence is critical. The dangers of unwitting side effects of maintenance (that is, the introduction of regression faults) are too great for that argument to hold water; regression testing is an essential aspect of maintenance in all situations.

14.10 CASE Tools for Postdelivery Maintenance

It is unreasonable to expect maintenance programmers to keep track manually of the various revision numbers and assign the next revision number each time a code artifact is updated. Unless the operating system incorporates version control, a version-control tool such as the UNIX tools *sccs* (source code control system) [Rochkind, 1975] and *rcs* (revision control system) [Tichy, 1985], or open-source product CVS (concurrent versions system) [Loukides and Oram, 1997], is needed. It is equally unreasonable to expect manual control of the freezing technique described in Chapter 5 or any other manual way of ensuring that revisions are updated appropriately. A configuration-control tool is needed. Typical examples of commercial tools are CCC (change and configuration control) and IBM Rational ClearCase. Even if the software organization does not wish to purchase a complete configuration-control tool, at the very least a build tool must be used in conjunction with a version-control tool. Another category of CASE tool virtually essential during postdelivery maintenance is a defect-tracking tool that keeps a record of reported defects not yet fixed.

Section 14.8 described some categories of CASE tools that can assist in reverse engineering and reengineering. Examples of such tools that assist by creating visual displays of the structure of the product include IBM Rational Rose and Together. Doxygen is an open-source tool that generates documentation in HTML.

Defect tracking is an important aspect of postdelivery maintenance. It is vital to be able to determine the current status of every reported defect. IBM Rational ClearQuest is a commercial **defect-tracking tool**, and Bugzilla is a popular open-source tool. Such tools can be used to record the severity of a defect (Section 14.5.1) and its status (essentially, whether or not the defect has been fixed). In addition, some defect-tracking tools can link a defect report to the configuration management tool so that, when a new version is built, the maintenance programmer can select specific defect report fixes to be included in the build.

Postdelivery maintenance is difficult and frustrating. The very least that management can do is to provide the maintenance team the tools needed for efficient and effective product maintenance.

14.11 Metrics for Postdelivery Maintenance

The activities of postdelivery maintenance essentially are analysis, design, implementation, testing, and documentation. Therefore, the metrics that measure these activities are equally applicable to maintenance. For example, the complexity metrics of Section 13.12.2 are relevant to postdelivery maintenance, in that a code artifact with high complexity is a likely candidate for inducing a regression fault. Particular care must be taken in modifying such a code artifact.

In addition, metrics specific to postdelivery maintenance include measures relating to software defect reports, such as the total number of defects reported and classification of those defects by severity and type. In addition, information regarding the current status of the defect reports is needed. For example, there is a considerable difference between having 13 critical defects reported and fixed during 2007 and having only 2 critical defects reported during that year but neither of them fixed.

14.12 Postdelivery Maintenance: The MSG Foundation Case Study

A number of faults have been seeded in the source code of the MSG Foundation case study. In addition, perfective maintenance must be performed. These maintenance tasks are left as exercises (Problems 14.11 through 14.16).

14.13 Challenges of Postdelivery Maintenance

This chapter describes numerous challenges of postdelivery maintenance. The toughest one to change is that maintenance is generally harder than development, yet maintenance programmers are often looked down on by developers and all too frequently are paid less than developers.

**Chapter
Review**

The chapter begins with a comparison of development and maintenance (Section 14.1). Postdelivery maintenance is an important and challenging software activity (Sections 14.2 and 14.3). This is illustrated by means of the mini case study of Section 14.4. Issues relating to the management of postdelivery maintenance are described (Section 14.5), including the problem of repeated maintenance (Section 14.5.4). Postdelivery maintenance of object-oriented software is discussed in Section 14.6. The skills that a maintenance programmer needs are the same as those of a developer; the difference is that a developer can specialize in one aspect of the software process, whereas the maintainer must be an expert in all aspects of software production (Section 14.7). A description of reverse engineering is given in Section 14.8. Next follows a description of testing during postdelivery maintenance (Section 14.9) and CASE tools for postdelivery maintenance (Section 14.10). Metrics for postdelivery maintenance are described in Section 14.11. Postdelivery maintenance of the MSG Foundation case study, discussed in Section 14.12, is left as an exercise. The chapter concludes with a discussion of the challenges of postdelivery maintenance (Section 14.13).

**For
Further
Reading**

A classic source of information on postdelivery maintenance is [Lientz, Swanson, and Tompkins, 1978], although some of the results are now being questioned (see Just in Case You Wanted to Know Box 1.3). Regression test case selection is discussed in [Harrold, Rosenblum, Rothermel, and Weyuker, 2001] and setting priorities of regression test cases in [Rothermel, Untch, Chu, and Harrold, 2001]. Regression testing in an industrial environment is discussed in [Onoma, Tsai, Poonawala, and Suganuma, 1998]. A method for estimating staffing needs during postdelivery maintenance is described in [Antoniol, Cimitile, Di Lucca, and Di Penta, 2004].

Planning reengineering is covered in [Sneed, 1995], one of the many articles on reengineering in the January 1995 issue of *IEEE Software*. The costs and benefits of reengineering are discussed in [Adolph, 1996]. Charette, Adams, and White [1997] describe risk management within the framework of postdelivery maintenance, and von Mayrhauser and Vana [1997] discuss various mechanisms of program comprehension for postdelivery maintenance of large-scale products.

A profile of successful reengineering projects is given in [Teng, Jeong, and Grover, 1998]. Maintenance of legacy software products is described in [Bisbal, Lawless, Wu, and Grimson, 1999]. Fioravanti and Nesi [2001] present metrics for estimating adaptive maintenance effort. Problems of comprehension of legacy systems are discussed in [Rajlich, Wilde, Buckellew, and Page, 2001]. The importance of traceability within the context of reengineering is the subject of [Ebner and Kaindl, 2002]. The use of metrics within the context of maintainability is discussed in [Bandi, Vaishnavi, and Turk, 2003]. Problems that can arise in the maintenance of open-source software are presented in [Samoladas, Stamelos, Angelis, and Oikonomou, 2005].

The impact on postdelivery maintenance of the use of objects is described in [Henry and Humphrey, 1990] and [Mancl and Havanas, 1990]. Postdelivery maintenance of specific object-oriented products is described in [Lejter, Meyers, and Reiss, 1992] and [Wilde, Matthews, and Huitt, 1993]. Briand, Bunse, and Daly [2001] discuss the maintainability of object-oriented designs. Experiments to assess the impact of design pattern documentation on postdelivery maintenance are described in [Prechelt, Unger-Lamprecht, Philippsen, and Tichy, 2002]. The maintainability of object-oriented software is discussed in [Lim, Jeong, and Schach, 2005] and [Freeman and Schach, 2005].

Papers on software maintenance appear in the May 1994 issue of *Communications of the ACM*. The July/August 1998 issue of *IEEE Software* contains a number of articles on legacy systems, especially [Rugaber and White, 1998]. The proceedings of the annual Conference on Software Maintenance are a broadly based source of information on all aspects of maintenance.

Key Terms

adaptive maintenance 464
corrective maintenance 464
defect 465
defect report 468
defect-tracking tool 477
encapsulation 471
evolution 464

forward engineering 475
fragile base class
   problem 474
inheritance 473
legacy system 474
moving-target problem 471
perfective maintenance 464

postdelivery maintenance 462
reengineering 475
refactoring 475
regression fault 465
regression testing 465
restructuring 475
reverse engineering 474

Problems

14.1   Why do you think that the mistake is frequently made of considering postdelivery software maintenance to be inferior to software development?

14.2   Consider a product that determines whether a computer is virus free. Describe why such a product is likely to have multiple variations of many of its code artifacts. What are the implications for postdelivery maintenance? How can the resulting problems be solved?

14.3   Repeat Problem 14.2 for the automated library circulation system of Problem 8.7.

14.4   Repeat Problem 14.2 for the product of Problem 8.8 that checks whether a bank statement is correct.

14.5   Repeat Problem 14.2 for the automated teller machine of Problem 8.9.

14.6   You are the manager in charge of postdelivery maintenance in a large software organization. What qualities do you look for when hiring new employees?

14.7   What are the implications of postdelivery maintenance for a one-person software production organization?

14.8   You have been asked to build a computerized defect report file. What sort of data would you store in the file? What sort of queries could be answered by your tool? What sort of queries could not be answered by your tool?

14.9   You receive a memo from the vice-president for software maintenance of Ye Olde Fashioned Software Corporation (Problem 13.24), pointing out that, for the foreseeable future, Olde Fashioned will have to maintain tens of millions of lines of COBOL code and asking your advice with regard to CASE tools for such postdelivery maintenance. What do you reply?

14.10 (Term Project) Suppose that the product for Osric's Office Appliances and Decor of Appendix A has been implemented exactly as described. Now Osric wants the product to be modified so that the priority of a customer in the queue can be manually changed. In what ways will the existing product have to be modified? Would it be better to discard everything and start again from scratch? Compare your answer to the answer you gave to Problem 1.17.

14.11 (Case Study) Improve the aesthetic appearance of the reports in the implementation of Section 13.7 by adjusting the horizontal alignment of the various components.

14.12 (Case Study) Suppose that the requirements of the MSG Foundation are changed so that a couple will never have to pay more than 26 percent of their gross income each week to the MSG Foundation (rather than the 28 percent as currently stipulated). In how many places does the implementation of Section 13.7 have to be changed?

14.13 (Case Study) The MSG Foundation has decided that it will now operate on a monthly basis, rather than a weekly basis. Modify the implementation of Section 13.7 accordingly.

14.14 (Case Study) Replace the menu-driven input routines in the implementation of Section 13.7 with a graphical user interface (GUI).

14.15 (Case Study) Modify the implementation of Section 13.7 to make it Web-based.

14.16 (Readings in Software Engineering) Your instructor will distribute copies of [Freeman and Schach, 2005]. Do you feel that the paper resolves the question of whether object orientation promotes maintainability? Justify your answer.

References

[Adolph, 1996] W. S. ADOLPH, "Cash Cow in the Tar Pit: Reengineering a Legacy System," *IEEE Software* **13** (May 1996), pp. 41–47.

[Antoniol, Cimitile, Di Lucca, and Di Penta, 2004] G. ANTONIOL, A. CIMITILE, G. A. DI LUCCA, AND M. DI PENTA, "Assessing Staffing Needs for a Software Maintenance Project through Queuing Simulation," *IEEE Transactions on Software Engineering* **30** (January 2004), pp. 43–58.

[Bandi, Vaishnavi, and Turk, 2003] R. K. Bandi, V. K. Vaishnavi, and D. E. Turk, "Predicting Maintenance Performance Using Object-Oriented Design Complexity Metrics," *IEEE Transactions on Software Engineering* **29** (January 2003), pp. 77–87.

[Bisbal, Lwawless, Wu, and Grimson, 1999] J. Bisbal, D. Lawless, B. Wu, and J. Grimson, "Legacy Software Products: Issues and Directions," *IEEE Software* **16** (September/October 1999), pp. 103–111.

[Briand, Bunse, and Daly, 2001] L. C. Briand, C. Bunse, and J. W. Daly, "A Controlled Experiment for Evaluating Quality Guidelines on the Maintainability of Object-Oriented Designs," *IEEE Transactions on Software Engineering* **27** (June 2001), pp. 513–30.

[Charette, Adams, and White, 1997] R. N. Charette, K. M. Adams, and M. B. White, "Managing Risk in Software Maintenance," *IEEE Software* **14** (May/June 1997), pp. 43–50.

[Ebner and Kaindl, 2002] G. Ebner and H. Kaindl, "Tracing All Around in Reengineering," *IEEE Software* **19** (May/June 2002), pp. 70–77.

[Fioravanti and Nesi, 2001] F. Fioravanti and P. Nesi, "Estimation and Prediction Metrics for Adaptive Maintenance Effort of Object-Oriented Systems," *IEEE Transactions on Software Engineering* **27** (December 2001), pp. 1062–84.

[Freeman and Schach, 2005] G. L. Freeman, Jr., and S. R. Schach, "The Task-Dependent Nature of the Maintenance of Object-Oriented Programs," *Journal of Systems and Software* **76** (May 2005), pp. 195–206.

[Harrold, Rosenblum, Rothermel, and Weyuker, 2001] M. J. Harrold, D. Rosenblum, G. Rothermel, and E. Weyuker, "Empirical Studies of a Prediction Model for Regression Test Selection," *IEEE Transactions on Software Engineering* **27** (March 2001), pp. 248–63.

[Henry and Humphrey, 1990] S. M. Henry and M. Humphrey, "A Controlled Experiment to Evaluate Maintainability of Object-Oriented Software," *Proceedings of the IEEE Conference on Software Maintenance*, San Diego, CA, November 1990, pp. 258–65.

[Jacobson, Booch, and Rumbaugh, 1999] I. Jacobson, G. Booch, and J. Rumbaugh, The Unified Software Development Process, Addison-Wesley, Reading, MA, 1999.

[Lejter, Meyers, and Reiss, 1992] M. Lejter, S. Meyers, and S. P. Reiss, "Support for Maintaining Object-Oriented Programs," *IEEE Transactions on Software Engineering* **18** (December 1992), pp. 1045–52.

[Lientz, Swanson, and Tompkins, 1978] B. P. Lientz, E. B. Swanson, and G. E. Tompkins, "Characteristics of Application Software Maintenance," *Communications of the ACM* **21** (June 1978), pp. 466–71.

[Lim, Jeong, and Schach, 2005] J. S. Lim, S. R. Jeong, and S. R. Schach, "An Empirical Investigation of the Impact of the Object-Oriented Paradigm on the Maintainability of Real-World Mission-Critical Software," *Journal of Systems and Software* **77** (August 2005), pp. 131–38.

[Lotto, 1515] L. Lotto, *Giovanni Agostino della Torre and his Son, Niccolò*, oil on canvas, 1515, www.nationalgallery.org.uk/cgi-bin/WebObjects.dll/CollectionPublisher.woa/wa/largeImage?workNumber=NG699.

[Loukides and Oram, 1997] M. K. Loukides and A. Oram, *Programming with GNU Software*, O'Reilly and Associates, Sebastopol, CA, 1997.

[Magnus, 2005] A. P. Magnus "9th Kings, Popes, and Symphonies," www.math.ucl.ac.be/~magnus/onine/const9.jpg.

[Mancl and Havanas, 1990] D. Mancl and W. Havanas, "A Study of the Impact of C++ on Software Maintenance," *Proceedings of the IEEE Conference on Software Maintenance*, San Diego, CA, November 1990, pp. 63–69.

[Onoma, Tsai, Poonawala, and Suganuma, 1998] A. K. Onoma, W.-T. Tsai, M. H. Poonawala, and H. Suganuma, "Regression Testing in an Industrial Environment," *Communications of the ACM* **42** (May 1998), pp. 81–86.

[Parnas, 1999] D. L. Parnas, "Ten Myths about Y2K Inspections," *Communications of the ACM* **42** (May 1999), p. 128.

[Pigoski, 1996] T. M. Pigoski, *Practical Software Maintenance: Best Practices for Managing Your Software Investment*, John Wiley and Sons, New York, 1996.

[Prechelt, Unger-Lamprecht, Philippsen, and Tichy, 2002] L. Prechelt, B. Unger-Lamprecht, M. Philippsen, and W. F. Tichy, "Two Controlled Experiments in Assessing the Usefulness of Design Pattern Documentation in Program Maintenance," *IEEE Transactions on Software Engineering* **28** (June 2002), pp. 595–606.

[Rajlich, Wilde, Buckellew, and Page, 2001] V. Rajlich, N. Wilde, M. Buckellew, and H. Page, "Software Cultures and Evolution," *IEEE Computer* **34** (September 2001), pp. 24–28.

[Rochkind, 1975] M. J. Rochkind, "The Source Code Control System," *IEEE Transactions on Software Engineering* **SE-1** (October 1975), pp. 255–65.

[Rothermel, Untch, Chu, and Harrold, 2001] G. Rothermel, R. H. Untch, C. Chu, and M. J. Harrold, "Prioritizing Test Cases for Regression Test Cases," *IEEE Transactions on Software Engineering* **27** (October 2001), pp. 929–48.

[Rugaber and White, 1998] S. Rugaber and J. White, "Restoring a Legacy: Lessons Learned," *IEEE Software* **15** (July/August 1998), pp. 28–33.

[Samoladas, Stamelos, Angelis, and Oikonomou, 2005] I. Samoladas, I. Stamelos, L. Angelis, and A. Oikonomou, "Open Source Software Development Should Strive for Even Greater Code Maintainability," *Communications of the ACM* **47** (October 2004), pp. 83–87.

[Sneed, 1995] H. M. Sneed, "Planning the Reengineering of Legacy Systems," *IEEE Software* **12** (January 1995), pp. 24–34.

[Teng, Jeong, and Grover, 1998] J. T. C. Teng, S. R. Jeong, and V. Grover, "Profiling Successful Reengineering Projects," *Communications of the ACM* **41** (June 1999), pp. 96–102.

[Tichy, 1985] W. F. Tichy, "RCS—A System for Version Control," *Software—Practice and Experience* **15** (July 1985), pp. 637–54.

[von Mayrhauser and Vana, 1997] A. von Mayrhauser and A. M. Vana, "Identification of Dynamic Comprehension Processes during Large Scale Maintenance," *IEEE Transactions on Software Engineering* **22** (June 1996), pp. 424–37.

[Wilde, Matthews, and Huitt, 1993] N. Wilde, P. Matthews, and R. Huitt, "Maintaining Object-Oriented Software," *IEEE Software* **10** (January 1993), pp. 75–80.

Chapter 15

More on UML

Learning Objectives

After studying this chapter, you should be able to

- Model software using UML use cases, class diagrams, notes, use-case diagrams, interaction diagrams, statecharts, activity diagrams, packages, component diagrams, and deployment diagrams.
- Appreciate that UML is a language, *not* a methodology.

During the course of this book, various elements of UML [Booch, Rumbaugh, and Jacobson, 1999] have been introduced. Specifically, the notation for class diagrams, inheritance, aggregation, and association was described in Chapter 7. In Chapter 10, use cases, use-case diagrams, and notes were introduced; in Chapter 11, statecharts, communication diagrams, and sequence diagrams were added.

This subset of UML is adequate for understanding this book and for doing all the exercises, as well as the term project of Appendix A. However, real-world software products are, unfortunately, much larger and considerably more complex than the MSG Foundation case study or the term project of Appendix A. Accordingly, in this chapter more material on UML is presented, as preparation for entering the real world.

Before reading this chapter, it is necessary to be aware that UML, like all state-of-the-art computer languages, is constantly changing. When this book was written, the latest version of UML was Version 2.0. By this time, however, some aspects of UML may have changed. As explained in Just in Case You Wanted to Know Box 3.3, UML is now under the control of the Object Management Group. Before proceeding, it would probably be a good idea to check for updates to UML at the OMG website, www.omg.org.

15.1   UML Is *Not* a Methodology

Before looking at UML in more detail, it is essential to clarify what UML is and, more importantly, what UML is not. UML is an acronym for Unified Modeling Language. That is, UML is a *language*. Consider a language like English. English can be used to write novels, encyclopedias, poems, prayers, news reports, and even textbooks on software engineering. That is, a language is simply a tool for expressing ideas. A specific language does not constrain the types of ideas that can be described by that language or the way that they can be described.

As a language, UML can be used to describe software developed using the traditional paradigm or any of the many versions of the object-oriented paradigm, including the Unified Process. In other words, UML is a notation, not a methodology. It is a notation that can be used in conjunction with any methodology.

In fact, UML is not merely *a* notation; it is *the* notation. It is hard to imagine a modern book on software engineering that does not use UML to describe software. UML has become a world standard, so much so that someone unfamiliar with UML would have difficulty functioning today as a software professional.

The title of this chapter is "More on UML." Bearing in mind the central role played by UML, it would seem essential for all of UML to be presented here. However, the manual for Version 2.0 of UML is over 1200 pages long, so complete coverage would probably not be a good idea. But is it possible to be a competent software professional without knowing every single aspect of UML?

The key point is that UML is a language. The English language has over 100,000 words, but almost all speakers of English seem to manage perfectly well with just a subset of the complete English vocabulary. In the same way, in this chapter all the types of UML diagrams are described, together with many (but by no means all) of the various options for each of those diagrams. The small subset of UML presented in Chapters 7, 10, and 11 is adequate for the purposes of this book. In the same way, the larger subset of UML presented in this chapter is adequate for the development and maintenance of most software products.

15.2   Class Diagrams

The simplest possible **class diagram** is shown in Figure 15.1. It depicts the **Bank Account Class**. More details of **Bank Account Class** are shown in the class diagram of Figure 15.2. A key aspect of UML is that both Figures 15.1 and 15.2 are valid class

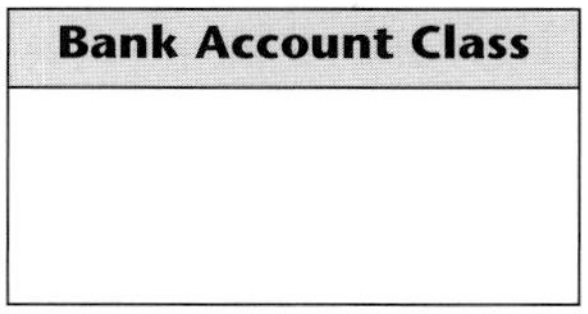

Figure 15.2   The class diagram of Figure 15.1 with an attribute and two operations added.

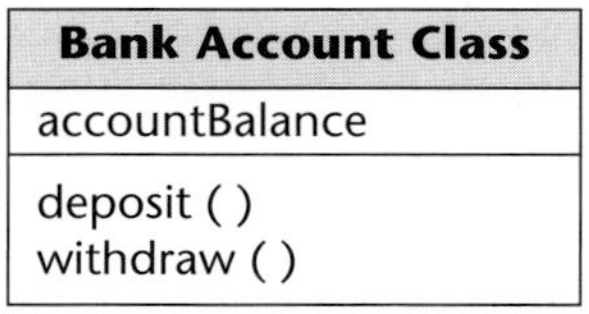

Figure 15.1   The simplest possible class diagram.

Bank Account Class

Bank Account Class
accountBalance
deposit ( ) withdraw ( )

diagrams. In other words, in UML as many or as few details may be added as are judged appropriate for the current iteration and incrementation.

This freedom of notation extends to objects. The notation **bank account** may be informally used for one specific object of this class. The full UML notation is

<u>**bank account : Bank Account Class**</u>

That is, <u>**bank account**</u> is an object, an instance of a class **Bank Account Class**. In more detail, the underlining denotes an object, the colon denotes "an instance of," and the boldface and initial uppercase letters in **Bank Account Class** denote this is a class. However, UML allows us to use a shorter notation, <u>**bank account**</u>, when there is no ambiguity.

Now suppose we wish to model the concept of an arbitrary bank account. That is, we do not wish to refer to one specific object of **Bank Account Class**. The UML notation for this is

<u>**: Bank Account Class**</u>

As just pointed out, the colon means "an instance of," so <u>**: Bank Account Class**</u> means "an instance of class **Bank Account Class**," which is precisely what we wanted to model. This notation is widely used in Chapter 11. Conversely, in Figure 11.48, a communication diagram for the realization of a scenario of the use case Update Estimated Annual Operating Expenses of the MSG Foundation software product, the actor is labeled **MSG Staff Member** and not <u>**: MSG Staff Member**</u> (the labeling of other items in that diagram) precisely because **MSG Staff Member** denotes that MSG Staff Member is an actor, whereas <u>**: MSG Staff Member**</u> would denote "an instance of the [nonexistent] **MSG Staff Member Class**."

Section 7.6 introduced the concept of information hiding. In UML, the prefix + indicates that an attribute or operation is **public**, and similarly the prefix – denotes that the attribute or operation is **private**. This notation is used in Figure 15.3. The attribute of **Bank Account Class** is declared to be **private** (so that we can achieve information hiding), whereas both the operations are **public** so that they can be invoked from anywhere in the software product. A third standard type of visibility, **protected**, uses the prefix #. If an attribute is **public**, it is visible everywhere; if it is **private**, it is visible only in the class in which it is defined, and if it is **protected**, it is visible either within the class in which it is defined or within subclasses of that class.

Up to now in this chapter, class diagrams containing only one class have been presented. Section 16.2.1 considers class diagrams with more than one class.

15.2.1 Aggregation

Consider Figure 15.4, which models the statement: "A car consists of a chassis, an engine, wheels, and seats." Recall that the open diamonds denote aggregation. **Aggregation** is the UML term for the **part–whole relationship**; the parts of a car are the chassis, engine,

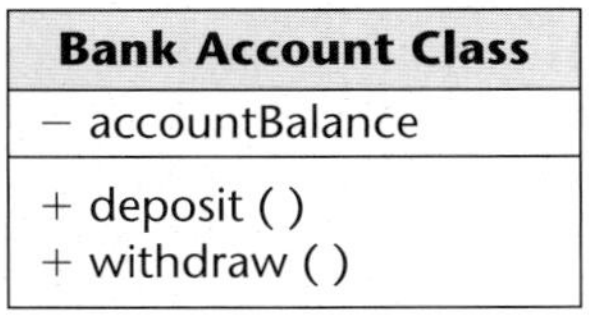

Figure 15.3
The class diagram of Figure 15.2 with visibility prefixes added.

Bank Account Class
− accountBalance
+ deposit ( )   + withdraw ( )

Figure 15.4   An aggregation example.

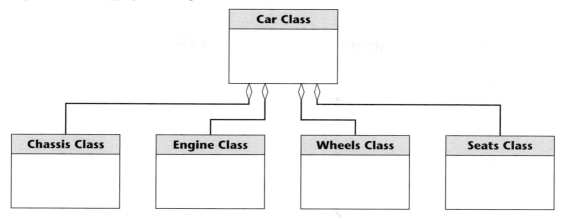

Figure 15.5   Aggregation example with multiplicities.

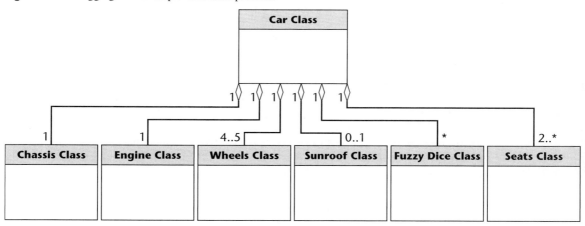

wheels, and seats. The diamond is placed at the "whole" (car) end, not the "part" (chassis, engine, wheels, or seats) end of the line connecting a part to the whole.

15.2.2   Multiplicity

Now suppose that we want to use UML to model the statement: "A car consists of one chassis, one engine, four or five wheels, an optional sunroof, zero or more fuzzy dice hanging from the rearview mirror, and two or more seats." This is shown in Figure 15.5. The numbers next to the ends of the lines denote ***multiplicity***, the number of times that the one class is associated with the other class.

First consider the line connecting **Chassis Class** to **Car Class**. The 1 at the "part" end of the line denotes that one chassis is involved in this relationship, and the 1 at the "whole" end denotes that one car is involved; that is, each car has one chassis. Similar observations hold for the line connecting **Engine Class** to **Car Class**.

Now consider the line connecting **Wheels Class** to **Car Class**. The 4..5 at the "part" end together with the 1 at the "whole" end denotes that each car has from four to five wheels (the fifth wheel is the spare). Because instances of classes come in whole numbers only, this means that the UML diagram models the statement that a car has four or five wheels, as required.

In general, the two dots .. denote a range. Accordingly, 0..1 means zero or one, which is the UML way of denoting "optional." That is why there is the 0..1 next to the line connecting **Sun Roof Class** to **Car Class**.

Now look at the line connecting **Fuzzy Dice Class** to **Car Class**. At the "part" end, the label is *. An asterisk by itself denotes "zero or more." Therefore, the * in Figure 15.5 means that a car has zero or more fuzzy dice hanging from the rearview mirror. (If you want to know more about that asterisk, see Just in Case You Wanted to Know Box 15.1.)

Now look at the line connecting **Seats Class** to **Car Class**. At the "part" end, the label is 2..*. An asterisk by itself denotes "zero or more"; an asterisk in a range denotes "or more." Accordingly, the 2..* in Figure 15.5 means that a car has two or more seats.

Therefore, in UML if the exact multiplicity is known, that number is used. An example is the 1 that appears in eight places in Figure 15.5. If the range is known, the range notation is used, as with the 0..1 or 4..5 in Figure 15.5. And if the number is unspecified, the asterisk is used. If the upper limit in a range is unspecified, the range notation is combined with the asterisk notation, as with the 2..* in Figure 15.5. In passing, the multiplicity notation of UML is based on the entity–relationship diagrams of traditional database theory [Date, 2003].

15.2.3   Composition

Another example of aggregation is shown in Figure 15.6, which models the relationship between a chessboard and its squares; every chessboard consists of 64 squares. In fact, this relationship goes further; it is an example of **composition**, a stronger form of aggregation. As previously stated, association models the part–whole relationship. When there is composition, then, in addition, every part may belong to only one whole, and if the whole is deleted, so are the parts. In the example, if there are a number of different chessboards, each square belongs to only one board, and if a chessboard is thrown away, all 64 squares

Figure 15.6
Another aggregation example (but see Figure 15.7).

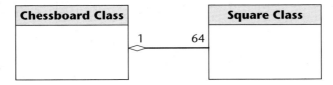

Figure 15.7
Composition
example.

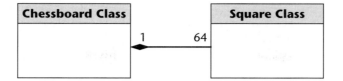

Figure 15.8
Generalization
(inheritance)
example with
an explicit
discriminator.

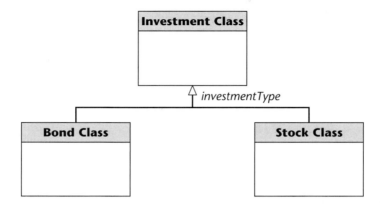

Figure 15.9
An association.

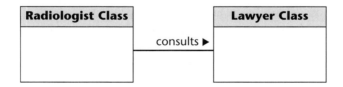

on that board go as well. Composition, an extension of aggregation, is depicted with a solid diamond, as in Figure 15.7.

15.2.4   Generalization

Inheritance is a required feature of object orientation. It is a special case of **_generalization_**. The UML notation for generalization is an open triangle. Sometimes we choose to label that open triangle with a **_discriminator_**. Consider Figure 15.8, which models two types of investments: bonds and stocks. The notation *investmentType* next to the open triangle means that every instance of **Investment Class** or its two subclasses has an attribute investmentType, and this attribute can be used to distinguish between instances of bonds and instances of stocks.

15.2.5   Association

In Section 7.7, an example of **_association_** involving two classes was presented in which the direction of the association had to be clarified by means of a navigation arrow in the form of a solid triangle. Figure 7.32 is reproduced here as Figure 15.9.

Figure 15.10   An association class.

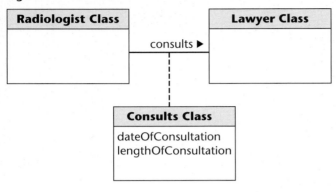

Figure 15.11
Generalization
of an actor.

In some cases, the association between the two classes may itself need to be modeled as a class. For example, suppose the radiologist in Figure 15.9 consults the lawyer on a number of different occasions, on each occasion for a different length of time. To enable the lawyer to bill the radiologist correctly, a class diagram such as that depicted in Figure 15.10 is needed. Now consults has become a class, **Consults Class**, called an ***association class*** (because it is both an association and a class).

15.3   Notes

When we want to include a comment in a UML diagram, we put it in a ***note*** (a rectangle with the top right-hand corner bent over). A dashed line is then drawn from the note to the item to which the note refers. Figure 11.38 shows a note.

15.4   Use-Case Diagrams

As described in Section 10.4.3, a ***use case*** is a model of the interaction between external users of a software product (***actors***) and the software product itself. More precisely, an actor is a user playing a specific role. A ***use-case diagram*** is a set of use cases.

In Section 10.4.3, generalization within the context of actors was described, as depicted in Figure 10.2. Figure 15.11 is another example; it shows that a **Manager** is a special case of an **Employee**. As with classes, the open triangle points toward the more general case.

15.5   Stereotypes

The three primary tax forms for U.S. personal income tax are Forms 1040, 1040A, and 1040EZ. Figure 15.12 shows that use cases Prepare Form 1040, Prepare Form 1040A, and Prepare Form 1040EZ all incorporate the use case Print Tax Form, as indicated by the include relationship, represented by a stereotype.

Figure 15.12
The use cases Prepare Form 1040, Prepare Form 1040A, and Prepare Form 1040EZ incorporate the use case Print Tax Form.

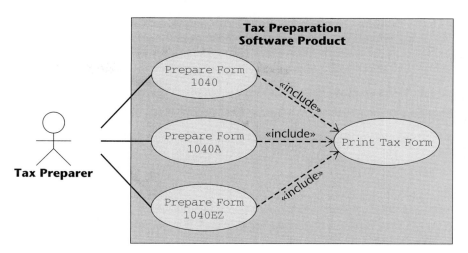

Figure 15.13   Use case Order a Burger showing the variation when the customer turns down the fries.

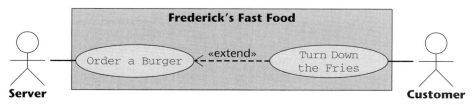

A *stereotype* in UML is a way of extending UML. That is, if we need to define a construct that is not in UML, we can do it. Three stereotypes were presented in Chapter 11: boundary, control, and entity classes. In general, the names of stereotypes appear between *guillemets*, for example, «this is my own construct». Consequently, instead of using the special symbol for a boundary class, the standard rectangular symbol for a class could have been used with the notation «boundary class» inside the rectangle and similarly for control and entity classes.

The **include** *relationship* shown in Figure 15.12 is treated in UML as a stereotype; hence the notation «include» in that figure to denote common functionality, in this instance the use case Print Tax Form (Figure 10.41). Another relationship is the **extend** *relationship*, where one use case is a variation of the standard use case. For example, we may wish to have a separate use case to model the situation of a customer ordering a burger but turning down the fries. The notation «extend» is similarly used for this purpose, as shown in Figure 15.13. However, for this relationship, the open-headed arrow goes in the other direction.

15.6   Interaction Diagrams

Interaction diagrams show the way that the objects in the software product interact with one another. In Chapter 11, both types of interaction diagram supported by UML were presented: sequence diagrams and communication diagrams.

First, consider **sequence diagrams**. Suppose that someone interactively orders an item over the Internet, but when the overall total, including sales tax and delivery charges, is displayed, the buyer decides that the price is too high and cancels the order. Figure 15.14 depicts the dynamic creation and subsequent dynamic destruction of the order.

1. Consider the lifelines in Figure 15.14. When an object is active, this is denoted by a thin rectangle (**activation box**) in place of the dashed line. For example, the **: Price Class** object is active from message 5: Determine price of order until message 6: Return price, and similarly for the other objects.

2. The **: Order Class** object is created only when the **: Assemble Order Control Class** sends message 3: Create order to the **: Order Class** object. This is denoted by the lifeline starting at only the point of dynamic creation,

3. Figure 15.14 also shows the destruction of the **: Order Class** object after the **: Order Class** object receives the message 9: Destroy object. The destruction is denoted by the large X.

Figure 15.14
A sequence diagram showing dynamic creation and destruction of an object, return, and explicit activation.

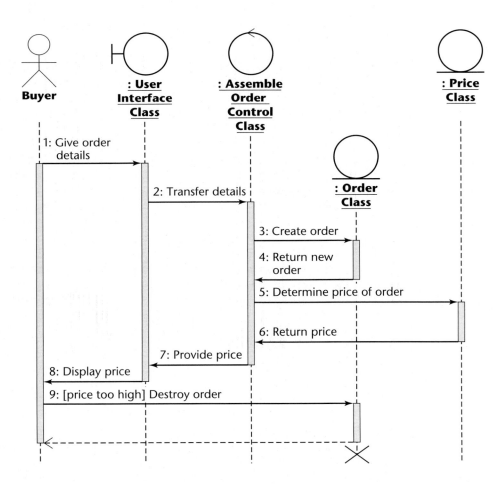

4. This destruction takes place after a return has taken place, denoted by the dashed horizontal line below event 9, terminated by an open arrow. In the rest of the sequence diagram, each message is eventually followed by a message sent back to the object that sent the original message. In fact, this reciprocity is optional; it is perfectly valid to send a message without eventually receiving any sort of reply. Even if there is a reply, it is not necessary that a specific new message be sent back. Instead, a dashed line ending in an open arrow is drawn (a ***return***) to indicate a return from the original message, as opposed to a new message.

5. There is a guard on message 9: [price too high] Destroy order. That is, message 9 is sent only if the buyer decides not to purchase the item because the price is too high. A ***guard*** (condition) is something that is true or false; only if it is true is the message sent. In Section 16.7, guards are described within the context of statecharts, but here they are used in a sequence diagram.

(In Figure 15.14, the message 9: [price too high] Destroy order should be sent from the **Buyer** to the **: User Interface Class** object, and the latter should then send a message to the **: Assemble Order Control Class** object. Next, the **: Assemble Order Control Class** object should send a message to the **: Order Class** object, instructing it to destroy the order. To highlight dynamic destruction of an object, these details have been suppressed in Figure 15.14.)

Many other options are supported by UML interaction diagrams. For example, suppose we model an elevator going up. We do not know in advance which elevator button will be pressed, so we have no idea how many floors up the elevator will go. We model this iteration by labeling the relevant message *move up one floor, as shown in Figure 15.15. The asterisk is, once again, the Kleene star (see Just in Case You Wanted to Know Box 15.1). So this message means, "move up zero or more floors."

An object can send a message to itself. This is termed a ***self-call***. For example, suppose that the elevator has arrived at a floor. The elevator controller sends a message to the elevator doors to open. Once the return has been received, the elevator controller sends a message to itself to start its timer; this self-call is also shown in Figure 15.15. At the end of the time period, the elevator controller sends a message to the doors to close. When the second return has been received (that is, when the doors have been safely closed), the elevator is instructed to move again.

Turning now to ***communication diagrams***, it was stated in Section 11.18.1 that communication diagrams are equivalent to sequence diagrams. So, all the features of sequence diagrams presented in this section are equally applicable to communication diagrams, such as Figure 11.33.

15.7   Statecharts

Consider the ***statechart*** of Figure 15.16. This is similar to the statechart of Figure 11.22, but modeled using guards instead of events. It shows the initial state (the solid circle) with an unlabeled ***transition*** leading to state **MSG Foundation Event Loop**. Five transitions lead from that state, each with a guard, that is, a condition that is true or false. When one of the guards becomes true, the corresponding transition takes place.

Figure 15.15
A sequence diagram showing iteration and self-call.

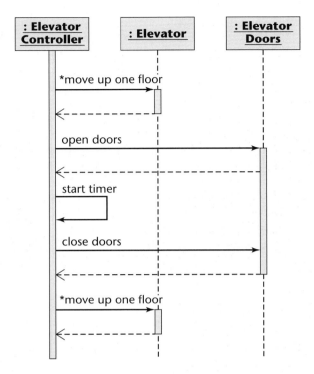

An *event* also causes transitions between states. A common event is the receipt of a message. Consider Figure 15.17, which depicts a part of a statechart for an elevator. The elevator is in state **Elevator Moving**. It stays in motion, performing operation Move up one floor, while guard [no message received yet] remains true, until it receives the message Elevator has arrived at floor. The receipt of this message (event) causes the guard to be false and also enables a transition to state **Stopped At Floor**. In this state, the activity Open the elevator doors is performed.

So far, transition labels have been in the form of [guard] or event. In fact, the most general form of a transition label is

event [guard] / action

That is, if event has taken place and [guard] is true, then the transition occurs and, while it is occurring, action is performed. An example of such a transition label is shown in Figure 15.18, which is equivalent to Figure 15.17. The transition label is Elevator has arrived at floor [a message has been received] / Open the elevator doors. The *guard* [a message has been received] is true when the *event* Elevator has arrived at floor has occurred and a message to this effect has been sent. The **action** to be taken, indicated by the instruction following the slash /, is Open the elevator doors.

Comparing Figures 15.17 and 15.18, we see that there are two places where an action can be performed in a statechart. First, as reflected in state **Stopped At Floor** in Figure 15.17, an action can be performed when a state is entered. Such an action is called an **activity** in UML. Second, as shown in Figure 15.18, an action can take place as part of

Figure 15.16   A statechart for the MSG Foundation case study.

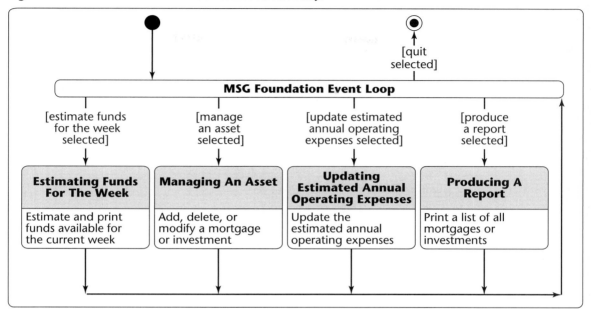

Figure 15.17   A portion of a statechart for an elevator.

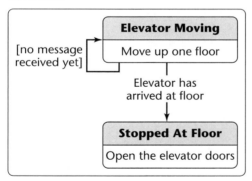

a transition. (Technically, there is a slight difference between an activity and an action. An action is assumed to take place essentially instantaneously, but an activity may take place less quickly, perhaps over several seconds.)

UML supports a wide variety of different types of actions and events in statecharts. For instance, an event can be specified in terms of words like when or after. Therefore, an event might stipulate when (cost > 1000) or after (2.5 seconds).

A statechart with a large number of states tends to have a large number of transitions. The many arrows representing these transitions soon make the statechart look like a large bowl of spaghetti. One technique for dealing with this is to use a ***superstate***. Consider

Figure 15.18   A statechart equivalent to
Figure 15.17.

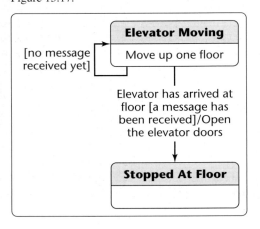

Figure 15.19   Statechart (a) without
and (b) with superstate.

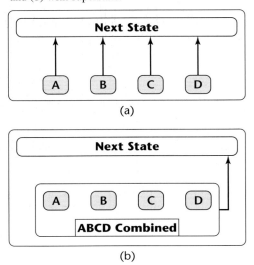

the statechart of Figure 15.19(a). The four states **A**, **B**, **C**, and **D** all have transitions to
Next State. Figure 15.19(b) shows how these four states can be combined into one
superstate, **ABCD Combined**, which needs only one transition, as opposed to the four
in Figure 15.19(a). This reduces the number of arrows from four to only one. At the same
time, states **A**, **B**, **C**, and **D** still exist in their own right, so any existing actions associated with those states are not affected nor are any existing transitions into those states.
Another example of a superstate is shown in Figure 15.20, where the four lower states of
Figure 15.16 are unified into one superstate, **MSG Foundation Combined**, leading to
a cleaner and clearer diagram.

15.8   Activity Diagrams

Activity diagrams show how various events are coordinated. They are therefore used
when activities are carried out in parallel.

Suppose a couple seated at a restaurant orders their meal. One orders a chicken dish;
the other orders fish. The waiter writes down their order and hands the order to the chef
so that she knows what dishes to prepare. It does not matter which dish is completed first
because the meal is served only when both dishes have been prepared. This is shown in
Figure 15.21. The upper heavy horizontal line is called a *fork,* and the lower one is called
a *join.* In general, a **fork** has one incoming transition and many outgoing transitions, each
of which starts an activity to be executed in parallel with the other activities. Conversely,
a **join** has many incoming transitions, each of which lead from an activity executed in
parallel with the other activities, and one outgoing transition that is started when all the
parallel activities have been completed.

Figure 15.20   Figure 15.16 with four states combined into a superstate, **MSG Foundation Combined**.

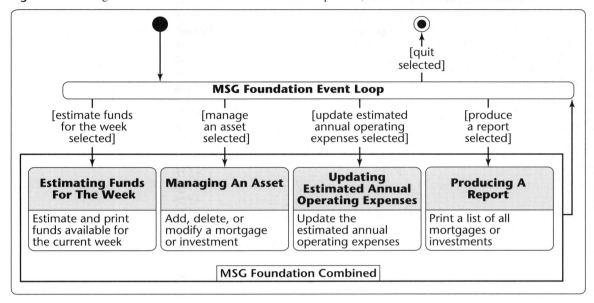

Figure 15.21
An activity
diagram for a
restaurant order
for two diners.

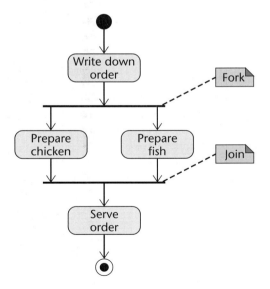

Activity diagrams are useful for modeling businesses where a number of activities are carried out in parallel. For example, consider a company that assembles computers as specified by the customer. As shown in the activity diagram of Figure 15.22, when an order is received, it is passed on to the **Assembly Department**. It is also passed to the **Accounts Receivable Department**. The order is complete when

Figure 15.22
An activity
diagram for
a computer
assembly
company.

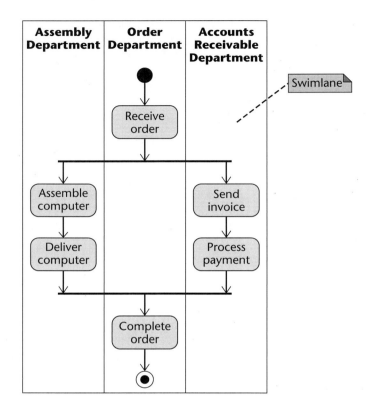

the computer has been assembled and delivered, and the customer's payment has been processed. Each of the three departments involved, the **Assembly Department**, the **Order Department**, and **Accounts Receivable Department**, is in its own *swimlane*. In general, the combination of forks, joins, and swimlanes shows clearly which branches of an organization are involved in each specific activity, which tasks are carried out in parallel, and which tasks have to be completed in parallel before the next task can be started.

15.9   Packages

As explained in Section 12.4, the way to handle a large software product is to decompose it into relatively independent **packages**. The UML notation for a package is a rectangle with a name tag, as shown in Figure 15.23. This figure shows that My Package is a package, but the rectangle is empty. This is a valid UML diagram—the diagram simply models the fact that My Package is a package. Figure 15.24 is more interesting—it shows the contents of My Package, including a class, an entity class, and another package. We can continue to supply more details until the package is at the appropriate level of detail for the current iteration and incrementation.

Figure 15.23 The UML notation for a package.

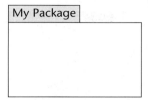

Figure 15.24 The package of Figure 15.23 with more details shown.

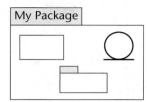

Figure 15.25 Component diagram.

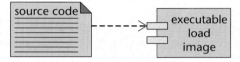

15.10 Component Diagrams

A ***component diagram*** shows dependencies among software components, including source code, compiled code, and executable load images. For example, the component diagram of Figure 15.25 shows source code (represented by a note) and the executable load image created from the source code.

15.11 Deployment Diagrams

A ***deployment diagram*** shows on which hardware component each software component is installed (or deployed). It also shows the communication links among the hardware components. A simple deployment diagram is shown in Figure 15.26.

Figure 15.26 A deployment diagram.

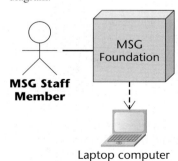

15.12 Review of UML Diagrams

A wide variety of different UML diagrams have been presented in this chapter. In the interests of clarity, here is a list of some of the diagram types that might be confused:

- A *use case* models the interaction between actors (external users of a software product) and the software product itself.
- A *use-case diagram* is a single diagram that incorporates a number of use cases.
- A *class diagram* is a model of the classes showing the static relationships among them, including association and generalization.
- A *statechart* shows states (specific values of attributes of objects), events that cause transitions between states (subject to guards), and actions and activities performed by objects. A statechart is therefore a dynamic model—it reflects the behavior of objects, that is, the way they react to specific events.
- An *interaction diagram (sequence diagram* or *communication diagram)* shows the way that objects interact with one another as messages are passed between them. This is another dynamic model; that is, it also shows how objects behave.
- An *activity diagram* shows how events that occur at the same time are coordinated. This is yet another dynamic model.

15.13 UML and Iteration

Consider a statechart. The transitions can be labeled with a guard, an event, an action, or all three. Now consider a sequence diagram. The lifelines may or may not include activation boxes, there may or may not be returns, and there may or may not be guards on the messages.

A wide range of options are available for every UML diagram. That is, a valid UML diagram consists of a small required part plus any number of options. UML diagrams have so many options for two reasons. First, not every feature of UML is applicable to every software product, so there has to be freedom with regard to choice of options. Second, we cannot perform the iteration and incrementation of the Unified Process unless we are permitted to add features stepwise to diagrams, rather than create the complete final diagram at the beginning. That is, UML allows us to start with a basic diagram. We can then add optional features as we wish, bearing in mind that, at all times, the resulting UML diagram is still valid. This is one of the many reasons why UML is so well suited to the Unified Process.

Chapter Review

It is explained in Section 15.1 that UML is a language, not a methodology. Class diagrams are described in Section 15.2. Specific aspects of class diagrams are discussed, including aggregation (Section 15.2.1), multiplicity (Section 15.2.2), composition (Section 15.2.3), generalization (Section 15.2.4), and association (Section 15.2.5). Next, a variety of UML diagrams are presented, including notes (Section 15.3), use-case diagrams (Section 15.4), stereotypes (Section 15.5), interaction diagrams (both sequence diagrams and communication diagrams; Section 15.6), statecharts (Section 15.7), activity diagrams (Section 15.8), packages (Section 15.9), component diagrams (Section 15.10), and deployment diagrams (Section 15.11). The chapter concludes with a review of UML diagrams (Section 15.12) and a discussion of why UML is so suitable for the Unified Process (Section 15.13).

For Further Reading

There is no substitute for reading the current version of the UML manual, to be found at the OMG website, www.omg.org. Two good introductory texts on UML are [Fowler and Scott, 2000] and [Stevens and Pooley, 2000].

Key Terms

action 492	deployment diagram 497	package 496
activation box 490	discriminator 487	part–whole
activity 492	event 492	relationship 484
activity diagram 494	extend relationship 489	return 491
actor 488	fork 494	self-call 491
aggregation 484	generalization 487	sequence diagram 490
association 487	guard 491	statechart 491
association class 488	guillemets 489	stereotype 489
class diagram 483	include relationship 489	superstate 493
communication	interaction diagram 489	swimlane 496
diagram 491	join 494	transition 491
component diagram 497	multiplicity 485	use case 488
composition 486	note 488	use-case diagram 488

Problems

15.1   Use UML to model airports. (Hint: Do not show any more details than are strictly needed to answer the question.)

15.2   Use UML to model chocolate cakes. A chocolate cake is made with eggs, flour, sugar, baking powder, milk, and cocoa. A chocolate cake is mixed, baked, frosted, and then eaten. To prevent unauthorized individuals from baking a chocolate cake, the ingredients are private, as are all but the last operation.

15.3   Use UML to model dining rooms. Every dining room has to have a table, four or more chairs, and a sideboard. Optionally, it may also have a fireplace.

15.4   Model the dining rooms of Problem 15.3 using a combination of aggregation and composition.

15.5   Modify your UML model of Problem 15.3 to reflect that a dining room is a specific type of room.

15.6   Add a note to your diagram of Problem 15.2 pointing out that the cake you modeled is a chocolate cake.

15.7   Use UML to model John Cage's somewhat controversial 1952 piano composition entitled *4'33"*. The piece consists of three silent movements, of length 30 seconds, 2 minutes 23 seconds, and 1 minute 40 seconds, respectively. (The title of the piece comes from its total length.) The pianist walks onto the stage holding a stopwatch and the score (in conventional music notation but with blank measures). The pianist sits down on the piano stool, puts the score and the stopwatch on the piano, opens the score, starts the stopwatch, and then signals the start of the first movement by lowering the lid of the piano. At the end of the first movement (that is, after 30 seconds of silence during which the pianist carefully follows the blank score, turning the page when necessary), the lid of the piano is raised to signal the end of the first movement. These actions are repeated for the second movement (2 minutes 23 seconds) and the third movement (1 minute 40 seconds). The pianist then closes the score, picks up the score and the stopwatch, gets up, and leaves the stage.

References   [Booch, Rumbaugh, and Jacobson, 1999] G. Booch, J. Rumbaugh, and I. Jacobson, *The UML Users Guide,* Addison-Wesley, Reading, MA, 1999.

[Date, 2003] C. J. Date, An Introduction to Database Systems, 8th ed., Addison-Wesley, Reading, MA, 2003.

[Fowler and Scott, 2000] M. Fowler with K. Scott, UML Distilled, 2nd ed., Addison-Wesley, Upper Saddle River, NJ, 2000.

[Stevens and Pooley, 2000] P. Stevens with R. Pooley, Using UML: Software Engineering with Objects and Components, updated edition, Addison-Wesley, Upper Saddle River, NJ, 2000.

Bibliography

[Ackerman, Buchwald, and Lewski, 1989] A. F. ACKERMAN, L. S. BUCHWALD, AND F. H. LEWSKI, "Software Inspections: An Effective Verification Process," *IEEE Software* **6** (May 1989), pp. 31–36. (Chapter 6)

[Adolph, 1996] W. S. ADOLPH, "Cash Cow in the Tar Pit: Reengineering a Legacy System," *IEEE Software* **13** (May 1996), pp. 41–47. (Chapter 14)

[Albrecht, 1979] A. J. ALBRECHT, "Measuring Application Development Productivity," *Proceedings of the IBM SHARE/GUIDE Applications Development Symposium*, Monterey, CA, October 1979, pp. 83–92. (Chapter 9)

[Alexander, 1999] C. ALEXANDER, "The Origins of Pattern Theory," *IEEE Software* **16** (September/October 1999), pp. 71–82. (Chapter 8)

[I. Alexander, 2003] I. ALEXANDER, "Misuse Cases: Use Cases with Hostile Intent," *IEEE Software* **20** (January/February 2003), pp. 58–66. (Chapter 10)

[R. Alexander, 2003] R. ALEXANDER, "The Real Costs of Aspect-Oriented Programming," *IEEE Software* **20** (November/December 2003), pp. 92–93. (Chapter 7)

[Alexander et al., 1977] C. ALEXANDER, S. ISHIKAWA, M. SILVERSTEIN, M. JACOBSON, I. FIKSDAHL-KING, AND S. ANGEL, *A Pattern Language*, Oxford University Press, New York, 1977. (Chapter 8)

[Alshayeb and Li, 2003] M. ALSHAYEB, AND W. LI "An Empirical Validation of Object-Oriented Metrics in Two Different Iterative Software Processes," *IEEE Transactions on Software Engineering* **29** (November 2003), pp. 1043–49. (Chapters 5 and 13)

[ANSI/IEEE 754, 1985] *Standard for Binary Floating Point Arithmetic*, ANSI/IEEE 754, American National Standards Institute, Institute of Electrical and Electronic Engineers, New York, 1985. (Chapter 8)

[ANSI/IEEE 829, 1991] *Software Test Documentation*, ANSI/IEEE 829-1991, American National Standards Institute, Institute of Electrical and Electronic Engineers, New York, 1991. (Chapter 9)

[ANSI/MIL-STD-1815A, 1983] *Reference Manual for the Ada Programming Language*, ANSI/MIL-STD-1815A, American National Standards Institute, United States Department of Defense, Washington, DC, 1983. (Chapter 8)

[Antoniol, Cimitile, Di Lucca, and Di Penta, 2004] G. ANTONIOL, A. CIMITILE, G. A. DI LUCCA, AND M. DI PENTA, "Assessing Staffing Needs for a Software Maintenance Project through Queuing Simulation," *IEEE Transactions on Software Engineering* **30** (January 2004), pp. 43–58. (Chapter 14)

[Awad, Kuusela, and Ziegler, 1996] M. AWAD, J. KUUSELA, AND J. ZIEGLER, *Object-Oriented Technology for Real-Time Systems: A Practical Approach Using OMT and Fusion,* Prentice Hall, Upper Saddle River, NJ, 1996. (Chapter 11)

[Baber, 1987] R. L. BABER, *The Spine of Software: Designing Provably Correct Software: Theory and Practice*, John Wiley and Sons, New York, 1987. (Chapter 6)

[Babich, 1986] W. A. BABICH, *Software Configuration Management: Coordination for Team Productivity*, Addison-Wesley, Reading, MA, 1986. (Chapter 5)

[Baetjer, 1996] H. BAETJER, *Software as Capital: An Economic Perspective on Software Engineering,* IEEE Computer Society Press, Los Alamitos, CA, 1996. (Chapter 1)

[Baker, 1972] F. T. BAKER, "Chief Programmer Team Management of Production Programming," *IBM Systems Journal* **11** (No. 1, 1972), pp. 56–73. (Chapter 4)

[Bamberger, 1997] J. BAMBERGER, "Essence of the Capability Maturity Model," *IEEE Computer* **30** (June 1997), pp. 112–14. (Chapter 3)

[Bamford and Deibler, 1993a] R. C. BAMFORD AND W. J. DEIBLER, II, "Comparing, Contrasting ISO 9001 and the SEI Capability Maturity Model," *IEEE Computer* **26** (October 1993), pp. 68–70. (Chapter 3)

[Bamford and Deibler, 1993b] R. C. BAMFORD AND W. J. DEIBLER, II, "A Detailed Comparison of the SEI Software Maturity Levels and Technology Stages to the Requirements for ISO 9001 Registration," Software Systems Quality Consulting, San Jose, CA, 1993. (Chapter 3)

[Bandi, Vaishnavi, and Turk, 2003] R. K. BANDI, V. K. VAISHNAVI, AND D. E. TURK, "Predicting Maintenance Performance Using Object-Oriented Design Complexity Metrics," *IEEE Transactions on Software Engineering* **29** (January 2003), pp. 77–87. (Chapter 14)

[Banks, Carson, Nelson, and Nichol, 2001] J. BANKS, J. S. CARSON, B. L. NELSON, AND D. M. NICHOL, *Discrete-Event System Simulation,* 3rd ed., Prentice Hall, Upper Saddle River, NJ, 1995. (Chapter 11)

[Bansiya and Davis, 2002] J. BANSIYA AND C. G. DAVIS, "A Hierarchical Model for Object-Oriented Design Quality Assessment," *IEEE Transactions on Software Engineering* **28** (January 2002), pp. 4–17. (Chapter 12)

[Barnard and Price, 1994] J. BARNARD AND A. PRICE, "Managing Code Inspection Information," *IEEE Software* **11** (March 1994), pp. 59–69. (Chapter 13)

[Barnes and Bollinger, 1991] B. H. BARNES AND T. B. BOLLINGER, "Making Reuse Cost-Effective," *IEEE Software* **8** (January 1991), pp. 13–24. (Chapter 8)

[Basili and Hutchens, 1983] V. R. BASILI AND D. H. HUTCHENS, "An Empirical Study of a Syntactic Complexity Family," *IEEE Transactions on Software Engineering* **SE-9** (November 1983), pp. 664–72. (Chapter 13)

[Basili and Selby, 1987] V. R. BASILI AND R. W. SELBY, "Comparing the Effectiveness of Software Testing Strategies," *IEEE Transactions on Software Engineering* **SE-13** (December 1987), pp. 1278–96. (Chapter 13)

[Basili and Weiss, 1984] V. R. BASILI AND D. M. WEISS, "A Methodology for Collecting Valid Software Engineering Data," *IEEE Transactions on Software Engineering* **SE-10** (November 1984), pp. 728–38. (Chapter 13)

[Bass, Clements, and Kazman, 2003] L. BASS, P. CLEMENTS, AND R. KAZMAN, *Software Architecture in Practice,* 2nd ed., Addison-Wesley, Reading, MA, 2003. (Chapter 8)

[Baster, Konana, and Scott, 2001] G. BASTER, P. KONANA, AND J. E. SCOTT, "Business Components: A Case Study of Bankers Trust Australia Limited," Communications of the ACM 44 (May 2001), pp. 92–98. (Chapter 8)

[Beck, 2000] K. BECK, *Extreme Programming Explained: Embrace Change,* Addison-Wesley Longman, Reading, MA, 2000. (Chapters 2 and 4)

[Beck and Cunningham, 1989] K. BECK AND W. CUNNINGHAM, "A Laboratory for Teaching Object-Oriented Thinking," Proceedings of OOPSLA '89, *ACM SIGPLAN Notices* **24** (October 1989), pp. 1–6. (Chapter 11)

[Beck et al., 2001] K. BECK, M. BEEDLE, A. COCKBURN, W. CUNNINGHAM, M. FOWLER, J. GRENNING, J. HIGHSMITH, A. HUNT, R. JEFFRIES, J. KERN, B. MARICK, R. C. MARTIN, S. MELLOR, K. SCHWABER, J. SUTHERLAND, D. THOMAS, AND A. VAN BENNEKUM, *Manifesto for Agile Software Development,* at agilemanifesto.org, 2001. (Chapters 2 and 4)

[Beizer, 1990] B. BEIZER, *Software Testing Techniques,* 2nd ed., Van Nostrand Reinhold, New York, 1990. (Chapters 3, 6, 12, and 13)

[Beizer, 1995] B. BEIZER, *Black-Box Testing: Techniques for Functional Testing of Software and Systems,* John Wiley and Sons, New York, 1995. (Chapter 13)

[Beizer, 1997] B. BEIZER, "Cleanroom Process Model: A Critical Examination," *IEEE Software* **14** (March/April 1997), pp. 14–16. (Chapter 13)

[Bellinzona, Fugini, and Pernici, 1995] R. BELLINZONA, M. G. FUGINI, AND B. PERNICI, "Reusing Specifications in OO Applications," *IEEE Software* **12** (March 1995), pp. 656–75. (Chapter 11)

[Bennatan, 2000] E. M. BENNATAN, *On Time Within Budget: Software Project Management Practices and Techniques,* 3rd ed., John Wiley and Sons, New York, 2000. (Chapter 9)

[Berry and Wing, 1985] D. M. BERRY AND J. M. WING, "Specifying and Prototyping: Some Thoughts on Why They Are Successful," in: *Formal Methods and Software Development, Proceedings of the International Joint Conference on Theory and Practice of Software Development,* Vol. 2, Springer-Verlag, Berlin, 1985, pp. 117–28. (Chapter 6)

[Berry, 2004] D. M. BERRY, "The Inevitable Pain of Software Development: Why There Is No Silver Bullet," in: *Radical Innovations of Software and Systems Engineering in the Future,* Lecture Notes in Computer Science, Vol. 2941, Springer-Verlag, Berlin, 2004, pp. 50–74. (Chapter 10)

[Bianchi, Caivano, Marengo, and Visaggio, 2003] A. BIANCHI, D. CAIVANO, V. MARENGO, AND G. VISAGGIO, "Iterative Reengineering of Legacy Systems," *IEEE Transactions on Software Engineering* **29** (March 2003), pp. 225–41. (Chapter 2)

[Bias, 1991] R. BIAS, "Walkthroughs: Efficient Collaborative Testing," *IEEE Software* **8** (September 1991), pp. 94–95. (Chapter 12)

[Binkley and Schach, 1996] A. B. BINKLEY AND S. R. SCHACH, "A Comparison of Sixteen Quality Metrics for Object-Oriented Design," *Information Processing Letters* **57** (No. 6 (June 1996), pp. 271–75. (Chapters 12 and 13)

[Binkley and Schach, 1997] A. B. BINKLEY AND S. R. SCHACH, "Toward a Unified Approach to

Object-Oriented Coupling," *Proceedings of the 35th Annual ACM Southeast Conference*, Murfreesboro, TN, April 2-4, 1997, pp. 91–97. (Chapters 7, 12, and 13)

[Binkley and Schach, 1998] A. B. BINKLEY AND S. R. SCHACH, "Validation of the Coupling Dependency Metric as a Predictor of Run-Time Failures and Maintenance Measures," *Proceedings of the 20th International Conference on Software Engineering*, Kyoto, Japan, April 1988, pp. 542–55. (Chapter 12)

[Birk et al. 2003] A. BIRK, G. HELLER, I. JOHN, K. SCHMID, T. VON DER MASSEN, AND K. MULLER, "Product Line Engineering, the State of the Practice," *IEEE Software* **20** (November/December 2003), pp. 52–60. (Chapter 8)

[Bisbal, Lawless, Wu, and Grimson, 1999] J. BISBAL, D. LAWLESS, B. WU, AND J. GRIMSON, "Legacy Software Products: Issues and Directions," *IEEE Software* **16** (September/October 1999), pp. 103–11. (Chapter 14)

[Blaha, Premerlani, and Rumbaugh, 1988] M. R. BLAHA, W. J. PREMERLANI, AND J. E. RUMBAUGH, "Relational Database Design Using an Object-Oriented Methodology," *Communications of the ACM* **31** (April 1988), pp. 414–27. (Chapter 7)

[Blanco, Gutiérrez, and Satriani, 2001] M. BLANCO, P. GUTIÉRREZ, AND G. SATRIANI, "SPI Patterns: Learning from Experience," *IEEE Software* **18** (May/June 2001), pp. 28–35. (Chapter 3)

[Bockle et al., 2004] G. BOCKLE, P. CLEMENTS, J. D. MCGREGOR, D. MUTHIG, AND K. SCHMID, "Calculating ROI for Software Product Lines," *IEEE Software* **21** (May/June 2004), pp. 23–31. (Chapters 5 and 8)

[Boehm, 1976] B. W. BOEHM, "Software Engineering," *IEEE Transactions on Computers* C-25 (December 1976), pp. 1226–41. (Chapters 1 and 3)

[Boehm, 1979] B. W. BOEHM, "Software Engineering, R & D Trends and Defense Needs," in: *Research Directions in Software Technology*, P. Wegner (Editor), The MIT Press, Cambridge, MA, 1979. (Chapter 1)

[Boehm, 1980] B. W. BOEHM, "Developing Small-Scale Application Software Products: Some Experimental Results," *Proceedings of the Eighth IFIP World Computer Congress,* October 1980, pp. 321–26. (Chapter 1)

[Boehm, 1981] B. W. BOEHM, *Software Engineering Economics,* Prentice Hall, Englewood Cliffs, NJ, 1981. (Chapters 1 and 9)

[Boehm, 1984] B. W. BOEHM, "Software Engineering Economics," *IEEE Transactions on Software Engineering* **SE-10** (January 1984), pp. 4–21. (Chapter 9)

[Boehm, 1988] B. W. BOEHM, "A Spiral Model of Software Development and Enhancement," *IEEE Computer* **21** (May 1988), pp. 61–72. (Chapter 2)

[Boehm, 1997] R. BOEHM (EDITOR), "Function Point FAQ," at ourworld.compuserve.com/homepages/softcomp/fpfaq.htm, June 25, 1997. (Chapter 9)

[Boehm, 2002] B. W. BOEHM, "Get Ready for Agile Methods, with Care," *IEEE Computer* **35** (January 2002), pp. 64–69. (Chapters 2 and 4)

[Boehm and Basili, 2001] B. BOEHM AND V. R. BASILI, "Software Defect Reduction Top Ten List," *IEEE Computer* **34** (January 2001), pp. 135–37. (Chapter 6)

[Boehm and Huang, 2003] B. BOEHM AND L. G. HUANG, "Value-Based Software Engineering: A Case Study," *IEEE Computer* **36** (March 2003), pp. 33–41. (Chapter 1)

[Boehm and Turner, 2003] B. BOEHM AND R. TURNER, *Balancing Agility and Discipline: A Guide for the Perplexed*, Addison-Wesley Professional, Boston, MA, 2003. (Chapter 2)

[Boehm et al., 1984] B. W. BOEHM, M. H. PENEDO, E. D. STUCKLE, R. D. WILLIAMS, AND A. B. PYSTER, "A Software Development Environment for Improving Productivity," *IEEE Computer* **17** (June 1984), pp. 30–44. (Chapters 2 and 9)

[Boehm et al., 2000] B. W. BOEHM, C. ABTS, A. W. BROWN, S. CHULANI, B. K. CLARK, E. HOROWITZ, R. MADACHY, D. REIFER, AND B. STEECE, *Software Cost Estimation with COCOMO II*, Prentice Hall, Upper Saddle River, NJ, 2000. (Chapter 9)

[Booch, 1994] G. BOOCH, *Object-Oriented Analysis and Design with Applications,* 2nd ed., Benjamin/Cummings, Redwood City, CA, 1994. (Chapters 3 and 11)

[Booch, 2000] G. BOOCH, "The Future of Software Engineering," keynote address, International Conference on Software Engineering, Limerick, Ireland, May 2000. (Chapter 2)

[Booch, Rumbaugh, and Jacobson, 1999] G. BOOCH, J. RUMBAUGH, AND I. JACOBSON, *The UML Users Guide*, Addison-Wesley, Reading, MA, 1999. (Chapters 3, 11, and 15)

[Borjesson and Mathiassen, 2004] A. BORJESSON AND L. MATHIASSEN, "Successful Process Implementation," *IEEE Software* **21** (July/August 2004), pp. 36–44. (Chapter 3)

[Borland, 2002] BORLAND, "Press Release: Borland Unveils C++ Application Development Strategy for 2002," at www.borland.com/news/press_releases /2002/01_28_02_cpp.strategy.html, January 28, 2002. (Chapter 13)

[Bosch, 2000] J. BOSCH, *Design and Use of Software Architectures,* Addison-Wesley, Reading, MA, 2000. (Chapter 8)

[Brereton and Budgen, 2000] P. BRERETON AND D. BUDGEN, "Component-Based Systems: A Classification of Issues," *IEEE Computer* **33** (November 2000), pp. 54–62. (Chapter 8)

[Brereton et al., 1999] P. BRERETON, D. BUDGEN, K. BENNETT, M. MUNRO, P. LAYZELL, L. MACAULAY, D. GRIFFITHS, AND C. STANNETT, "The Future of Software," *Communications of the ACM* **42** (December 1999), pp. 78–84. (Chapter 1)

[Briand and Wüst, 2001] L. C. BRIAND AND J. WÜST, "Modeling Development Effort in Object-Oriented Systems Using Design Properties," *IEEE Transactions on Software Engineering* **27** (November 2001), pp. 963–86. (Chapters 5 and 9)

[Briand, Bunse, and Daly, 2001] L. C. BRIAND, C. BUNSE, AND J. W. DALY, "A Controlled Experiment for Evaluating Quality Guidelines on the Maintainability of Object-Oriented Designs," *IEEE Transactions on Software Engineering* **27** (June 2001), pp. 513–30. (Chapters 12 and 14)

[Briand, Daly, Porter, and Wüst, 1998] L. C. BRIAND, J. DALY, V. PORTER, AND J. WÜST, "A Comprehensive Empirical Validation of Design Measures for Object-Oriented Systems," *Proceedings of the Fifth International Metrics Symposium,* Bethesda, MD, November 1998, pp. 246–257. (Chapter 7)

[Brooks, 1975] F. P. BROOKS, Jr., *The Mythical Man-Month: Essays on Software Engineering,* Addison-Wesley, Reading, MA, 1975; Twentieth Anniversary Edition, Addison-Wesley, Reading, MA, 1995. (Chapters 1, 3, 4, and 10)

[Brooks, 1986] F. P. BROOKS, JR., "No Silver Bullet," in: *Information Processing '86,* H.-J. Kugler (Editor), Elsevier North-Holland, New York, 1986; reprinted in *IEEE Computer* **20** (April 1987), pp. 10–19. (Chapters 3 and 12)

[Brooks et al., 1987] F. P. BROOKS, V. BASILI, B. BOEHM, E. BOND, N. EASTMAN, D. L. EVANS, A. K. JONES, M. SHAW, AND C. A. ZRAKET, "Report of the Defense Science Board Task Force on Military Software," Department of Defense, Office of the Under Secretary of Defense for Acquisition, Washington, DC, September 1987. (Chapter 3)

[Brown et al., 1998] W. J. BROWN, R. C. MALVEAU, W. H. BROWN, H. W. MCCORMICK, III, AND T. J. MOWBRAY, *AntiPatterns: Refactoring Software, Architectures, and Projects in Crisis,* John Wiley and Sons, New York, 1998. (Chapter 8)

[Brownsword, Oberndorf, and Sledge, 2000] L. BROWNSWORD, T. OBERNDORF, AND C. A. SLEDGE, "Developing New Process for COTS-Based Systems," *IEEE Software* **17** (July/August 2000), pp. 40–47. (Chapter 1)

[Bruegge, Blythe, Jackson, and Shufelt, 1992] B. BRUEGGE, J. BLYTHE, J. JACKSON, AND J. SHUFELT, "Object-Oriented Modeling with OMT," Proceedings of the Conference on Object-Oriented Programming, Languages, and Systems, OOPSLA '92, *ACM SIGPLAN Notices* **27** (October 1992), pp. 359–76. (Chapter 7)

[Budd, 2002] T. A. BUDD, *An Introduction to Object-Oriented Programming*, 3rd ed., Addison-Wesley, Reading, MA, 2002. (Chapter 1)

[Bush, 1990] M. BUSH, "Improving Software Quality: The Use of Formal Inspections at the Jet Propulsion Laboratory," *Proceedings of the 12th International Conference on Software Engineering*, Nice, France, March 1990, pp. 196–99. (Chapter 6)

[Business Week Online, 1999] *Business Week Online,* at www.businessweek.com/1999/99_08/b3617025. htm, February 2, 1999. (Chapter 4)

[Caldiera and Basili, 1991] G. CALDIERA AND V. R. BASILI, "Identifying and Qualifying Reusable Software Components," *IEEE Computer* **24** (February 1991), pp. 61–70. (Chapter 8)

[Capper, Colgate, Hunter, and James, 1994] N. P. CAPPER, R. J. COLGATE, J. C. HUNTER, AND M. F. JAMES, "The Impact of Object-Oriented Technology on Software Quality: Three Case Histories," *IBM Systems Journal* **33** (No. 1, 1994), pp. 131–57. (Chapters 1 and 7)

[Cartwright and Shepperd, 2000] M. CARTWRIGHT AND M. SHEPPERD, "An Empirical Investigation of an Object-Oriented Software System," *IEEE Transactions on Software Engineering* **26** (August 2000), pp. 786–95. (Chapters 7 and 9)

[Ceschi, Sillitti, Succi, and De Panfilis, 2005] M. CESCHI, A. SILLITTI, G. SUCCI, AND S. DE PANFILIS, "Project Management in Plan-Based and Agile Companies," *IEEE Software* **22** (May/June 2005), pp. 21–27. (Chapter 2)

[Charette, Adams, and White, 1997] R. N. CHARETTE, K. M. ADAMS, AND M. B. WHITE, "Managing Risk in Software Maintenance," *IEEE Software* **14** (May/June 1997), pp. 43–50. (Chapter 14)

[Chidamber and Kemerer, 1994] S. R. CHIDAMBER AND C. F. KEMERER, "A Metrics Suite for Object Oriented Design," *IEEE Transactions on Software Engineering* **20** (June 1994), pp. 476–93. (Chapters 12 and 13)

[Ciolkowski, Laitenberger, and Biffl, 2003] M. CIOLKOWSKI, O. LAITENBERGER, S. BIFFL, "Software Reviews, the State of the Practice," *IEEE Software* **20** (November/December 2003), pp. 46–51. (Chapter 6)

[Clarke, Podgurski, Richardson, and Zeil, 1989] L. A. CLARKE, A. PODGURSKI, D. J. RICHARDSON, AND S. J. ZEIL, "A Formal Evaluation of Data Flow Path Selection Criteria," *IEEE Transactions on Software Engineering* **15** (November 1989), pp. 1318–32. (Chapter 13)

[Clements and Northrop, 2002] P. CLEMENTS AND L. NORTHROP, *Software Product Lines: Practices and Patterns*, Addison-Wesley, Reading, MA, 2002. (Chapter 8)

[CNN.com, 2003] "Russia: Software Bug Made Soyuz Stray," at edition.cnn.com/2003/TECH/space/05/06/soyuz.landing.ap/. (Chapter 3)

[Coad and Yourdon, 1991a] P. COAD AND E. YOURDON, *Object-Oriented Analysis,* 2nd ed., Yourdon Press, Englewood Cliffs, NJ, 1991. (Chapter 11)

[Coad and Yourdon, 1991b] P. COAD AND E. YOURDON, *Object-Oriented Design*, Yourdon Press, Englewood Cliffs, NJ, 1991. (Chapter 12)

[Cockburn, 2001] A. COCKBURN, *Agile Software Development*, Addison-Wesley Professional, Reading, MA, 2001. (Chapter 2)

[Coleman et al., 1994] D. COLEMAN, P. ARNOLD, S. BODOFF, C. DOLLIN, H. GILCHRIST, F. HAYES, AND P. JEREMAES, *Object-Oriented Development: The Fusion Method*, Prentice Hall, Englewood Cliffs, NJ, 1994. (Chapter 11)

[Computer Gripes, 2004] "Gripes about Web Sites That Don't Work Well With Firefox," at www.computer-gripes.com/firefoxsites.html, 2004. (Chapter 8)

[Connell and Shafer, 1989] J. L. CONNELL AND L. SHAFER, *Structured Rapid Prototyping: An Evolutionary Approach to Software Development*, Yourdon Press, Englewood Cliffs, NJ, 1989. (Chapters 2 and 10)

[Conradi and Fuggetta, 2002] R. CONRADI AND A. FUGGETTA, "Improving Software Process Improvement," *IEEE Software* **19** (July/August 2002), pp. 92–99. (Chapter 3)

[Costagliola, Ferrucci, Tortora, and Vitiello, 2005] G. COSTAGLIOLA, F. FERRUCCI, G. TORTORA, AND G. VITIELLO, "Class Point: An Approach for the Size Estimation of Object-Oriented Systems," *IEEE Transactions on Software Engineering* **31** (January 2005), pp. 52–74. (Chapter 9)

[Crossman, 1982] T. D. CROSSMAN, "Inspection Teams, Are They Worth It?" *Proceedings of the Second National Symposium on EDP Quality Assurance*, Chicago, November 1982. (Chapter 13)

[Curtis, Hefley, and Miller, 2002] B. CURTIS, W. E. HEFLEY, AND S. A. MILLER, *The People Capability Maturity Model: Guidelines for Improving the Workforce*, Addison-Wesley, Reading, MA, 2002 (Chapter 4)

[Cusumano and Selby, 1995] M. A. CUSUMANO AND R. W. SELBY, *Microsoft Secrets: How the World's Most Powerful Software Company Creates Technology, Shapes Markets, and Manages People*, The Free Press/Simon and Schuster, New York, 1995. (Chapters 2 and 4)

[Cusumano and Selby, 1997] M. A. CUSUMANO AND R. W. SELBY, "How Microsoft Builds Software," *Communications of the ACM* **40** (June 1997), pp. 53–61. (Chapters 2 and 4)

[Cutter Consortium, 2002] Cutter Consortium, "78% of IT Organizations Have Litigated," *The Cutter Edge*, at www.cutter.com/research/2002/edge020409.html, April 09, 2002. (Chapter 1)

[Cysneiros and do Prado Leite, 2004] L. M. CYSNEIROS AND J. C. S. DO PRADO LEITE, "Nonfunctional Requirements: From Elicitation to Conceptual Models," *IEEE Transactions on Software Engineering* **30** (May 2004), pp. 328–50. (Chapter 10)

[D'Souza and Wills, 1999] D. D'SOUZA AND A. WILLS, *Objects, Components, and Frameworks with UML: The Catalysis Approach*, Addison-Wesley, Reading, MA, 1999. (Chapters 8 and 11)

[Dahl and Nygaard, 1966] O.-J. DAHL AND K. NYGAARD, "SIMULA—An ALGOL-Based Simulation Language," *Communications of the ACM* **9** (September 1966), pp. 671–78. (Chapter 7)

[Daly, 1977] E. B. DALY, "Management of Software Development," *IEEE Transactions on Software Engineering* **SE-3** (May 1977), pp. 229–42. (Chapter 1)

[Date, 2003] C. J. DATE, *An Introduction to Database Systems,* 8th ed., Addison-Wesley, Reading, MA, 2003. (Chapters 13 and 15)

[Dawood, 1994] M. DAWOOD, "It's Time for ISO 9000," *CrossTalk* (March 1994), pp. 26–28. (Chapter 3) [de Champeaux and Faure, 1992] D. DE CHAMPEAUX AND P. FAURE, "A Comparative Study of Object-Oriented Analysis Methods," *Journal of Object-Oriented Programming* **5** (March/April 1992), pp. 21–33. (Chapter 11)

[DeMarco and Boehm, 2002] T. DEMARCO AND B. BOEHM, "The Agile Methods Fray," *IEEE Computer* **35** (June 2002), pp. 90–92. (Chapters 2 and 4)

[DeMarco and Lister, 1987] T. DEMARCO AND T. LISTER, *Peopleware: Productive Projects and Teams*, Dorset House, New York, 1987. (Chapters 1 and 4)

[DeMillo, Lipton, and Perlis, 1979] R. A. DEMILLO, R. J. LIPTON, AND A. J. PERLIS, "Social Processes and Proofs of Theorems and Programs," *Communications of the ACM* **22** (May 1979), pp. 271–80. (Chapter 6)

[DeMillo, Lipton, and Sayward, 1978] R. A. DEMILLO, R. J. LIPTON, AND F. G. SAYWARD, "Hints on Test Data Selection: Help for the Practicing Programmer," *IEEE Computer* **11** (April 1978), pp. 34–43. (Chapter 6)

[Deming, 1986] W. E. DEMING, *Out of the Crisis*, MIT Center for Advanced Engineering Study, Cambridge, MA, 1986. (Chapter 3)

[DeRemer and Kron, 1976] F. DEREMER AND H. H. KRON, "Programming-in-the-Large versus Programming-in-the-Small," *IEEE Transactions on Software Engineering* **SE-2** (June 1976), pp. 80–86. (Chapter 5)

[Devenny, 1976] T. DEVENNY, "An Exploratory Study of Software Cost Estimating at the Electronic Systems Division," Thesis No. GSM/SM/765–4, Air Force Institute of Technology, Dayton, OH, 1976. (Chapter 9)

[Devlin, 2001] K. DEVLIN, "The Real Reason Why Software Engineers Need Math," *Communications of the ACM* **44** (October 2001), pp. 21–22. (Chapter 1)

[Diaz and Sligo, 1997] M. DIAZ AND J. SLIGO, "How Software Process Improvement Helped Motorola," *IEEE Software* **14** (September/October 1997), pp. 75–81. (Chapter 3)

[Dijkstra, 1968] E. W. DIJKSTRA, "A Constructive Approach to the Problem of Program Correctness," *BIT* **8** (No. 3, 1968), pp. 174–86. (Chapter 6)

[Dijkstra, 1972] E. W. DIJKSTRA, "The Humble Programmer," *Communications of the ACM* **15** (October 1972), pp. 859–66. (Chapter 6)

[Dijkstra, 1976] E. W. DIJKSTRA, *A Discipline of Programming,* Prentice Hall, Englewood Cliffs, NJ, 1976. (Chapter 5)

[Dion, 1993] R. DION, "Process Improvement and the Corporate Balance Sheet," *IEEE Software* **10** (July 1993), pp. 28–35. (Chapter 3)

[Dolado, 2000] J. J. DOLADO, "A Validation of the Component-Based Method for Software Size estimation," *IEEE Transactions on Software Engineering* **26** (October 2000), pp. 1006–21. (Chapter 9)

[Donohoe, 2000] P. DONOHOE (EDITOR), *Software Product Lines: Experience and Research Directions*, Kluwer Academic Publishers, Boston, 2000. (Chapter 8)

[Dooley and Schach, 1985] J. W. M. DOOLEY AND S. R. SCHACH, "FLOW: A Software Development Environment Using Diagrams," *Journal of Systems and Software* **5** (August 1985), pp. 203–19. (Chapter 5)

[Drobka, Noftz, and Raghu, 2004] J. DROBKA, D. NOFTZ, AND R. RAGHU, "Piloting XP on Four Mission-Critical Projects," *IEEE Software* **21** (November/December 2004), pp. 70–75. (Chapters 2 and 4)

[Dunn, 1984] R. H. DUNN, *Software Defect Removal*, McGraw-Hill, New York, 1984. (Chapter 13)

[Dunsmore, Roper, and Wood, 2003] A. DUNSMORE, M. ROPER, AND M. WOOD, "The Development and Evaluation of Three Diverse Techniques for Object-Oriented Code Inspection," *IEEE Transactions on Software Engineering* **29** (August 2003), pp. 677–86. (Chapter 6)

[Dybå, 2005] T. DYBÅ, "An Empirical Investigation of the Key Factors for Success in Software Process Improvement," *IEEE Transactions in Software Engineering* **31** (May 2005), pp. 410–24. (Chapter 3)

[Ebert, Matsubara, Pezzé, and Bertelsen, 1997] C. EBERT, T. MATSUBARA, M. PEZZÉ, AND O. W. BERTELSEN, "The Road to Maturity: Navigating between Craft and Science," *IEEE Software* **14** (November/December 1997), pp. 77–88. (Chapters 1 and 3)

[Ebner and Kaindl, 2002] G. EBNER AND H. KAINDL, "Tracing All Around in Reengineering," *IEEE Software* **19** (May/June 2002), pp. 70–77. (Chapter 14)

[Eickelmann, 2003] N. EICKELMANN, "An Insider's View of CMM Level 5," *IEEE Software* **20** (July/August 2003), pp. 79–81. (Chapter 3)

[Eickelmann and Anant, 2003] N. EICKELMANN AND A. ANANT, "Statistical Process Control: What You Don't Know Can Hurt You!" *IEEE Software* **20** (March/April 2003), pp. 49–51. (Chapter 3)

[El Emam, Benlarbi, Goel, and Rai, 2001] K. EL EMAM, S. BENLARBI, N. GOEL, AND S. N. RAI, "The Confounding Effect of Class Size on the Validity of Object-Oriented Metrics," *IEEE Transactions on Software Engineering* **27** (July 2001), pp. 630–50. (Chapter 5)

[Elbaum, Malishevsky, and Rothermel, 2002] A. Elbaum, A. G. Malishevsky, and G. Rothermel, "Test Case Prioritization: A Family of Empirical Studies," *IEEE Transactions on Software Engineering* **28** (2002), pp. 159–82. (Chapters 6 and 13)

[Elrad et al., 2001] T. Elrad, M. Aksit, G. Kiczales, K. Lieberherr, and H. Ossher, "Discussing Aspects of AOP," *Communications of the ACM* **44** (October 2001), pp. 33–38. (Chapter 7)

[El-Rewini et al., 1995] H. El-Rewini, S. Hamilton, Y.-P. Shan, R. Earle, S. McGaughey, A. Helal, R. Badrachalam, A. Chien, A. Grimshaw, B. Lee, A. Wade, D. Morse, A. Elmagramid, E. Pitoura, R. Binder, and P. Wegner, "Object Technology," *IEEE Computer* **28** (October 1995), pp. 58–72. (Chapter 7)

[Elshoff, 1976] J. L. Elshoff, "An Analysis of Some Commercial PL/I Programs," *IEEE Transactions on Software Engineering* **SE-2** (June 1976), pp. 113–20. (Chapter 1)

[Embley, Jackson, and Woodfield, 1995] D. W. Embley, R. B. Jackson, and S. N. Woodfield, "OO Systems Analysis: Is It or Isn't It?" *IEEE Software* **12** (July 1995), pp. 18–33. (Chapter 11)

[Endres, 1975] A. Endres, "An Analysis of Errors and their Causes in System Programs," *IEEE Transactions on Software Engineering* **SE-1** (June 1975), pp. 140–49. (Chapter 13)

[Erdogmus, Morisio, and Torchiano, 2005] H. Erdogmus, M. Morisio, and M. Torchiano, "On the Effectiveness of the Test-First Approach to Programming," *IEEE Transactions on Software Engineering* **31** (March 2005), pp. 226–237. (Chapter 2)

[Fach, 2001] P. W. Fach, "Design Reuse through Frameworks and Patterns," *IEEE Software* **18** (September/October 2001), pp. 71–76. (Chapter 8)

[Fagan, 1974] M. E. Fagan, "Design and Code Inspections and Process Control in the Development of Programs," Technical Report IBM-SSD TR 21.572, IBM Corporation, December 1974. (Chapter 1)

[Fagan, 1976] M. E. Fagan, "Design and Code Inspections to Reduce Errors in Program Development," *IBM Systems Journal* **15** (No. 3, 1976), pp. 182–211. (Chapters 6 and 12)

[Fagan, 1986] M. E. Fagan, "Advances in Software Inspections," *IEEE Transactions on Software Engineering* **SE-12** (July 1986), pp. 744–51. (Chapters 6 and 12)

[Fayad and Johnson, 1999] M. Fayad and R. Johnson, *Domain-Specific Application Frameworks: Frameworks Experience by Industry,* John Wiley and Sons, New York, 1999. (Chapter 8)

[Fayad and Schmidt, 1999] M. Fayad and D. C. Schmidt, *Building Application Frameworks: Object-Oriented Foundations of Framework Design,* John Wiley and Sons, New York, 1999. (Chapter 8)

[Fayad, Schmidt, and Johnson, 1999] M. Fayad, D. C. Schmidt, and R. Johnson, *Implementing Application Frameworks: Object-Oriented Frameworks at Work,* John Wiley and Sons, New York, 1999. (Chapter 8)

[Fayad, Tsai, and Fulghum, 1996] M. E. Fayad, W.-T. Tsai, and M. L. Fulghum, "Transition to Object-Oriented Software Development," *Communications of the ACM* **39** (February 1996), pp. 108–21. (Chapter 7)

[Feldman, 1979] S. I. Feldman, "Make—A Program for Maintaining Computer Programs," *Software—Practice and Experience* **9** (April 1979), pp. 225–65. (Chapter 5)

[Fenton and Pfleeger, 1997] N. E. Fenton and S. L. Pfleeger, *Software Metrics: A Rigorous and Practical Approach,* 2nd ed., IEEE Computer Society, Los Alamitos, CA, 1997. (Chapter 5)

[Ferguson and Sheard, 1998] J. Ferguson and S. Sheard, "Leveraging Your CMM Efforts for IEEE/EIA 12207," *IEEE Software* **15** (September/October 1998), pp. 23–28. (Chapter 3)

[Ferguson et al., 1997] P. Ferguson, W. S. Humphrey, S. Khajenoori, S. Macke, and A. Matvya, "Results of Applying the Personal Software Process," *IEEE Computer* **30** (May 1997), pp. 24–31. (Chapter 3)

[Fichman and Kemerer, 1992] R. G. Fichman and C. F. Kemerer, "Object-Oriented and Conventional Analysis and Design Methodologies: Comparison and Critique," *IEEE Computer* **25** (October 1992), pp. 22–39. (Chapters 11 and 12)

[Fichman and Kemerer, 1997] R. G. Fichman and C. F. Kemerer, "Object Technology and Reuse: Lessons from Early Adopters," *IEEE Computer* **30** (July 1997), pp. 47–57. (Chapters 1 and 8)

[Fingar, 2000] P. Fingar, "Component-Based Frameworks for e-Commerce," *Communications of the ACM* **43** (October 2000), pp. 61–66. (Chapter 8)

[Finkelstein, 2000] A. Finkelstein (Editor), *The Future of Software Engineering*, IEEE Computer Society Press, Los Alamitos, CA, 2000. (Chapter 1)

[Fioravanti and Nesi, 2001] F. Fioravanti and P. Nesi, "Estimation and Prediction Metrics for Adaptive Maintenance Effort of Object-Oriented Systems," *IEEE Transactions on Software Engineering* **27** (December 2001), pp. 1062–84. (Chapter 14)

[Flanagan, 2005] D. Flanagan, *Java in a Nutshell: A Desktop Quick Reference*, 5th ed., O'Reilly and Associates, Sebastopol, CA, 2005. (Chapters 7, 8, and 12)

[Florac, Carleton, and Barnard, 2000] W. A. Florac, A. D. Carleton, and J. Barnard, "Statistical Process Control: Analyzing a Space Shuttle Onboard Software Process," *IEEE Software* **17** (July/August 2000), pp. 97–106. (Chapter 3)

[*Florida Today*, 1999] "Milstar Satellite Lost during Air Force Titan 4b Launch from Cape," *Florida Today*, at **www.floridatoday.com/space/explore/uselv/titan/b32/**, June 5, 1999. (Chapter 3)

[Fowler, 1986] P. J. Fowler, "In-Process Inspections of Workproducts at AT&T," *AT&T Technical Journal* **65** (March/April 1986), pp. 102–12. (Chapter 6)

[Fowler, 1997] M. Fowler, *Analysis Patterns: Reusable Object Models*, Addison-Wesley, Reading, MA, 1997. (Chapter 8)

[Fowler and Scott, 2000] M. Fowler with K. Scott, UML Distilled, 2nd ed., Addison-Wesley, Upper Saddle River, NJ, 2000. (Chapter 15)

[Fowler et al., 1999] M. Fowler with K. Beck, J. Brant, W. Opdyke, and D. Roberts, *Refactoring: Improving the Design of Existing Code*, Addison-Wesley, Reading, MA, 1999. (Chapter 2)

[Freeman and Schach, 2005] G. L. Freeman, Jr. and S. R. Schach, "The Task-Dependent Nature of the Maintenance of Object-Oriented Programs," *Journal of Systems and Software* **76** (May 2005), pp. 195–206. (Chapter 14)

[Fuggetta, 1993] A. Fuggetta, "A Classification of CASE Technology," *IEEE Computer* **26** (December 1993), pp. 25–38. (Chapter 5)

[Furey and Kitchenham, 1997] S. Furey and B. Kitchenham, "Function Points," *IEEE Software* **14** (March/April 1997), pp. 28–32. (Chapter 9)

[Gamma, Helm, Johnson, and Vlissides, 1995] E. Gamma, R. Helm, R. Johnson, and J. Vlissides, *Design Patterns: Elements of Reusable Object-Oriented Software*, Addison-Wesley, Reading, MA, 1995. (Chapter 8)

[Gane and Sarsen, 1979] C. Gane and T. Sarsen, *Structured Systems Analysis: Tools and Techniques*, Prentice Hall, Englewood Cliffs, NJ, 1979. (Chapter 1)

[Gane, 1989] C. Gane, *Rapid System Development: Using Structured Techniques and Relational Technology*, Prentice Hall, Englewood Cliffs, NJ, 1989. (Chapter 10)

[Garman, 1981] J. R. Garman, "The 'Bug' Heard 'Round the World," *ACM SIGSOFT Software Engineering Notes* **6** (October 1981), pp. 3–10. (Chapter 3)

[Gelperin and Hetzel, 1988] D. Gelperin and B. Hetzel, "The Growth of Software Testing," *Communications of the ACM* **31** (June 1988), pp. 687–95. (Chapter 6)

[Gerald and Wheatley, 1999] C. F. Gerald and P. O. Wheatley, *Applied Numerical Analysis*, 6th ed., Addison-Wesley, Reading, MA, 1999. (Chapter 7)

[Gifford and Spector, 1987] D. Gifford and A. Spector, "Case Study: IBM's System/360–370 Architecture," *Communications of the ACM* **30** (April 1987), pp. 292–307. (Chapter 8)

[GJSentinel.com, 2003] "Sallie Mae's Errors Double Some Bills," at **www.gjsentinel.com/news/content/coxnet/headlines/0522_salliemae.html**, May 22, 2003. (Chapter 1)

[Glass, 1998] R. L. Glass, "Is There Really a Software Crisis?" *IEEE Software* **15** (January/February 1998), pp. 104–5. (Chapter 1)

[Goldberg and Robson, 1989] A. Goldberg and D. Robson, *Smalltalk-80: The Language*, Addison-Wesley, Reading, MA, 1989. (Chapters 7 and 12)

[Goldstein, 2005] H. Goldstein, "Who Killed the Virtual Case File?" *IEEE Spectrum* **43** (September 2005), pp. 24–35. (Chapter 1)

[Gomaa, 2000] H. Gomaa, *Designing Concurrent, Distributed, and Real-time Applications with UML*, Addison-Wesley, Reading, MA, 2000. (Chapter 12)

[Goodenough and Gerhart, 1975] J. B. Goodenough and S. L. Gerhart, "Toward a Theory of Test Data Selection," *Proceedings of the Third International Conference on Reliable Software*, Los Angeles, 1975, pp. 493–510; also published in *IEEE Transactions on Software Engineering* **SE-1** (June 1975), pp. 156–73. Revised version: J. B. Goodenough, and S. L. Gerhart, "Toward a Theory of Test Data Selection: Data Selection Criteria," in: *Current Trends in Programming Methodology,* Vol. 2, R. T. Yeh (Editor), Prentice Hall, Englewood Cliffs, NJ, 1977, pp. 44–79. (Chapters 6 and 11)

[Goodenough, 1979] J. B. Goodenough, "A Survey of Program Testing Issues," in: *Research Directions in Software Technology*, P. Wegner (Editor), The MIT Press, Cambridge, MA, 1979, pp. 316–40. (Chapter 6)

[Gorla and Lam, 2004] N. Gorla and Y. W. Lam, "Who Should Work with Whom?" *Communications of the ACM* **47** (June 2004), pp. 79–82. (Chapter 4)

[Goth, 2000] G. Goth, "New Air Traffic Control Software Takes an Incremental Approach," *IEEE Software* **17** (July/August 2000), pp. 108–111. (Chapter 2)

[Grady, 1992] R. B. Grady, *Practical Software Metrics for Project Management and Process Improvement*, Prentice Hall, Englewood Cliffs, NJ, 1992. (Chapter 13)

[Grady, 1994] R. B. Grady, "Successfully Applying Software Metrics," *IEEE Computer* **27** (September 1994), pp. 18–25. (Chapters 1 and 2)

[Gramlich, 1997] E. M. Gramlich, *A Guide to Benefit–Cost Analysis*, 2nd ed., Waveland Books, Prospect Heights, IL, 1997. (Chapter 5)

[Green, 2000] P. Green, "FW: Here's an Update to the Simulated Kangaroo Story," *The Risks Digest* 20 (January 23, 2000), at catless.ncl.ac.uk/Risks/20.76.html. (Chapter 8)

[Griss, 1993] M. L. Griss, "Software Reuse: From Library to Factory," *IBM Systems Journal* **32** (No. 4, 1993), pp. 548–66. (Chapter 8)

[Guerrero and Eterovic, 2004] F. Guerrero and Y. Eterovic, "Adopting the SW-CMM in a Small IT Organization," *IEEE Software* **21** (July/August 2004), pp. 29–35. (Chapter 3)

[Guinan, Cooprider, and Sawyer, 1997] P. J. Guinan, J. G. Cooprider, and S. Sawyer, "The Effective Use of Automated Application Development Tools," *IBM Systems Journal* **36** (No. 1, 1997), pp. 124–39. (Chapter 5)

[Guttag, 1977] J. Guttag, "Abstract Data Types and the Development of Data Structures," *Communications of the ACM* **20** (June 1977), pp. 396–404. (Chapter 7)

[Hagge and Lappe, 2005] L. Hagge and K. Lappe, "Sharing Requirements Engineering Experience Using Patterns," *IEEE Software* **22** (January/February 2005), pp. 24–31. (Chapter 8)

[Haley, 1996] T. J. Haley, "Raytheon's Experience in Software Process Improvement," *IEEE Software* **13** (November 1996), pp. 33–41. (Chapter 3)

[Harel and Gery, 1997] D. Harel and E. Gery, "Executable Object Modeling with Statecharts," *IEEE Computer* **30** (July 1997), pp. 31–42. (Chapter 11)

[Harel et al., 1990] D. Harel, H. Lachover, A. Naamad, A. Pnueli, M. Politi, R. Sherman, A. Shtull-Trauring, and M. Trakhtenbrot, "STATEMATE: A Working Environment for the Development of Complex Reactive Systems," *IEEE Transactions on Software Engineering* **16** (April 1990), pp. 403–14. (Chapter 13)

[Harrold and Soffa, 1991] M. J. Harrold and M. L. Soffa, "Selecting and Using Data for Integration Testing," *IEEE Software* **8** (1991), pp. 58–65 (Chapter 13)

[Harrold, McGregor, and Fitzpatrick, 1992] M. J. Harrold, J. D. McGregor, and K. J. Fitzpatrick, "Incremental Testing of Object-Oriented Class Structures," *Proceedings of the 14th International Conference on Software Engineering*, Melbourne, Australia, May 1992, pp. 68–80. (Chapter 13)

[Harrold, Rosenblum, Rothermel and Weyuker, 2001] M. J. Harrold, D. Rosenblum, G. Rothermel, and E. Weyuker, "Empirical Studies of a Prediction Model for Regression Test Selection," *IEEE Transactions on Software Engineering* **27** (March 2001), pp. 248–63. (Chapter 14)

[Hatton, 1998] L. Hatton, "Does OO Sync with How We Think?" *IEEE Software* **15** (May/June 1998), pp. 46–54. (Chapter 1)

[Hayes, 2004] F. Hayes, "Chaos Is Back," *Computerworld*, at www.computerworld.com/managementtopics/management/project/story/0,10801,97283,00.html, November 8, 2004 (Chapters 1 and 2)

[Heineman and Councill, 2001] G. T. Heineman and W. T. Councill, *Component-Based Software Engineering: Putting the Pieces Together*, Addison-Wesley, Reading, MA, 2001. (Chapter 8)

[Henry and Humphrey, 1990] S. M. Henry and M. Humphrey, "A Controlled Experiment to Evaluate Maintainability of Object-Oriented Software," *Proceedings of the IEEE Conference on Software Maintenance*, San Diego, CA, November 1990, pp. 258–65. (Chapter 14)

[Henry and Kafura, 1981] S. M. Henry and D. Kafura, "Software Structure Metrics Based on Information Flow," *IEEE Transactions on Software Engineering* **SE-7** (September 1981), pp. 510–18. (Chapter 12)

[Herbsleb et al., 1997] J. Herbsleb, D. Zubrow, D. Goldenson, W. Hayes, and M. Paulk, "Software Quality and the Capability Maturity Model," *Communications of the ACM* **40** (June 1997), pp. 30–40. (Chapter 3)

[Hetzel, 1988] W. Hetzel, *The Complete Guide to Software Testing*, 2nd ed., QED Information Systems, Wellesley, MA, 1988. (Chapter 6)

[Highsmith and Coburn, 2001] J. HIGHSMITH AND A. COCKBURN, "Agile Software Development: The Business of Innovation," *IEEE Computer* **34** (September 2001), pp. 120–22. (Chapter 2)

[Hoare, 1969] C. A. R. HOARE, "An Axiomatic Basis for Computer Programming," *Communications of the ACM* **12** (October 1969), pp. 576–83. (Chapter 6)

[Hoare, 1981] C. A. R. HOARE, "The Emperor's Old Clothes," *Communications of the ACM* **24** (February 1981), pp. 75–83. (Chapter 6)

[Hoare, 1987] C. A. R. HOARE, "An Overview of Some Formal Methods for Program Design," *IEEE Computer* **20** (September 1987), pp. 85–91. (Chapter 12)

[Holzinger, 2005] A. HOLZINGER, "Usability Engineering Methods for Software Developers," *Communications of the ACM* **48** (January 2005), pp. 71–74. (Chapter 10)

[Horgan, London, and Lyu, 1994] J. R. HORGAN, S. LONDON, AND M. R. LYU, "Achieving Software Quality with Testing Coverage Measures," *IEEE Computer* **27** (1994), pp. 60–69. (Chapter 13)

[Howden, 1987] W. E. HOWDEN, *Functional Program Testing and Analysis*, McGraw-Hill, New York, 1987. (Chapter 13)

[HTML, 2006] "W3C HTML Homepage," at www.w3.org/MarkUp, 2006. (Chapter 8)

[Humphrey, 1989] W. S. HUMPHREY, *Managing the Software Process*, Addison-Wesley, Reading, MA, 1989. (Chapter 3)

[Humphrey, 1996] W. S. HUMPHREY, "Using a Defined and Measured Personal Software Process," *IEEE Software* **13** (May 1996), pp. 77–88. (Chapter 3)

[Humphrey, 1999] W. S. HUMPHREY, "Pathways to Process Maturity: The Personal Software Process and Team Software Process," *SEI Interactive* 2 (No. 4, December 1999), at interactive.sei.cmu.edu/Features/1999/June/Background/Background.jun99.htm. (Chapter 3)

[Humphrey, Snider, and Willis, 1991] W. S. HUMPHREY, T. R. SNIDER, AND R. R. WILLIS, "Software Process Improvement at Hughes Aircraft," *IEEE Software* **8** (July 1991), pp. 11–23. (Chapter 3)

[Hwang, 1981] S.-S. V. HWANG, "An Empirical Study in Functional Testing, Structural Testing, and Code Reading Inspection," Scholarly Paper 362, Department of Computer Science, University of Maryland, College Park, 1981. (Chapter 13)

[IEEE 1028, 1997] *Standard for Software Reviews*, IEEE 1028, Institute of Electrical and Electronic Engineers, New York, 1997. (Chapter 6)

[IEEE 1058, 1998] "IEEE Standard for Software Project Management Plans." IEEE Std. 1058-1998, Institute of Electrical and Electronic Engineers, New York, 1998. (Chapter 9)

[IEEE 610.12, 1990] *A Glossary of Software Engineering Terminology*, IEEE 610.12-1990, Institute of Electrical and Electronic Engineers, Inc., 1990. (Chapters 1 and 6)

[IEEE Standards, 2003] "Products and Projects Status Report," at standards.ieee.org/db/status/status.txt, June 3, 2003. (Chapter 1)

[IEEE/ACM, 1999] "Software Engineering Code of Ethics and Professional Practice, Version 5.2, as Recommended by the IEEE-CS/ACM Joint Task Force on Software Engineering Ethics and Professional Practice," at www.computer.org/tab/seprof/code.htm, 1999. (Chapter 1)

[IEEE/EIA 12207, 1998] "IEEE/EIA 12207.0-1996 Industry Implementation of International Standard ISO/IEC 12207:1995," Institute of Electrical and Electronic Engineers, Electronic Industries Alliance, New York, 1998. (Chapter 3)

[IEEE/EIA 12207.0-1996, 1998] "IEEE/EIA 12207.0-1996 Industry Implementation of International Standard ISO/IEC 12207:1995," Institute of Electrical and Electronic Engineers, Electronic Industries Alliance, New York, 1998. (Chapter 1)

[Isakowitz and Kauffman, 1996] T. ISAKOWITZ AND R. J. KAUFFMAN, "Supporting Search for Reusable Software Objects," *IEEE Transactions on Software Engineering* **22** (June 1996), pp. 407–23. (Chapter 8)

[ISO 9000-3, 1991] "ISO 9000-3, Guidelines for the Application of ISO 9001 to the Development, Supply, and Maintenance of Software," International Organization for Standardization, Geneva, 1991. (Chapter 3)

[ISO 9001, 1987] "ISO 9001, Quality Systems—Model for Quality Assurance in Design/Development, Production, Installation, and Servicing," International Organization for Standardization, Geneva, 1987. (Chapter 3)

[ISO/IEC 12207, 1995] "ISO/IEC 12207:1995, Information Technology—Software Life-Cycle Processes," International Organization for Standardization, International Electrotechnical Commission, Geneva, 1995. (Chapters 1, 2, and 3)

[ISO/IEC 14882, 1998] *Programming Language C++*, ISO/IEC 14882, International Organization for Standardization, International Electrotechnical Commission, Geneva, 1998. (Chapter 8)

[ISO/IEC 1539–1, 2004] *Information Technology—Programming Languages—Fortran—Part 1: Base Language*, ISO/IEC 1539–1, International Organization for Standardization, International Electrotechnical Commission, Geneva, 2004. (Chapter 8)

[ISO/IEC 1989, 2002] *Information Technology—Programming Language COBOL*, ISO 1989:2002, International Organization for Standardization, International Electrotechnical Commission, Geneva, 2002. (Chapter 8)

[ISO/IEC 8652, 1995] *Programming Language Ada: Language and Standard Libraries*, ISO/IEC 8652, International Organization for Standardization, International Electrotechnical Commission, Geneva, 1995. (Chapters 6, 7, 8, 12)

[IWSSD, 1986] Call for Papers, Fourth International Workshop on Software Specification and Design, *ACM SIGSOFT Software Engineering Notes* **11** (April 1986), pp. 94–96. (Chapter 11)

[Jackson and Chapin, 2000] D. JACKSON AND J. CHAPIN, "Redesigning Air Traffic Control: An Exercise in Software Design," *IEEE Software* **17** (May/June 2000), pp. 63–70. (Chapter 12)

[Jackson, 1975] M. A. JACKSON, *Principles of Program Design*, Academic Press, New York, 1975. (Chapters 1, 12)

[Jackson, 1995] M. JACKSON, *Software Requirements and Specifications: A Lexicon of Practice, Principles and Prejudices,* Addison-Wesley Longman, Reading, MA, 1995. (Chapter 10)

[Jacobson, Booch, and Rumbaugh, 1999] G. BOOCH, I. JACOBSON, AND J. RUMBAUGH, *The Unified Software Development Process*, Addison-Wesley, Reading, MA, 1999. (Chapters 2, 3, 10, 11, 12, 13, and 14)

[Jacobson, Christerson, Jonsson, and Overgaard, 1992] I. JACOBSON, M. CHRISTERSON, P. JONSSON, AND G. OVERGAARD, *Object-Oriented Software Engineering: A Use Case Driven Approach*, ACM Press, New York, 1992. (Chapter 11)

[Jalote, Palit, Kurien, and Peethamber, 2004] P. JALOTE, A. PALIT, P. KURIEN AND V. T. PEETHAMBER, "Timeboxing: A Process Model for Iterative Software Development," *Journal of Systems and Software* **70** (February 2004), pp. 117–27. (Chapter 2)

[Jazayeri, Ran, and van der Linden, 2000] M. JAZAYERI, A. RAN, AND F. VAN DER LINDEN, *Software Architecture for Product Families: Principles and Practice,* Addison-Wesley, Reading, MA, 2000. (Chapter 8)

[Jézéquel and Meyer, 1997] J.-M. JÉZÉQUEL AND B. MEYER, "Put It in the Contract: The Lessons of Ariane," *IEEE Computer* **30** (January 1997), pp. 129–30. (Chapter 8)

[Johnson, 2000] R. A. JOHNSON, "The Ups and Downs of Object-Oriented System Development," *Communications of the ACM* **43** (October 2000), pp. 69–73. (Chapters 1 and 7)

[Johnson and Brodman, 2000] D. JOHNSON AND J. G. BRODMAN, "Applying CMM Project Planning Practices to Diverse Environments," *IEEE Software* **17** (July/August 2000), pp. 40–47. (Chapter 3)

[Johnson and Disney, 1998] P. M. JOHNSON AND A. M. DISNEY, "The Personal Software Process: A Cautionary Tale," *IEEE Software* 15 (November/December 1998), pp. 85–88. (Chapter 3)

[Johnson and Ritchie, 1978] S. C. JOHNSON AND D. M. RITCHIE, "Portability of C Programs and the UNIX System," *Bell System Technical Journal* **57** (No. 6, Part 2, 1978), pp. 2021–48. (Chapter 8)

[Jones, 1978] T. C. JONES, "Measuring Programming Quality and Productivity," *IBM Systems Journal* **17** (No. 1, 1978), pp. 39–63. (Chapter 6)

[Jones, 1984] T. C. JONES, "Reusability in Programming: A Survey of the State of the Art," *IEEE Transactions on Software Engineering* **SE-10** (September 1984), pp. 488–94. (Chapter 8)

[Jones, 1986a] C. JONES, *Programming Productivity,* McGraw-Hill, New York, 1986. (Chapter 9)

[Jones, 1987] C. JONES, Letter to the Editor, *IEEE Computer* **20** (December 1987), p. 4. (Chapter 9)

[Jones, 1994] C. JONES, "Software Metrics: Good, Bad, and Missing," *IEEE Computer* **27** (September 1994), pp. 98–100. (Chapter 5)

[Jones, 1996] C. JONES, *Applied Software Measurement,* McGraw-Hill, New York, 1996. (Chapter 3)

[Jorgensen and Erickson, 1994] P. C. JORGENSEN AND C. ERICKSON, "Object-Oriented Integration Testing," *Communications of the ACM* 37 (September 1994), pp. 30–38. (Chapter 13)

[Jorgensen and Molokken-Ostvold, 2004] M. Jorgensen and K. Molokken-Ostvold, "Reasons for Software Effort Estimation Error: Impact of Respondent Role, Information Collection Approach, and Data Analysis Method," *IEEE Transactions on Software Engineering* 30 (December 2004), pp. 993–1007. (Chapter 9)

[Josephson, 1992] M. Josephson, *Edison, A Biography*, John Wiley and Sons, New York, 1992. (Chapter 1)

[Juran, 1988] J. M. Juran, *Juran on Planning for Quality*, Macmillan, New York, 1988. (Chapter 3)

[Juristo, Moreno, and López, 2000] N. Juristo, A. M. Moreno, and M. López, "How to Use Linguistic Instruments for Object-Oriented Analysis," *IEEE Software* 17 (May/June 2000), pp. 80–89. (Chapter 11)

[Kan et al., 1994] S. H. Kan, S. D. Dull, D. N. Amundson, R. J. Lindner, and R. J. Hedger, "AS/400 Software Quality Management," *IBM Systems Journal* 33 (No. 1, 1994), pp. 62–88. (Chapter 1)

[Karlsson and Ryan, 1997] J. Karlsson and K. Ryan, "A Cost-Value Approach for Prioritizing Requirements," *IEEE Software* 14 (September/October 1997), pp. 67–74. (Chapter 10)

[Karlström and Runeson, 2005] D. Karlström and P. Runeson, "Combining Agile Methods with Stage-Gate Project Management," *IEEE Software* 22 (May/June 2005), pp. 43–49. (Chapter 2)

[Keeni, 2000] G. Keeni, "The Evolution of Quality Processes at Tata Consultancy Services," *IEEE Software* 17 (July/August 2000), pp. 79–88. (Chapter 3)

[Keil and Tiwana, 2005] M. Keil and A. Tiwana, "Beyond Cost: The Drivers of COTS Application Value," IEEE Software 22 (May/June 2005), pp. 64–69. (Chapter 1)

[Kelly and Sherif, 1992] J. C. Kelly and J. S. Sherif, "A Comparison of Four Design Methods for Real-Time Software Development," *Information and Software Technology* 34 (February 1992), pp. 74–82. (Chapter 12)

[Kelly, Sherif, and Hops, 1992] J. C. Kelly, J. S. Sherif, and J. Hops, "An Analysis of Defect Densities Found during Software Inspections," *Journal of Systems and Software* 17 (January 1992), pp. 111–17. (Chapters 1 and 6)

[Kemerer, 1993] C. F. Kemerer, "Reliability of Function Points Measurement: A Field Experiment," *Communications of the ACM* 36 (February 1993), pp. 85–97. (Chapter 9)

[Kemerer and Porter, 1992] C. F. Kemerer and B. S. Porter, "Improving the Reliability of Function Point Measurement: An Empirical Study," *IEEE Transactions on Software Engineering* 18 (November 1992), pp. 1011–24. (Chapter 9)

[Kernighan and Plauger, 1974] B. W. Kernighan and P. J. Plauger, *The Elements of Programming Style,* McGraw-Hill, New York, 1974. (Chapter 13)

[Khan, Al-A'ali, and Girgis, 1995] E. H. Khan, M. Al-A'ali, and M. R. Girgis, "Object-Oriented Programming for Structured Procedural Programming," *IEEE Computer* 28 (October 1995), pp. 48–57. (Chapter 1)

[Kilpi, 2001] T. Kilpi, "Implementing a Software Metrics Program at Nokia," *IEEE Software* 18 (November/December 2001), pp. 72–76. (Chapter 5)

[Kitchenham, 1997] B. Kitchenham, "The Problem with Function Points," *IEEE Software* 14 (March/April 1997), pp. 29, 31. (Chapter 9)

[Kitchenham and Mendes, 2004] B. Kitchenham and E. Mendes, "Software Productivity Measurement Using Multiple Size Measures," *IEEE Transactions on Software Engineering* 30 (December 2004), pp. 1023–35. (Chapter 9)

[Kitchenham, Pickard, and Linkman, 1990] B. A. Kitchenham, L. M. Pickard, and S. J. Linkman, "An Evaluation of Some Design Metrics," *Software Engineering Journal* 5 (January 1990), pp. 50–58. (Chapter 12)

[Kitchenham, Pickard, and Pfleeger, 1995] B. Kitchenham, L. Pickard, and S. L. Pfleeger. "Case Studies for Method and Tool Evaluation," *IEEE Software* 12 (July 1995), pp. 52–62. (Chapter 5)

[Kleinrock and Gail, 1996] L. Kleinrock and R. Gail, *Queuing Systems: Problems and Solutions*, John Wiley and Sons, New York, 1996. (Chapter 11)

[Klunder, 1988] D. Klunder, "Hungarian Naming Conventions," Technical Report, Microsoft Corporation, Redmond, WA, January 1988. (Chapter 13)

[Knauber, Muthig, Schmid, and Widen, 2000] P. Knauber, D. Muthig, K. Schmid, and T. Widen, "Applying Product Line Concepts in Small and Medium-Sized Companies," *IEEE Software* 17 (September/October 2000), pp. 88–95. (Chapter 8)

[Knuth, 1968] D. E. Knuth, *The Art of Computer Programming, Vol. I, Fundamental Algorithms*, Addison-Wesley, Reading, MA, 1968. (Chapter 11)

[Knuth, 1974] D. E. Knuth, "Structured Programming with go to Statements," *ACM Computing Surveys* 6 (December 1974), pp. 261–301. (Chapter 7)

[Kobryn, 2000] C. Kobryn, "Modeling Components and Frameworks with UML," *Communications of the ACM* 43 (October 2000), pp. 31–38. (Chapter 8)

[Kroeker et al., 1999] K. K. Kroeker, L. Wall, D. A. Taylor, C. Horn, P. Bassett, J. K. Ousterhout, M. L. Griss, R. M. Soley, J. Waldo, and C. Simonyi, "Software [R]evolution: A Roundtable," *IEEE Computer* 32 (May 1999), pp. 48–57. (Chapter 1)

[Kung, Hsia, and Gao, 1998] D. C. KUNG, P. HSIA, AND J. GAO, *Testing Object-Oriented Software*, IEEE Computer Society Press, Los Alamitos, CA, 1998. (Chapter 6)

[Kurki-Suonio, 1993] R. KURKI-SUONIO, "Stepwise Design of Real-Time Systems," *IEEE Transactions on Software Engineering* **19** (January 1993), pp. 56–69. (Chapter 5)

[Lai, Weiss, and Parnas, 1999] C. T. R. LAI, D. M. WEISS, AND D. L. PARNAS, *Software Product-Line Engineering: A Family-Based Software Development Process,* Addison-Wesley, Reading, MA, 1999. (Chapter 8)

[Landwehr, 1983] C. E. LANDWEHR, "The Best Available Technologies for Computer Security," *IEEE Computer* **16** (July 1983), pp. 86–100. (Chapter 6)

[Lanergan and Grasso, 1984] R. G. LANERGAN AND C. A. GRASSO, "Software Engineering with Reusable Designs and Code," *IEEE Transactions on Software Engineering* **SE-10** (September 1984), pp. 498–501. (Chapter 8)

[LAPACK++, 2000] "LAPACK++: Linear Algebra Package in C++," at math.nist.gov/lapack++, 2000. (Chapter 8)

[Larman and Basili, 2003] C. LARMAN AND V. R. BASILI, "Iterative and Incremental Development: A Brief History," *IEEE Computer* **36** (June 2003), pp. 47–56. (Chapter 2)

[Leavenworth, 1970] B. LEAVENWORTH, Review #19420, *Computing Reviews* **11** (July 1970), pp. 396–97. (Chapters 6 and 11)

[Lejter, Meyers, and Reiss, 1992] M. LEJTER, S. MEYERS, AND S. P. REISS, "Support for Maintaining Object-Oriented Programs," *IEEE Transactions on Software Engineering* **18** (December 1992), pp. 1045–52. (Chapter 14)

[Leveson and Turner, 1993] N. G. LEVESON AND C. S. TURNER, "An Investigation of the Therac-25 Accidents," *IEEE Computer* **26** (July 1993), pp. 18–41. (Chapter 1)

[Lewis et al., 1995] T. LEWIS, L. ROSENSTEIN, W. PREE, A. WEINAND, E. GAMMA, P. CALDER, G. ANDERT, J. VLISSIDES, AND K. SCHMUCKER, *Object-Oriented Application Frameworks*, Manning, Greenwich, CT, 1995. (Chapter 8)

[Lieberman and Fry, 2001] H. LIEBERMAN AND C. FRY, "Will Software Ever Work?" *Communications of the ACM* **44** (March 2001), pp. 122–24. (Chapter 6)

[Lientz, Swanson, and Tompkins, 1978] B. P. LIENTZ, E. B. SWANSON, AND G. E. TOMPKINS, "Characteristics of Application Software Maintenance," *Communications of the ACM* **21** (June 1978), pp. 466–71. (Chapters 1 and 14)

[Lim, 1994] W. C. LIM, "Effects of Reuse on Quality, Productivity, and Economics," *IEEE Software* **11** (September 1994), pp. 23–30. (Chapters 8 and 9)

[Lim, 1998] W. C. LIM, *Managing Software Reuse*, Prentice Hall, Upper Saddle River, NJ, 1998. (Chapter 8)

[Lim, Jeong, and Schach, 2005] J. S. LIM, S. R. JEONG, AND S. R. SCHACH, "An Empirical Investigation of the Impact of the Object-Oriented Paradigm on the Maintainability of Real-World Mission-Critical Software," *Journal of Systems and Software* **77** (August 2005), pp. 131–38. (Chapter 14)

[Linger, 1994] R. C. LINGER, "Cleanroom Process Model," *IEEE Software* **11** (March 1994), pp. 50–58. (Chapter 13)

[Liskov and Zilles, 1974] B. LISKOV AND S. ZILLES, "Programming with Abstract Data Types," *ACM SIGPLAN Notices* **9** (April 1974), pp. 50–59. (Chapter 7)

[Liskov, Snyder, Atkinson, and Schaffert, 1977] B. LISKOV, A. SNYDER, R. ATKINSON, AND C. SCHAFFERT, "Abstraction Mechanisms in CLU," *Communications of the ACM* **20** (August 1977), pp. 564–76. (Chapter 8)

[Liu, 2000] J. W. S. LIU, *Real Time Systems*, Prentice Hall, Upper Saddle River, NJ, 2000. (Chapter 12)

[London, 1971] R. L. LONDON, "Software Reliability through Proving Programs Correct," *Proceedings of the IEEE International Symposium on Fault-Tolerant Computing,* March 1971. (Chapters 6 and 11)

[Long and Morris, 1993] F. LONG AND E. MORRIS, "An Overview of PCTE: A Basis for a Portable Common Tool Environment," Technical Report CMU/SEI–93–TR–1, Software Engineering Institute, Carnegie Mellon University, Pittsburgh, January 1993. (Chapter 13)

[Longstaff, Chittister, Pethia, and Haimes, 2000] T. A. LONGSTAFF, C. CHITTISTER, R. PETHIA, AND Y. Y. HAIMES, "Are We Forgetting the Risks of Information Technology?" *IEEE Computer* **33** (December 2000), pp. 43–51. (Chapters 1 and 2)

[Lotto, 1515] L. LOTTO, *Giovanni Agostino della Torre and his Son, Niccolò*, oil on canvas, 1515, at www.nationalgallery.org.uk/cgi-bin/WebObjects.dll/CollectionPublish-er.woa/wa/largeImage?workNumber=NG699. (Chapter 14)

[Loukides and Oram, 1997] M. K. LOUKIDES AND A. ORAM, *Programming with GNU Software*, O'Reilly and Associates, Sebastopol, CA, 1997. (Chapters 5 and 14)

[Low and Jeffrey, 1990] G. C. LOW AND D. R. JEFFREY, "Function Points in the Estimation and Evaluation of the Software Process," *IEEE Transactions on Software Engineering* **16** (January 1990), pp. 64–71. (Chapter 9)

[Luqi, Zhang, Berzins, and Qiao, 2004] LUQI, L. ZHANG, V. BERZINS, AND Y. QIAO, "Documentation Driven Development for Complex Real-Time Systems," *IEEE Transactions on Software Engineering* **30** (December 2004), pp. 936–52. (Chapter 12)

[Mackenzie, 1980] C. E. MACKENZIE, *Coded Character Sets: History and Development*, Addison-Wesley, Reading, MA, 1980. (Chapter 8)

[Mackey, 1999] K. MACKEY, "Stages of Team Development," *IEEE Software* **16** (July/August 1999), pp. 90–91. (Chapter 4)

[Madanmohan and De', 2004] T. R. MADANMOHAN AND R. DE', "Open Source Reuse in Commercial Firms," *IEEE Software* **21** (November/December 2004), pp. 62–69. (Chapter 1)

[Magee and Kramer, 1999] J. MAGEE AND J. KRAMER, *Concurrency: State Models & Java Programs*, John Wiley and Sons, New York, 1999. (Chapter 12)

[Magnus, 2005] A. P. MAGNUS, "9th Kings, Popes, and Symphonies," at www.math.ucl.ac.be/~magnus/onine/const9.jpg. (Chapter 14)

[Mancl and Havanas, 1990] D. MANCL AND W. HAVANAS, "A Study of the Impact of C++ on Software Maintenance," *Proceedings of the IEEE Conference on Software Maintenance,* San Diego, CA, November 1990, pp. 63–69. (Chapter 14)

[Manna and Pnueli, 1992] Z. MANNA AND A. PNUELI, *The Temporal Logic of Reactive and Concurrent Systems,* Springer-Verlag, New York, 1992. (Chapter 6)

[Manna and Waldinger, 1978] Z. MANNA AND R. WALDINGER, "The Logic of Computer Programming," *IEEE Transactions on Software Engineering* **SE-4** (1978), pp. 199–229. (Chapter 6)

[Mantei, 1981] M. MANTEI, "The Effect of Programming Team Structures on Programming Tasks," *Communications of the ACM* **24** (March 1981), pp. 106–13. (Chapter 4)

[Manzoni and Price, 2003] L. V. MANZONI AND R. T. PRICE, "Identifying Extensions Required by RUP (Rational Unified Process) to Comply with CMM (Capability Maturity Model) Levels 2 and 3," *IEEE Transactions on Software Engineering* **29** (February 2003), pp. 181–92. (Chapter 3)

[Maranzano et al., 2005] J. F. MARANZANO, S. A. ROZSYPAL, G. H. ZIMMERMAN, G. W. WARNKEN, P. E. WIRTH, AND D. M. WEISS, "Architecture Reviews: Practice and Experience," *IEEE Software* **22** (March/April 2005), pp. 34–43. (Chapter 12)

[Maring, 1996] B. MARING, "Object-Oriented Development of Large Applications," *IEEE Software* **13** (May 1996), pp. 33–40. (Chapter 1)

[Matsumoto, 1984] Y. MATSUMOTO, "Management of Industrial Software Production," *IEEE Computer* **17** (February 1984), pp. 59–72. (Chapter 8)

[Matsumoto, 1987] Y. MATSUMOTO, "A Software Factory: An Overall Approach to Software Production," in: *Tutorial: Software Reusability*, P. Freeman (Editor), Computer Society Press, Washington, DC, 1987, pp. 155–78. (Chapter 8)

[Maxwell and Forselius, 2000] K. D. MAXWELL AND P. FORSELIUS, "Benchmarking Software Development Productivity," *IEEE Software* **17** (January/February 2000), pp. 80–88. (Chapter 9)

[McCabe, 1976] T. J. MCCABE, "A Complexity Measure," *IEEE Transactions on Software Engineering* **SE-2** (December 1976), pp. 308–20. (Chapters 12 and 13)

[McCabe and Butler, 1989] T. J. MCCABE AND C. W. BUTLER, "Design Complexity Measurement and Testing," *Communications of the ACM* **32** (December 1989), pp. 1415–25. (Chapter 13)

[McConnell, 1993] S. MCCONNELL, *Code Complete: A Practical Handbook of Software Construction,* Microsoft Press, Redmond, WA, 1993. (Chapter 13)

[McConnell, 1996] S. MCCONNELL, "Daily Build and Smoke Test," *IEEE Software* **13** (July/August 1996), pp. 144, 143. (Chapters 2 and 4)

[McConnell, 2001] S. MCCONNELL, "The Nine Deadly Sins of Project Planning," *IEEE Software* **18** (November/December 2001), pp. 5–7. (Chapter 9)

[McGarry and Decker, 2002] F. MCGARRY AND B. DECKER, "Attaining Level 5 in CMM Process Maturity," *IEEE Software* **19** (2002), pp. 87–96. (Chapter 3)

[Mellor, 1994] P. MELLOR, "CAD: Computer-Aided Disaster," Technical Report, Centre for Software Reliability, City University, London, July 1994. (Chapter 1)

[Memon, Pollack, and Soffa, 2001] A. M. MEMON, M. E. POLLACK, AND M. L. SOFFA, "Hierarchical GUI Test

Case Generation Using Automated Planning," *IEEE Transactions on Software Engineering* **27** (February 2001), pp. 144–55. (Chapter 13)

[Mens, 2002] T. MENS, "A State-of-the-Art Survey on Software Merging," *IEEE Transactions on Software Engineering* **28** (May 2002), pp. 449–62. (Chapter 5)

[Mens and Tourwe, 2004] T. MENS AND T. TOURWE, "A Survey of Software Refactoring," *IEEE Transactions on Software Engineering* **30** (February 2004), pp. 126–39. (Chapter 2)

[Meyer, 1985] B. MEYER, "On Formalism in Specifications," *IEEE Software* **2** (January 1985), pp. 6–26. (Chapter 11)

[Meyer, 1986] B. MEYER, "Genericity versus Inheritance," Proceedings of the Conference on Object-Oriented Programming Systems, Languages and Applications, *ACM SIGPLAN Notices* **21** (November 1986), pp. 391–405. (Chapter 7)

[Meyer, 1987] B. MEYER, "Reusability: The Case for Object-Oriented Design," *IEEE Software* **4** (March 1987), pp. 50–64. (Chapter 8)

[Meyer, 1992] B. MEYER, "Applying 'Design by Contract'," *IEEE Computer* **25** (October 1992), pp. 40–51. (Chapters 1 and 7)

[Meyer, 1996a] B. MEYER, "The Reusability Challenge," *IEEE Computer* **29** (February 1996), pp. 76–78. (Chapter 8)

[Meyer, 1996b] B. MEYER, "The Many Faces of Inheritance: A Taxonomy of Taxonomy," *IEEE Computer* **29** (May 1996), pp. 105–8. (Chapter 7)

[Meyer, 1997] B. MEYER, *Object-Oriented Software Construction*, 2nd ed., Prentice Hall, Upper Saddle River, NJ, 1997. (Chapters 1 and 7)

[Miller, 1956] G. A. MILLER, "The Magical Number Seven, Plus or Minus Two: Some Limits on Our Capacity for Processing Information," *The Psychological Review* **63** (March 1956), pp. 81–97; reprinted in: at www.well.com/user/smalin/miller.html. (Chapters 2, 3, and 5)

[Miller and Yin, 2004] J. MILLER AND Z. YIN, "A Cognitive-Based Mechanism for Constructing Software Inspection Teams," *IEEE Transactions on Software Engineering* **30** (November 30), pp. 811–25. (Chapter 6)

[Mills, Dyer, and Linger, 1987] H. D. MILLS, M. DYER, AND R. C. LINGER, "Cleanroom Software Engineering," *IEEE Software* **4** (September 1987), pp. 19–25. (Chapter 13)

[Monarchi and Puhr, 1992] D. E. MONARCHI AND G. I. PUHR, "A Research Typology for Object-Oriented Analysis and Design," *Communications of the ACM* **35** (September 1992), pp. 35–47. (Chapters 11 and 12)

[Mooney, 1990] J. D. MOONEY, "Strategies for Supporting Application Portability," *IEEE Computer* **23** (November 1990), pp. 59–70. (Chapter 8)

[Moran, 1981] T. P. MORAN (Editor), Special Issue: The Psychology of Human-Computer Interaction, *ACM Computing Surveys* **13** (March 1981). (Chapter 5)

[Morisio, Ezran, and Tully, 2002] M. MORISIO, M. EZRAN, AND C. TULLY, "Success and Failure Factors in Software Reuse," *IEEE Transactions on Software Engineering* **28** (April 2002), pp. 340–57. (Chapter 8)

[Morisio, Tully, and Ezran, 2000] M. MORISIO, C. TULLY, AND M. EZRAN, "Diversity in Reuse Processes," *IEEE Software* **17** (July/August 2000), pp. 56–63. (Chapter 8)

[Murphy et al., 2001] G. C. MURPHY, R. J. WALKER, E. L. A. BANNIASSAD, M. P. ROBILLARD, A. LIA, AND M. A. KERSTEN, "Does Aspect-Oriented Programming Work?" *Communications of the ACM* **44** (October 2001), pp. 75–78. (Chapter 7)

[Murru, Deias, and Mugheddu, 2003] O. MURRU, R. DEIAS, AND G. MUGHEDDU, "Assessing XP at a European Internet Company," *IEEE Software* **20** (May/June, 2003), pp. 37–43. (Chapters 2 and 4)

[Murugappan and Keeni, 2003] M. MURUGAPPAN AND G. KEENI, "Blending CMM and Six Sigma to Meet Business Goals," *IEEE Software* **20** (March/April 2003), pp. 42–48. (Chapter 3)

[Musa and Everett, 1990] J. D. MUSA AND W. W. EVERETT, "Software-Reliability Engineering: Technology for the 1990s," *IEEE Software* **7** (November 1990), pp. 36–43. (Chapter 13)

[Musa, Iannino, and Okumoto, 1987] J. D. MUSA, A. IANNINO, AND K. OKUMOTO, *Software Reliability: Measurement, Prediction, Application*, McGraw-Hill, New York, 1987. (Chapter 13)

[Musser and Saini, 1996] D. R. MUSSER AND A. SAINI, *STL Tutorial and Reference Guide: C++ Programming with the Standard Template Library*, Addison-Wesley, Reading, MA, 1996. (Chapter 8)

[Myers, 1976] G. J. MYERS, *Software Reliability: Principles and Practices,* Wiley-Interscience, New York, 1976. (Chapter 13)

[Myers, 1978a] G. J. MYERS, "A Controlled Experiment in Program Testing and Code Walkthroughs/

Inspections," *Communications of the ACM* **21** (September 1978), pp. 760–68. (Chapter 13)

[Myers, 1978b] G. J. MYERS, *Composite/Structured Design*, Van Nostrand Reinhold, New York, 1978. (Chapter 7)

[Myers, 1979] G. J. MYERS, *The Art of Software Testing*, John Wiley and Sons, New York, 1979. (Chapters 6 and 13)

[Myers, 1992] W. MYERS, "Good Software Practices Pay off—or Do They?" *IEEE Software* **9** (March 1992), pp. 96–97. (Chapter 5)

[NAG, 2003] "NAG The Numerical Algorithms Group Ltd," at www.nag.co.uk, 2003. (Chapter 8)

[Naur, 1969] P. NAUR, "Programming by Action Clusters," *BIT* **9** (No. 3, 1969), pp. 250–58. (Chapters 6 and 11)

[Naur, Randell, and Buxton, 1976] P. NAUR, B. RANDELL, AND J. N. BUXTON (Editors), *Software Engineering: Concepts and Techniques: Proceedings of the NATO Conferences*, Petrocelli-Charter, New York, 1976. (Chapter 1)

[Nerur, Mahapatra, and Mangalaraj, 2005] S. NERUR, R. MAHAPATRA, G. MANGALARAJ, "Challenges of Migrating to Agile Methodologies," *Communications of the ACM* **48** (May 2005), pp. 72–78. (Chapter 2)

[Nesi, 1998] P. NESI, "Managing OO Projects Better," *IEEE Software* **15** (July/August 1998), pp. 50–60. (Chapter 9)

[Neumann, 1980] P. G. NEUMANN, Letter from the Editor, *ACM SIGSOFT Software Engineering Notes* **5** (July 1980), p. 2. (Chapter 1)

[Neumann, 1995] P. G. NEUMANN, *Computer-Related Risks*, Addison-Wesley, Reading, MA, 1995. (Chapter 1)

[NIST 151, 1988] "POSIX: Portable Operating System Interface for Computer Environments," Federal Information Processing Standard 151, National Institute of Standards and Technology, Washington, DC, 1988. (Chapter 8)

[Norden, 1958] P. V. NORDEN, "Curve Fitting for a Model of Applied Research and Development Scheduling," *IBM Journal of Research and Development* **2** (July 1958), pp. 232–48. (Chapter 9)

[Norušis, 2005] M. J. NORUŠIS, *SPSS 13.0 Guide to Data Analysis,* Prentice Hall, Upper Saddle Valley River, NJ, 2005. (Chapter 8)

[Norwig, 1996] P. NORWIG, "Design Patterns in Dynamic Programming," at norvig.com/design-patterns/ppframe.htm/, 1996. (Chapter 8)

[OMG, 2005] "Software Process Engineering Metamodel Specification," Version 2.0, August 2005, at www.omg.org/cgi-bin/doc?formal/05-07-04. (Chapter 3)

[Onoma, Tsai, Poonawala, and Suganuma, 1998] A. K. ONOMA, W.-T. TSAI, M. H. POONAWALA, AND H. SUGANUMA, "Regression Testing in an Industrial Environment," *Communications of the ACM* **42** (May 1998), pp. 81–86. (Chapter 14)

[Parnas and Lawford, 2003] D. L. PARNAS AND M. LAWFORD, "The Role of Inspection in Software Quality Assurance," *IEEE Transactions on Software Engineering* **29** (August 2003), pp. 674–76. (Chapter 6)

[Parnas, 1971] D. L. PARNAS, "Information Distribution Aspects of Design Methodology," *Proceedings of the IFIP Congress*, Ljubljana, Yugoslavia, 1971, pp. 339–44. (Chapter 7)

[Parnas, 1972a] D. L. PARNAS, "A Technique for Software Module Specification with Examples," *Communications of the ACM* **15** (May 1972), pp. 330–36. (Chapter 7)

[Parnas, 1972b] D. L. PARNAS, "On the Criteria to Be Used in Decomposing Systems into Modules," *Communications of the ACM* **15** (December 1972), pp. 1053–58. (Chapter 7)

[Parnas, 1994] D. L. PARNAS, "Software Aging," *Proceedings of the 16th International Conference on Software Engineering*, Sorrento, Italy, May 1994, pp. 279–87. (Chapter 1)

[Parnas, 1999] D. L. PARNAS, "Ten Myths about Y2K Inspections," *Communications of the ACM* **42** (May 1999), p. 128. (Chapter 14)

[Paulk, 1995] M. C. PAULK, "How ISO 9001 Compares with the CMM," *IEEE Software* **12** (January 1995), pp. 74–83. (Chapter 3)

[Paulk, Weber, Curtis, and Chrissis, 1995] M. C. PAULK, C. V. WEBER, B. CURTIS, AND M. B. CHRISSIS, *The Capability Maturity Model: Guidelines for Improving the Software Process*, Addison-Wesley, Reading, MA, 1995. (Chapter 3)

[Paulson, Succi, and Eberlein, 2004] J. W. PAULSON, G. SUCCI, AND A. EBERLEIN, "An Empirical Study of Open-Source and Closed-Source Software Products," *IEEE Transactions on Software Engineering* **30** (April 2004), pp. 246–56. (Chapter 1)

[Perry and Kaiser, 1990] D. E. PERRY AND G. E. KAISER, "Adequate Testing and Object-Oriented Programming," *Journal of Object-Oriented Programming* **2** (January/February 1990), pp. 13–19. (Chapter 13)

[Perry et al., 2002] D. E. PERRY, A. PORTER, M. W. WADE, L G. VOTTA, AND J. PERPICH, "Reducing Inspection Interval in Large-Scale Software Development," *IEEE Transactions on Software Engineering* **28** (July 2002), pp. 695–705. (Chapter 6)

[Pfleeger, Jeffrey, Curtis, and Kitchenham, 1997] S. L. PFLEEGER, R. JEFFREY, B. CURTIS, AND B. KITCHENHAM, "Status Report on Software Measurement," *IEEE Software* **14** (March/April 1997), pp. 33–44. (Chapter 5)

[Pigoski, 1996] T. M. PIGOSKI, *Practical Software Maintenance: Best Practices for Managing Your Software Investment*, John Wiley and Sons, New York, 1996. (Chapter 14)

[Pitterman, 2000] B. PITTERMAN, "Telecordia Technologies: The Journey to High Maturity," *IEEE Software* **17** (July/August 2000), pp. 89–96. (Chapter 3)

[Pittman, 1993] M. PITTMAN, "Lessons Learned in Managing Object-Oriented Development," *IEEE Software* **10** (January 1993), pp. 43–53. (Chapter 9)

[Ponder and Bush, 1994] C. PONDER AND B. BUSH, "Polymorphism Considered Harmful," *ACM SIGSOFT Software Engineering Notes* **19** (April, 1994), pp. 35–38. (Chapter 7)

[Pont and Banner, 2004] M. J. PONT AND M. P. BANNER, "Designing Embedded Systems Using Patterns: A Case Study," *Journal of Systems and Software* **71** (May 2004), pp. 201–213. (Chapter 8)

[Poulin, 1997] J. S. POULIN, *Measuring Software Reuse: Principles, Practice, and Economic Models*, Addison-Wesley, Reading, MA, 1997. (Chapter 8)

[Prechelt and Unger, 2000] L. PRECHELT AND B. UNGER, "An Experiment Measuring the Effects of Personal Software Process (PSP) Training," *IEEE Transactions on Software Engineering* **27** (May 2000), pp. 465–72. (Chapter 3)

[Prechelt, Unger-Lamprecht, Philippsen, and Tichy, 2002] L. PRECHELT, B. UNGER-LAMPRECHT, M. PHILIPPSEN, AND W. F. TICHY, "Two Controlled Experiments in Assessing the Usefulness of Design Pattern Documentation in Program Maintenance," *IEEE Transactions on Software Engineering* **28** (June 2002), pp. 595–606. (Chapters 8 and 14)

[Prieto-Díaz, 1991] R. PRIETO-DÍAZ, "Implementing Faceted Classification for Software Reuse," *Communications of the ACM* **34** (May 1991), pp. 88–97. (Chapter 8)

[Putnam, 1978] L. H. PUTNAM, "A General Empirical Solution to the Macro Software Sizing and Estimating Problem," *IEEE Transactions on Software Engineering* **SE-4** (July 1978), pp. 345–61. (Chapter 9)

[Radin, 1996] G. RADIN, "Object Technology in Perspective," *IBM Systems Journal* **35** (No. 2, 1996), pp. 124–26. (Chapter 1)

[Rajlich and Bennett, 2000] V. RAJLICH AND K. H. BENNETT, "A Staged Model for the Software Life Cycle," *IEEE Computer* **33** (July 2000), pp. 66–71. (Chapter 2)

[Rajlich, Wilde, Buckellew, and Page, 2001] V. RAJLICH, N. WILDE, M. BUCKELLEW, AND H. PAGE, "Software Cultures and Evolution," *IEEE Computer* **34** (September 2001), pp. 24–28. (Chapter 14)

[Rapps and Weyuker, 1985] S. RAPPS AND E. J. WEYUKER, "Selecting Software Test Data Using Data Flow Information," *IEEE Transactions on Software Engineering* **SE-11** (April 1985), pp. 367–75. (Chapter 13)

[Rasmussen, 2003] J. RASMUSSON, "Introducing XP into Greenfield Projects: Lessons Learned," *IEEE Software* **20** (May/June, 2003), pp. 21–29. (Chapter 2)

[Ravichandran and Rothenberger, 2003] T. RAVICHANDRAN AND M. A. ROTHENBERGER, "Software Reuse Strategies and Component Markets," *Communications of the ACM* **46** (August 2003), pp. 109-14 (Chapter 8)

[Raymond, 2000] E. S. RAYMOND, *The Cathedral and the Bazaar: Musings on Linux and Open Source by an Accidental Revolutionary*, O'Reilly & Associates, Sebastopol, CA, 2000; also available at www.catb.org/~esr/writings/cathedral-bazaar/cathedral-bazaar/. (Chapters 1 and 2)

[Reifer, 2000] D. J. REIFER, "Software Management: The Good, the Bad, and the Ugly," *IEEE Software* **17** (March/April 2000), pp. 73–75. (Chapter 9)

[Reifer, 2003] D. REIFER, "XP and the CMM," *IEEE Software* **20** (May/June 2003), pp. 14–15. (Chapter 4)

[Reifer, Maurer, and Erdogmus, 2003] D. REIFER, F. MAURER, AND H. ERDOGMUS, "Scaling Agile Methods," *IEEE Software* **20** (July/August 2004), pp. 12–14. (Chapter 2)

[Rochkind, 1975] M. J. ROCHKIND, "The Source Code Control System," *IEEE Transactions on Software Engineering* **SE-1** (October 1975), pp. 255–65. (Chapters 5 and 14)

[Ropponen and Lyttinen, 2000] J. ROPPONEN AND K. LYTTINEN, "Components of Software Development Risk: How to Address Them? A Project Manager Survey," *IEEE Transactions on Software Engineering* **26** (February 2000), pp. 96–111. (Chapter 2)

[Rothermel, Untch, Chu, and Harrold, 2001] G. ROTHERMEL, R. H. UNTCH, C. CHU, AND M. J. HARROLD, "Prioritizing Test Cases for Regression Test Cases," *IEEE*

Transactions on Software Engineering **27** (October 2001), pp. 929–48. (Chapter 14)

[Royce, 1970] W. W. ROYCE, "Managing the Development of Large Software Systems: Concepts and Techniques," *1970 WESCON Technical Papers, Western Electronic Show and Convention*, Los Angeles, August 1970, pp. A/1-1–A/1-9; reprinted in: *Proceedings of the 11th International Conference on Software Engineering*, Pittsburgh, May 1989, IEEE, pp. 328–38. (Chapter 2)

[Royce, 1998] W. ROYCE, *Software Project Management: A Unified Framework*, Addison-Wesley, Reading, MA, 1998. (Chapters 2 and 4)

[Rugaber and White, 1998] S. RUGABER AND J. WHITE, "Restoring a Legacy: Lessons Learned," *IEEE Software* **15** (July/August 1998), pp. 28–33. (Chapter 14)

[Rumbaugh et al., 1991] J. RUMBAUGH, M. BLAHA, W. PREMERLANI, F. EDDY, AND W. LORENSEN, *Object-Oriented Modeling and Design*, Prentice Hall, Englewood Cliffs, NJ, 1991. (Chapters 3 and 11)

[Rumbaugh, Jacobson, and Booch, 1999] J. RUMBAUGH, I. JACOBSON, AND G. BOOCH, *The Unified Modeling Language Reference Manual,* Addison-Wesley, Reading, MA, 1999. (Chapter 11)

[Sackman, 1970] H. SACKMAN, *Man–Computer Problem Solving: Experimental Evaluation of Time-Sharing and Batch Processing,* Auerbach, Princeton, NJ, 1970. (Chapter 9)

[Sackman, Erikson, and Grant, 1968] H. SACKMAN, W. J. ERIKSON, AND E. E. GRANT, "Exploratory Experimental Studies Comparing Online and Offline Programming Performance," *Communications of the ACM* **11** (January 1968), pp. 3–11. (Chapter 9)

[Saiedian and Kuzara, 1995] H. SAIEDIAN AND R. KUZARA, "SEI Capability Maturity Model's Impact on Contractors," *IEEE Computer* **28** (January 1995), pp. 16–26. (Chapter 3)

[Sammet, 1978] J. E. SAMMET, "The Early History of COBOL," *Proceedings of the History of Programming Languages Conference,* Los Angeles, 1978, pp. 199–276. (Chapter 13)

[Samoladas, Stamelos, Angelis, and Oikonomou, 2005] I. SAMOLADAS, I. STAMELOS, L. ANGELIS, AND A. OIKONOMOU, "Open Source Software Development Should Strive for Even Greater Code Maintainability," *Communications of the ACM* **47** (October 2004), pp. 83–87. (Chapter 14)

[Schach, 1992] S. R. SCHACH, *Software Reuse: Past, Present, and Future*, videotape, 150 min, US-VHS format, IEEE Computer Society Press, Los Alamitos, CA, November 1992. (Chapter 8)

[Schach, 1994] S. R. SCHACH, "The Economic Impact of Software Reuse on Maintenance," *Journal of Software Maintenance—Research and Practice* **6** (July/August 1994), pp. 185–96. (Chapter 8)

[Schach, 1994] S. R. SCHACH, "The Economic Impact of Software Reuse on Maintenance," *Journal of Software Maintenance: Research and Practice* **6** (July/August 1994), pp. 185–96. (Chapter 9)

[Schach, 1997] S. R. SCHACH, *Software Engineering with Java*, Richard D. Irwin, Chicago, 1997. (Chapter 8)

[Schach and Stevens-Guille, 1979] S. R. SCHACH AND P. D. STEVENS-GUILLE, "Two Aspects of Computer-Aided Design," *Transactions of the Royal Society of South Africa* **44** (Part 1, 1979), 123–26. (Chapter 7)

[Schach and Wood, 1986] S. R. SCHACH AND P. T. WOOD, "An Almost Path-Free Very High-Level Interactive Data Manipulation Language for a Microcomputer-Based Database System," *Software–Practice and Experience* **16** (March 1986), pp. 243–68. (Chapter 10)

[Schach et al., 2002] S, R. SCHACH, B. JIN, D. R. WRIGHT, G. Z. HELLER, AND A. J. OFFUTT, "Maintainability of the Linux Kernel," *IEE Proceedings—Software* **149** (February 2002), pp. 18–23. (Chapters 1 and 7)

[Schach et al., 2003a] S. R. SCHACH, B. JIN, DAVID R. WRIGHT, G. Z. HELLER, AND J. OFFUTT, "Quality Impacts of Clandestine Common Coupling," *Software Quality Journal* **11** (July 2003), pp. 211–18. (Chapter 7)

[Schach et al., 2003b] S. R. SCHACH, B. JIN, G. Z. HELLER, L. YU, AND J. OFFUTT, "Determining the Distribution of Maintenance Categories: Survey versus Measurement," *Empirical Software Engineering* **8** (December 2003), pp. 351–66. (Chapter 1)

[Schrage, 2004] M. SCHRAGE, "Never Go to a Client Meeting without a Prototype," *IEEE Software* **21** (2004), pp. 42–45. (Chapter 10)

[Schricker, 2000] D. SCHRICKER, "Cobol for the Next Millennium," *IEEE Software* **17** (March/April 2000), pp. 48–52. (Chapter 8)

[Schwaber, 2001] K. SCHWABER, *Agile Software Development with Scrum*, Prentice Hall, Upper Saddle River, NJ, 2001. (Chapter 2)

[Scott and Vessey, 2002] J. E. SCOTT AND I. VESSEY, "Managing Risks in Enterprise Systems

Implementations," *Communications of the ACM* **45** (April 2002), pp. 74–81. (Chapters 1 and 2)

[Sedigh-Ali and Paul, 2001] S. SEDIGH-ALI AND R. A. PAUL, "Software Engineering Metrics for COTS-Based Systems," *IEEE Computer* **34** (May 2001), pp. 44–50. (Chapter 5)

[SEI, 2002] "CMMI Frequently Asked Questions (FAQ)," Software Engineering Institute, Carnegie Mellon University, Pittsburgh, June 2002. (Chapter 3)

[Selby, 1989] R. W. SELBY, "Quantitative Studies of Software Reuse," in: *Software Reusability,* Vol. 2, *Applications and Experience*, T. J. Biggerstaff and A. J. Perlis (Editors), ACM Press, New York, 1989, pp. 213–33. (Chapter 8)

[Selic, Gullekson, and Ward, 1995] B. SELIC, G. GULLEKSON, AND P. T. WARD, *Real-Time Object-Oriented Modeling*, John Wiley and Sons, New York, 1995. (Chapter 11)

[Shapiro, 1994] F. R. SHAPIRO, "The First Bug," *Byte* **19** (April 1994), p. 308. (Chapter 1)

[Sharma and Rai, 2000] S. SHARMA AND A. RAI, "CASE Deployment in IS Organizations," *Communications of the ACM* **43** (January 2000), pp. 80–88. (Chapter 5)

[Shaw and Garlan, 1996] M. SHAW AND D. GARLAN, *Software Architecture: Perspectives on an Emerging Discipline*, Prentice Hall, Upper Saddle River, NJ, 1996. (Chapter 8)

[Shepperd, 1988] M. SHEPPERD, "A Critique of Cyclomatic Complexity as a Software Metric," *Software Engineering Journal* **3** (March 1988), pp. 30–36. (Chapter 13)

[Shepperd, 1990] M. SHEPPERD, "Design Metrics: An Empirical Analysis," *Software Engineering Journal* **5** (January 1990), pp. 3–10. (Chapter 12)

[Shepperd, 1996] M. SHEPPERD, *Foundations of Software Measurement,* Prentice Hall, Upper Saddle River, NJ, 1996. (Chapter 5)

[Shepperd and Ince, 1994] M. SHEPPERD AND D. C. INCE, "A Critique of Three Metrics," *Journal of Systems and Software* **26** (September 1994), pp. 197–210. (Chapter 13)

[Sherer, Kouchakdjian, and Arnold, 1996] S. W. SHERER, A. KOUCHAKDJIAN, AND P. G. ARNOLD, "Experience Using Cleanroom Software Engineering," *IEEE Software* **13** (May 1996), pp. 69–76. (Chapter 13)

[Shlaer and Mellor, 1992] S. SHLAER AND S. MELLOR, *Object Lifecycles: Modeling the World in States,* Yourdon Press, Englewood Cliffs, NJ, 1992. (Chapter 11 and 12)

[Shneiderman, 1980] B. SHNEIDERMAN, *Software Psychology: Human Factors in Computer and Information Systems,* Winthrop Publishers, Cambridge, MA, 1980. (Chapter 1)

[Shneiderman, 2003] B. SHNEIDERMAN, *Designing the User Interface: Strategies for Effective Human-Computer Interaction,* 4th ed., Addison-Wesley Longman, Reading, MA, 2003. (Chapter 10)

[Shneiderman and Mayer, 1975] B. SHNEIDERMAN AND R. MAYER, "Towards a Cognitive Model of Programmer Behavior," Technical Report TR-37, Indiana University, Bloomington, 1975. (Chapter 7)

[Silberschatz, Galvin, and Gagne, 2002] A. SILBERSCHATZ, P. B. GALVIN, AND G. GAGNE, *Operating System Concepts,* 6th ed., Addison-Wesley, Reading, MA, 2002. (Chapter 12)

[Smith, Hale, and Parrish, 2001] R. K. SMITH, J. E. HALE, AND A. S. PARRISH, "An Empirical Study Using Task Assignment Patterns to Improve the Accuracy of Software Effort Estimation," *IEEE Transactions on Software Engineering* **27** (March 2001), pp. 264–71. (Chapter 9)

[Sneed, 1995] H. M. SNEED, "Planning the Reengineering of Legacy Systems," *IEEE Software* **12** (January 1995), pp. 24–34. (Chapter 14)

[Snyder, 1993] A. SNYDER, "The Essence of Objects: Concepts and Terms," *IEEE Software* **10** (January 1993), pp. 31–42. (Chapter 7)

[Sobell, 1995] M. G. SOBELL, *A Practical Guide to the UNIX System,* 3rd ed., Benjamin/Cummings, Menlo Park, CA, 1995. (Chapter 5)

[Softwaremag.com, 2004] "Standish: Project Success Rates Improved Over 10 Years," at www.softwaremag.com/L.cfm?Doc=newsletter/2004-01-15/Standish, January 15, 2004. (Chapter 2)

[Sparling, 2000] M. SPARLING, "Lessons Learned through Six Years of Component-Based Development," *Communications of the ACM* **43** (October 2000), pp. 47–53. (Chapter 8)

[Spiegel Online, 2004] "Rheinbrücke mit Treppe - 54 Zentimeter Höhenunterschied," at www.spiegel.de/panorama/0,1518,281837,00.html. (Chapter 1)

[Spivey, 1992] J. M. SPIVEY, *The Z Notation: A Reference Manual*, Prentice Hall, New York, 1992. (Chapter 2)

[St. Petersburg Times Online, 2003] "Thousands of Federal Checks Uncashable," at www.sptimes.com/2003/02/07/Worldandnation/Thousands_of_federal_.shtml, February 07, 2003. (Chapter 1)

[Standish, 2003] STANDISH GROUP INTERNATIONAL, "Introduction," at www.standishgroup.com/chaos/introduction.pdf, 2003. (Chapter 2)

[Stephens and Rosenberg, 2003] M. STEPHENS AND D. ROSENBERG, *Extreme Programming Refactored: The Case against XP*, Apress, Berkeley, CA, 2003. (Chapter 2)

[Stephenson, 1976] W. E. STEPHENSON, "An Analysis of the Resources Used in Safeguard System Software Development," Bell Laboratories, Draft Paper, August 1976. (Chapter 1)

[Stevens and Pooley, 2000] P. STEVENS WITH R. POOLEY, *Using UML: Software Engineering with Objects and Components*, updated edition, Addison-Wesley, Upper Saddle River, NJ, 2000. (Chapter 15)

[Stevens, Myers, and Constantine, 1974] W. P. STEVENS, G. J. MYERS, AND L. L. CONSTANTINE, "Structured Design," *IBM Systems Journal* **13** (No. 2, 1974), pp. 115–39. (Chapter 7)

[Stocks and Carrington, 1996] P. STOCKS AND D. CARRINGTON, "A Framework for Specification-Based Testing," *IEEE Transactions on Software Engineering* **22** (November 1996), pp. 777–93. (Chapter 13)

[Stolper, 1999] S. A. STOLPER, "Streamlined Design Approach Lands Mars Pathfinder," *IEEE Software* 16 (September/October 1999), pp. 52–62. (Chapter 12)

[Stroustrup, 2003] B. STROUSTRUP, *The C++ Standard: Incorporating Technical Corrigendum No. 1*, 2nd ed., John Wiley and Sons, New York, 2003. (Chapters 7 and 12)

[Sykes and McGregor, 2000] D. A. SYKES AND J. D. MCGREGOR, *Practical Guide to Testing Object-Oriented Software*, Addison-Wesley, Reading, MA, 2000. (Chapter 6)

[Symons, 1991] C. R. SYMONS, *Software Sizing and Estimating: Mk II FPA*, John Wiley and Sons, Chichester, UK, 1991. (Chapter 9)

[Takahashi and Kamayachi, 1985] M. TAKAHASHI AND Y. KAMAYACHI, "An Empirical Study of a Model for Program Error Prediction," *Proceedings of the Eighth International Conference on Software Engineering*, London, 1985, pp. 330–36. (Chapter 13)

[Tanenbaum, 2002] A. S. TANENBAUM, *Computer Networks,* 4th ed., Prentice Hall, Upper Saddle River, NJ, 2002. (Chapter 8)

[Teng, Jeong, and Grover, 1998] J. T. C. TENG, S. R. JEONG, AND V. GROVER, "Profiling Successful Reengineering Projects," *Communications of the ACM* **41** (June 1999), pp. 96–102. (Chapter 14)

[Thayer and Dorfman, 1999] R. H. THAYER AND M. DORFMAN, *Software Requirements Engineering*, revised 2nd ed., IEEE Computer Society Press, Los Alamitos, CA, 1999. (Chapter 10)

[Tichy, 1985] W. F. TICHY, "RCS—A System for Version Control," *Software—Practice and Experience* **15** (July 1985), pp. 637–54. (Chapters 5 and 14)

[Toft, Coleman, and Ohta, 2000] P. TOFT, D. COLEMAN, AND J. OHTA, "A Cooperative Model for Cross-Divisional Product Development for a Software Product Line," in: *Software Product Lines: Experience and Research Directions*, P. Donohoe (Editor), Kluwer Academic Publishers, Boston, 2000, pp. 111–32. (Chapter 8)

[Tomer and Schach, 2000] A. TOMER AND S. R. SCHACH, "The Evolution Tree: A Maintenance-Oriented Software Development Model," in: *Proceedings of the Fourth European Conference on Software Maintenance and Reengineering (CSMR 2000)*, Zürich, Switzerland, February/March 2000, pp. 209–14. (Chapter 2)

[Tomer and Schach, 2002] A. TOMER AND S. R. SCHACH, "A Three-Dimensional Model for System Design Evolution," *Systems Engineering* **5** (No. 4, 2002), pp. 264–273 (Chapter 5)

[Tomer et al., 2004] A. TOMER, L. GOLDIN, T. KUFLIK, E. KIMCHI, AND S. R. SCHACH, "Evaluating Software Reuse Alternatives: A Model and Its Application to an Industrial Case Study," *IEEE Transactions on Software Engineering* **30** (September 2004), 601–12. (Chapter 8)

[Tracz, 1979] W. J. TRACZ, "Computer Programming and the Human Thought Process," *Software—Practice and Experience* **9** (February 1979), pp. 127–37. (Chapter 5)

[Tracz, 1994] W. TRACZ, "Software Reuse Myths Revisited," *Proceedings of the 16th International Conference on Software Engineering*, Sorrento, Italy, May 1994, pp. 271–72. (Chapter 8)

[Trammel, Binder, and Snyder, 1992] C. J. TRAMMEL, L. H. BINDER, AND C. E. SNYDER, "The Automated Production Control Documentation System: A Case Study in Cleanroom Software Engineering," *ACM Transactions on Software Engineering and Methodology* **1** (January 1992), pp. 81–94. (Chapter 13)

[Turner, 1994] C. D. TURNER, "State-Based Testing: A New Method for the Testing of Object-Oriented Programs," Ph.D. thesis, Computer Science Division, University of Durham, Durham, UK, November, 1994. (Chapter 13)

[Tyran and George, 2002] C. K. TYRAN AND J. F. GEORGE, "Improving Software Inspections with Group Process Support," *Communications of the ACM* **45** (September 2002), pp. 87–92. (Chapter 6)

[Ulkuniemi and Seppanen, 2004] P. ULKUNIEMI, AND V. SEPPANEN, "COTS Component Acquisition in an Emerging Market," *IEEE Software* **21** (November/December 2004), pp. 76–82. (Chapter 1)

[USNO, 2000] "The 21st Century and the Third Millennium—When Will They Begin?" U.S. Naval Observatory, Astronomical Applications Department, at aa.usno.navy.mil/AA/faq/docs/millennium.html, February 22, 2000. (Chapter 11)

[van der Hoek, Carzaniga, Heimbigner, and Wolf, 2002] A. VAN DER HOEK, A. CARZANIGA, D. HEIMBIGNER, AND A. L. WOLF, "A Testbed for Configuration Management Policy Programming," *IEEE Transactions on Software Engineering* **28** (January 2002), pp. 79–99. (Chapter 5)

[van der Poel and Schach, 1983] K. G. VAN DER POEL AND S. R. SCHACH, "A Software Metric for Cost Estimation and Efficiency Measurement in Data Processing System Development," *Journal of Systems and Software* **3** (September 1983), pp. 187–91. (Chapter 9)

[van Solingen, 2004] R. VAN SOLINGEN, "Measuring the ROI of Software Process Improvement," *IEEE Software* **21** (May/June 2004), pp. 32–38. (Chapters 3 and 5)

[van Wijngaarden et al., 1975] A. VAN WIJNGAARDEN, B. J. MAILLOUX, J. E. L. PECK, C. H. A. KOSTER, M. SINTZOFF, C. H. LINDSEY, L. G. L. T. MEERTENS, AND R. G. FISKER, "Revised Report on the Algorithmic Language ALGOL 68," *Acta Informatica* **5** (1975), pp. 1–236. (Chapter 3)

[Vitharana, 2003] P. VITHARANA, "Risks and Challenges of Component-Based Software Development," *Communications of the ACM* **46** (August 2003), pp. 67–72. (Chapter 8)

[Vitharana and Ramamurthy, 2003] P. VITHARANA AND K. RAMAMURTHY, "Computer-Mediated Group Support, Anonymity and the Software Inspection Process: An Empirical Investigation," *IEEE Transactions on Software Engineering* **29** (March 2003), pp. 167–80. (Chapter 6)

[Vlissides, 1998] J. VLISSIDES, *Pattern Hatching: Design Patterns Applied,* Addison-Wesley, Reading, MA, 1998. (Chapter 8)

[Voas, 1999] J. VOAS, "Software Quality's Eight Greatest Myths," *IEEE Software* 16 (September/October 1999), pp. 118–20. (Chapter 6)

[Vokac, 2004] M. VOKAC, "Defect Frequency and Design Patterns: An Empirical Study of Industrial Code," *IEEE Transactions on Software Engineering* **30** (December 2004), pp. 904–17. (Chapter 8)

[von Mayrhauser and Vana, 1997] A. VON MAYRHAUSER AND A. M. VANA, "Identification of Dynamic Comprehension Processes during Large Scale Maintenance," *IEEE Transactions on Software Engineering* **22** (June 1996), pp. 424–37. (Chapter 14)

[Walker, 1992] I. J. WALKER, "Requirements of an Object-Oriented Design Method," *Software Engineering Journal* **7** (March 1992), pp. 102–13. (Chapter 12)

[Walrad and Strom, 2002] C. WALRAD AND D. STROM, "The Importance of Branching Models in SCM," *IEEE Computer* **35** (September 2002), pp. 31–38. (Chapter 5)

[Walsh, 1979] T. J. WALSH, "A Software Reliability Study Using a Complexity Measure," *Proceedings of the AFIPS National Computer Conference*, New York, 1979, pp. 761–68. (Chapter 13)

[Ward and Mellor, 1985] P. T. WARD AND S. MELLOR, *Structured Development for Real-Time Systems.* Vols. 1, 2, and 3, Yourdon Press, New York, 1985. (Chapter 12)

[Wasserman, 1996] A. I. WASSERMAN, "Toward a Discipline of Software Engineering," *IEEE Software* **13** (November/December 1996), pp. 23–31. (Chapters 1 and 3)

[Watson and McCabe, 1996] A. H. WATSON AND T. J. MCCABE, "Structured Testing: A Testing Methodology Using the Cyclomatic Complexity Metric," NIST Special Publication 500–235, Computer Systems Laboratory, National Institute of Standards and Technology, Gaithersburg, MD, 1996. (Chapter 13)

[Webster, 1995] B. F. WEBSTER, *Pitfalls of Object-Oriented Development*, M&T Books, New York, 1995. (Chapter 1)

[Weinberg, 1971] G. M. WEINBERG, *The Psychology of Computer Programming*, Van Nostrand Reinhold, New York, 1971. (Chapters 1 and 4)

[Weinberg, 1992] G. M. WEINBERG, *Quality Software Management: Systems Thinking*, Vol. 1, Dorset House, New York, 1992. (Chapter 9)

[Weinberg, 1993] G. M. WEINBERG, *Quality Software Management: First-Order Measurement*, Vol. 2, Dorset House, New York, 1993. (Chapter 9)

[Weinberg, 1994] G. M. WEINBERG, *Quality Software Management: Congruent Action*, Vol. 3, Dorset House, New York, 1994. (Chapter 9)

[Weinberg, 1997] G. M. WEINBERG, *Quality Software Management: Anticipating Change*, Vol. 4, Dorset House, New York, 1997. (Chapter 9)

[Weller, 1994] E. F. WELLER, "Using Metrics to Manage Software Projects," *IEEE Computer* **27** (September 1994), pp. 27–34. (Chapter 9)

[Weller, 2000] E. F. WELLER, "Practical Applications of Statistical Process Control," *IEEE Software* **18** (May/June 2000), pp. 48–55. (Chapter 3)

[Weyuker, 1988a] E. J. WEYUKER, "An Empirical Study of the Complexity of Data Flow Testing," *Proceedings of the Second Workshop on Software Testing, Verification, and Analysis*, Banff, Canada, July 1988, pp. 188–95. (Chapter 13)

[Weyuker, 1988b] E. WEYUKER, "Evaluating Software Complexity Measures," *IEEE Transactions on Software Engineering* **14** (September 1988), pp. 1357–65. (Chapter 13)

[Weyuker, 1998] E. J. WEYUKER, "Testing Component-Based Software: A Cautionary Tale," *IEEE Software* **15** (September/October 1998), pp. 54–59. (Chapter 8)

[Whitgift, 1991] D. WHITGIFT, *Methods and Tools for Software Configuration Management*, John Wiley and Sons, New York, 1991. (Chapter 5)

[Whittaker and Voas, 2000] J. A. WHITTAKER AND J. VOAS, "Toward a More Reliable Theory of Software Reliability," *IEEE Computer* **33** (December 2000), pp. 36–42. (Chapter 6)

[Whittaker, 2000] J. A. WHITTAKER, "What Is Software Testing? And Why Is It So Hard?" *IEEE Software* **17** (January/February 2000), pp. 70–79. (Chapter 6)

[Wilde, Matthews, and Huitt, 1993] N. WILDE, P. MATTHEWS, AND R. HUITT, "Maintaining Object-Oriented Software," *IEEE Software* **10** (January 1993), pp. 75–80. (Chapters 13 and 14)

[Williams, 1996] J. D. WILLIAMS, "Managing Iteration in OO Projects," *IEEE Computer* **29** (September 1996), pp. 39–43. (Chapter 11)

[Williams, Kessler, Cunningham, and Jeffries, 2000] L. WILLIAMS, R. R. KESSLER, W. CUNNINGHAM, AND R. JEFFRIES, "Strengthening the Case for Pair Programming," *IEEE Software* **17** (July/August 2000), pp. 19–25. (Chapter 2)

[Williams, Kessler, Cunningham, and Jeffries, 2000] L. WILLIAMS, R. R. KESSLER, W. CUNNINGHAM, AND R. JEFFRIES, "Strengthening the Case for Pair Programming," *IEEE Software* **17** (July/August 2000), pp. 19–25. (Chapter 4)

[Wirfs-Brock, Wilkerson, and Wiener, 1990] R. WIRFS-BROCK, B. WILKERSON, AND L. WIENER, *Designing Object-Oriented Software*, Prentice Hall, Englewood Cliffs, NJ, 1990. (Chapters 1, 11, and 12)

[Wirth, 1971] N. WIRTH, "Program Development by Stepwise Refinement," *Communications of the ACM* **14** (April 1971), pp. 221–27. (Chapters 5 and 6)

[Wirth, 1975] N. WIRTH, *Algorithms + Data Structures = Programs,* Prentice Hall, Englewood Cliffs, NJ, 1975. (Chapter 5)

[Wohlwend and Rosenbaum, 1993] H. WOHLWEND AND S. ROSENBAUM, "Software Improvements in an International Company," *Proceedings of the 15th International Conference on Software Engineering*, Baltimore, MD, May 1993, pp. 212–20. (Chapter 3)

[Woodward, Hedley, and Hennell, 1980] M. R. WOODWARD, D. HEDLEY, AND M. A. HENNELL, "Experience with Path Analysis and Testing of Programs," *IEEE Transactions on Software Engineering* **SE-6** (May 1980), pp. 278–86. (Chapter 13)

[W3C, 2006] "World Wide Web Consortium," at www.w3.org, 2006.

[XML, 2003] "Extensible Markup Language (XML)," at www.w3.org/XML, 2003.

[Yamaura, 1998] T. YAMAURA, "How to Design Practical Test Cases," *IEEE Software* **15** (November/December 1998), pp. 30–36. (Chapter 13)

[Yourdon and Constantine, 1979] E. YOURDON AND L. L. CONSTANTINE, *Structured Design: Fundamentals of a Discipline of Computer Program and Systems Design*, Prentice Hall, Englewood Cliffs, NJ, 1979. (Chapter 1)

[Yourdon and Constantine, 1979] E. YOURDON AND L. L. CONSTANTINE, *Structured Design: Fundamentals of a Discipline of Computer Program and Systems Design*, Prentice Hall, Englewood Cliffs, NJ, 1979. (Chapter 7)

[Yourdon and Constantine, 1979] E. YOURDON AND L. L. CONSTANTINE, *Structured Design: Fundamentals of a Discipline of Computer Program and Systems Design*, Prentice Hall, Englewood Cliffs, NJ, 1979. (Chapter 12)

[Yourdon, 1989] E. YOURDON, *Modern Structured Analysis*, Yourdon Press, Englewood Cliffs, NJ, 1989. (Chapter 13)

[Yourdon, 1992] E. YOURDON, *The Decline and Fall of the American Programmer*, Yourdon Press, Upper Saddle River, NJ, 1992. (Chapter 1)

[Yu, Schach, Chen, and Offutt, 2004] L. Yu, S. R. Schach, K. Chen, and J. Offutt, "Categorization of Common Coupling and Its Application to the Maintainability of the Linux Kernel," *IEEE Transactions on Software Engineering* **30** (October 2004), pp. 694–706. (Chapters 2 and 7)

[Zage and Zage, 1993] W. M. Zage and D. M. Zage, "Evaluating Design Metrics on Large-Scale Software," *IEEE Software* **10** (July 1993), pp. 75–81. (Chapter 12)

[Zelkowitz, Shaw, and Gannon, 1979] M. V. Zelkowitz, A. C. Shaw, and J. D. Gannon, *Principles of Software Engineering and Design,* Prentice Hall, Englewood Cliffs, NJ, 1979. (Chapter 1)

[Zvegintzov, 1998] N. Zvegintzov, "Frequently Begged Questions and How to Answer Them," *IEEE Software* **15** (January/February 1998), pp. 93–96. (Chapter 1)

A

Term Project: Osric's Office Appliances and Decor

Osric Ormondsey owns Osric's Office Appliances and Decor (OOA&D). Osric has a highly successful career decorating the offices of top business executives. He employs a number of subcontractors and technicians so that he can provide a complete turnkey service, including telecommunications (telephone, fax, high-speed data link, and so on). His success is largely due to the speed with which he responds to a customer's request; he has been known to completely redecorate a large executive suite in only two days.

Osric's customers frequently comment effusively about the skills of his two telecommunications technicians, in the light of their many bad experiences with technicians of the local telephone company. Osric realizes that he can expand his business by adding a telecommunications division. He decides to hire the best technicians he can find, offer them an exorbitant salary plus bonuses, and advertise their services to the executives whose offices he has decorated. The executives realize that it is far more effective for their companies to pay Osric's high rates for a highly skilled technician who arrives within an hour or two and fixes the problem quickly than to wait two or three days for an incompetent technician to come and make the problem worse.

Osric's idea has succeeded beyond his wildest dreams. His technicians are in constant high demand, so much so that the waiting time for an OOA&D technician is sometimes more than two days, despite the fact that Osric has technicians on call 24 hours a day. This is unacceptable to both Osric and his customers, so Osric tries to rectify the situation. He has been unable to hire enough technicians with the necessary high level of skills, so he has decided to ration their services. Specifically, he decides to prioritize his customers so that, when someone calls to request service, Osric can decide where to put them on the waiting list for a technician.

Each customer company has a five-digit customer number and is assigned a priority.

Priority 4: A company that has hired Osric to decorate an executive office.

Priority 3: A company that has had three or more previous telecommunications service calls.

Priority 2: A company that has had one or two previous telecommunications service calls.

Priority 1: A company calling for service for the first time

When someone calls for service, the assistant asks the caller for his or her company's customer number. If the customer does not know the customer number, the assistant asks for the company name. If the name is not found, the software assumes that this is a new customer. A new customer is assigned a number only if it is put on the waiting list (see the following).

When there is a request for service, the company is added to the waiting list. The companies on the waiting list are sorted by priority, and by date and time of call within priority.

Osric's technicians work 8-hour shifts. He currently has seven technicians on the day shift, and two on each of the two night shifts, but this could change. Osric has observed that the durations of the service calls are normally distributed with a mean of 5.5 hours and a standard deviation of 9.8 hours. However, the shortest time for a job was 1.9 hours, and the longest time was 23.1 hours.[2] At 8 A.M. a technician is assigned to each of the top seven companies on the waiting list, and similarly at 12 noon, provided that there are no incomplete jobs, as described in the next paragraph.

If a job is completed within its assigned 4-hour *block*, the customer is charged for the 4-hour block and the technician returns to OOA&D. If a job has not been completed by 12 noon, the same technician is assigned a further 4-hour block to complete it, reducing the number of technicians available for new jobs.

Osric provides service 24 hours a day. At night, however, the assistant on duty does not accept new service requests; his or her sole task is to supervise the night technicians. At 4 P.M. the assistant on duty checks if there are jobs that have not been completed. If so, he or she calls each company to ask if they want a night technician to continue the job (at double rates), or whether they want the same technician to continue in the morning. Because there are fewer night technicians than day technicians, it may not be possible to honor all requests for night service. Accordingly, the assistant calls the companies with outstanding jobs in waiting list order, that is, by priority, and by date and time of call within priority.

---

[2]Many programming languages support pseudorandom number generators. In Java, function nextGaussian generates numbers from a distribution that is normally distributed with mean 0 and standard deviation 1. In C++, function rand generates numbers uniformly distributed between 0 and 1; the Box-Muller transformation can then be used to generate normally distributed pseudorandom numbers (see G. E. P. Box and M. E. Muller, "A Note on the Generation of Random Normal Deviates," *Annals of Mathematical Statistics* **29** (1958), pp. 610–11). Alternatively, many free Gaussian pseudorandom number generators for C++ can be downloaded from the Web, including gsl_ran_Gaussian in the GNU Scientific Library (GSL).

If x is a number generated from a distribution that is normally distributed with mean 0 and standard deviation 1, then $\mu + x \times \sigma$ will be from a distribution that is normally distributed with mean μ and standard deviation σ. Outliers (numbers that are too high or too low) can then be rejected.

Osric, the foppish courtier, appears for the first time in the final scene (Act V, Scene 2) of William Shakespeare's *The Tragedy of Hamlet, Prince of Denmark*, which is set in Kronberg Castle in Helsingør (Elsinore in English). I have always felt sorry for the actor playing Osric. He has nothing to do for the first three hours of the play, he has only one worthwhile line ("A hit, a very palpable hit"), and he is mercilessly mocked by Hamlet and Laertes. Tom Stoppard made Hamlet's friends Rosencrantz and Guildenstern the protagonists of his version of *Hamlet*, which he called *Rosencrantz and Guildenstern Are Dead*. In the same spirit, I have made Osric the protagonist of this term project.

Again, work is assigned and charged at night on the basis of 4-hour blocks. A night job can continue the following day, if necessary, at day rates. In this case, too, the same day technician as before will be assigned to the job.

After a company has been on the waiting list for 2 full day blocks, its priority is *temporarily* increased by 1 before technicians are assigned to their next job. As a result, Priority-4 customers usually get service within 4 hours, but new (Priority 1) customers may have to wait until the fourth day for service.

When a customer calls for service, the software product estimates how soon service will be available based on the time taken so far on each of the current jobs, the length of the current waiting list, and the average time to complete a job. It also gives a worst-case estimate, based on the time it will take if the company has to reach Priority 4 before receiving service. The assistant gives this information to the customer, and asks if the company is prepared to wait, if necessary. Each morning the assistant calls all the customers on the waiting list to inform them how soon they can expect service. Again, this information is computed by the product, using the information available at that time.

If a new company requests a service call, this must first be approved by a manager. Ordinarily, such approval will not be given if the number of customers on the waiting list exceeds twice the number of day technicians. Occasionally, however, Osric will want to add a specific new company to his customer list. Accordingly, decisions regarding new customers have to be made by a manager who will give an immediate response when called by the assistant.

When the technician has completed the service call, he or she hands the job card to the assistant, who enters the customer number, and the number of day and night blocks that the job required. The software product first uses this information to update the company's priority, if applicable. Then the data are used to generate a bill to be mailed to the customer; the cost per block is $480 during the day, and $960 at night. Osric's billing address is Suite 16, Kronborg Castle, Helsingør, Sjælland, Denmark (see Just in Case You Wanted to Know Box A.1).

You are required to determine the effectiveness of Osric's scheme by simulating it. First, generate a job mix, that is, a set of jobs. For each job in the mix, specify the necessary attributes, including the time the call is made, the company priority, and the duration; other attributes will also be needed. As each job is called in, it is added to the queue. At the start of each block, jobs are removed from the queue and assigned to available technicians. When a job is finished, the technician is released, either to begin a job at the start of the second block of the shift or to go home.

In order to assess the effectiveness of the scheme, certain statistics need to be kept, including the average waiting time before a job is started; the average queue length; the percentage of time the queue is empty, both day and night; the number of blocks when a technician is idle (and hence no income accrues to OOA&D); and the number of jobs that cannot be continued at night because no technician is available.

Now, using the same job mix, determine the same statistics without Osric's scheme, that is, on a pure first-come-first-served basis, including new customers. Determine the average waiting time for customers with each priority. Repeat with different sets of jobs and different numbers of technicians. Decide whether Osric's scheme is cost effective for Osric, and whether it reduces the customers' waiting time.

Appendix B

Software Engineering Resources

There are two good ways to get more information on software engineering topics: by reading journals and conference proceedings, and via the Internet and World Wide Web.

Journals dedicated exclusively to software engineering are available, such as *IEEE Transactions on Software Engineering*, as well as journals of a more general nature, such as *Communications of the ACM*, in which significant articles on software engineering are published. For reasons of space, only a selection of journals of both classes follows. The journals have been chosen on a subjective basis, those I currently find to be the most useful.

ACM Computing Reviews
ACM Computing Surveys
ACM SIGSOFT Software Engineering Notes
ACM Transactions on Computer Systems
ACM Transactions on Programming Languages and Systems
ACM Transactions on Software Engineering and Methodology
Communications of the ACM
Computer Journal
Empirical Software Engineering
IBM Systems Journal
IEEE Computer
IEEE Software
IEEE Transactions on Software Engineering
Journal of Systems and Software
Software Engineering Journal
Software—Practice and Experience
Software Quality Journal

In addition, proceedings of many conferences contain important articles on software engineering topics. Again, a subjective selection follows. Most of the conferences are referred to by their acronym or name of sponsoring organization; these appear in parentheses.

ACM SIGPLAN Annual Conference (SIGPLAN)

ACM SIGSOFT Symposium on the Foundations of Software Engineering (FSE)

Conference on Human Factors in Computing Systems (CHI)

Conference on Object-Oriented Programming Systems, Languages, and Applications (OOPSLA)

International Computer Software and Applications Conference (COMPSAC)

International Conference on Software Engineering (ICSE)

International Conference on Software Maintenance (ICSM)

International Conference on Software Reuse (ICSR)

International Conference on the Software Process (ICSP)

International Software Architecture Workshop (ISAW)

International Symposium on Software Testing and Analysis (ISSTA)

International Workshop on Software Configuration Management (SCM)

International Workshop on Software Specification and Design (IWSSD)

The Internet is another valuable source of information on software engineering. With regard to Usenet news groups, the following two have been consistently useful to me:

comp.object
comp.software-eng

Other newsgroups that sometimes have items that I find relevant include the following:

comp.lang.c++.moderated
comp.lang.java.programmer
comp.risks
comp.software.config-mgmt

The Requirements Workflow: The MSG Foundation Case Study

The requirements workflow for the MSG Foundation case study appears in Chapter 10.

D

The Analysis Workflow: The MSG Foundation Case Study

The analysis workflow is presented in Chapter 11.

Appendix E

Software Project Management Plan: The MSG Foundation Case Study

The plan presented here is for development of the MSG product by a small software organization consisting of three individuals: Almaviva, the owner of the company, and two software engineers, Bartolo and Cherubini.

1 Overview.

1.1 Project Summary.

1.1.1 Purpose, Scope, and Objectives. The objective of this project is to develop a software product that will assist the Martha Stockton Greengage (MSG) Foundation in making decisions regarding home mortgages for married couples. The product will allow the client to add, modify, and delete information regarding the Foundation's investments, operating expenses, and individual mortgage information. The product will perform the required calculations in these areas and produce reports listing investments, mortgages, and weekly operating expenses.

1.1.2 Assumptions and Constraints. Constraints include the following:

The deadline must be met.
The budget constraint must be met.
The product must be reliable.

The architecture must be open so that additional functionality may be added later. The product must be user-friendly.

1.1.3 Project Deliverables. The complete product, including user manual, will be delivered 10 weeks after the project commences.

1.1.4 Schedule and Budget Summary. The duration, personnel requirements, and budget of each workflow are as follows:

Requirements workflow (1 week, two team members, $3740)
Analysis workflow (2 weeks, two team members, $7480)
Design workflow (2 weeks, two team members, $7480)
Implementation workflow (3 weeks, three team members, $16,830)
Testing workflow (2 weeks, three team members, $11,220)

The total development time is 10 weeks, and the total internal cost is $46,750.

1.2 Evolution of the Project Management Plan. All changes in the project management plan must be agreed to by Almaviva before they are implemented. All changes should be documented in order to keep the project management plan correct and up to date.

2 Reference Materials. All artifacts will conform to the company's programming, documentation, and testing standards.

3 Definitions and Acronyms. MSG—Martha Stockton Greengage; the MSG Foundation is our client.

4 Project Organization.

4.1 External Interfaces. All the work on this project will be performed by Almaviva, Bartolo, and Cherubini. Almaviva will meet weekly with the client to report progress and discuss possible changes and modifications.

4.2 Internal Structure. The development team consists of Almaviva (owner), Bartolo, and Cherubini.

4.3 Roles and Responsibilities. Bartolo and Cherubini will perform the design workflow. Almaviva will implement the class definitions and report artifacts, Bartolo will construct the artifacts to handle investments and operating expenses, and Cherubini will develop the artifacts that handle mortgages. Each member is responsible for the quality of the artifacts he or she produces. Almaviva will oversee integration and the overall quality of the software product and will liaise with the client.

5 Managerial Process Plans.

5.1 Start-up Plan.

5.1.1 Estimation Plan. As previously stated, the total development time is estimated to be 10 weeks and the total internal cost to be $46,750. These figures were obtained by expert judgment by analogy, that is, by comparison with similar projects.

5.1.2 Staffing Plan. Almaviva is needed for the entire 10 weeks, for the first 5 weeks in only a managerial capacity and the second 5 weeks as both manager and programmer. Bartolo and Cherubini are needed for the entire 10 weeks, for the first 5 weeks as systems analysts and designers, and for the second 5 weeks as programmers and testers.

5.1.3 Resource Acquisition Plan. All necessary hardware, software, and CASE tools for the project are already available. The product will be delivered to the MSG Foundation installed on a desktop computer that will be leased from our usual supplier.

5.1.4 Project Staff Training Plan. No additional staff training is needed for this project.

5.2 Work Plan.

5.2.1–2 Work Activities and Schedule Allocation.

Week 1.	(Completed) Met with client, and determined requirements artifacts. Inspected requirements artifacts.
Weeks 2, 3.	(Completed) Produced analysis artifacts, and inspected analysis artifacts. Showed artifacts to client, who approved them. Produced software project management plan, and inspected software project management plan.
Weeks 4, 5.	Produce design artifacts, inspect design artifacts.
Weeks 6–10.	Implementation and inspection of each class, unit testing and documentation, integration of each class, integration testing, product testing, and documentation inspection.

5.2.3 Resource Allocation. The three team members will work separately on their assigned artifacts. Almaviva's assigned role will be to monitor the daily progress of the other two, oversee implementation, be responsible for overall quality, and interact with the client. Team members will meet at the end of each day and discuss problems and progress. Formal meetings with the client will be held at the end of each week to report progress and determine if any changes need to be made. Almaviva will ensure that schedule and budget requirements are met. Risk management will also be Almaviva's responsibility.

Minimizing faults and maximizing user-friendliness will be Almaviva's top priorities. Almaviva has overall responsibility for all documentation and has to ensure that it is up to date.

5.2.4 Budget Allocation. The budget for each workflow is as follows:

Requirements workflow	$ 3,740
Analysis workflow	7,480
Design workflow	7,480
Implementation workflow	16,830
Testing workflow	11,220
Total	$46,750

5.3 Control Plan. Any major changes that affect the milestones or the budget have to be approved by Almaviva and documented. No outside quality assurance personnel are involved. The benefits of having someone other than the individual who carried out the development task do the testing will be accomplished by each person testing another person's work products.

Almaviva will be responsible for ensuring that the project is completed on time and within budget. This will be accomplished through daily meetings with the team members. At each meeting, Bartolo and Cherubini will present the day's progress and problems. Almaviva will determine whether they are progressing as expected and whether they are following the specification document and the project management plan. Any major problems faced by the team members will immediately be reported to Almaviva.

5.4 Risk Management Plan.   The risk factors and the tracking mechanisms are as follows.

There is no existing product with which the new product can be compared. Accordingly, it will not be possible to run the product in parallel with an existing one. Therefore, the product should be subjected to extensive testing.

The client is assumed to be inexperienced with computers. Therefore, special attention should be paid to the analysis workflow and communication with the client. The product has to be made as user-friendly as possible.

Because of the ever-present possibility of a major design fault, extensive testing will be performed during the design workflow. Also, each of the team members will initially test his or her own code and then test the code of another member. Almaviva will be responsible for integration testing and in charge of product testing.

The information must meet the specified storage requirements and response times. This should not be a major problem because of the small size of the product, but it will be monitored by Almaviva throughout development.

There is a slim chance of hardware failure, in which case another machine will be leased. If there is a fault in the compiler, it will be replaced. These are covered in the warranties received from the hardware and compiler suppliers.

5.5 Project Close-out Plan.   Not applicable here.

6 Technical Process Plans.

6.1 Process Model.   The Unified Process will be used.

6.2 Methods, Tools, and Techniques.   The workflows will be performed in accordance with the Unified Process. The product will be implemented in Java.

6.3 Infrastructure Plan.   The product will be developed using ArgoUML running under Linux on a personal computer.

6.4 Product Acceptance Plan.   Acceptance of the product by our client will be achieved by following the steps of the Unified Process.

7 Supporting Process Plan

7.1 Configuration Management Plan.   CVS will be used throughout for all artifacts.

7.2 Testing Plan.   The testing workflow of the Unified Process will be performed.

7.3 Documentation Plan.   Documentation will be produced as specified in the Unified Process.

7.4–5 Quality Assurance Plan and Reviews and Audits Plan. Bartolo and Cherubini will test each other's code, and Almaviva will conduct integration testing. Extensive product testing will then be performed by all three.

7.6 Problem Resolution Plan. As stated in 5.3, any major problems faced by the team members will immediately be reported to Almaviva.

7.7 Subcontractor Management Plan. Not applicable here.

7.8 Process Improvement Plan. All activities will be conducted in accord with the company plan to advance from CMM level 2 to level 3 within 2 years.

8 Additional Plans. Additional components:

Security. A password will be needed to use the product.

Training. Training will be performed by Almaviva at time of delivery. Because the product is straightforward to use, 1 day should be sufficient for training. Almaviva will answer questions at no cost for the first year of use.

Maintenance. Corrective maintenance will be performed by the team at no cost for a period of 12 months. A separate contract will be drawn up regarding enhancement.

Appendix **F**

The Design Workflow: The MSG Foundation Case Study

This appendix contains the final version of the class diagram for the MSG Foundation case study. The overall class diagram is followed by UML diagrams for the 10 component classes, in alphabetical order. These UML diagrams show the attributes and the methods. As explained in Section 15.2, the UML visibility prefixes are – for **private**, + for **public**, and # for **protected**. The attributes and methods are shown in a PDL for Java. Accordingly, there is no **Date Class** (see Section 12.3).

Figure F.1
The final class
diagram for
the MSG
Foundation
case study.

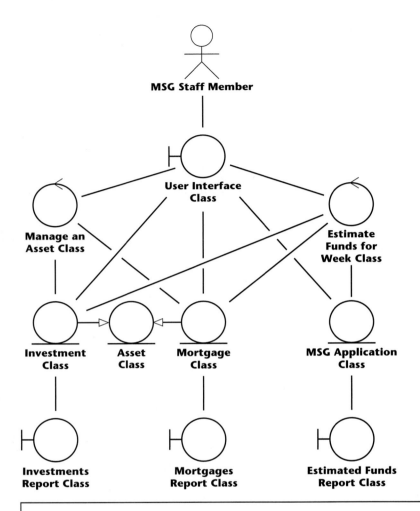

«entity class»
Asset Class

assetNumber : string

+ getAssetNumber ( ) : string
+ setAssetNumber (a : string) : void
+ **abstract** read (fileName : RandomAccessFile) : void
+ **abstract** obtainNewData ( ) : void
+ **abstract** performDeletion ( ) : void
+ **abstract** write (fileName : RandomAccessFile) : void
+ **abstract** save ( ) : void
+ **abstract** print ( ) : void
+ **abstract** find (s : string) : Boolean
+ delete ( ) : void
+ add ( ) : void

«control class»
Estimate Funds for Week Class
+ <<static>> compute ( ) : void

«boundary class»
Estimate Funds Report Class
+ <<static>> printReport ( ) : void

«entity class»
Investment Class
– investmentName : string – expectedAnnualReturn : float – expectedAnnualReturnUpdated : string
+ getInvestmentName ( ) : string + setInvestmentName (n : string) : void + getExpectedAnnualReturn ( ) : float + setExpectedAnnualReturn (r : float) : void + getExpectedAnnualReturnUpdated ( ) : string + setExpectedAnnualReturnUpdated (d : string) : void + totalWeeklyReturnOnInvestment ( ) : float + find (findInvestmentID : string) : Boolean + read (fileName : RandomAccessFile) : void + write (fileName : RandomAccessFile) : void + save ( ) : void + print ( ) : void + printAll ( ) : void + obtainNewData ( ) : void + performDeletion ( ) : void + readInvestmentData ( ) : void + updateInvestmentName ( ) : void + updateExpectedReturn ( ) : void

«boundary class»
Investments Report Class
+ <<static>> printReport ( ) : void

| «control class» |
| **Manage an Asset Class** |
| |
| + <<static>> manageInvestment ( ) : void
+ <<static>> manageMortgage ( ) : void |

| «entity class» |
| **Mortgage Class** |
| – mortgageeName : string
– price : float
– dateMortgageIssued : string
– currentWeeklyIncome : float
– weeklyIncomeUpdated : string
– annualPropertyTax : float
– annualInsurancePremium : float
– mortgageBalance : float
+ <<static final>> INTEREST_RATE : float
+ <<static final>> MAX_PER_OF_INCOME : float
+ <<static final>> NUMBER_OF_MORTGAGE_PAYMENTS : int
+ <<static final>> WEEKS_IN_YEAR : float
+ getMortgageeName ( ) : string
+ setMortgageeName (n : string) : void
+ getPrice ( ) : float
+ setPrice (p : float) : void
+ getDateMortgageIssued ( ) : string
+ setDateMortgageIssued (w : string) : void
+ getCurrentWeeklyIncome ( ) : float
+ setCurrentWeeklyIncome (i : float) : void
+ getWeeklyIncomeUpdated ( ) : string
+ setWeeklyIncomeUpdated (w : string) : void
+ getAnnualPropertyTax ( ) : float
+ setAnnualPropertyTax (t : float) : void
+ getAnnualInsurancePremium ( ) : float
+ setAnnualInsurancePremium (p : float) : void
+ getMortgageBalance ( ) : float
+ setMortgageBalance (m : float) : void
+ totalWeeklyNetPayments ( ) : float
+ find (findMortgageID : string) : Boolean
+ read (fileName : RandomAccessFile) : void
+ write (fileName : RandomAcessFile) : void
+ obtainNewData ( ) : void
+ performDeletion ( ) : void
+ print ( ) : void
+ <<static>> printAll ( ) : void
+ save ( ) : void |

+ readMortgageData ( ) : void
+ updateBalance ( ) : void
+ updateDate ( ) : void
+ updateInsurancePremium ( ) : void
+ updateMortgageeName ( ) : void
+ updatePrice ( ) : void
+ updatePropertyTax ( ) : void
+ updateWeeklyIncome ( ) : void

«boundary class»
Mortgages Report Class

+ <<static>> printReport ( ) : void

«entity class»
MSG Application Class

– <<static>> estimatedAnnualOperatingExpenses : float
– <<static>> estimatedFundsForWeek : float

– <<static>> getAnnualOperatingExpenses ( ) : float
– <<static>> setAnnuallOperatingExpenses (e : float) : void
+ <<static>> getEstimatedFundsForWeek ( ) : float
+ <<static>> setEstimatedFundsForWeek (e : float) : void
+ <<static>> initializeApplication ( ) : void
+ <<static>> updateAnnualOperatingExpenses ( ) : void
+ <<static>> main ( )

«boundary class»
User Interface Class

+ <<static>> clearScreen ( ) : void
+ <<static>> pressEnter ( ) : void
+ <<static>> displayMainMenu ( ) : void
+ <<static>> displayInvestmentMenu ( ) : void
+ <<static>> displayMortgageMenu ( ) : void
+ <<static>> displayReportMenu ( ) : void
+ <<static>> getChar ( ) : char
+ <<static>> getString ( ) : string
+ <<static>> getInt ( ) : int

G

The Implementation Workflow: The MSG Foundation Case Study (C++ Version)

The complete C++ source code for the MSG Foundation product is available on the World Wide Web at www.mhhe.com/schach.

Appendix

H

The Implementation Workflow: The MSG Foundation Case Study (Java Version)

The complete Java source code for the MSG Foundation product is available on the World Wide Web at www.mhhe.com/schach.

The Test Workflow: The MSG Foundation Case Study

The test workflow of the MSG Foundation case study is presented in four sections:

Section 10.11 (requirements)

Section 11.21 (analysis)

Section 12.6 (design)

Section 13.22 (implementation)

Author Index

This index includes only authors cited in the actual text.

A

Ackerman, A. F., 152
Albrecht, A. J., 261
Alexander, C., 224, 225
Alshayeb, M., 56, 454
Atkinson, R., 241

B

Babich, W. A., 136
Baker, F. T., 105, 106, 107
Banks, J., 332
Basili, V. R., 39, 440, 441
Beck, K., 54, 55, 112
Beizer, B., 404
Berry, D. M., 163, 180
Binder, L. H., 442
Binkley, A. B., 409, 454
Blaha, M. R., 203
Blythe, J., 210
Boehm, B., 56
Boehm, B. W., 12, 13, 14, 58,
    59, 61, 257, 265, 266, 268,
    269, 279
Boehm, R., 263
Booch, G., 39, 56, 71, 84, 85, 86, 288,
    335, 385, 451
Briand, L. C., 188
Brooks, F. P., 8, 89, 95, 102, 104,
    324, 410
Brown, W. J., 226
Bruegge, B., 210
Buchwald, L. S., 152
Budd, T., 20
Bush, M., 152
Buxton, J. N., 5
Capper, N. P., 209

C

Carson, J. S., 332
Chidamber, S. R., 409, 454
Chrissis, M. B., 89
Cockburn, A., 55

Coleman, D., 226
Colgate, R. J., 209
Constantine, L. L., 174, 176
Cooprider, J. G., 140
Councill, W. T., 227
Crossman, T. D., 441
Cunningham, W., 54, 56, 112
Curtis, B., 89, 113
Cusumano, M. A., 57, 111
Cutter Consortium, 6

D

Dahl, O.-J., 174, 201
Daly, E. B., 12, 13
Daly, J., 188
Dawood, M., 93
Deming, W. E., 90
DeRemer, F., 130
Devenny, T., 258
Diaz, M., 94
Dijkstra, E. W., 154, 162
Dion, R., 94
Dooley, J. W. M., 133
Drobka, J., 54
Dunn, R. H., 441
Dyer, M., 442

E

Elshoff, J. L., 12
Endres, A., 446
Erdogmus, H., 56
Erikson, W. J., 259

F

Fagan, M. E., 13, 150, 151, 152
Feldman, S. I., 139
Fenton, N., 127
Ferguson, J., 95
Fitzpatrick, J., 445
Flanagan, D., 201, 223, 393
Forselius, P., 263
Fowler, M., 225

Fowler, P. J., 152
Fuggetta, A., 129

G

Gagne, G., 406
Gail, R., 332
Galvin, P. B., 406
Gamma, E., 224, 225, 229, 234, 235,
    237, 238
Gane, C., 18
Gannon, J. D., 12
Garlan, D., 226
Garman, J. R., 87
Gerald, C. F., 176
Gerhart, S. L., 162, 334, 335
Gifford, D., 240
Goldberg, A., 201, 393
Gomaa, H., 407
Goodenough, J. B., 154, 155, 157,
    162, 334, 335
Grady, R. B., 13, 41, 446
Grant, E. E., 259
Grasso, C. A., 220
Green, P., 219
Griss, M. L., 218
Guinan, P. J., 140

H

Harel, D., 451
Harrold, M. J., 445
Hatton, L., 12, 19
Hayes, F., 6, 45
Hedley, D., 439
Heineman, G. T., 227
Helfey, W. E., 113
Helm, R., 224, 225, 229, 234, 235,
    237, 238
Hennell, M. A., 439
Henry, S. M., 409
Hoare, C. A. R., 165
Hops, J., 15, 152
Howden, W. E., 435, 436

Huitt, R., 443
Humphrey, W. S., 89, 93
Hunter, J. C., 209
Hutchens, D. H., 440
Hwang, S.-S. V., 441

I

Iannino, A., 441
Ince, D. C., 441

J

Jackson, J., 210
Jacobson, I., 39, 71, 84, 85, 86, 288, 335, 385, 451
Jalote, P., 55
James, M. F., 209
Jazayeri, M., 226
Jeffries, R., 54, 56, 112
Jézéquel, J.-M., 221, 222
Johnson, R., 224, 225, 229, 234, 235, 237, 238
Johnson, R. A., 209
Johnson, S. C., 246
Jones, C., 94, 152, 217, 262, 263, 279
Josephson, M., 24
Juran, J. M., 90

K

Kafura, D. G., 409
Kaiser, G. E., 445
Kamayachi, Y., 440
Kan, S. H., 14
Keeni, G., 94
Kelly, J. C., 15, 152
Kemerer, C. F., 409, 454
Kessler, R. R., 54, 56, 112
Kitchenham, B. A., 409
Kleinrock, L., 332
Klunder, D., 418
Knuth, D. E., 186, 337
Kron, H. H., 130
Kurien, P., 55

L

Lai, C. T. R., 226
Landwehr, C. E., 163
Lanergan, R. G., 220
Larman, V., 39
Leavenworth, B., 162, 334
Leveson, N. G., 5
Lewski, F. H., 152
Li, W., 56, 454

Lientz, B. P., 10
Lim, W. C., 218, 219, 271
Linger, R. C., 442, 443
Linkman, S. J., 409
Liskov, B., 241
Liu, J. W. S., 407
London, R. L., 162, 334
Long, F., 452
Loukides, M., 138, 476

M

Mackenzie, C. E., 240
Manna, Z., 163, 164
Mantei, M., 104
Matsumoto, Y., 219
Matthews, P., 443
Maurer, F., 56
Maxwell, K. D., 263
Mayer, R., 177
McCabe, T. J., 409, 440
McGregor, J. D., 445
Mellor, P., 5
Mellor, S., 407
Meyer, B., 20, 201, 218, 221, 222, 334
Miller, 113
Miller, G. A., 39, 88
Miller, S. A., 113
Mills, H. D., 442
Mooney, J. D., 239
Morris, E., 452
Murphy, G. C., 210
Musa, J. D., 441
Musser, D. R., 217
Myers, G. J., 166, 176, 178, 427, 432, 441, 446
Myers, W., 139

N

Naur, P., 5, 162, 334
Nelson, B. L., 332
Neumann, P. G., 4
New, R., 149
Nichol, D. M., 332
Noftz, D., 54
Norden, P. V., 271
Norušis, M. J., 217
Nygaard, K., 174, 201

O

Ohta, J., 226
Okumoto, K., 441
Oram, A., 138, 476

P

Palit, A., 55
Parnas, D. L., 199, 226, 470
Paulk, M. C., 89
Peethamber, V. T., 55
Perry, D. E., 445
Pfleeger, S. L., 127
Pickard, L. M., 409
Pigorski, T., 467
Pittman, M., 270
Pnueli, A., 163
Porter, V., 188
Premerlani, W. J., 203
Prieto-Díaz, R., 218, 219
Putnam, L. H., 271

R

Raghu, R., 54
Ran, A., 226
Randell, B., 5
Rapps, S., 439
Raymond, E. S., 22, 53
Reifer, D. J., 56
Ritchie, D. M., 246
Robson, D., 201, 393
Rochkind, M. J., 138, 476
Royce, W. W., 35, 48
Rumbaugh, J., 39, 71, 84, 85, 86, 203, 288, 335, 385, 451

S

Sackman, H., 259
Saini, A., 217
Sammet, J. E., 416
Sarsen, T., 18
Sawyer, S., 140
Schach, S. R., 10, 33, 127, 133, 183, 184, 238, 243, 260, 261, 270, 323, 409, 454
Schaffert, C., 241
Schricker, D., 243
Schwaber, K., 55
Selby, R. W., 57, 111, 125, 219, 441
Shapiro, F. R., 24
Shaw, A. C., 12
Shaw, M., 226
Sheard, S., 95
Shepperd, M., 409, 441
Sherif, J. S., 15, 152
Shneiderman, B., 177
Shufelt, J., 210
Silberschatz, A., 406

Sligo, J., 94
Snider, T. R., 93
Snyder, A., 241
Snyder, C. E., 442
Sobell, M. G., 130, 132
Spector, A., 240
Spivey, J. M., 49
Stephenson, W. E., 13
Stevens, W. P., 176
Stevens-Guille, P. D., 184
Stroustrup, B., 201, 393
Swanson, E. B., 10
Symons, C. R., 263

T
Takahashi, M., 440
Tanenbaum, A. S., 246
Tichy, W. F., 138, 476
Toft, P., 226
Tomer, A., 33, 127

Tompkins, G. E., 10
Tracz, W., 218
Trammel, C. J., 442
Turner, C. S., 5
Turner, R., 56

V
van der Linden, F., 226
van der Poel, K. G., 260, 261
van Wijngaarden, A., 80
Vlissides, J., 224, 225, 229, 234, 235, 237, 238

W
Waldinger, R., 164
Walsh, T. J., 440
Ward, P. T., 407
Watson, A. H., 440
Weber, C. V., 89
Weinberg, G. M., 103

Weiss, D. M., 226, 441
Weyuker, E. J., 439
Wheatley, P. O., 176
Wiener, L., 20, 343
Wilde, N., 443
Wilkerson, B., 20, 343
Williams, L., 54, 56, 112
Willis, R. R., 93
Wing, J. M., 163
Wirfs-Brock, R., 20, 343
Wirth, N., 124
Wood, P. T., 323
Woodward, M. R., 439
Wüst, J., 188

Y
Yourdon, E., 12, 19, 174

Z
Zelkowitz, M. V., 12

Subject Index

A

abstract method, 473
abstract class, 229
abstract data type, 181, 197–98, 199, 443
abstract data type design, 393
Abstract Factory design pattern, 233–34
abstract method, 229
abstract noun, 341
abstraction, 191–97
acceptance criteria, 332
acceptance testing, 9, 80, 149, 448, 449–50
accessor, 401
accidental reuse, 216
action, 492
   definition, 492
activation box, 490
activity, 129, 272, 492
   definition, 492
activity diagram, 495, 494–96, 498
actor, 292–93, 297–99, 338, 383–84, 488, 498
   definition, 292
   elevator problem case study, 338
   MSG Foundation case study, 297–99
Ada, 184, 244, 243–44, 263, 452
Ada 83 (language), 243, 244
Ada 95 (language), 244, 393
Ada Joint Program Office (AJPO), 243, 244
Ada reference manual, 243
Ada standard, 243–44
Adapter design pattern, 225, 230
adaptive maintenance, 9, 134, 464, 466, 469, 474
   definition, 464
aggregate, 233
aggregation, 203, 484
Agile Alliance, 55
agile process, 55, 54–56, 112
Alexander, Christopher, 225
ALGOL, 244
algorithm, 302–3
all-definition-use-path coverage, 439
alpha release, 81
alpha testing, 81, 448

alter verb, 182
ambiguity, 334
analysis. *See* analysis workflow, object-oriented analysis
analysis artifacts, 79
   review, 79
analysis fault, 13–15, 464
analysis phase, 9
analysis testing, 79
analysis workflow, 39–42, 74–76, 352–82, 336–84, 331–85, 531
   challenges, 385
   elevator problem case study, 338–51
   MSG Foundation case study, 352–82, 531
analytic network modeling, 332
Ant, 139
antipattern, 226
Apache project, 139
Apache Web server, 21
application composition model, 269
application domain, 70, 73, 289–90
application framework, 224
application programming interface (API), 217
architect, 403
architectural design, 9
architecture, 44, 84. *See also* software architecture
architecture pattern, 226–27
ArgoUML, 325, 385, 407
Ariane 5 rocket, 221–22
artifact, 19, 36, 127
ASCII, 240
aspect-oriented programming (AOP), 210
assembler, 246, 263, 447, 475
assert statement, 165, 222
assertion, 159, 161, 165
association, 203, 487
association class, 488
asterisk, 486
AT&T Bell Laboratories, 242
ATM, 266
attribute, 19–21, 202, 341, 443

B

Babbage, Charles, 244
back-end CASE tool, 128, 407

backtrack, 315, 355
backup programmer, 105–6, 107
baseline, 36, 137–38, 272, 470
Basili, 39
Beethoven, Ludwig van, 216
behavioral design pattern, 236
behavioral testing, 430
beta release, 81, 86
beta testing, 81, 448
binding, 176
black-box testing, 278, 430. *See also* black-box unit testing
   origin of term, 430
black-box unit testing, 433–36, 441–43
Booch's method, 71
Borland, 21
bottom-up integration, 426
   strengths, 426
   weaknesses, 426
boundary class, 351, 360–61
   definition, 335
   MSG Foundation case study, 360–61
boundary value analysis, 434–35
bounds checking, 165
branch coverage, 439
Bridge design pattern, 230
Brooks's Law, 102
browser, 217
budget, 76, 258, 272
bug, 23, 24, 103
   first use in computer context, 24
Bugzilla, 477
build tool, 138–39, 476
business case, 84–86
business logic tier, 227
business model, 73, 290–93, 297–99
   definition, 290
   MSG Foundation case study, 297–99
business-oriented environment, 452
Byron, Lord Alfred, 244

C

C, 139, 165, 186, 191, 202, 204, 242–43, 244, 246, 393, 416, 452
   history, 242

C/SD. *See* composite structured design
C++, 12, 23, 131, 132, 135, 139, 157,
    165, 174, 186, 192–201, 202,
    204, 205, 217, 220, 241, 242–43,
    244, 393, 415, 416–17, 421, 422,
    428, 429, 445, 450, 452
    history, 242–43
    popularity, 416–17
C++ standard, 243
California Institute of Technology, 337
capability maturity model (CMM),
    89–95, 113, 140, 453
capital, 295
CASE, 118, 127–40, 217, 263,
    279–80, 324–25, 383, 385, 407,
    447, 450–53, 471, 475, 476–77
    scope, 130–33
    tools for analysis workflow, 385
    tools for design workflow, 407
    tools for implementation, 130–33
    tools for implementation work-
    flow, 450–53
    tools for management, 279–80
    tools for object-oriented analysis,
    385
    tools for planning and estimating,
    279–80
    tools for post-delivery mainte-
    nance, 476–77
    tools for requirements workflow,
    324–25
    tools for test workflow, 453
    tools for the complete life cycle,
    450–53
case study. *See* elevator problem case
    study, MSG case study
CCC, 476
challenges
    of object-oriented analysis, 385
    of post-delivery maintenance, 478
    of the analysis workflow, 385
    of the design workflow, 409–10
    of the implementation workflow,
    454–55
    of the requirements workflow,
    325–26
CHAOS Report, 45, 46
chief programmer, 105–11
chief programmer team, 104–7,
    104–11
    impracticality, 107
    modern, 107–11
choice of programming language, 403
chunk, 124

clandestine common coupling, 183
class, 192–210, 443–45
class diagram, 338–51, 354–55,
    483–88, 498
    elevator problem case study,
    338–51
    MSG Foundation case study,
    354–55
class extraction, 337–62
class library, 217
class testing, 443
classical paradigm, 18–19, 205,
    207–10
    strengths, 207–10
    weaknesses, 207–10
class-responsibility-collaboration
    (CRC) card, 343–44, 347
    elevator problem case study,
    347–51
Cleanroom, 442–43
clickware, 21
client, 20
client–server, 226
CLU, 241
CMM. *See* capability maturity model
CMMI, 89
COBOL, 182, 220–21, 224, 244,
    393, 417. *See also* OO-COBOL
    history, 416
    object-oriented, 416, 417
COBOL program logic structure, 220
Coca-Cola, 147
COCOMO, 266, 265–70, 279
    example, 266–68
    experimentation, 268
COCOMO II, 269, 279
CODASYL, 242
code artifact, 77, 429
code generator, 452
code inspection, 441–43
code reuse, 222–27, 423
code review, 80, 107
code walkthrough, 441–43
code-and-fix model, 47–48, 208, 324
coding. *See* implementation
coding fault, 464
coding standard, 422–23
coding tool, 130
cohesion, 176–81, 208, 408
    example, 181
coincidental cohesion, 177, 181, 422
collaboration diagram, 365
collection, 233
comments, 419

commercial off-the-shelf software.
    See COTS
common coupling, 183–85, 187, 195
communication diagram, 489–91,
    498
communicational cohesion, 179–80
compiler, 243–69
    incompatibility, 243–69
complexity, 20, 440
component, 216
component diagram, 497
    definition, 497
component-based software
    engineering, 227
composite/structured design (C/SD),
    176–88, 222
composition, 486–87
computer crime, 184, 186
computer-aided software engineering.
    See CASE
concept exploration, 74
conceptual independence, 20, 192,
    222, 471
cone of uncertainty, 258
configuration, 135
configuration control, 135–39,
    476–77
    during development, 138
    during maintenance, 137–38
    during post-delivery maintenance,
    476–77
configuration-control tool, 135, 137,
    450, 476
consistency checker, 129, 451
consistent variable names, 417–18
constraints, 156, 332, 406, 449, 450
    deadline, 73, 77, 332
    hard time, 156, 406
    parallel running, 332, 450
    portability, 332
    reliability, 73, 332
    response time, 449
    security, 449
    size of object code, 73
    storage, 449
    timing, 332, 406
construction phase, 83, 86
container, 233
content coupling, 182–83
contract software development, 21
control class, 336, 351, 361
    definition, 336
    MSG Foundation case study, 361
control coupling, 185, 187

core workflows, 73
corrective maintenance, 9, 134, 441, 464, 465, 466, 469, 471, 474
    definition, 464
correctness, 157
    necessity, 157
    sufficiency, 157
correctness proof, 158–65
    and testing, 162
    example, 158–61
    mini case study, 163, 334–35
    strengths, 164–65
    weaknesses, 164
correctness proof mini case study, 163, 334–35
correctness testing, 80, 157–58, 449
cost, 73, 126, 257–60
    external, 259
    internal, 259
cost estimation, 75–76, 257–60
    algorithmic models, 265–69
    bottom-up approach, 265
    expert judgment by analogy, 264
cost–benefit analysis, 124–25, 164, 246, 445
    example, 124–25
COTS, 21, 57, 81, 218, 336, 448
coupling, 176, 181–89, 195, 208, 408
    example, 187–88
    importance, 188–89
CppUnit, 453
CRC card. *See* class-responsibility-collaboration card
creational design pattern, 235
Cresti, Domenico, 322
cursor, 233
Cutter Consortium, 6
cvs tool, 138
cyclomatic complexity, 409, 440–41, 453
    strengths, 409
    weaknesses, 409

D

data abstraction, 192, 198, 204
data access logic tier, 227
data coupling, 186, 187
data dictionary, 128–29, 407, 451
data encapsulation, 191, 189–96
    and development, 191–92
    and maintenance, 192–96
data processing, 220–21, 261, 415
data-driven testing, 430
data-oriented design, 392

date and time stamp, 139
dbx tool, 133
debugging, 132–33, 166, 446
defect
    terminology, 23, 146, 465
defect report, 468–69
defect tracking, 477
defect-tracking tool, 477
defensive programming, 426, 427
defined level, 90
deliberate reuse, 216
deliverables, 76, 82, 85, 86
della Torre, Giovanni Agostino, 464
della Torre, Niccolò, 464
Delphi technique, 264
delta, 137
democratic team, 103–4, 107–11
    strengths, 104
    weaknesses, 104
Department of Defense (DoD), 91, 416
Department of Redundant Information Department, 266
deployment diagram, 497
    definition, 497
deposit, 295
derivation, 136
derived class, 202
design, 392–410. *See also* design workflow, object-oriented design of real-time systems, 406–7
design artifacts, 79
design by contract, 20
design document, 9, 474
design fault, 13–15, 79, 404, 464
design inspection, 404–5
design pattern, 224–38
    Abstract Factory, 233–34
    Adapter, 225, 230
    behavioral, 236
    Bridge, 230
    creational, 235
    Iterator, 231–33
    strengths, 237
    structural, 235
    weaknesses, 237–38
design pattern mini case study, 228–29
design phase, 9
design reuse, 222–27, 222–27
design testing, 404–5
design walkthrough, 404
design workflow, 39–42, 76–77, 402–5, 409–10, 537–41
    challenges, 409–10

MSG Foundation case study, 537–41
desk checking, 166
detailed design, 9, 394, 398, 402, 405
    elevator problem case study, 398
    formal techniques, 405
    MSG Foundation case study, 402
developers, 20
development, 19, 20
development-then-maintenance model, 10–11
direct observation, 291
discriminator, 487
distributed software, 406
documentation, 22, 40, 68, 69, 76, 80, 81, 82, 85, 130, 247, 279, 449, 465, 466, 469, 470, 474, 476
    checking, 449
documentation fault, 464
documentation phase, 18
documentation standard, 247, 279
doghouse, 56
domain, 73, 289–90. *See also* application domain
DOS/VS, 447
Doxygen, 280, 476
driver, 230, 424–26
    definition, 424
DTSTTCPW, 55
duration, 127, 257–60
duration estimation, 75–76, 257–60
dynamic binding, 205–7, 210, 473
dynamic model, 344–47, 357–58
    elevator problem case study, 344–47
    MSG Foundation case study, 357–58
dynamic modeling, 357–58
    definition, 337

E

early design model, 269
EBCDIC, 240
Eclipse, 133, 451, 453
e-Components, 224
economics, 7–8
Edison, Thomas Alva, 24
efficiency, 261
effort, 127
egoless programming, 103–4
elaboration phase, 83, 85–86
element access, 233
element traversal, 233
elephant, 102

elevator button, 338
elevator controller, 342
elevator door, 338
elevator door malfunction, 349
elevator problem
    history, 337
elevator problem case study, 338–51,
    397–99
    class diagram, 338–51
    class-responsibility-collaboration
    (CRC) card, 347–51
    constraints, 338
    detailed design, 398
    dynamic model, 344–47
    entity class model, 340–44
    entity classes, 338–51
    functional model, 338–40
    noun extraction, 343
    object-oriented analysis,
    338–51
    object-oriented design, 397–99
    scenarios, 339–40
    statechart, 344–47
    statement of problem, 337
    test workflow, 347–51
    use case, 338
e-mail, 130
embedded software, 156
Emeraude, 452
encapsulation, 20, 192, 189–96,
    222, 471
enhancement, 9, 471
Enterprise JavaBeans, 224
entity class, 352–60
    definition, 335
    MSG Foundation case study,
    352–60
entity class model, 340–44
    elevator problem case study,
    340–44
entity class modeling
    definition, 337
environment, 129, 450–53. *See also*
    CASE
    potential problems, 452
equivalence class, definition, 434
equivalence testing, 434–35
error
    terminology, 23, 146
escrow account, 296
estimation. *See* cost estimation, size
    estimation, duration estimation
ethics, 24–25
European Space Agency, 221–22

European Strategic Programme for
    Research in Information
    Technology (ESPRIT), 452
event, 344, 357
event (UML), 492
evolution, 463
evolution-tree model, 35–37, 38,
    42–43
Excel, 279
exception, 221
exception scenario, 339
executable load image, 139
execution-based testing, 146,
    153–58, 167, 430–39, 441–43
    who should perform it, 166–67
experimentation, 152, 259, 262, 268,
    441–42
    on COCOMO, 268
    on function points, 262
    on inspection, 152
    on programmer performance, 259
    on unit testing, 441–42
extend relationship, 489
external cost, 259
extreme programming, 54–55,
    111–12
failure
    terminology, 23, 146

F

fan-in, 409
fan-out, 409
fault
    terminology, 23, 146
fault density, 153
fault detection, 148–55, 157–58,
    442–45
fault detection efficiency, 153
fault detection rate, 153
fault distribution, 441, 446–47
fault isolation, 180, 426, 424–27
fault statistics, 151–52, 277–78,
    453, 477
faults
    maximum permitted number, 447
feature creep, 38
FFP metric, 261, 263
    strengths, 261
    weaknesses, 261, 263
field, 23
Firefox, 130
first-generation language, 452
Flintstock Life Insurance Company
    mini case study, 228–29

floating-point standard, 241
floor button, 338
FLOW, 133
flowchart, 50, 124, 475
flowchart cohesion, 180
follow-up, 151
fork, 496
    definition, 494
formal method, 451
formal specification, 49, 334
formal technique, 405, 451
formatter, 131
forms, 291
FORTRAN, 243, 244, 393. *See also*
    Fortran 2003
    spelling, 244
Fortran 2003, 243
Fortran standard, 242
forward engineering, 475
fourth-generation language, 452
FoxBASE, 442
fragile base class problem, 209, 474
framework, 224, 225
freeze, 137
front-end CASE tool, 128, 407
function points, 261–63, 270
    experimentation, 262
    strengths, 263
    weaknesses, 263
functional analysis, 436
functional cohesion, 176, 180, 222
functional model, 338–40, 352–53
    elevator problem case study,
    338–40
    MSG Foundation case study,
    352–53
functional modeling
    definition, 337
functional module, 220
functional requirement, 403
    definition, 294
functional testing, 430, 435–36

G

Gang of Four, 225
generalization, 203, 293, 487
glass-box testing, 430
    origin of term, 430
glass-box unit testing, 440, 436–43
glossary, 290
    MSG Foundation case study, 296
good programming practice, 195,
    417–22
Gosling, James, 242, 243

graphical user interface (GUI), 209, 223, 247, 323, 447–48
graphical user interface (GUI) generator, 452
Gregorian calendar, 344
GTE, 13
guard, 491–93
    definition, 491
GUI, 358
guillemet, 489

H

Hagia Sophia Museum, 464
Hamlet, Prince of Denmark, The Tragedy of, 526
hardware, 239–40
    incompatibility, 239–40
Hayakawa, S. I., 288
Hewlett-Packard, 218, 226
hierarchy, 105
high-level language, 245, 246
history
    of C, 242
    of C++, 242–43
    of COBOL, 416
    of elevator problem, 337
    of Java, 242–43
    of reuse, 217
Hopper, Grace Murray, 24
hot spot, 224
How to Perform
    equivalence testing, 435
    object-oriented analysis, 384
    object-oriented design, 402
    requirements workflow, 327
    sandwich integration, 428
HTML, 248
Hughes Aircraft, 93
human factors, 259, 323, 322–23, 322–23
human–computer interface (HCI), 322–23
Hungarian Naming Conventions, 418, 419
Hypertext Markup Language. *See* HTML

I

IBM, 13, 14, 106, 152, 209, 240, 243, 452
IBM Rational ClearCase, 476
IBM Rational ClearQuest, 477
IBM Rational Functional Tester, 453
IBM Rational Purify, 453

IBM Rational Rose, 325, 385, 407, 451, 476
illuminated (button), 338
implementation, 131–33, 414–55. *See also* implementation workflow
implementation artifacts, 79–81
implementation phase, 9
implementation testing. *See* unit testing
implementation workflow, 39–42, 77–78, 429, 542, 543
    challenges, 454–55
    MSG Foundation case study, 542, 543
inception phase, 83–85
include relationship, 304–12, 317, 489
incrementation, 39, 38–47, 82–87, 355
    management, 46–47
infeasible path, 439
informal specification, 333–35
    example, 333–34
information hiding, 19, 174, 199–201, 222, 230, 443–44, 470, 471
informational cohesion, 176, 180–81, 190, 222
inheritance, 209–10, 201–11, 293, 342, 443, 444–45, 471–72
initial level, 90
initial requirements, 293–94, 300–301
input specification, 157, 159–62, 163–64
input/output-driven testing, 430
inspection, 150–53, 277–78, 441–43
    code, 441–43
    comparison with walkthrough, 152–53
    experimentation, 152
    possible danger, 152
    strength, 153
    transaction-driven, 405
    weakness, 153
inspection rate, 153
instance variable, 23
insurance premium, 296
integrated environment, 278, 451–52
integration, 9, 80–81, 423–29, 447–50
    of object-oriented products, 428
integration testing, 80, 86, 423–27, 447–50, 474
interaction diagram, 489–91, 498

interactive source-level debugger, 133
interconnection diagram, 425
interface, 178
Intermediate COCOMO. *See* CO-COMO
internal cost, 259
internal software development, 21
International Organization for Standardization (ISO), 12, 92
interview, 290–91, 325
IPD–CMM, 89
isA relation, 202
ISO. *See* International Organization for Standardization
ISO 9000-3, 93
ISO 9001, 93
ISO/IEC 15504 (SPICE), 93
iteration, 38, 43–47, 355, 393
    management, 46–47
iterative and incremental life-cycle model, 312
iterative and incremental model, 38–42, 43–47, 72, 337, 498
    strengths, 44–45
iterator, 233
Iterator design pattern, 231–33

J

Jackpot Source Code Metrics, 453
Java, 12, 132, 135, 165, 174, 201, 217, 241, 242–43, 244, 395, 416, 417, 421, 422, 428, 429, 450, 452
    history, 242–43
    origin of name, 242
Java Abstract Windowing Toolkit, 223
Java interpreter, 16
Java loader, 16
JavaBeans, 224
Javadoc, 280
JBuilder, 131
job control language (JCL), 105, 240
Johannesburg, 418
join, 496
    definition, 494
Julian Days, 344
JUnit, 453
Just in Case You Wanted to Know, 5, 6, 10, 12, 21, 24, 33, 46, 69, 70, 71, 87, 95, 103, 127, 147, 156, 165, 174, 186, 195, 199, 216, 219, 225, 226, 242–43, 244, 266, 267, 288, 295, 322, 336, 337, 344, 349, 416, 418, 419, 427, 430, 447, 451, 464, 467, 486, 526

K

kangaroos, 219
KDSI. *See* lines of code
key process area (KPA), 91, 113
Kleene star, 486, 491
Kleene, Stephen, 486
KLOC. *See* lines of code
Kokomo, Indiana, 266

L

learning curve, 209
legacy system, 11, 336, 474
levels of abstraction, 452, 475
librarian, 106
library, 223
life cycle, 8–9, 13–15
life-cycle model, 8, 35, 32–62
    agile processes, 54–56
    code-and-fix, 47–48
    comparison, 61–62
    evolution-tree, 35–37
    extreme programming, 54–55
    iterative and incremental, 43–47
    open source, 51–54
    rapid prototyping, 50–51
    spiral, 57–61
    synchronize-and-stabilize, 57
Lilio, Luigi, 344
linear path sequences, 439
line-editing problem. *See* text-
    processing problem
lines of code (LOC, KLOC, KDSI),
    126, 260, 262, 265, 440, 441, 453
Linus's Law, 22
Linux, 21, 44, 233, 247
LISP, 202, 260, 415, 417
LOC. *See* lines of code
logic artifact, 425–27
    definition, 425
logical cohesion, 178, 181, 185
logic-driven testing, 430
lookahead, 123
loop invariant, 160–62, 163–64
Lotto, Lorenzo, 464
Lotus 1-2-3, 279
lowerCASE tool, 128, 407

M

Mac OS, 233, 234
Mac OS X, 217
Macintosh, 323, 451
MacProject, 280
maintainability, 464, 470
    techniques, 470

maintenance, 10, 8–13, 19, 20, 69,
    81–82, 177, 178, 180, 186, 209.
    See also post-delivery mainte-
    nance
    modern, 11
    operational definition, 11
    postdelivery, 69, 81–82
    temporal definition, 10
maintenance programmer, 418–19,
    465–70
maintenance team, 137–38
maintenance testing, 81–82
maintenance tool, 476–77
make tool, 139
managed level, 90
management, 69, 149–50, 271–78,
    428–29, 445–46, 468–71. *See
    also* software project manage-
    ment plan
    of integration, 428–29
    of post-delivery maintenance,
    468–71
    of unit testing, 445–46
    of walkthrough, 149–50
managerial independence, 147
*Manifesto for Agile Software
    Development,* 55, 56
manual. *See* documentation
manual pages, 130
maturity, 89
maturity level, 89–95, 113
mean time between failures,
    126, 155
mean time to repair, 155
meaningful variable names, 417–18
MEASL. *See* million equivalent
    assembler source lines
member, 23
member function, 23
menu, 358
message, 208, 428, 471
method, 443, 451
    multiple meanings, 451
method-based environment, 451
methodology, 22
    correct meaning, 22
metrics, 126–27, 153, 176–89, 325,
    409, 440–41, 453–54, 477
    cohesion, 176–81
    complexity, 409, 440–41
    cost, 126, 258–60
    coupling, 181–89
    cyclomatic complexity, 440–41
    duration, 127, 258–60

effort, 127
    for design, 409
    for implementation, 440–41,
    453–54
    for inspections, 153
    for post-delivery maintenance,
    477
    for requirements, 325
    object-oriented, 409
    quality, 127, 408
    size, 126, 260–63, 408
Microsoft, 21, 57, 111, 419, 453
Microsoft Project, 280
milestone, 76, 272
millennium bug, 336
Miller's Law, 39, 72, 88, 118–19
million equivalent assembler source
    lines (MEASL), 94
Milstar satellite, 87
mini case study. *See* correctness
    proof mini case study, design pat-
    tern mini case study, Flintstock
    Life Insurance Company mini
    case study, post-delivery mainte-
    nance mini case study, stepwise
    refinement mini case study, Teal
    Tractors mini case study, Winburg
    mini case study
mistake
    terminology, 23, 146
mitigate risk. *See* risk mitigation
Mk II function points, 263
modal logic, 163, 164
model (UML), 292
model, life cycle. *See* life-cycle
    model
model, UML, 72
model-view-controller (MVC)
    architecture pattern, 226
modern chief programmer team,
    107–11
modern maintenance, 11
module, 9, 174–210, 222
    context, 176
    definition, 174
    logic, 176
    operation, 176
money, 272
mortgage, 295, 294–96
    pronunciation, 295
Motif, 247
Motorola, 94
moving target problem, 38, 471
Mozart, Wolfgang Amadeus, 216

MSG Foundation case study,
294–321, 338, 382–83, 393,
400–402, 403, 405, 429, 436,
450, 477, 530–44
actors, 297–99
algorithm, 302–3
analysis workflow, 352–82, 531
black-box test cases, 436
boundary classes, 360–61
C++ implementation, 542
class diagram, 354–55
control classes, 361
design workflow, 400–402, 537–41
detailed design, 402
dynamic model, 357–58
entity classes, 352–60
functional model, 352–53
implementation workflow, 429,
542, 543
initial business model, 297–99
initial requirements, 300–301
initial understanding of the
domain, 294–96
Java implementation, 543
noun extraction, 354
object-oriented design, 400–402
post-delivery maintenance, 477
requirements workflow, 294–321,
530
software project management
plan, 338, 532–36
statechart, 357–58
test workflow, 321, 382, 405,
450, 544
use cases, 294–321, 351–56,
362–78
use-case diagram, 304–20
use-case diagram, 355
multiplicity, 485–86
mutator, 401

N

NAG, 217
NASA, 14
National Gallery, 464
natural language, 333
Naur, Peter, 162, 334–35
navigation triangle, 204, 487
negotiation, 326
nested **if** statement, 421–22
Netscape, 130
New York Times, 106–7
No Silver Bullet, 95, 410
nominal effort, 266

non-execution-based testing, 146,
148–53, 158–65, 430, 441–43
nonfunctional requirement, 294, 403
normal scenario, 339
not invented here (NIH) syndrome,
218
note, 202, 488
noun extraction, 341–43, 354
elevator problem case study, 343
MSG Foundation case study, 354
numerical software, 241
incompatibility, 241

O

object, 19–21, 173, 181, 201, 208,
201–10, 222, 428, 443–45, 471
advantages, 204
object code, 138–39
Object Management Group (OMG),
70, 71, 482
object points, 269
object testing, 443–45
object-oriented analysis (OOA). *See
also* analysis workflow
elevator problem case study,
338–51
MSG Foundation case study,
352–82, 531
object-oriented architecture, 226
object-oriented CASE tool, 385, 451
object-oriented design (OOD), 20,
340, 393–402, 407. *See also*
design workflow
elevator problem case study,
397–99
MSG Foundation case study,
400–402
object-oriented language, 393
object-oriented metrics, 409
object-oriented paradigm, 19, 18–21,
173, 176, 192–210, 222, 270–71,
278, 289–321, 331–85, 393–405,
416–17, 428, 429, 443–45, 451,
471–74
strengths, 21, 207–10
weaknesses, 21, 207–10, 471–74
object-oriented programming language, 416–17, 428
hybrid, 417, 428
pure, 417, 428
object-oriented software engineering
definition, 23
Objectory, 71
OMG. *See* Object Management Group

OMT, 71
one-dimensional life-cycle model,
87. *See also* waterfall model
online documentation, 130, 133
online interface checker, 131–32, 133
OO-COBOL, 243, 416, 417
open-ended design, 77
open-source CASE tool
Ant, 139
ArgoUML, 325, 385, 407
Bugzilla, 477
cvs, 138, 450, 476
Doxygen, 280, 476
Eclipse, 133
open-source life-cycle model, 51–54
open-source software, 21, 139
open-source software development,
51–54
operating system, 246
incompatibility, 240–41, 247
operating system front end, 132, 133
operation, 19–21
operational artifact, 425–27
definition, 425
operation-oriented design, 392
opportunistic reuse, 216
optimization, 186
optimizing level, 91
Oracle Developer Suite, 452
OS/370, 446
OS/VS2, 178
output specification, 157, 159–62,
163–64
overview, 150

P

P & I. *See* principal and interest
package, 403, 496
definition, 496
pair programming, 54, 56, 112
Palm Pilot, 290
paradigm, 22
correct meaning, 23
parameter, 420
Parasoft, 453
part–whole relationship, 484
Pascal, 241, 244
Pascal, Blaise, 244
path coverage, 433, 439
path-oriented testing, 430
Patriot missile, 5
pattern, 224–38. *See* architecture
pattern, design pattern
architecture, 226–27

pattern language for architecture, 225
P–CMM, 89, 113
PCTE. *See* portable common tool environment
PDL. *See* pseudocode
people capability maturity model. *See* P–CMM
perfective maintenance, 9, 134, 464, 466, 469, 474
performance appraisal, 107–8, 150, 152
performance testing, 156–57, 449
person-month
    definition, 126
phase, 8–9, 16–18. *See also* construction phase, elaboration phase, inception phase, transition phase
    Unified Process, 82–87
physical independence, 20, 222, 471
PIN, 266
pipes and filters, 226, 451
PL/I, 106–7, 243
planning, 16–17, 40, 85, 91, 256–80
planning phase, 16–17
platform constraint, 294
point and click, 323
points, 296
polymorphism, 205–7, 210, 473
portability, 239–69, 403, 452
    definition, 239
    description, 216
    impediments, 244, 248
    strengths, 245, 248
portable application software, 246–47
portable common tool environment (PCTE), 452
portable compiler, 243–44
portable data, 247–48
portable database, 247
portable numerical software, 241
portable operating system, 246
portable operating system interface for computer environments (POSIX), 247
portable system software, 246
POSIX. *See* portable operating system interface for computer environments
postarchitecture model, 269
postdelivery maintenance, 9, 10, 11, 8–13, 69, 81–82, 137–38, 238–39
post-delivery maintenance, 462–78. *See also* maintenance
    attitude toward, 467

challenges, 478
difficulty, 465–66
management of, 468–71
mini case study, 467–68
of object-oriented software, 471–74
repeated, 471
scope, 463
skills, 474
thanklessness, 466
post-delivery maintenance mini case study, 467–68
post-delivery maintenance testing, 475–76
pragma statement, 165, 222
predicate, 344
predicate calculus, 163
PREfast, 453
PREfix, 453
preparation, 150
presentation logic tier, 227
pretty printer, 131, 475
price, 259
principal, 295
principal and interest, 295
private visibility modifier, 200
private workspace, 137, 470
procedural abstraction, 192, 198
procedural cohesion, 179
process. *See* software process
process improvement, 89–95
process integration, 451
process maturity level, 89–95
process metric, 126
product
    terminology, 22
product line, 226
product metric, 126
product testing, 80, 86, 277, 448–49, 474
productivity, 139–40, 221, 222, 260, 261, 262
program, 22
program description language. *See* pseudocode (PDL)
programming languages. *See specific languages*
programming secretary, 105, 106, 107
programming team, 15–16
programming workbench, 133
programming-in-the-large, 130
programming-in-the-many, 130, 132, 414

programming-in-the-small, 130
project function, 272
prologue comments, 419, 469
proof of correctness. *See* correctness proof
proof-of-concept prototype, 40, 57, 85
prototype, 57–59, 85, 332. *See also* rapid prototype
pseudocode (PDL), 124, 395, 410
public visibility modifier, 183, 198, 200
public tool infrastructure, 452
PureCoverage, 438
PVCS, 138, 450

Q

QARun, 448
quality. *See* software quality
    terminology, 147
questionnaire, 291

R

rapid prototype, 50–51, 58, 321–22
rapid prototyping model, 50–51, 321–22, 324
Rational, 71
Rational Unified Process, 71
Rayleigh distribution, 271
Raytheon, 94, 220–21, 224
rcs tool, 138, 476
readability, 419, 421
reader, 151
real-time software, 87, 157
real-time system, 12, 154, 157, 406–7
    difficulties, 406–7
real-time system design, 406–7
    extension of nonreal-time techniques, 407
recorder, 151
reengineering, 475
refactoring, 54, 475
refine, 293, 361, 383
    definition, 290
regression fault, 19, 38, 48, 186, 208, 465, 471, 477
regression testing, 49, 82, 167, 465, 469, 471, 475–76
reliability, 155, 294, 403
reliability analysis, 446
reliability testing, 155
repeatable level, 90
report generator, 129, 383, 407
requirements, 287–326. *See also* requirements workflow

requirements analysis, 289
requirements artifacts, 78
requirements capture, 289
requirements elicitation, 289, 290–92
requirements fault, 14
requirements management, 91
requirements phase, 9
requirements workflow, 39–42,
    73–74, 289–321, 324–26, 530
    actors, 292–93
    business model, 290–93
    challenges, 325–26
    intial requirements, 293–94
    MSG Foundation case study,
    294–321, 530
    understanding the domain,
    289–90
    use cases, 292–93
RequisitePro, 129
resources, 271, 272
response time, 294
responsibility-driven design, 20, 21,
    394
restructuring, 475
retirement, 9, 82, 167
return, 491
reuse, 20, 177, 178, 179, 180, 183,
    208, 216–39, 270–71, 403, 423,
    425–26, 427
    and postdelivery maintenance,
    238–39
    case studies, 219–22
    code, 222–27, 423
    description, 216
    design, 222–27
    history, 217
    impediments, 248
    object-oriented paradigm, 222
    savings, 270
    statistics, 221
    strengths, 248
    theoretical upper limit, 217
reverse engineering, 474–75
review, 79, 80. *See also* walkthrough,
    inspection
revision, 134
rework, 151
risk, 45, 57–61, 81, 84–85
risk analysis, 416
risk mitigation, 58
Ritchie, Dennis, 242
robustness, 44, 80, 85, 156, 403, 448
robustness testing, 80, 156, 449
role, 383

Romeo and Juliet, 216
Romney, George, 288

S

Sallie Mae, 5
San Francisco (framework), 224
sandwich integration, 426–27
    origin of term, 427
SBC Communications, 243
Scaliger, Joseph, 344
Scaliger, Julius Caesar, 344
sccs tool, 138, 476
scenario, 337, 339–40
    elevator problem case study,
    339–40
scheduling tool, 280
Schubert, Franz, 216
scientific software, 223
scratch, 33
screen generator, 129, 383, 407
SDRTS, 407
second-generation language, 452
secretary, 106
SEI. *See* Software Engineering
    Institute
self-call, 491
self-documenting code, 418
semiformal specification, 335
separate implementation and
    integration, 423–24
sequence diagram, 489–91, 498
Shakespeare, William, 216
Shoo-Bug, 103
shrink-wrapped software, 21
SilkTest, 447, 453
Simula 67 (language), 174, 201
simulator, 155
size, 260–63
SLAM, 453
Smalltalk, 201, 217, 393, 414, 416
software, 22
software architecture, 226–27, 403–4
software crisis, 5–7
    financial implications, 6–7
software depression, 7
software development effort
    multipliers, 266
software development environment.
    See CASE
software engineering
    definition, 4
    economic aspects, 7–8
    historical aspects, 5–7
    maintenance aspects, 8–13

requirements, analysis and design
    aspects, 13–15
    scope of, 3–16
    team development aspects, 15–16
Software Engineering Institute (SEI),
    89–91
software engineering resources,
    528–29
software process, 68–95
Software Process Engineering
    Metamodel (SPEM), 70
software process improvement, 89–95
    costs and benefits, 93–95
software product line, 226
software production
    terminology, 22
software project management plan
    (SPMP), 9, 16, 76, 270, 271–78,
    280, 429, 449, 532–36
    components, 271–72
    IEEE standard, 271, 274–77
    MSG Foundation case study,
    532–36
    terminology, 271–72
    testing, 280
software quality, 18, 126, 127, 146,
    147, 146–48, 164
software quality assurance (SQA),
    57, 91, 147–48, 470
software quality assurance (SQA)
    group, 18, 48, 76, 79, 134, 149,
    151, 166, 277, 419, 423, 447–49,
    470
software repair, 9
Software through Pictures, 129, 325,
    407, 451
software tool. *See* CASE, tool
software update, 9
solution strategy, 332–33
source code, 139, 465
source computer, 239
source-level debugger, 133
SourceSafe, 138, 450
Soyuz TMA-1 spaceship, 87
space shuttle, 87
specialization, 105, 203, 293

specification document, 9, 49, 75,
    331–32, 382–83, 407, 474
    ambiguity, 334
    correctness, 157–58, 164
    feasibility, 79
    MSG Foundation case study,
    382–83

SPICE. *See* ISO/IEC 15504
spiral model, 57–61
    strengths, 59–60, 61
    weaknesses, 61
spreadsheet, 130
SPSS, 217
SQA. *See* software quality assurance
stabilize, 57
stamp coupling, 185–86, 187
Standish Group, 5, 45, 46
stand-up meeting, 55
state (attribute value), 344
state variable, 344, 443
statechart, 344–47, 357–58, 491–94,
    498
    elevator problem case study,
    344–47
    MSG Foundation case study,
    357–58
statement coverage, 438–39
statistical-based testing, 445–46
stepwise refinement, 39, 118–24,
    191–92, 405
    mini case study, 119–24
stepwise refinement mini case study,
    118–24
stereotype, 304–12, 488–89
    definition, 336
stories, 54
strength, 176
stress testing, 448
Stroustrup, Bjarne, 243
structural design pattern, 235
structural testing, 430, 439
structure editor, 131–33
structured interview
    definition, 290
structured paradigm, 18–19
structured programming, 18, 180,
    183
structured systems analysis, 18
structured testing, 18, 440
stub, 423–28
    definition, 423
subclass, 202

subsystem, 403
Sun Microsystems, 242, 244
Sun ONE Java Studio, 133
superprogrammer, 107
superstate, 493
SW–CMM, 89–92
swimlane, 496
    definition, 496

synchronization, 406
synchronize, 57
synchronize-and-stabilize model,
    57, 111
synchronize-and-stabilize team, 111
system
    terminology, 22
System Architect, 325, 343
systematic reuse, 216
systematic testing, 166
systems analysis, 208
    definition, 22
systems design
    definition, 22
systems engineering, 127

T
target computer, 239
task, 54, 112, 272
Teal Tractors mini case study, 37–38
team, 101–15
team leader, 108–11
team manager, 108–11
team organization, 101–15
    communication channels, 102
    comparison, 114–15
    managerial aspects, 102, 107–12
technical complexity factor, 262
technique, 23
technique-based environment, 451,
    452
technology, 174
Temperate Fruit Committee, 467–68
temporal cohesion, 178–79
temporal logic, 163
terminology, 21–24
test case, 167
    successful, 166
test case selection, 430–39
test driven development, 54
test plan, 277–78, 444
test workflow, 39–42, 78–81, 85,
    321, 382, 404–5, 450, 453,
    475–76, 544
    analysis artifacts, 79
    design artifacts, 79
    during analysis, 382
    during design, 404–5
    during implementation, 429–41,
    447–50
    during integration, 447–50
    during post-delivery maintenance,
    470, 475–76
    during requirements, 321

elevator problem case study,
    347–51
graphical user interface (GUI),
    447–48
implementation, 430
implementation artifacts, 79–81
MSG Foundation case study, 321,
    382, 405, 450, 544
    requirements artifacts, 78
testing, 17–18, 40, 57, 69, 79, 80–82,
    85, 154–55, 145–67, 423–27.
    See also test workflow
    classes, 443
    destructiveness, 166
    during implementation, 429–41
    during integration, 423–27
    execution-based, 146, 153–58,
    167
    non-execution-based, 146,
    148–53, 158–65
    objects, 443–45
    when it stops, 167
testing fault rate, 442
testing phase, 17–18
testing to code, 430, 431–33
    feasibility, 431–33
    reliability, 432, 433
    validity, 433
testing to specifications, 430,
    431–33
    feasibility, 431–33
text-processing problem, 162–63,
    334–35
theorem prover, 163–64
Therac-25, 5
third-generation language, 452
Three Amigos, 71
time. *See* duration
timeboxing, 55
timeout, 338
Together, 325, 385, 407, 476
tool, 128–29, 450. *See also* CASE
tool integration, 451
toolkit, 223, 224, 225
top-down integration, 424–26
    strengths, 425
    weaknesses, 425–26
Torvalds, Linus, 22
traceability, 78, 79, 277
tracing, 132
trade-offs, 403
traditional paradigm. *See* classical
    paradigm
training, 278

transaction
  definition, 404
transaction-driven inspection, 405
transition (UML), 493
  definition, 491
transition phase, 83, 86–87
TRW, 13
two-dimensional life-cycle model,
  87–88. *See also* evolution tree
  model, iterative and ncremental
  life-cycle model

U

U.S. Air Force, 91
UML, 70, 72, 202–6, 289, 292–321,
  336–84, 393–405, 482–98
  aggregation, 203
  association, 203
  inheritance, 202
  navigation triangle, 204
  not a methodology, 483
  note, 202
unadjusted function points, 261
understanding the domain, 289–90,
  294–96
  MSG Foundation case study,
  294–96
Unified Modeling Language. *See*
  UML
Unified Process, 70–81, 82–87, 88,
  146, 274, 289–321, 335–37,
  382–84, 402–5, 451, 463, 483,
  498
  analysis workflow, 335–37,
  382–84
  construction phase, 86
  design workflow, 402–5
  elaboration phase, 85–86
  history, 71
  implementation workflow, 429
  inception phase, 83–85
  phases, 82–87
  requirements workflow, 289–321
  transition phase, 86–87
unit testing, 9, 79, 86, 429–47
  comparison, 441–42
  experimentation, 441–42
  statistical techniques, 445–46

UNIX, 44, 130, 132, 138, 139, 226,
  246, 247, 451, 452, 476
UNIX Programmer's Workbench, 451
unstructured interview
  definition, 290
upperCASE tool, 128, 407
upward compatibility, 245
urban myth, 219
use case, 292–93, 297, 294–321,
  338, 351–56, 362–78, 383–84,
  488, 498
  definition, 338
  elevator problem case study, 338
  MSG Foundation case study,
  351–56, 362–78
use-case description, 297
use-case diagram, 299, 304–20, 350,
  488, 498
  MSG Foundation case study, 299,
  304–20, 355
use-case realization
  definition, 362
user, 21
user friendliness, 322–23
user interface, 358, 383
user interface integration, 451
utility, 155
utility testing, 155, 156

V

V & V, 146
validation, 17, 146
variable names
  consistent, 417–18
  meaningful, 417–18
variation, 136–37, 136–37
  multiple, 136–37
verification, 17, 146, 158
version, 133–39, 471
version control, 136–39, 476–77
version-control tool, 136, 138, 136
videotape, 291
virtual method, 205
Virtual Case File, 5
Visual Basic .NET, 23
Visual C++, 131, 139
Visual Java, 139
volume testing, 449

W

walkthrough, 149–50, 152–53,
  441–43
  code, 441–43
  comparison with inspection,
  152–53
  possible danger, 150
  strength, 153
  weakness, 153
WarGames, 4
waterfall life-cycle model. *See* waterfall model
waterfall model, 8, 35–36, 44, 46
  strengths, 49
Web-based applications, 248
WebSphere, 224
West Side Story, 216
white-box testing, 430
widget, 233
Win32, 217
Winburg mini case study, 33–37, 39,
  42–43, 45
Windows, 233, 247
word processor, 130
work package, 272
work product, 272
workbench, 129, 450. *See also* CASE
worker, 384
workflow, 39, 72. *See also* analysis
  workflow, core workflows, design
  workflow, implementation workflow, requirements workflow, test
  workflow
wrapper, 225
WWMCCS, 4

X

X11, 247
XML, 248
XRunner, 448

Y

Y2K problem, 336
YAGNI, 55

Z

Zoe
  Empress, 464